THIS *bible* BELONGS TO:

THIS CATHOLIC JOURNALING BIBLE IS DESIGNED FOR CREATIVE AND INSPIRED PRAYER. FILL THESE PAGES WITH NOTES, PRAYERS, DOODLES & DRAWINGS.

Drawn to Faith

ISBN-13: 978-1-945888-69-4
ISBN-10: 1-945888-69-5

Free Prints!

www.drawntofaith.com/catholicjournaling

YOUR DOWNLOAD CODE: CPDV3258

@drawntofaith

Drawn To Faith

TABLE OF CONTENTS

THE SACRED BIBLE: THE BOOK OF PSALMS

CHAPTER 1

[1] Blessed is the man who has not followed the counsel of the impious, and has not remained in the way of sinners, and has not sat in the chair of pestilence. [2] But his will is with the law of the Lord, and he will meditate on his law, day and night. [3] And he will be like a tree that has been planted beside running waters, which will provide its fruit in its time, and its leaf will not fall away, and all things whatsoever that he does will prosper. [4] Not so the impious, not so. For they are like the dust that the wind casts along the face of the earth. [5] Therefore, the impious will not prevail again in judgment, nor sinners in the council of the just. [6] For the Lord knows the way of the just. And the path of the impious will pass away.

CHAPTER 2

[1] Why have the Gentiles been seething, and why have the people been pondering nonsense? [2] The kings of the earth have stood up, and the leaders have joined together as one, against the Lord and against his Christ: [3] "Let us shatter their chains and cast their yoke away from us." [4] He who dwells in heaven will ridicule them, and the Lord will mock them. [5] Then will he speak to them in his anger and trouble them with his fury. [6] Yet I have been appointed king by him over Zion, his holy mountain, preaching his precepts. [7] The Lord has said to me: You are my son, this day have I begotten you. [8] Ask of me and I will give to you: the Gentiles for your inheritance, and the ends of the earth for your possession. [9] You will rule them with an iron rod, and you will shatter them like a potter's vessel. [10] And now, O kings, understand. Receive instruction, you who judge the earth. [11] Serve the Lord in fear, and exult in him with trembling. [12] Embrace discipline, lest at any time the Lord might become angry, and you would perish from the way of the just. [13] Though his wrath can flare up in a short time, blessed are all those who trust in him.

CHAPTER 3

[1] A Psalm of David. When he fled from the face of his son, Absalom. [2] Lord, why have those who trouble me been multiplied? Many rise up against me. [3] Many say to my soul, "There is no salvation for him in his God." [4] But you, Lord, are my supporter, my glory, and the one who raises up my head. [5] I have cried out to the Lord with my voice, and he has heard me from his holy mountain. [6] I have slept, and I have been stupefied. But I awakened because the Lord has taken me up. [7] I will not fear the thousands of people surrounding me. Rise up, Lord. Save me, my God. [8] For you have struck all those who oppose me without cause. You have broken the teeth of sinners. [9] Salvation is of the Lord, and your blessing is upon your people.

CHAPTER 4

[1] In parts according to verses. A Psalm of David. [2] When I called upon him, the God of my justice heeded me. In tribulation, you have enlarged me. Have mercy on me, and heed my prayer. [3] Sons of men, how long will you be dull in heart, so that whatever you love is in vain, and whatever you seek is false? [4] And know this: the Lord has made wondrous his holy one. The Lord will heed me when I cry out to him. [5] Be angry, and do not be willing to sin. The things that you say in your hearts: be sorry for them on your beds. [6] Offer the sacrifice of justice, and hope in the Lord. Many say, "Who reveals to us what is good?" [7] The light of your countenance, Lord, has been sealed upon us. You have given joy to my heart. [8] By the fruit of their grain, wine, and oil, they have been multiplied. [9] In peace itself, I will sleep and I will rest. [10] For you, O Lord, have established me singularly in hope.

CHAPTER 5

[1] Unto the end. For her who pursues the inheritance. A Psalm of David. [2] O Lord, listen closely to my words. Understand my outcry. [3] Attend to the voice of my prayer, my King and my God. [4] For to you, I will pray. In the morning, Lord, you

will hear my voice. ⁵In the morning, I will stand before you, and I will see. For you are not a God who wills iniquity. ⁶And the malicious will not dwell close to you, nor will the unjust endure before your eyes. ⁷You hate all who work iniquity. You will destroy all who speak a lie. The bloody and deceitful man, the Lord will abominate. ⁸But I am in the multitude of your mercy. I will enter your house. I will show adoration toward your holy temple, in your fear. ⁹Lord, lead me in your justice. Because of my enemies, direct my way in your sight. ¹⁰For there is no truth in their mouth: their heart is vain. ¹¹Their throat is an open sepulcher. They have acted deceitfully with their tongues. Judge them, O God. Let them fall by their own intentions: according to the multitude of their impiety, expel them. For they have provoked you, O Lord. ¹²But let all those who hope in you rejoice. They will exult in eternity, and you will dwell in them. And all those who love your name will glory in you. ¹³For you will bless the just. You have crowned us, O Lord, as if with a shield of your good will.

CHAPTER 6

¹In parts according to verses. A Psalm of David. For the octave. ²O Lord, do not rebuke me in your fury, nor chastise me in your anger. ³Have mercy on me, Lord, for I am weak. Heal me, Lord, for my bones have become disturbed, ⁴and my soul has been very troubled. But as for you, Lord, when? ⁵Turn to me, Lord, and rescue my soul. Save me because of your mercy. ⁶For there is no one in death who would be mindful of you. And who will confess to you in Hell? ⁷I have labored in my groaning. Every night, with my tears, I will wash my bed and drench my blanket. ⁸My eye has been troubled by rage. I have grown old among all my enemies. ⁹Scatter before me, all you who work iniquity, for the Lord has heard the voice of my weeping. ¹⁰The Lord has heard my supplication. The Lord has accepted my prayer. ¹¹Let all my enemies be ashamed and together be greatly troubled. May they be converted and become ashamed very quickly.

CHAPTER 7

¹A Psalm of David, which he sang to the Lord because of the words of Cush, the son of Jemini. ²O Lord, my God, in you I have hoped. Save me from all those who persecute me, and free me: ³lest at any time, like a lion, he might seize my soul, while there is no one to redeem me, nor any who can save. ⁴O Lord, my God, if there is iniquity in my hands, if I have done this: ⁵if I have repaid those who rendered evils to me, may I deservedly fall away empty before my enemies: ⁶let the enemy pursue my soul, and take hold of it, and trample my life into the earth, and drag down my glory into the dust. ⁷Rise up, Lord, in your anger. And be exalted to the borders of my enemies. And rise up, O Lord my God, according to the precept that you commanded, ⁸and a congregation of people will surround you. And, because of this, return on high. ⁹The Lord judges the people. Judge me, O Lord, according to my justice and according to my innocence within me. ¹⁰The wickedness of sinners will be consumed, and you will direct the just: the examiner of hearts and temperaments is God. ¹¹Just is my help from the Lord, who saves the upright of heart. ¹²God is a just judge, strong and patient. How could he be angry throughout every day? ¹³Unless you will be converted, he will brandish his sword. He has extended his bow and made it ready. ¹⁴And with it, he has prepared instruments of death. He has produced his arrows for those on fire. ¹⁵Behold him who has given birth to injustice: he has conceived sorrow and has begotten iniquity. ¹⁶He has opened a pit and enlarged it. And he has fallen into the hole that he made. ¹⁷His sorrow will be turned upon his own head, and his iniquity will descend upon his highest point. ¹⁸I will confess to the Lord according to his justice, and I will sing a psalm to the name of the Lord Most High.

CHAPTER 8

¹Unto the end. For the oil and wine presses. A Psalm of David. ²O Lord, our Lord, how admirable is your name throughout all the earth! For your magnificence is elevated above the heavens. ³Out of the mouths of babes and infants, you have perfected praise, because of your enemies, so that you may destroy the enemy and the revenger. ⁴For I will behold your heavens, the works of your fingers: the moon and the stars, which you have founded. ⁵What is man, that you are mindful of him, or the son of man, that you visit him? ⁶You reduced him to a little less than the Angels; you have crowned him with glory and honor, ⁷and you have set him

over the works of your hands. [8]You have subjected all things under his feet, all sheep and oxen, and in addition: the beasts of the field, [9]the birds of the air, and the fish of the sea, which pass through the paths of the sea. [10]O Lord, our Lord, how admirable is your name throughout all the earth!

CHAPTER 9 (9 - 10)

[1]Unto the end. For the secrets of the Son. A Psalm of David. [2]I will confess to you, Lord, with my whole heart. I will recount all your wonders. [3]I will rejoice and exult in you. I will sing a psalm to your name, O Most High. [4]For my enemy will be turned back. They will be weakened and perish before your face. [5]For you have accomplished my judgment and my cause. You have sat upon the throne that judges justice. [6]You have rebuked the Gentiles, and the impious one has perished. You have deleted their name in eternity and for all generations. [7]The spears of the enemy have failed in the end, and their cities, you have destroyed. Their memory has perished with a loud noise. [8]But the Lord remains in eternity. He has prepared his throne in judgment. [9]And he will judge the whole world in equity. He will judge the people in justice. [10]And the Lord has become a refuge for the poor, a helper in opportunity, in tribulation. [11]And may they hope in you, who know your name. For you have not abandoned those seeking you, Lord. [12]Sing a psalm to the Lord, who dwells in Zion. Announce his study among the Gentiles. [13]Because of those who yearned for their blood, he has remembered them. He has not forgotten the cry of the poor. [14]Have mercy on me, Lord. See my humiliation from my enemies. [15]You lift me up from the gates of death, so that I may announce all your praises at the gates of the daughter of Zion. [16]I will exult in your salvation. The Gentiles have become trapped in the ruin that they made. Their foot has been caught in the same snare that they themselves had hidden. [17]The Lord will be recognized when making judgments. The sinner has been caught in the works of his own hands. [18]The sinners will be turned into Hell: all the Gentiles who have forgotten God. [19]For the poor will not be forgotten in the end. The patience of the poor will not perish in the end. [20]Rise up, Lord: do not let man be strengthened. Let the Gentiles be judged in your sight. [21]O Lord, establish a lawgiver over them, so that the Gentiles may know that they are only men. [22]So then, why, O Lord, have you withdrawn far away? Why have you overlooked us in opportunity, in tribulation? [23]While the impious is arrogant, the poor is enflamed. They are held by the counsels that they devise. [24]For the sinner is praised by the desires of his soul, and the iniquitous is blessed. [25]The sinner has provoked the Lord; according to the multitude of his wrath, he will not seek him. [26]God is not before his sight. His ways are stained at all times. Your judgments are removed from his face. He will be master of all his enemies. [27]For he has said in his heart, "I will not be disturbed: from generation to generation without evil." [28]His mouth is full of curses, and bitterness, and deceit. Under his tongue are hardship and sorrow. [29]He sits in ambush, with resources in hidden places, so that he may execute the innocent. [30]His eyes catch sight of the poor. He lies in ambush, in hiding like a lion in his den. He lies in ambush, so that he may seize the poor, to seize the poor as he draws him in. [31]With his snare, he will bring him down. He will crouch down and pounce, when he has power over the poor. [32]For he has said in his heart, "God has forgotten, he has turned away his face, lest he see to the end." [33]O Lord God, rise up. Let your hand be exalted. Do not forget the poor. [34]How has the impious one provoked God? For he has said in his heart, "He will not inquire." [35]You do see, for you examine hardship and sorrow, so that you may deliver them into your hands. The poor one has been abandoned to you. You will be a helper to the orphan. [36]Break the arm of the sinner and the malicious. His sin will be sought, and it will not be found. [37]The Lord shall reign in eternity, even forever and ever. You will perish the Gentiles from his land. [38]The Lord has heeded the desire of the poor. Your ear has listened to the preparation of their heart, [39]so as to judge for the orphan and the humble, so that man may no longer presume to magnify himself upon the earth.

CHAPTER 10 (11)

[1]Unto the end. A Psalm of David. [2]I trust in the Lord. How can you say to my soul, "Sojourn to the mountain, like a sparrow." [3]For behold, the sinners have bent their bow. They have prepared their arrows in the quiver, so as to shoot arrows in the dark at the upright of heart. [4]For they have destroyed the things that you have completed. But what has the just one done? [5]The Lord is in his

holy temple. The Lord's throne is in heaven. His eyes look upon the poor. His eyelids question the sons of men. [6]The Lord questions the just and the impious. Yet he who loves iniquity, hates his own soul. [7]He will rain down snares upon sinners. Fire and brimstone and windstorms will be the portion of their cup. [8]For the Lord is just, and he has chosen justice. His countenance has beheld equity.

CHAPTER 11 (12)

[1]Unto the end. For the octave. A Psalm of David. [2]Save me, O Lord, because holiness has passed away, because truths have been diminished, before the sons of men. [3]They have been speaking emptiness, each one to his neighbor; they have been speaking with deceitful lips and a duplicitous heart. [4]May the Lord scatter all deceitful lips, along with the tongue that speaks malice. [5]They have said: "We will magnify our tongue; our lips belong to us. What is Lord to us?" [6]Because of the misery of the destitute and the groaning of the poor, now I will arise, says the Lord. I will place him in safety. I will act faithfully toward him. [7]The eloquence of the Lord is pure eloquence, silver tested by fire, purged from the earth, refined seven times. [8]You, O Lord, will preserve us, and you will guard us from this generation into eternity. [9]The impious wander aimlessly. According to your loftiness, you have multiplied the sons of men.

CHAPTER 12 (13)

[1]Unto the end. A Psalm of David. How long, O Lord? Will you forget me until the end? How long will you turn your face away from me? [2]How long can I take counsel in my soul, sorrowing in my heart throughout the day? [3]How long will my enemy be exalted over me? [4]Look upon me and listen to me, O Lord my God. Enlighten my eyes, lest I fall asleep forever in death, [5]lest at any time my enemy may say, "I have prevailed against him." Those who trouble me will exult, if I have been disturbed. [6]But I have hoped in your mercy. My heart will exult in your salvation. I will sing to the Lord, who assigns good things to me. And I will sing psalms to the name of the Lord Most High.

CHAPTER 13 (14)

[1]Unto the end. A Psalm of David. The fool has said in his heart, "There is no God." They were corrupted, and they have become abominable in their studies. There is no one who does good; there is not even one. [2]The Lord has looked down from heaven upon the sons of men, to see if there were any who were considering or seeking God. [3]They have all gone astray; together they have become useless. There is no one who does good; there is not even one. [4]Their throat is an open sepulcher. With their tongues, they have been acting deceitfully; the venom of asps is under their lips. Their mouth is full of curses and bitterness. [5]Their feet are swift to shed blood. Grief and unhappiness are in their ways; and the way of peace, they have not known. [6]There is no fear of God before their eyes. [7]Will they never learn: all those who work iniquity, who devour my people like a meal of bread? [8]They have not called upon the Lord. There, they have trembled in fear, where there was no fear. [9]For the Lord is with the just generation. You have confounded the counsel of the needy because the Lord is his hope. [10]Who will grant the salvation of Israel from Zion? When the Lord turns away the captivity of his people, Jacob will exult, and Israel will rejoice.

CHAPTER 14 (15)

[1]A Psalm of David. O Lord, who will dwell in your tabernacle? Or who will rest on your holy mountain? [2]He who walks without blemish and who works justice. [3]He who speaks the truth in his heart, who has not acted deceitfully with his tongue, and has not done evil to his neighbor, and has not taken up a reproach against his neighbors. [4]In his sight, the malicious one has been reduced to nothing, but he glorifies those who fear the Lord. He who swears to his neighbor and does not deceive. [5]He who has not given his money in usury, nor accepted bribes against the innocent. He who does these things will be undisturbed for eternity.

CHAPTER 15 (16)

[1]The inscription of a title: of David himself. Preserve me, O Lord, because I have hoped in you. [2]I have said to the Lord: "You are my God, so you have no need of my goodness." [3]As for the saints, who are in his land: he has made

all my desires wonderful in them. ⁴Their infirmities have been multiplied; after this, they acted more quickly. I will not gather for their convocations of blood, nor will I remember their names with my lips. ⁵The Lord is the portion of my inheritance and my cup. It is you who will restore my inheritance to me. ⁶The lots have fallen upon me with clarity. And, indeed, my inheritance has been very clear to me. ⁷I will bless the Lord, who has bestowed understanding upon me. Moreover, my temperament has also corrected me, even through the night. ⁸I have made provision for the Lord always in my sight. For he is at my right hand, so that I may not be disturbed. ⁹Because of this, my heart has been joyful, and my tongue has exulted. Moreover, even my body will rest in hope. ¹⁰For you will not abandon my soul to Hell, nor will you allow your holy one to see corruption. ¹¹You have made known to me the ways of life; you will fill me with joy by your countenance. At your right hand are delights, even to the end.

CHAPTER 16 (17)

¹A Prayer of David. Lord, listen to my justice, attend to my supplication. Pay attention to my prayer, which is not from deceitful lips. ²Let my judgment proceed from your presence. Let your eyes behold fairness. ³You have tested my heart and visited it by night. You have examined me by fire, and iniquity has not been found in me. ⁴Therefore, may my mouth not speak the works of men. I have kept to difficult ways because of the words of your lips. ⁵Perfect my steps in your paths, so that my footsteps may not be disturbed. ⁶I have cried out because you, O God, have listened to me. Incline your ear to me and heed my words. ⁷Make your mercies wonderful, for you save those who hope in you. ⁸From those who resist your right hand, preserve me like the pupil of your eye. Protect me under the shadow of your wings, ⁹from the face of the impious who have afflicted me. My enemies have surrounded my soul. ¹⁰They have concealed their fatness; their mouth has been speaking arrogantly. ¹¹They have cast me out, and now they have surrounded me. They have cast their eyes down to the earth. ¹²They have taken me, like a lion ready for the prey, and like a young lion dwelling in hiding. ¹³Rise up, O Lord, arrive before him and displace him. Deliver my soul from the impious one: your spear from the enemies of your hand. ¹⁴Lord, divide them from the few of the earth in their life. Their gut has been filled from your hidden stores. They have been filled with sons, and they have bequeathed to their little ones the remainder. ¹⁵But as for me, I will appear before your sight in justice. I will be satisfied when your glory appears.

CHAPTER 17 (18)

¹Unto the end. For David, the servant of the Lord, who spoke the words of this canticle to the Lord, in the day that the Lord delivered him from the hand of all his enemies and from the hand of Saul. And he said: ²I will love you, O Lord my strength. ³The Lord is my firmament, my refuge, and my liberator. My God is my helper, and I hope in him: my protector, and the horn of my salvation, and my support. ⁴Praising, I will call upon the Lord. And I will be saved from my enemies. ⁵The sorrows of death surrounded me, and the torrents of iniquity dismayed me. ⁶The sorrows of Hell encompassed me, and the snares of death intercepted me. ⁷In my tribulation, I called upon the Lord, and I cried out to my God. And he listened to my voice from his holy temple. And my cry in his presence entered into his ears. ⁸The earth was shaken, and it trembled. The foundations of the mountains were disturbed, and they were shaken, because he was angry with them. ⁹A smoke ascended by his wrath, and a fire flared up from his face: coals were kindled by it. ¹⁰He bent the heavens, and they descended. And darkness was under his feet. ¹¹And he ascended upon the cherubim, and he flew: he flew upon the feathers of the winds. ¹²And he set darkness as his hiding place, with his tabernacle all around him: dark waters in the clouds of the air. ¹³At the brightness that was before his sight, the clouds crossed by, with hail and coals of fire. ¹⁴And the Lord thundered from heaven, and the Most High uttered his voice: hail and coals of fire. ¹⁵And he sent forth his arrows and scattered them. He multiplied lightnings, and he set them in disarray. ¹⁶Then the fountains of waters appeared, and the foundations of the world were revealed, by your rebuke, O Lord, by the inspiration of the Spirit of your wrath. ¹⁷He sent from on high, and he accepted me. And he took me up, out of many waters. ¹⁸He rescued me from my strongest enemies, and from those who hated me. For they had been too strong for me. ¹⁹They intercepted me in the day of my

affliction, and the Lord became my protector. ²⁰ And he led me out, into a wide place. He accomplished my salvation, because he willed me. ²¹ And the Lord will reward me according to my justice, and he will repay me according to the purity of my hands. ²² For I have preserved the ways of the Lord, and I have not behaved impiously before my God. ²³ For all his judgments are in my sight, and his justice, I have not pushed away from me. ²⁴ And I will be immaculate together with him, and I will keep myself from my iniquity. ²⁵ And the Lord will reward me according to my justice and according to the purity of my hands before his eyes. ²⁶ With the holy, you will be holy, and with the innocent, you will be innocent, ²⁷ and with the elect, you will be elect, and with the perverse, you will be perverse. ²⁸ For you will save the humble people, but you will bring down the eyes of the arrogant. ²⁹ For you illuminate my lamp, O Lord. My God, enlighten my darkness. ³⁰ For in you, I will be delivered from temptation; and with my God, I will climb over a wall. ³¹ As for my God, his way is undefiled. The eloquence of the Lord has been examined by fire. He is the protector of all who hope in him. ³² For who is God, except the Lord? And who is God, except our God? ³³ It is God who has wrapped me with virtue and made my way immaculate. ³⁴ It is he who has perfected my feet, like the feet of deer, and who stations me upon the heights. ³⁵ It is he who trains my hands for battle. And you have set my arms like a bow of brass. ³⁶ And you have given me the protection of your salvation. And your right hand sustains me. And your discipline has corrected me unto the end. And your discipline itself will teach me. ³⁷ You have expanded my footsteps under me, and my tracks have not been weakened. ³⁸ I will pursue my enemies and apprehend them. And I will not turn back until they have failed. ³⁹ I will break them, and they will not be able to stand. They will fall under my feet. ⁴⁰ And you have wrapped me with virtue for the battle. And those rising up against me, you have subdued under me. ⁴¹ And you have given the back of my enemies to me, and you have destroyed those who hated me. ⁴² They cried out, but there was none to save them, to the Lord, but he did not heed them. ⁴³ And I will crush them into dust before the face of the wind, so that I will obliterate them like the mud in the streets. ⁴⁴ You will rescue me from the contradictions of the people. You will set me at the head of the Gentiles. ⁴⁵ A people I did not know has served me. As soon as their ears heard, they were obedient to me. ⁴⁶ The sons of foreigners have been deceitful to me, the sons of foreigners have grown weak with time, and they have wavered from their paths. ⁴⁷ The Lord lives, and blessed is my God, and may the God of my salvation be exalted: ⁴⁸ O God, who vindicates me and who subdues the people under me, my liberator from my enraged enemies. ⁴⁹ And you will exalt me above those who rise up against me. From the iniquitous man, you will rescue me. ⁵⁰ Because of this, O Lord, I will confess to you among the nations, and I will compose a psalm to your name: ⁵¹ magnifying the salvation of his king, and showing mercy to David, his Christ, and to his offspring, even for all time.

CHAPTER 18 (19)

¹ Unto the end. A Psalm of David. ² The heavens describe the glory of God, and the firmament announces the work of his hands. ³ Day proclaims the word to day, and night to night imparts knowledge. ⁴ There are no speeches or conversations, where their voices are not being heard. ⁵ Their sound has gone forth through all the earth, and their words to the ends of the world. ⁶ He has placed his tabernacle in the sun, and he is like a bridegroom coming out of his bedroom. He has exulted like a giant running along the way; ⁷ his departure is from the summit of heaven. And his course reaches all the way to its summit. Neither is there anyone who can hide himself from his heat. ⁸ The law of the Lord is immaculate, converting souls. The testimony of the Lord is faithful, providing wisdom to little ones. ⁹ The justice of the Lord is right, rejoicing hearts. The precepts of the Lord are brilliant, enlightening the eyes. ¹⁰ The fear of the Lord is holy, enduring for all generations. The judgments of the Lord are true, justified in themselves: ¹¹ desirable beyond gold and many precious stones, and sweeter than honey and the honeycomb. ¹² For, indeed, your servant keeps them, and in keeping them, there are many rewards. ¹³ Who can understand transgression? From my hidden faults, cleanse me, O Lord, ¹⁴ and from those of others, spare your servant. If they will have no dominion over me, then I will be immaculate, and I will be cleansed from the greatest transgression. ¹⁵ And the eloquence of my mouth will be so as to please, along with the meditation of my heart, in your sight, forever, O Lord, my helper and my redeemer.

CHAPTER 19 (20)

[1] Unto the end. A Psalm of David. [2] May the Lord hear you in the day of tribulation. May the name of the God of Jacob protect you. [3] May he send you help from the sanctuary and watch over you from Zion. [4] May he be mindful of all your sacrifices, and may your burnt-offerings be fat. [5] May he grant to you according to your heart, and confirm all your counsels. [6] We will rejoice in your salvation, and in the name of our God, we will be magnified. [7] May the Lord fulfill all your petitions. Now I know that the Lord has saved his Christ. He will hear him from his holy heaven. The salvation of his right hand is in his power. [8] Some trust in chariots, and some in horses, but we will call upon the name of the Lord our God. [9] They have been bound, and they have fallen. But we have risen up, and we have been set upright. [10] O Lord, save the king, and hear us on the day that we will call upon you.

CHAPTER 20 (21)

[1] Unto the end. A Psalm of David. [2] In your virtue, Lord, the king will rejoice, and over your salvation, he will exult exceedingly. [3] You have granted him the desire of his heart, and you have not cheated him of the wish of his lips. [4] For you have gone ahead of him with blessings of sweetness. You have placed a crown of precious stones on his head. [5] He petitioned you for life, and you have granted him length of days, in the present time, and forever and ever. [6] Great is his glory in your salvation. Glory and great adornment, you will lay upon him. [7] For you will give him as a blessing forever and ever. You will make him rejoice with gladness in your presence. [8] Because the king hopes in the Lord, and in the mercy of the Most High, he will not be disturbed. [9] May your hand be found by all your enemies. May your right hand discover all those who hate you. [10] You will make them like an oven of fire, in the time of your presence. The Lord will stir them up with his wrath, and fire will devour them. [11] You will destroy their fruit from the earth and their offspring from the sons of men. [12] For they have turned evils upon you; they have devised plans, which they have not been able to accomplish. [13] For you will make them turn their back; with your remnants, you will prepare their countenance. [14] Be exalted, Lord, by your own power. We will play music and sing psalms to your virtues.

CHAPTER 21 (22)

[1] Unto the end. For the tasks of early morning. A Psalm of David. [2] O God, my God, look upon me. Why have you forsaken me? Far from my salvation are the words of my offenses. [3] My God, I will cry out by day, and you will not heed, and by night, and it will not be foolishness for me. [4] But you dwell in holiness, O Praise of Israel. [5] In you, our fathers have hoped. They hoped, and you freed them. [6] They cried out to you, and they were saved. In you, they hoped and were not confounded. [7] But I am a worm and not a man: a disgrace among men, and an outcast of the people. [8] All those who saw me have derided me. They have spoken with the lips and shook the head. [9] He has hoped in the Lord, let him rescue him. Let him save him because he chooses him. [10] For you are the one who has drawn me out of the womb, my hope from the breasts of my mother. [11] I have been thrown upon you from the womb; from the womb of my mother, you are my God. [12] Do not depart from me. For tribulation is near, since there is no one who may help me. [13] Many calves have surrounded me; fat bulls have besieged me. [14] They have opened their mouths over me, just like a lion seizing and roaring. [15] And so, I have been poured out like water, and all my bones have been scattered. My heart has become like wax, melting in the midst of my chest. [16] My strength has dried up like clay, and my tongue has adhered to my jaws. And you have pulled me down, into the dust of death. [17] For many dogs have surrounded me. The council of the malicious has besieged me. They have pierced my hands and feet. [18] They have numbered all my bones. And they have examined me and stared at me. [19] They divided my garments among them, and over my vestment, they cast lots. [20] But you, O Lord, do not take your help far from me; be attentive to my defense. [21] O God, rescue my soul from the spear, and my only one from the hand of the dog. [22] Save me from the mouth of the lion, and my humility from the horns of the single-horned beast. [23] I will declare your name to my brothers. In the midst of the Church, I will praise you. [24] You who fear the Lord, praise him. All the offspring of Jacob, glorify him. [25] May all the offspring of Israel fear him. For he has neither spurned nor despised the pleas of the poor.

Neither has he turned his face away from me. And when I cried out to him, he heeded me. [26] My praise is with you, within a great church. I will pay my vows in the sight of those who fear him. [27] The poor will eat and be satisfied, and those who yearn for the Lord will praise him. Their hearts will live forever and ever. [28] All the ends of the earth will remember, and they will be converted to the Lord. And all the families of the Gentiles will adore in his sight. [29] For the kingdom belongs to the Lord, and he will have dominion over the Gentiles. [30] All the fat of the earth have gnashed their teeth, and they have adored. In his sight, they will fall down, all those who descend to the ground. [31] And my soul will live for him, and my offspring will serve him. [32] There will be announced for the Lord a future generation, and the heavens will announce his justice to a people who will be born, whom the Lord has made.

CHAPTER 22 (23)

[1] A Psalm of David. The Lord directs me, and nothing will be lacking to me. [2] He has settled me here, in a place of pasture. He has led me out to the water of refreshment. [3] He has converted my soul. He has led me away on the paths of justice, for the sake of his name. [4] For, even if I should walk in the midst of the shadow of death, I will fear no evils. For you are with me. Your rod and your staff, they have given me consolation. [5] You have prepared a table in my sight, opposite those who trouble me. You have anointed my head with oil, and my cup, which inebriates me, how brilliant it is! [6] And your mercy will follow me all the days of my life, and so may I dwell in the house of the Lord for length of days.

CHAPTER 23 (24)

[1] For the First Sabbath. A Psalm of David. The earth and all its fullness belong to the Lord: the whole world and all that dwells in it. [2] For he has founded it upon the seas, and he has prepared it upon the rivers. [3] Who will ascend to the mountain of the Lord? And who will stand in his holy place? [4] The innocent of hands and the clean of heart, who has not received his soul in vain, nor sworn deceitfully to his neighbor. [5] He will receive a blessing from the Lord, and mercy from God, his Savior. [6] This is the generation that seeks him, that seeks the face of the God of Jacob. [7] Lift up your gates, you princes, and be lifted up, eternal gates. And the King of Glory shall enter. [8] Who is this King of Glory? The Lord who is strong and powerful; the Lord powerful in battle. [9] Lift up your gates, you princes, and be lifted up, eternal gates. And the King of Glory shall enter. [10] Who is this King of Glory? The Lord of virtue. He himself is the King of Glory.

CHAPTER 24 (25)

[1] Unto the end. A Psalm of David. To you, Lord, I have lifted up my soul. [2] In you, my God, I trust. Let me not be put to shame. [3] And do not let my enemies laugh at me. For all who remain with you will not be confounded. [4] May all those who act unjustly over nothing be confounded. O Lord, demonstrate your ways to me, and teach me your paths. [5] Direct me in your truth, and teach me. For you are God, my Savior, and I remain with you all day long. [6] O Lord, remember your compassion and your mercies, which are from ages past. [7] Do not remember the offenses of my youth and my ignorances. Remember me according to your mercy, because of your goodness, O Lord. [8] The Lord is sweet and righteous. Because of this, he will grant a law to those who fall short in the way. [9] He will direct the mild in judgment. He will teach the meek his ways. [10] All the ways of the Lord are mercy and truth, to those who yearn for his covenant and his testimonies. [11] Because of your name, O Lord, you will pardon my sin, for it is great. [12] Which is the man who fears the Lord? He has established a law for him, on the way that he has chosen. [13] His soul will dwell upon good things, and his offspring will inherit the earth. [14] The Lord is a firmament to those who fear him, and his covenant will be made manifest to them. [15] My eyes are ever toward the Lord, for he will pull my feet from the snare. [16] Look upon me and have mercy on me; for I am alone and poor. [17] The troubles of my heart have been multiplied. Deliver me from my needfulness. [18] See my lowliness and my hardship, and release all my offenses. [19] Consider my enemies, for they have been multiplied, and they have hated me with an unjust hatred. [20] Preserve my soul and rescue me. I will not be ashamed, for I have hoped in you. [21] The innocent and the righteous have adhered to me, because I have remained with you. [22] Free Israel, O God, from all his tribulations.

CHAPTER 25 (26)

[1] Unto the end. A Psalm of David. Judge me, Lord, for I have been walking in my innocence, and by hoping in the Lord, I will not be weakened. [2] Examine me, Lord, and test me: enkindle my temperament and my heart. [3] For your mercy is before my eyes, and I am serene in your truth. [4] I have not sat with the council of emptiness, and I will not enter with those who carry out injustice. [5] I have hated the assembly of the malicious; and I will not sit with the impious. [6] I will wash my hands among the innocent, and I will surround your altar, O Lord, [7] so that I may hear the voice of your praise and describe all your wonders. [8] O Lord, I have loved the beauty of your house and the dwelling place of your glory. [9] O God, do not let my soul perish with the impious, nor my life with the men of blood, [10] in whose hands are iniquities: their right hand has been filled by bribes. [11] But as for me, I have been walking in my innocence. Redeem me, and have mercy on me. [12] My foot has stood firm in the straight path. In the churches, I will bless you, O Lord.

CHAPTER 26 (27)

[1] A Psalm of David, before he was sealed. The Lord is my light and my salvation, whom shall I fear? The Lord is the protector of my life, of whom shall I be afraid? [2] Meanwhile, the guilty draw near to me, so as to eat my flesh. Those who trouble me, my enemies, have themselves been weakened and have fallen. [3] If entrenched armies were to stand together against me, my heart would not fear. If a battle were to rise up against me, I would have hope in this. [4] One thing I have asked of the Lord, this I will seek: that I may dwell in the house of the Lord all the days of my life, so that I may behold the delight of the Lord, and may visit his temple. [5] For he has hidden me in his tabernacle. In the day of evils, he has protected me in the hidden place of his tabernacle. [6] He has exalted me upon the rock, and now he has exalted my head above my enemies. I have circled around and offered a sacrifice of loud exclamation in his tabernacle. I will sing, and I will compose a psalm, to the Lord. [7] Hear my voice, O Lord, with which I have cried out to you. Have mercy on me, and hear me. [8] My heart has spoken to you; my face has sought you. I yearn for your face, O Lord. [9] Do not turn your face away from me. In your wrath, do not turn aside from your servant. Be my helper. Do not abandon me, and do not despise me, O God, my Savior. [10] For my father and my mother have left me behind, but the Lord has taken me up. [11] O Lord, establish a law for me in your way, and direct me in the right path, because of my enemies. [12] Do not surrender me to the souls of those who trouble me. For unjust witnesses have risen up against me, and iniquity has lied to itself. [13] I believe that I shall see the good things of the Lord in the land of the living. [14] Wait for the Lord, act manfully; and let your heart be strengthened, and remain with the Lord.

CHAPTER 27 (28)

[1] A Psalm of David himself. To you, Lord, I will cry out. My God, do not be silent toward me. For if you remain silent toward me, I will become like those who descend into the pit. [2] Hear, O Lord, the voice of my supplication, when I pray to you, when I lift up my hands toward your holy temple. [3] Do not draw me away together with sinners; and let me not perish with those who work iniquity, who speak peacefully to their neighbor, yet evils are in their hearts. [4] Give to them according to their works and according to the wickedness of their inventions. Assign to them according to the works of their hands. Repay them with their own retribution. [5] Since they have not understood the works of the Lord and the works of his hands, you will destroy them, and you will not build them up. [6] Blessed is the Lord, for he has heard the voice of my supplication. [7] The Lord is my helper and my protector. In him, my heart has hoped and I have been helped. And my flesh has flourished again. And from my will, I shall confess to him. [8] The Lord is the strength of his people and the protector of the salvation of his Christ. [9] O Lord, save your people and bless your inheritance, and reign over them and exalt them, even unto eternity.

CHAPTER 28 (29)

[1] A Psalm of David, at the completion of the tabernacle. Bring to the Lord, O sons of God, bring to the Lord the sons of rams. [2] Bring to the Lord, glory and honor. Bring to the Lord, glory for his name. Adore the Lord in his holy court. [3] The voice of the Lord is over the waters. The God of majesty has thundered. The Lord is over many waters. [4] The voice of the Lord is in virtue. The voice of the

Lord is in magnificence. ⁵The voice of the Lord shatters the cedars. And the Lord will shatter the cedars of Lebanon. ⁶And it will break them into pieces, like a calf of Lebanon, and in the same way as the beloved son of the single-horned beast. ⁷The voice of the Lord cuts through the flame of fire. ⁸The voice of the Lord shakes the desert. And the Lord will quake the desert of Kadesh. ⁹The voice of the Lord is preparing the stags, and he will reveal the dense woods. And in his temple, all will speak his glory. ¹⁰The Lord causes the great flood to dwell. And the Lord will sit as King in eternity. ¹¹The Lord will give virtue to his people. The Lord will bless his people in peace.

CHAPTER 29 (30)

¹A Canticle Psalm. In dedication to the house of David. ²I will extol you, Lord, for you have sustained me, and you have not allowed my enemies to delight over me. ³O Lord my God, I have cried out to you, and you have healed me. ⁴Lord, you led my soul away from Hell. You have saved me from those who descend into the pit. ⁵Sing a psalm to the Lord, you his saints, and confess with remembrance of his holiness. ⁶For wrath is in his indignation, and life is in his will. Toward evening, weeping will linger, and toward morning, gladness. ⁷But I have said in my abundance: "I will never be disturbed." ⁸O Lord, in your will, you made virtue preferable to beauty for me. You turned your face away from me, and I became disturbed. ⁹To you, Lord, I will cry out. And I will make supplication to my God. ¹⁰What use would there be in my blood, if I descend into corruption? Will dust confess to you or announce your truth? ¹¹The Lord has heard, and he has been merciful to me. The Lord has become my helper. ¹²You have turned my mourning into gladness for me. You have cut off my sackcloth, and you have surrounded me with joy. ¹³So then, may my glory sing to you, and may I not regret it. O Lord, my God, I will confess to you for eternity.

CHAPTER 30 (31)

¹Unto the end. A Psalm of David according to an ecstasy. ²In you, Lord, I have hoped; let me never be confounded. In your justice, deliver me. ³Incline your ear to me. Hasten to rescue me. Be for me a protector God and a house of refuge, so as to accomplish my salvation. ⁴For you are my strength and my refuge; and for the sake of your name, you will lead me and nourish me. ⁵You will lead me out of this snare, which they have hidden for me. For you are my protector. ⁶Into your hands, I commend my spirit. You have redeemed me, O Lord, God of truth. ⁷You have hated those who practice emptiness to no purpose. But I have hoped in the Lord. ⁸I will exult and rejoice in your mercy. For you have looked upon my humility; you have saved my soul from needfulness. ⁹And you have not enclosed me in the hands of the enemy. You have set my feet in a spacious place. ¹⁰Have mercy on me, Lord, for I am troubled. My eye has been disturbed by wrath, along with my soul and my gut. ¹¹For my life has fallen into sorrow, and my years into sighing. My virtue has been weakened in poverty, and my bones have been disturbed. ¹²I have become a disgrace among all my enemies, and even more so to my neighbors, and a dread to my acquaintances. Those who catch sight of me, flee away from me. ¹³I have become forgotten, like one dead to the heart. I have become like a damaged utensil. ¹⁴For I have heard the harsh criticism of many who linger in the area. While assembled together against me in that place, they deliberated on how to take away my life. ¹⁵But I have hoped in you, O Lord. I said, "You are my God." ¹⁶My fate is in your hands. Rescue me from the hand of my enemies and from those who are persecuting me. ¹⁷Shine your face upon your servant. Save me in your mercy. ¹⁸Do not let me be confounded, Lord, for I have called upon you. Let the impious be ashamed and be drawn down into Hell. ¹⁹May deceitful lips be silenced: those that speak iniquity against the just, in arrogance and in abusiveness. ²⁰How great is the multitude of your sweetness, O Lord, which you keep hidden for those who fear you, which you have perfected for those who hope in you, in the sight of the sons of men. ²¹You hide them in the concealment of your face, from the disturbance of men. You protect them in your tabernacle, from the contradiction of tongues. ²²Blessed is the Lord. For he has shown his wonderful mercy to me, in a fortified city. ²³But I said in the excess of my mind: "I have been cast away from the glance of your eyes." And so, you heeded the voice of my prayer, while I was still crying out to you. ²⁴Love the Lord, all you his saints. For the Lord will require truth, and he will abundantly repay those who act with arrogance. ²⁵Act manfully, and let your heart be strengthened, all you who hope in the Lord.

CHAPTER 31 (32)

[1] The understanding of David himself. Blessed are they whose iniquities have been forgiven and whose sins have been covered. [2] Blessed is the man to whom the Lord has not imputed sin, and in whose spirit there is no deceit. [3] Because I was silent, my bones grew old, while still I cried out all day long. [4] For, day and night, your hand was heavy upon me. I have been converted in my anguish, while still the thorn is piercing. [5] I have acknowledged my offense to you, and I have not concealed my injustice. I said, "I will confess against myself, my injustice to the Lord," and you forgave the impiety of my sin. [6] For this, everyone who is holy will pray to you in due time. Yet truly, in a flood of many waters, they will not draw near to him. [7] You are my refuge from the tribulation that has surrounded me. You are my exultation: rescue me from those who are surrounding me. [8] I will give you understanding, and I will instruct you in this way, in which you will walk. I will fix my eyes upon you. [9] Do not become like the horse and the mule, which have no understanding. Their jaws are constrained with bit and bridle, so as not to draw near to you. [10] Many are the scourges of the sinner, but mercy will surround him that hopes in the Lord. [11] Rejoice in the Lord and exult, you just ones, and glory, all you upright of heart.

CHAPTER 32 (33)

[1] A Psalm of David. Exult in the Lord, you just ones; together praise the upright. [2] Confess to the Lord with stringed instruments; sing psalms to him with the psaltery, the instrument of ten strings. [3] Sing to him a new song. Sing psalms to him skillfully, with loud exclamation. [4] For the word of the Lord is upright, and all his works are in faith. [5] He loves mercy and judgment. The earth is full of the mercy of the Lord. [6] By the word of the Lord, the heavens were established, and all their power, by the Spirit of his mouth: [7] gathering together the waters of the sea, as if in a container, placing the depths in storage. [8] Let all the earth fear the Lord, and may all the inhabitants of the world quake before him. [9] For he spoke, and they became. He commanded, and they were created. [10] The Lord scatters the counsels of the nations. Moreover, he reproves the thoughts of the people, and he rejects the counsels of the leaders. [11] But the counsel of the Lord remains for eternity, the thoughts of his heart from generation to generation. [12] Blessed is the nation whose God is the Lord, the people whom he has chosen as his inheritance. [13] The Lord has looked down from heaven. He has seen all the sons of men. [14] From his well-prepared dwelling place, he has gazed upon all who dwell on the earth. [15] He has formed the hearts of each one of them; he understands all their works. [16] The king is not saved by great power, nor will the giant be saved by his many powers. [17] The horse is false safety; for he will not be saved by the abundance of his powers. [18] Behold, the eyes of the Lord are on those who fear him and on those who hope in his mercy, [19] so as to rescue their souls from death and to feed them during famine. [20] Our soul remains with the Lord. For he is our helper and protector. [21] For in him, our heart will rejoice, and in his holy name, we have hoped. [22] Let your mercy be upon us, O Lord, just as we have hoped in you.

CHAPTER 33 (34)

[1] To David, when he changed his appearance in the sight of Abimelech, and so he dismissed him, and he went away. [2] I will bless the Lord at all times. His praise will be ever in my mouth. [3] In the Lord, my soul will be praised. May the meek listen and rejoice. [4] Magnify the Lord with me, and let us extol his name in itself. [5] I sought the Lord, and he heeded me, and he carried me away from all my tribulations. [6] Approach him and be enlightened, and your faces will not be confounded. [7] This poor one cried out, and the Lord heeded him, and he saved him from all his tribulations. [8] The Angel of the Lord will encamp around those who fear him, and he will rescue them. [9] Taste and see that the Lord is sweet. Blessed is the man who hopes in him. [10] Fear the Lord, all you his saints. For there is no destitution for those who fear him. [11] The rich have been needy and hungry, but those who seek the Lord will not be deprived of any good thing. [12] Come forward, sons. Listen to me. I will teach you the fear of the Lord. [13] Which is the man who wills life, who chooses to see good days? [14] Prohibit your tongue from evil and your lips from speaking deceit. [15] Turn away from evil, and do good. Inquire about peace, and pursue it. [16] The eyes of the Lord are on the just, and his ears are with their prayers. [17] But the countenance of the Lord is upon those who do evil, to perish the remembrance of them from the earth.

[18]The just cried out, and the Lord heard them, and he freed them from all their tribulations. [19]The Lord is near to those who are troubled in heart, and he will save the humble in spirit. [20]Many are the afflictions of the just, but from them all the Lord will free them. [21]The Lord preserves all of their bones, not one of them shall be broken. [22]The death of a sinner is very harmful, and those who hate the just will fare badly. [23]The Lord will redeem the souls of his servants, and none of those who hope in him will fare badly.

CHAPTER 34 (35)

[1]Of David himself. O Lord, judge those who harm me; assail those who attack me. [2]Take hold of weapons and a shield, and rise up in assistance to me. [3]Bring forth the spear, and close in on those who persecute me. Say to my soul, "I am your salvation." [4]Let them be confounded and in awe, who pursue my soul. Let them be turned back and be confounded, who think up evil against me. [5]May they become like dust before the face of the wind, and let the Angel of the Lord hem them in. [6]May their way become dark and slippery, and may the Angel of the Lord pursue them. [7]For, without cause, they have concealed their snare for me unto destruction. Over nothing, they have rebuked my soul. [8]Let the snare, of which he is ignorant, come upon him, and let the deception, which he has hidden, take hold of him: and may he fall into that very snare. [9]But my soul will exult in the Lord and delight over his salvation. [10]All my bones will say, "Lord, who is like you?" He rescues the needy from the hand of the stronger one, the indigent and the poor from those who plunder him. [11]Unfair witnesses have risen up, interrogating me about things of which I am ignorant. [12]They repaid me evil for good, to the deprivation of my soul. [13]But as for me, when they were harassing me, I was clothed with haircloth. I humbled my soul with fasting, and my prayer will become my sinews. [14]Like a neighbor, and like our brother, so did I please; like one mourning and contrite, so was I humbled. [15]And they have been joyful against me, and they joined together. Scourges have been gathered over me, and I was ignorant of it. [16]They have been scattered, yet they were unremorseful. They have tested me. They scoffed at me with scorn. They gnashed their teeth over me. [17]Lord, when will you look down upon me? Restore my soul from before their malice, my only one from before the lions. [18]I will confess to you in a great Church. I will praise you among a weighty people. [19]May those who are my unjust adversaries not be glad over me: those who have hated me without cause, and who nod agreement with their eyes. [20]For indeed, they spoke peacefully to me; and speaking with passion to the earth, they intended deceit. [21]And they opened their mouth wide over me. They said, "Well, well, our eyes have seen." [22]You have seen, O Lord, do not be silent. Lord, do not depart from me. [23]Rise up and be attentive to my judgment, to my cause, my God and my Lord. [24]Judge me according to your justice, O Lord, my God, and do not let them be glad over me. [25]Do not let them say in their hearts, "Well, well, to our soul." Neither let them say, "We have devoured him." [26]Let them blush and be in awe together, those who congratulate at my misfortunes. Let them be clothed with confusion and awe, who speak great things against me. [27]Let them exult and rejoice, who wish my justice, and let them ever say, "The Lord be magnified," who will the peace of his servant. [28]And so my tongue will express your justice: your praise all day long.

CHAPTER 35 (36)

[1]Unto the end. To the servant of the Lord, David himself. [2]The unjust one has said within himself that he would commit offenses. There is no fear of God before his eyes. [3]For he has acted deceitfully in his sight, such that his iniquity will be found to be hatred. [4]The words of his mouth are iniquity and deceit. He is unwilling to understand, so that he may act well. [5]He has been considering iniquity on his bed. He has set himself on every way that is not good; moreover, he has not hated evil. [6]Lord, your mercy is in heaven, and your truth is even to the clouds. [7]Your justice is like the mountains of God. Your judgments are a great abyss. Men and beasts, you will save, O Lord. [8]How you have multiplied your mercy, O God! And so the sons of men will hope under the cover of your wings. [9]They will be inebriated with the fruitfulness of your house, and you will give them to drink from the torrent of your enjoyment. [10]For with you is the fountain of life; and within your light, we will see the light. [11]Extend your mercy before those who know you, and your justice to these, who are upright in heart. [12]May arrogant feet not approach me, and may the hand of the sinner not disturb me.

¹³In that place, those who work iniquity have fallen. They have been expelled; they were not able to stand.

CHAPTER 36 (37)

¹A Psalm of David himself. Do not choose to imitate the malicious; neither should you envy those who work iniquity. ²For they will quickly wither away like dry grass, and in like manner to kitchen herbs, they will soon droop. ³Hope in the Lord and do good, and dwell in the land, and so you shall be pastured with its riches. ⁴Delight in the Lord, and he will grant to you the petitions of your heart. ⁵Reveal your way to the Lord, and hope in him, and he will accomplish it. ⁶And he will bring forth your justice like the light, and your judgment like the midday. ⁷Be subject to the Lord and pray to him. Do not choose to compete with him who prospers in his way, with the man who does injustice. ⁸Cease from wrath and leave behind rage. Do not choose to imitate the malicious. ⁹For those who are malicious will be exterminated. But those who remain with the Lord, these will inherit the land. ¹⁰Yet still a little while, and the sinner will not be. And you will search his place and find nothing. ¹¹But the meek shall inherit the earth, and they will delight in the multitude of peace. ¹²The sinner will observe the just, and he will gnash his teeth over him. ¹³But the Lord will laugh at him: for he knows in advance that his day will come. ¹⁴The sinners have drawn the sword, they have bent their bow, so as to cast down the poor and the needy, so as to massacre the upright of heart. ¹⁵Let their sword enter into their own hearts, and let their bow be broken. ¹⁶A little is better to the just than the many riches of sinners. ¹⁷For the arms of sinners will be crushed, but the Lord confirms the just. ¹⁸The Lord knows the days of the immaculate, and their inheritance will be in eternity. ¹⁹They will not be confounded in an evil time; and in days of famine, they will be satisfied: ²⁰for sinners will perish. Truly, the adversaries of the Lord, soon after they have been honored and exalted, will fade away, in the same way that smoke fades away. ²¹The sinner will lend and not release, but the just one shows compassion and donates. ²²For those who bless him will inherit the earth, but those who curse him will perish. ²³The steps of a man will be directed by the Lord, and he will choose his way. ²⁴When he falls, he will not be harmed, because the Lord places his hand under him. ²⁵I have been young, and now I am old; and I have not seen the just forsaken, nor his offspring seeking bread. ²⁶He shows compassion and lends, all day long, and his offspring will be in blessing. ²⁷Turn away from evil and do good, and dwell forever and ever. ²⁸For the Lord loves judgment, and he will not abandon his saints. They will be kept safe in eternity. The unjust will be punished, and the offspring of the impious will perish. ²⁹But the just will inherit the earth, and they will dwell upon it forever and ever. ³⁰The mouth of the just one will express wisdom, and his tongue will speak judgment. ³¹The law of his God is in his heart, and his steps shall not be supplanted. ³²The sinner considers the just one and seeks to put him to death. ³³But the Lord will not abandon him into his hands, nor condemn him, when he will be judged. ³⁴Wait for the Lord, and keep to his way. And he will exalt you, so as to inherit the land that you may seize. When the sinners will have passed away, then you shall see. ³⁵I have seen the impious over-exalted, and lifted up like the cedars of Lebanon. ³⁶And I passed by, and behold, he was not. And I sought him, and his place was not found. ³⁷Keep to innocence, and gaze upon fairness: because there are allotments for the peaceful man. ³⁸But the unjust will be destroyed together: the allotments of the impious will pass away. ³⁹But the salvation of the just is from the Lord, and he is their protector in time of tribulation. ⁴⁰And the Lord will help them and free them. And he will rescue them from sinners and save them, because they have hoped in him.

CHAPTER 37 (38)

¹A Psalm of David, in commemoration of the Sabbath. ²O Lord, do not rebuke me in your fury, nor chastise me in your wrath. ³For your arrows have been driven into me, and your hand has been confirmed over me. ⁴There is no health in my flesh before the face of your wrath. There is no peace for my bones before the face of my sins. ⁵For my iniquities have walked over my head, and they have been like a heavy burden weighing upon me. ⁶My sores have putrefied and been corrupted before the face of my foolishness. ⁷I have become miserable, and I have been bent down, even to the end. I have walked with contrition all day long. ⁸For my loins have been filled with illusions, and there is no health in my flesh. ⁹I have been afflicted and greatly humbled. I bellowed from the groaning of my heart.

[10] O Lord, all my desire is before you, and my groaning before you has not been hidden. [11] My heart has been disturbed. My strength has abandoned me, and the light of my eyes has abandoned me, and it is not with me. [12] My friends and my neighbors have drawn near and stood against me. And those who were next to me stood far apart. And those who sought my soul used violence. [13] And those who sought evil accusations against me were speaking emptiness. And they practiced deceitfulness all day long. [14] But, like someone deaf, I did not hear. And I was like someone mute, not opening his mouth. [15] And I became like a man who does not hear, and who has no reproofs in his mouth. [16] For in you, Lord, I have hoped. You will listen to me, O Lord my God. [17] For I said, "Lest at any time, my enemies might rejoice over me," and, "While my feet are being shaken, they have spoken great things against me." [18] For I have been prepared for scourges, and my sorrow is ever before me. [19] For I will announce my iniquity, and I will think about my sin. [20] But my enemies live, and they have been stronger than me. And those who have wrongfully hated me have been multiplied. [21] Those who render evil for good have dragged me down, because I followed goodness. [22] Do not forsake me, O Lord my God. Do not depart from me. [23] Be attentive to my help, O Lord, the God of my salvation.

CHAPTER 38 (39)

[1] Unto the end. For Jeduthun himself. A Canticle of David. [2] I said, "I will keep to my ways, so that I will not offend with my tongue." I posted a guard at my mouth, when a sinner took up a position against me. [3] I was silenced and humbled, and I was quiet before good things, and my sorrow was renewed. [4] My heart grew hot within me, and, during my meditation, a fire would flare up. [5] I spoke with my tongue, "O Lord, make me know my end, and what the number of my days will be, so that I may know what is lacking to me." [6] Behold, you have made my days measurable, and, before you, my substance is as nothing. Yet truly, all things are vanity: every living man. [7] So then, truly man passes by like an image; even so, he is disquieted in vain. He stores up, and he knows not for whom he will gather these things. [8] And now, what is it that awaits me? Is it not the Lord? And my substance is with you. [9] Rescue me from all my iniquities. You have handed me over as a reproach to the foolish. [10] I was silenced, and I did not open my mouth, because it was you who acted. [11] Remove your scourges from me. [12] I fall short at corrections from the strength of your hand. For you have chastised man for iniquity. And you have made his soul shrink away like a spider. Nevertheless, it is in vain that any man be disquieted. [13] O Lord, heed my prayer and my supplication. Pay attention to my tears. Do not be silent. For I am a newcomer with you, and a sojourner, just as all my fathers were. [14] Forgive me, so that I may be refreshed, before I will go forth and be no more.

CHAPTER 39 (40)

[1] Unto the end. A Psalm of David himself. [2] I have waited expectantly for the Lord, and he was attentive to me. [3] And he heard my prayers and he led me out of the pit of misery and the quagmire. And he stationed my feet upon a rock, and he directed my steps. [4] And he sent a new canticle into my mouth, a song to our God. Many will see, and they will fear; and they will hope in the Lord. [5] Blessed is the man whose hope is in the name of the Lord, and who has no respect for vanities and absurd falsehoods. [6] You have accomplished your many wonders, O Lord my God, and there is no one similar to you in your thoughts. I have announced and I have spoken: they are multiplied beyond number. [7] Sacrifice and oblation, you did not want. But you have perfected ears for me. Holocaust and sin offering, you did not require. [8] Then I said, "Behold, I draw near." At the head of the book, it has been written of me: [9] that I should do your will. My God, I have willed it. And your law is in the midst of my heart. [10] I have announced your justice in a great Church: behold, I will not restrain my lips. O Lord, you have known it. [11] I have not concealed your justice within my heart. I have spoken your truth and your salvation. I have not concealed your mercy and your truth from a great assembly. [12] O Lord, do not take your tender mercies far from me. Your mercy and your truth ever sustain me. [13] For evils without number have surrounded me. My iniquities have taken hold of me, and I was not able to see. They have been multiplied beyond the hairs of my head. And my heart has forsaken me. [14] Be pleased, O Lord, to rescue me. Look down, O Lord, to help me. [15] Let them together be confounded and awed, who seek after my soul to steal it away. Let them be turned back and be in awe, who wish evils upon me.

¹⁶Let them bear their confusion all at once, who say to me, "Well, well." ¹⁷Let all who seek you exult and rejoice over you. And let those who love your salvation always say, "May the Lord be magnified." ¹⁸But I am a beggar and poor. The Lord has been concerned about me. You are my helper and my protector. My God, do not delay.

CHAPTER 40 (41)

¹Unto the end. A Psalm of David himself. ²Blessed is he who shows understanding toward the needy and the poor. The Lord will deliver him in the evil day. ³May the Lord preserve him and give him life, and make him blessed upon the earth. And may he not hand him over to the will of his adversaries. ⁴May the Lord bring him help on his bed of sorrow. In his infirmity, you have changed his entire covering. ⁵I said, "O Lord, be merciful to me. Heal my soul, because I have sinned against you." ⁶My enemies have spoken evils against me. When will he die and his name perish? ⁷And when he came in to see me, he was speaking emptiness. His heart gathered iniquity to itself. He went outside, and he was speaking in the same way. ⁸All my enemies were whispering against me. They were thinking up evils against me. ⁹They established an unjust word against me. Will he that sleeps no longer rise again? ¹⁰For even the man of my peace, in whom I hoped, who ate my bread, has greatly supplanted me. ¹¹But you, O Lord, have mercy on me, and raise me up again. And I will requite them. ¹²By this, I knew that you preferred me: because my adversary will not rejoice over me. ¹³But you have sustained me, because of my innocence, and you have confirmed me in your sight in eternity. ¹⁴Blessed is the Lord God of Israel, for all generations and even forever. Amen. Amen.

CHAPTER 41 (42)

¹Unto the end. The understanding of the sons of Korah. ²As the deer longs for fountains of water, so my soul longs for you, O God. ³My soul has thirsted for the strong living God. When will I draw close and appear before the face of God? ⁴My tears have been my bread, day and night. Meanwhile, it is said to me daily: "Where is your God?" ⁵These things I have remembered; and my soul within me, I have poured out. For I will cross into the place of the wonderful tabernacle, all the way to the house of God, with a voice of exultation and confession, the sound of feasting. ⁶Why are you sad, my soul? And why do you disquiet me? Hope in God, for I will still confess to him: the salvation of my countenance, ⁷and my God. My soul has been troubled within myself. Because of this, I will remember you from the land of the Jordan and from Hermon, from the little mountain. ⁸Abyss calls upon abyss, with the voice of your floodgate. All your heights and your waves have passed over me. ⁹In the daylight, the Lord has ordered his mercy; and in the night, a canticle to him. With me is a prayer to the God of my life. ¹⁰I will say to God, "You are my supporter. Why have you forgotten me? And why do I walk in mourning, while my adversary afflicts me?" ¹¹While my bones are being broken, my enemies, who trouble me, have reproached me. Meanwhile, they say to me every single day, "Where is your God?" ¹²My soul, why are you saddened? And why do you disquiet me? Hope in God, for I will still confess to him: the salvation of my countenance and my God.

CHAPTER 42 (43)

¹A Psalm of David. Judge me, O God, and discern my cause from that of a nation not holy; rescue me from a man unjust and deceitful. ²For you are God, my strength. Why have you rejected me? And why do I walk in sadness, while the adversary afflicts me? ³Send forth your light and your truth. They have guided me and led me, to your holy mountain and into your tabernacles. ⁴And I will enter, up to the altar of God, to God who enlivens my youthfulness. To you, O God, my God, I will confess upon a stringed instrument. ⁵Why are you sad, my soul? And why do you disquiet me? Hope in God, for I will still give praise to him: the salvation of my countenance and my God.

CHAPTER 43 (44)

¹Unto the end. To the sons of Korah, toward understanding. ²We have heard, O God, with our own ears. Our fathers have announced to us the work that you wrought in their days and in the days of antiquity. ³Your hand dispersed the Gentiles, and you transplanted them. You afflicted a people, and you expelled

them. ⁴ For they did not take possession of the land by their sword, and their own arm did not save them. But your right hand and your arm, and the light of your countenance did so, because you were pleased with them. ⁵ You yourself are my king and my God, who commands the salvation of Jacob. ⁶ With you, we will brandish a horn before our enemies; and in your name, we will spurn those rising up against us. ⁷ For I will not hope in my bow, and my sword will not save me. ⁸ For you have saved us from those who afflict us, and you have bewildered those who hate us. ⁹ In God, we will give praise all day long; and in your name, we will confess forever. ¹⁰ But now, you have rejected and bewildered us, and you will not go forth with our armies, O God. ¹¹ You have turned our back to our enemies, and those who hated us have plundered for themselves. ¹² You have given us over like sheep for food. You have scattered us among the Gentiles. ¹³ You have sold your people without a price, and no great number was exchanged for them. ¹⁴ You have set us as a disgrace to our neighbors, a scoff and a derision to those who are around us. ¹⁵ You have set us as a parable among the Gentiles, a shaking of the head among the peoples. ¹⁶ All day long my shame is before me, and the confusion of my face has covered me, ¹⁷ before the voice of the reproacher and the commentator, before the face of the adversary and the pursuer. ¹⁸ All these things have come upon us, yet we have not forgotten you, and we have not acted unjustly in your covenant. ¹⁹ And our heart has not turned back. And you have not diverted our steps from your way. ²⁰ For you humbled us in a place of affliction, and the shadow of death has covered us. ²¹ If we have forgotten the name of our God, and if we have extended our hands to a foreign god, ²² will not God find this out? For he knows the secrets of the heart. For, because of you, we are being killed all day long. We are considered as sheep for the slaughter. ²³ Rise up. Why do you fall asleep, O Lord? Rise up, and do not reject us in the end. ²⁴ Why do you turn your face away, and why do you forget our needfulness and our tribulation? ²⁵ For our soul has been humbled into the dust. Our belly has been bound to the earth. ²⁶ Rise up, O Lord. Help us and redeem us, because of your name.

CHAPTER 44 (45)

¹ Unto the end. For those who will be changed. To the sons of Korah, toward understanding. A Canticle for the Beloved. ² My heart has uttered a good word. I speak of my works to the king. My tongue is like the pen of a scribe who writes quickly. ³ You are a brilliant form before the sons of men. Grace has been poured freely into your lips. Because of this, God has blessed you in eternity. ⁴ Fasten your sword to your thigh, O most powerful one. ⁵ With your splendor and your excellence extended, proceed prosperously, and reign for the sake of truth and meekness and justice, and so will your right hand lead you wondrously. ⁶ Your arrows are sharp; the people will fall under you, with the hearts of the enemies of the king. ⁷ Your throne, O God, is forever and ever. The scepter of your kingdom is a scepter of true aim. ⁸ You have loved justice and hated iniquity. Because of this, God, your God, has anointed you, before your co-heirs, with the oil of gladness. ⁹ Myrrh and balsam and cinnamon perfume your garments, from the houses of ivory. From these, they have delighted you: ¹⁰ the daughters of kings in your honor. The queen assisted at your right hand, in clothing of gold, encircled with diversity. ¹¹ Listen, daughter, and see, and incline your ear. And forget your people and your father's house. ¹² And the king will desire your beauty. For he is the Lord your God, and they will adore him. ¹³ And the daughters of Tyre will entreat your countenance with gifts: all the rich men of the people. ¹⁴ All the glory of the daughter of its king is inside, in golden fringes, ¹⁵ clothed all around with diversities. After her, virgins will be led to the king. Her neighbors will be brought to you. ¹⁶ They will be brought with gladness and exultation. They will be led into the temple of the king. ¹⁷ For your fathers, sons have been born to you. You will establish them as leaders over all the earth. ¹⁸ They will remember your name always, for generation after generation. Because of this, people will confess to you in eternity, even forever and ever.

CHAPTER 45 (46)

¹ Unto the end. To the sons of Korah, for confidants. A Psalm. ² Our God is our refuge and strength, a helper in the tribulations that have greatly overwhelmed us. ³ Because of this, we will not be afraid when the earth will be turbulent and the mountains will be transferred into the heart of the sea. ⁴ They thundered, and the waters were stirred up among them; the mountains have been disturbed by his strength. ⁵ The frenzy of the river rejoices the city of God. The Most High has

sanctified his tabernacle. [6] God is in its midst; it will not be shaken. God will assist it in the early morning. [7] The peoples have been disturbed, and the kingdoms have been bowed down. He uttered his voice: the earth has been moved. [8] The Lord of hosts is with us. The God of Jacob is our supporter. [9] Draw near and behold the works of the Lord: what portents he has set upon the earth, [10] carrying away wars even to the end of the earth. He will crush the bow and break the weapons, and he will burn the shield with fire. [11] Be empty, and see that I am God. I will be exalted among the peoples, and I will be exalted upon the earth. [12] The Lord of hosts is with us. The God of Jacob is our supporter.

CHAPTER 46 (47)

[1] Unto the end. A Psalm for the sons of Korah. [2] All nations, clap your hands. Shout joyfully to God with a voice of exultation. [3] For the Lord is exalted and terrible: a great King over all the earth. [4] He has subjected the peoples to us and subdued the nations under our feet. [5] He has chosen us for his inheritance: the splendor of Jacob, whom he has loved. [6] God ascends with jubilation, and the Lord with the voice of the trumpet. [7] Sing psalms to our God, sing psalms. Sing psalms to our King, sing psalms. [8] For God is the King of all the earth. Sing psalms wisely. [9] God will reign over the peoples. God sits upon his holy throne. [10] The leaders of the peoples have been gathered together by the God of Abraham. For the strong gods of the earth have been exceedingly exalted.

CHAPTER 47 (48)

[1] A Canticle Psalm. To the sons of Korah, on the second Sabbath. [2] The Lord is great and exceedingly praiseworthy, in the city of our God, on his holy mountain. [3] Mount Zion is being founded with the exultation of the whole earth, on the north side, the city of the great king. [4] In her houses, God will be known, since he will support her. [5] For behold, the kings of the earth have been gathered together; they have convened as one. [6] Such did they see, and they were astonished: they were disturbed, they were moved. [7] Trembling took hold of them. In that place, their pains were that of a woman in labor. [8] With a vehement spirit, you will crush the ships of Tarshish. [9] As we have heard, so we have seen, in the city of the Lord of hosts, in the city of our God. God has founded it in eternity. [10] We have received your mercy, O God, in the midst of your temple. [11] According to your name, O God, so does your praise reach to the ends of the earth. Your right hand is full of justice. [12] Let mount Zion rejoice, and let the daughters of Judah exult, because of your judgments, O Lord. [13] Encircle Zion and embrace her. Discourse in her towers. [14] Set your hearts on her virtue. And distribute her houses, so that you may discourse of it in another generation. [15] For this is God, our God, in eternity and forever and ever. He will rule us forever.

CHAPTER 48 (49)

[1] Unto the end. A Psalm to the sons of Korah. [2] Hear these things, all nations. Pay attention, all inhabitants of the world: [3] whoever is earth-born, you sons of men, together as one, the rich and the poor. [4] My mouth will speak wisdom, and the meditation of my heart will speak prudence. [5] I will incline my ear to a parable. I will open my case with the psaltery. [6] Why should I fear in the evil day? The iniquity at my heel will surround me. [7] Those who trust in their own strength and who glory in the multitude of their riches, [8] no brother redeems, nor will man buy back. He will not give to God his appeasement, [9] nor the price for the redemption of his soul. And he will labor continuously, [10] and he will still live, until the end. [11] He will not see death, when he sees the wise dying: the foolish and the senseless will perish together. And they will leave their riches to strangers. [12] And their sepulchers will be their houses forever, their tabernacles from generation to generation. They have called their names in their own lands. [13] And man, when he was held in honor, did not understand. He has been compared to the senseless beasts, and he has become like them. [14] This way of theirs is a scandal to them. And afterwards, they will delight in their mouth. [15] They have been placed in Hell like sheep. Death will feed on them. And the just will have dominion over them in the morning. And their help will grow old in Hell for their glory. [16] Even so, truly God will redeem my soul from the hand of Hell, when he will receive me. [17] Do not be afraid, when a man will have been made rich, and when the glory of his house will have been multiplied. [18] For when he dies, he will take nothing away, and his glory will not descend with him. [19] For his soul will be blessed in his

lifetime, and he will admit to you when you do good to him. [20] He will even enter with the progeny of his fathers, but, even in eternity, he will not see the light. [21] Man, when he was in honor, did not understand. He has been compared to the senseless beasts, and he has become like them.

CHAPTER 49 (50)

[1] A Psalm of Asaph. The God of gods, the Lord has spoken, and he has called the earth, from the rising of the sun even to its setting, [2] from Zion, the brilliance of his beauty. [3] God will arrive manifestly. Our God also will not keep silence. A fire will flare up in his sight, and a mighty tempest will surround him. [4] He will call to heaven from above, and to the earth, to discern his people. [5] Gather his holy ones to him, you who order his covenant above sacrifices. [6] And the heavens will announce his justice. For God is the judge. [7] Listen, my people, and I will speak. Listen, Israel, and I will testify for you. I am God, your God. [8] I will not reprove you for your sacrifices. Moreover, your holocausts are ever in my sight. [9] I will not accept calves from your house, nor he-goats from your flocks. [10] For all the wild beasts of the forest are mine: the cattle on the hills and the oxen. [11] I know all the flying things of the air, and the beauty of the field is with me. [12] If I should be hungry, I would not tell you: for the whole world is mine, and all its plentitude. [13] Shall I gnaw on the flesh of bulls? Or would I drink the blood of goats? [14] Offer to God the sacrifice of praise, and pay your vows to the Most High. [15] And call upon me in the day of tribulation. I will rescue you, and you will honor me. [16] But to the sinner, God has said: Why do you discourse on my justices, and take up my covenant through your mouth? [17] Truly, you have hated discipline, and you have cast my sermons behind you. [18] If you saw a thief, you ran with him, and you have placed your portion with adulterers. [19] Your mouth has abounded with malice, and your tongue has concocted deceits. [20] Sitting, you spoke against your brother, and you set up a scandal against your mother's son. [21] These things you have done, and I was silent. You thought, unjustly, that I ought to be like you. But I will reprove you, and I will set myself against your face. [22] Understand these things, you who forget God; lest at any time, he might quickly take you away, and there would be no one to rescue you. [23] The sacrifice of praise will honor me. And in that place is the journey by which I will reveal to him the salvation of God.

CHAPTER 50 (51)

[1] Unto the end. A Psalm of David, [2] when Nathan the prophet came to him, after he went to Bathsheba. [3] Be merciful to me, O God, according to your great mercy. And, according to the plentitude of your compassion, wipe out my iniquity. [4] Wash me once again from my iniquity, and cleanse me from my sin. [5] For I know my iniquity, and my sin is ever before me. [6] Against you only have I sinned, and I have done evil before your eyes. And so, you are justified in your words, and you will prevail when you give judgment. [7] For behold, I was conceived in iniquities, and in sinfulness did my mother conceive me. [8] For behold, you have loved truth. The obscure and hidden things of your wisdom, you have manifested to me. [9] You will sprinkle me with hyssop, and I will be cleansed. You will wash me, and I will be made whiter than snow. [10] In my hearing, you will grant gladness and rejoicing. And the bones that have been humbled will exult. [11] Turn your face away from my sins, and erase all my iniquities. [12] Create a clean heart in me, O God. And renew an upright spirit within my inmost being. [13] Do not cast me away from your face; and do not take your Holy Spirit from me. [14] Restore to me the joy of your salvation, and confirm me with an unsurpassed spirit. [15] I will teach the unjust your ways, and the impious will be converted to you. [16] Free me from blood, O God, the God of my salvation, and my tongue will extol your justice. [17] O Lord, you will open my lips, and my mouth will announce your praise. [18] For if you had desired sacrifice, I would certainly have given it, but with holocausts, you will not be delighted. [19] A crushed spirit is a sacrifice to God. A contrite and humbled heart, O God, you will not spurn. [20] Act kindly, Lord, in your good will toward Zion, so that the walls of Jerusalem may be built up. [21] Then you will accept the sacrifice of justice, oblations, and holocausts. Then they will lay calves upon your altar.

CHAPTER 51 (52)

[1] Unto the end. The understanding of David. [2] When Doeg the Edomite came and reported to Saul, David went to the house of Ahimelech. [3] Why do you glory

in malice, you who are powerful in iniquity? [4] All day long your tongue thinks up injustice. Like a sharp razor, you have wrought deceit. [5] You have loved malice above goodness, and iniquity more than speaking righteousness. [6] You have loved all precipitous words, you deceitful tongue. [7] Because of this, God will destroy you in the end. He will pull you up, and he will remove you from your tabernacle and your root from the land of the living. [8] The just will see and be afraid, and they will laugh over him, and say: [9] "Behold the man who did not set God as his helper. But he hoped in the multitude of his riches, and so he prevailed in his emptiness." [10] But I, like a fruitful olive tree in the house of God, have hoped in the mercy of God unto eternity, and forever and ever. [11] I will confess to you forever, because you have accomplished it. And I will wait on your name, for it is good in the sight of your saints.

CHAPTER 52 (53)

[1] Unto the end. For Mahalath: the thoughts of David. The fool has said in his heart, "There is no God." [2] They were corrupted, and they became abominable with iniquities. There is no one who does good. [3] God gazed down from heaven on the sons of men, to see if there were any who were considering or seeking God. [4] All have gone astray; together they have become useless. There is no one who does good; there is not even one. [5] Will they never learn: all those who work iniquity, who devour my people like a meal of bread? [6] They have not called upon God. In that place, they have trembled in fear, where there was no fear. For God has scattered the bones of those who please men. They have been confounded, because God has spurned them. [7] Who will grant from Zion the salvation of Israel? Jacob will exult, when God will convert the captivity of his people; and Israel will rejoice.

CHAPTER 53 (54)

[1] Unto the end. In verses, the understanding of David, [2] when the Ziphites had arrived and they said to Saul, "Has not David been hidden with us?" [3] Save me, O God, by your name, and judge me in your virtue. [4] O God, listen to my prayer. Pay attention to the words of my mouth. [5] For strangers have risen up against me, and the strong have sought my soul. And they have not set God before their eyes. [6] For behold, God is my helper, and the Lord is the protector of my soul. [7] Turn back the evils upon my adversaries, and ruin them by your truth. [8] I will freely sacrifice to you, and I will confess your name, O God, because it is good. [9] For you have quickly rescued me from all tribulation, and my eye has looked down upon my enemies.

CHAPTER 54 (55)

[1] Unto the end. In verses, the understanding of David. [2] Listen to my prayer, O God, and despise not my supplication. [3] Be attentive to me, and heed me. I have been grieved in my training, and I have been disturbed [4] at the voice of the adversary and at the tribulation of the sinner. For they have diverted iniquities toward me, and they have been harassing me with rage. [5] My heart has become disturbed within me, and the dread of death has fallen over me. [6] Fear and trembling have overwhelmed me, and darkness has buried me. [7] And I said, "Who will give me wings like the dove, so that I may fly away and take rest?" [8] Behold, I have fled far away, and I linger in solitude. [9] I waited for him who saved me from a weak-minded spirit and from a tempest. [10] Cast them down, O Lord, and divide their tongues. For I have seen iniquity and contradiction in the city. [11] Day and night, iniquity will surround it upon its walls, and hardship is in its midst, [12] with injustice. And usury and deceit have not fallen away from its streets. [13] For if my enemy had spoken evil about me, certainly, I would have sustained it. And if he who hated me had been speaking great things against me, I would perhaps have hidden myself from him. [14] Truly, you are a man of one mind: my leader and my acquaintance, [15] who took sweet food together with me. In the house of God, we walked side-by-side. [16] Let death come upon them, and let them descend alive into Hellfire. For there is wickedness in their dwellings, in their midst. [17] But I have cried out to God, and the Lord will save me. [18] Evening and morning and midday, I will discourse and announce, and he will heed my voice. [19] He will redeem my soul in peace from those who draw near to me. For, among the many, they were with me. [20] God will hear, and He who is before time will

humble them. For there is no change with them, and they have not feared God. [21] He has stretched forth his hand in retribution. They have contaminated his covenant. [22] They were divided by the wrath of his countenance, and his heart has drawn near. His words are smoother than oil, and they are arrows. [23] Cast your cares upon the Lord, and he will nurture you. He will not allow the just to be tossed about forever. [24] Truly, O God, you will lead them away into the well of death. Bloody and deceitful men will not divide their days in half. But I will hope in you, O Lord.

CHAPTER 55 (56)

[1] Unto the end. For the people who have become far removed from the Sacred. Of David, with the inscription of a title, when the Philistines held him in Gath. [2] Have mercy on me, O God, because man has trampled over me. All day long, he has afflicted me by fighting against me. [3] My enemies have trampled over me all day long. For those who make war against me are many. [4] From the height of the day, I will be afraid. But truly, I will hope in you. [5] In God, I will praise my words. In God, I have put my trust. I will not fear what flesh can do to me. [6] All day long, they curse my words. All their intentions are for evil against me. [7] They will dwell and hide themselves. They will watch my heel, just as they waited for my soul; [8] because of this, nothing will save them. In your anger, you will crush the people. [9] O God, I have announced my life to you. You have placed my tears in your sight, and even in your promise. [10] Then my enemies will be turned back. On whatever day that I call upon you, behold, I know that you are my God. [11] In God, I will praise the word. In the Lord, I will praise his speech. In God, I have hoped. I will not fear what man can do to me. [12] My vows to you, O God, are in me. I will repay them. Praises be to you. [13] For you have rescued my soul from death and my feet from slipping, so that I may be pleasing in the sight of God, in the light of the living.

CHAPTER 56 (57)

[1] Unto the end. May you not destroy. Of David, with the inscription of a title, when he fled from Saul into a cave. [2] Be merciful to me, O God, be merciful to me. For my soul trusts in you. And I will hope in the shadow of your wings, until iniquity passes away. [3] I will cry out to God Most High, to God who has been kind to me. [4] He sent from heaven and freed me. He has surrendered into disgrace those who trampled me. God has sent his mercy and his truth. [5] And he has rescued my soul from the midst of the young lions. I slept troubled. The sons of men: their teeth are weapons and arrows, and their tongue is a sharp sword. [6] Be exalted above the heavens, O God, and your glory above all the earth. [7] They prepared a snare for my feet, and they bowed down my soul. They dug a pit before my face, yet they have fallen into it. [8] My heart is prepared, O God, my heart is prepared. I will sing, and I will compose a psalm. [9] Rise up, my glory. Rise up, psaltery and harp. I will arise in early morning. [10] I will confess to you, O Lord, among the peoples. I will compose a psalm to you among the nations. [11] For your mercy has been magnified, even to the heavens, and your truth, even to the clouds. [12] Be exalted above the heavens, O God, and your glory above all the earth.

CHAPTER 57 (58)

[1] Unto the end. May you not destroy. Of David, with the inscription of a title. [2] If, truly and certainly, you speak justice, then judge what is right, you sons of men. [3] For, even in your heart, you work iniquity. Your hands construct injustice on the earth. [4] Sinners have become foreigners from the womb; they have gone astray from conception. They have been speaking falsehoods. [5] Their fury is similar to that of a serpent; it is like a deaf asp, who even blocks her ears, [6] who will not listen to the voice of charmers, nor even to the enchanter who chants wisely. [7] God will crush their teeth within their own mouth. The Lord will break the molars of the lions. [8] They will come to nothing, like water flowing away. He has aimed his bow, while they are being weakened. [9] Like wax that flows, they will be carried away. Fire has fallen upon them, and they will not see the sun. [10] Before your thorns could know the brier, he consumes them alive, as if in rage. [11] The just one will rejoice when he sees vindication. He will wash his hands in the blood of the sinner. [12] And man will say, "If the just one is fruitful, then, truly, there is a God judging them on earth."

CHAPTER 58 (59)

[1] Unto the end. May you not destroy. Of David, with the inscription of a title, when Saul sent and watched his house, in order to execute him. [2] Rescue me from my enemies, my God, and free me from those who rise up against me. [3] Rescue me from those who work iniquity, and save me from men of blood. [4] For behold, they have seized my soul. The strong have rushed upon me. [5] And it is neither my iniquity, nor my sin, O Lord. I have run and gone directly, without iniquity. [6] Rise up to meet me, and see: even you, O Lord, the God of hosts, the God of Israel. Reach out to visit all nations. Do not take pity on all those who work iniquity. [7] They will return toward evening, and they will suffer hunger like dogs, and they will wander around the city. [8] Behold, they will speak with their mouth, and a sword is in their lips: "For who has heard us?" [9] And you, O Lord, will laugh at them. You will lead all the Gentiles to nothing. [10] I will guard my strength toward you, for you are God, my supporter. [11] My God, his mercy will precede me. [12] God will oversee my enemies for me. Do not slay them, lest at times my people may forget them. Scatter them by your virtue. And depose them, O Lord, my protector, [13] by the offense of their mouth and by the speech of their lips. And may they be caught in their arrogance. And, for their cursing and lying, they will be made known [14] at the consummation, in the fury of the consummation, and so they will be no more. And they will know that God will rule over Jacob, even to the ends of the earth. [15] They will return toward evening, and they will suffer hunger like dogs, and they will wander around the city. [16] They will be dispersed in order to gnaw, and truly, when they will not have been satisfied, they will murmur. [17] But I will sing your strength, and I will extol your mercy, in the morning. For you have been my supporter and my refuge in the day of my tribulation. [18] To you, my helper, I will sing psalms. For you are God, my supporter. My God is my mercy.

CHAPTER 59 (60)

[1] Unto the end. For those who will be changed, with the inscription of a title, of David himself, for instruction: [2] when he set fire to Mesopotamia of Syria and Sobal, and Joab turned back and struck Idumea, in the valley of the salt pits, twelve thousand men. [3] O God, you have rejected us, and you have ruined us. You became angry, and yet you have been merciful to us. [4] You have moved the earth, and you have disturbed it. Heal its breaches, for it has been moved. [5] You have revealed to your people difficulties. You have made us drink the wine of remorse. [6] You have given a warning sign to those who fear you, so that they may flee from before the face of the bow, so that your beloved may be delivered. [7] Save me with your right hand, and hear me. [8] God has spoken in his holy place: I will rejoice, and I will divide Shechem, and I will measure the steep valley of the tabernacles. [9] Gilead is mine, and Manasseh is mine. And Ephraim is the strength of my head. Judah is my king. [10] Moab is the cooking pot of my hope. Into Idumea, I will extend my shoe. To me, the foreigners have been made subject. [11] Who will lead me into the fortified city? Who will lead me all the way to Idumea? [12] Will not you, O God, who has rejected us? And will not you, O God, go out with our armies? [13] Grant us help from tribulation. For salvation from man is empty. [14] In God, we will act virtuously. And those who trouble us, he will lead to nothing.

CHAPTER 60 (61)

[1] Unto the end. With hymns, of David. [2] O God, pay attention to my supplication. Be attentive to my prayer. [3] I cried out to you from the ends of the earth. When my heart was in anguish, you exalted me on a rock. You have led me, [4] for you have been my hope, a tower of strength before the face of the enemy. [5] I will dwell in your tabernacle forever. I will be protected under the cover of your wings. [6] For you, my God, have listened to my prayer. You have granted an inheritance to those who fear your name. [7] You will add days to the days of the king, to his years, even to the time of generation after generation. [8] He remains in eternity, in the sight of God. Who will long for his mercy and truth? [9] So I will compose a psalm to your name, forever and ever, so that I may repay my vows from day to day.

CHAPTER 61 (62)

[1] Unto the end. For Jeduthun. A Psalm of David. [2] Will my soul not be subject to God? For from him is my salvation. [3] Yes, he himself is my God and my salvation. He is my supporter; I will be moved no more. [4] How is it that you rush against a man? Every one of you puts to death, as if you were pulling down a ruined

wall, leaning over and falling apart. ⁵So, truly, they intended to reject my price. I ran in thirst. They blessed with their mouth and cursed with their heart. ⁶Yet, truly, my soul will be subject to God. For from him is my patience. ⁷For he is my God and my Savior. He is my helper; I will not be expelled. ⁸In God is my salvation and my glory. He is the God of my help, and my hope is in God. ⁹All peoples gathered together: trust in him. Pour out your hearts in his sight. God is our helper for eternity. ¹⁰So, truly, the sons of men are untrustworthy. The sons of men are liars in the scales, so that, by emptiness, they may deceive among themselves. ¹¹Do not trust in iniquity, and do not desire plunder. If riches flow toward you, do not be willing to set your heart on them. ¹²God has spoken once. I have heard two things: that power belongs to God, ¹³and that mercy belongs to you, O Lord. For you will repay each one according to his works.

CHAPTER 62 (63)

¹A Psalm of David, when he was in the desert of Idumea. ²O God, my God: to you, I keep vigil until first light. For you, my soul has thirsted, to you my body, in so many ways. ³By a deserted land, both inaccessible and waterless, so I have appeared in the sanctuary before you, in order to behold your virtue and your glory. ⁴For your mercy is better than life itself. It is you my lips will praise. ⁵So will I bless you in my life, and I will lift up my hands in your name. ⁶Let my soul be filled, as if with marrow and fatness; and my mouth will give praise with exultant lips. ⁷When I have remembered you on my bed in the morning, I will meditate on you. ⁸For you have been my helper. And I will exult under the cover of your wings. ⁹My soul has clung close to you. Your right hand has supported me. ¹⁰Truly, these ones have sought my soul in vain. They will enter into the lower parts of the earth. ¹¹They will be delivered into the hand of the sword. They will be the portions of foxes. ¹²Truly, the king will rejoice in God: all those who swear by him will be praised, because the mouth of those who speak iniquity has been blocked.

CHAPTER 63 (64)

¹Unto the end. A Psalm of David. ²Hear, O God, my prayer of supplication. Rescue my soul from the fear of the enemy. ³You have protected me from the assembly of the malignant, from a multitude of workers of iniquity. ⁴For they have sharpened their tongues like a sword; they have formed their bow into a bitter thing, ⁵so that they may shoot arrows from hiding at the immaculate. ⁶They will suddenly shoot arrows at him, and they will not be afraid. They are resolute in their wicked talk. They have discussed hidden snares. They have said, "Who will see them?" ⁷They have been searching carefully for iniquities. Their exhaustive search has failed. Man will approach with a deep heart, ⁸and God will be exalted. The arrows of the little ones have become their wounds, ⁹and their tongues have been weakened against them. All those who saw them have been troubled; ¹⁰and every man was afraid. And they announced the works of God, and they understood his acts. ¹¹The just will rejoice in the Lord, and they will hope in him. And all the upright of heart will be praised.

CHAPTER 64 (65)

¹Unto the end. A Psalm of David. A Canticle of Jeremiah and Ezekiel to the people of the captivity, when they began to go into exile. ²O God, a hymn adorns you in Zion, and a vow will be repaid to you in Jerusalem. ³Hear my prayer: all flesh will come to you. ⁴Words of iniquity have prevailed over us. And you will pardon our impieties. ⁵Blessed is he whom you have chosen and taken up. He will dwell in your courts. We will be filled with the good things of your house. Holy is your temple: ⁶wonderful in equity. Hear us, O God our Savior, the hope of all the ends of the earth and of a sea far away. ⁷You prepare the mountains in your virtue, wrapped with power. ⁸You stir up the depths of the sea, the noise of its waves. The nations will be troubled, ⁹and those who dwell at the limits will be afraid, before your signs. You will make the passing of morning and evening enjoyable. ¹⁰You have visited the earth, and you have saturated it. You have enriched it in so many ways. The river of God has been filled with water. You have prepared their food. For thus is its preparation. ¹¹Drench its streams, multiply its fruits; it will spring up and rejoice in its showers. ¹²You will bless the crown of the year with your kindness, and your fields will be filled with abundance. ¹³The beauty of the desert will fatten, and the hills will be wrapped with exultation. ¹⁴The rams of the sheep

have been clothed, and the valleys will abound with grain. They will cry out; yes, they will even utter a hymn.

CHAPTER 65 (66)

[1] Unto the end. A Canticle Psalm of the Resurrection. Shout joyfully to God, all the earth. [2] Proclaim a psalm to his name. Give glory to his praise. [3] Exclaim to God, "How terrible are your works, O Lord!" According to the fullness of your virtue, your enemies will speak lies about you. [4] Let all the earth adore you and sing psalms to you. May it sing a psalm to your name. [5] Draw near and see the works of God, who is terrible in his counsels over the sons of men. [6] He converts the sea into dry land. They will cross the river on foot. There, we will rejoice in him. [7] He rules by his virtue for eternity. His eyes gaze upon the nations. May those who exasperate him, not be exalted in themselves. [8] Bless our God, you Gentiles, and make the voice of his praise be heard. [9] He has set my soul toward life, and he has granted that my feet may not be shaken. [10] For you, O God, have tested us. You have examined us by fire, just as silver is examined. [11] You have led us into a snare. You have placed tribulations on our back. [12] You have set men over our heads. We have crossed through fire and water. And you have led us out to refreshment. [13] I will enter your house with holocausts. I will repay my vows to you, [14] which my lips discerned and my mouth spoke, in my tribulation. [15] I will offer to you holocausts full of marrow, with the burnt offerings of rams. I will offer to you bulls as well as goats. [16] Draw near and listen, all you who fear God, and I will describe to you how much he has done for my soul. [17] I cried out to him with my mouth, and I extolled him under my breath. [18] If I have seen iniquity in my heart, the Lord would not heed me. [19] And yet, God has heeded me and he has attended to the voice of my supplication. [20] Blessed is God, who has not removed my prayer, nor his mercy, from me.

CHAPTER 66 (67)

[1] Unto the end. With hymns, a Canticle Psalm of David. [2] May God have mercy on us and bless us. May he shine his countenance upon us, and may he have mercy on us. [3] So may we know your way upon the earth, your salvation among all nations. [4] Let the peoples confess to you, O God. Let all the peoples confess to you. [5] May the nations rejoice and exult. For you judge the peoples with equity, and you direct the nations on earth. [6] Let the peoples confess to you, O God. Let all the peoples confess to you. [7] The earth has provided her fruit. May God, our God, bless us. [8] May God bless us, and may all the ends of the earth fear him.

CHAPTER 67 (68)

[1] Unto the end. A Canticle Psalm of David himself. [2] May God rise up, and may his enemies be scattered, and may those who hate him flee from before his face. [3] Just as smoke vanishes, so may they vanish. Just as wax flows away before the face of fire, so may sinners pass away before the face of God. [4] And so, let the just feast, and let them exult in the sight of God and be delighted in gladness. [5] Sing to God, sing a psalm to his name. Make a path for him, who ascends over the west. The Lord is his name. Exult in his sight; they will be stirred up before his face, [6] the father of orphans and the judge of widows. God is in his holy place. [7] It is God who makes men dwell in a house under one custom. He leads out those who are strongly bound, and similarly, those who exasperate, who dwell in sepulchers. [8] O God, when you departed in the sight of your people, when you passed through the desert, [9] the earth was moved, for the heavens rained down before the face of the God of Sinai, before the face of the God of Israel. [10] You will set aside for your inheritance, O God, a willing rain. And though it was weak, truly, you have made it perfect. [11] Your animals will dwell in it. O God, in your sweetness, you have provided for the poor. [12] The Lord will give the word to evangelizers, along with great virtue. [13] The King of virtue is beloved among the beloved. And the beauty of the house will divide spoils. [14] If you take your rest in the midst of the clergy, you will be like a dove whose wings are covered with fine silver and edged with pale gold. [15] When heaven discerns kings to be over her, they will be whitened with the snows of Zalmon. [16] The mountain of God is a fat mountain, a dense mountain, a thick mountain. [17] So then, why are you distrustful of dense mountains? The mountain on which God is well pleased to dwell, even there, the Lord will dwell until the end. [18] The chariot of God is ten thousand fold: thousands rejoice. The Lord is with them in Sinai, in the holy place. [19] You

have ascended on high; you have taken captivity captive. You have accepted gifts among men. For even those who do not believe dwell with the Lord God. ²⁰Blessed is the Lord, day after day. The God of our salvation will make our journey prosper for us. ²¹Our God is the God who will bring about our salvation, and our Lord is the Lord who has brought an end to death. ²²So then, truly, God will break the heads of his enemies, the hairy skull of those who wander around in their offenses. ²³The Lord said: I will turn them away from Bashan, I will turn them into the depths of the sea, ²⁴so that your feet may be soaked in the blood of your enemies, so that the tongue of your dogs may be soaked with the same. ²⁵O God, they have seen your arrival, the arrival of my God, of my king who is in a holy place. ²⁶The leaders went ahead, united with the singers of psalms, in the midst of girls playing on timbrels. ²⁷In the churches, bless the Lord God from the fountains of Israel. ²⁸In that place, Benjamin is a youth in ecstasy of mind. The leaders of Judah are their governors: the leaders of Zebulun, the leaders of Naphtali. ²⁹Command by your virtue, O God. Confirm in this place, O God, what you have wrought in us. ³⁰Before your temple in Jerusalem, kings will offer gifts to you. ³¹Rebuke the wild beasts of the reeds, a congregation of bulls with the cows of the people, for they seek to exclude those who have been tested like silver. Scatter the nations that are pleased by wars. ³²Ambassadors will come out of Egypt. Ethiopia will offer in advance her hands to God. ³³Sing to God, O kingdoms of the earth. Sing psalms to the Lord. Sing psalms to God. ³⁴He ascends, up to the heaven of the heavens, toward the east. Behold, he will utter his voice, the voice of virtue. ³⁵Give glory to God beyond Israel. His magnificence and his virtue is in the clouds. ³⁶God is wonderful in his saints. The God of Israel himself will give virtue and strength to his people. Blessed is God.

CHAPTER 68 (69)

¹Unto the end. For those who will be changed: of David. ²Save me, O God, for the waters have entered, even to my soul. ³I have become stuck in a deep quagmire, and there is no firm footing. I have arrived at the height of the sea, and a tempest has overwhelmed me. ⁴I have endured hardships, while crying out. My jaws have become hoarse; my eyes have failed. Meanwhile, I hope in my God. ⁵Those who hate me without cause have been multiplied beyond the hairs of my head. My enemies, who persecuted me unjustly, have been strengthened. Then I was required to pay for what I did not take. ⁶O God, you know my foolishness, and my offenses have not been hidden from you. ⁷Let those who wait for you, O Lord, the Lord of hosts, not be shamed in me. Let those who seek you, O God of Israel, not be confounded over me. ⁸For because of you, I have endured reproach; confusion has covered my face. ⁹I have become a stranger to my brothers and a sojourner to the sons of my mother. ¹⁰For zeal for your house has consumed me, and the reproaches of those who reproached you have fallen upon me. ¹¹And I covered my soul with fasting, and it has become a reproach to me. ¹²And I put on a haircloth as my garment, and I became a parable to them. ¹³Those who sat at the gate spoke against me, and those who drank wine made me their song. ¹⁴But as for me, truly, my prayer is to you, O Lord. This time has pleased you well, O God. In the multitude of your mercy, in the truth of your salvation, hear me. ¹⁵Rescue me from the quagmire, so that I may not become trapped. Free me from those who hate me and from deep waters. ¹⁶Do not allow the tempest of water to submerge me, nor the deep to absorb me. And do not allow the well to close in on me. ¹⁷Hear me, O Lord, for your mercy is kind. Look upon me, according to the fullness of your compassion. ¹⁸And do not turn your face away from your servant, for I am in trouble: heed me quickly. ¹⁹Attend to my soul, and free it. Rescue me, because of my enemies. ²⁰You know my reproach, and my confusion, and my reverence. ²¹All those who trouble me are in your sight; my heart has anticipated reproach and misery. And I sought for one who might grieve together with me, but there was no one, and for one who might console me, and I found no one. ²²And they gave me gall for my food. And in my thirst, they gave me vinegar to drink. ²³Let their table be a snare before them, and a retribution, and a scandal. ²⁴Let their eyes be darkened, so that they may not see, and may their back always be crooked. ²⁵Pour out your indignation upon them, and may the fury of your anger take hold of them. ²⁶May their dwelling place be deserted, and may there be no one who dwells in their tabernacles. ²⁷For they persecuted whomever you struck. And they have added to the grief of my wounds. ²⁸Assign an iniquity upon their iniquity, and may they not enter into your justice. ²⁹Delete them from the Book of the Living, and let them not be written down with the

just. [30] I am poor and sorrowful, but your salvation, O God, has taken me up. [31] I will praise the name of God with a canticle, and I will magnify him with praise. [32] And it will please God more than a new calf producing horns and hoofs. [33] Let the poor see and rejoice. Seek God, and your soul will live. [34] For the Lord has heard the poor, and he has not despised his prisoners. [35] Let the heavens and the earth praise him: the sea, and everything that crawls in it. [36] For God will save Zion, and the cities of Judah will be built up. And they will dwell there, and they will acquire it by inheritance. [37] And the offspring of his servants will possess it; and those who love his name will dwell in it.

CHAPTER 69 (70)

[1] Unto the end. A Psalm of David, in remembrance that the Lord had saved him. [2] O God, reach out to help me. O Lord, hasten to assist me. [3] May those who seek my soul be confounded and awed. [4] May those who wish evils upon me be turned back and blush with shame. May they be turned away immediately, blushing with shame, who say to me: "Well, well." [5] Let all who seek you exult and rejoice in you, and let those who love your salvation forever say: "The Lord be magnified." [6] I am truly destitute and poor. O God, assist me. You are my helper and my deliverer. O Lord, do not delay.

CHAPTER 70 (71)

[1] A Psalm of David. Of the sons of Jonadab and the former captives. In you, O Lord, I have hoped; do not let me be brought to ruin forever. [2] Free me by your justice, and rescue me. Incline your ear to me, and save me. [3] Be a God of protection and a place of strength for me, so that you may accomplish my salvation. For you are my firmament and my refuge. [4] Rescue me, O my God, from the hand of the sinner, and from the hand of the unjust and those who act against the law. [5] For you, O Lord, are my patience: my hope from my youth, O Lord. [6] In you, I have been confirmed from conception. From my mother's womb, you are my protector. In you, I will sing forever. [7] I have become to many as if I were a portent, but you are a strong helper. [8] Let my mouth be filled with praise, so that I may sing your glory, your greatness all day long. [9] Do not cast me off in the time of old age. Do not abandon me when my strength will fail. [10] For my enemies have spoken against me. And those who watched for my soul have taken counsel as one, [11] saying: "God has abandoned him. Pursue and overtake him. For there is no one to rescue him." [12] O God, do not be far from me. O my God, provide for my assistance. [13] May they be confounded, and may they fail, who drag down my soul. Let them be covered with confusion and shame, who seek evils for me. [14] But I will always have hope. And I will add more to all your praise. [15] My mouth will announce your justice, your salvation all day long. For I have not known letters. [16] I will enter into the powers of the Lord. I will be mindful of your justice alone, O Lord. [17] You have taught me from my youth, O God. And so I will declare your wonders continuously, [18] even in old age and with grey hairs. Do not abandon me, O God, while I announce your arm to every future generation: your power [19] and your justice, O God, even to the highest great things that you have done. O God, who is like you? [20] How great is the tribulation that you have revealed to me: very great and evil. And so, turning back, you have brought me to life, and you have led me back again from the abyss of the earth. [21] You have multiplied your magnificence. And so, turning back to me, you have consoled me. [22] Therefore, I will confess your truth to you, with the instruments of the Psalter. O God, I will sing psalms to you with stringed instruments, O Holy One of Israel. [23] My lips will exult, when I sing to you, and also my soul, which you have redeemed. [24] And even my tongue will meditate on your justice all day long, when those who seek evils for me have been confounded and set in awe.

CHAPTER 71 (72)

[1] A Psalm according to Solomon. [2] Give your judgment, O God, to the king, and your justice to the king's son, to judge your people with justice and your poor with judgment. [3] Let the mountains take up peace for the people, and the hills, justice. [4] He will judge the poor of the people, and he will bring salvation to the sons of the poor. And he will humble the false accuser. [5] And he will remain, with the sun and before the moon, from generation to generation. [6] He will descend like rain upon fleece, and like showers showering upon the earth. [7] In his days, justice will rise like the sun, with abundance of peace, until the moon is taken away. [8] And he

will rule from sea to sea and from the river to the limits of the whole world. [9] In his sight, the Ethiopians will fall prostrate, and his enemies will lick the ground. [10] The kings of Tarshish and the islands will offer gifts. The kings of Arabia and of Seba will bring gifts. [11] And all the kings of the earth shall adore him. All nations will serve him. [12] For he will free the poor from the powerful, and the poor one who has no helper. [13] He will spare the poor and the indigent, and he will bring salvation to the souls of the poor. [14] He will redeem their souls from usuries and from iniquity, and their names shall be honorable in his sight. [15] And he will live, and to him will be given from the gold of Arabia, and by him they will always adore. They will bless him all day long. [16] And there will be a firmament on earth, at the summits of mountains: its fruits will be extolled above Lebanon, and those of the city will flourish like the grass of the earth. [17] May his name be blessed forever; may his name remain before the sun. And all the tribes of the earth will be blessed in him. All nations will magnify him. [18] Blessed is the Lord, God of Israel, who alone does wondrous things. [19] And blessed is the name of his majesty in eternity. And all the earth will be filled with his majesty. Amen. Amen. [20] The praises of David, the son of Jesse, have reached an end.

CHAPTER 72 (73)

[1] A Psalm of Asaph. How good is God to Israel, to those who are upright in heart. [2] But my feet were nearly moved; my steps had nearly slipped. [3] For I was zealous over the iniquitous, seeing the peacefulness of sinners. [4] For they have no respect for their death, nor do they have support in their wounds. [5] They are not with the hardships of men, nor will they be scourged with men. [6] Therefore, arrogance has held on to them. They have been covered with their iniquity and impiety. [7] Their iniquity has proceeded, as if from fat. They have parted from the affection of the heart. [8] They have thought and spoken wickedness. They have spoken iniquity in high places. [9] They have set their mouth against heaven, and their tongue has traversed the earth. [10] Therefore, my people will be converted here, and fullness of days will be found in them. [11] And they said, "How would God know?" and, "Isn't there knowledge in high places?" [12] Behold, these are sinners, and, abounding in this age, they have obtained riches. [13] And I said: So then, it is without purpose that I have justified my heart and washed my hands among the innocent. [14] And I have been scourged all day long, and I have received my chastisement in the mornings. [15] If I were to say that I would explain this: Behold, I would condemn this nation of your sons. [16] I considered, so that I might know this. It is a hardship before me, [17] until I may enter into the Sanctuary of God, and understand it to its last part. [18] So, because of deceitfulness, truly, you have placed it before them. While they were being lifted up, you were casting them down. [19] How have they been brought to desolation? They have suddenly failed. They have perished because of their iniquity. [20] As a dream is to those who awaken, O Lord, so will you reduce their image to nothing in your city. [21] For my heart has been inflamed, and my temperament has been changed. [22] And so, I have been reduced to nothing, and I did not know it. [23] I have become like a beast of burden to you, and I am always with you. [24] You have held my right hand. And in your will, you have conducted me, and with your glory, you have taken me up. [25] For what is there for me in heaven? And what do I wish for on earth before you? [26] My body has failed, and my heart: O God of my heart, and God my portion, into eternity. [27] For behold, those who put themselves far from you will perish. You have perished all those who fornicate away from you. [28] But it is good for me to adhere to God, to put my hope in the Lord God, so that I may announce all your prophecies, at the gates of the daughter of Zion.

CHAPTER 73 (74)

[1] The understanding of Asaph. O God, why have you rejected us to the end. Why has your fury become enraged over the sheep of your pasture? [2] Be mindful of your congregation, which you have possessed from the beginning. You redeemed the scepter of your inheritance, mount Zion, in which you have dwelt. [3] Lift up your hands against their arrogance in the end. How great the malice of the enemy has been in the sanctuary! [4] And those who hate you have been glorified, in the midst of your solemnity. They have set up their own signs as a proof, [5] as if it had been issued from on high; yet they did not understand. As in a forest of chopped wood, [6] they have cut down the entrances themselves. With axe and hatchet, they have brought it down. [7] They have set fire to your Sanctuary. They have polluted the tabernacle of your name on earth. [8] They have said in their heart, the whole

group of them together: "Let us cause all the feast days of God to cease from the land. ⁹ We have not seen our proof; there is now no prophet. And he will no longer know us." ¹⁰ How long, O God, will the enemy place blame? Is the adversary to provoke your name until the end? ¹¹ Why do you turn your hand away, even your right hand, from the midst of your sinews, until the end? ¹² But God is our king before all ages. He has wrought salvation in the midst of the earth. ¹³ In your virtue, you confirmed the sea. You crushed the heads of the serpents in the waters. ¹⁴ You have broken the heads of the serpent. You have given him as food for the people of the Ethiopians. ¹⁵ You have disrupted the fountains and the torrents. You have dried up the rivers of Ethan. ¹⁶ Yours is the day, and yours is the night. You have made the morning light and the sun. ¹⁷ You have made all the limits of the earth. The summer and the spring were formed by you. ¹⁸ Be mindful of this: the enemy placed blame against the Lord, and a foolish people has incited against your name. ¹⁹ Do not hand over to beasts the souls that confess to you; and do not forget the souls of your poor until the end. ²⁰ Consider your covenant. For those who have been darkened upon the earth have been filled by the iniquity of the houses. ²¹ Do not allow the humble to be turned away in confusion. The poor and the needy will praise your name. ²² Rise up, O God, judge your own case. Call to mind the accusations against you, which are made by the foolish all day long. ²³ Do not forget the voices of your adversaries. The arrogance of those who hate you rises up continually.

CHAPTER 74 (75)

¹ Unto the end. May you not be corrupted. A Canticle Psalm of Asaph. ² We will confess to you, O God. We will confess, and we will call upon your name. We will describe your wonders. ³ While I have time, I will judge justices. ⁴ The earth has been dissolved, with all who dwell in it. I have confirmed its pillars. ⁵ I said to the iniquitous: "Do not act unjustly," and to the offenders: "Do not exalt the horn." ⁶ Do not exalt your horn on high. Do not speak iniquity against God. ⁷ For it is neither from the east, nor from the west, nor before the desert mountains. ⁸ For God is judge. This one he humbles and that one he exalts. ⁹ For, in the hand of the Lord, there is a cup of undiluted wine, full of consternation. And he has tipped it from here to there. So, truly, its dregs have not been emptied. All the sinners of the earth will drink. ¹⁰ But I will announce it in every age. I will sing to the God of Jacob. ¹¹ And I will break all the horns of sinners. And the horns of the just will be exalted.

CHAPTER 75 (76)

¹ Unto the end. With Praises. A Psalm of Asaph. A Canticle to the Assyrians. ² In Judea, God is known. In Israel, his name is great. ³ And his place has been formed with peace. And his dwelling place is in Zion. ⁴ In that place, he has broken the powers of the bows, the shield, the sword, and the battle. ⁵ You illuminate wondrously from the mountains of eternity. ⁶ All the foolish of heart have been disturbed. They have slept their sleep, and all the men of riches have found nothing in their hands. ⁷ At your rebuke, O God of Jacob, those who were mounted on horseback have fallen asleep. ⁸ You are terrible, and so, who can withstand you? From thence is your wrath. ⁹ You have caused judgment to be heard from heaven. The earth trembled and was quieted, ¹⁰ when God rose up in judgment in order to bring salvation to all the meek of the earth. ¹¹ For the thinking of man will confess to you, and the legacy of his thinking will keep a feast day to you. ¹² Make vows and pay them to the Lord, your God. All you who surround him bring gifts: to him who is terrible, ¹³ even to him who takes away the spirit of leaders, to him who is terrible with the kings of the earth.

CHAPTER 76 (77)

¹ Unto the end. For Jeduthun. A Psalm of Asaph. ² I cried out to the Lord with my voice, to God with my voice, and he attended to me. ³ In the days of my tribulation, I sought God, with my hands opposite him in the night, and I was not deceived. My soul refused to be consoled. ⁴ I was mindful of God, and I was delighted, and I was distressed, and my spirit fell away. ⁵ My eyes anticipated the vigils. I was disturbed, and I did not speak. ⁶ I considered the days of antiquity, and I held the years of eternity in my mind. ⁷ And I meditated in the night with my heart, and I was distressed, and I examined my spirit. ⁸ So then, will God reject for eternity? Will he not continue to allow himself to show favor? ⁹ Or,

will he cut off his mercy in the end, from generation to generation? ¹⁰ And would God ever forget to be merciful? Or, would he, in his wrath, restrict his mercies? ¹¹ And I said, "Now I have begun. This change is from the right hand of the Most High." ¹² I was mindful of the works of the Lord. For I will be mindful from the beginning of your wonders, ¹³ and I will meditate on all your works. And I will take part in your intentions. ¹⁴ Your way, O God, is in what is holy. Which God is great like our God? ¹⁵ You are the God who performs miracles. You have made your virtue known among the peoples. ¹⁶ With your arm, you have redeemed your people, the sons of Jacob and of Joseph. ¹⁷ The waters saw you, O God, the waters saw you, and they were afraid, and the depths were stirred up. ¹⁸ Great was the sound of the waters. The clouds uttered a voice. For your arrows also pass by. ¹⁹ The voice of your thunder is like a wheel. Your flashes have illuminated the whole world. The earth has quaked and trembled. ²⁰ Your way is through the sea, and your paths are through many waters. And your traces will not be known. ²¹ You have conducted your people like sheep, by the hand of Moses and Aaron.

CHAPTER 77 (78)

¹ The understanding of Asaph. O my people, attend to my law. Incline your ears to the words of my mouth. ² I will open my mouth in parables. I will speak about concepts that are from the beginning. ³ We have heard and known such great things, as our fathers have described to us. ⁴ These things have not been hidden from their sons in any generation: declaring the praises of the Lord, and his virtues, and the wonders that he has done. ⁵ And he has received testimony with Jacob, and he has set a law within Israel. Such great things, he has commanded our fathers, so as to make these things known to their sons, ⁶ so that another generation might know them, and so that the sons, who will be born and who will grow up, shall describe them to their sons. ⁷ So then, may they put their hope in God, and may they not forget the works of God, and may they seek his commandments. ⁸ May they not become like their fathers, a perverse and exasperating generation: a generation that does not straighten their heart and whose spirit is not trustworthy with God. ⁹ The sons of Ephraim, who bend and shoot the bow, have been turned back in the day of battle. ¹⁰ They have not kept the covenant of God. And they were not willing to walk in his law. ¹¹ And they have been forgetful of his benefits, and of his miracle, which he revealed to them. ¹² He performed miracles in the sight of their fathers, in the land of Egypt, in the field of Tanis. ¹³ He broke the sea and he led them through. And he stationed the waters, as if in a vessel. ¹⁴ And he led them with a cloud by day, and with illumination by fire throughout the night. ¹⁵ He broke through the rock in the wasteland, and he gave them to drink, as if from the great abyss. ¹⁶ He brought forth water from the rock, and he conducted the waters, as if they were rivers. ¹⁷ And yet, they continued to sin against him. In a waterless place, they provoked the Most High with resentment. ¹⁸ And they tempted God in their hearts, by asking for food according to their desires. ¹⁹ And they spoke badly about God. They said, "Would God be able to prepare a table in the desert? ²⁰ He struck the rock, and so waters flowed and the torrents flooded, but would even he be able to provide bread, or provide a table, for his people?" ²¹ Therefore, the Lord heard, and he was dismayed, and a fire was kindled within Jacob, and an anger ascended into Israel. ²² For they neither put their trust in God, nor did they hope in his salvation. ²³ And he commanded the clouds from above, and he opened the doors of heaven. ²⁴ And he rained down manna upon them to eat, and he gave them the bread of heaven. ²⁵ Man ate the bread of Angels. He sent them provisions in abundance. ²⁶ He transferred the south wind from heaven, and, in his virtue, he brought in the Southwest wind. ²⁷ And he rained down flesh upon them, as if it were dust, and feathered birds, as if they were the sand of the sea. ²⁸ And they fell down in the midst of their camp, encircling their tabernacles. ²⁹ And they ate until they were greatly satisfied, and he brought to them according to their desires. ³⁰ They were not cheated out of what they wanted. Their food was still in their mouth, ³¹ and then the wrath of God came upon them. And he slew the fat ones among them, and he impeded the elect of Israel. ³² In all these things, they continued to sin, and they were not trustworthy with his miracles. ³³ And their days faded away into vanity, and their years with haste. ³⁴ When he slew them, then they sought him. And they returned, and they drew near to him in the early morning. ³⁵ And they were mindful that God is their helper and that the Most High God is their redeemer. ³⁶ And they chose him with their mouth, and then they lied to him

with their tongue. [37] For their heart was not upright with him, nor have they been living faithfully in his covenant. [38] Yet he is merciful, and he will pardon their sins. And he will not destroy them. And he has abundantly turned aside his own wrath. And he did not enflame his wrath entirely. [39] And he remembered that they are flesh: with a spirit that goes forth and does not return. [40] How often did they provoke him in the desert and stir him to wrath in a waterless place? [41] And they turned back and tempted God, and they exasperated the Holy One of Israel. [42] They did not remember his hand, in the day that he redeemed them from the hand of the one troubling them. [43] Thus, he positioned his signs in Egypt and his wonders in the field of Tanis. [44] And he turned their rivers into blood, along with their rain showers, so that they could not drink. [45] He sent among them the common fly, and it devoured them, and the frog, and it scattered them. [46] And he gave up their fruits to mold and their labors to the locust. [47] And he slew their vineyards with hail and their mulberry trees with severe frost. [48] And he delivered their cattle to the hail and their possessions to fire. [49] And he sent the wrath of his indignation among them: indignation and wrath and tribulation, sent forth by evil angels. [50] He made way for the path of his anger. He did not spare their souls from death. And he enclosed their beasts of burden in death. [51] And he struck all the first-born in the land of Egypt: the first-fruits of all their labor in the tabernacles of Ham. [52] And he took away his own people like sheep, and he led them through the wilderness like a flock. [53] And he led them out in hope, and they did not fear. And the sea covered their enemies. [54] And he led them to the mountain of his sanctification: the mountain that his right hand had acquired. And he cast out the Gentiles before their face. And he divided their land by lot to them, with a line of distribution. [55] And he caused the tribes of Israel to dwell in their tabernacles. [56] Yet they tempted and aggravated God Most High, and they did not keep his testaments. [57] And they turned themselves aside, and they did not serve the covenant. In the same manner as their fathers, they were turned backwards, like a crooked bow. [58] They impelled him to anger on their hills, and they provoked him to rivalry with their graven images. [59] God listened, and he spurned them, and he reduced Israel greatly, almost to nothing. [60] And he rejected the tabernacle of Shiloh, his tabernacle where he had dwelt among men. [61] And he delivered their virtue into captivity, and their beauty into the hands of the enemy. [62] And he enclosed his people with the sword, and he spurned his inheritance. [63] Fire consumed their young men, and their virgins were not lamented. [64] Their priests fell by the sword, and their widows did not weep. [65] And the Lord was awakened, as if out of sleep, and like a powerful man impaired by wine. [66] And he struck his enemies on the back. He gave them over to everlasting disgrace. [67] And he rejected the tabernacle of Joseph, and he did not choose the tribe of Ephraim. [68] But he chose the tribe of Judah: mount Zion, which he loved. [69] And he built up his sanctuary, like a single-horned beast, in the land that he founded for all ages. [70] And he chose his servant David, and he took him from the flocks of the sheep: he received him from following the ewes with their young, [71] in order to pasture Jacob his servant and Israel his inheritance. [72] And he fed them with the innocence of his heart. And he led them with the understanding of his hands.

CHAPTER 78 (79)

[1] A Psalm of Asaph. O God, the Gentiles have entered into your inheritance; they have polluted your holy temple. They have set Jerusalem as a place to tend fruit trees. [2] They have placed the dead bodies of your servants as food for the birds of the sky, the flesh of your saints for the beasts of the earth. [3] They have poured out their blood like water all around Jerusalem, and there was no one who would bury them. [4] We have become a disgrace to our neighbors, an object of ridicule and mockery to those who are around us. [5] How long, O Lord? Will you be angry until the end? Will your zeal be kindled like a fire? [6] Pour out your wrath among the Gentiles, who have not known you, and upon the kingdoms that have not invoked your name. [7] For they have devoured Jacob, and they have desolated his place. [8] Do not remember our iniquities of the past. May your mercies quickly intercept us, for we have become exceedingly poor. [9] Help us, O God, our Savior. And free us, Lord, for the glory of your name. And forgive us our sins for the sake of your name. [10] Let them not say among the Gentiles, "Where is their God?" And may your name become known among the nations before our eyes. For the retribution of your servants' blood, which has been poured out: [11] may the groans of the shackled enter before you. According to the greatness of your arm, take

possession of the sons of those who have been killed. ¹²And repay our neighbors sevenfold within their sinews. It is the reproach of the same ones who brought reproach against you, O Lord. ¹³But we are your people and the sheep of your pasture: we will give thanks to you in all ages. From generation to generation, we will announce your praise.

CHAPTER 79 (80)

¹Unto the end. For those who will be changed. The testimony of Asaph. A Psalm. ²The One who reigns over Israel: Be attentive. For you lead Joseph like a sheep. The One who sits upon the cherubim: Shine forth ³in the presence of Ephraim, Benjamin, and Manasseh. Awaken your power and draw near, so as to accomplish our salvation. ⁴Convert us, O God. And reveal your face, and we will be saved. ⁵O Lord, God of hosts, how long will you be angry over the prayer of your servant? ⁶How long will you feed us the bread of tears, and give us to drink a full measure of tears? ⁷You have set us as a contradiction to our neighbors. And our enemies have ridiculed us. ⁸O God of hosts, convert us. And reveal your face, and we will be saved. ⁹You have transferred a vineyard from Egypt. You have cast out the Gentiles, and planted it. ¹⁰You were the leader of the journey in its sight. You planted its roots, and it filled the earth. ¹¹Its shadow covered the hills, and its branches covered the cedars of God. ¹²It extended its new branches even to the sea, and its new seedlings even to the river. ¹³So then, why have you destroyed its walls, so that all those who pass by the way gather its grapes? ¹⁴The wild boar of the forest has trampled it, and a single wild beast has laid waste to it. ¹⁵Turn back, O God of hosts. Look down from heaven, and see, and visit this vineyard; ¹⁶and complete what your right hand has planted, and look upon the son of man, whom you have confirmed for yourself. ¹⁷Whatever has been set on fire and dug under will perish at the rebuke of your countenance. ¹⁸Let your hand be over the man on your right, and over the son of man, whom you have confirmed for yourself. ¹⁹For we do not depart from you, and you will revive us. And we will invoke your name. ²⁰O Lord, God of hosts, convert us. And reveal your face, and we will be saved.

CHAPTER 80 (81)

¹Unto the end. For the wine and oil presses. A Psalm of Asaph himself. ²Exult before God our helper. Sing joyfully to the God of Jacob. ³Take up a psalm, and bring forth the timbrel: a pleasing Psalter with stringed instruments. ⁴Sound the trumpet at the new moon, on the noteworthy day of your solemnity, ⁵for it is a precept in Israel and a judgment for the God of Jacob. ⁶He set it as a testimony with Joseph, when he went out of the land of Egypt. He heard a tongue that he did not know. ⁷He turned the burdens away from his back. His hands had been a slave to baskets. ⁸You called upon me in tribulation, and I freed you. I heard you within the hidden tempest. I tested you with waters of contradiction. ⁹My people, listen and I will call you to testify. If, O Israel, you will pay heed to me, ¹⁰then there will be no new god among you, nor will you adore a foreign god. ¹¹For I am the Lord your God, who led you out of the land of Egypt. Widen your mouth, and I will fill it. ¹²But my people did not hear my voice, and Israel was not attentive to me. ¹³And so, I sent them away, according to the desires of their heart. They will go forth according to their own inventions. ¹⁴If my people had heard me, if Israel had walked in my ways, ¹⁵I would have humbled their enemies, as if it were nothing, and I would have sent my hand upon those who troubled them. ¹⁶The enemies of the Lord have lied to him, and their time will come, in every age. ¹⁷And he fed them from the fat of the grain, and he saturated them with honey from the rock.

CHAPTER 81 (82)

¹A Psalm of Asaph. God has stood in the synagogue of gods, but, in their midst, he decides between gods. ²How long will you judge unjustly and favor the faces of sinners? ³Judge for the indigent and the orphan. Do justice to the humble and the poor. ⁴Rescue the poor, and free the needy from the hand of the sinner. ⁵They did not know and did not understand. They wander in darkness. All the foundations of the earth will be moved. ⁶I said: You are gods, and all of you are sons of the Most High. ⁷But you will die like men, and you will fall just like one of the princes. ⁸Rise up, O God. Judge the earth. For you will inherit it with all the nations.

CHAPTER 82 (83)

[1] A Canticle Psalm of Asaph. [2] O God, who will ever be like you? Do not be silent, and do not be unmoved, O God. [3] For behold, your enemies have sounded off, and those who hate you have carried out a head. [4] They have acted with malice in counsel over your people, and they have plotted against your holy ones. [5] They have said, "Come, let us scatter them from the nations and not allow the name of Israel to be remembered any longer." [6] For they plotted unanimously. Joined together against you, they ordained a covenant: [7] the tabernacle of Edomites and Ishmaelites, and Moab and the Hagarites, [8] and Gebal, and Ammon, and Amalek, the foreigners among the inhabitants of Tyre. [9] For even Assur comes with them. They have become the helpers of the sons of Lot. [10] Do to them as you did to Midian and Sisera, just as to Jabin at the torrent of Kishon. [11] They perished at Endor, and they became like the dung of the earth. [12] Set their leaders to be like Oreb and Zeeb, and Zebah and Zalmunna: all their leaders [13] who said, "Let us possess the Sanctuary of God for an inheritance." [14] My God, set them like a wheel, and like stubble before the face of the wind. [15] Set them like a fire burning up the forest, and like a flame burning up the mountains. [16] So will you pursue them in your tempest, and disturb them in your wrath. [17] Fill their faces with shame, and they will seek your name, O Lord. [18] Let them be ashamed and troubled, from age to age, and let them be confounded and perish. [19] And let them know that the Lord is your name. You alone are the Most High in all the earth.

CHAPTER 83 (84)

[1] Unto the end. For the wine and oil presses. A Psalm to the sons of Korah. [2] How beloved are your tabernacles, O Lord of hosts! [3] My soul longs and faints for the courts of the Lord. My heart and my flesh have exulted in the living God. [4] For even the sparrow has found a home for himself, and the turtle-dove a nest for herself, where she may lay her young: your altars, O Lord of hosts, my king and my God. [5] Blessed are those who dwell in your house, O Lord. They will praise you from age to age. [6] Blessed is the man whose help is from you. In his heart, he is disposed to ascend [7] from the valley of tears, from the place which he has determined. [8] For even the lawgiver will provide a blessing; they will go from virtue to virtue. The God of gods will be seen in Zion. [9] O Lord, God of hosts, hear my prayer. Pay attention, O God of Jacob. [10] O God, gaze upon our protector, and look upon the face of your Christ. [11] For one day in your courts is better than thousands elsewhere. I have chosen to be lowly in the house of my God, rather than to dwell in the tabernacles of sinners. [12] For God loves mercy and truth. The Lord will give grace and glory. [13] He will not withhold good things from those who walk in innocence. O Lord of hosts, blessed is the man who hopes in you.

CHAPTER 84 (85)

[1] Unto the end. A Psalm to the sons of Korah. [2] O Lord, you have blessed your land. You have turned aside the captivity of Jacob. [3] You have released the iniquity of your people. You have covered all their sins. [4] You have mitigated all your wrath. You have turned aside from the wrath of your indignation. [5] Convert us, O God, our Savior, and turn your anger away from us. [6] Will you be angry with us forever? And will you extend your wrath from generation to generation? [7] O God, you will turn back and revive us. And your people will rejoice in you. [8] O Lord, reveal to us your mercy, and grant to us your salvation. [9] I will listen to what the Lord God may be saying to me. For he will speak peace to his people, and to his saints, and to those who are being converted to the heart. [10] So then, truly his salvation is near to those who fear him, so that glory may inhabit our land. [11] Mercy and truth have met each other. Justice and peace have kissed. [12] Truth has risen from the earth, and justice has gazed down from heaven. [13] For so will the Lord give goodness, and our earth will give her fruit. [14] Justice will walk before him, and he will set his steps upon the way.

CHAPTER 85 (86)

[1] A Prayer of David himself. Incline your ear, O Lord, and hear me. For I am needy and poor. [2] Preserve my soul, for I am holy. My God, bring salvation to your servant who hopes in you. [3] O Lord, be merciful to me, for I have cried out to you all day long. [4] Give joy to the soul of your servant, for I have lifted up my soul to you, Lord. [5] For you are sweet and mild, Lord, and plentiful in mercy to

all who call upon you. [6]Pay attention, Lord, to my prayer, and attend to the voice of my supplication. [7]In the day of my tribulation, I cried out to you, because you heeded me. [8]There is no one like you among the gods, O Lord, and there is no one like you in your works. [9]All the nations, which you have made, will draw near and adore in your presence, O Lord. And they will glorify your name. [10]For you are great, and you perform wonders. You alone are God. [11]Lead me, O Lord, in your way, and I will walk in your truth. May my heart rejoice, so that it will fear your name. [12]I will confess to you, O Lord my God, with my whole heart. And I will glorify your name in eternity. [13]For your mercy toward me is great, and you have rescued my soul from the lower part of Hell. [14]O God, the iniquitous have risen up against me, and the synagogue of the powerful have sought my soul, and they have not placed you in their sight. [15]And you, Lord God, are compassionate and merciful, being patient and full of mercy and truthful. [16]Look down upon me and have mercy on me. Grant your authority to your servant, and bring salvation to the son of your handmaid. [17]Make me a sign of what is good, so that those who hate me, may look and be confounded. For you, O Lord, have helped me and consoled me.

CHAPTER 86 (87)

[1]A Canticle Psalm to the sons of Korah. Its foundations are in the holy mountains: [2]the Lord loves the gates of Zion above all the tabernacles of Jacob. [3]Glorious things are being said of you, O City of God. [4]I will be mindful of Rahab and of Babylon knowing me. Behold, the foreigners, and Tyre, and the people of the Ethiopians: these have been there. [5]Will not Zion say that this man and that man were born in her? And the Most High himself has founded her. [6]The Lord will explain, in the writings of peoples and of leaders, about those who have been in her. [7]For so the dwelling place within you is with all rejoicing.

CHAPTER 87 (88)

[1]A Canticle Psalm to the sons of Korah. Unto the end. For Mahalath, to answer the understanding of Heman the Ezrahite. [2]O Lord, God of my salvation: I have cried out, day and night, in your presence. [3]Let my prayer enter in your sight. Incline your ear to my petition. [4]For my soul has been filled with evils, and my life has drawn near to Hell. [5]I am considered to be among those who will descend into the pit. I have become like a man without assistance, [6]idle among the dead. I am like the wounded sleeping in sepulchers, whom you no longer remember, and who have been repelled by your hand. [7]They have lain me in the lower pit: in dark places and in the shadow of death. [8]Your fury has been confirmed over me. And you have brought all your waves upon me. [9]You have sent my acquaintances far from me. They have set me as an abomination to themselves. I was handed over, yet I did not depart. [10]My eyes languished before destitution. All day long, I cried out to you, O Lord. I stretched out my hands to you. [11]Will you perform wonders for the dead? Or will physicians raise to life, and so confess to you? [12]Could anyone declare your mercy in the sepulcher, or your truth from within perdition? [13]Will your wonders be known in the darkness, or your justice in the land of oblivion? [14]And I have cried out to you, O Lord, and in early morning, my prayer will come before you. [15]Lord, why do you reject my prayer? Why do you turn your face away from me? [16]I am poor, and I have been amid hardships from my youth. And, though I have been exalted, I am humbled and disturbed. [17]Your wrath has crossed into me, and your terrors have disturbed me. [18]They have surrounded me like water, all day long. They have surrounded me, all at once. [19]Friend and neighbor, and my acquaintances, you have sent far away from me, away from misery.

CHAPTER 88 (89)

[1]The understanding of Ethan the Ezrahite. [2]I will sing the mercies of the Lord in eternity. I will announce your truth with my mouth, from generation to generation. [3]For you have said: Mercy will be built in the heavens, unto eternity. Your truth will be prepared there. [4]I have set up a covenant with my elect. I have sworn to David my servant: [5]I will prepare your offspring, even in eternity. And I will build up your throne, from generation to generation. [6]The heavens will confess your miracles, Lord, and also your truth, in the Church of the saints. [7]For who among the clouds is equal to the Lord? Who among the sons of God is like God? [8]God is glorified by the counsel of the saints. He is great and terrible above

all those who are around him. [9] O Lord, God of hosts, who is like you? You are powerful, Lord, and your truth is all around you. [10] You rule over the power of the sea, and you even mitigate the movement of its waves. [11] You have humbled the arrogant one, like one who has been wounded. You have scattered your enemies with the arm of your strength. [12] Yours are the heavens, and yours is the earth. You founded the whole world in all its fullness. [13] You created the north and the sea. Tabor and Hermon will exult in your name. [14] Your arm acts with power. Let your hand be strengthened, and let your right hand be exalted. [15] Justice and judgment are the preparation of your throne. Mercy and truth will precede your face. [16] Blessed is the people that knows jubilation. They will walk in the light of your countenance, O Lord, [17] and they will exult in your name all day long, and they will be exalted in your justice. [18] For you are the glory of their virtue, and in your goodness, our horn will be exalted. [19] For our assumption is of the Lord, and it is of our king, the holy one of Israel. [20] Then you spoke in a vision to your holy ones, and you said: I have stationed help with the powerful one, and I have exalted the elect one from my people. [21] I have found my servant David. I have anointed him with my holy oil. [22] For my hand will assist him, and my arm will fortify him. [23] The enemy will have no advantage over him, nor will the son of iniquity be positioned to harm him. [24] And I will cut down his enemies before his face. And those who hate him, I will turn to flight. [25] And my truth and my mercy will be with him. And his horn will be exalted in my name. [26] And I will place his hand on the sea and his right hand on the rivers. [27] He will invoke me: "You are my father, my God, and the support of my salvation." [28] And I will make him the first-born, preeminent before the kings of the earth. [29] I will preserve my mercy for him eternally, and my covenant for him faithfully. [30] And I will set his offspring from generation to generation, and his throne like the days of heaven. [31] But if his sons abandon my law, and if they do not walk in my judgments, [32] if they profane my justices, and if they do not keep my commandments: [33] I will visit their iniquities with a rod, and their sins with a beating. [34] But I will not scatter my mercy from him, and I will not do harm to my truth. [35] And I will not profane my covenant, and I will not make void that which proceeds from my lips. [36] I have sworn by my holiness one time: I will not lie to David, [37] his offspring will remain for eternity. And his throne will be like the sun in my sight, [38] and, like the moon, it is perfected in eternity, and it is a faithful witness in heaven. [39] Yet, truly, you have rejected and despised, you have pushed away, my Christ. [40] You have overthrown the covenant of your servant. You have profaned his sanctuary on earth. [41] You have destroyed all his fences. You have made his territory dreadful. [42] All who pass by the way have plundered him. He has become a disgrace to his neighbors. [43] You have exalted the right hand of those who oppress him. You have brought joy to all his enemies. [44] You have diverted the help of his sword, and you have not assisted him in battle. [45] You have torn him away from cleansing, and you have smashed his throne down to the ground. [46] You have reduced the days of his time. You have flooded him with confusion. [47] How long, O Lord? Will you turn away unto the end? Will your wrath flare up like a fire? [48] Remember what my substance is. For could you really have appointed all the sons of men in vain? [49] Who is the man that will live, and yet not see death? Who will rescue his own soul from the hand of the underworld? [50] O Lord, where are your mercies of antiquity, just as you swore to David in your truth? [51] Be mindful, O Lord, of the disgrace of your servants (which I have sustained in my sinews) among many nations. [52] With these, your enemies have reproached you, O Lord; with these, they have reproached the commutation of your Christ. [53] Blessed is the Lord for all eternity. Amen. Amen.

CHAPTER 89 (90)

[1] A prayer of Moses, the man of God. O Lord, you have been our refuge from generation to generation. [2] Before the mountains became, or the land was formed along with the world: from ages past, even to all ages, you are God. [3] And, lest man be turned aside in humiliation, you have said: Be converted, O sons of men. [4] For a thousand years before your eyes are like the days of yesterday, which have passed by, and they are like a watch of the night, [5] which was held for nothing: so their years shall be. [6] In the morning, he may pass away like grass; in the morning, he may flower and pass away. In the evening, he will fall, and harden, and become dry. [7] For, at your wrath, we have withered away, and we have been disturbed by your fury. [8] You have placed our iniquities in your sight, our age in the illumination of your countenance. [9] For all our days have faded away, and at

your wrath, we have fainted. Our years will be considered to be like a spider's web. [10] The days of our years in them are seventy years. But in the powerful, they are eighty years, and more of these are with hardship and sorrow. For mildness has overwhelmed us, and we shall be corrected. [11] Who knows the power of your wrath? And, before fear, can your wrath [12] be numbered? So make known your right hand, along with men learned in heart, in wisdom. [13] Return, O Lord, how long? And may you be persuaded on behalf of your servants. [14] We were filled in the morning with your mercy, and we exulted and delighted all our days. [15] We have been rejoicing, because of the days in which you humbled us, because of the years in which we saw evils. [16] Look down upon your servants and upon their works, and direct their sons. [17] And may the splendor of the Lord our God be upon us. And so, direct the works of our hands over us; direct even the work of our hands.

CHAPTER 90 (91)

[1] The Praise of a Canticle, of David. Whoever dwells with the assistance of the Most High will abide in the protection of the God of heaven. [2] He will say to the Lord, "You are my supporter and my refuge." My God, I will hope in him. [3] For he has freed me from the snare of those who go hunting, and from the harsh word. [4] He will overshadow you with his shoulders, and you will hope under his wings. [5] His truth will surround you with a shield. You will not be afraid: before the terror of the night, [6] before the arrow flying in the day, before the troubles that wander in the darkness, nor of invasion and the midday demon. [7] A thousand will fall before your side and ten thousand before your right hand. Yet it will not draw near you. [8] So then, truly, you will consider with your eyes, and you will see the retribution of sinners. [9] For you, O Lord, are my hope. You have set the Most High as your refuge. [10] Disaster will not draw near to you, and the scourge will not approach your tabernacle. [11] For he has given his Angels charge over you, so as to preserve you in all your ways. [12] With their hands, they will carry you, lest you hurt your foot against a stone. [13] You will walk over the asp and the king serpent, and you will trample the lion and the dragon. [14] Because he has hoped in me, I will free him. I will protect him because he has known my name. [15] He will cry out to me, and I will heed him. I am with him in tribulation. I will rescue him, and I will glorify him. [16] I will fill him with length of days. And I will reveal to him my salvation.

CHAPTER 91 (92)

[1] A Canticle Psalm. On the day of the Sabbath. [2] It is good to confess to the Lord and to sing psalms to your name, O Most High: [3] to announce your mercy in the morning, and your truth throughout the night, [4] upon the ten strings, upon the psaltery, with a canticle, upon stringed instruments. [5] For you, O Lord, have delighted me with your doings, and I will exult in the works of your hands. [6] How great are your works, O Lord! Your thoughts have been made exceedingly deep. [7] A foolish man will not know these things, and a senseless one will not understand: [8] when sinners will have risen up like grass, and when all those who work iniquity will have appeared, that they shall pass away, age after age. [9] But you, O Lord, are the Most High for all eternity. [10] For behold your enemies, O Lord, for behold your enemies will perish, and all those who work iniquity will be dispersed. [11] And my horn will be exalted like that of the single-horned beast, and my old age will be exalted in fruitful mercy. [12] And my eye has looked down upon my enemies, and my ear will hear of the malignant rising up against me. [13] The just one will flourish like the palm tree. He will be multiplied like the cedar of Lebanon. [14] Those planted in the house of the Lord will flourish in the courts of the house of our God. [15] They will still be multiplied in a fruitful old age, and they will endure well, [16] so that they may announce that the Lord our God is righteous and that there is no iniquity in him.

CHAPTER 92 (93)

[1] The Praise of a Canticle, of David himself. In the time before the Sabbath, when the earth was founded. [2] The Lord has reigned. He has been clothed with beauty. [3] The Lord has been clothed with strength, and he has girded himself. Yet he has also confirmed the world, which will not be moved. [4] My throne is prepared from of old. You are from everlasting. [5] The floods have lifted up, O Lord, the floods have lifted up their voice. The floods have lifted up their waves, [6] before the noise

of many waters. Wondrous are the surges of the sea; wondrous is the Lord on high. [7] Your testimonies have been made exceedingly trustworthy. Sanctity befits your house, O Lord, with length of days.

CHAPTER 93 (94)

[1] A Psalm of David himself. The Fourth Sabbath. The Lord is the God of retribution. The God of retribution acts in order to deliver. [2] Lift yourself up, for you judge the earth. Repay the arrogant with retribution. [3] How long will sinners, O Lord, how long will sinners glory? [4] How long will they utter and speak iniquity? How long will all who work injustice speak out? [5] They have humiliated your people, O Lord, and they have harassed your inheritance. [6] They have executed the widow and the new arrival, and they have slaughtered the orphan. [7] And they have said, "The Lord will not see, nor will the God of Jacob understand." [8] Understand, you senseless ones among the people. And be wise at last, you foolish ones. [9] He who formed the ear, will he not hear? And he who forged the eye, does he not look closely? [10] He who chastises nations, he who teaches man knowledge, will he not rebuke? [11] The Lord knows the thoughts of men: that these are in vain. [12] Blessed is the man whom you will instruct, O Lord. And you will teach him from your law. [13] So may you soothe him from the evil days, until a pit may be dug for sinners. [14] For the Lord will not drive away his people, and he will not abandon his inheritance, [15] even until the time when justice is being converted into judgment, and when those who are close to justice are all those who are upright of heart. [16] Who will rise up with me against the malignant? Or who will stand with me against the workers of iniquity? [17] Except that the Lord assisted me, my soul almost would have dwelt in Hell. [18] If ever I said, "My foot is slipping," then your mercy, O Lord, assisted me. [19] According to the multitude of my sorrows in my heart, your consolations have given joy to my soul. [20] Does the seat of iniquity adhere to you, you who contrive hardship within a commandment? [21] They will hunt down the soul of the just, and they will condemn innocent blood. [22] And the Lord has been made into a refuge for me, and my God into the assistance of my hope. [23] And he will repay them their iniquity, and he will destroy them in their malice. The Lord our God will utterly destroy them.

CHAPTER 94 (95)

[1] The Praise of a Canticle, of David himself. Come, let us exult in the Lord. Let us shout joyfully to God, our Savior. [2] Let us anticipate his presence with confession, and let us sing joyfully to him with psalms. [3] For the Lord is a great God and a great King over all gods. [4] For in his hand are all the limits of the earth, and the heights of the mountains are his. [5] For the sea is his, and he made it, and his hands formed the dry land. [6] Come, let us adore and fall prostrate, and let us weep before the Lord who made us. [7] For he is the Lord our God, and we are the people of his pasture and the sheep of his hand. [8] If today you hear his voice, harden not your hearts: [9] as in the provocation, according to the day of temptation in the wilderness, where your fathers tempted me; they tested me, though they had seen my works. [10] For forty years, I was offended by that generation, and I said: These have always strayed in heart. [11] And these have not known my ways. So I swore in my wrath: They shall not enter into my rest.

CHAPTER 95 (96)

[1] A Canticle of David himself, when the house was built after the captivity. Sing to the Lord a new song. Sing to the Lord, all the earth. [2] Sing to the Lord and bless his name. Announce his salvation from day to day. [3] Announce his glory among the Gentiles, his miracles among all peoples. [4] For the Lord is great and greatly to be praised. He is terrible, beyond all gods. [5] For all the gods of the Gentiles are demons, but the Lord made the heavens. [6] Confession and beauty are in his sight. Sanctity and magnificence are in his sanctuary. [7] Bring to the Lord, you natives of the nations, bring to the Lord glory and honor. [8] Bring to the Lord glory for his name. Lift up sacrifices, and enter into his courts. [9] Adore the Lord in his holy court. Let the entire earth be shaken before his face. [10] Say among the Gentiles: The Lord has reigned. For he has even corrected the whole world, which will not be shaken. He will judge the peoples with fairness. [11] Let the heavens rejoice, and let the earth exult; let the sea and all its fullness be moved. [12] The fields and all the things that are in them will be glad. Then all the

trees of the forest will rejoice ¹³before the face of the Lord: for he arrives. For he arrives to judge the earth. He will judge the whole world with fairness and the peoples with his truth.

CHAPTER 96 (97)

¹This is to David, when his land was restored to him. The Lord has reigned, let the earth exult. Let the many islands rejoice. ²Clouds and mist are all around him. Justice and judgment are corrections from his throne. ³A fire will precede him, and it will enflame his enemies all around. ⁴His lightnings have enlightened the whole world. The earth saw, and it was shaken. ⁵The mountains flowed like wax before the face of the Lord, before the face of the Lord of all the earth. ⁶The heavens announced his justice, and all peoples saw his glory. ⁷May all those who adore graven images be confounded, along with those who glory in their false images. All you his Angels: Adore him. ⁸Zion heard, and was glad. And the daughters of Judah exulted because of your judgments, O Lord. ⁹For you are the Most High Lord over all the earth. You are greatly exalted above all gods. ¹⁰You who love the Lord: hate evil. The Lord watches over the souls of his holy ones. He will free them from the hand of the sinner. ¹¹The light has risen for the just, and joy for the upright of heart. ¹²Rejoice in the Lord, you just ones, and confess to the memory of his sanctuary.

CHAPTER 97 (98)

¹A Psalm of David himself. Sing to the Lord a new song, for he has performed wonders. His right hand has accomplished salvation for him, with his holy arm. ²The Lord has made known his salvation. He has revealed his justice in the sight of the nations. ³He has remembered his mercy and his truth toward the house of Israel. All the ends of the earth have seen the salvation of our God. ⁴Sing joyfully to God, all the earth. Sing and exult, and sing psalms. ⁵Sing psalms to the Lord with stringed instruments, with strings and the voice of a psalmist, ⁶with subtle wind instruments and the voice of woodwinds. Make a joyful noise before the Lord our king. ⁷Let the sea be moved and all its fullness, the whole world and all who dwell in it. ⁸The rivers will clap their hands, the mountains will exult together, ⁹before the presence of the Lord. For he comes to judge the earth. He will judge the whole world with justice, and the peoples with fairness.

CHAPTER 98 (99)

¹A Psalm of David himself. The Lord has reigned: let the peoples be angry. He sits upon the cherubim: let the earth be moved. ²The Lord is great in Zion, and he is high above all peoples. ³May they confess to your great name, for it is terrible and holy. ⁴And the honor of the king loves judgment. You have prepared guidance. You have accomplished judgment and justice in Jacob. ⁵Exalt the Lord our God, and adore the footstool of his feet, for it is holy. ⁶Moses and Aaron are among his priests, and Samuel is among those who call upon his name. They called upon the Lord, and he heeded them. ⁷He spoke to them in the pillar of the cloud. They kept his testimonies and the precept that he gave them. ⁸You heeded them, O Lord our God. You were a forgiving God to them, though taking vengeance on all their inventions. ⁹Exalt the Lord our God, and adore on his holy mountain. For the Lord our God is holy.

CHAPTER 99 (100)

¹A Psalm of Confession. ²Shout joyfully to God, all the earth. Serve the Lord with rejoicing. Enter into his sight in exultation. ³Know that the Lord himself is God. He made us, and we ourselves did not. We are his people and the sheep of his pasture. ⁴Enter his gates with confession, his courts with hymns, and acknowledge him. Praise his name. ⁵For the Lord is sweet, his mercy is in eternity, and his truth is from generation to generation.

CHAPTER 100 (101)

¹A Psalm of David himself. I will sing mercy and judgment to you, O Lord. I will sing psalms. ²And I will have understanding within the immaculate way, when you will draw near to me. I wandered about in the innocence of my heart, in the midst of my house. ³I will not display any unjust thing before my eyes. I have hated those carrying out betrayals. ⁴The perverse heart did not adhere to me. And

the malignant, who turned away before me, I would not recognize. ⁵ The one who secretly detracted his neighbor, this one I pursued. The one with an arrogant eye and an insatiable heart, with that one I would not eat. ⁶ My eyes looked toward the faithful of the earth, to sit with me. The one walking in the immaculate way, this one ministered to me. ⁷ He who has acted arrogantly will not dwell in the midst of my house. He who has spoken iniquity was not guided with the sight of my eyes. ⁸ In the morning, I executed all the sinners of the earth, so that I might scatter all the workers of iniquity from the city of the Lord.

CHAPTER 101 (102)

¹ The prayer of the pauper, when he was anxious, and so he poured out his petition in the sight of the Lord. ² O Lord, hear my prayer, and let my outcry reach you. ³ Do not turn your face away from me. In whatever day that I am in trouble, incline your ear to me. In whatever day that I will call upon you, heed me quickly. ⁴ For my days have faded away like smoke, and my bones have dried out like firewood. ⁵ I have been cut down like hay, and my heart has withered, for I had forgotten to eat my bread. ⁶ Before the voice of my groaning, my bone has adhered to my flesh. ⁷ I have become like a pelican in solitude. I have become like a night raven in a house. ⁸ I have kept vigil, and I have become like a solitary sparrow on a roof. ⁹ All day long my enemies reproached me, and those who praised me swore oaths against me. ¹⁰ For I chewed on ashes like bread, and I mixed weeping into my drink. ¹¹ By the face of your anger and indignation, you lifted me up and threw me down. ¹² My days have declined like a shadow, and I have dried out like hay. ¹³ But you, O Lord, endure for eternity, and your memorial is from generation to generation. ¹⁴ You will rise up and take pity on Zion, for it is time for its mercy, for the time has come. ¹⁵ For its stones have pleased your servants, and they will take pity on its land. ¹⁶ And the Gentiles will fear your name, O Lord, and all the kings of the earth your glory. ¹⁷ For the Lord has built up Zion, and he will be seen in his glory. ¹⁸ He has noticed the prayer of the humble, and he has not despised their petition. ¹⁹ Let these things be written in another generation, and the people who will be created will praise the Lord. ²⁰ For he has gazed from his high sanctuary. From heaven, the Lord has beheld the earth. ²¹ So may he hear the groans of those in shackles, in order that he may release the sons of the slain. ²² So may they announce the name of the Lord in Zion and his praise in Jerusalem: ²³ while the people convene, along with kings, in order that they may serve the Lord. ²⁴ He responded to him in the way of his virtue: Declare to me the brevity of my days. ²⁵ Do not call me back in the middle of my days: your years are from generation to generation. ²⁶ In the beginning, O Lord, you founded the earth. And the heavens are the work of your hands. ²⁷ They will perish, but you remain. And all will grow old like a garment. And, like a blanket, you will change them, and they will be changed. ²⁸ Yet you are ever yourself, and your years will not decline. ²⁹ The sons of your servants will live, and their offspring will be guided aright in every age.

CHAPTER 102 (103)

¹ To David himself. Bless the Lord, O my soul, and bless his holy name, all that is within me. ² Bless the Lord, O my soul, and do not forget all his recompenses. ³ He forgives all your iniquities. He heals all your infirmities. ⁴ He redeems your life from destruction. He crowns you with mercy and compassion. ⁵ He satisfies your desire with good things. Your youth will be renewed like that of the eagle. ⁶ The Lord accomplishes mercies, and his judgment is for all who patiently endure injuries. ⁷ He has made his ways known to Moses, his will to the sons of Israel. ⁸ The Lord is compassionate and merciful, patient and full of mercy. ⁹ He will not be angry forever, and he will not threaten for eternity. ¹⁰ He has not dealt with us according to our sins, and he has not repaid us according to our iniquities. ¹¹ For according to the height of the heavens above the earth, so has he reinforced his mercy toward those who fear him. ¹² As far as the east is from the west, so far has he removed our iniquities from us. ¹³ As a father is compassionate to his sons, so has the Lord been compassionate to those who fear him. ¹⁴ For he knows our form. He has called to mind that we are dust. ¹⁵ Man: his days are like hay. Like the flower of the field, so will he flourish. ¹⁶ For the spirit in him will pass away, and it will not remain, and he will know his place no longer. ¹⁷ But the mercy of the Lord is from eternity, and even unto eternity, upon those who fear him. And his justice is with the sons of the sons, ¹⁸ with those who serve his covenant and have been mindful of his commandments by doing them. ¹⁹ The Lord has

prepared his throne in heaven, and his kingdom will rule over all. ²⁰Bless the Lord, all you his Angels: powerful in virtue, doing his word, in order to heed the voice of his discourse. ²¹Bless the Lord, all his hosts: his ministers who do his will. ²²Bless the Lord, all his works: in every place of his dominion. Bless the Lord, O my soul.

CHAPTER 103 (104)

¹To David himself. Bless the Lord, O my soul. O Lord my God, you are exceedingly great. You have clothed yourself with confession and beauty; ²you are dressed with light like a garment, while you stretch out heaven like a tent. ³You cover its heights with water. You set the clouds as your stairs. You walk upon the wings of the winds. ⁴You make your Angels a breath of life, and your ministers a burning fire. ⁵You founded the earth upon its stable base. It will not be bent from age to age. ⁶The abyss, like a garment, is its clothing. The waters will remain standing above the mountains. ⁷At your rebuke, they will flee. At the voice of your thunder, they will dread. ⁸The mountains ascend, and the plains descend, to the place which you have founded for them. ⁹You have set a limit that they will not cross. And they will not return to cover the earth. ¹⁰You spring forth fountains in steep valleys. The waters will cross through the midst of the mountains. ¹¹All the wild beasts of the field will drink. The wild donkeys will anticipate in their thirst. ¹²Above them, the flying things of the air will dwell. From the midst of the rocks, they will utter voices. ¹³You irrigate the mountains from your heights. The earth will be satiated from the fruit of your works, ¹⁴producing grass for cattle and herbs for the service of men. So may you draw bread from the earth, ¹⁵and wine, in order to cheer the heart of man. Then he may gladden his face with oil, and bread will confirm the heart of man. ¹⁶The trees of the field will be saturated, along with the cedars of Lebanon, which he planted. ¹⁷There, the sparrows will make their nests. The leader of them is the house of the heron. ¹⁸The heights of the hills are for the deer; the rock is a refuge for the hedgehog. ¹⁹He has made the moon for seasons; the sun knows its setting. ²⁰You appointed darkness, and it has become night; all the beasts of the forest will cross through it. ²¹The young lions will roar, while searching for and seizing their meal from God. ²²The sun arose, and they were gathered together; and in their dens, they will lie down together. ²³Man will go forth to his work and to his activities, until the evening. ²⁴How great are your works, O Lord! You have made all things in wisdom. The earth has been filled with your possessions. ²⁵This sea is great and its hands are spacious. There are creeping things without number: the small animals with the great. ²⁶There, the ships will pass by this sea-serpent that you have formed to mock them. ²⁷All these expect you to give them food in due time. ²⁸What you give to them, they will gather. When you open your hand, they will all be filled with goodness. ²⁹But if you turn your face away, they will be disturbed. You will take away their breath, and they will fail, and they will return to their dust. ³⁰You will send forth your Spirit, and they will be created. And you will renew the face of the earth. ³¹May the glory of the Lord be for all ages. The Lord will rejoice in his works. ³²He considers the earth, and he makes it tremble. He touches the mountains, and they smoke. ³³I will sing to the Lord with my life. I will sing psalms to my God, as long as I am. ³⁴May my speech be pleasing to him. Truly, I will take delight in the Lord. ³⁵Let sinners fade away from the earth, along with the unjust, so that they may not be. Bless the Lord, O my soul.

CHAPTER 104 (105)

¹Alleluia. Confess to the Lord, and invoke his name. Announce his works among the nations. ²Sing to him, and sing psalms to him. Describe all his wonders. ³Be praised in his holy name. Let the heart of those who seek the Lord rejoice. ⁴Seek the Lord, and be confirmed. Seek his face always. ⁵Remember his miracles, which he has done, his portents and the judgments of his mouth: ⁶you offspring of Abraham his servant, you sons of Jacob his elect. ⁷He is the Lord our God. His judgments are throughout the entire earth. ⁸He has remembered his covenant for all ages: the word that he entrusted to a thousand generations, ⁹which he assigned to Abraham, and his oath to Isaac. ¹⁰And he stationed the same for Jacob with a precept, and for Israel with an eternal testament, ¹¹saying: To you, I will give the land of Canaan, the allotment of your inheritance. ¹²Though they may have been but a small number, very few and foreigners there, ¹³and though they passed from nation to nation, and from one kingdom to another people, ¹⁴he allowed no

man to harm them, and he reproved kings on their behalf. [15] Do not be willing to touch my Christ, and do not be willing to malign my prophets. [16] And he called a famine upon the land, and he crushed every foundation of the bread. [17] He sent a man before them: Joseph, who had been sold as a slave. [18] They humbled his feet in shackles; the iron pierced his soul, [19] until his word arrived. The eloquence of the Lord inflamed him. [20] The king sent and released him; he was the ruler of the people, and he dismissed him. [21] He established him as master of his house and ruler of all his possessions, [22] so that he might instruct his princes as himself, and teach his elders prudence. [23] And Israel entered into Egypt, and Jacob became a sojourner in the land of Ham. [24] And he helped his people greatly, and he strengthened them over their enemies. [25] He turned their heart to hate his people, and to deal deceitfully with his servants. [26] He sent Moses, his servant, and Aaron, the one whom he chose. [27] He placed with them signs of his word, and portents in the land of Ham. [28] He sent darkness and made it conceal, and he did not afflict them with his speech. [29] He turned their waters into blood, and he slaughtered their fish. [30] Their land brought forth frogs, even in the inner chambers of their kings. [31] He spoke, and there came forth common flies and gnats, in every region. [32] He gave them a shower of hail and a burning fire, in the same land. [33] And he struck their vineyards and their fig trees, and he crushed the trees of their region. [34] He spoke, and the locust came forth, and the caterpillar, of which there was no number. [35] And it devoured all the grass in their land, and it consumed all the fruit of their land. [36] And he struck all the first-born in their land, the first-fruits of all their labor. [37] And he led them out with silver and gold, and there was not an infirm one among their tribes. [38] Egypt was joyful at their departure, for the fear of them lay heavy upon them. [39] He spread a cloud for their protection, and a fire, to give them light through the night. [40] They petitioned, and the quail came; and he satisfied them with the bread of heaven. [41] He ruptured the rock and the waters flowed: rivers gushed in the dry land. [42] For he had called to mind his holy word, which he kept near to his servant Abraham. [43] And he led forth his people in exultation, and his elect in rejoicing. [44] And he gave them the regions of the Gentiles, and they possessed the labors of the peoples, [45] so that they might observe his justifications, and inquire about his law.

CHAPTER 105 (106)

[1] Alleluia. Confess to the Lord, for he is good, for his mercy is with every generation. [2] Who will declare the powers of the Lord? Who make a hearing for all his praises? [3] Blessed are those who keep judgment and who do justice at all times. [4] Remember us, O Lord, with good will for your people. Visit us with your salvation, [5] so that we may see the goodness of your elect, so that we may rejoice in the joy of your nation, so that you may be praised along with your inheritance. [6] We have sinned, as have our fathers. We have acted unjustly; we have wrought iniquity. [7] Our fathers did not understand your miracles in Egypt. They did not remember the multitude of your mercies. And they provoked you, while going up to the sea, even the Red Sea. [8] And he saved them for the sake of his name, so that he might make known his power. [9] And he rebuked the Red Sea, and it dried up. And he led them into the abyss, as if into a desert. [10] And he saved them from the hand of those who hated them. And he redeemed them from the hand of the enemy. [11] And the water covered those who troubled them. Not one of them remained. [12] And they believed his words, and they sang his praises. [13] As soon as they had finished, they forgot his works, and they would not endure his counsel. [14] And they coveted their desire in the desert, and they tempted God in a waterless place. [15] And he granted to them their request, and he sent abundance into their souls. [16] And they provoked Moses in the camp, and Aaron, the holy one of the Lord. [17] The earth opened and swallowed Dathan, and it covered the congregation of Abiram. [18] And a fire broke out in their congregation. A flame burned up the sinners. [19] And they fashioned a calf at Horeb, and they adored a graven image. [20] And they exchanged their glory for the likeness of a calf that eats hay. [21] They forgot God, who saved them, who did great things in Egypt: [22] miracles in the land of Ham, terrible things at the Red Sea. [23] And he said that he would destroy them, yet Moses, his elect, stood firm before him in the breach, in order to avert his wrath, lest he destroy them. [24] And they held the desirable land to be nothing. They did not trust in his word. [25] And they murmured in their tabernacles. They did not heed the voice of the Lord. [26] And he lifted up his hand over them, in order to prostrate them in the desert, [27] and in order to cast their offspring among the nations, and to scatter them among the regions. [28] And

they were initiated into Baal of Peor, and they ate the sacrifices of the dead. ²⁹ And they provoked him with their inventions, and ruination was multiplied in them. ³⁰ Then Phinehas stood up and placated him: and so the violent disturbance ceased. ³¹ And it was reputed to him unto justice, from generation to generation, even forever. ³² And they provoked him at the Waters of Contradiction, and Moses was afflicted because of them, ³³ for they exasperated his spirit. And so he divided them with his lips. ³⁴ They did not destroy the nations, about which the Lord had spoken to them. ³⁵ And they were mixed among the Gentiles. And they learned their works, ³⁶ and they served their graven images, and it became a scandal to them. ³⁷ And they sacrificed their sons and their daughters to demons. ³⁸ And they shed innocent blood: the blood of their sons and of their daughters, which they sacrificed to the graven images of Canaan. And the land was infected with bloodshed, ³⁹ and was contaminated with their works. And they fornicated according to their own inventions. ⁴⁰ And the Lord became furiously angry with his people, and he abhorred his inheritance. ⁴¹ And he delivered them into the hands of the nations. And those who hated them became rulers over them. ⁴² And their enemies afflicted them, and they were humbled under their hands. ⁴³ Many times, he delivered them. Yet they provoked him with their counsel, and they were brought low by their iniquities. ⁴⁴ And he saw that they were in tribulation, and he heard their prayer. ⁴⁵ And he was mindful of his covenant, and he repented according to the multitude of his mercies. ⁴⁶ And he provided for them with mercies, in the sight of all those who had seized them. ⁴⁷ Save us, O Lord our God, and gather us from the nations, so that we may confess your holy name and glory in your praise. ⁴⁸ Blessed is the Lord God of Israel, from ages past, even to all ages. And let all the people say: Amen. Amen.

CHAPTER 106 (107)

¹ Alleluia. Confess to the Lord, for he is good, for his mercy is with every generation. ² Let those who have been redeemed by the Lord say so: those whom he redeemed from the hand of the enemy and gathered from the regions, ³ from the rising of the sun and its setting, from the north and from the sea. ⁴ They wandered into solitude in a waterless place. They did not find the way of the city to be their dwelling place. ⁵ They were hungry, and they were thirsty. Their soul fainted within them. ⁶ And they cried out to the Lord in tribulation, and he rescued them in their necessity. ⁷ And he led them in the right way, so that they might go forth to a city of habitation. ⁸ Let his mercies confess to the Lord, and let his miracles confess to the sons of men. ⁹ For he has satisfied the empty soul, and he has satisfied the hungry soul with good things: ¹⁰ those sitting in darkness and in the shadow of death, shackled by extreme poverty and by iron. ¹¹ For they exasperated the eloquence of God, and they irritated the deliberation of the Most High. ¹² And their heart was brought low with hardships. They were weakened, and there was no one to help them. ¹³ And they cried out to the Lord in their tribulation, and he freed them from their distress. ¹⁴ And he led them out of darkness and the shadow of death, and he broke apart their chains. ¹⁵ Let his mercies confess to the Lord, and let his miracles confess to the sons of men. ¹⁶ For he has crushed the gates of brass and broken the iron bars. ¹⁷ He has taken them up, from the way of their iniquity. For they were brought low, because of their injustices. ¹⁸ Their soul abhorred all food, and they drew near even to the gates of death. ¹⁹ And they cried out to the Lord in their tribulation, and he delivered them in their necessity. ²⁰ He sent his word, and he healed them, and he rescued them from their utter destruction. ²¹ Let his mercies confess to the Lord, and let his miracles confess to the sons of men. ²² And let them offer sacrifice with the sacrifice of praise, and let them announce his works in exultation. ²³ Those who descend to the sea in ships, making their livelihood in the great waters: ²⁴ these have seen the works of the Lord and his wonders in the deep. ²⁵ He spoke: and a windstorm stood up, and its waves were exalted. ²⁶ They ascend even to the heavens, and they descend even to the abyss. Their soul will waste away in distress. ²⁷ They were troubled, and they moved like a drunkard, and all their wisdom was consumed. ²⁸ And they cried out to the Lord in their tribulation, and he led them out of their distress. ²⁹ And he replaced the storm with a breeze, and its waves were stilled. ³⁰ And they were joyful that it was stilled, and he led them into the haven that they desired. ³¹ Let his mercies confess to the Lord, and let his miracles confess to the sons of men. ³² And let them exalt him in the Church of the people, and praise him in the chair of the elders. ³³ He has placed rivers in the desert and sources of water in dry places, ³⁴ a fruit-bearing land in the midst

of brine, before the malice of those who dwell in it. ³⁵ He has placed a desert in the midst of pools of waters, and a land without water in the midst of sources of water. ³⁶ And he has gathered the hungry together there, and they constructed a city of habitation. ³⁷ And they sowed fields and planted vineyards, and they produced the fruit of nativity. ³⁸ And he blessed them, and they were multiplied exceedingly. And he did not diminish their beasts of burden. ³⁹ And they became few, and they were afflicted by the tribulation of evils and of sorrow. ⁴⁰ Contempt was poured over their leaders, and he caused them to wander in an impassable place, and not on the way. ⁴¹ And he helped the poor out of destitution, and he stationed families like sheep. ⁴² The upright will see, and they will rejoice. And every iniquity will block its mouth. ⁴³ Who is wise and will keep these things? And who will understand the mercies of the Lord?

CHAPTER 107 (108)

¹ A Canticle Psalm, of David himself. ² My heart is prepared, O God, my heart is prepared. I will sing songs, and I will sing psalms in my glory. ³ Rise up, my glory. Rise up, Psalter and harp. I will arise in early morning. ⁴ I will confess to you, O Lord, among the peoples. And I will sing psalms to you among the nations. ⁵ For your mercy is great, beyond the heavens, and your truth, even to the clouds. ⁶ Be exalted, O God, beyond the heavens, and your glory, beyond all the earth, ⁷ so that your beloved may be freed. Save with your right hand, and heed me. ⁸ God has spoken in his holiness. I will exult, and I will divide Shechem, and I will divide by measure the steep valley of tabernacles. ⁹ Gilead is mine, and Manasseh is mine, and Ephraim is the supporter of my head. Judah is my king. ¹⁰ Moab is the cooking pot of my hope. I will extend my shoe in Idumea; the foreigners have become my friends. ¹¹ Who will lead me into the fortified city? Who will lead me, even into Idumea? ¹² Will not you, O God, who had rejected us? And will not you, O God, go out with our armies? ¹³ Grant us help from tribulation, for vain is the help of man. ¹⁴ In God, we will act virtuously, and he will bring our enemies to nothing.

CHAPTER 108 (109)

¹ Unto the end. A Psalm of David. ² O God, do not be silent toward my praise, for the mouth of the sinner and the mouth of the deceitful one have been opened against me. ³ They have spoken against me with deceitful tongues, and they have surrounded me with hateful words, and they fought against me over nothing. ⁴ Instead of choosing to act on my behalf, they detracted me. But I gave myself to prayer. ⁵ And they set evil against me, instead of good, and hatred, in return for my love. ⁶ Establish the sinner over him, and let the devil stand at his right hand. ⁷ When he is judged, may he go forth in condemnation, and may his prayer be counted as sin. ⁸ May his days be few, and let another take his episcopate. ⁹ May his sons be orphans, and his wife a widow. ¹⁰ May his sons be carried by those who walk unsteadily, and may they go begging. And may they be cast out of their dwelling places. ¹¹ May the money lenders scrutinize all his belongings, and let foreigners plunder his labors. ¹² May there be no one to assist him, nor anyone to be compassionate to his orphaned children. ¹³ May his posterity be in utter ruin. In one generation, may his name be wiped away. ¹⁴ May the iniquity of his fathers return in memory before the sight of the Lord, and do not let the sin of his mother be wiped away. ¹⁵ May these be opposite the Lord always, but let their memory perish from the earth. ¹⁶ For certain things are not remembered about them, in order to be merciful. ¹⁷ And so the destitute man was pursued, with the beggar and the remorseful in heart, so as to be put to death. ¹⁸ And he loved a curse, and it came to him. And he was unwilling to have a blessing, and it went far from him. And he clothed himself with curses like a garment, and it entered his inner self like water, and it entered his bones like oil. ¹⁹ May it be to him like a garment that covers him, and like a belt that always cinches him. ²⁰ This is the work of those who detract me with the Lord and who speak evils against my soul. ²¹ But as for you, Lord, O Lord: act on my behalf for your name's sake. For your mercy is sweet. ²² Free me, for I am destitute and poor, and my heart has been disquieted within me. ²³ I have been taken away like a shadow when it declines, and I have been shaken off like locusts. ²⁴ My knees have been weakened by fasting, and my flesh has been replaced by oil. ²⁵ And I have become a disgrace to them. They saw me, and they shook their heads. ²⁶ Help me, O Lord, my God. Save me according to your mercy. ²⁷ And let them know that this is your hand, and that you, O Lord, have done this. ²⁸ They will curse, and you will bless. May

those who rise up against me be confounded. But your servant will rejoice. ²⁹ May those who detract me be clothed with shame, and may they be covered with their confusion, as if with a double cloak. ³⁰ I will confess exceedingly to the Lord with my mouth. And I will praise him in the midst of the multitude. ³¹ For he stands at the right hand of the poor, in order to save my soul from persecutors.

CHAPTER 109 (110)

¹ A Psalm of David. The Lord said to my Lord, "Sit at my right hand, until I make your enemies your footstool." ² The Lord will send forth the scepter of your virtue from Zion. Rule in the midst of your enemies. ³ It is with you from the beginning, in the day of your virtue, in the splendor of the saints. From conception, before the light-bearer, I begot you. ⁴ The Lord has sworn, and he will not repent: "You are a priest forever, according to the order of Melchizedek." ⁵ The Lord is at your right hand. He has broken kings in the day of his wrath. ⁶ He will judge between the nations; he will fill up ruination. He will shatter heads in the land of the many. ⁷ He will drink from the torrent on the way. Because of this, he will exalt the head.

CHAPTER 110 (111)

¹ Alleluia. I will confess to you, O Lord, with my whole heart, in the council of the just and in the congregation. ² Great are the works of the Lord, exquisite in all his intentions. ³ Confession and magnificence are his work. And his justice remains from age to age. ⁴ He has created a memorial to his wonders; he is a merciful and compassionate Lord. ⁵ He has given food to those who fear him. He will be mindful of his covenant in every age. ⁶ He will announce the virtue of his works to his people, ⁷ so that he may give them the inheritance of the nations. The works of his hands are truth and judgment. ⁸ All his commands are faithful: confirmed from age to age, created in truth and fairness. ⁹ He has sent redemption upon his people. He has commanded his covenant for all eternity. Holy and terrible is his name. ¹⁰ The fear of the Lord is the beginning of wisdom. A good understanding is for all who do it. His praise remains from age to age.

CHAPTER 111 (112)

¹ Alleluia. Of the return of Haggai and Zachariah. Blessed is the man who fears the Lord. He will prefer his commandments exceedingly. ² His offspring will be powerful on the earth. The generation of the upright will be blessed. ³ Glory and wealth will be in his house, and his justice shall remain from age to age. ⁴ For the upright, a light has risen up in the darkness. He is merciful and compassionate and just. ⁵ Pleasing is the man who shows mercy and lends. He will order his words with judgment. ⁶ For he will not be disturbed in eternity. ⁷ The just one will be an everlasting memorial. He will not fear a report of disasters. His heart is prepared to hope in the Lord. ⁸ His heart has been confirmed. He will not be disturbed, until he looks down upon his enemies. ⁹ He has distributed, he has given to the poor. His justice shall remain from age to age. His horn shall be exalted in glory. ¹⁰ The sinner will see and become angry. He will gnash his teeth and waste away. The desire of sinners will perish.

CHAPTER 112 (113)

¹ Alleluia. Praise the Lord, children. Praise the name of the Lord. ² Blessed is the name of the Lord, from this time forward and even forever. ³ From the rising of the sun, even to its setting, praiseworthy is the name of the Lord. ⁴ The Lord is high above all nations, and his glory is high above the heavens. ⁵ Who is like the Lord, our God, who dwells on high, ⁶ and who gazes upon the humble things in heaven and on earth? ⁷ He lifts up the needy from the ground, and he urges the poor away from filth, ⁸ so that he may place him with the leaders, with the leaders of his people. ⁹ He causes a barren woman to live in a house, as the joyful mother of sons.

CHAPTER 113 (114-115)

¹ Alleluia. At the departure of Israel from Egypt, the house of Jacob from a barbarous people: ² Judea was made his sanctuary; Israel was made his power. ³ The sea looked, and it fled. The Jordan was turned back again. ⁴ The mountains exulted like rams, and the hills like lambs among the sheep. ⁵ What happened to

you, O sea, so that you fled, and to you, O Jordan, so that you were turned back again? ⁶ What happened to you, O mountains, so that you exulted like rams, and to you, O hills, so that you exulted like lambs among the sheep? ⁷ Before the face of the Lord, the earth was moved, before the face of the God of Jacob. ⁸ He converted the rock into pools of water, and the cliff into fountains of waters. ⁹ Not to us, O Lord, not to us, but to your name give glory. ¹⁰ Give glory to your mercy and your truth, lest the Gentiles should say, "Where is their God?" ¹¹ But our God is in heaven. All things whatsoever that he has willed, he has done. ¹² The idols of the nations are silver and gold, the works of the hands of men. ¹³ They have mouths, and do not speak; they have eyes, and do not see. ¹⁴ They have ears, and do not hear; they have noses, and do not smell. ¹⁵ They have hands, and do not feel; they have feet, and do not walk. Neither will they cry out with their throat. ¹⁶ Let those who make them become like them, along with all who trust in them. ¹⁷ The house of Israel has hoped in the Lord. He is their helper and their protector. ¹⁸ The house of Aaron has hoped in the Lord. He is their helper and their protector. ¹⁹ Those who fear the Lord have hoped in the Lord. He is their helper and their protector. ²⁰ The Lord has been mindful of us, and he has blessed us. He has blessed the house of Israel. He has blessed the house of Aaron. ²¹ He has blessed all who fear the Lord, the small with the great. ²² May the Lord add blessings upon you: upon you, and upon your sons. ²³ Blessed are you by the Lord, who made heaven and earth. ²⁴ The heaven of heaven is for the Lord, but the earth he has given to the sons of men. ²⁵ The dead will not praise you, Lord, and neither will all those who descend into Hell. ²⁶ But we who live will bless the Lord, from this time forward, and even forever.

CHAPTER 114 (116A)

¹ Alleluia. I have loved: therefore, the Lord will heed the voice of my prayer. ² For he has inclined his ear to me. And in my days, I will call upon him. ³ The sorrows of death have surrounded me, and the perils of Hell have found me. I have found tribulation and sorrow. ⁴ And so, I called upon the name of the Lord. O Lord, free my soul. ⁵ Merciful is the Lord, and just. And our God is compassionate. ⁶ The Lord is the keeper of little ones. I was humbled, and he freed me. ⁷ Turn again, my soul, to your rest. For the Lord has done good to you. ⁸ For he has rescued my soul from death, my eyes from tears, my feet from slipping. ⁹ I will please the Lord in the land of the living.

CHAPTER 115 (116B)

¹ Alleluia. I had confidence, because of what I was saying, but then I was greatly humbled. ² I said in my excess, "Every man is a liar." ³ What shall I repay to the Lord, for all the things that he has repaid to me? ⁴ I will take up the cup of salvation, and I will call upon the name of the Lord. ⁵ I will repay my vows to the Lord, in the sight of all his people. ⁶ Precious in the sight of the Lord is the death of his holy ones. ⁷ O Lord, because I am your servant, your servant and the son of your handmaid, you have broken my bonds. ⁸ I will sacrifice to you the sacrifice of praise, and I will invoke the name of the Lord. ⁹ I will repay my vows to the Lord in the sight of all his people, ¹⁰ in the courts of the house of the Lord, in your midst, O Jerusalem.

CHAPTER 116 (117)

¹ Alleluia. All nations, praise the Lord. All peoples, praise him. ² For his mercy has been confirmed over us. And the truth of the Lord remains for all eternity.

CHAPTER 117 (118)

¹ Alleluia. Confess to the Lord, for he is good, for his mercy is forever. ² Let Israel now say: For he is good, for his mercy is forever. ³ Let the house of Aaron now say: For his mercy is forever. ⁴ Let those who fear the Lord now say: For his mercy is forever. ⁵ In my tribulation, I called upon the Lord. And the Lord heeded me with generosity. ⁶ The Lord is my helper. I will not fear what man can do to me. ⁷ The Lord is my helper. And I will look down upon my enemies. ⁸ It is good to trust in the Lord, rather than to trust in man. ⁹ It is good to hope in the Lord, rather than to hope in leaders. ¹⁰ All the nations have surrounded me. And, in the name of the Lord, I have been avenged over them. ¹¹ Surrounding me, they closed in on me. And, in the name of the Lord, I have been avenged over them. ¹² They surrounded me like a swarm, and they burned like fire among the thorns.

And, in the name of the Lord, I have been avenged over them. [13] Having been pushed, I was overturned so as to fall. But the Lord took me up. [14] The Lord is my strength and my praise. And he has become my salvation. [15] A voice of exultation and salvation is in the tabernacles of the just. [16] The right hand of the Lord has wrought virtue. The right hand of the Lord has exalted me. The right hand of the Lord has wrought virtue. [17] I will not die, but I will live. And I will declare the works of the Lord. [18] When chastising, the Lord chastised me. But he has not delivered me over to death. [19] Open the gates of justice to me. I will enter them, and I will confess to the Lord. [20] This is the gate of the Lord. The just will enter by it. [21] I will confess to you because you have heard me. And you have become my salvation. [22] The stone which the builders have rejected, this has become the head of the corner. [23] By the Lord has this been done, and it is a wonder before our eyes. [24] This is the day that the Lord has made. Let us exult and rejoice in it. [25] O Lord, grant salvation to me. O Lord, grant good prosperity. [26] Blessed is he who arrives in the name of the Lord. We have blessed you from the house of the Lord. [27] The Lord is God, and he has enlightened us. Establish a solemn day amid a dense crowd, even to the horn of the altar. [28] You are my God, and I will confess to you. You are my God, and I will exalt you. I will confess to you, for you have heeded me. And you have become my salvation. [29] Confess to the Lord, for he is good, for his mercy is forever.

CHAPTER 118 (119)

[1] Alleluia. ALEPH. Blessed are the immaculate in the way, who walk in the law of the Lord. [2] Blessed are those who examine his testimonies. They seek him with their whole heart. [3] For those who work iniquity have not walked in his ways. [4] You have ordered your commandments to be kept most diligently. [5] I wish that my ways may be directed so as to keep your justifications. [6] Then I will not be confounded, when I will look into all your commandments. [7] I will confess to you with honesty of heart. In this way, I have learned the judgments of your justice. [8] I will keep your justifications. Do not utterly abandon me. [9] BETH. By what does an adolescent correct his way? By keeping to your words. [10] With my whole heart, I have sought you. Do not let me be driven away from your commandments. [11] I have hidden your eloquence in my heart, so that I may not sin against you. [12] Blessed are you, O Lord. Teach me your justifications. [13] With my lips, I have pronounced all the judgments of your mouth. [14] I have been delighted in the way of your testimonies, as if in all riches. [15] I will be trained in your commandments, and I will consider your ways. [16] I will meditate on your justifications. I will not forget your words. [17] GHIMEL. Repay your servant, revive me; and I will keep your words. [18] Reveal to my eyes, and I will consider the wonders of your law. [19] I am a sojourner on the earth. Do not hide your commandments from me. [20] My soul has longed to desire your justifications at all times. [21] You have rebuked the arrogant. Those who decline from your commandments are accursed. [22] Take me away from disgrace and contempt, for I have sought your testimonies. [23] For even the leaders sat and spoke against me. But your servant has been trained in your justifications. [24] For your testimonies are also my meditation, and your justifications are my counsel. [25] DALETH. My soul has adhered to the pavement. Revive me according to your word. [26] I have declared my ways, and you have heeded me. Teach me your justifications. [27] Instruct me in the way of your justifications, and I will be trained in your wonders. [28] My soul has slumbered because of weariness. Confirm me in your words. [29] Remove the way of iniquity from me, and have mercy on me by your law. [30] I have chosen the way of truth. I have not forgotten your judgments. [31] I have adhered to your testimonies, O Lord. Do not be willing to confound me. [32] I have run by way of your commandments, when you enlarged my heart. [33] HE. O Lord, place the law before me, the way of your justifications, and I will always inquire into it. [34] Give me understanding, and I will examine your law. And I will keep it with my whole heart. [35] Lead me according to the path of your commandments, for I have desired this. [36] Bend my heart with your testimonies, and not with avarice. [37] Turn my eyes away, lest they see what is vain. Revive me in your way. [38] Station your eloquence with your servant, along with your fear. [39] Cut off my disgrace, which I have taken up, for your judgments are delightful. [40] Behold, I have longed for your commandments. Revive me in your fairness. [41] VAU. And let your mercy overwhelm me, O Lord: your salvation according to your eloquence. [42] And I will respond to those who reproach me by word, for I have hoped in your words. [43] And do not utterly take away the word of truth from my mouth. For in your

judgments, I have hoped beyond hope. ⁴⁴And I will always keep your law, in this age and forever and ever. ⁴⁵And I have wandered far and wide, because I was seeking your commandments. ⁴⁶And I spoke of your testimonies in the sight of kings, and I was not confounded. ⁴⁷And I meditated on your commandments, which I loved. ⁴⁸And I lifted up my hands to your commandments, which I loved. And I was trained in your justifications. ⁴⁹ZAIN. Be mindful of your word to your servant, by which you have given me hope. ⁵⁰This has consoled me in my humiliation, for your word has revived me. ⁵¹The arrogant act altogether iniquitously, but I have not turned aside from your law. ⁵²I called to mind your judgments of antiquity, O Lord, and I was consoled. ⁵³Faintness has taken hold of me, because of the sinners, those who abandon your law. ⁵⁴Your justifications were the subject of my worthy singing, in the place of my pilgrimage. ⁵⁵During the night, I remembered your name, O Lord, and I kept your law. ⁵⁶This has happened to me because I sought your justifications. ⁵⁷HETH. O Lord, my portion, I have said that I would keep your law. ⁵⁸I have beseeched your face with my whole heart. Be merciful to me according to your word. ⁵⁹I have considered my ways, and I have turned my feet toward your testimonies. ⁶⁰I have been prepared, and I have not been disturbed, so that I may keep your commandments. ⁶¹The ropes of the impious have encircled me, and I have not forgotten your law. ⁶²I arose in the middle of the night to confess to you, over the judgments of your justification. ⁶³I am a partaker with all those who fear you and who keep your commandments. ⁶⁴The earth, O Lord, is full of your mercy. Teach me your justifications. ⁶⁵TETH. You have done well with your servant, O Lord, according to your word. ⁶⁶Teach me goodness and discipline and knowledge, for I have trusted your commandments. ⁶⁷Before I was humbled, I committed offenses; because of this, I have kept to your word. ⁶⁸You are good, so in your goodness teach me your justifications. ⁶⁹The iniquity of the arrogant has been multiplied over me. Yet I will examine your commandments with all my heart. ⁷⁰Their heart has been curdled like milk. Truly, I have meditated on your law. ⁷¹It is good for me that you humbled me, so that I may learn your justifications. ⁷²The law of your mouth is good for me, beyond thousands of gold and silver pieces. ⁷³IOD. Your hands have created me and formed me. Give me understanding, and I will learn your commandments. ⁷⁴Those who fear you will see me, and they will rejoice. For I have greatly hoped in your words. ⁷⁵I know, O Lord, that your judgments are fairness. And in your truth, you have humbled me. ⁷⁶Let it be your mercy that consoles me, according to your eloquence to your servant. ⁷⁷Let your compassion draw near to me, and I will live. For your law is my meditation. ⁷⁸Let the arrogant be confounded, for unjustly they have done iniquity to me. But I will be trained in your commandments. ⁷⁹Let those who fear you turn to me, along with those who know your testimonies. ⁸⁰Let my heart be immaculate in your justifications, so that I may not be confounded. ⁸¹CAPH. My soul has faltered in your salvation, yet in your word, I have hoped beyond hope. ⁸²My eyes have failed in your eloquence, saying, "When will you console me?" ⁸³For I have become like a wineskin in the frost. I have not forgotten your justifications. ⁸⁴How many are the days of your servant? When will you bring judgment against those who persecute me? ⁸⁵The iniquitous have spoken fables to me. But these are unlike your law. ⁸⁶All your commandments are truth. They have been persecuting me unjustly: assist me. ⁸⁷They have nearly consumed me on earth. Yet I have not forsaken your commandments. ⁸⁸Revive me according to your mercy. And I will keep the testimonies of your mouth. ⁸⁹LAMED. O Lord, your word remains firm in heaven, for all eternity. ⁹⁰Your truth is from generation to generation. You have founded the earth, and it remains firm. ⁹¹By your ordinance, the day perseveres. For all things are in service to you. ⁹²If your law had not been my meditation, then perhaps I would have perished in my humiliation. ⁹³I will not forget your justifications, for eternity. For by them, you have enlivened me. ⁹⁴I am yours. Accomplish my salvation. For I have inquired into your justifications. ⁹⁵The sinners have waited for me, in order to destroy me. I have understood your testimonies. ⁹⁶I have seen the end of the consummation of all things. Your commandment is exceedingly broad. ⁹⁷MEM. How have I loved your law, O Lord? It is my meditation all day long. ⁹⁸By your commandment, you have made me able to see far, beyond my enemies. For it is with me for eternity. ⁹⁹I have understood beyond all my teachers. For your testimonies are my meditation. ¹⁰⁰I have understood beyond the elders. For I have searched your commandments. ¹⁰¹I have prohibited my feet from every evil way, so that I may keep your words. ¹⁰²I have not declined from your judgments, because you have stationed a law for me. ¹⁰³How sweet is your eloquence to my palate, more so than honey to my mouth! [104] I obtained understanding by your commandments. Because of this, I have hated every way of iniquity. [105] NUN. Your word is a lamp to my feet and a light to my paths. [106] I have sworn it, and so I am determined to keep the judgments of your justice. [107] I have been altogether humbled, Lord. Revive me according to your word. [108] Make the willing offerings of my mouth well pleasing, Lord, and teach me your judgments. [109] My soul is always in my hands, and I have not forgotten your law. [110] Sinners have set a snare for me, yet I have not strayed from your commandments. [111] I have acquired your testimonies as an inheritance unto eternity, because they are the exultation of my heart. [112] I have inclined my heart to do your justifications for eternity, as a recompense. [113] SAMECH. I have hated the iniquitous, and I have loved your law. [114] You are my helper and my supporter. And in your word, I have greatly hoped. [115] Turn away from me, you malignant ones. And I will examine the commandments of my God. [116] Uphold me according to your eloquence, and I will live. And let me not be confounded in my expectation. [117] Help me, and I will be saved. And I will meditate always on your justifications. [118] You have despised all those who fell away from your judgments. For their intention is unjust. [119] I have considered all the sinners of the earth to be transgressors. Therefore, I have loved your testimonies. [120] Pierce my flesh with your fear, for I am afraid of your judgments. [121] AIN. I have accomplished judgment and justice. Do not hand me over to those who slander me. [122] Uphold your servant in what is good. And do not allow the arrogant to slander me. [123] My eyes have failed in your salvation and in the eloquence of your justice. [124] Deal with your servant according to your mercy, and teach me your justifications. [125] I am your servant. Give me understanding, so that I may know your testimonies. [126] It is time to act, O Lord. They have dissipated your law. [127] Therefore, I have loved your commandments beyond gold and topaz. [128] Because of this, I was directed toward all your commandments. I held hatred for every iniquitous way. [129] PHE. Your testimonies are wonderful. Therefore, my soul has been examined by them. [130] The declaration of your words illuminates, and it gives understanding to little ones. [131] I opened my mouth and drew breath, for I desired your commandments. [132] Gaze upon me and be merciful to me, according to the judgment of those who love your name. [133] Direct my steps according to your eloquence, and let no injustice rule over me. [134] Redeem me from the slanders of men, so that I may keep your commandments. [135] Make your face shine upon your servant, and teach me your justifications. [136] My eyes have gushed like springs of water, because they have not kept your law. [137] SADE. You are just, O Lord, and your judgment is right. [138] You have commanded justice: your testimonies and your truth even more so. [139] My zeal has caused me to pine away, because my enemies have forgotten your words. [140] Your eloquence has been greatly enflamed, and your servant has loved it. [141] I am young and treated with contempt. But I have not forgotten your justifications. [142] Your justice is justice for all eternity, and your law is truth. [143] Tribulation and anguish have found me. Your commandments are my meditation. [144] Your testimonies are fairness unto eternity. Give me understanding, and I will live. [145] COPH. I cried out with my whole heart. Heed me, O Lord. I will ask for your justifications. [146] I cried out to you. Save me, so that I may keep your commandments. [147] I arrived first in maturity, and so I cried out. For in your words, I have hoped beyond hope. [148] My eyes preceded the dawn for you, so that I might meditate on your eloquence. [149] Hear my voice according to your mercy, O Lord. And revive me according to your judgment. [150] Those who persecute me have drawn near to iniquity, but they have been brought far from your law. [151] You are near, O Lord, and all your ways are truth. [152] I have known from the beginning about your testimonies. For you founded them in eternity. [153] RES. See my humiliation and rescue me, for I have not forgotten your law. [154] Judge my judgment and redeem me. Revive me because of your eloquence. [155] Salvation is far from sinners, because they have not inquired about your justifications. [156] Many are your mercies, O Lord. Enliven me according to your judgment. [157] Many are those who persecute me and who trouble me. I have not turned away from your testimonies. [158] I saw the prevaricators, and I pine away. For they have not kept your word. [159] O Lord, see how I have loved your commandments. Revive me in your mercy. [160] The beginning of your words is truth. All the judgments of your justice are for eternity. [161] SIN. The leaders have persecuted me without cause. And my heart has been awed by your words. [162] I will rejoice over your eloquence, like one who has found many spoils. [163] I have held hatred for iniquity, and I have abhorred it. Yet I have loved your law. [164] Seven times a day, I uttered praise to you about the judgments of your justice. [165] Those who love your law have great peace, and there is no scandal for them. [166] I have waited for your salvation, O Lord. And I have loved your commandments. [167] My soul has kept to your testimonies and has loved them exceedingly. [168] I have served your commandments and your testimonies. For all my ways are before your sight. [169] TAU. O Lord, let my supplication draw near in your sight. Grant understanding to me according to your eloquence. [170] Let my petition enter before you. Rescue me according to your word. [171] A hymn will burst forth from my lips, when you will teach me your justifications. [172] My tongue will pronounce your eloquence. For all your commandments are fairness. [173] Let it be your hand that saves me. For I have chosen your commandments. [174] O Lord, I have longed for your salvation, and your law is my meditation. [175] My soul will live and will praise you, and your judgments will assist me. [176] I have gone astray like a sheep that is lost. Seek out your servant, for I have not forgotten your commandments.

CHAPTER 119 (120)

[1] A Canticle in steps. When troubled, I cried out to the Lord, and he heard me. [2] O Lord, free my soul from lips of iniquity and from the deceitful tongue. [3] What will be given to you, or what will be added to you, for a deceitful tongue?: [4] the sharp arrows of the powerful, along with the burning coals of desolation. [5] Woe to me, for my sojourning has been prolonged. I have lived with the inhabitants of Kedar. [6] My soul has long been a sojourner. [7] With those who hated peace, I was peaceful. When I spoke to them, they fought against me without cause.

CHAPTER 120 (121)

[1] A Canticle in steps. I have lifted up my eyes to the mountains; from thence help will come to me. [2] My help is from the Lord, who made heaven and earth. [3] May he not allow your foot to be moved, and may he not slumber, who guards you. [4] Behold, he who guards Israel will neither sleep, nor slumber. [5] The Lord is your keeper, the Lord is your protection, above your right hand. [6] The sun will not burn you by day, nor the moon by night. [7] The Lord guards you from all evil. May the Lord guard your soul. [8] May the Lord guard your entrance and your exit, from this time forward and even forever.

CHAPTER 121 (122)

[1] A Canticle in steps. I rejoiced in the things that were said to me: "We shall go into the house of the Lord." [2] Our feet were standing in your courts, O Jerusalem. [3] Jerusalem has been built as a city, whose participation is unto itself. [4] For to that place, the tribes ascended, the tribes of the Lord: the testimony of Israel, to confess to the name of the Lord. [5] For in that place, seats have sat down in judgment, seats above the house of David. [6] Petition for the things that are for the peace of Jerusalem, and for abundance for those who love you. [7] Let peace be in your virtue, and abundance in your towers. [8] For the sake of my brothers and my neighbors, I spoke peace about you. [9] For the sake of the house of the Lord our God, I sought good things for you.

CHAPTER 122 (123)

[1] A Canticle in steps. I have lifted up my eyes to you, who dwells in the heavens. [2] Behold, as the eyes of the servants are on the hands of their masters, as the eyes of the handmaid are on the hands of her mistress, so our eyes are upon the Lord our God, until he may be merciful to us. [3] Have mercy on us, O Lord, have mercy on us. For we have been filled with utter disdain. [4] For our soul has been greatly filled. We are the disgrace of those who have abundance and the disdain of the arrogant.

CHAPTER 123 (124)

[1] A Canticle in steps. If the Lord had not been with us, let Israel now say it: [2] if the Lord had not been with us, when men rose up against us, [3] perhaps they would have swallowed us alive. When their fury was enraged against us, [4] perhaps the waters would have engulfed us. [5] Our soul has passed through a torrent. Perhaps, our soul had even passed through intolerable water. [6] Blessed is the Lord, who has not given us into the harm of their teeth. [7] Our soul has been snatched away like a sparrow from the snare of the hunters. The snare has been broken, and we have been freed. [8] Our help is in the name of the Lord, who made heaven and earth.

CHAPTER 124 (125)

[1] A Canticle in steps. Those who trust in the Lord will be like the mountain of Zion. He will not be disturbed for eternity, who dwells [2] in Jerusalem. Mountains surround it. And the Lord surrounds his people, from this time forward and even forever. [3] For the Lord will not allow the rod of sinners to remain over the lot of the just, so that the just may not extend their hands toward iniquity. [4] Do good, O Lord, to the good and to the upright of heart. [5] But those who turn away into obligation, the Lord will lead away with the workers of iniquity. Peace be upon Israel.

CHAPTER 125 (126)

[1] A Canticle in steps. When the Lord turned back the captivity of Zion, we became like those who are consoled. [2] Then our mouth was filled with gladness and our tongue with exultation. Then they will say among the nations: "The Lord has done great things for them." [3] The Lord has done great things for us. We have become joyful. [4] Convert our captivity, O Lord, like a torrent in the south. [5] Those who sow in tears shall reap in exultation. [6] When departing, they went forth and wept, sowing their seeds. [7] But when returning, they will arrive with exultation, carrying their sheaves.

CHAPTER 126 (127)

[1] A Canticle in steps: of Solomon. Unless the Lord has built the house, those who build it have labored in vain. Unless the Lord has guarded the city, he who guards it watches in vain. [2] It is in vain that you rise before daylight, that you rise up after you have sat down, you who chew the bread of sorrow. Whereas, to his beloved, he will give sleep. [3] Behold, the inheritance of the Lord is sons, the reward is the fruit of the womb. [4] Like arrows in the hand of the powerful, so are the sons of those who have been cast out. [5] Blessed is the man who has filled his desire from these things. He will not be confounded when he speaks to his enemies at the gate.

CHAPTER 127 (128)

[1] A Canticle in steps. Blessed are all those who fear the Lord, who walk in his ways. [2] For you will eat by the labors of your hands. Blessed are you, and it will be well with you. [3] Your wife is like an abundant vine on the sides of your house. Your sons are like young olive trees surrounding your table. [4] Behold, so will the man be blessed who fears the Lord. [5] May the Lord bless you from Zion, and may you see the good things of Jerusalem, all the days of your life. [6] And may you see the sons of your sons. Peace be upon Israel.

CHAPTER 128 (129)

[1] A Canticle in steps. They have often fought against me from my youth, let Israel now say: [2] they have often fought against me from my youth, yet they could not prevail over me. [3] The sinners have made fabrications behind my back. They have prolonged their iniquity. [4] The just Lord will cut the necks of sinners. [5] Let all those who hate Zion be confounded and turned backwards. [6] Let them be like grass on the rooftops, which withers before it can be pulled up: [7] with it, he who reaps does not fill his hand and he who gathers sheaves does not fill his bosom. [8] And those who were passing by have not said to them: "The blessing of the Lord be upon you. We have blessed you in the name of the Lord."

CHAPTER 129 (130)

[1] A Canticle in steps. From the depths, I have cried out to you, O Lord. [2] O Lord, hear my voice. Let your ears be attentive to the voice of my supplication. [3] If you, O Lord, were to heed iniquities, who, O Lord, could persevere? [4] For with you, there is forgiveness, and because of your law, I persevered with you, Lord. My soul has persevered in his word. [5] My soul has hoped in the Lord. [6] From the morning watch, even until night, let Israel hope in the Lord. [7] For with the Lord there is mercy, and with him there is bountiful redemption. [8] And he will redeem Israel from all his iniquities.

CHAPTER 130 (131)

[1] A Canticle in steps: of David. O Lord, my heart has not been exalted, and my eyes have not been raised up. Neither have I walked in greatness, nor in

wonders beyond me. [2] When I was not humble in thought, then I lifted up my soul. Like one who has been weaned from his mother, so was I recompensed in my soul. [3] Let Israel hope in the Lord, from this time forward and even forever.

CHAPTER 131 (132)

[1] A Canticle in steps. O Lord, remember David and all his meekness, [2] how he swore to the Lord, how he made a vow to the God of Jacob: [3] I shall not enter into the tabernacle of my house, nor climb into the bed where I lie down; [4] I shall not give sleep to my eyes, nor slumber to my eyelids [5] and rest to my temples, until I find a place for the Lord, a tabernacle for the God of Jacob. [6] Behold, we heard of it in Ephrathah. We discovered it in the fields of the forest. [7] We will enter into his tabernacle. We will adore in the place where his feet stood. [8] Rise up, O Lord, into your resting place. You and the ark of your sanctification. [9] Let your priests be clothed with justice, and let your saints exult. [10] For the sake of your servant David, do not turn away the face of your Christ. [11] The Lord has sworn the truth to David, and he will not disappoint: I will set upon your throne from the fruit of your lineage. [12] If your sons will keep my covenant and these, my testimonies, which I will teach to them, then their sons will sit upon your throne even forever. [13] For the Lord has chosen Zion. He has chosen it as his dwelling place. [14] This is my resting place, forever and ever. Here I will dwell, for I have chosen it. [15] When blessing, I will bless her widow. I will satisfy her poor with bread. [16] I will clothe her priests with salvation, and her saints will rejoice with great joy. [17] There, I will produce a horn to David. There, I have prepared a lamp for my Christ. [18] I will clothe his enemies with confusion. But my sanctification will flourish over him.

CHAPTER 132 (133)

[1] A Canticle in steps: of David. Behold, how good and how pleasing it is for brothers to dwell in unity. [2] It is like the ointment on the head that descended to the beard, the beard of Aaron, which descended to the hem of his garment. [3] It is like the dew of Hermon, which descended from mount Zion. For in that place, the Lord has commanded a blessing, and life, even unto eternity.

CHAPTER 133 (134)

[1] A Canticle in steps. Behold, bless the Lord now, all you servants of the Lord, who stand in the house of the Lord, in the courts of the house of our God. [2] In the nights, lift up your hands in sanctity, and bless the Lord. [3] May the Lord, who made heaven and earth, bless you from Zion.

CHAPTER 134 (135)

[1] Alleluia. Praise the name of the Lord. You servants, praise the Lord. [2] You who stand in the house of the Lord, in the courts of the house of our God: [3] praise the Lord, for the Lord is good. Sing psalms to his name, for it is sweet. [4] For the Lord has chosen Jacob for himself, Israel for his own possession. [5] For I have known that the Lord is great, and our God is before all gods. [6] All things whatsoever that he willed, the Lord did: in heaven, on earth, in the sea, and in all the deep places. [7] He leads clouds from the ends of the earth. He has created lightnings in the rain. He has produced winds from his storehouses. [8] He struck the first-born of Egypt, from man even to cattle. [9] He sent signs and wonders into your midst, O Egypt: upon Pharaoh and upon all his servants. [10] He has struck many nations, and he has slaughtered strong kings: [11] Sihon, king of the Amorites, and Og, king of Bashan, and all the kingdoms of Canaan. [12] And he gave their land as an inheritance, as an inheritance for his people Israel. [13] Your name, O Lord, is in eternity. Your memorial, O Lord, is from generation to generation. [14] For the Lord will judge his people, and he will be petitioned by his servants. [15] The idols of the Gentiles are silver and gold, the works of the hands of men. [16] They have a mouth, and do not speak. They have eyes, and do not see. [17] They have ears, and do not hear. For neither is there any breath in their mouths. [18] Let those who make them become like them, along with all who trust in them. [19] Bless the Lord, O house of Israel. Bless the Lord, O house of Aaron. [20] Bless the Lord, O house of Levi. You who fear the Lord, bless the Lord. [21] The Lord is blessed from Zion, by those who dwell in Jerusalem.

CHAPTER 135 (136)

[1] Alleluia. Confess to the Lord, for he is good: for his mercy is eternal. [2] Confess to the God of gods, for his mercy is eternal. [3] Confess to the Lord of lords, for his mercy is eternal. [4] He alone performs great miracles, for his mercy is eternal. [5] He made the heavens with understanding, for his mercy is eternal. [6] He established the earth above the waters, for his mercy is eternal. [7] He made the great lights, for his mercy is eternal: [8] the sun to rule the day, for his mercy is eternal: [9] the moon and the stars to rule the night, for his mercy is eternal. [10] He struck Egypt along with their first-born, for his mercy is eternal. [11] He led Israel away from their midst, for his mercy is eternal: [12] with a powerful hand and an outstretched arm, for his mercy is eternal. [13] He divided the Red Sea into separate parts, for his mercy is eternal. [14] And he led out Israel through the middle of it, for his mercy is eternal. [15] And he shook off Pharaoh and his army in the Red Sea, for his mercy is eternal. [16] He led his people through the desert, for his mercy is eternal. [17] He has struck great kings, for his mercy is eternal. [18] And he has slaughtered strong kings, for his mercy is eternal: [19] Sihon, king of the Amorites, for his mercy is eternal: [20] and Og, king of Bashan, for his mercy is eternal. [21] And he granted their land as an inheritance, for his mercy is eternal: [22] as an inheritance for his servant Israel, for his mercy is eternal. [23] For he was mindful of us in our humiliation, for his mercy is eternal. [24] And he redeemed us from our enemies, for his mercy is eternal. [25] He gives food to all flesh, for his mercy is eternal. [26] Confess to the God of heaven, for his mercy is eternal. [27] Confess to the Lord of lords, for his mercy is eternal.

CHAPTER 136 (137)

[1] A Psalm of David: to Jeremiah. Above the rivers of Babylon, there we sat and wept, while we remembered Zion. [2] By the willow trees, in their midst, we hung up our instruments. [3] For, in that place, those who led us into captivity questioned us about the words of the songs. And those who carried us away said: "Sing us a hymn from the songs of Zion." [4] How can we sing a song of the Lord in a foreign land? [5] If I ever forget you, Jerusalem, let my right hand be forgotten. [6] May my tongue adhere to my jaws, if I do not remember you, if I do not set Jerusalem first, as the beginning of my joy. [7] O Lord, call to mind the sons of Edom, in the day of Jerusalem, who say: "Despoil it, despoil it, even to its foundation." [8] O daughter of Babylon, have pity. Blessed is he who will repay you with your payment, which you have paid to us. [9] Blessed is he who will take hold of your little ones and dash them against the rock.

CHAPTER 137 (138)

[1] Of David himself. O Lord, I will confess to you with my whole heart, for you have heard the words of my mouth. I will sing psalms to you in the sight of the Angels. [2] I will adore before your holy temple, and I will confess your name: it is above your mercy and your truth. For you have magnified your holy name above all. [3] On whatever day that I will call upon you: hear me. You will multiply virtue in my soul. [4] May all the kings of the earth confess to you, O Lord. For they have heard all the words of your mouth. [5] And let them sing in accordance with the ways of the Lord. For great is the glory of the Lord. [6] For the Lord is exalted, and he looks with favor on the humble. But the lofty he knows from a distance. [7] If I wander into the midst of tribulation, you will revive me. For you extended your hand against the wrath of my enemies. And your right hand has accomplished my salvation. [8] The Lord will provide retribution on my behalf. O Lord, your mercy is forever. Do not disdain the works of your hands.

CHAPTER 138 (139)

[1] Unto the end. A Psalm of David. O Lord, you have examined me, and you have known me. [2] You have known my sitting down and my rising up again. [3] You have understood my thoughts from afar. My path and my fate, you have investigated. [4] And you have foreseen all my ways. For there is no word in my tongue. [5] Behold, O Lord, you have known all things: the newest and the very old. You have formed me, and you have placed your hand over me. [6] Your knowledge has become a wonder to me. It has been reinforced, and I am not able to prevail against it. [7] Where will I go from your Spirit? And where will I flee from your face? [8] If I ascend into heaven, you are there. If I descend into Hell, you are near. [9] If I assume my feathers in early morning, and dwell in the utmost parts of the

sea, [10] even there, your hand will lead me forth, and your right hand will hold me. [11] And I said: Perhaps darkness will overwhelm me, and the night will be my illumination, to my delight. [12] But darkness will not be impenetrable to you, and night will illuminate like the day: for just as its darkness is, so also is its light. [13] For you have possessed my temperament. You have supported me from the womb of my mother. [14] I will confess to you, for you have been magnified terribly. Your works are miraculous, as my soul knows exceedingly well. [15] My bone, which you have made in secret, has not been hidden from you, and my substance is in accord with the lower parts of the earth. [16] Your eyes saw my imperfection, and all this shall be written in your book. Days will be formed, and no one shall be in them. [17] But to me, O God, your friends have been greatly honored. Their first ruler has been exceedingly strengthened. [18] I will number them, and they will be more numerous than the sand. I rose up, and I am still with you. [19] O God, if only you would cut down sinners. You men of blood: depart from me. [20] For you say in thought: They will accept your cities in vain. [21] Have I not hated those who hated you, Lord, and wasted away because of your enemies? [22] I have hated them with a perfect hatred, and they have become enemies to me. [23] Examine me, O God, and know my heart. Question me, and know my paths. [24] And see if there might be in me the way of iniquity, and lead me in the way of eternity.

CHAPTER 139 (140)

[1] Unto the end. A Psalm of David. [2] Rescue me, O Lord, from the evil man. Rescue me from the iniquitous leader. [3] Those who have devised iniquities in their hearts: all day long they constructed conflicts. [4] They have sharpened their tongues like a serpent. The venom of asps is under their lips. [5] Preserve me, O Lord, from the hand of the sinner, and rescue me from men of iniquity. They have decided to supplant my steps. [6] The arrogant have hidden a snare for me. And they have stretched out cords for a snare. They have placed a stumbling block for me near the road. [7] I said to the Lord: You are my God. O Lord, heed the voice of my supplication. [8] Lord, O Lord, the strength of my salvation: you have overshadowed my head in the day of war. [9] O Lord, do not hand me over to the sinner by my desire. They have plotted against me. Do not abandon me, lest they should triumph. [10] The head of those who encompass me, the labor of their lips, will overwhelm them. [11] Burning coals will fall upon them. You will cast them down into the fire, into miseries that they will not be able to withstand. [12] A talkative man will not be guided aright upon the earth. Evils will drag the unjust man unto utter ruin. [13] I know that the Lord will accomplish justice for the needy and vindication for the poor. [14] So then, truly, the just will confess your name, and the upright will dwell with your countenance.

CHAPTER 140 (141)

[1] A Psalm of David. O Lord, I have cried out to you, hear me. Attend to my voice, when I cry out to you. [2] Let my prayer be guided like incense in your sight: the lifting up of my hands, like the evening sacrifice. [3] O Lord, station a guard over my mouth and a door enclosing my lips. [4] Do not turn aside my heart to words of malice, to making excuses for sins, with men who work iniquity; and I will not communicate, even with the best of them. [5] The just one will correct me with mercy, and he will rebuke me. But do not allow the oil of the sinner to fatten my head. For my prayer will still be toward their good will. [6] Their judges have been engulfed, joined to the rocks. They will hear my words, which have prevailed, [7] as when the lava of the earth has erupted above ground. Our bones have been scattered beside Hell. [8] For Lord, O Lord, my eyes look to you. In you, I have hoped. Do not take away my soul. [9] Protect me from the snare that they have set up for me and from the scandals of those who work iniquity. [10] The sinners will fall into his net. I am alone, until I pass over.

CHAPTER 141 (142)

[1] The understanding of David. A prayer, when he was in the cave. [2] With my voice, I cried out to the Lord. With my voice, I made supplication to the Lord. [3] In his sight, I pour out my prayer, and before him, I declare my tribulation. [4] Though my spirit may become faint within me, even then, you have known my paths. Along this way, which I have been walking, they have hidden a snare for me. [5] I considered toward the right, and I looked, but there was no one who would know me. Flight has perished before me, and there is no one who has concern

for my soul. ⁶I cried out to you, O Lord. I said: You are my hope, my portion in the land of the living. ⁷Attend to my supplication. For I have been humbled exceedingly. Free me from my persecutors, for they have been fortified against me. ⁸Lead my soul out of confinement in order to confess your name. The just are waiting for me, until you repay me.

CHAPTER 142 (143)

¹A Psalm of David, when his son Absalom was pursuing him. O Lord, hear my prayer. Incline your ear to my supplication in your truth. Heed me according to your justice. ²And do not enter into judgment with your servant. For all the living will not be justified in your sight. ³For the enemy has pursued my soul. He has lowered my life to the earth. He has stationed me in darkness, like the dead of ages past. ⁴And my spirit has been in anguish over me. My heart within me has been disturbed. ⁵I have called to mind the days of antiquity. I have been meditating on all your works. I have meditated on the workings of your hands. ⁶I have extended my hands to you. My soul is like a land without water before you. ⁷O Lord, heed me quickly. My spirit has grown faint. Do not turn your face away from me, lest I become like those who descend into the pit. ⁸Make me hear your mercy in the morning. For I have hoped in you. Make known to me the way that I should walk. For I have lifted up my soul to you. ⁹O Lord, rescue me from my enemies. I have fled to you. ¹⁰Teach me to do your will. For you are my God. Your good Spirit will lead me into the righteous land. ¹¹For the sake of your name, O Lord, you will revive me in your fairness. You will lead my soul out of tribulation. ¹²And you will scatter my enemies in your mercy. And you will destroy all those who afflict my soul. For I am your servant.

CHAPTER 143 (144)

¹A Psalm of David versus Goliath. Blessed is the Lord, my God, who trains my hands for the battle and my fingers for the war. ²My mercy and my refuge, my supporter and my deliverer, my protector and him in whom I have hoped: he subdues my people under me. ³O Lord, what is man that you have become known to him? Or the son of man that you consider him? ⁴Man has been made similar to vanity. His days pass by like a shadow. ⁵O Lord, incline your heavens and descend. Touch the mountains, and they will smoke. ⁶Send a flash of lightning, and you will scatter them. Shoot your arrows, and you will set them in disarray. ⁷Send forth your hand from on high: rescue me, and free me from many waters, from the hand of the sons of foreigners. ⁸Their mouth has been speaking vain things, and their right hand is the right hand of iniquity. ⁹To you, O God, I will sing a new song. On the psaltery, with an instrument of ten strings, I will sing psalms to you. ¹⁰He gives salvation to kings. He has redeemed your servant David from the malignant sword. ¹¹Rescue me, and deliver me from the hand of the sons of foreigners. Their mouth has been speaking vain things, and their right hand is the right hand of iniquity. ¹²Their sons are like new plantings in their youth. Their daughters are dressed up: adorned all around like the idols of a temple. ¹³Their cupboards are full: overflowing from one thing into another. Their sheep bear young, brought forth in abundance. ¹⁴Their cattle are fat. There is no ruined wall or passage, nor anyone crying out in their streets. ¹⁵They have called the people that has these things: blessed. But blessed is the people whose God is the Lord.

CHAPTER 144 (145)

¹The Praise of David himself. I will extol you, O God, my king. And I will bless your name, in this time and forever and ever. ²Throughout every single day, I will bless you. And I will praise your name, in this time and forever and ever. ³The Lord is great and exceedingly praiseworthy. And there is no end to his greatness. ⁴Generation after generation will praise your works, and they will declare your power. ⁵They will tell of the magnificent glory of your sanctity. And they will discourse of your wonders. ⁶And they will talk about the virtue of your terrible acts. And they will describe your greatness. ⁷They will shout about the memory of your abundant sweetness. And they will exult in your justice. ⁸The Lord is compassionate and merciful, patient and full of mercy. ⁹The Lord is sweet to all things, and his compassion is upon all his works. ¹⁰O Lord, may all your works confess to you, and let your holy ones bless you. ¹¹They will speak of the glory of your kingdom, and they will declare your power, ¹²so as to make known to the sons of men your power and the glory of your magnificent kingdom. ¹³Your

kingdom is a kingdom for all ages, and your dominion is with all, from generation to generation. The Lord is faithful in all his words and holy in all his works. [14]The Lord lifts up all who have fallen down, and he sets upright all who have been thrown down. [15]O Lord, all eyes hope in you, and you provide their food in due time. [16]You open your hand, and you fill every kind of animal with a blessing. [17]The Lord is just in all his ways and holy in all his works. [18]The Lord is near to all who call upon him, to all who call upon him in truth. [19]He will do the will of those who fear him, and he will heed their supplication and accomplish their salvation. [20]The Lord watches over all who love him. And he will destroy all sinners. [21]My mouth will speak the praise of the Lord, and may all flesh bless his holy name, in this time and forever and ever.

CHAPTER 145 (146)

[1]Alleluia. Of Haggai and Zachariah. [2]Praise the Lord, O my soul. I will praise the Lord with my life. I will sing psalms to my God as long as I shall be. Do not trust in the leaders, [3]in the sons of men, in whom there is no salvation. [4]His spirit will depart, and he will return to his earth. In that day, all their thoughts will perish. [5]Blessed is he whose help is the God of Jacob: his hope is in the Lord God himself, [6]who made heaven and earth, the sea, and all the things that are in them. [7]He preserves the truth forever. He executes judgment for those who suffer injury. He provides food for the hungry. The Lord releases those who are bound. [8]The Lord enlightens the blind. The Lord sets upright those who have been thrown down. The Lord loves the just. [9]The Lord watches over new arrivals. He will support the orphan and the widow. And he will destroy the ways of sinners. [10]The Lord shall reign forever: your God, O Zion, from generation to generation.

CHAPTER 146 (147A)

[1]Alleluia. Praise the Lord, because the psalm is good. Delightful and beautiful praise shall be for our God. [2]The Lord builds up Jerusalem. He will gather together the dispersed of Israel. [3]He heals the contrite of heart, and he binds up their sorrows. [4]He numbers the multitude of the stars, and he calls them all by their names. [5]Great is our Lord, and great is his virtue. And of his wisdom, there is no number. [6]The Lord lifts up the meek, but he brings down the sinner, even to the ground. [7]Sing before the Lord with confession. Play psalms to our God on a stringed instrument. [8]He covers heaven with clouds, and he prepares rain for the earth. He produces grass on the mountains and herbs for the service of men. [9]He gives their food to beasts of burden and to young ravens that call upon him. [10]He will not have good will for the strength of the horse, nor will he be well pleased with the legs of a man. [11]The Lord is well pleased with those who fear him and with those who hope in his mercy.

CHAPTER 147 (147B)

[1]Alleluia. Praise the Lord, O Jerusalem. Praise your God, O Zion. [2]For he has reinforced the bars of your gates. He has blessed your sons within you. [3]He has stationed peace at your borders, and he has satisfied you with the fat of the grain. [4]He sends forth his eloquence to the earth. His word runs swiftly. [5]He provides snow like wool. He strews clouds like ashes. [6]He sends his ice crystals like morsels. Who can stand firm before the face of his cold? [7]He will send forth his word, and it will melt them. His Spirit will breathe out, and the waters will flow. [8]He announces his word to Jacob, his justices and his judgments to Israel. [9]He has not done so much for every nation, and he has not made his judgments manifest to them. Alleluia.

CHAPTER 148

[1]Alleluia. Praise the Lord from the heavens. Praise him on the heights. [2]Praise him, all his Angels. Praise him, all his hosts. [3]Praise him, sun and moon. Praise him, all stars and light. [4]Praise him, heavens of the heavens. And let all the waters that are above the heavens [5]praise the name of the Lord. For he spoke, and they became. He commanded, and they were created. [6]He has stationed them in eternity, and for age after age. He has established a precept, and it will not pass away. [7]Praise the Lord from the earth: you dragons and all deep places, [8]fire, hail, snow, ice, windstorms, which do his word, [9]mountains and all hills, fruitful trees and all cedars, [10]wild beasts and all cattle, serpents and feathered flying things, [11]kings of the earth and all peoples, leaders and all judges of the earth, [12]young men and virgins. Let the older men with the younger men, praise the name of the Lord. [13]For his name alone is exalted. [14]Confession of him is beyond heaven and earth, and he has exalted the horn of his people. A hymn to all his holy ones, to the sons of Israel, to a people close to him. Alleluia.

CHAPTER 149

[1]Alleluia. Sing to the Lord a new song. His praise is in the Church of the saints. [2]Let Israel rejoice in him who made them, and let the sons of Zion exult in their king. [3]Let them praise his name in chorus. Let them sing psalms to him with the timbrel and the psaltery. [4]For the Lord is well pleased with his people, and he will exalt the meek unto salvation. [5]The saints will exult in glory. They will rejoice upon their couches. [6]The exultations of God will be in their throat, and two-edged swords will be in their hands: [7]to obtain vindication among the nations, chastisements among the peoples, [8]to bind their kings with shackles and their nobles with manacles of iron, [9]to obtain judgment over them, as it has been written. This is glory for all his saints. Alleluia.

CHAPTER 150

[1]Alleluia. Praise the Lord in his holy places. Praise him in the firmament of his power. [2]Praise him for his virtues. Praise him according to the multitude of his greatness. [3]Praise him with the sound of the trumpet. Praise him with psaltery and stringed instrument. [4]Praise him with timbrel and choir. Praise him with strings and organ. [5]Praise him with sweet-sounding cymbals. Praise him with cymbals of jubilation. [6]Let every spirit praise the Lord. Alleluia.

THE SACRED BIBLE:
THE BOOK OF PROVERBS

CHAPTER 1

[1] The parables of Solomon, son of David, king of Israel, [2] in order to know wisdom and discipline, [3] to understand words of prudence, and to accept the instruction of doctrine, justice and judgment, and equity, [4] so as to give discernment to little ones, knowledge and understanding to adolescents. [5] By listening, the wise shall become wiser and the intelligent shall possess governments. [6] He shall turn his soul to a parable and to its interpretation, to the words of the wise and their enigmas. [7] The fear of the Lord is the beginning of wisdom. The foolish despise wisdom as well as doctrine. [8] Listen, my son, to the discipline of your father, and forsake not the law of your mother, [9] so that grace may be added to your head and a collar to your neck. [10] My son, if sinners should entice you, do not consent to them. [11] If they should say: "Come with us. We will lie in wait for blood. We will lay traps against the innocent, without cause. [12] Let us swallow him alive, like Hell, and whole, like one descending into the pit. [13] We will discover every precious substance. We will fill our houses with spoils. [14] Cast your lot with us. One purse will be for us all." [15] My son, do not walk with them. Preclude your feet from their paths. [16] For their feet rush to evil, and they hurry to shed blood. [17] But a net is thrown in vain before the eyes of those who have wings. [18] Likewise, they lie in ambush against their own blood, and they undertake deceits against their own souls. [19] Thus, the ways of all those who are greedy seize the souls of those who possess. [20] Wisdom forewarns far and wide; she bestows her voice in the streets. [21] She cries out at the head of crowds; at the entrance of the gates of the city, she offers her words, saying: [22] "Little ones, how long will you choose to be childish, and how long will the foolish desire what is harmful to themselves, and how long will the imprudent hate knowledge? [23] Be converted by my correction. Lo, I will offer my spirit to you, and I will reveal my words to you. [24] For I called, and you refused. I extended my hand, and there was no one who watched. [25] You have despised all my counsels, and you have neglected my rebukes. [26] Similarly, I will ridicule you at your demise, and I will mock you, when that which you feared shall overcome you. [27] When sudden calamity rushes upon you, and your demise advances like a tempest, when tribulation and anguish overcome you, [28] then they will call to me, and I will not heed, they will arise in the morning, and not find me. [29] For they held hatred for discipline, and they would not accept the fear of the Lord; [30] they would not consent to my counsel, but they detracted from all of my corrections. [31] Therefore, they shall eat the fruit of their way, and they shall have their fill of their own counsels. [32] The loathing of the little ones shall destroy them, and the prosperity of the foolish shall perish them. [33] But whoever will listen to me shall rest without terror, and shall have full enjoyment of abundance, without fear of evils."

CHAPTER 2

[1] My son, if you would accept my words, and conceal my commandments within you, [2] so that your ears may listen to wisdom, then bend your heart in order to know prudence. [3] For if you would call upon wisdom and bend your heart to prudence, [4] if you will seek her like money, and dig for her as if for treasure, [5] then you will understand the fear of the Lord, and you will discover the knowledge of God. [6] For the Lord bestows wisdom, and out of his mouth, prudence and knowledge. [7] He will preserve the salvation of the righteous, and he will protect those who walk in simplicity: [8] serving the paths of justice, and guarding the ways of sanctity. [9] Then you shall understand justice and judgment, and equity, and every good path. [10] If wisdom is to enter into your heart, and if knowledge is to become pleasing to your soul, [11] then counsel must guard you, and prudence must serve you, [12] so that you may be rescued from the evil way, and from the man who speaks perversities, [13] from those who leave the straight path to walk in dark ways, [14] who rejoice when they have done evil, and who exult in the most wicked things. [15] Their ways are perverse, and their steps are infamous. [16] So may you be rescued from the foreign woman, and from the outsider, who softens her speech, [17] and who leaves behind the Guide of her youth, [18] and who has forgotten the covenant of her God. For her household inclines toward death, and her paths toward Hell. [19] All those who enter to her will not return again, nor will they take hold of the

paths of life. [20] So may you walk in the good way, and keep to the difficult paths of the just. [21] For those who are upright shall live upon the earth, and the simple shall continue upon it. [22] Yet truly, the impious shall perish from the earth, and those who act unjustly shall be taken away from it.

CHAPTER 3

[1] My son, do not forget my law, but let your heart guard my precepts. [2] For they shall set before you length of days, and years of life, and peace. [3] Let not mercy and truth abandon you: encircle them around your throat, and inscribe them on the tablets of your heart. [4] And so shall you discover grace and good discipline, in the sight of God and men. [5] Have confidence in the Lord with all your heart, and do not depend upon your own prudence. [6] In all your ways, consider him, and he himself will direct your steps. [7] Do not seem wise to yourself. Fear God, and withdraw from evil. [8] Certainly, it shall be health to your navel, and refreshment to your bones. [9] Honor the Lord with your substance, and give to him from the first of all your fruits, [10] and then your storehouses will be filled with abundance, and your presses shall overflow with wine. [11] My son, do not discard the discipline of the Lord, and do not fall away when you are corrected by him. [12] For whomever the Lord loves, he corrects, and just as a father does with a son, he wins him over. [13] Blessed is the man who finds wisdom and who advances to prudence. [14] Her acquisition is better than trading in silver, and her fruit is better than the first and purest gold. [15] She is more precious than all riches, and all that can be desired cannot prevail in comparison to her. [16] Length of days is at her right hand, and at her left hand is wealth and glory. [17] Her ways are beautiful ways, and all her paths are peaceful. [18] She is a tree of life to those who overtake her, and he who shall take hold of her is blessed. [19] The Lord founded the earth on wisdom. He secured the heavens with prudence. [20] By his wisdom, the abyss erupted and the clouds increased with dew. [21] My son, let not these things move away from your eyes. Preserve law as well as counsel. [22] And so shall there be life in your soul and grace in your voice. [23] Then you shall walk confidently in your way, and your feet will not stumble. [24] When you slumber, you shall not fear. When you rest, your sleep also will be sweet. [25] Do not fear unexpected terror, nor the power of the impious falling upon you. [26] For the Lord will be at your side, and he will guard your feet, so that you may not be seized. [27] Do not prevent him who is able from doing good. When you are able, do good yourself too. [28] Do not say to your friend: "Go away, and then return. Tomorrow I will give to you." When you are able to do so, give in the present. [29] Do not undertake evil against your friend, even though he has trust in you. [30] Do not contend against a man without cause, even though he has done no evil to you. [31] Do not rival an unjust man, and do not imitate his ways. [32] For everyone who ridicules is an abomination to the Lord, and his communication is for the simple. [33] Destitution in the house of the impious is from the Lord. But the habitations of the just shall be blessed. [34] He will ridicule those who ridicule, but he will bestow grace upon the mild. [35] The wise will possess glory. The exaltation of the foolish is disgraceful.

CHAPTER 4

[1] Listen, sons, to the discipline of a father, and pay attention, so that you may know prudence. [2] I will bestow upon you a good gift. Do not relinquish my law. [3] For I, too, was the son of my father, tender and an only son in the sight of my mother. [4] And he taught me, and he also said: "Let your heart accept my words. Keep my precepts, and you shall live. [5] Obtain wisdom, obtain prudence. May you neither forget, nor turn away from, the words of my mouth. [6] Do not send her away, and she will guard you. Love her, and she will preserve you. [7] The beginning of wisdom is to obtain wisdom, and, with all that you possess, to acquire prudence. [8] Grasp her, and she will exalt you. You will be glorified by her, when you have embraced her. [9] She will bestow upon your head an increase in graces, and she will protect you with a noble crown. [10] Listen, my son, and accept my words, so that years of life may be multiplied for you. [11] I will demonstrate to you the way of wisdom. I will lead you along the paths of equity. [12] When you have entered by these, your steps will not be constrained, and when running, you will have no obstacle. [13] Take hold of discipline. Do not dismiss it. Guard it, for it is your life. [14] Do not delight in the paths of the impious, nor permit the way of evil-doers to please you. [15] Take flight from it. Do not pass close to it. Turn away and abandon it. [16] For they do not sleep, unless they have done evil. And their sleep is quickly taken away from them, unless they have overthrown. [17] They eat the bread of

impiety, and they drink the wine of iniquity. ¹⁸ But the path of the just is like a shining light: it advances and increases, even to the day of completion. ¹⁹ The way of the impious is darkened. They do not know where they may fall. ²⁰ My son, pay attention to my sermons, and incline your ear to my eloquent words. ²¹ Let them not recede from your eyes. Keep them in the midst of your heart. ²² For they are life to those who find them and health to all that is flesh. ²³ Preserve your heart with all watchfulness, for life proceeds from this. ²⁴ Remove from yourself a corrupt mouth, and let detracting lips be far from you. ²⁵ Let your eyes look straight ahead, and let your eyelids precede your steps. ²⁶ Direct the path of your feet, and all your ways shall be secure. ²⁷ Turn aside, neither to the right, nor to the left; yet turn your foot away from evil. For the Lord knows the ways that are on the right, and truly, those that are on the left are perverse. But he himself will make your courses straight. Then your journey will advance in peace.

CHAPTER 5

¹ My son, pay attention to my wisdom, and incline your ear to my prudence, ² so that you may guard your thinking, and so that your lips may preserve discipline. Do not pay attention to the deceit of a woman. ³ For the lips of a loose woman are like a dripping honeycomb, and her voice is smoother than oil. ⁴ But in the end, she is as bitter as wormwood, and as sharp as a two-edged sword. ⁵ Her feet descend into death, and her steps reach even to Hell. ⁶ They do not walk along the path of life; her steps are wandering and untraceable. ⁷ Therefore, my son, listen to me now, and do not withdraw from the words of my mouth. ⁸ Make your way at a distance from her, and do not approach the doors of her house. ⁹ Do not give your honor to foreigners, and your years to the cruel. ¹⁰ Otherwise, outsiders may be filled with your strength, and your labors may be in a foreign house, ¹¹ and you may mourn in the end, when you will have consumed your flesh and your body. And so you may say: ¹² "Why have I detested discipline, and why has my heart not been quieted by correction? ¹³ And why have I not listened to the voice of those who guided me? And why has my ear not inclined to my teachers? ¹⁴ I have almost been with all evil in the midst of the church and of the assembly." ¹⁵ Drink water from your own cistern and from the springs of your own well. ¹⁶ Let your fountains be diverted far and wide, and divide your waters in the streets. ¹⁷ Hold them for yourself alone, and do not let strangers be partakers with you. ¹⁸ Let your spring be blessed, and rejoice with the wife of your youth: ¹⁹ a beloved doe and most pleasing fawn. Let her breasts inebriate you at all times. Be delighted continually by her love. ²⁰ Why are you seduced, my son, by a strange woman, and why are you kept warm by the bosom of another? ²¹ The Lord beholds the ways of man, and he considers all his steps. ²² His own iniquities take hold of the impious, and he is bound by the cords of his own sins. ²³ He shall die, for he has not held to discipline. And by the multitude of his foolishness, he shall be deceived.

CHAPTER 6

¹ My son, if you have taken a pledge on behalf of your friend, then you have bound your hand to an outsider, ² then you are ensnared by the words of your own mouth, and taken captive by your own words. ³ Therefore, my son, do what I say, and free yourself, for you have fallen into the hand of your neighbor. Run, hurry, awaken your friend. ⁴ Do not grant sleep to your eyes, nor let your eyelids slumber. ⁵ Rescue yourself like a gazelle from the hand, and like a bird from the hand of the fowler. ⁶ Go to the ant, you lazy one, and consider her ways, and so learn wisdom. ⁷ For though she has no ruler, nor instructor, nor leader, ⁸ she provides meals for herself in the summer, and she gathers at the harvest what she may eat. ⁹ How long will you slumber, you lazy one? When will you rise up from your sleep? ¹⁰ You will sleep a little, you will slumber a little, you will fold your hands a little to sleep, ¹¹ and then destitution will meet with you, like a traveler, and poverty, like an armed man. Yet truly, if you would be diligent, then your harvest will arrive like a fountain, and destitution will flee far from you. ¹² An apostate man, a harmful man, walks with a perverse mouth; ¹³ he winks with the eyes, touches with the foot, speaks with the finger. ¹⁴ With a depraved heart he devises evil, and at all times he sows conflict. ¹⁵ To this one, his perdition will arrive promptly, and he shall be crushed suddenly: he will no longer have any remedy. ¹⁶ Six things there are that the Lord hates, and the seventh, his soul detests: ¹⁷ haughty eyes, a lying tongue, hands that shed innocent blood, ¹⁸ a heart that devises the most wicked thoughts, feet running swiftly unto evil, ¹⁹ a deceitful witness bringing forth lies, and he who sows discord among brothers. ²⁰ My son, preserve the

precepts of your father, and do not dismiss the law of your mother. ²¹Bind them to your heart unceasingly, and encircle them around your throat. ²²When you walk, let them keep step with you. When you sleep, let them guard you. And when you keep watch, speak with them. ²³For commandment is a lamp, and law is a light, and the reproofs of discipline are the way of life. ²⁴So may they guard you from an evil woman, and from the flattering tongue of the outsider. ²⁵Let not your heart desire her beauty; do not be captivated by her winks. ²⁶For the price of a prostitute is only one loaf. Yet the woman seizes the precious soul of a man. ²⁷Would a man be able to conceal fire in his bosom, so that his garments would not burn? ²⁸Or could he walk over burning coals, so that his feet would not be burned? ²⁹So also, he who enters to the wife of his neighbor shall not be clean when he touches her. ³⁰Not so great is the fault when someone has stolen. For he steals so as to satisfy a hungry soul. ³¹Also, if he is apprehended, he shall repay sevenfold and hand over all the substance of his house. ³²But whoever is an adulterer, because of the emptiness of his heart, will destroy his own soul. ³³He gathers shame and dishonor to himself, and his disgrace will not be wiped away. ³⁴For the jealousy and fury of the husband will not spare him on the day of vindication, ³⁵nor will he agree to the pleadings of anyone, nor will he accept, as repayment, a multitude of gifts.

CHAPTER 7

¹My son, guard my words and conceal my precepts within you. ²Son, preserve my commandments, and you shall live. And keep my law as the pupil of your eye. ³Bind it with your fingers; write it on the tablets of your heart. ⁴Say to wisdom, "You are my sister," and call prudence your friend. ⁵So may she guard you from the woman who is an outsider, and from the stranger who sweetens her words. ⁶For I gaze from the window of my house, through the lattice, ⁷and I see little ones. I consider a frenzied youth, ⁸who crosses the street at the corner and close to the way of that house. ⁹He steps into shadows, as day becomes evening, into the darkness and gloom of the night. ¹⁰And behold, a woman meets him, dressed like a harlot, prepared to captivate souls: chattering and rambling, ¹¹unwilling to bear silence, unable to keep her feet at home, ¹²now outside, now in the streets, now lying in ambush near the corners. ¹³And overtaking the youth, she kisses him, and with a provocative face, she flatters him, saying: ¹⁴"I vowed sacrifices for well-being. Today I have repaid my vows. ¹⁵Because of this, I have gone out to meet you, desiring to see you, and I have found you. ¹⁶I have woven my bed with cords. I have strewn it with embroidered tapestries from Egypt. ¹⁷I have sprinkled my bed with myrrh, aloe, and cinnamon. ¹⁸Come, let us be inebriated in abundance, and let us delight in the embraces of desire, until the day begins to dawn. ¹⁹For my husband is not in his house. He has gone away on a very long journey. ²⁰He took with him a bag of money. He will return to his house on the day of the full moon." ²¹She enmeshed him with many words, and she drew him forward with the flattery of her lips. ²²Immediately, he follows her, like an ox being led to the sacrifice, and like a lamb acting lasciviously, and not knowing that he is being drawn foolishly into chains, ²³until the arrow pierces his liver. It is just as if a bird were to hurry into the snare. And he does not know that his actions endanger his own soul. ²⁴Therefore, my son, hear me now, and attend to the words of my mouth. ²⁵Do not let your mind be pulled into her ways. And do not be deceived by her paths. ²⁶For she has tossed aside many wounded, and some of those who were very strong have been slain by her. ²⁷Her household is the way to Hell, reaching even to the inner places of death.

CHAPTER 8

¹Does not wisdom call out, and prudence bestow her voice? ²At the summits and the tops of exalted places, standing above the ways, in the midst of the paths, ³beside the gates of the city, at the very doors, she speaks, saying: ⁴"O men, to you I call out, and my voice is to the sons of men. ⁵O little ones, understand discernment. And you who are unwise, turn your souls. ⁶Listen, for I will speak about great things, and my lips will be opened, so as to foretell what is right. ⁷My throat shall practice truth, and my lips shall detest the impious. ⁸All my words are just. There is no depravity in them, and no perversity. ⁹They are upright to those who understand, and equitable to those who discover knowledge. ¹⁰Accept my discipline, and not money. Choose the doctrine that is greater than gold. ¹¹For wisdom is better than all that is most precious, and everything that is desirable cannot compare to her. ¹²I, wisdom, dwell in counsel, and I am inside

learned thoughts. [13]The fear of the Lord hates evil. I detest arrogance, and pride, and every wicked way, and a mouth with a double tongue. [14]Counsel is mine, and equity. Prudence is mine. Strength is mine. [15]Through me, kings reign and legislators decree just conditions. [16]Through me, princes rule and the powerful decree justice. [17]I love those who love me. And those who stand watch for me until morning shall discover me. [18]With me, are wealth and glory, superb riches and justice. [19]For my fruit is better than gold and precious stones, and my progeny better than choice silver. [20]I walk in the way of justice, in the midst of the paths of judgment, [21]so that I may enrich those who love me, and thus complete their treasures. [22]The Lord possessed me in the beginning of his ways, before he made anything, from the beginning. [23]I was ordained from eternity, and out of antiquity, before the earth was formed. [24]The abyss did not yet exist, and I was already conceived; neither had the fountains of waters yet erupted. [25]The mountains, with their great mass, had not yet been established. Before the hills, I was brought forth. [26]Still he had not made the earth, and the rivers, and the poles of the globe of the earth. [27]I was already present: when he prepared the heavens; when, with a certain law and a circuit, he fortified the abyss; [28]when he made firm the sky above, and set free the fountains of waters; [29]when he encompassed the sea within its limits, and laid down a law for the waters, lest they transgress their limits; when he weighed the foundations of the earth. [30]I was with him in composing all things. And I was delighted, throughout every day, by playing in his sight at all times, [31]playing in globe of the earth. And my delight was to be with the sons of men. [32]Therefore, sons, hear me now. Blessed are those who preserve my ways. [33]Listen to discipline, and become wise, and do not be willing to cast it aside. [34]Blessed is the man who listens to me, and who stands watch at my gates every day, and who observes at the posts of my doors. [35]He who finds me, finds life, and he will draw salvation from the Lord. [36]But he who sins against me will wound his own soul. All who hate me love death."

CHAPTER 9

[1]Wisdom has built a house for herself. She has hewn seven columns. [2]She has immolated her victims. She has mixed her wine and set forth her table. [3]She has sent her maids to call out to the tower and to the fortified walls of the city, [4]"If anyone is little, let him come to me." And to the unwise, she has said: [5]"Approach. Eat my bread, and drink the wine that I have mixed for you. [6]Leave behind childishness. And live and walk by the ways of prudence." [7]Whoever teaches a mocker causes injury to himself. And whoever argues with the impious produces a blemish on himself. [8]Do not be willing to argue with a mocker, lest he hate you. Dispute with the wise, and he will love you. [9]Present an opportunity to the wise, and wisdom shall be added to him. Teach the just, and he will hurry to receive it. [10]The fear of the Lord is the beginning of wisdom, and knowledge of holiness is prudence. [11]For by me, your days will be multiplied and years of life will be added to you. [12]If you would be wise, you will be so for yourself. But if you would be one who ridicules, you alone shall carry the evil. [13]A foolish and loud woman, who is full of enticements and who knows nothing at all, [14]sat at the entrance of her house on a seat, in a high place of the city, [15]so as to call to those who were passing by the way and continuing on their journey: [16]"Whoever is little, let him turn aside to me." And to the frenzied, she said, [17]"Stolen waters are more soothing, and secret bread is more pleasant." [18]And he did not know that giants are there, and that her companions are in the depths of Hell.

CHAPTER 10

[1]A wise son gladdens the father. Yet truly, a foolish son is the grief of his mother. [2]Treasures of impiety will profit nothing. Truly, justice shall liberate from death. [3]The Lord will not afflict with famine the soul of the just, and he will overthrow the treacheries of the impious. [4]The neglectful hand has wrought destitution. But the hand of the steadfast prepares riches. He who advances by lies, this one feeds on the wind. For he is the same as one who runs after flying birds. [5]He who gathers the harvest is a wise son. But he who snores in warm weather is a son of confusion. [6]The blessing of the Lord is on the head of the just. But iniquity covers the mouth of the impious. [7]The remembrance of the just is with praises. And the name of the impious shall decay. [8]The wise of heart accept precepts. The foolish are cut down by the lips. [9]He who walks in simplicity walks in confidence. But he who corrupts his ways shall be discovered. [10]He who winks with the eye gives sorrow. And the foolish in lips shall be beaten. [11]The mouth of the just is

a vein of life. And the mouth of the impious covers iniquity. ¹²Hatred rises up from disputes. And charity covers all offenses. ¹³In the lips of the wise, wisdom is discovered. And a rod is for the back of one who lacks heart. ¹⁴The wise store away knowledge. But the mouth of the foolish is a neighbor to confusion. ¹⁵The substance of the rich is the city of his strength. The fear of the poor is their destitution. ¹⁶The work of the just is unto life. But the fruit of the impious is unto sin. ¹⁷The way of life is for those who observe discipline. But whoever abandons correction wanders astray. ¹⁸Lying lips conceal hatred; whoever brings forth contempt is unwise. ¹⁹In a multitude of speaking, sin will not be lacking. But whoever tempers his lips is most prudent. ²⁰The tongue of the just is choice silver. But the heart of the impious is exchanged for nothing. ²¹The lips of the just instruct many. But those who are unlearned shall die in destitution of heart. ²²The blessing of the Lord causes riches. Affliction will not be a companion to them. ²³The foolish work wickedness as if in jest. But wisdom is prudence to a man. ²⁴What the impious fear will overwhelm them. The just shall be given their desire. ²⁵Like a passing tempest, so the impious one will be no more. But the just one is like an everlasting foundation. ²⁶Like vinegar to the teeth, and smoke to the eyes, so is a lazy one to those who sent him. ²⁷The fear of the Lord adds days. And the years of the impious will be shortened. ²⁸The expectation of the just is rejoicing. But the hope of the impious will perish. ²⁹The strength of the simple is the way of the Lord, and it is fear to those who work evil. ³⁰The just in eternity shall not be moved. But the impious will not live upon the earth. ³¹The mouth of the just shall bring forth wisdom. The tongue of the depraved will perish. ³²The lips of the just consider what is acceptable. And the mouth of the impious considers perversities.

CHAPTER 11

¹A deceitful scale is an abomination with the Lord, and a fair weighing is his will. ²Wherever arrogance may be, there too is insult. But wherever humility is, there too is wisdom. ³The simplicity of the just shall direct them, and the rebellion of the perverse will devastate them. ⁴Wealth will not profit in the day of vengeance. But justice shall liberate from death. ⁵The justice of the simple shall direct his way. And the impious will fall in his impiety. ⁶The justice of the upright shall free them. And the iniquitous will be seized by their own treachery. ⁷When the impious man is dead, there will no longer be any hope. And the expectation of the anxious will perish. ⁸The just one is freed from anguish. And the impious one will be handed over instead of him. ⁹The pretender deceives his friend by mouth. But the just shall be freed by knowledge. ¹⁰In the good of the just, the city shall exult. And in the perdition of the impious, there shall be praise. ¹¹By the blessing of the just, the city shall be exalted. And by the mouth of the impious, it will be subverted. ¹²Whoever despises his friend is destitute in heart. But the prudent man will remain silent. ¹³Whoever walks dishonestly reveals secrets. But whoever is of a faithful soul conceals what is confided by a friend. ¹⁴Where there is no governor, the people shall fall. But where there is much counsel, well-being shall be. ¹⁵He will be afflicted with evil, who provides a guarantee for an outsider. But whoever is wary of traps shall be secure. ¹⁶A gracious woman shall discover glory. And the robust will have wealth. ¹⁷A merciful man benefits his own soul. But whoever is cruel casts out even his close relatives. ¹⁸The impious does work with inconstancy. But for the sower of justice, there is the reward of faithfulness. ¹⁹Clemency prepares life. And the pursuit of evils prepares death. ²⁰A depraved heart is abominable to the Lord. And his will is with those who walk in simplicity. ²¹Hand in hand, the evil shall not be innocent. But the offspring of the just shall be saved. ²²A beautiful and senseless woman is like a gold ring in the snout of a swine. ²³The desire of the just is entirely good. The anticipation of the impious is fury. ²⁴Some distribute their own goods, and they become wealthier. Others seize what is not their own, and they are always in need. ²⁵The soul that blesses shall be made fat. And whoever inebriates will likewise be inebriated himself. ²⁶Whoever hides away grain shall be cursed among the people. But a blessing is upon the head of those who sell it. ²⁷He does well to rise early, who seeks what is good. But whoever is a seeker of evils shall be oppressed by them. ²⁸Whoever trusts in his riches will fall. But the just shall spring up like a green leaf. ²⁹Whoever troubles his own house will possess the winds. And whoever is foolish will serve the wise. ³⁰The fruit of the just one is the tree of life. And whoever receives souls is wise. ³¹If the just are repaid upon the earth, how much more the impious and the sinner!

CHAPTER 12

¹Whoever loves discipline loves knowledge. But whoever hates correction is unwise. ²Whoever is good shall draw grace from the Lord. But whoever trusts in his own thoughts acts impiously. ³Man will not be made strong from impiety. And the root of the just shall not be moved. ⁴A diligent woman is a crown to her husband. And she who acts with confusion as to which things are worthy is decay to his bones. ⁵The thoughts of the just are judgments. And the counsels of the impious are dishonest. ⁶The words of the impious lie in wait for blood. The mouth of the just shall free them. ⁷Turn from the impious, and they will not be. But the house of the just shall stand firm. ⁸A man will be known by his doctrine. But whoever is vain and heartless will suffer contempt. ⁹Better is a pauper who has what he needs, than someone glorious and in need of bread. ¹⁰The just one knows the lives of his beasts. But the inner most parts of the impious are cruel. ¹¹Whoever works his land shall be satisfied with bread. But whoever continually pursues leisure is most foolish. Whoever is soothed by lingering over wine leaves behind contempt in his strongholds. ¹²The desire of the impious is the fortification of what is most wicked. But the root of the just shall prosper. ¹³For the sins of the lips draw ruin to the evil. But the just shall escape from distress. ¹⁴By the fruit of his own mouth, each one shall be filled with good things, and according to the works of his own hands, it will be distributed to him. ¹⁵The way of the foolish is right in his own eyes. But whoever is wise listens to counsels. ¹⁶The senseless immediately reveals his anger. But whoever ignores injuries is clever. ¹⁷He is a sign of justice, who speaks what he knows. But whoever deceives is a dishonest witness. ¹⁸He who makes promises is also jabbed, as if with a sword, in conscience. But the tongue of the wise is reasonable. ¹⁹The lips of truth shall be steadfast forever. But a hasty witness readies a lying tongue. ²⁰Deceit is in the heart of those who devise evils. But gladness follows those who take up counsels of peace. ²¹Whatever may befall the just, it will not discourage him. But the impious will be filled with disasters. ²²Lying lips are an abomination to the Lord. But whoever acts faithfully pleases him. ²³A resourceful man conceals knowledge. And the heart of the unwise provokes foolishness. ²⁴The hand of the strong will rule. But anyone who is neglectful will pay tribute. ²⁵Grief in the heart of a man humbles him. And with a good word he shall be made glad. ²⁶He who ignores a loss for the sake of a friend is just. But the way of the impious will deceive them. ²⁷The dishonest will not discover gain. But the substance of a man will be like precious gold. ²⁸In the path of justice, there is life. But the devious way leads to death.

CHAPTER 13

¹A wise son is the doctrine of his father. But he who ridicules does not listen when he is reproved. ²From the fruit of his own mouth, a man shall be satisfied with good things. But the soul of betrayers is iniquity. ³Whoever guards his mouth guards his soul. But whoever gives no consideration to his speech shall experience misfortunes. ⁴The lazy one is willing and then not willing. But the soul of he who labors shall be made fat. ⁵The just shall detest a lying word. But the impious confound and will be confounded. ⁶Justice guards the way of the innocent. But impiety undermines the sinner. ⁷One is like the rich, though he has nothing. And another is like the poor, though he has many riches. ⁸The redemption of a man's life is his riches. But he who is poor cannot tolerate correction. ⁹The light of the just enriches. But the lamp of the impious will be extinguished. ¹⁰Among the arrogant, there are always conflicts. But those who do everything with counsel are ruled by wisdom. ¹¹Substance obtained in haste will be diminished. But what is collected by hand, little by little, shall be multiplied. ¹²Hope, when it is delayed, afflicts the soul. The arrival of the desired is a tree of life. ¹³Whoever denounces something obligates himself for the future. But whoever fears a lesson shall turn away in peace. Deceitful souls wander into sins. The just are merciful and compassionate. ¹⁴The law of the wise is a fountain of life, so that he may turn aside from the ruin of death. ¹⁵Good doctrine bestows grace. In the way of the contemptuous, there is a chasm. ¹⁶The discerning do everything with counsel. But whoever is senseless discloses his stupidity. ¹⁷The messenger of the impious will fall into evil. But a faithful ambassador shall prosper. ¹⁸Destitution and disgrace are for those who abandon discipline. But whoever agrees with a reproof shall be glorified. ¹⁹The desired, when perfected, shall delight the soul. The foolish detest those who flee from evils. ²⁰Whoever keeps step with the wise shall be wise. A friend of the foolish will become like them. ²¹Evil pursues sinners. And good

things shall be distributed to the just. ²²The good leave behind heirs: children and grandchildren. And the substance of the sinner is preserved for the just. ²³Much nourishment is in the fallow land of the fathers. But for others, it is gathered without judgment. ²⁴He who spares the rod hates his son. But he who loves him urgently instructs him. ²⁵The just eats and fills his soul. But the belly of the impious is never satisfied.

CHAPTER 14

¹A wise woman builds up her household. But a foolish one will pull down with her own hands what has been built up. ²One who walks on a virtuous journey, and who fears God, is despised by him who advances along a disreputable way. ³In the mouth of the foolish, there is a rod of arrogance. But the lips of the wise guard them. ⁴Where there are no oxen, the feeding trough is empty. But where there are many crops, there the strength of the ox is manifest. ⁵A faithful witness will not lie. But a deceitful witness offers a lie. ⁶A mocker seeks wisdom and does not find it. The doctrine of the prudent is accessible. ⁷Go against a foolish man, and he does not acknowledge lips of prudence. ⁸The wisdom of a discerning man is to understand his way. And the imprudence of the foolish is to be wandering astray. ⁹The foolish will speak mockingly of sin. But grace lingers among the just. ¹⁰The heart that knows the bitterness of its own soul, in its gladness the outsider shall not meddle. ¹¹The house of the impious will be wiped away. Yet truly, the tabernacles of the just shall spring forth. ¹²There is a way which seems just to a man, but its conclusion leads to death. ¹³Laughter shall be mingled with sorrow, and mourning occupies the limits of joy. ¹⁴The foolish will be filled up by his own ways. And the good man shall be above him. ¹⁵The innocent trust every word. The astute one considers his own steps. Nothing good will be for the deceitful son. But the wise servant shall act prosperously and his way will be set in order. ¹⁶The wise fear, and so turn away from evil. The foolish leap ahead with confidence. ¹⁷The impatient will work foolishness. And a resourceful man is hated. ¹⁸The childish will possess foolishness, and the discerning will anticipate knowledge. ¹⁹The evil will fall down before the good. And the impious will fall down before the gates of the just. ²⁰The pauper will be hated, even by his own neighbor. Yet truly, the friends of the wealthy are many. ²¹Whoever despises his neighbor, sins. But whoever pities the poor shall be blessed. Whoever trusts in the Lord loves mercy. ²²They wander astray who work evil. But mercy and truth prepare good things. ²³In every work, there shall be abundance. But where there are many words, there is often need. ²⁴The crown of the wise is their wealth. The senselessness of the foolish is imprudence. ²⁵A faithful witness frees souls. And the chameleon utters lies. ²⁶In the fear of the Lord is the faithfulness of strength, and there shall be hope for his sons. ²⁷The fear of the Lord is a fountain of life, so as to turn aside from the ruin of death. ²⁸In a multitude of people, there is dignity for the king. And in a paucity of people, there is disgrace for the prince. ²⁹Whoever is patient is governed by much prudence. But whoever is impatient exalts his foolishness. ³⁰The well-being of the heart is life for the flesh. But envy is decay for the bones. ³¹Whoever slanders the indigent argues against his Maker. But he who has compassion on the poor honors his Maker. ³²The impious will be expelled in his malice. But the just finds hope even in his own death. ³³In the heart of the prudent, wisdom finds rest. And so shall he instruct all the uneducated. ³⁴Justice elevates a nation. But sin makes the peoples miserable. ³⁵An intelligent minister is acceptable to the king. Whoever is useless shall bear his wrath.

CHAPTER 15

¹A mild response shatters anger. But a harsh word stirs up fury. ²The tongue of the wise adorns knowledge. But the mouth of the senseless gushes with foolishness. ³In every place, the eyes of the Lord consider good and evil. ⁴A peaceful tongue is a tree of life. But that which is immoderate will crush the spirit. ⁵A fool laughs at the discipline of his father. But whoever preserves rebukes will become astute. In abundant justice, there is very great virtue. But the intentions of the impious will be eradicated. ⁶The house of the just has very great strength. And in the fruits of the impious, there is disorder. ⁷The lips of the wise shall disseminate knowledge. The heart of the foolish will be dissimilar. ⁸The sacrifices of the impious are abominable to the Lord. The vows of the just are appeasing. ⁹The way of the impious is an abomination to the Lord. Whoever

pursues justice is loved by him. ¹⁰ Doctrine is evil to those who abandon the way of life. Whoever hates correction shall die. ¹¹ Hell and perdition are in the sight of the Lord. How much more the hearts of the sons of men! ¹² He who corrupts himself does not love the one who afflicts him, nor will he step toward the wise. ¹³ A rejoicing heart gladdens the face. But by the grief of the soul, the spirit is cast down. ¹⁴ The heart of the wise seeks doctrine. And the mouth of the foolish feeds on ignorance. ¹⁵ All the days of the poor are evil. A secure mind is like a continual feast. ¹⁶ Better is a little with the fear of the Lord, than great treasures and dissatisfaction. ¹⁷ It is better to be called to vegetables with charity, than to a fatted calf with hatred. ¹⁸ A short-tempered man provokes conflicts. Whoever is patient tempers those who are stirred up. ¹⁹ The way of the slothful is like a hedge of thorns. The way of the just is without offense. ²⁰ A wise son gladdens the father. But the foolish man despises his mother. ²¹ Folly is gladness to the foolish. And the prudent man sets his own steps in order. ²² Intentions dissipate where there is no counsel. Yet truly, they are confirmed where there are many counselors. ²³ A man rejoices in the verdict of his own mouth. And a word at the right time is best. ²⁴ The path of life is for the wise above, so that he may turn away from the end of Hell. ²⁵ The Lord will demolish the house of the arrogant. And He will make firm the borders of the widow. ²⁶ Evil intentions are an abomination to the Lord. And pure conversation, most beautiful, shall be confirmed by him. ²⁷ Whoever pursues avarice disturbs his own house. But whoever hates bribes shall live. Through mercy and faith, sins are purged. But through the fear of the Lord, each one turns aside from evil. ²⁸ The mind of the just meditates on obedience. The mouth of the impious overflows with evils. ²⁹ The Lord is distant from the impious. And he will heed the prayers of the just. ³⁰ The light of the eyes rejoices the soul. A good reputation fattens the bones. ³¹ The ear that listens to the reproofs of life shall abide in the midst of the wise. ³² Whoever rejects discipline despises his own soul. But whoever agrees to correction is a possessor of the heart. ³³ The fear of the Lord is the discipline of wisdom. And humility precedes glory.

CHAPTER 16

¹ It is for man to prepare the soul, and for the Lord to govern the tongue. ² All the ways of a man are open to his eyes; the Lord is the one who weighs spirits. ³ Open your works to the Lord, and your intentions will be set in order. ⁴ The Lord has wrought all things because of himself. Likewise the impious is for the evil day. ⁵ All the arrogant are an abomination to the Lord. Even if hand will be joined to hand, he is not innocent. The beginning of a good way is to do justice. And this is more acceptable with God than to immolate sacrifices. ⁶ By mercy and truth, iniquity is redeemed. And by the fear of the Lord, one turns away from evil. ⁷ When the ways of man will please the Lord, he will convert even his enemies to peace. ⁸ Better is a little with justice, than many fruits with iniquity. ⁹ The heart of man disposes his way. But it is for Lord to direct his steps. ¹⁰ Foreknowledge is in the lips of the king. His mouth shall not err in judgment. ¹¹ Weights and scales are judgments of the Lord. And all the stones in the bag are his work. ¹² Those who act impiously are abominable to the king. For the throne is made firm by justice. ¹³ Just lips are the will of kings. He who speaks honestly shall be loved. ¹⁴ The indignation of a king is a herald of death. And the wise man will appease it. ¹⁵ In the cheerfulness of the king's countenance, there is life. And his clemency is like belated rain. ¹⁶ Possess wisdom, for it is better than gold. And acquire prudence, for it is more precious than silver. ¹⁷ The path of the just turns away from evils. He who guards his soul preserves his way. ¹⁸ Arrogance precedes destruction. And the spirit is exalted before a fall. ¹⁹ It is better to be humbled with the meek, than to divide spoils with the arrogant. ²⁰ The learned in word shall find good things. And whoever hopes in the Lord is blessed. ²¹ Whoever is wise in heart shall be called prudent. And whoever is sweet in eloquence shall attain to what is greater. ²² Learning is a fountain of life to one who possesses it. The doctrine of the foolish is senseless. ²³ The heart of the wise shall instruct his mouth and add grace to his lips. ²⁴ Careful words are a honeycomb: sweet to the soul and healthful to the bones. ²⁵ There is a way which seems right to a man, and its end result leads to death. ²⁶ The soul of the laborer labors for himself, because his mouth has driven him to it. ²⁷ The impious man digs up evil, and in his lips is a burning fire. ²⁸ A perverse man stirs up lawsuits. And one who is verbose divides leaders. ²⁹ A man of iniquity entices his friend, and he leads him along a way that is not good. ³⁰ Whoever, with astonished eyes, thinks up depravities, biting his lips, accomplishes evil. ³¹ Old age is a crown of dignity, when it is found in the

ways of justice. ³²A patient man is better than a strong one. And whoever rules his soul is better than one who assaults cities. ³³Lots are cast into the lap, but they are tempered by the Lord.

CHAPTER 17

¹A dry morsel with gladness is better than a house full of sacrifices along with conflict. ²A wise servant shall rule over foolish sons, and he will divide the inheritance among brothers. ³Just as silver is tested by fire, and gold is tested in the furnace, so also does the Lord test hearts. ⁴The evil obey an unjust tongue. And the false are submissive to lying lips. ⁵Whoever despises the poor rebukes his Maker. And whoever rejoices in the ruin of another will not go unpunished. ⁶Sons of sons are the crown of old age. And the glory of sons is their fathers. ⁷Well-chosen words are not fitting for the foolish, nor are lying lips fitting for a leader. ⁸The expectation of those who stand ready is a most pleasing jewel. Whichever way he turns himself, he understands prudently. ⁹Whoever conceals an offense seeks friendships. Whoever repeats the words of another separates allies. ¹⁰A correction benefits more with a wise man, than a hundred stripes with a fool. ¹¹The evil one continually seeks conflicts. But a cruel Angel shall be sent against him. ¹²It is more expedient to meet a bear robbed of her young, than the foolish trusting in his own folly. ¹³Whoever repays evil for good, evil shall not withdraw from his house. ¹⁴Whoever releases the water is the head of the conflict. And just before he suffers contempt, he abandons judgment. ¹⁵Those who justify the impious, and those who condemn the just, both are abominable with God. ¹⁶What does it profit the foolish to have riches, when he is not able to buy wisdom? Whoever makes his house high seeks ruin. And whoever shuns learning shall fall into evils. ¹⁷Whoever is a friend loves at all times. And a brother is proved by distress. ¹⁸A foolish man will clap his hands, when he makes a pledge for his friend. ¹⁹Whoever dwells on discord loves disputes. And whoever exalts his door seeks ruin. ²⁰Whoever is of a perverse heart shall not find good. And whoever turns his tongue shall fall into evil. ²¹A foolish one is born into his own disgrace. But his father will not rejoice in one who is senseless. ²²A joyful soul makes a lifetime flourish. A gloomy spirit dries out the bones. ²³The impious receives gifts from the bosom, so that he may pervert the paths of judgment. ²⁴Prudence shines from the face of the wise. The eyes of the foolish are on the ends of the earth. ²⁵A foolish son is the anger of the father and the grief of the mother who conceived him. ²⁶It is not good to inflict damage on the just, nor to strike the leader who judges uprightly. ²⁷Whoever moderates his words is learned and prudent. And a man of learning has a precious spirit. ²⁸If he would remain silent, even the foolish would be considered wise, and if he closes his lips, intelligent.

CHAPTER 18

¹Whoever has a will to withdraw from a friend, seeks occasions; he shall be reproached at all times. ²The foolish do not accept words of prudence, unless you say what is already turning in his heart. ³The impious, when he has arrived within the depths of sin, thinks little of it. But ill repute and disgrace follow him. ⁴Words from the mouth of a man are deep waters. And the fountain of wisdom is a torrent overflowing. ⁵It is not good to accept the character of the impious, so as to turn away from true judgment. ⁶The lips of the foolish meddle in disputes. And his mouth provokes conflicts. ⁷The mouth of the foolish is his destruction, and his own lips are the ruin of his soul. ⁸The words of the double-tongued seem simple. And they reach even to the interior of the gut. Fear casts down the lazy, but the souls of the effeminate shall go hungry. ⁹Whoever is dissolute and slack in his work is the brother of him who wastes his own works. ¹⁰The name of the Lord is a very strong tower. The just one rushes to it, and he shall be exalted. ¹¹The substance of the wealthy is the city of his strength, and it is like a strong wall encircling him. ¹²The heart of a man is exalted before it is crushed and humbled before it is glorified. ¹³Whoever responds before he listens, demonstrates himself to be foolish and deserving of confusion. ¹⁴The spirit of a man sustains his weakness. Yet who can sustain a spirit that is easily angered? ¹⁵A prudent heart shall possess knowledge. And the ear of the wise seeks doctrine. ¹⁶A man's gift expands his way and makes space for him before leaders. ¹⁷The just is the first accuser of himself; his friend arrives and shall investigate him. ¹⁸Casting a lot suppresses contentions and passes judgment, even among the powerful. ¹⁹A brother who is helped by a brother is like a reinforced city, and

judgments are like the bars of cities. ²⁰ From the fruit of a man's mouth shall his belly be filled. And the harvest of his own lips shall satisfy him. ²¹ Death and life are in the power of the tongue. Whoever values it shall eat from its fruits. ²² He who has found a good wife has found goodness, and he shall draw contentment from the Lord. He who expels a good wife expels goodness. But he who holds on to an adulteress is foolish and impious. ²³ The poor will speak with supplications. And the rich will express themselves roughly. ²⁴ A man amiable to society shall be more friendly than a brother.

CHAPTER 19

¹ Better is the poor who walks in his simplicity, than the rich who twists his lips and is unwise. ² Where there is no knowledge of the soul, there is no good. And whoever hurries with his feet will stumble. ³ The foolishness of a man undermines his steps. And then he seethes in his soul against God. ⁴ Riches add many friends. But from the pauper, even those whom he had become separated. ⁵ A false witness shall not go unpunished. And whoever speaks lies will not escape. ⁶ Many honor the character of one who is powerful, and there are friends for a giver of gifts. ⁷ The brothers of the poor man hate him. Moreover, even his friends have withdrawn far from him. Whoever pursues only words shall have nothing. ⁸ But whoever possesses reason loves his own soul. And one who guards prudence shall discover good things. ⁹ A false witness shall not go unpunished. And whoever speaks lies will perish. ¹⁰ Fine things are not fitting for the foolish, nor is it fitting for a servant to rule over princes. ¹¹ The doctrine of a man is known through patience. And his glory is to pass beyond iniquities. ¹² Like the roaring of a lion, so also is the wrath of a king. And his cheerfulness is like the dew upon the grass. ¹³ A foolish son is the grief of his father. And an argumentative wife is like a roof that is continually leaking. ¹⁴ A house and its riches are given by parents. But a prudent wife is particularly from the Lord. ¹⁵ Laziness sends one into a deep sleep, and a dissolute soul will go hungry. ¹⁶ Whoever guards a commandment guards his own soul. But whoever neglects his own way will die. ¹⁷ Whoever is merciful to the poor lends to the Lord. And he will repay him for his efforts. ¹⁸ Teach your son; do not despair. But do not set your soul toward putting him to death. ¹⁹ Whoever is impatient will sustain damage. And when it has been taken away, he will set up another. ²⁰ Listen to counsel and take up discipline, so that you may be wise in your latter days. ²¹ There are many intentions in the heart of a man. But the will of the Lord shall stand firm. ²² An indigent man is merciful. And a pauper is better than a deceitful man. ²³ The fear of the Lord is unto life. And he shall linger in plentitude, without being visited by disaster. ²⁴ The lazy conceals his hand under his arm, and he will not so much as bring it to his mouth. ²⁵ When the pestilent are scourged, the foolish will become wiser. But if you chastise the wise, he will understand discipline. ²⁶ Whoever afflicts his father and flees from his mother is disreputable and unhappy. ²⁷ Son, do not cease listening to doctrine, and do not be ignorant of the sermons of knowledge. ²⁸ An unjust witness ridicules judgment. And the mouth of the impious devours iniquity. ²⁹ Judgments are prepared for those who ridicule. And striking hammers are prepared for the bodies of the foolish.

CHAPTER 20

¹ It is a luxurious thing, wine, and inebriation is tumultuous. Anyone who is delighted by this will not be wise. ² Just like the roaring of a lion, so also is the dread of a king. Whoever provokes him sins in his own soul. ³ Honor is for the man who separates himself from contentions. But all the foolish meddle in altercations. ⁴ Because of the cold, the lazy one was not willing to plough. Therefore, in the summer, he will beg, and it will not be given to him. ⁵ Counsel in the heart of a man is like deep waters. But a wise man will draw it out. ⁶ Many men are called merciful. But who will find a faithful man? ⁷ The just who walks in his simplicity shall leave behind him blessed sons. ⁸ The king who sits on the throne of judgment scatters all evil with his gaze. ⁹ Who is able to say: "My heart is clean. I am pure from sin?" ¹⁰ Diverse weights, diverse measures: both are abominable with God. ¹¹ A child may be understood by his interests: whether his works may be clean and upright. ¹² The hearing ear and the seeing eye: the Lord has made them both. ¹³ Do not love sleep, lest deprivation oppress you. Open your eyes and be satisfied with bread. ¹⁴ "It is bad, it is bad," says every buyer; and when he has withdrawn, then he will boast. ¹⁵ There is gold, and there are a multitude of jewels. But lips of knowledge are a precious vessel. ¹⁶ Take away

the vestments of him who stands up to vouch for a stranger, and take a pledge from him instead of from outsiders. ¹⁷The bread of lies is sweet to a man. But afterwards, his mouth will be filled with pebbles. ¹⁸Plans are strengthened by counsels. And wars are to be handled by governments. ¹⁹Do not become involved with him who reveals mysteries, and who walks deceitfully, and who enlarges his lips. ²⁰Whoever curses his father and mother, his lamp will be extinguished in the midst of darkness. ²¹When an inheritance is obtained hastily in the beginning, in the end it will be without a blessing. ²²Do not say, "I will repay evil." Wait for the Lord, and he will free you. ²³Diverse weights are an abomination with the Lord. A deceitful balance is not good. ²⁴The steps of men are directed by the Lord. But who is the man able to understand his own way? ²⁵It is ruin for a man to devour what is holy, or, after making vows, to retract them. ²⁶A wise king scatters the impious and bends an archway over them. ²⁷The spirit of a man is a lamp to the Lord, which investigates all the secrets of the inner self. ²⁸Mercy and truth guard the king, and his throne is strengthened by clemency. ²⁹The joy of youths is their strength. And the dignity of old men is their grey hairs. ³⁰The bruise of a wound, as well as scourges, shall wipe away evils in the more secret places of the inner self.

CHAPTER 21

¹Just as with the dividing of the waters, so also is the heart of the king in the hand of the Lord. He shall bend it whichever way he wills. ²Every way of a man seems right to himself. But the Lord weighs hearts. ³To do mercy and judgment is more pleasing to the Lord than sacrifices. ⁴To lift up the eyes is to enlarge the heart. The lamp of the impious is sin. ⁵The intentions of the robust continually bring forth abundance. But all the lazy are continually in need. ⁶Whoever gathers treasures by a lying tongue is vain and heartless. And he will stumble into the snares of death. ⁷The robberies of the impious will drag them down, because they were not willing to do judgment. ⁸The perverse way of a man is foreign. But whoever is pure: his work is upright. ⁹It is better to sit in a corner of the attic, than with a contentious woman and in a shared house. ¹⁰The soul of the impious desires evil; he will not take pity on his neighbor. ¹¹When the pestilent is punished, a little one will become wiser. And if he pursues what is wise, he will receive knowledge. ¹²The just thinks carefully about the house of the impious, so that he may draw the impious away from evil. ¹³Whoever blocks his ears to the outcry of the poor shall also cry out himself, and he will not be heeded. ¹⁴A surprise gift extinguishes anger. And a gift concealed in the bosom extinguishes the greatest indignation. ¹⁵It is gladness for the just to do judgment; and it is dread for those who work iniquity. ¹⁶A man who wanders astray from the way of doctrine will linger in the company of the giants. ¹⁷Whoever loves a feast will be in deprivation. Whoever loves wine and fatness will not be enriched. ¹⁸The impious is given over instead of the just, and the iniquitous is given over in place of the upright. ¹⁹It is better to live in a deserted land, than with a quarrelsome and emotional woman. ²⁰There is desirable treasure, as well as oil, in the habitations of the just. And the imprudent man will waste it. ²¹Whoever follows justice and mercy shall discover life, justice, and glory. ²²The wise has ascended the city of the strong, and he has torn down the bulwark of its confidence. ²³Whoever guards his mouth and his tongue guards his soul from anguish. ²⁴A proud and arrogant one is also called ignorant, if he, in anger, acts according to pride. ²⁵Desires kill the lazy, for his hands are not willing to work at all. ²⁶He covets and desires all day long. But whoever is just shall distribute and shall not cease. ²⁷The sacrifices of the impious are abominable, because they are offered out of wickedness. ²⁸A lying witness will perish. An obedient man shall speak of victory. ²⁹The impious man insolently hardens his face. But whoever is upright corrects his own way. ³⁰There is no wisdom, there is no prudence, there is no counsel, which is against the Lord. ³¹The horse is prepared for the day of battle. But the Lord bestows salvation.

CHAPTER 22

¹A good name is better than many riches. And good esteem is above silver and gold. ²The rich and poor have met one another. The Lord is the maker of them both. ³The clever saw evil and hid himself. The innocent continued on and was afflicted with damage. ⁴The end of moderation is the fear of the Lord, riches and glory and life. ⁵Weapons and swords are on the way of the perverse. But he who guards his own soul withdraws far from them. ⁶The proverb is: A youth is close to his way; even when he is old, he will not withdraw from it. ⁷The rich rule over

the poor. And the borrower is servant to the lender. [8] Whoever sows iniquity will reap evils, and by the rod of his own wrath he will be consumed. [9] Whoever is inclined to mercy shall be blessed, for from his bread he has given to the poor. Whoever gives gifts will acquire victory and honor. But he carries away the soul of the receiver. [10] Cast out the one who ridicules, and conflict will go out with him, and accusations and insults will cease. [11] Whoever loves cleanness of heart, because of the grace of his lips, will have the king as his friend. [12] The eyes of the Lord watch over knowledge. And the words of the iniquitous are supplanted. [13] The lazy one says: "There is a lion outside. I might be slain in the midst of the streets." [14] The mouth of a foreign woman is a deep pit; the Lord was angry with him who will fall into it. [15] Foolishness has been bound to the heart of a child, and a rod of discipline shall cause it to flee. [16] Whoever slanders the poor, so as to augment his own riches, will give it away to one who is richer, and will be in need. [17] Incline your ear, and listen to the words of the wise. Then apply your heart to my doctrine. [18] It shall be beautiful to you, if you preserve it in your inner self, and it shall overflow from your lips, [19] so that your confidence may be in the Lord. Therefore, I also have revealed it to you this day. [20] Behold, I have written it for you in three ways, and with meditations and knowledge, [21] so that I might reveal to you, firmly and with words of truth, in order to respond about these things to those who sent you. [22] Do not act with violence toward the pauper because he is poor. And do not weary the needy at the gate. [23] For the Lord will judge his case, and he will pierce those who have pierced his soul. [24] Do not be willing to be a friend to an angry man, and do not walk with a furious man, [25] lest perhaps you learn his ways, and take up a stumbling block to your soul. [26] Do not be willing to be with those who certify with their hands, and who offer themselves as a guarantee against debts. [27] For if you do not have the means to restore, what reason should there be for him to take the covering from your bed? [28] Do not cross beyond the ancient limits that your fathers have set. [29] Have you seen a man swift in his work? He shall stand in the sight of kings, and not before those who are disreputable.

CHAPTER 23

[1] When you sit down to eat with a leader, pay close attention to what has been set before your face, [2] and put a knife to your throat, if, in such a way, you could hold your soul in your own power. [3] Do not desire his foods, in which is the bread of deceit. [4] Do not be willing to labor so that you may be enriched. But set limits by your prudence. [5] Do not raise your eyes toward wealth that you are not able to have. For they will make themselves wings, like those of an eagle, and they will fly in the sky. [6] Do not eat with an envious man, and do not desire his foods. [7] For, like a seer and an interpreter of dreams, he presumes what he does not know. "Eat and drink," he will say to you; and his mind is not with you. [8] The foods that you had eaten, you will vomit up. And you will lose the beauty in your words. [9] Do not speak into the ears of the unwise. They will despise the doctrine of your eloquence. [10] Do not touch the boundaries of little ones, and do not enter into the field of the fatherless. [11] For their close relative is strong, and he will judge their case against you. [12] Let your heart enter into doctrine, and let your ears enter into words of knowledge. [13] Do not be willing to take away discipline from a child. For if you strike him with the rod, he will not die. [14] You will strike him with the rod, and so shall you deliver his soul from Hell. [15] My son, if your soul will become wise, my heart will be glad with you. [16] And my temperament will exult, when your lips will have spoken what is upright. [17] Let not your heart compete with sinners. But be in the fear of the Lord all day long. [18] For you will have hope in the end, and your expectation will not be taken away. [19] Listen, my son, and be wise, and direct your soul along the way. [20] Do not be willing to be in the feasts of great drinkers, nor in the carousings of those who gather to feed on flesh. [21] For those who waste time drinking, and who surrender themselves to symbols, will be consumed. And those who sleep will be clothed in rags. [22] Listen to your father, who conceived you. And do not despise your mother, when she is old. [23] Purchase truth, and do not sell wisdom, or doctrine, or understanding. [24] The father of the just exults in gladness; he who has conceived the wise will rejoice in him. [25] Let your father and your mother be joyful, and may she who conceived you exult. [26] My son, offer me your heart, and let your eyes keep to my ways. [27] For a loose woman is a deep pit, and a foreign woman is a constricted well. [28] She lies in wait along the way like a robber. And the incautious one whom she sees, she will put to death. [29] Who has woe? Whose father has woe? Who has quarrels?

Who falls into pits? Who has wounds without cause? Who has watery eyes? [30] Is it not those who linger over wine, and who strive to be drinking from their cups? [31] Do not gaze into the wine when it turns gold, when its color shines in the glass. It enters pleasantly, [32] but in the end, it will bite like a snake, and it will spread poison like a king of snakes. [33] Your eyes will see women who are outsiders, and your heart will utter perversities. [34] And you will be like someone sleeping in the middle of the sea, and like a pilot, fast asleep, who has lost his hold on the helm. [35] And you will say: "They have beaten me, but I did not feel pain. They have dragged me, and I did not realize it. When will I awaken and find more wine?"

CHAPTER 24

[1] Do not imitate evil men, nor desire to be among them. [2] For their mind meditates on robberies, and their lips speak deceptions. [3] By wisdom shall a house be built, and by prudence shall it be strengthened. [4] By doctrine, the storerooms shall be filled with every substance that is precious and most beautiful. [5] A wise man is strong, and a well-taught man is robust and valiant. [6] For war is undertaken in an orderly manner, and safety shall be where there are many counsels. [7] Wisdom is beyond the foolish; at the gate he will not open his mouth. [8] Whoever intends to do evil shall be called foolish. [9] The intention of the foolish is sin. And the detractor is an abomination among men. [10] If you despair, being weary in the day of anguish, your strength will be diminished. [11] Rescue those who are led away to death. And do not cease from delivering those who are dragged away to a violent death. [12] If you would say: "I do not have sufficient strength." He who inspects the heart, the same one understands, and nothing slips past the one who preserves your soul. And he shall repay a man according to his works. [13] My son, eat honey, because it is good, and the honeycomb, because it is so sweet to your throat. [14] So, too, is the doctrine of wisdom to your soul. When you have found it, you will have hope in the end, and your hope shall not perish. [15] Do not lie in wait, and do not seek impiety in the house of the just, nor spoil his rest. [16] For the just one will fall seven times, and he shall rise again. But the impious will fall into evil. [17] When your enemy will fall, do not be glad, and do not let your heart exult in his ruin, [18] lest perhaps the Lord see, and it displease him, and he may take away his wrath from him. [19] Do not contend with the most wicked, and do not be a rival to the impious. [20] For the evil hold no hope in the future, and the lamp of the impious will be extinguished. [21] My son, fear the Lord, as well as the king. And do not mingle with detractors. [22] For their perdition shall rise up suddenly. And who knows what ruin will be for each of them? [23] Likewise, these things are for the wise. It is not good to base judgment on knowledge of character. [24] Those who say to the impious, "You are just," shall be cursed by the people, and the tribes shall detest them. [25] Those who argue against the impious shall be praised, and a blessing shall come upon them. [26] He shall kiss the lips, who responds with upright words. [27] Prepare your outdoor work, and diligently cultivate your field, so that afterward, you may build your house. [28] Do not be a witness without cause against your neighbor. And do not mislead anyone with your lips. [29] Do not say, "I will do to him as he has done to me." I will repay each one according to his work. [30] I passed by the field of a lazy man, and by the vineyard of a foolish man, [31] and behold, it was entirely filled with nettles, and thorns had covered its surface, and the stonewall was destroyed. [32] When I had seen this, I laid it up in my heart, and by this example, I received discipline. [33] You will sleep a little," I said. "You will slumber briefly. You will fold your hands a little, so as to rest. [34] And destitution will overtake you like a runner, and begging will overtake you like an armed man."

CHAPTER 25

[1] These, too, are parables of Solomon, which the men of Hezekiah, king of Judah, transferred. [2] It is to the glory of God to conceal a word, and it is to the glory of kings to investigate speech. [3] Heaven above, and earth below, and the heart of kings are each unsearchable. [4] Take away the tarnish from silver, and a most pure vessel will go forth. [5] Take away impiety from the face of the king, and his throne shall be made firm by justice. [6] Do not appear glorious before the king, and do not stand in the place of the great. [7] For it is better that it should be said to you, "Ascend to here," than that you should be humbled before the prince. [8] The things that your eyes have seen, do not offer hastily in a quarrel, lest afterward you may not be able to make amends, when you have dishonored your friend. [9] Argue your case with your friend, and do not reveal the secret to an outsider,

¹⁰lest perhaps he may insult you, when he has heard it, and he might not cease to reproach you. Grace and friendship free a man; preserve these for yourself, lest you fall under reproach. ¹¹Whoever speaks a word at an opportune time is like apples of gold on beds of silver. ¹²Whoever reproves the wise and obedient ear is like an earring of gold with a shining pearl. ¹³Just like the cold of snow in a time of harvest, so also is a faithful messenger to him who sent him: he causes his soul to rest. ¹⁴A man who boasts and does not fulfill his promises is like clouds and wind, when rain does not follow. ¹⁵By patience, a leader shall be appeased, and a soft tongue shall break hardness. ¹⁶You have discovered honey; eat what is sufficient for you, lest perhaps, being filled up, you may vomit it. ¹⁷Withdraw your feet from the house of your neighbor, lest, when he has had his fill, he may hate you. ¹⁸A man who speaks false testimony against his neighbor is like a dart and a sword and a sharp arrow. ¹⁹Whoever sets his hopes on the unfaithful in a day of anguish is like a rotten tooth and weary foot, ²⁰and like one who loosens his garment in cold weather. Whoever sings verses to a wicked heart is like vinegar on baking soda. Just like a moth to a garment, and a worm to wood, so too does the sadness of a man do harm to the heart. ²¹If your enemy is hungry, feed him. If he is thirsty, give him water to drink. ²²For you will gather hot coals upon his head, and the Lord will repay you. ²³The north wind brings forth the rain, and a sorrowful face brings forth a detracting tongue. ²⁴It is better to sit in a corner of the attic, than with an argumentative woman and in a shared house. ²⁵Like cold water to a thirsty soul, so too are good reports from a far away land. ²⁶The just falling down before the impious is like a fountain stirred up by feet and like a corrupted spring. ²⁷Just as whoever eats too much honey, it is not good for him, so also whoever is an investigator of what is majestic will be overwhelmed by glory. ²⁸Just like a city lying in the open and without surrounding walls, so also is a man who is unable to restrain his own spirit in speaking.

CHAPTER 26

¹In the manner of snow in the summer, and rain at the harvest, so also is glory unfit for the foolish. ²Like a bird flying away to another place, and like a sparrow that hurries away freely, so also a curse uttered against someone without cause will pass away. ³A whip is for a horse, and a muzzle is for donkey, and a rod is for the back of the imprudent. ⁴Do not respond to the foolish according to his folly, lest you become like him. ⁵Respond to the foolish according to his folly, lest he imagine himself to be wise. ⁶Whoever sends words by a foolish messenger has lame feet and drinks iniquity. ⁷In the manner of a lame man who has beautiful legs to no purpose, so also is a parable unfit for the mouth of the foolish. ⁸Just like one who casts a stone into the pile of Mercury, so also is he who gives honor to the foolish. ⁹In the manner of a thorn, if it were to spring up from the hand of a drunkard, so also is a parable in the mouth of the foolish. ¹⁰Judgment determines cases. And whoever imposes silence on the foolish mitigates anger. ¹¹Like a dog that returns to his vomit, so also is the imprudent who repeats his foolishness. ¹²Have you seen a man who seems wise to himself? There will be greater hope held for the unwise than for him. ¹³The lazy one says, "There is a lion along the way, and a lioness in the roads." ¹⁴Just as a door turns upon its hinges, so also does the lazy one turn upon his bed. ¹⁵The lazy one conceals his hand under his arms, and it is a labor for him to move it to his mouth. ¹⁶The lazy one seems wiser to himself than seven men speaking judgments. ¹⁷Just like one who takes hold of a dog by the ears, so also is he who crosses impatiently and meddles in the quarrels of another. ¹⁸Just as he is guilty who let loose the arrows and the lances unto death, ¹⁹so also is the man who harms his friend by deceitfulness. And when he has been apprehended, he says, "I did it jokingly." ²⁰When the wood fails, the fire will be extinguished. And when the gossiper is taken away, conflicts will be quelled. ²¹Just as charcoals are to burning coals, and wood is to fire, so also is an angry man who stirs up quarrels. ²²The words of a whisperer seem simple, but they penetrate to the innermost parts of the self. ²³In the same manner as an earthen vessel, if it were adorned with impure silver, conceited lips are allied with a wicked heart. ²⁴An enemy is known by his lips, though it is from his heart that he draws out deceit. ²⁵When he will have lowered his voice, do not believe him, for there are seven vices in his heart. ²⁶Whoever covers hatred with deceit, his malice shall be revealed in the assembly. ²⁷Whoever digs a pit will fall into it. And whoever rolls a stone, it will roll back to him. ²⁸A false tongue does not love truth. And a slippery mouth works ruin.

CHAPTER 27

¹Do not boast about tomorrow, for you do not know what the future day may bring. ²Let another praise you, and not your own mouth: an outsider, and not your own lips. ³A stone is weighty, and sand is burdensome; but the wrath of the foolish is heavier than both. ⁴Anger holds no mercy, nor does fury when it erupts. And who can bear the assault of one who has been provoked? ⁵An open rebuke is better than hidden love. ⁶The wounds of a loved one are better than the deceitful kisses of a hateful one. ⁷A sated soul will trample the honeycomb. And a hungry soul will accept even bitter in place of sweet. ⁸Just like a bird migrating from her nest, so also is a man who abandons his place. ⁹Ointment and various perfumes delight the heart. And the good advice of a friend is sweet to the soul. ¹⁰Do not dismiss your friend or your father's friend. And do not enter your brother's house in the day of your affliction. A close neighbor is better than a distant brother. ¹¹My son, study wisdom, and rejoice my heart, so that you may be able to respond to the one who reproaches. ¹²The discerning man, seeing evil, hides himself. The little ones, continuing on, sustain losses. ¹³Take away the garment of him who has vouched for an outsider. And take a pledge from him on behalf of foreigners. ¹⁴Whoever blesses his neighbor with a grand voice, rising in the night, shall be like one who curses. ¹⁵A roof leaking on a cold day, and an argumentative woman, are comparable. ¹⁶He who would restrain her, he is like one who would grasp the wind, or who would gather together oil with his right hand. ¹⁷Iron sharpens iron, and a man sharpens the countenance of his friend. ¹⁸Whoever maintains the fig tree shall eat its fruit. And whoever is the keeper of his master shall be glorified. ¹⁹In the manner of faces looking into shining water, so are the hearts of men made manifest to the prudent. ²⁰Hell and perdition are never filled; similarly the eyes of men are insatiable. ²¹In the manner of silver being tested in the refinery, and gold in the furnace, so also is a man tested by the mouth of one who praises. The heart of the iniquitous inquires after evils, but the heart of the righteous inquires after knowledge. ²²Even if you were to crush the foolish with a mortar, as when a pestle strikes over pearled barley, his foolishness would not be taken from him. ²³Be diligent to know the countenance of your cattle, and consider your own flocks, ²⁴for you will not always hold this power. But a crown shall be awarded from generation to generation. ²⁵The meadows are open, and the green plants have appeared, and the hay has been collected from the mountains. ²⁶Lambs are for your clothing, and goats are for the price of a field. ²⁷Let the milk of goats be sufficient for your food, and for the necessities of your household, and for the provisions of your handmaids.

CHAPTER 28

¹The impious flees, though no one pursues. But the just, like a confident lion, shall be without dread. ²Because of the sins of the land, it has many princes. And because of the wisdom of a man, and the knowledge of those things that are said, the life of the leader shall be prolonged. ³A poor man slandering the poor is like a violent rainstorm in advance of a famine. ⁴Those who abandon the law praise the impious. Those who guard it are inflamed against him. ⁵Evil men do not intend judgment. But those who inquire after the Lord turn their souls toward all things. ⁶Better is the pauper walking in his simplicity, than the rich walking in ways of depravity. ⁷Whoever keeps the law is a wise son. But whoever feeds gluttons brings shame to his father. ⁸Whoever piles up riches by usury and profit gathers them for him who will give freely to the poor. ⁹Whoever turns away his ears from listening to the law: his prayer will be detestable. ¹⁰Whoever deceives the just in a malicious way will fall into his own perdition. And the simple shall possess his goods. ¹¹The rich one seems wise to himself. But the poor one, being prudent, shall evaluate him. ¹²In the exultation of the just, there is great glory. When the impious reign, men are brought to ruin. ¹³Whoever hides his crimes will not be guided. But whoever will have confessed and abandoned them shall overtake mercy. ¹⁴Blessed is the man who is ever fearful. Yet truly, whoever is hardened in mind will fall into evil. ¹⁵An impious leader over a poor people is like a roaring lion and a hungry bear. ¹⁶A leader destitute of prudence will oppress many through false accusations. But whoever hates avarice shall prolong his days. ¹⁷A man who slanders the blood of a life, even if he flees to the pit, no one will tolerate him. ¹⁸Whoever walks simply shall be saved. Whoever is perverse in his steps will fall all at once. ¹⁹Whoever works his land shall be satisfied with bread. But whoever pursues leisure will be filled with need. ²⁰A faithful man shall be greatly praised. But whoever rushes to become rich will not be innocent. ²¹Whoever shows favoritism in judgment does

not do well; even if it is for a morsel of bread, he forsakes the truth. ²² A man who hurries to become rich, and who envies others, does not know that destitution will overwhelm him. ²³ Whoever corrects a man, afterward he shall find favor with him, more so than he who deceives him with a flattering tongue. ²⁴ Whoever takes away anything from his father or mother, and who says, "This is not a sin," is the associate of a murderer. ²⁵ Whoever boasts and enlarges himself stirs up conflicts. Yet truly, whoever trusts in the Lord will be healed. ²⁶ Whoever trusts in his own heart is a fool. But whoever treads wisely, the same shall be saved. ²⁷ Whoever gives to the poor shall not be in need. Whoever despises his petition will suffer scarcity. ²⁸ When the impious rise up, men will hide themselves. When they perish, the just shall be multiplied.

CHAPTER 29

¹ The man who, with a stiff neck, treats the one who corrects him with contempt will be suddenly overwhelmed to his own destruction, and reason shall not follow him. ² When just men are multiplied, the common people shall rejoice. When the impious take up the leadership, the people shall mourn. ³ The man who loves wisdom rejoices his father. But whoever nurtures promiscuous women will lose his substance. ⁴ A just king guides the land. A man of avarice will destroy it. ⁵ A man who speaks to his friend with flattering and feigned words spreads a net for his own feet. ⁶ A snare will entangle the iniquitous when he sins. And the just shall praise and be glad. ⁷ The just knows the case of the poor. The impious is ignorant of knowledge. ⁸ Pestilent men squander a city. Yet truly, the wise avert fury. ⁹ A wise man, if he were to contend with the foolish, whether in anger or in laughter, would find no rest. ¹⁰ Bloodthirsty men hate the simple one; but the just seek out his soul. ¹¹ A foolish one offers everything on his mind. A wise one reserves and defers until later. ¹² A leader who freely listens to lying words has only impious servants. ¹³ The pauper and the creditor have met one another. The Lord is the illuminator of them both. ¹⁴ The king who judges the poor in truth, his throne shall be secured in eternity. ¹⁵ The rod and its correction distribute wisdom. But the child who is left to his own will, brings shame to his mother. ¹⁶ When the impious are multiplied, crimes will be multiplied. But the just shall see their ruin. ¹⁷ Teach your son, and he will refresh you, and he will give delight to your soul. ¹⁸ When prophecy fails, the people will be scattered. Yet truly, whoever guards the law is blessed. ¹⁹ A servant cannot be taught by words, because he understands what you say, but he disdains to respond. ²⁰ Have you seen a man rushing to speak? Foolishness has more hope than his correction. ²¹ Whoever nurtures his servant delicately from childhood, afterwards will find him defiant. ²² A short-tempered man provokes quarrels. And whoever is easily angered is more likely to sin. ²³ Humiliation follows the arrogant. And glory shall uphold the humble in spirit. ²⁴ Whoever participates with a thief hates his own soul; for he listens to his oath and does not denounce him. ²⁵ Whoever fears man will quickly fall. Whoever hopes in the Lord shall be lifted up. ²⁶ Many demand the face of the leader. But the judgment of each one proceeds from the Lord. ²⁷ The just abhor an impious man. And the impious abhor those who are on the right way. By keeping the word, the son shall be free from perdition.

CHAPTER 30

¹ The words of the Gatherer, the son of the Vomiter. The vision that the man spoke. God is with him, and he, being strengthened by God and abiding with him, said: ² "I am the most foolish among men, and the wisdom of men is not with me. ³ I have not learned wisdom, and I have not known the knowledge of sanctity. ⁴ Who has ascended to heaven and also descended? Who has grasped the wind in his hands? Who has tied the waters together, as with a garment? Who has raised all the limits of the earth? What is his name, and what is the name of his son, if you know? ⁵ Every word of God is fire-tested. He is a bronze shield to those who hope in him. ⁶ Do not add anything to his words, lest you be reproved and be discovered to be a liar. ⁷ Two things I have asked of you; do not deny them to me before I die. ⁸ Remove, far from me, vanity and lying words. Give me neither begging, nor wealth. Apportion to me only the necessities of my life, ⁹ lest perhaps, being filled, I might be enticed into denial, and say: 'Who is the Lord?' Or, being compelled by destitution, I might steal, and then perjure myself in the name of my God. ¹⁰ Do not accuse a servant to his lord, lest he curse you, and you fall. ¹¹ There is a generation which curses their father, and

which does not bless their mother. [12]There is a generation which seems pure to themselves, and yet they are not even washed from their filthiness. [13]There is a generation, whose eyes have been elevated, and their eyelids are lifted on high. [14]There is a generation which has swords in place of teeth, and which commands their molars to devour the indigent from the earth and the poor from among men. [15]The leech has two daughters, who say, 'Bring, bring.' Three things are insatiable, and a fourth never says 'Enough': [16]Hell, and the mouth of the womb, and a land that is not filled with water. And truly, fire never says, 'Enough.' [17]The eye of one who mocks his father and who despises the childbearing of his mother, let the ravens of the torrent tear it out, and let the sons of the eagles consume it. [18]Three things are difficult for me, and about a fourth, I am nearly ignorant: [19]the way of an eagle in the sky, the way of a serpent on a rock, the way of a ship in the middle of the sea, and the way of a man in adolescence. [20]Such is the way also of an adulterous woman, who eats, and wiping her mouth, says: "I have done no evil." [21]By three things, the earth is moved, and a fourth it is not able to sustain: [22]by a slave when he reigns, by the foolish when he has been filled with food, [23]by a hateful woman when she has been taken in matrimony, and by a handmaid when she has been heir to her mistress. [24]Four things are least upon the earth, and they are wiser than the wise: [25]the ants, an infirm people who provide food for themselves at the harvest, [26]the rabbit, a sickened people who make their bed upon the rock. [27]The locust has no king, but they all depart by their troops. [28]The lizard supports itself on hands and dwells in the buildings of kings. [29]There are three things that advance well, and a fourth that marches happily on: [30]a lion, the strongest of beasts, who fears nothing that he meets, [31]a rooster prepared at the loins, likewise a ram, and a king, whom none can resist. [32]There is one who has appeared foolish, after he was lifted up on high; for if he had understood, he would have placed his hand over his mouth. [33]But whoever strongly squeezes the udder to bring out the milk, presses out butter. And whoever violently blows his nose, brings out blood. And whoever provokes wrath, brings forth discord."

CHAPTER 31

[1]The words of king Lamuel. The vision by which his mother instructed him: [2]"What, O my beloved? What, O beloved of my womb? What, O beloved of my vows? [3]Do not give your substance to women, or your riches to overthrow kings. [4]Not to kings, O Lamuel, not to kings give wine. For there are no secrets where drunkenness reigns. [5]And perhaps they may drink and forget judgments, and alter the case of the sons of the poor. [6]Give strong drink to the grieving, and wine to those who are bitter in soul. [7]Let them drink, and forget their needs, and remember their sorrow no more. [8]Open your mouth for the mute and for all the cases of the sons who are passing through. [9]Open your mouth, declare what is just, and do justice to the indigent and the poor. [10]Who shall find a strong woman? Far away, and from the furthest parts, is her price. [11]The heart of her husband confides in her, and he will not be deprived of spoils. [12]She will repay him with good, and not evil, all the days of her life. [13]She has sought wool and flax, and she has worked these by the counsel of her hands. [14]She has become like a merchant's ship, bringing her bread from far away. [15]And she has risen in the night, and given a prey to her household, and provisions to her maids. [16]She has considered a field and bought it. From the fruit of her own hands, she has planted a vineyard. [17]She has wrapped her waist with fortitude, and she has strengthened her arm. [18]She has tasted and seen that her tasks are good; her lamp shall not be extinguished at night. [19]She has put her hand to strong things, and her fingers have taken hold of the spindle. [20]She has opened her hand to the needy, and she has extended her hands to the poor. [21]She shall not fear, in the cold of snow, for her household. For all those of her household have been clothed two-fold. [22]She has made embroidered clothing for herself. Fine linen and purple is her garment. [23]Her husband is noble at the gates, when he sits among the senators of the land. [24]She has made finely woven cloth and sold it, and she has delivered a waistband to the Canaanite. [25]Strength and elegance are her clothing, and she will laugh in the final days. [26]She has opened her mouth to wisdom, and the law of clemency is on her tongue. [27]She has considered the paths of her household, and she has not eaten her bread in idleness. [28]Her sons rose up and predicted great happiness; her husband rose up and praised her. [29]Many daughters have gathered together riches; you have surpassed them all. [30]Charm is false, and beauty is vain. The woman who fears the Lord, the same shall be praised. [31]Give to her from the fruit of her own hands. And let her works praise her at the gates.

THE SACRED BIBLE:
THE GOSPEL OF MATTHEW

CHAPTER 1

[1] The book of the lineage of Jesus Christ, the son of David, the son of Abraham. [2] Abraham conceived Isaac. And Isaac conceived Jacob. And Jacob conceived Judah and his brothers. [3] And Judah conceived Perez and Zerah by Tamar. And Perez conceived Hezron. And Hezron conceived Ram. [4] And Ram conceived Amminadab. And Amminadab conceived Nahshon. And Nahshon conceived Salmon. [5] And Salmon conceived Boaz by Rahab. And Boaz conceived Obed by Ruth. And Obed conceived Jesse. [6] And Jesse conceived king David. And king David conceived Solomon, by her who had been the wife of Uriah. [7] And Solomon conceived Rehoboam. And Rehoboam conceived Abijah. And Abijah conceived Asa. [8] And Asa conceived Jehoshaphat. And Jehoshaphat conceived Joram. And Joram conceived Uzziah. [9] And Uzziah conceived Jotham. And Jotham conceived Ahaz. And Ahaz conceived Hezekiah. [10] And Hezekiah conceived Manasseh. And Manasseh conceived Amos. And Amos conceived Josiah. [11] And Josiah conceived Jechoniah and his brothers in the transmigration of Babylon. [12] And after the transmigration of Babylon, Jechoniah conceived Shealtiel. And Shealtiel conceived Zerubbabel. [13] And Zerubbabel conceived Abiud. And Abiud conceived Eliakim. And Eliakim conceived Azor. [14] And Azor conceived Zadok. And Zadok conceived Achim. And Achim conceived Eliud. [15] And Eliud conceived Eleazar. And Eleazar conceived Matthan. And Matthan conceived Jacob. [16] And Jacob conceived Joseph, the husband of Mary, of whom was born Jesus, who is called Christ. [17] And so, all the generations from Abraham to David are fourteen generations; and from David to the transmigration of Babylon, fourteen generations; and from the transmigration of Babylon to the Christ, fourteen generations. [18] Now the procreation of the Christ occurred in this way. After his mother Mary had been betrothed to Joseph, before they lived together, she was found to have conceived in her womb by the Holy Spirit. [19] Then Joseph, her husband, since he was just and was not willing to hand her over, preferred to send her away secretly. [20] But while thinking over these things, behold, an Angel of the Lord appeared to him in his sleep, saying: "Joseph, son of David, do not be afraid to accept Mary as your wife. For what has been formed in her is of the Holy Spirit. [21] And she shall give birth to a son. And you shall call his name JESUS. For he shall accomplish the salvation of his people from their sins." [22] Now all this occurred in order to fulfill what was spoken by the Lord through the prophet, saying: [23] "Behold, a virgin shall conceive in her womb, and she shall give birth to a son. And they shall call his name Emmanuel, which means: God is with us." [24] Then Joseph, arising from sleep, did just as the Angel of the Lord had instructed him, and he accepted her as his wife. [25] And he knew her not, yet she bore her son, the firstborn. And he called his name JESUS.

CHAPTER 2

[1] And so, when Jesus had been born in Bethlehem of Judah, in the days of king Herod, behold, Magi from the east arrived in Jerusalem, [2] saying: "Where is he who was born king of the Jews? For we have seen his star in the east, and we have come to adore him." [3] Now king Herod, hearing this, was disturbed, and all Jerusalem with him. [4] And gathering together all the leaders of the priests, and the scribes of the people, he consulted with them as to where the Christ would be born. [5] And they said to him: "In Bethlehem of Judea. For so it has been written by the prophet: [6] 'And you, Bethlehem, the land of Judah, are by no means least among the leaders of Judah. For from you shall go forth the ruler who shall guide my people Israel.'" [7] Then Herod, quietly calling the Magi, diligently learned from them the time when the star appeared to them. [8] And sending them into Bethlehem, he said: "Go and diligently ask questions about the boy. And when you have found him, report back to me, so that I, too, may come and adore him." [9] And when they had heard the king, they went away. And behold, the star that they had seen in the east went before them, even until, arriving, it stood still above the place where the child was. [10] Then, seeing the star, they were gladdened by a very great joy. [11] And entering the home, they found the boy with his mother Mary. And so, falling prostrate, they adored him. And opening their treasures, they offered him gifts: gold, frankincense, and myrrh. [12] And having received a response in sleep that they should not return to Herod, they went back by another

way to their own region. ¹³ And after they had gone away, behold, an Angel of the Lord appeared in sleep to Joseph, saying: "Rise up, and take the boy and his mother, and flee into Egypt. And remain there until I tell you. For it will happen that Herod will seek the boy to destroy him." ¹⁴ And getting up, he took the boy and his mother by night, and withdrew into Egypt. ¹⁵ And he remained there, until the death of Herod, in order to fulfill what was spoken by the Lord through the prophet, saying: "Out of Egypt, I called my son." ¹⁶ Then Herod, seeing that he had been fooled by the Magi, was very angry. And so he sent to kill all the boys who were in Bethlehem, and in all its borders, from two years of age and under, according to the time that he had learned by questioning the Magi. ¹⁷ Then what was spoken through the prophet Jeremiah was fulfilled, saying: ¹⁸ "A voice has been heard in Ramah, great weeping and wailing: Rachel crying for her sons. And she was not willing to be consoled, because they were no more." ¹⁹ Then, when Herod had passed away, behold, an Angel of the Lord appeared in sleep to Joseph in Egypt, ²⁰ saying: "Rise up, and take the boy and his mother, and go into the land of Israel. For those who were seeking the life of the boy have passed away." ²¹ And rising up, he took the boy and his mother, and he went into the land of Israel. ²² Then, hearing that Archelaus reigned in Judea in place of his father Herod, he was afraid to go there. And being warned in sleep, he withdrew into parts of Galilee. ²³ And arriving, he lived in a city which is called Nazareth, in order to fulfill what was spoken through the prophets: "For he shall be called a Nazarene."

CHAPTER 3

¹ Now in those days, John the Baptist arrived, preaching in the desert of Judea, ² and saying: "Repent. For the kingdom of heaven has drawn near." ³ For this is the one who was spoken of through the prophet Isaiah, saying: "A voice crying out in the desert: Prepare the way of the Lord. Make straight his paths." ⁴ Now the same John had a garment made from the hair of camels, and a leather belt around his waist. And his food was locusts and wild honey. ⁵ Then Jerusalem, and all Judea, and the entire region around the Jordan went out to him. ⁶ And they were baptized by him in the Jordan, acknowledging their sins. ⁷ Then, seeing many of the Pharisees and Sadducees arriving for his baptism, he said to them: "Progeny of vipers, who warned you to flee from the approaching wrath? ⁸ Therefore, produce fruit worthy of repentance. ⁹ And do not choose to say within yourselves, 'We have Abraham as our father.' For I tell you that God has the power to raise up sons to Abraham from these stones. ¹⁰ For even now the axe has been placed at the root of the trees. Therefore, every tree that does not produce good fruit shall be cut down and cast into the fire. ¹¹ Indeed, I baptize you with water for repentance, but he who will come after me is more powerful than me. I am not worthy to carry his shoes. He will baptize you with the fire of the Holy Spirit. ¹² His winnowing fan is in his hand. And he will thoroughly cleanse his threshing floor. And he will gather his wheat into the barn. But the chaff he will burn with unquenchable fire." ¹³ Then Jesus came from Galilee, to John at the Jordan, in order to be baptized by him. ¹⁴ But John refused him, saying, "I ought to be baptized by you, and yet you come to me?" ¹⁵ And responding, Jesus said to him: "Permit this for now. For in this way it is fitting for us to fulfill all justice." Then he allowed him. ¹⁶ And Jesus, having been baptized, ascended from the water immediately, and behold, the heavens were opened to him. And he saw the Spirit of God descending like a dove, and alighting on him. ¹⁷ And behold, there was a voice from heaven, saying: "This is my beloved Son, in whom I am well pleased."

CHAPTER 4

¹ Then Jesus was led by the Spirit into the desert, in order to be tempted by the devil. ² And when he had fasted for forty days and forty nights, afterwards he was hungry. ³ And approaching, the tempter said to him, "If you are the Son of God, tell these stones to become bread." ⁴ And in response he said, "It has been written: 'Not by bread alone shall man live, but by every word that proceeds from the mouth of God.'" ⁵ Then the devil took him up, into the holy city, and set him on the pinnacle of the temple, ⁶ and said to him: "If you are the Son of God, cast yourself down. For it has been written: 'For he has given charge of you to his angels, and they shall take you into their hands, lest perhaps you may hurt your foot against a stone.'" ⁷ Jesus said to him, "Again, it has been written: 'You shall not tempt the Lord your God.'" ⁸ Again, the devil took him up, onto a very

high mountain, and showed him all the kingdoms of the world and their glory, [9] and said to him, "All these things I will give to you, if you will fall down and adore me." [10] Then Jesus said to him: "Go away, Satan. For it has been written: 'You shall adore the Lord your God, and him only shall you serve.'" [11] Then the devil left him. And behold, Angels approached and ministered to him. [12] And when Jesus had heard that John had been handed over, he withdrew into Galilee. [13] And leaving behind the city of Nazareth, he went and lived in Capernaum, near the sea, at the borders of Zebulun and of Naphtali, [14] in order to fulfill what was said through the prophet Isaiah: [15] "Land of Zebulun and land of Naphtali, the way of the sea across the Jordan, Galilee of the Gentiles: [16] A people who were sitting in darkness have seen a great light. And unto those sitting in the region of the shadow of death, a light has risen." [17] From that time, Jesus began to preach, and to say: "Repent. For the kingdom of heaven has drawn near." [18] And Jesus, walking near the Sea of Galilee, saw two brothers, Simon who is called Peter, and his brother Andrew, casting a net into the sea (for they were fishermen). [19] And he said to them: "Follow me, and I will make you fishers of men." [20] And at once, leaving behind their nets, they followed him. [21] And continuing on from there, he saw another two brothers, James of Zebedee, and his brother John, in a ship with their father Zebedee, repairing their nets. And he called them. [22] And immediately, leaving their nets and their father behind, they followed him. [23] And Jesus traveled throughout all of Galilee, teaching in their synagogues, and preaching the Gospel of the kingdom, and healing every sickness and every infirmity among the people. [24] And reports of him went out to all of Syria, and they brought to him all those who had maladies, those who were in the grasp of various sicknesses and torments, and those who were in the hold of demons, and the mentally ill, and paralytics. And he cured them. [25] And a great crowd followed him from Galilee, and from the Ten Cities, and from Jerusalem, and from Judea, and from across the Jordan.

CHAPTER 5

[1] Then, seeing the crowds, he ascended the mountain, and when he had sat down, his disciples drew near to him, [2] and opening his mouth, he taught them, saying: [3] "Blessed are the poor in spirit, for theirs is the kingdom of heaven. [4] Blessed are the meek, for they shall possess the earth. [5] Blessed are those who mourn, for they shall be consoled. [6] Blessed are those who hunger and thirst for justice, for they shall be satisfied. [7] Blessed are the merciful, for they shall obtain mercy. [8] Blessed are the pure in heart, for they shall see God. [9] Blessed are the peacemakers, for they shall be called sons of God. [10] Blessed are those who endure persecution for the sake of justice, for theirs is the kingdom of heaven. [11] Blessed are you when they have slandered you, and persecuted you, and spoken all kinds of evil against you, falsely, for my sake: [12] be glad and exult, for your reward in heaven is plentiful. For so they persecuted the prophets who were before you. [13] You are the salt of the earth. But if salt loses its saltiness, with what will it be salted? It is no longer useful at all, except to be cast out and trampled under by men. [14] You are the light of the world. A city set on a mountain cannot be hidden. [15] And they do not light a lamp and put it under a basket, but on a lampstand, so that it may shine to all who are in the house. [16] So then, let your light shine in the sight of men, so that they may see your good works, and may glorify your Father, who is in heaven. [17] Do not think that I have come to loosen the law or the prophets. I have not come to loosen, but to fulfill. [18] Amen I say to you, certainly, until heaven and earth pass away, not one iota, not one dot shall pass away from the law, until all is done. [19] Therefore, whoever will have loosened one of the least of these commandments, and have taught men so, shall be called the least in the kingdom of heaven. But whoever will have done and taught these, such a one shall be called great in the kingdom of heaven. [20] For I say to you, that unless your justice has surpassed that of the scribes and the Pharisees you shall not enter into the kingdom of heaven. [21] You have heard that it was said to the ancients: 'You shall not murder; whoever will have murdered shall be liable to judgment.' [22] But I say to you, that anyone who becomes angry with his brother shall be liable to judgment. But whoever will have called his brother, 'Idiot,' shall be liable to the council. Then, whoever will have called him, 'Worthless,' shall be liable to the fires of Hell. [23] Therefore, if you offer your gift at the altar, and there you remember that your brother has something against you, [24] leave your gift there, before the altar, and go first to be reconciled to your brother, and then you may approach and offer your gift. [25] Be reconciled with your adversary quickly, while you are still on the way with him,

lest perhaps the adversary may hand you over to the judge, and the judge may hand you over to the officer, and you will be thrown in prison. ²⁶ Amen I say to you, that you shall not go forth from there, until you have repaid the last quarter. ²⁷ You have heard that it was said to the ancients: 'You shall not commit adultery.' ²⁸ But I say to you, that anyone who will have looked at a woman, so as to lust after her, has already committed adultery with her in his heart. ²⁹ And if your right eye causes you to sin, root it out and cast it away from you. For it is better for you that one of your members perish, than that your whole body be cast into Hell. ³⁰ And if your right hand causes you to sin, cut it off and cast it away from you. For it is better for you that one of your members perish, than that your whole body go into Hell. ³¹ And it has been said: 'Whoever would dismiss his wife, let him give her a bill of divorce.' ³² But I say to you, that anyone who will have dismissed his wife, except in the case of fornication, causes her to commit adultery; and whoever will have married her who has been dismissed commits adultery. ³³ Again, you have heard that it was said to the ancients: 'You shall not swear falsely. For you shall repay your oaths to the Lord.' ³⁴ But I say to you, do not swear an oath at all, neither by heaven, for it is the throne of God, ³⁵ nor by earth, for it is his footstool, nor by Jerusalem, for it is the city of the great king. ³⁶ Neither shall you swear an oath by your own head, because you are not able to cause one hair to become white or black. ³⁷ But let your word 'Yes' mean 'Yes,' and 'No' mean 'No.' For anything beyond that is of evil. ³⁸ You have heard that it was said: 'An eye for an eye, and a tooth for a tooth.' ³⁹ But I say to you, do not resist one who is evil, but if anyone will have struck you on your right cheek, offer to him the other also. ⁴⁰ And anyone who wishes to contend with you in judgment, and to take away your tunic, release to him your cloak also. ⁴¹ And whoever will have compelled you for one thousand steps, go with him even for two thousand steps. ⁴² Whoever asks of you, give to him. And if anyone would borrow from you, do not turn away from him. ⁴³ You have heard that it was said, 'You shall love your neighbor, and you shall have hatred for your enemy.' ⁴⁴ But I say to you: Love your enemies. Do good to those who hate you. And pray for those who persecute and slander you. ⁴⁵ In this way, you shall be sons of your Father, who is in heaven. He causes his sun to rise upon the good and the bad, and he causes it to rain upon the just and the unjust. ⁴⁶ For if you love those who love you, what reward will you have? Do not even tax collectors behave this way? ⁴⁷ And if you greet only your brothers, what more have you done? Do not even the pagans behave this way? ⁴⁸ Therefore, be perfect, even as your heavenly Father is perfect."

CHAPTER 6

¹ "Pay attention, lest you perform your justice before men, in order to be seen by them; otherwise you shall not have a reward with your Father, who is in heaven. ² Therefore, when you give alms, do not choose to sound a trumpet before you, as the hypocrites do in the synagogues and in the towns, so that they may be honored by men. Amen I say to you, they have received their reward. ³ But when you give alms, do not let your left hand know what your right hand is doing, ⁴ so that your almsgiving may be in secret, and your Father, who sees in secret, will repay you. ⁵ And when you pray, you should not be like the hypocrites, who love standing in the synagogues and at the corners of the streets to pray, so that they may be seen by men. Amen I say to you, they have received their reward. ⁶ But you, when you pray, enter into your room, and having shut the door, pray to your Father in secret, and your Father, who sees in secret, will repay you. ⁷ And when praying, do not choose many words, as the pagans do. For they think that by their excess of words they might be heeded. ⁸ Therefore, do not choose to imitate them. For your Father knows what your needs may be, even before you ask him. ⁹ Therefore, you shall pray in this way: Our Father, who is in heaven: May your name be kept holy. ¹⁰ May your kingdom come. May your will be done, as in heaven, so also on earth. ¹¹ Give us this day our life-sustaining bread. ¹² And forgive us our debts, as we also forgive our debtors. ¹³ And lead us not into temptation. But free us from evil. Amen. ¹⁴ For if you will forgive men their sins, your heavenly Father also will forgive you your offenses. ¹⁵ But if you will not forgive men, neither will your Father forgive you your sins. ¹⁶ And when you fast, do not choose to become gloomy, like the hypocrites. For they alter their faces, so that their fasting may be apparent to men. Amen I say to you, that they have received their reward. ¹⁷ But as for you, when you fast, anoint your head and wash your face, ¹⁸ so that your fasting will not be apparent to men, but to your Father, who is in secret. And your Father, who sees in secret, will repay you. ¹⁹ Do not choose to store up for

yourselves treasures on earth: where rust and moth consume, and where thieves break in and steal. [20] Instead, store up for yourselves treasures in heaven: where neither rust nor moth consumes, and where thieves do not break in and steal. [21] For where your treasure is, there also is your heart. [22] The lamp of your body is your eye. If your eye is wholesome, your entire body will be filled with light. [23] But if your eye has been corrupted, your entire body will be darkened. If then the light that is in you is darkness, how great will that darkness be! [24] No one is able to serve two masters. For either he will have hatred for the one, and love the other, or he will persevere with the one, and despise the other. You cannot serve God and wealth. [25] And so I say to you, do not be anxious about your life, as to what you will eat, nor about your body, as to what you will wear. Is not life more than food, and the body more than clothing? [26] Consider the birds of the air, how they neither sow, nor reap, nor gather into barns, and yet your heavenly Father feeds them. Are you not of much greater value than they are? [27] And which of you, by thinking, is able to add one cubit to his stature? [28] And as for clothing, why are you anxious? Consider the lilies of the field, how they grow; they neither work nor weave. [29] But I say to you, that not even Solomon, in all his glory, was arrayed like one of these. [30] So if God so clothes the grass of the field, which is here today, and cast into the oven tomorrow, how much more will he care for you, O little in faith? [31] Therefore, do not choose to be anxious, saying: 'What shall we eat, and what shall we drink, and with what shall we be clothed?' [32] For the Gentiles seek all these things. Yet your Father knows that you need all these things. [33] Therefore, seek first the kingdom of God and his justice, and all these things shall be added to you as well. [34] Therefore, do not be anxious about tomorrow; for the future day will be anxious for itself. Sufficient for the day is its evil."

CHAPTER 7

[1] "Do not judge, so that you may not be judged. [2] For with whatever judgment you judge, so shall you be judged; and with whatever measure you measure out, so shall it be measured back to you. [3] And how can you see the splinter in your brother's eye, and not see the board in your own eye? [4] Or how can you say to your brother, 'Let me take the splinter from your eye,' while, behold, a board is in your own eye? [5] Hypocrite, first remove the board from your own eye, and then you will see clearly enough to remove the splinter from your brother's eye. [6] Do not give what is holy to dogs, and do not cast your pearls before swine, lest perhaps they may trample them under their feet, and then, turning, they may tear you apart. [7] Ask, and it shall be given to you. Seek, and you shall find. Knock, and it shall be opened to you. [8] For everyone who asks, receives; and whoever seeks, finds; and to anyone who knocks, it will be opened. [9] Or what man is there among you, who, if his son were to ask him for bread, would offer him a stone; [10] or if he were to ask him for a fish, would offer him a snake? [11] Therefore, if you, though you are evil, know how to give good gifts to your sons, how much more will your Father, who is in heaven, give good things to those who ask him? [12] Therefore, all things whatsoever that you wish that men would do to you, do so also to them. For this is the law and the prophets. [13] Enter through the narrow gate. For wide is the gate, and broad is the way, which leads to perdition, and many there are who enter through it. [14] How narrow is the gate, and how straight is the way, which leads to life, and few there are who find it! [15] Beware of false prophets, who come to you in sheep's clothing, but inwardly are ravenous wolves. [16] You shall know them by their fruits. Can grapes be gathered from thorns, or figs from thistles? [17] So then, every good tree produces good fruit, and the evil tree produces evil fruit. [18] A good tree is not able to produce evil fruit, and an evil tree is not able to produce good fruit. [19] Every tree which does not produce good fruit shall be cut down and cast into the fire. [20] Therefore, by their fruits you will know them. [21] Not all who say to me, 'Lord, Lord,' will enter into the kingdom of heaven. But whoever does the will of my Father, who is in heaven, the same shall enter into the kingdom of heaven. [22] Many will say to me in that day, 'Lord, Lord, did we not prophesy in your name, and cast out demons in your name, and perform many powerful deeds in your name?' [23] And then will I disclose to them: 'I have never known you. Depart from me, you workers of iniquity.' [24] Therefore, everyone who hears these words of mine and does them shall be compared to a wise man, who built his house upon the rock. [25] And the rains descended, and the floods rose up, and the winds blew, and rushed upon that house, but it did not fall, for it was founded on the rock. [26] And everyone who hears these words of mine and does not do them shall be like a foolish man, who built his house upon the sand. [27] And the rains

descended, and the floods rose up, and the winds blew, and rushed upon that house, and it did fall, and great was its ruin." [28] And it happened, when Jesus had completed these words, that the crowds were astonished at his doctrine. [29] For he was teaching them as one who has authority, and not like their scribes and Pharisees.

CHAPTER 8

[1] And when he had descended from the mountain, great crowds followed him. [2] And behold, a leper, drawing near, adored him, saying, "Lord, if you are willing, you are able to cleanse me." [3] And Jesus, extending his hand, touched him, saying: "I am willing. Be cleansed." And immediately his leprosy was cleansed. [4] And Jesus said to him: "See to it that you tell no one. But go, show yourself to the priest, and offer the gift that Moses instructed, as a testimony for them." [5] And when he had entered into Capernaum, a centurion approached, petitioning him, [6] and saying, "Lord, my servant lies at home paralyzed and badly tormented." [7] And Jesus said to him, "I will come and heal him." [8] And responding, the centurion said: "Lord, I am not worthy that you should enter under my roof, but only say the word, and my servant shall be healed. [9] For I, too, am a man placed under authority, having soldiers under me. And I say to one, 'Go,' and he goes, and to another, 'Come,' and he comes, and to my servant, 'Do this,' and he does it." [10] And, hearing this, Jesus wondered. And he said to those following him: "Amen I say to you, I have not found so great a faith in Israel. [11] For I say to you, that many shall come from the east and the west, and they shall sit at table with Abraham, and Isaac, and Jacob in the kingdom of heaven. [12] But the sons of the kingdom shall be cast into the outer darkness, where there will be weeping and gnashing of teeth." [13] And Jesus said to the centurion, "Go, and just as you have believed, so let it be done for you." And the servant was healed at that very hour. [14] And when Jesus had arrived at the house of Peter, he saw his mother-in-law lying ill with a fever. [15] And he touched her hand, and the fever left her, and she rose up and ministered to them. [16] And when evening arrived, they brought to him many who had demons, and he cast out the spirits with a word. And he healed all those having maladies, [17] in order to fulfill what was spoken through the prophet Isaiah, saying, "He took our infirmities, and he carried away our diseases." [18] Then Jesus, seeing the great crowds encircling him, gave orders to go across the sea. [19] And one scribe, approaching, said to him, "Teacher, I will follow you wherever you will go." [20] And Jesus said to him, "Foxes have dens, and the birds of the air have nests, but the Son of man has nowhere to rest his head." [21] Then another of his disciples said to him, "Lord, permit me first to go and bury my father." [22] But Jesus said to him, "Follow me, and allow the dead to bury their dead." [23] And climbing into a boat, his disciples followed him. [24] And behold, a great tempest occurred in the sea, so much so that the boat was covered with waves; yet truly, he was sleeping. [25] And his disciples drew near to him, and they awakened him, saying: "Lord, save us, we are perishing." [26] And Jesus said to them, "Why are you afraid, O little in faith?" Then rising up, he commanded the winds, and the sea. And a great tranquility occurred. [27] Moreover, the men wondered, saying: "What kind of man is this? For even the winds and the sea obey him." [28] And when he had arrived across the sea, into the region of the Gerasenes, he was met by two who had demons, who were so exceedingly savage, as they went out from among the tombs, that no one was able to cross by that way. [29] And behold, they cried out, saying: "What are we to you, O Jesus, the Son of God? Have you come here to torment us before the time?" [30] Now there was, not far from them, a herd of many swine feeding. [31] Then the demons petitioned him, saying: "If you cast us from here, send us into the herd of swine." [32] And he said to them, "Go." And they, going out, went into the swine. And behold, the entire herd suddenly rushed along a steep place into the sea. And they died in the waters. [33] Then the shepherds fled, and arriving in the city, they reported on all this, and on those who had had the demons. [34] And behold, the entire city went out to meet Jesus. And having seen him, they petitioned him, so that he would cross from their borders.

CHAPTER 9

[1] And climbing into a boat, he crossed the sea, and he arrived at his own city. [2] And behold, they brought to him a paralytic, lying on a bed. And Jesus, seeing their faith, said to the paralytic, "Be strengthened in faith, son; your sins are forgiven you." [3] And behold, some of the scribes said within themselves, "He is

blaspheming." [4] And when Jesus had perceived their thoughts, he said: "Why do you think such evil in your hearts? [5] Which is easier to say, 'Your sins are forgiven you,' or to say, 'Rise up and walk?' [6] But, so that you may know that the Son of man has authority on earth to forgive sins," he then said to the paralytic, "Rise up, take up your bed, and go into your house." [7] And he arose and went into his house. [8] Then the crowd, seeing this, was frightened, and they glorified God, who gave such power to men. [9] And when Jesus passed on from there, he saw, sitting at the tax office, a man named Matthew. And he said to him, "Follow me." And rising up, he followed him. [10] And it happened that, as he was sitting down to eat in the house, behold, many tax collectors and sinners arrived, and they sat down to eat with Jesus and his disciples. [11] And the Pharisees, seeing this, said to his disciples, "Why does your Teacher eat with tax collectors and sinners?" [12] But Jesus, hearing this, said: "It is not those who are healthy who are in need of a physician, but those who have maladies. [13] So then, go out and learn what this means: 'I desire mercy and not sacrifice.' For I have not come to call the just, but sinners." [14] Then the disciples of John drew near to him, saying, "Why do we and the Pharisees fast frequently, but your disciples do not fast?" [15] And Jesus said to them: "How can the sons of the groom mourn, while the groom is still with them? But the days will arrive when the groom will be taken away from them. And then they shall fast. [16] For no one would sew a patch of new cloth onto an old garment. For it pulls its fullness away from the garment, and the tear is made worse. [17] Neither do they pour new wine into old wineskins. Otherwise, the wineskins rupture, and the wine pours out, and the wineskins are destroyed. Instead, they pour new wine into new wineskins. And so, both are preserved." [18] As he was speaking these things to them, behold, a certain ruler approached and adored him, saying: "Lord, my daughter has recently passed away. But come and impose your hand upon her, and she will live." [19] And Jesus, rising up, followed him, with his disciples. [20] And behold, a woman, who had suffered from a flow of blood for twelve years, approached from behind and touched the hem of his garment. [21] For she said within herself, "If I will touch even his garment, I shall be saved." [22] But Jesus, turning and seeing her, said: "Be strengthened in faith, daughter; your faith has made you well." And the woman was made well from that hour. [23] And when Jesus had arrived in the house of the ruler, and he had seen the musicians and the tumultuous crowd, [24] he said, "Depart. For the girl is not dead, but asleep." And they derided him. [25] And when the crowd had been sent away, he entered. And he took her by the hand. And the girl rose up. [26] And the news of this went out to that entire land. [27] And as Jesus passed from there, two blind men followed him, crying out and saying, "Take pity on us, Son of David." [28] And when he had arrived at the house, the blind men approached him. And Jesus said to them, "Do you trust that I am able to do this for you?" They say to him, "Certainly, Lord." [29] Then he touched their eyes, saying, "According to your faith, so let it be done for you." [30] And their eyes were opened. And Jesus warned them, saying, "See to it that no one knows of this." [31] But going out, they spread the news of it to all that land. [32] Then, when they had departed, behold, they brought him a man who was mute, having a demon. [33] And after the demon was cast out, the mute man spoke. And the crowds wondered, saying, "Never has anything like this been seen in Israel." [34] But the Pharisees said, "By the prince of demons does he cast out demons." [35] And Jesus traveled throughout all of the cities and towns, teaching in their synagogues, and preaching the Gospel of the kingdom, and healing every illness and every infirmity. [36] Then, seeing the multitudes, he had compassion on them, because they were distressed and were reclining, like sheep without a shepherd. [37] Then he said to his disciples: "The harvest indeed is great, but the laborers are few. [38] Therefore, petition the Lord of the harvest, so that he may sent out laborers to his harvest."

CHAPTER 10

[1] And having called together his twelve disciples, he gave them authority over unclean spirits, to cast them out and to cure every sickness and every infirmity. [2] Now the names of the twelve Apostles are these: the First, Simon, who is called Peter, and Andrew his brother, [3] James of Zebedee, and John his brother, Philip and Bartholomew, Thomas and Matthew the tax collector, and James of Alphaeus, and Thaddaeus, [4] Simon the Canaanite, and Judas Iscariot, who also betrayed him. [5] Jesus sent these twelve, instructing them, saying: "Do not travel by the way of the Gentiles, and do not enter into the city of the Samaritans, [6] but instead go to the sheep who have fallen away from the house of Israel. [7] And

going forth, preach, saying: 'For the kingdom of heaven has drawn near.' [8] Cure the infirm, raise the dead, cleanse lepers, cast out demons. You have received freely, so give freely. [9] Do not choose to possess gold, nor silver, nor money in your belts, [10] nor provisions for the journey, nor two tunics, nor shoes, nor a staff. For the laborer deserves his portion. [11] Now, into whatever city or town you will enter, inquire as to who is worthy within it. And stay there until you depart. [12] Then, when you enter into the house, greet it, saying, 'Peace to this house.' [13] And if, indeed, that house is worthy, your peace will rest upon it. But if it is not worthy, your peace will return to you. [14] And whoever has neither received you, nor listened to your words, departing from that house or city, shake off the dust from your feet. [15] Amen I say to you, it will be more tolerable for the land of Sodom and Gomorrah in the day of judgment, than for that city. [16] Behold, I am sending you like sheep in the midst of wolves. Therefore, be as prudent as serpents and as simple as doves. [17] But beware of men. For they will hand you over to councils, and they will scourge you in their synagogues. [18] And you shall be led before both rulers and kings for my sake, as a testimony to them and to the Gentiles. [19] But when they hand you over, do not choose to think about how or what to speak. For what to speak shall be given to you in that hour. [20] For it is not you who will be speaking, but the Spirit of your Father, who will speak in you. [21] And brother will hand over brother to death, and father will hand over son. And children will rise up against parents and bring about their deaths. [22] And you will be hated by all for the sake of my name. But whoever will have persevered, even to the end, the same shall be saved. [23] Now when they persecute you in one city, flee into another. Amen I say to you, you will not have exhausted all the cities of Israel, before the Son of man returns. [24] The disciple is not above the teacher, nor is the servant above his master. [25] It is sufficient for the disciple that he be like his teacher, and the servant, like his master. If they have called the Father of the family, 'Beelzebub,' how much more those of his household? [26] Therefore, do not fear them. For nothing is covered that shall not be revealed, nor hidden that shall not be known. [27] What I tell you in darkness, speak in the light. And what you hear whispered in the ear, preach above the rooftops. [28] And do not be afraid of those who kill the body, but are not able to kill the soul. But instead fear him who is able to destroy both soul and body in Hell. [29] Are not two sparrows sold for one small coin? And yet not one of them will fall to the ground without your Father. [30] For even the hairs of your head have all been numbered. [31] Therefore, do not be afraid. You are worth more than many sparrows. [32] Therefore, everyone who acknowledges me before men, I also will acknowledge before my Father, who is in heaven. [33] But whoever will have denied me before men, I also will deny before my Father, who is in heaven. [34] Do not think that I came to send peace upon the earth. I came, not to send peace, but the sword. [35] For I came to divide a man against his father, and a daughter against her mother, and a daughter-in-law against her mother-in-law. [36] And the enemies of a man will be those of his own household. [37] Whoever loves father or mother more than me is not worthy of me. And whoever loves son or daughter above me is not worthy of me. [38] And whoever does not take up his cross and follow me is not worthy of me. [39] Whoever finds his life, will lose it. And whoever will have lost his life because of me, shall find it. [40] Whoever receives you, receives me. And whoever receives me, receives him who sent me. [41] Whoever receives a prophet, in the name of a prophet, shall receive the reward of a prophet. And whoever receives the just in the name of the just shall receive the reward of the just. [42] And whoever shall give, even to one of the least of these, a cup of cold water to drink, solely in the name of a disciple: Amen I say to you, he shall not lose his reward."

CHAPTER 11

[1] And it happened that, when Jesus had completed instructing his twelve disciples, he went away from there in order to teach and to preach in their cities. [2] Now when John had heard, in prison, about the works of Christ, sending two of his disciples, he said to him, [3] "Are you he who is to come, or should we expect another?" [4] And Jesus, responding, said to them: "Go and report to John what you have heard and seen. [5] The blind see, the lame walk, the lepers are cleansed, the deaf hear, the dead rise again, the poor are evangelized. [6] And blessed is he who has found no offense in me." [7] Then, after they departed, Jesus began to speak to the crowds about John: "What did you go out to the desert to see? A reed shaken by the wind? [8] So what did you go out to see? A man in soft garments? Behold, those who are clothed in soft garments are in the houses of kings. [9] Then what

did you go out to see? A prophet? Yes, I tell you, and more than a prophet. [10] For this is he, of whom it is written: 'Behold, I send my Angel before your face, who shall prepare your way before you.' [11] Amen I say to you, among those born of women, there has arisen no one greater than John the Baptist. Yet the least in the kingdom of heaven is greater than he. [12] But from the days of John the Baptist, even until now, the kingdom of heaven has endured violence, and the violent carry it away. [13] For all the prophets and the law prophesied, even until John. [14] And if you are willing to accept it, he is the Elijah, who is to come. [15] Whoever has ears to hear, let him hear. [16] But to what shall I compare this generation? It is like children sitting in the marketplace, [17] who, calling out to their companions, say: 'We played music for you, and you did not dance. We lamented, and you did not mourn.' [18] For John came neither eating nor drinking; and they say, 'He has a demon.' [19] The Son of man came eating and drinking; and they say, 'Behold, a man who eats voraciously and who drinks wine, a friend of tax collectors and sinners.' But wisdom is justified by her sons." [20] Then he began to rebuke the cities in which many of his miracles were accomplished, for they still had not repented. [21] "Woe to you, Chorazin! Woe to you, Bethsaida! For if the miracles that were done in you had been done in Tyre and Sidon, they would have repented long ago in haircloth and ashes. [22] Yet truly, I say to you, Tyre and Sidon shall be forgiven more than you, on the day of judgment. [23] And you, Capernaum, would you be exalted all the way to heaven? You shall descend all the way to Hell. For if the miracles that were done in you had been done in Sodom, perhaps it would have remained, even to this day. [24] Yet truly, I say to you, that the land of Sodom shall be forgiven more than you, on the day of judgment." [25] At that time, Jesus responded and said: "I acknowledge you, Father, Lord of Heaven and earth, because you have hidden these things from the wise and the prudent, and have revealed them to little ones. [26] Yes, Father, for this was pleasing before you. [27] All things have been delivered to me by my Father. And no one knows the Son except the Father, nor does anyone know the Father except the Son, and those to whom the Son is willing to reveal him. [28] Come to me, all you who labor and have been burdened, and I will refresh you. [29] Take my yoke upon you, and learn from me, for I am meek and humble of heart; and you shall find rest for your souls. [30] For my yoke is sweet and my burden is light."

CHAPTER 12

[1] At that time, Jesus went out through the ripe grain on the Sabbath. And his disciples, being hungry, began to separate the grain and to eat. [2] Then the Pharisees, seeing this, said to him, "Behold, your disciples are doing what is not lawful to do on the Sabbaths." [3] But he said to them: "Have you not read what David did, when he was hungry, and those who were with him: [4] how he entered the house of God and ate the bread of the Presence, which was not lawful for him to eat, nor for those who were with him, but only for the priests? [5] Or have you not read in the law, that on the Sabbaths the priests in the temple violate the Sabbath, and they are without guilt? [6] But I say to you, that something greater than the temple is here. [7] And if you knew what this means, 'I desire mercy, and not sacrifice,' you would never have condemned the innocent. [8] For the Son of man is Lord even of the Sabbath." [9] And when he had passed from there, he went into their synagogues. [10] And behold, there was a man who had a withered hand, and they questioned him, so that they might accuse him, saying, "Is it lawful to cure on the Sabbaths?" [11] But he said to them: "Who is there among you, having even one sheep, if it will have fallen into a pit on the Sabbath, would not take hold of it and lift it up? [12] How much better is a man than a sheep? And so, it is lawful to do good on the Sabbaths." [13] Then he said to the man, "Extend your hand." And he extended it, and it was restored to health, just like the other one. [14] Then the Pharisees, departing, took council against him, as to how they might destroy him. [15] But Jesus, knowing this, withdrew from there. And many followed him, and he cured them all. [16] And he instructed them, lest they make him known. [17] Then what was spoken through the prophet Isaiah was fulfilled, saying: [18] "Behold, my servant whom I have chosen, my beloved in whom my soul is well pleased. I will place my Spirit over him, and he shall announce judgment to the nations. [19] He shall not contend, nor cry out, neither shall anyone hear his voice in the streets. [20] He shall not crush the bruised reed, and he shall not extinguish the smoking wick, until he sends forth judgment unto victory. [21] And the Gentiles shall hope in his name." [22] Then one who had a demon, who was blind and mute, was brought to him. And he cured him, so that he spoke and saw. [23] And all the

crowds were stupefied, and they said, "Could this be the son of David?" [24] But the Pharisees, hearing it, said, "This man does not cast out demons, except by Beelzebub, the prince of the demons." [25] But Jesus, knowing their thoughts, said to them: "Every kingdom divided against itself will become desolate. And every city or house divided against itself will not stand. [26] So if Satan casts out Satan, then he is divided against himself. How then will his kingdom stand? [27] And if I cast out demons by Beelzebub, by whom do your own sons cast them out? Therefore, they shall be your judges. [28] But if I cast out demons by the Spirit of God, then the kingdom of God has arrived among you. [29] Or how can anyone enter into the house of a strong man, and plunder his belongings, unless he first restrains the strong man? And then he will plunder his house. [30] Whoever is not with me, is against me. And whoever does not gather with me, scatters. [31] For this reason, I say to you: Every sin and blasphemy shall be forgiven men, but blasphemy against the Spirit shall not be forgiven. [32] And anyone who will have spoken a word against the Son of man shall be forgiven. But whoever will have spoken against the Holy Spirit shall not be forgiven, neither in this age, nor in the future age. [33] Either make the tree good and its fruit good, or make the tree evil and its fruit evil. For certainly a tree is known by its fruit. [34] Progeny of vipers, how are you able to speak good things while you are evil? For out of the abundance of the heart, the mouth speaks. [35] A good man offers good things from a good storehouse. And an evil man offers evil things from an evil storehouse. [36] But I say to you, that for every idle word which men will have spoken, they shall render an account in the day of judgment. [37] For by your words shall you be justified, and by your words shall you be condemned." [38] Then certain ones from the scribes and the Pharisees responded to him, saying, "Teacher, we want to see a sign from you." [39] And answering, he said to them: "An evil and adulterous generation seeks a sign. But a sign will not be given to it, except the sign of the prophet Jonah. [40] For just as Jonah was in the belly of the whale for three days and three nights, so shall the Son of man be in the heart of the earth for three days and three nights. [41] The men of Nineveh shall arise in judgment with this generation, and they shall condemn it. For, at the preaching of Jonah, they repented. And behold, there is a greater than Jonah here. [42] The Queen of the South shall arise in judgment with this generation, and she shall condemn it. For she came from the ends of the earth to hear the wisdom of Solomon. And behold, there is a greater than Solomon here. [43] Now when an unclean spirit departs from a man, he walks through dry places, seeking rest, and he does not find it. [44] Then he says, 'I will return to my house, from which I departed'. And arriving, he finds it vacant, swept clean, and decorated. [45] Then he goes and takes with him seven other spirits more wicked than himself, and they enter in and live there. And in the end, the man becomes worse than he was at first. So, too, shall it be with this most wicked generation." [46] While he was still speaking to the crowds, behold, his mother and his brothers were standing outside, seeking to speak with him. [47] And someone said to him: "Behold, your mother and your brothers are standing outside, seeking you." [48] But responding to the one speaking to him, he said, "Which one is my mother, and who are my brothers?" [49] And extending his hand to his disciples, he said: "Behold: my mother and my brothers. [50] For anyone who does the will of my Father, who is in heaven, the same is my brother, and sister, and mother."

CHAPTER 13

[1] In that day, Jesus, departing from the house, sat down beside the sea. [2] And such great crowds were gathered to him that he climbed into a boat and he sat down. And the entire multitude stood on the shore. [3] And he spoke many things to them in parables, saying: "Behold, a sower went out to sow seed. [4] And while he was sowing, some fell beside the road, and the birds of the air came and ate it. [5] Then others fell in a rocky place, where they did not have much soil. And they sprung up promptly, because they had no depth of soil. [6] But when the sun rose up, they were scorched, and because they had no roots, they withered. [7] Still others fell among thorns, and the thorns increased and suffocated them. [8] Yet some others fell upon good soil, and they produced fruit: some one hundred fold, some sixty fold, some thirty fold. [9] Whoever has ears to hear, let him hear." [10] And his disciples drew near to him and said, "Why do you speak to them in parables?" [11] Responding, he said to them: "Because it has been given to you to know the mysteries of the kingdom of heaven, but it has not been given to them. [12] For whoever has, it shall be given to him, and he shall have in abundance.

But whoever has not, even what he has shall be taken away from him. ¹³For this reason, I speak to them in parables: because seeing, they do not see, and hearing they do not hear, nor do they understand. ¹⁴And so, in them is fulfilled the prophecy of Isaiah, who said, 'Hearing, you shall hear, but not understand; and seeing, you shall see, but not perceive. ¹⁵For the heart of this people has grown fat, and with their ears they hear heavily, and they have closed their eyes, lest at any time they might see with their eyes, and hear with their ears, and understand with their heart, and be converted, and then I would heal them.' ¹⁶But blessed are your eyes, because they see, and your ears, because they hear. ¹⁷Amen I say to you, certainly, that many of the prophets and the just desired to see what you see, and yet they did not see it, and to hear what you hear, and yet they did not hear it. ¹⁸Listen, then, to the parable of the sower. ¹⁹With anyone who hears the word of the kingdom and does not understand it, evil comes and carries away what was sown in his heart. This is he who received the seed by the side of the road. ²⁰Then whoever has received the seed upon a rocky place, this is one who hears the word and promptly accepts it with joy. ²¹But he has no root in himself, so it is only for a time; then, when tribulation and persecution occur because of the word, he promptly stumbles. ²²And whoever has received the seed among thorns, this is he who hears the word, but the cares of this age and the falseness of riches suffocate the word, and he is effectively without fruit. ²³Yet truly, whoever has received the seed into good soil, this is he who hears the word, and understands it, and so he bears fruit, and he produces: some a hundred fold, and another sixty fold, and another thirty fold." ²⁴He proposed another parable to them, saying: "The kingdom of heaven is like a man who sowed good seed in his field. ²⁵But while the men were sleeping, his enemy came and sowed weeds amid the wheat, and then went away. ²⁶And when the plants had grown, and had produced fruit, then the weeds also appeared. ²⁷So the servants of the Father of the family, approaching, said to him: 'Lord, did you not sow good seed in your field? Then how is it that it has weeds?' ²⁸And he said to them, 'A man who is an enemy has done this.' So the servants said to him, 'Is it your will that we should go and gather them up?' ²⁹And he said: 'No, lest perhaps in gathering the weeds, you might also root out the wheat together with it. ³⁰Permit both to grow until the harvest, and at the time of the harvest, I will say to the reapers: Gather first the weeds, and bind them into bundles to burn, but the wheat gather into my storehouse.' " ³¹He proposed another parable to them, saying: "The kingdom of heaven is like a grain of mustard seed, which a man took and sowed in his field. ³²It is, indeed, the least of all seeds, but when it has grown, it is greater than all the plants, and it becomes a tree, so much so that the birds of the air come and dwell in its branches." ³³He spoke another parable to them: "The kingdom of heaven is like leaven, which a woman took and hid in three measures of fine wheat flour, until it was entirely leavened." ³⁴All these things Jesus spoke in parables to the crowds. And he did not speak to them apart from parables, ³⁵in order to fulfill what was spoken through the prophet, saying: "I will open my mouth in parables. I will proclaim what has been hidden since the foundation of the world." ³⁶Then, dismissing the crowds, he went into the house. And his disciples drew near to him, saying, "Explain to us the parable of the weeds in the field." ³⁷Responding, he said to them: "He who sows the good seed is the Son of man. ³⁸Now the field is the world. And the good seeds are the sons of the kingdom. But the weeds are the sons of wickedness. ³⁹So the enemy who sowed them is the devil. And truly, the harvest is the consummation of the age; while the reapers are the Angels. ⁴⁰Therefore, just as weeds are gathered up and burned with fire, so shall it be at the consummation of the age. ⁴¹The Son of man shall send out his Angels, and they shall gather from his kingdom all who lead astray and those who work iniquity. ⁴²And he shall cast them into the furnace of fire, where there shall be weeping and gnashing of teeth. ⁴³Then the just ones shall shine like the sun, in the kingdom of their Father. Whoever has ears to hear, let him hear. ⁴⁴The kingdom of heaven is like a treasure hidden in a field. When a man finds it, he hides it, and, because of his joy, he goes and sells everything that he has, and he buys that field. ⁴⁵Again, the kingdom of heaven is like a merchant seeking good pearls. ⁴⁶Having found one pearl of great value, he went away and sold all that he had, and he bought it. ⁴⁷Again, the kingdom of heaven is like a net cast into the sea, which gathers together all kinds of fish. ⁴⁸When it has been filled, drawing it out and sitting beside the shore, they selected the good into vessels, but the bad they threw away. ⁴⁹So shall it be at the consummation of the age. The Angels shall go forth and separate the bad from the midst of the just. ⁵⁰And they shall cast them into the furnace of fire, where there will be weeping and gnashing of teeth. ⁵¹ Have you understood all these things?" They say to him, "Yes." ⁵² He said to them, "Therefore, every scribe well-taught about the kingdom of heaven, is like a man, the father of a family, who offers from his storehouse both the new and the old." ⁵³ And it happened that, when Jesus had completed these parables, he went away from there. ⁵⁴ And arriving in his own country, he taught them in their synagogues, so much so that they wondered and said: "How can such wisdom and power be with this one? ⁵⁵ Is this not the son of a workman? Is not his mother called Mary, and his brothers, James, and Joseph, and Simon, and Jude? ⁵⁶ And his sisters, are they not all with us? Therefore, from where has this one obtained all these things?" ⁵⁷ And they took offense at him. But Jesus said to them, "A prophet is not without honor, except in his own country and in his own house." ⁵⁸ And he did not work many miracles there, because of their unbelief.

CHAPTER 14

¹ In that time, Herod the Tetrarch heard the news about Jesus. ² And he said to his servants: "This is John the Baptist. He has risen from the dead, and that is why miracles are at work in him." ³ For Herod had apprehended John, and bound him, and put him in prison, because of Herodias, the wife of his brother. ⁴ For John was telling him, "It is not lawful for you to have her." ⁵ And though he wanted to kill him, he feared the people, because they held him to be a prophet. ⁶ Then, on Herod's birthday, the daughter of Herodias danced in their midst, and it pleased Herod. ⁷ And so he promised with an oath to give her whatever she would ask of him. ⁸ But, having been advised by her mother, she said, "Give me here, on a platter, the head of John the Baptist." ⁹ And the king was greatly saddened. But because of his oath, and because of those who sat at table with him, he ordered it to be given. ¹⁰ And he sent and beheaded John in prison. ¹¹ And his head was brought on a platter, and it was given to the girl, and she brought it to her mother. ¹² And his disciples approached and took the body, and they buried it. And arriving, they reported it to Jesus. ¹³ When Jesus had heard it, he withdrew from there by boat, to a deserted place by himself. And when the crowds had heard of it, they followed him on foot from the cities. ¹⁴ And going out, he saw a great multitude, and he took pity on them, and he cured their sick. ¹⁵ And when evening had arrived, his disciples approached him, saying: "This is a deserted place, and the hour has now passed. Dismiss the crowds, so that, by going into the towns, they may buy food for themselves." ¹⁶ But Jesus said to them: "They have no need to go. Give them something to eat yourselves." ¹⁷ They answered him, "We have nothing here, except five loaves and two fish." ¹⁸ He said to them, "Bring them here to me." ¹⁹ And when he had ordered the multitude to sit down upon the grass, he took the five loaves and the two fish, and gazing up to heaven, he blessed and broke and gave the bread to the disciples, and then the disciples to the multitudes. ²⁰ And they all ate and were satisfied. And they took up the remnants: twelve baskets full of fragments. ²¹ Now the number of those who ate was five thousand men, besides women and children. ²² And Jesus promptly compelled his disciples to climb into the boat, and to precede him in crossing the sea, while he dismissed the crowds. ²³ And having dismissed the multitude, he ascended alone onto a mountain to pray. And when evening arrived, he was alone there. ²⁴ But in the midst of the sea, the boat was being tossed about by the waves. For the wind was against them. ²⁵ Then, in the fourth watch of the night, he came to them, walking upon the sea. ²⁶ And seeing him walking upon the sea, they were disturbed, saying: "It must be an apparition." And they cried out, because of fear. ²⁷ And immediately, Jesus spoke to them, saying: "Have faith. It is I. Do not be afraid." ²⁸ Then Peter responded by saying, "Lord, if it is you, order me to come to you over the waters." ²⁹ And he said, "Come." And Peter, descending from the boat, walked over the water, so as to go to Jesus. ³⁰ Yet truly, seeing that the wind was strong, he was afraid. And as he began to sink, he cried out, saying: "Lord, save me." ³¹ And immediately Jesus extended his hand and took hold of him. And he said to him, "O little in faith, why did you doubt?" ³² And when they had ascended into the boat, the wind ceased. ³³ Then those who were in the boat drew near and adored him, saying: "Truly, you are the Son of God." ³⁴ And having crossed the sea, they arrived in the land of Genesaret. ³⁵ And when the men of that place had recognized him, they sent into all that region, and they brought to him all who had maladies. ³⁶ And they petitioned him, so that they might touch even the hem of his garment. And as many as touched it were made whole.

CHAPTER 15

[1] Then the scribes and the Pharisees came to him from Jerusalem, saying: [2] "Why do your disciples transgress the tradition of the elders? For they do not wash their hands when they eat bread." [3] But responding, he said to them: "And why do you transgress the commandment of God for the sake of your tradition? For God said: [4] 'Honor your father and mother,' and, 'Whoever will have cursed father or mother shall die a death.' [5] But you say: 'If anyone will have said to father or mother, "It is dedicated, so that whatever is from me will benefit you," [6] then he shall not honor his father or his mother.' So have you nullified the commandment of God, for the sake of your tradition. [7] Hypocrites! How well did Isaiah prophesy about you, saying: [8] 'This people honors me with their lips, but their heart is far from me. [9] For in vain do they worship me, teaching the doctrines and commandments of men.'" [10] And having called the multitudes to him, he said to them: "Listen and understand. [11] A man is not defiled by what enters into the mouth, but by what proceeds from the mouth. This is what defiles a man." [12] Then his disciples drew near and said to him, "Do you know that the Pharisees, upon hearing this word, were offended?" [13] But in response he said: "Every plant which has not been planted by my heavenly Father shall be uprooted. [14] Leave them alone. They are blind, and they lead the blind. But if the blind are in charge of the blind, both will fall into the pit." [15] And responding, Peter said to him, "Explain this parable to us." [16] But he said: "Are you, even now, without understanding? [17] Do you not understand that everything that enters into the mouth goes into the gut, and is cast into the sewer? [18] But what proceeds from the mouth, goes forth from the heart, and those are the things that defile a man. [19] For from the heart go out evil thoughts, murders, adulteries, fornications, thefts, false testimonies, blasphemies. [20] These are the things that defile a man. But to eat without washing hands does not defile a man." [21] And departing from there, Jesus withdrew into the areas of Tyre and Sidon. [22] And behold, a woman of Canaan, going out from those parts, cried out, saying to him: "Take pity on me, Lord, Son of David. My daughter is badly afflicted by a demon." [23] He did not say a word to her. And his disciples, drawing near, petitioned him, saying: "Dismiss her, for she is crying out after us." [24] And responding, he said, "I was not sent except to the sheep who have fallen away from the house of Israel." [25] But she approached and adored him, saying, "Lord, help me." [26] And responding, he said, "It is not good to take the bread of the children and cast it to the dogs." [27] But she said, "Yes, Lord, but the young dogs also eat from the crumbs that fall from the table of their masters." [28] Then Jesus, responding, said to her: "O woman, great is your faith. Let it be done for you just as you wish." And her daughter was healed from that very hour. [29] And when Jesus had passed from there, he arrived beside the sea of Galilee. And ascending onto a mountain, he sat down there. [30] And great multitudes came to him, having with them the mute, the blind, the lame, the disabled, and many others. And they cast them down at his feet, and he cured them, [31] so much so that the crowds wondered, seeing the mute speaking, the lame walking, the blind seeing. And they magnified the God of Israel. [32] And Jesus, calling together his disciples, said: "I have compassion on the crowds, because they have persevered with me now for three days, and they do not have anything to eat. And I am not willing to dismiss them, fasting, lest they faint along the way." [33] And the disciples said to him: "From where, then, in the desert, would we obtain enough bread to satisfy so a great multitude?" [34] And Jesus said to them, "How many loaves of bread do you have?" But they said, "Seven, and a few little fish." [35] And he instructed the crowds to recline upon the ground. [36] And taking the seven loaves and the fish, and giving thanks, he broke and gave to his disciples, and the disciples gave to the people. [37] And they all ate and were satisfied. And, from what was left over of the fragments, they took up seven full baskets. [38] But those who ate were four thousand men, plus children and women. [39] And having dismissed the crowd, he climbed into a boat. And he went into the coastal region of Magadan.

CHAPTER 16

[1] And Pharisees and Sadducees approached him to test him, and they asked him to show them a sign from heaven. [2] But he responded by saying to them: "When evening arrives, you say, 'It will be calm, for the sky is red,' [3] and in the morning, 'Today there will be a storm, for the sky is red and gloomy.' So then, you know how to judge the appearance of the sky, but you are unable to know the signs of the times? [4] An evil and adulterous generation seeks a sign. And a sign shall not

be given to it, except the sign of the prophet Jonah." And leaving them behind, he went away. [5] And when his disciples went across the sea, they forgot to bring bread. [6] And he said to them, "Consider and beware of the leaven of the Pharisees and the Sadducees." [7] But they were thinking within themselves, saying, "It is because we have not brought bread." [8] Then Jesus, knowing this, said: "Why do you consider within yourselves, O little in faith, that it is because you have no bread? [9] Do you not yet understand, nor remember, the five loaves among the five thousand men, and how many containers you took up? [10] Or the seven loaves among the four thousand men, and how many baskets you took up? [11] Why do you not understand that it was not because of bread that I said to you: Beware of the leaven of the Pharisees and the Sadducees?" [12] Then they understood that he was not saying that they should beware of the leaven of bread, but of the doctrine of the Pharisees and the Sadducees. [13] Then Jesus went into parts of Caesarea Philippi. And he questioned his disciples, saying, "Who do men say that the Son of man is?" [14] And they said, "Some say John the Baptist, and others say Elijah, still others say Jeremiah or one of the prophets." [15] Jesus said to them, "But who do you say that I am?" [16] Simon Peter responded by saying, "You are the Christ, the Son of the living God." [17] And in response, Jesus said to him: "Blessed are you, Simon son of Jonah. For flesh and blood has not revealed this to you, but my Father, who is in heaven. [18] And I say to you, that you are Peter, and upon this rock I will build my Church, and the gates of Hell shall not prevail against it. [19] And I will give you the keys of the kingdom of heaven. And whatever you shall bind on earth shall be bound, even in heaven. And whatever you shall release on earth shall be released, even in heaven." [20] Then he instructed his disciples that they should tell no one that he is Jesus the Christ. [21] From that time, Jesus began to reveal to his disciples that it was necessary for him to go to Jerusalem, and to suffer much from the elders and the scribes and the leaders of the priests, and to be killed, and to rise again on the third day. [22] And Peter, taking him aside, began to rebuke him, saying, "Lord, may it be far from you; this shall not happen to you." [23] And turning away, Jesus said to Peter: "Get behind me, Satan; you are an obstacle to me. For you are not behaving according to what is of God, but according to what is of men." [24] Then Jesus said to his disciples: "If anyone is willing to come after me, let him deny himself, and take up his cross, and follow me. [25] For whoever would save his life, will lose it. But whoever will have lost his life for my sake, shall find it. [26] For how does it benefit a man, if he gains the whole world, yet truly suffers damage to his soul? Or what shall a man give in exchange for his soul? [27] For the Son of man will arrive in the glory of his Father, with his Angels. And then he will repay each one according to his works. [28] Amen I say to you, there are some among those standing here, who shall not taste death, until they see the Son of man arriving in his reign."

CHAPTER 17

[1] And after six days, Jesus took Peter and James and his brother John, and he led them onto a lofty mountain separately. [2] And he was transfigured before them. And his face shined brightly like the sun. And his garments were made white like snow. [3] And behold, there appeared to them Moses and Elijah, speaking with him. [4] And Peter responded by saying to Jesus: "Lord, it is good for us to be here. If you are willing, let us make three tabernacles here, one for you, one for Moses, and one for Elijah." [5] And while he was still speaking, behold, a shining cloud overshadowed them. And behold, there was a voice from the cloud, saying: "This is my beloved Son, with whom I am well pleased. Listen to him." [6] And the disciples, hearing this, fell prone on their face, and they were very afraid. [7] And Jesus drew near and touched them. And he said to them, "Rise up and do not be afraid." [8] And lifting up their eyes, they saw no one, except Jesus alone. [9] And as they were descending from the mountain, Jesus instructed them, saying, "Tell no one about the vision, until the Son of man has risen from the dead." [10] And his disciples questioned him, saying, "Why then do the scribes say that it is necessary for Elijah to arrive first?" [11] But in response, he said to them: "Elijah, indeed, shall arrive and restore all things. [12] But I say to you, that Elijah has already arrived, and they did not recognize him, but they did whatever they wanted to him. So also shall the Son of man suffer from them." [13] Then the disciples understood that he had spoken to them about John the Baptist. [14] And when he had arrived at the multitude, a man approached him, falling to his knees before him, saying: "Lord, take pity on my son, for he is an epileptic, and he suffers harm. For he frequently falls into fire, and often also into water. [15] And I brought him to your disciples,

but they were not able to cure him." ¹⁶Then Jesus responded by saying: "What an unbelieving and perverse generation! How long shall I be with you? How long shall I endure you? Bring him here to me." ¹⁷And Jesus rebuked him, and the demon went out of him, and the boy was cured from that hour. ¹⁸Then the disciples approached Jesus privately and said, "Why were we unable to cast him out?" ¹⁹Jesus said to them: "Because of your unbelief. Amen I say to you, certainly, if you will have faith like a grain of mustard seed, you will say to this mountain, 'Move from here to there,' and it shall move. And nothing will be impossible for you. ²⁰But this kind is not cast out, except through prayer and fasting." ²¹And when they were conversing together in Galilee, Jesus said to them: "The Son of man shall be delivered into the hands of men. ²²And they will kill him, but he will rise again on the third day." And they were extremely saddened. ²³And when they had arrived at Capernaum, those who collected the half shekel approached Peter, and they said to him, "Doesn't your Teacher pay the half shekel?" ²⁴He said, "Yes." And when he had entered into the house, Jesus went before him, saying: "How does it seem to you, Simon? The kings of the earth, from whom do they receive tribute or the census tax: from their own sons or from foreigners?" ²⁵And he said, "From foreigners." Jesus said to him: "Then the sons are free. ²⁶But so that we may not become an obstacle to them: go to the sea, and cast in a hook, and take the first fish that is brought up, and when you have opened its mouth, you will find a shekel. Take it and give it to them, for me and for you."

CHAPTER 18

¹In that hour, the disciples drew near to Jesus, saying, "Whom do you consider to be greater in the kingdom of heaven?" ²And Jesus, calling to himself a little child, placed him in their midst. ³And he said: "Amen I say to you, unless you change and become like little children, you shall not enter into the kingdom of heaven. ⁴Therefore, whoever will have humbled himself like this little child, such a one is greater in the kingdom of heaven. ⁵And whoever shall accept one such little child in my name, accepts me. ⁶But whoever will have led astray one of these little ones, who trust in me, it would be better for him to have a great millstone hung around his neck, and to be submerged in the depths of the sea. ⁷Woe to a world that leads people astray! Although it is necessary for temptations to arise, nevertheless: Woe to that man through whom temptation arises! ⁸So if your hand or your foot leads you to sin, cut it off and cast it away from you. It is better for you to enter into life disabled or lame, than to be sent into eternal fire having two hands or two feet. ⁹And if your eye leads you to sin, root it out and cast it away from you. It is better for you to enter into life with one eye, than to be sent into the fires of Hell having two eyes. ¹⁰See to it that you do not despise even one of these little ones. For I say to you, that their Angels in heaven continually look upon the face of my Father, who is in heaven. ¹¹For the Son of man has come to save what had been lost. ¹²How does it seem to you? If someone has one hundred sheep, and if one of them has gone astray, should he not leave behind the ninety-nine in the mountains, and go out to seek what has gone astray? ¹³And if he should happen to find it: Amen I say to you, that he has more joy over that one, than over the ninety-nine which did not go astray. ¹⁴Even so, it is not the will before your Father, who is in heaven, that one of these little ones should be lost. ¹⁵But if your brother has sinned against you, go and correct him, between you and him alone. If he listens to you, you will have regained your brother. ¹⁶But if he will not listen you, invite with you one or two more, so that every word may stand by the mouth of two or three witnesses. ¹⁷And if he will not listen to them, tell the Church. But if he will not listen to the Church, let him be to you like the pagan and the tax collector. ¹⁸Amen I say to you, whatever you will have bound on earth, shall be bound also in heaven, and whatever you will have released on earth, shall be released also in heaven. ¹⁹Again I say to you, that if two of those among you have agreed on earth, about anything whatsoever that they have requested, it shall be done for them by my Father, who is in heaven. ²⁰For wherever two or three are gathered in my name, there am I, in their midst." ²¹Then Peter, drawing near to him, said: "Lord, how many times shall my brother sin against me, and I forgive him? Even seven times?" ²²Jesus said to him: "I do not say to you, even seven times, but even seventy times seven times. ²³Therefore, the kingdom of heaven is compared to a man who was king, who wanted to take account of his servants. ²⁴And when he had begun taking account, one was brought to him who owed him ten thousand talents. ²⁵But since he did not have any way to repay it, his lord ordered him to be sold, with his wife and children, and all that he had, in

order to repay it. ²⁶ But that servant, falling prostrate, begged him, saying, 'Have patience with me, and I will repay it all to you.' ²⁷ Then the lord of that servant, being moved with pity, released him, and he forgave his debt. ²⁸ But when that servant departed, he found one of his fellow servants who owed him one hundred denarius. And taking hold of him, he choked him, saying: 'Repay what you owe.' ²⁹ And his fellow servant, falling prostrate, petitioned him, saying: 'Have patience with me, and I will repay it all to you.' ³⁰ But he was not willing. Instead, he went out and had him sent to prison, until he would repay the debt. ³¹ Now his fellow servants, seeing what was done, were greatly saddened, and they went and reported to their lord all that was done. ³² Then his lord called him, and he said to him: 'You wicked servant, I forgave you all your debt, because you pleaded with me. ³³ Therefore, should you not also have had compassion on your fellow servant, just as I also had compassion on you?' ³⁴ And his lord, being angry, handed him over to the torturers, until he repaid the entire debt. ³⁵ So, too, shall my heavenly Father do to you, if each one of you will not forgive his brother from your hearts."

CHAPTER 19

¹ And it happened that, when Jesus had completed these words, he moved away from Galilee, and he arrived within the borders of Judea, across the Jordan. ² And great crowds followed him, and he healed them there. ³ And the Pharisees approached him, testing him, and saying, "Is it lawful for a man to separate from his wife, no matter what the cause?" ⁴ And he said to them in response, "Have you not read that he who made man from the beginning, made them male and female?" And he said: ⁵ "For this reason, a man shall separate from father and mother, and he shall cling to his wife, and these two shall become one flesh. ⁶ And so, now they are not two, but one flesh. Therefore, what God has joined together, let no man separate." ⁷ They said to him, "Then why did Moses command him to give a bill of divorce, and to separate?" ⁸ He said to them: "Although Moses permitted you to separate from your wives, due to the hardness of your heart, it was not that way from the beginning. ⁹ And I say to you, that whoever will have separated from his wife, except because of fornication, and who will have married another, commits adultery, and whoever will have married her who has been separated, commits adultery." ¹⁰ His disciples said to him, "If such is the case for a man with a wife, then it is not expedient to marry." ¹¹ And he said to them: "Not everyone is able to grasp this word, but only those to whom it has been given. ¹² For there are chaste persons who were born so from their mother's womb, and there are chaste persons who have been made so by men, and there are chaste persons who have made themselves chaste for the sake of the kingdom of heaven. Whoever is able to grasp this, let him grasp it." ¹³ Then they brought to him little children, so that he would place his hands upon them and pray. But the disciples rebuked them. ¹⁴ Yet truly, Jesus said to them: "Allow the little children to come to me, and do not choose to prohibit them. For the kingdom of heaven is among such as these." ¹⁵ And when he had imposed his hands upon them, he went away from there. ¹⁶ And behold, someone approached and said to him, "Good Teacher, what good should I do, so that I may have eternal life?" ¹⁷ And he said to him: "Why do you question me about what is good? One is good: God. But if you wish to enter into life, observe the commandments." ¹⁸ He said to him, "Which?" And Jesus said: "You shall not murder. You shall not commit adultery. You shall not steal. You shall not give false testimony. ¹⁹ Honor your father and your mother. And, you shall love your neighbor as yourself." ²⁰ The young man said to him: "All these I have kept from my childhood. What is still lacking for me?" ²¹ Jesus said to him: "If you are willing to be perfect, go, sell what you have, and give to the poor, and then you will have treasure in heaven. And come, follow me." ²² And when the young man had heard this word, he went away sad, for he had many possessions. ²³ Then Jesus said to his disciples: "Amen, I say to you, that the wealthy shall enter with difficulty into the kingdom of heaven. ²⁴ And again I say to you, it is easier for a camel to pass through the eye of a needle, than for the wealthy to enter into the kingdom of heaven." ²⁵ And upon hearing this, the disciples wondered greatly, saying: "Then who will be able to be saved?" ²⁶ But Jesus, gazing at them, said to them: "With men, this is impossible. But with God, all things are possible." ²⁷ Then Peter responded by saying to him: "Behold, we have left behind all things, and we have followed you. So then, what will be for us?" ²⁸ And Jesus said to them: "Amen I say to you, that at the resurrection, when the Son of man shall sit on the seat of his majesty, those of you who have followed me shall also sit on twelve seats, judging the twelve tribes of Israel. ²⁹ And anyone

who has left behind home, or brothers, or sisters, or father, or mother, or wife, or children, or land, for the sake of my name, shall receive one hundred times more, and shall possess eternal life. [30] But many of those who are first shall be last, and the last shall be first."

CHAPTER 20

[1] "The kingdom of heaven is like the father of a family who went out in early morning to lead workers into his vineyard. [2] Then, having made an agreement with the workers for one denarius per day, he sent them into his vineyard. [3] And going out about the third hour, he saw others standing idle in the marketplace. [4] And he said to them, 'You may go into my vineyard, too, and what I will give you will be just.' [5] So they went forth. But again, he went out about the sixth, and about the ninth hour, and he acted similarly. [6] Yet truly, about the eleventh hour, he went out and found others standing, and he said to them, 'Why have you stood here idle all day?' [7] They say to him, 'Because no one has hired us.' He said to them, 'You also may go into my vineyard.' [8] And when evening had arrived, the lord of the vineyard said to his manager, 'Call the workers and pay them their wages, beginning from the last, even to the first.' [9] And so, when those who had arrived about the eleventh hour came forward, each received a single denarius. [10] Then when the first ones also came forward, they considered that they would receive more. But they, too, received one denarius. [11] And upon receiving it, they murmured against the father of the family, [12] saying, 'These last have worked for one hour, and you have made them equal to us, who worked bearing the weight and heat of the day.' [13] But responding to one of them, he said: 'Friend, I caused you no injury. Did you not agree with me to one denarius? [14] Take what is yours and go. But it is my will to give to this last, just as to you. [15] And is it not lawful for me to do what I will? Or is your eye wicked because I am good?' [16] So then, the last shall be first, and the first shall be last. For many are called, but few are chosen." [17] And Jesus, ascending to Jerusalem, took the twelve disciples aside in private and said to them: [18] "Behold, we are ascending to Jerusalem, and the Son of man shall be handed over to the leaders of the priests and to the scribes. And they shall condemn him to death. [19] And they shall hand him over to the Gentiles to be mocked and scourged and crucified. And on the third day, he shall rise again." [20] Then the mother of the sons of Zebedee approached him, with her sons, adoring him, and petitioning something from him. [21] And he said to her, "What do you want?" She said to him, "Declare that these, my two sons, may sit, one at your right hand, and the other at your left, in your kingdom." [22] But Jesus, responding, said: "You do not know what you are asking. Are you able to drink from the chalice, from which I will drink?" They said to him, "We are able." [23] He said to them: "From my chalice, indeed, you shall drink. But to sit at my right or my left is not mine to give to you, but it is for those for whom it has been prepared by my Father." [24] And the ten, upon hearing this, became indignant with the two brothers. [25] But Jesus called them to himself and said: "You know that the first ones among the Gentiles are their rulers, and that those who are greater exercise power among them. [26] It shall not be this way among you. But whoever will want to be greater among you, let him be your minister. [27] And whoever will want to be first among you, he shall be your servant, [28] even as the Son of man has not come to be served, but to serve, and to give his life as a redemption for many." [29] And as they were departing from Jericho, a great crowd followed him. [30] And behold, two blind men, sitting by the way, heard that Jesus was passing by; and they cried out, saying, "Lord, Son of David, take pity on us." [31] But the crowd rebuked them to be quiet. But they cried out all the more, saying, "Lord, Son of David, take pity on us." [32] And Jesus stood still, and he called them and said, "What do you want, that I might do for you?" [33] They said to him, "Lord, that our eyes be opened." [34] Then Jesus, taking pity on them, touched their eyes. And immediately they saw, and they followed him.

CHAPTER 21

[1] And when they had drawn near to Jerusalem, and had arrived at Bethphage, at the Mount of Olives, then Jesus sent two disciples, [2] saying to them: "Go into the town that is opposite you, and immediately you will find a donkey tied, and a colt with her. Release them, and lead them to me. [3] And if anyone will have said anything to you, say that the Lord has need of them. And he will promptly dismiss them." [4] Now all this was done in order to fulfill what was spoken through

the prophet, saying, [5]"Tell the daughter of Zion: Behold, your king comes to you meekly, sitting on a donkey and on a colt, the son of one accustomed to the yoke." [6]Then the disciples, going out, did just as Jesus instructed them. [7]And they brought the donkey and the colt, and they laid their garments on them, and they helped him sit upon them. [8]Then a very numerous crowd spread their garments on the way. But others cut branches from the trees and scattered them on the way. [9]And the crowds that preceded him, and those that followed, cried out, saying: "Hosanna to the Son of David! Blessed is he who comes in the name of the Lord. Hosanna in the highest!" [10]And when he had entered into Jerusalem, the entire city was stirred up, saying, "Who is this?" [11]But the people were saying, "This is Jesus, the Prophet from Nazareth of Galilee." [12]And Jesus entered into the temple of God, and he cast out all who were selling and buying in the temple, and he overturned the tables of the money changers and the chairs of the vendors of doves. [13]And he said to them: "It is written: 'My house shall be called a house of prayer. But you have made it into a den of robbers.'" [14]And the blind and the lame drew near to him in the temple; and he healed them. [15]Then the leaders of the priests and the scribes became indignant, seeing the miracles that he wrought, and the children crying out in the temple, saying, "Hosanna to the Son of David!" [16]And they said to him, "Do you hear what these ones are saying?" But Jesus said to them, "Certainly. Have you never read: For out of the mouth of babes and infants, you have perfected praise?" [17]And leaving them behind, he went out, beyond the city, into Bethania, and he lodged here. [18]Then, as he was returning to the city in the morning, he was hungry. [19]And seeing a certain fig tree beside the way, he approached it. And he found nothing on it, except only leaves. And he said to it, "May fruit never spring forth from you, for all time." And immediately the fig tree was dried up. [20]And seeing this, the disciples wondered, saying, "How did it dry up so quickly?" [21]And Jesus responded to them by saying: "Amen I say to you, if you have faith and do not hesitate, not only shall you do this, concerning the fig tree, but even if you would say to this mountain, 'Take and cast yourself into the sea,' it shall be done. [22]And all things whatsoever that you shall ask for in prayer: believing, you shall receive." [23]And when he had arrived at the temple, as he was teaching, the leaders of the priests and the elders of the people approached him, saying: "By what authority do you do these things? And who has given this authority to you?" [24]In response, Jesus said to them: "I also will question you with one word: if you tell me this, I also will tell you by what authority I do these things. [25]The baptism of John, where was it from? Was it from heaven, or from men?" But they thought within themselves, saying: [26]"If we say, 'From heaven,' he will say to us, 'Then why did you not believe him?' But if we say, 'From men,' we have the crowd to fear, for they all hold John to be a prophet." [27]And so, they answered Jesus by saying, "We do not know." So he also said to them: "Neither will I tell you by what authority I do these things. [28]But how does it seem to you? A certain man had two sons. And approaching the first, he said: 'Son, go out today to work in my vineyard.' [29]And responding, he said, 'I am not willing.' But afterwards, being moved by repentance, he went. [30]And approaching the other, he spoke similarly. And answering, he said, 'I am going, lord.' And he did not go. [31]Which of the two did the will of the father?" They said to him, "The first." Jesus said to them: "Amen I say to you, that tax collectors and prostitutes shall precede you, into the kingdom of God. [32]For John came to you in the way of justice, and you did not believe him. But the tax collectors and the prostitutes believed him. Yet even after seeing this, you did not repent, so as to believe him. [33]Listen to another parable. There was a man, the father of a family, who planted a vineyard, and surrounded it with a hedge, and dug a press in it, and built a tower. And he loaned it out to farmers, and he set out to sojourn abroad. [34]Then, when the time of the fruits drew near, he sent his servants to the farmers, so that they might receive its fruits. [35]And the farmers apprehended his servants; they struck one, and killed another, and stoned yet another. [36]Again, he sent other servants, more than before; and they treated them similarly. [37]Then, at the very end, he sent his son to them, saying: 'They will revere my son.' [38]But the farmers, seeing the son, said among themselves: 'This is the heir. Come, let us kill him, and then we will have his inheritance.' [39]And apprehending him, they cast him outside the vineyard, and they killed him. [40]Therefore, when the lord of the vineyard arrives, what will he do to those farmers?" [41]They said to him, "He will bring those evil men to an evil end, and he will loan out his vineyard to other farmers, who shall repay to him the fruit in its time." [42]Jesus said to them: "Have you never read in the Scriptures: 'The stone that the builders have rejected has become the cornerstone. By the Lord has this been done, and it is wonderful in our eyes?'

⁴³Therefore, I say to you, that the kingdom of God will be taken away from you, and it shall be given to a people who shall produce its fruits. ⁴⁴And whoever will have fallen on this stone shall be broken, yet truly, on whomever it shall fall, it will crush him." ⁴⁵And when the leaders of the priests, and the Pharisees had heard his parables, they knew that he was speaking about them. ⁴⁶And though they sought to take hold of him, they feared the crowds, because they held him to be a prophet.

CHAPTER 22

¹And responding, Jesus again spoke to them in parables, saying: ²"The kingdom of heaven is like a man who was king, who celebrated a wedding for his son. ³And he sent his servants to call those who were invited to the wedding. But they were not willing to come. ⁴Again, he sent other servants, saying, 'Tell the invited: Behold, I have prepared my meal. My bulls and fatlings have been killed, and all is ready. Come to the wedding.' ⁵But they ignored this and they went away: one to his country estate, and another to his business. ⁶Yet truly, the rest took hold of his servants and, having treated them with contempt, killed them. ⁷But when the king heard this, he was angry. And sending out his armies, he destroyed those murderers, and he burned their city. ⁸Then he said to his servants: 'The wedding, indeed, has been prepared. But those who were invited were not worthy. ⁹Therefore, go out to the ways, and call whomever you will find to the wedding.' ¹⁰And his servants, departing into the ways, gathered all those whom they found, bad and good, and the wedding was filled with guests. ¹¹Then the king entered to see the guests. And he saw a man there who was not clothed in a wedding garment. ¹²And he said to him, 'Friend, how is it that you have entered here without having a wedding garment?' But he was dumbstruck. ¹³Then the king said to the ministers: 'Bind his hands and feet, and cast him into the outer darkness, where there will be weeping and gnashing of teeth. ¹⁴For many are called, but few are chosen.'" ¹⁵Then the Pharisees, going out, took counsel as to how they might entrap him in speech. ¹⁶And they sent their disciples to him, with the Herodians, saying: "Teacher, we know that you are truthful, and that you teach the way of God in truth, and that the influence of others is nothing to you. For you do not consider the reputation of men. ¹⁷Therefore, tell us, how does it seem to you? Is it lawful to pay the census tax to Caesar, or not?" ¹⁸But Jesus, knowing their wickedness, said: "Why do you test me, you hypocrites? ¹⁹Show me the coin of the census tax." And they offered him a denarius. ²⁰And Jesus said to them, "Whose image is this, and whose inscription?" ²¹They said to him, "Caesar's." Then he said to them, "Then render to Caesar what is of Caesar; and to God what is of God." ²²And hearing this, they wondered. And having left him behind, they went away. ²³In that day, the Sadducees, who say there is to be no resurrection, approached him. And they questioned him, ²⁴saying: "Teacher, Moses said: If anyone will have died, having no son, his brother shall marry his wife, and he shall raise up offspring to his brother. ²⁵Now there were seven brothers with us. And the first, having taken a wife, died. And having no offspring, he left his wife to his brother: ²⁶similarly with the second, and the third, even to the seventh. ²⁷And last of all, the woman also passed away. ²⁸In the resurrection, then, whose wife of the seven will she be? For they all had her." ²⁹But Jesus responded to them by saying: "You have gone astray by knowing neither the Scriptures, nor the power of God. ³⁰For in the resurrection, they shall neither marry, nor be given in marriage. Instead, they shall be like the Angels of God in heaven. ³¹But concerning the resurrection of the dead, have you not read what was spoken by God, saying to you: ³²'I am the God of Abraham, and the God of Isaac, and the God of Jacob?' He is not the God of the dead, but of the living." ³³And when the crowds heard this, they wondered at his doctrine. ³⁴But the Pharisees, hearing that he had caused the Sadducees to be silent, came together as one. ³⁵And one of them, a doctor of the law, questioned him, to test him: ³⁶"Teacher, which is the great commandment in the law?" ³⁷Jesus said to him: " 'You shall love the Lord your God from all your heart, and with all your soul and with all your mind.' ³⁸This is the greatest and first commandment. ³⁹But the second is similar to it: 'You shall love your neighbor as yourself.' ⁴⁰On these two commandments the entire law depends, and also the prophets." ⁴¹Then, when the Pharisees were gathered together, Jesus questioned them, ⁴²saying: "What do you think about the Christ? Whose son is he?" They said to him, "David's." ⁴³He said to them: "Then how can David, in the Spirit, call him Lord, saying: ⁴⁴'The Lord said to my Lord: Sit at my right hand, until I make your enemies your

footstool?' ⁴⁵ So then, if David calls him Lord, how can he be his son?" ⁴⁶ And no one was able to respond to him a word. And neither did anyone dare, from that day forward, to question him.

CHAPTER 23

¹ Then Jesus spoke to the crowds, and to his disciples, ² saying: "The scribes and the Pharisees have sat down in the chair of Moses. ³ Therefore, all things whatsoever that they shall say to you, observe and do. Yet truly, do not choose to act according to their works. For they say, but they do not do. ⁴ For they bind up heavy and unbearable burdens, and they impose them on men's shoulders. But they are not willing to move them with even a finger of their own. ⁵ Truly, they do all their works so that they may be seen by men. For they enlarge their phylacteries and glorify their hems. ⁶ And they love the first places at feasts, and the first chairs in the synagogues, ⁷ and greetings in the marketplace, and to be called Master by men. ⁸ But you must not be called Master. For One is your Master, and you are all brothers. ⁹ And do not choose to call anyone on earth your father. For One is your Father, who is in heaven. ¹⁰ Neither should you be called teachers. For One is your Teacher, the Christ. ¹¹ Whoever is greater among you shall be your minister. ¹² But whoever has exalted himself, shall be humbled. And whoever has humbled himself, shall be exalted. ¹³ So then: Woe to you, scribes and Pharisees, you hypocrites! For you close the kingdom of heaven before men. For you yourselves do not enter, and those who are entering, you would not permit to enter. ¹⁴ Woe to you scribes and Pharisees, you hypocrites! For you consume the houses of widows, praying long prayers. Because of this, you shall receive the greater judgment. ¹⁵ Woe to you, scribes and Pharisees, you hypocrites! For you travel around by sea and by land, in order to make one convert. And when he has been converted, you make him twice the son of Hell that you are yourselves. ¹⁶ Woe to you, blind guides, who say: 'Whoever will have sworn by the temple, it is nothing. But whoever will have sworn by the gold of the temple is obligated.' ¹⁷ You are foolish and blind! For which is greater: the gold, or the temple that sanctifies the gold? ¹⁸ And you say: 'Whoever will have sworn by the altar, it is nothing. But whoever will have sworn by the gift that is on the altar is obligated.' ¹⁹ How blind you are! For which is greater: the gift, or the altar that sanctifies the gift? ²⁰ Therefore, whoever swears by the altar, swears by it, and by all that is on it. ²¹ And whoever will have sworn by the temple, swears by it, and by him who dwells in it. ²² And whoever swears by heaven, swears by the throne of God, and by him who sits upon it. ²³ Woe to you, scribes and Pharisees, you hypocrites! For you collect tithes on mint and dill and cumin, but you have abandoned the weightier things of the law: judgment and mercy and faith. These you ought to have done, while not omitting the others. ²⁴ You blind guides, straining out a gnat, while swallowing a camel! ²⁵ Woe to you, scribes and Pharisees, you hypocrites! For you clean what is outside the cup and the dish, but on the inside you are full of avarice and impurity. ²⁶ You blind Pharisee! First clean the inside of the cup and the dish, and then what is outside becomes clean. ²⁷ Woe to you, scribes and Pharisees, you hypocrites! For you are like whitewashed sepulchers, which outwardly appear brilliant to men, yet truly, inside, they are filled with the bones of the dead and with all filth. ²⁸ So also, you certainly appear to men outwardly to be just. But inwardly you are filled with hypocrisy and iniquity. ²⁹ Woe to you, scribes and Pharisees, you hypocrites, who build the sepulchers of the prophets and adorn the monuments of the just. ³⁰ And then you say, 'If we had been there in the days of our fathers, we would not have joined with them in the blood of the prophets.' ³¹ And so you are witnesses against yourselves, that you are the sons of those who killed the prophets. ³² Complete, then, the measure of your fathers. ³³ You serpents, you brood of vipers! How will you escape from the judgment of Hell? ³⁴ For this reason, behold, I send to you prophets and wise men, and scribes. And some of these you will put to death and crucify; and some you will scourge in your synagogues and persecute from city to city, ³⁵ so that upon you may fall all the blood of the just, which has been shed upon the earth, from the blood of Abel the just, even to the blood of Zechariah the son of Barachiah, whom you killed between the temple and the altar. ³⁶ Amen I say to you, all these things shall fall upon this generation. ³⁷ Jerusalem, Jerusalem! You kill the prophets and stone those who have been sent to you. How often I have wanted to gather your children together, in the way that a hen gathers her young under her wings. But you were not willing! ³⁸ Behold, your house shall be abandoned to you, having been deserted. ³⁹ For I say to you, you shall not see me again, until you say: 'Blessed is he who comes in the name of the Lord.'"

CHAPTER 24

¹ And Jesus departed from the temple and went away. And his disciples approached him, so as to show him the buildings of the temple. ² But he said to them in response: "Do you see all these things? Amen I say to you, there shall not remain here stone upon stone, which is not torn down." ³ Then, when he was seated at the Mount of Olives, the disciples drew near to him privately, saying: "Tell us, when will these things be? And what will be the sign of your advent and of the consummation of the age?" ⁴ And answering, Jesus said to them: "Pay attention, lest someone lead you astray. ⁵ For many will come in my name saying, 'I am the Christ.' And they will lead many astray. ⁶ For you will hear of battles and rumors of battles. Take care not to be disturbed. For these things must be, but the end is not so soon. ⁷ For nation will rise against nation, and kingdom against kingdom. And there will be pestilences, and famines, and earthquakes in places. ⁸ But all these things are just the beginning of the sorrows. ⁹ Then they will hand you over to tribulation, and they will kill you. And you will be hated by all nations for the sake of my name. ¹⁰ And then many will be led into sin, and will betray one another, and will have hatred for one another. ¹¹ And many false prophets will arise, and they will lead many astray. ¹² And because iniquity has abounded, the charity of many will grow cold. ¹³ But whoever will have persevered until the end, the same shall be saved. ¹⁴ And this Gospel of the kingdom shall be preached throughout the entire world, as a testimony to all nations. And then the consummation will occur. ¹⁵ Therefore, when you will have seen the abomination of desolation, which was spoken of by the prophet Daniel, standing in the holy place, may he who reads understand, ¹⁶ then those who are in Judea, let them flee to the mountains. ¹⁷ And whoever is on the roof, let him not descend to take anything from his house. ¹⁸ And whoever is in the field, let him not turn back to take his tunic. ¹⁹ So then, woe to those who are pregnant or nursing in those days. ²⁰ But pray that your flight may not be in winter, or on the Sabbath. ²¹ For then there will be a great tribulation, such as has not been from the beginning of the world until the present, and such as will not be. ²² And unless those days had been shortened, no flesh would be saved. But for the sake of the elect, those days shall be shortened. ²³ Then if anyone will have said to you, 'Behold, here is the Christ,' or 'he is there,' do not be willing to believe it. ²⁴ For there will arise false Christs and false prophets. And they will produce great signs and wonders, so much so as to lead into error even the elect (if this could be). ²⁵ Behold, I have warned you beforehand. ²⁶ Therefore, if they will have said to you, 'Behold, he is in the desert,' do not choose to go out, or, 'Behold, he is in the inner rooms,' do not be willing to believe it. ²⁷ For just as lightning goes out from the east, and appears even in the west, so shall it be also at the advent of the Son of man. ²⁸ Wherever the body shall be, there also will the eagles be gathered together. ²⁹ And immediately after the tribulation of those days, the sun will be darkened, and the moon will not give its light, and the stars will fall from heaven, and the powers of the heavens will be shaken. ³⁰ And then the sign of the Son of man shall appear in heaven. And then all tribes of the earth shall mourn. And they shall see the Son of man coming on the clouds of heaven, with great power and majesty. ³¹ And he shall send out his Angels with a trumpet and a great voice. And they shall gather together his elect from the four winds, from the heights of the heavens, even to their furthest limits. ³² So, from the fig tree learn a parable. When its branch has now become tender and the leaves have sprung forth, you know that summer is near. ³³ So also, when you will have seen all these things, know that it is near, even at the threshold. ³⁴ Amen I say to you, that this lineage shall not pass away, until all these things have been done. ³⁵ Heaven and earth shall pass away, but my words shall not pass away. ³⁶ But concerning that day and hour, no one knows, not even the Angels of the heavens, but only the Father. ³⁷ And just as in the days of Noah, so also will be the advent of the Son of man. ³⁸ For it will be just as it was in the days before the flood: eating and drinking, marrying and being given in marriage, even until that day when Noah entered into the ark. ³⁹ And they did not realize it, until the flood came and took them all away. So also will the advent of the Son of man be. ⁴⁰ Then two men will be in a field: one will be taken up, and one will be left behind. ⁴¹ Two women will be grinding at a millstone: one will be taken up, and one will be left behind. ⁴² Therefore, be vigilant. For you do not know at what hour your Lord will return. ⁴³ But know this: if only the father of the family knew at what hour the thief would arrive, he would certainly keep vigil and not permit his house to be broken into. ⁴⁴ For this reason, you also must be prepared,

for you do not know at what hour the Son of man will return. ⁴⁵ Consider this: who is a faithful and prudent servant, who has been appointed by his lord over his family, to give them their portion in due time? ⁴⁶ Blessed is that servant, if, when his lord has arrived, he shall find him doing so. ⁴⁷ Amen I say to you, he shall appoint him over all of his goods. ⁴⁸ But if that evil servant has said in his heart, 'My lord has been delayed in returning,' ⁴⁹ and so, he begins to strike his fellow servants, and he eats and drinks with the inebriated: ⁵⁰ then the lord of that servant will arrive on a day that he does not expect, and at an hour that he does not know. ⁵¹ And he shall separate him, and he shall place his portion with the hypocrites, where there shall be weeping and gnashing of teeth."

CHAPTER 25

¹ "Then the kingdom of heaven shall be like ten virgins, who, taking their lamps, went out to meet the groom and the bride. ² But five of them were foolish, and five were prudent. ³ For the five foolish, having brought their lamps, did not take oil with them. ⁴ Yet truly, the prudent ones brought the oil, in their containers, with the lamps. ⁵ Since the bridegroom was delayed, they all fell asleep, and they were sleeping. ⁶ But in the middle of the night, a cry went out: 'Behold, the groom is arriving. Go out to meet him.' ⁷ Then all those virgins rose up and trimmed their lamps. ⁸ But the foolish ones said to the wise, 'Give to us from your oil, for our lamps are being extinguished.' ⁹ The prudent responded by saying, 'Lest perhaps there may not be enough for us and for you, it would be better for you to go to the vendors and buy some for yourselves.' ¹⁰ But while they were going to buy it, the groom arrived. And those who were prepared entered with him to the wedding, and the door was closed. ¹¹ Yet truly, at the very end, the remaining virgins also arrived, saying, 'Lord, Lord, open to us.' ¹² But he responded by saying, 'Amen I say to you, I do not know you.' ¹³ And so you must be vigilant, because you do not know the day or the hour. ¹⁴ For it is like a man setting out on a long journey, who called his servants and delivered to them his goods. ¹⁵ And to one he gave five talents, and to another two, yet to another he gave one, to each according to his own ability. And promptly, he set out. ¹⁶ Then he who had received five talents went out, and he made use of these, and he gained another five. ¹⁷ And similarly, he who had received two gained another two. ¹⁸ But he who had received one, going out, dug into the earth, and he hid the money of his lord. ¹⁹ Yet truly, after a long time, the lord of those servants returned and he settled accounts with them. ²⁰ And when he who had received five talents approached, he brought another five talents, saying: 'Lord, you delivered five talents to me. Behold, I have increased it by another five.' ²¹ His lord said to him: 'Well done, good and faithful servant. Since you have been faithful over a few things, I will appoint you over many things. Enter into the gladness of your lord.' ²² Then he who had received two talents also approached, and he said: 'Lord, you delivered two talents to me. Behold, I have gained another two.' ²³ His lord said to him: 'Well done, good and faithful servant. Since you have been faithful over a few things, I will appoint you over many things. Enter into the gladness of your lord.' ²⁴ Then he who had received one talent, approaching, said: 'Lord, I know that you are a hard man. You reap where you have not sown, and gather where you have not scattered. ²⁵ And so, being afraid, I went out and hid your talent in the earth. Behold, you have what is yours.' ²⁶ But his lord said to him in response: 'You evil and lazy servant! You knew that I reap where I have not sown, and gather where I have not scattered. ²⁷ Therefore, you should have deposited my money with the bankers, and then, at my arrival, at least I would have received what is mine with interest. ²⁸ And so, take the talent away from him and give it to the one who has ten talents. ²⁹ For to everyone who has, more shall be given, and he shall have in abundance. But from him who has not, even what he seems to have, shall be taken away. ³⁰ And cast that useless servant into the outer darkness, where there will be weeping and gnashing of teeth.' ³¹ But when the Son of man will have arrived in his majesty, and all the Angels with him, then he will sit upon the seat of his majesty. ³² And all the nations shall be gathered together before him. And he shall separate them from one another, just as a shepherd separates the sheep from the goats. ³³ And he shall station the sheep, indeed, on his right, but the goats on his left. ³⁴ Then the King shall say to those who will be on his right: 'Come, you blessed of my Father. Possess the kingdom prepared for you from the foundation of the world. ³⁵ For I was hungry, and you gave me to eat; I was thirsty, and you gave me to drink; I was a stranger, and you took me in; ³⁶ naked, and you covered me; sick,

and you visited me; I was in prison, and you came to me.' [37] Then the just will answer him, saying: 'Lord, when have we seen you hungry, and fed you; thirsty, and given you drink? [38] And when have we seen you a stranger, and taken you in? Or naked, and covered you? [39] Or when did we see you sick, or in prison, and visit to you?' [40] And in response, the King shall say to them, 'Amen I say to you, whenever you did this for one of these, the least of my brothers, you did it for me.' [41] Then he shall also say, to those who will be on his left: 'Depart from me, you accursed ones, into the eternal fire, which was prepared for the devil and his angels. [42] For I was hungry, and you did not give me to eat; I was thirsty, and you did not give me to drink; [43] I was a stranger and you did not take me in; naked, and you did not cover me; sick and in prison, and you did not visit me.' [44] Then they will also answer him, saying: 'Lord, when did we see you hungry, or thirsty, or a stranger, or naked, or sick, or in prison, and did not minister to you?' [45] Then he shall respond to them by saying: 'Amen I say to you, whenever you did not do it to one of these least, neither did you do it to me.' [46] And these shall go into eternal punishment, but the just shall go into eternal life."

CHAPTER 26

[1] And it happened that, when Jesus had completed all these words, he said to his disciples, [2] "You know that after two days the Passover will begin, and the Son of man will be handed over to be crucified." [3] Then the leaders of the priests and the elders of the people were gathered together in the court of the high priest, who was called Caiaphas. [4] And they took counsel so that by deceitfulness they might take hold of Jesus and kill him. [5] But they said, "Not on the feast day, lest perhaps there may be a tumult among the people." [6] And when Jesus was in Bethania, in the house of Simon the leper, [7] a woman drew near to him, holding an alabaster box of precious ointment, and she poured it over his head while he was reclining at table. [8] But the disciples, seeing this, were indignant, saying: "What is the purpose of this waste? [9] For this could have been sold for a great deal, so as to be given to the poor." [10] But Jesus, knowing this, said to them: "Why are you bothering this woman? For she has done a good deed to me. [11] For the poor you will always have with you. But you will not always have me. [12] For in pouring this ointment on my body, she has prepared for my burial. [13] Amen I say to you, wherever this Gospel will be preached in the whole world, what she has done also shall be told, in memory of her." [14] Then one of the twelve, who was called Judas Iscariot, went to the leaders of the priests, [15] and he said to them, "What are you willing to give me, if I hand him over to you?" So they appointed thirty pieces of silver for him. [16] And from then on, he sought an opportunity to betray him. [17] Then, on the first day of Unleavened Bread, the disciples approached Jesus, saying, "Where do you want us to prepare for you to eat the Passover?" [18] So Jesus said, "Go into the city, to a certain one, and say to him: 'The Teacher said: My time is near. I am observing the Passover with you, along with my disciples.'" [19] And the disciples did just as Jesus appointed to them. And they prepared the Passover. [20] Then, when evening arrived, he sat at table with his twelve disciples. [21] And while they were eating, he said: "Amen I say to you, that one of you is about to betray me." [22] And being greatly saddened, each one of them began to say, "Surely, it is not I, Lord?" [23] But he responded by saying: "He who dips his hand with me into the dish, the same will betray me. [24] Indeed, the Son of man goes, just as it has been written about him. But woe to that man by whom the Son of man will be betrayed. It would be better for that man if he had not been born." [25] Then Judas, who betrayed him, responded by saying, "Surely, it is not I, Master?" He said to him, "You have said it." [26] Now while they were eating the meal, Jesus took bread, and he blessed and broke and gave it to his disciples, and he said: "Take and eat. This is my body." [27] And taking the chalice, he gave thanks. And he gave it to them, saying: "Drink from this, all of you. [28] For this is my blood of the new covenant, which shall be shed for many as a remission of sins. [29] But I say to you, I will not drink again from this fruit of the vine, until that day when I will drink it new with you in the kingdom of my Father." [30] And after a hymn was sung, they went out to the Mount of Olives. [31] Then Jesus said to them: "You will all fall away from me in this night. For it has been written: 'I will strike the shepherd, and the sheep of the flock will be scattered.' [32] But after I have risen again, I will go before you to Galilee." [33] Then Peter responded by saying to him, "Even if everyone else has fallen away from you, I will never fall away." [34] Jesus said to him, "Amen I say to you, that in this night, before the rooster crows, you will deny me three times." [35] Peter said to

him, "Even if it is necessary for me to die with you, I will not deny you." And all the disciples spoke similarly. [36] Then Jesus went with them to a garden, which is called Gethsemani. And he said to his disciples, "Sit down here, while I go there and pray." [37] And taking with him Peter and the two sons of Zebedee, he began to be sorrowful and saddened. [38] Then he said to them: "My soul is sorrowful, even unto death. Stay here and keep vigil with me." [39] And continuing on a little further, he fell prostrate on his face, praying and saying: "My Father, if it is possible, let this chalice pass away from me. Yet truly, let it not be as I will, but as you will." [40] And he approached his disciples and found them sleeping. And he said to Peter: "So, were you not able to keep vigil with me for one hour? [41] Be vigilant and pray, so that you may not enter into temptation. Indeed, the spirit is willing, but the flesh is weak." [42] Again, a second time, he went and prayed, saying, "My Father, if this chalice cannot pass away, unless I drink it, let your will be done." [43] And again, he went and found them sleeping, for their eyes were heavy. [44] And leaving them behind, again he went and prayed for the third time, saying the same words. [45] Then he approached his disciples and said to them: "Sleep now and rest. Behold, the hour has drawn near, and the Son of man will be delivered into the hands of sinners. [46] Rise up; let us go. Behold, he who will betray me draws near." [47] While he was still speaking, behold, Judas, one of the twelve, arrived, and with him was a large crowd with swords and clubs, sent from the leaders of the priests and the elders of the people. [48] And he who betrayed him gave them a sign, saying: "Whomever I will kiss, it is he. Take hold of him." [49] And quickly drawing close to Jesus, he said, "Hail, Master." And he kissed him. [50] And Jesus said to him, "Friend, for what purpose have you come?" Then they approached, and they put their hands on Jesus, and they held him. [51] And behold, one of those who were with Jesus, extending his hand, drew his sword and struck the servant of the high priest, cutting off his ear. [52] Then Jesus said to him: "Put your sword back in its place. For all who take up the sword shall perish by the sword. [53] Or do you think that I cannot ask my Father, so that he would give me, even now, more than twelve legions of Angels? [54] How then would the Scriptures be fulfilled, which say that it must be so?" [55] In that same hour, Jesus said to the crowds: "You went out, as if to a robber, with swords and clubs to seize me. Yet I sat daily with you, teaching in the temple, and you did not take hold of me. [56] But all this has happened so that the Scriptures of the prophets may be fulfilled." Then all the disciples fled, abandoning him. [57] But those who were holding Jesus led him to Caiaphas, the high priest, where the scribes and the elders had joined together. [58] Then Peter followed him from a distance, as far as the court of the high priest. And going inside, he sat down with the servants, so that he might see the end. [59] Then the leaders of the priests and the entire council sought false testimony against Jesus, so that they might deliver him to death. [60] And they did not find any, even though many false witnesses had come forward. Then, at the very end, two false witnesses came forward, [61] and they said, "This man said: 'I am able to destroy the temple of God, and, after three days, to rebuild it.'" [62] And the high priest, rising up, said to him, "Have you nothing to respond to what these ones testify against you?" [63] But Jesus was silent. And the high priest said to him, "I bind you by an oath to the living God to tell us if you are the Christ, the Son of God." [64] Jesus said to him: "You have said it. Yet truly I say to you, hereafter you shall see the Son of man sitting at the right hand of the power of God, and coming on the clouds of heaven." [65] Then the high priest tore his garments, saying: "He has blasphemed. Why do we still need witnesses? Behold, you have now heard the blasphemy. [66] How does it seem to you?" So they responded by saying, "He is guilty unto death." [67] Then they spit in his face, and they struck him with fists. And others struck his face with the palms of their hands, [68] saying: "Prophesy for us, O Christ. Who is the one that struck you?" [69] Yet truly, Peter sat outside in the courtyard. And a maidservant approached him, saying, "You also were with Jesus the Galilean." [70] But he denied it in the sight of them all, saying, "I do not know what you are saying." [71] Then, as he exited by the gate, another maidservant saw him. And she said to those who were there, "This man also was with Jesus of Nazareth." [72] And again, he denied it with an oath, "For I do not know the man." [73] And after a little while, those who were standing nearby came and said to Peter: "Truly, you also are one of them. For even your manner of speaking reveals you." [74] Then he began to curse and to swear that he had not known the man. And immediately the rooster crowed. [75] And Peter remembered the words of Jesus, which he had said: "Before the rooster crows, you will deny me three times." And going outside, he wept bitterly.

CHAPTER 27

¹Then, when morning arrived, all the leaders of the priests and the elders of the people took counsel against Jesus, so that they might deliver him to death. ²And they led him, bound, and handed him over to Pontius Pilate, the procurator. ³Then Judas, who betrayed him, seeing that he had been condemned, regretting his conduct, brought back the thirty pieces of silver to the leaders of the priests and the elders, ⁴saying, "I have sinned in betraying just blood." But they said to him: "What is that to us? See to it yourself." ⁵And throwing down the pieces of silver in the temple, he departed. And going out, he hanged himself with a snare. ⁶But the leaders of the priests, having taken up the pieces of silver, said, "It is not lawful to put them into the temple offerings, because it is the price of blood." ⁷Then, having taken counsel, they bought the potter's field with it, as a burying place for sojourners. ⁸For this reason, that field is called Haceldama, that is, 'The Field of Blood,' even to this very day. ⁹Then what was spoken by the prophet Jeremiah was fulfilled, saying, "And they took the thirty pieces of silver, the price of the one being appraised, whom they appraised before the sons of Israel, ¹⁰and they gave it for the potter's field, just as the Lord appointed to me." ¹¹Now Jesus stood before the procurator, and the procurator questioned him, saying, "You are the king of the Jews?" Jesus said to him, "You are saying so." ¹²And when he was accused by the leaders of the priests and the elders, he responded nothing. ¹³Then Pilate said to him, "Do you not hear how much testimony they speak against you?" ¹⁴And he did not respond any word to him, so that the procurator wondered greatly. ¹⁵Now on the solemn day, the procurator was accustomed to release to the people one prisoner, whomever they wished. ¹⁶And at that time, he had a notorious prisoner, who was called Barabbas. ¹⁷Therefore, having been gathered together, Pilate said to them, "Who is it that you want me to release to you: Barabbas, or Jesus, who is called Christ?" ¹⁸For he knew that it was out of envy they had handed him over. ¹⁹But as he was sitting in the place for the tribunal, his wife sent to him, saying: "It is nothing to you, and he is just. For I have experienced many things today through a vision for his sake." ²⁰But the leaders of the priests and the elders persuaded the people, so that they would ask for Barabbas, and so that Jesus would perish. ²¹Then, in response, the procurator said to them, "Which of the two do you want to be released to you?" But they said to him, "Barabbas." ²²Pilate said to them, "Then what shall I do about Jesus, who is called Christ?" They all said, "Let him be crucified." ²³The procurator said to them, "But what evil has he done?" But they cried out all the more, saying, "Let him be crucified." ²⁴Then Pilate, seeing that he was able to accomplish nothing, but that a greater tumult was occurring, taking water, washed his hands in the sight of the people, saying: "I am innocent of the blood of this just man. See to it yourselves." ²⁵And the entire people responded by saying, "May his blood be upon us and upon our children." ²⁶Then he released Barabbas to them. But Jesus, having been scourged, he handed over to them, so that he would be crucified. ²⁷Then the soldiers of the procurator, taking Jesus up to the praetorium, gathered the entire cohort around him. ²⁸And stripping him, they put a scarlet cloak around him. ²⁹And plaiting a crown of thorns, they placed it on his head, with a reed in his right hand. And genuflecting before him, they mocked him, saying, "Hail, King of the Jews." ³⁰And spitting on him, they took the reed and struck his head. ³¹And after they had mocked him, they stripped him of the cloak, and clothed him with his own garments, and they led him away to crucify him. ³²But as they were going out, they came upon a man of Cyrene, named Simon, whom they compelled to take up his cross. ³³And they arrived at the place which is called Golgotha, which is the place of Calvary. ³⁴And they gave him wine to drink, mixed with gall. And when he had tasted it, he refused to drink it. ³⁵Then, after they had crucified him, they divided his garments, casting lots, in order to fulfill what was spoken by the prophet, saying: "They divided my garments among them, and over my vestment they cast lots." ³⁶And sitting down, they observed him. ³⁷And they set his accusation above his head, written as: THIS IS JESUS, KING OF THE JEWS. ³⁸Then two robbers were crucified with him: one on the right and one on the left. ³⁹But those passing by blasphemed him, shaking their heads, ⁴⁰and saying: "Ah, so you would destroy the temple of God and in three days rebuild it! Save your own self. If you are the Son of God, descend from the cross." ⁴¹And similarly, the leaders of the priests, with the scribes and the elders, mocking him, said: ⁴²"He saved others; he cannot save himself. If he is the King of Israel, let him descend now from the cross, and we will believe in him. ⁴³He trusted in God; so now, let God free him, if he wills him. For he said, 'I am the Son of God.'" ⁴⁴Then, the robbers who were crucified with him

also reproached him with the very same thing. [45] Now from the sixth hour, there was darkness over the entire earth, even until the ninth hour. [46] And about the ninth hour, Jesus cried out with a loud voice, saying: "Eli, Eli, lamma sabacthani?" that is, "My God, My God, why have you forsaken me?" [47] Then certain ones who were standing and listening there said, "This man calls upon Elijah." [48] And one of them, running quickly, took a sponge and filled it with vinegar, and he set it on a reed and he gave it to him to drink. [49] Yet truly, the others said, "Wait. Let us see whether Elijah will come to free him." [50] Then Jesus, crying out again with a loud voice, gave up his life. [51] And behold, the veil of the temple was torn into two parts, from top to bottom. And the earth was shaken, and the rocks were split apart. [52] And the tombs were opened. And many bodies of the saints, which had been sleeping, arose. [53] And going out from the tombs, after his resurrection, they went into the holy city, and they appeared to many. [54] Now the centurion and those who were with him, guarding Jesus, having seen the earthquake and the things that were done, were very fearful, saying: "Truly, this was the Son of God." [55] And in that place, there were many women, at a distance, who had followed Jesus from Galilee, ministering to him. [56] Among these were Mary Magdalene and Mary the mother of James and Joseph, and the mother of the sons of Zebedee. [57] Then, when evening had arrived, a certain wealthy man from Arimathea, named Joseph, arrived, who himself was also a disciple of Jesus. [58] This man approached Pilate and asked for the body of Jesus. Then Pilate ordered the body to be released. [59] And Joseph, taking the body, wrapped it in a clean finely-woven linen cloth, [60] and he placed it in his own new tomb, which he had hewn out of a rock. And he rolled a great stone to the door of the tomb, and he went away. [61] Now Mary Magdalene and the other Mary were there, sitting opposite the sepulcher. [62] Then the next day, which is after the Preparation day, the leaders of the priests and the Pharisees went to Pilate together, [63] saying: "Lord, we have remembered that this seducer said, while he was still alive, 'After three days, I will rise again.' [64] Therefore, order the sepulcher to be guarded until the third day, lest perhaps his disciples may come and steal him, and say to the people, 'He has risen from the dead.' And this last error would be worse than the first." [65] Pilate said to them: "You have a guard. Go, guard it as you know how." [66] Then, going out, they secured the sepulcher with guards, sealing the stone.

CHAPTER 28

[1] Now on the morning of the Sabbath, when it began to grow light on the first Sabbath, Mary Magdalene and the other Mary went to see the sepulcher. [2] And behold, a great earthquake occurred. For an Angel of the Lord descended from heaven, and as he approached, he rolled back the stone and sat down on it. [3] Now his appearance was like lightning, and his vestment was like snow. [4] Then, out of fear of him, the guards were terrified, and they became like dead men. [5] Then the Angel responded by saying to the women: "Do not be afraid. For I know that you are seeking Jesus, who was crucified. [6] He is not here. For he has risen, just as he said. Come and see the place where the Lord was placed. [7] And then, go quickly, and tell his disciples that he has risen. And behold, he will precede you to Galilee. There you shall see him. Lo, I have told you beforehand." [8] And they went out of the tomb quickly, with fear and in great joy, running to announce it to his disciples. [9] And behold, Jesus met them, saying, "Hail." But they drew near and took hold of his feet, and they adored him. [10] Then Jesus said to them: "Do not be afraid. Go, announce it to my brothers, so that they may go to Galilee. There they shall see me." [11] And when they had departed, behold, some of the guards went into the city, and they reported to the leaders of the priests all that had happened. [12] And gathering together with the elders, having taken counsel, they gave an abundant sum of money to the soldiers, [13] saying: "Say that his disciples arrived at night and stole him away, while we were sleeping. [14] And if the procurator hears about this, we will persuade him, and we will protect you." [15] Then, having accepted the money, they did as they were instructed. And this word has been spread among the Jews, even to this day. [16] Now the eleven disciples went on to Galilee, to the mountain where Jesus had appointed them. [17] And, seeing him, they worshipped him, but certain ones doubted. [18] And Jesus, drawing near, spoke to them, saying: "All authority has been given to me in heaven and on earth. [19] Therefore, go forth and teach all nations, baptizing them in the name of the Father and of the Son and of the Holy Spirit, [20] teaching them to observe all that I have ever commanded you. And behold, I am with you always, even to the consummation of the age."

THE SACRED BIBLE: THE GOSPEL OF MARK

CHAPTER 1

[1] The beginning of the Gospel of Jesus Christ, the Son of God. [2] As it has been written by the prophet Isaiah: "Behold, I send my Angel before your face, who shall prepare your way before you. [3] The voice of one crying out in the desert: Prepare the way of the Lord; make straight his paths." [4] John was in the desert, baptizing and preaching a baptism of repentance, as a remission of sins. [5] And there went out to him all the region of Judea and all those of Jerusalem, and they were baptized by him in the river Jordan, confessing their sins. [6] And John was clothed with camel's hair and with a leather belt around his waist. And he ate locusts and wild honey. [7] And he preached, saying: "One stronger than me comes after me. I am not worthy to reach down and loosen the laces of his shoes. [8] I have baptized you with water. Yet truly, he will baptize you with the Holy Spirit." [9] And it happened that, in those days, Jesus arrived from Nazareth of Galilee. And he was baptized by John in the Jordan. [10] And immediately, upon ascending from the water, he saw the heavens opened and the Spirit, like a dove, descending, and remaining with him. [11] And there was a voice from heaven: "You are my beloved Son; in you I am well pleased." [12] And immediately the Spirit prompted him into the desert. [13] And he was in the desert for forty days and forty nights. And he was tempted by Satan. And he was with the wild animals, and the Angels ministered to him. [14] Then, after John was handed over, Jesus went into Galilee, preaching the Gospel of the kingdom of God, [15] and saying: "For the time has been fulfilled and the kingdom of God has drawn near. Repent and believe in the Gospel." [16] And passing by the shore of the Sea of Galilee, he saw Simon and his brother Andrew, casting nets into the sea, for they were fishermen. [17] And Jesus said to them, "Come after me, and I will make you fishers of men." [18] And at once abandoning their nets, they followed him. [19] And continuing on a little ways from there, he saw James of Zebedee and his brother John, and they were mending their nets in a boat. [20] And immediately he called them. And leaving behind their father Zebedee in the boat with his hired hands, they followed him. [21] And they entered into Capernaum. And entering into the synagogue promptly on the Sabbaths, he taught them. [22] And they were astonished over his doctrine. For he was teaching them as one who has authority, and not like the scribes. [23] And in their synagogue, there was a man with an unclean spirit; and he cried out, [24] saying: "What are we to you, Jesus of Nazareth? Have you come to destroy us? I know who you are: the Holy One of God." [25] And Jesus admonished him, saying, "Be silent, and depart from the man." [26] And the unclean spirit, convulsing him and crying out with a loud voice, departed from him. [27] And they were all so amazed that they inquired among themselves, saying: "What is this? And what is this new doctrine? For with authority he commands even the unclean spirits, and they obey him." [28] And his fame went out quickly, throughout the entire region of Galilee. [29] And soon after departing from the synagogue, they went into the house of Simon and Andrew, with James and John. [30] But the mother-in-law of Simon lay ill with a fever. And at once they told him about her. [31] And drawing near to her, he raised her up, taking her by the hand. And immediately the fever left her, and she ministered to them. [32] Then, when evening arrived, after the sun had set, they brought to him all who had maladies and those who had demons. [33] And the entire city was gathered together at the door. [34] And he healed many who were troubled with various illnesses. And he cast out many demons, but he would not permit them to speak, because they knew him. [35] And rising up very early, departing, he went out to a deserted place, and there he prayed. [36] And Simon, and those who were with him, followed after him. [37] And when they had found him, they said to him, "For everyone is seeking you." [38] And he said to them: "Let us go into the neighboring towns and cities, so that I may preach there also. Indeed, it was for this reason that I came." [39] And he was preaching in their synagogues and throughout all of Galilee, and casting out demons. [40] And a leper came to him, begging him. And kneeling down, he said to him, "If you are willing, you are able to cleanse me." [41] Then Jesus, taking pity on him, reached out his hand. And touching him, he said to him: "I am willing. Be cleansed." [42] And after he had spoken, immediately the leprosy departed from him, and he was cleansed. [43] And he admonished him, and he promptly sent him away. [44] And he said to him: "See to it that you tell no one. But go and show yourself to the high

priest, and offer for your cleansing that which Moses instructed, as a testimony for them." [45] But having departed, he began to preach and to disseminate the word, so that he was no longer able to openly enter a city, but had to remain outside, in deserted places. And they were gathered to him from every direction.

CHAPTER 2

[1] And after some days, he again entered into Capernaum. [2] And it was heard that he was in the house. And so many gathered that there was no room left, not even at the door. And he spoke the word to them. [3] And they came to him, bringing a paralytic, who was being carried by four men. [4] And when they were not able to present him to him because of the crowd, they uncovered the roof where he was. And opening it, they lowered down the stretcher on which the paralytic was lying. [5] Then, when Jesus had seen their faith, he said to the paralytic, "Son, your sins are forgiven you." [6] But some of the scribes were sitting in that place and thinking in their hearts: [7] "Why is this man speaking in this way? He is blaspheming. Who can forgive sins, but God alone?" [8] At once, Jesus, realizing in his spirit that they were thinking this within themselves, said to them: "Why are you thinking these things in your hearts? [9] Which is easier, to say to the paralytic, 'Your sins are forgiven you,' or to say, 'Rise up, take up your stretcher, and walk?' [10] But so that you may know that the Son of man has authority on earth to forgive sins," he said to the paralytic: [11] "I say to you: Rise up, take up your stretcher, and go into your house." [12] And immediately he got up, and lifting up his stretcher, he went away in the sight of them all, so that they all wondered. And they honored God, by saying, "We have never seen anything like this." [13] And he departed again to the sea. And the entire crowd came to him, and he taught them. [14] And as he was passing by, he saw Levi of Alphaeus, sitting at the customs office. And he said to him, "Follow me." And rising up, he followed him. [15] And it happened that, as he sat at table in his house, many tax collectors and sinners sat at table together with Jesus and his disciples. For those who followed him were many. [16] And the scribes and the Pharisees, seeing that he ate with tax collectors and sinners, said to his disciples, "Why does your Teacher eat and drink with tax collectors and sinners?" [17] Jesus, having heard this, said to them: "The healthy have no need of a doctor, but those who have maladies do. For I came not to call the just, but sinners." [18] And the disciples of John, and the Pharisees, were fasting. And they arrived and said to him, "Why do the disciples of John and of the Pharisees fast, but your disciples do not fast?" [19] And Jesus said to them: "How can the sons of the wedding fast while the groom is still with them? During whatever time they have the groom with them, they are not able to fast. [20] But the days will arrive when the groom will be taken away from them, and then they shall fast, in those days. [21] No one sews a patch of new cloth onto an old garment. Otherwise, the new addition pulls away from the old, and the tear becomes worse. [22] And no one puts new wine into old wineskins. Otherwise, the wine will burst the wineskins, and the wine will pour out, and the wineskins will be lost. Instead, new wine must be put into new wineskins." [23] And again, while the Lord was walking through the ripe grain on the Sabbath, his disciples, as they advanced, began to separate the ears of grains. [24] But the Pharisees said to him, "Behold, why are they doing what is not lawful on the Sabbaths?" [25] And he said to them: "Have you never read what David did, when he had need and was hungry, both he and those who were with him? [26] How he went into the house of God, under the high priest Abiathar, and ate the bread of the Presence, which it was not lawful to eat, except for the priests, and how he gave it to those who were with him?" [27] And he said to them: "The Sabbath was made for man, and not man for the Sabbath. [28] And so, the Son of man is Lord, even of the Sabbath."

CHAPTER 3

[1] And again, he entered into the synagogue. And there was a man there who had a withered hand. [2] And they observed him, to see if he would cure on the Sabbaths, so that they might accuse him. [3] And he said to the man who had the withered hand, "Stand up in the middle." [4] And he said to them: "Is it lawful to do good on the Sabbaths, or to do evil, to give health to a life, or to destroy?" But they remained silent. [5] And looking around at them with anger, being very saddened over the blindness of their hearts, he said to the man, "Extend your hand." And he extended it, and his hand was restored to him. [6] Then the Pharisees, going out, immediately took counsel with the Herodians against him, as to how they might

destroy him. [7] But Jesus withdrew with his disciples to the sea. And a great crowd followed him from Galilee and Judea, [8] and from Jerusalem, and from Idumea and across the Jordan. And those around Tyre and Sidon, upon hearing what he was doing, came to him in a great multitude. [9] And he told his disciples that a small boat would be useful to him, because of the crowd, lest they press upon him. [10] For he healed so many, that as many of them as had wounds would rush toward him in order to touch him. [11] And the unclean spirits, when they saw him, fell prostrate before him. And they cried out, saying, [12] "You are the Son of God." And he strongly admonished them, lest they make him known. [13] And ascending onto a mountain, he called to himself those whom he willed, and they came to him. [14] And he acted so that the twelve would be with him, and so that he might send them out to preach. [15] And he gave them authority to cure infirmities, and to cast out demons: [16] and he imposed on Simon the name Peter; [17] and also he imposed on James of Zebedee, and John the brother of James, the name 'Boanerges,' that is, 'Sons of Thunder;' [18] and Andrew, and Philip, and Bartholomew, and Matthew, and Thomas, and James of Alphaeus, and Thaddeus, and Simon the Canaanite, [19] and Judas Iscariot, who also betrayed him. [20] And they went to a house, and the crowd gathered together again, so much so that they were not even able to eat bread. [21] And when his own had heard of it, they went out to take hold of him. For they said: "Because he has gone mad." [22] And the scribes who had descended from Jerusalem said, "Because he has Beelzebub, and because by the prince of demons does he cast out demons." [23] And having called them together, he spoke to them in parables: "How can Satan cast out Satan? [24] For if a kingdom is divided against itself, that kingdom is not able to stand. [25] And if a house is divided against itself, that house is not able to stand. [26] And if Satan has risen up against himself, he would be divided, and he would not be able to stand; instead he reaches the end. [27] No one is able to plunder the goods of a strong man, having entered into the house, unless he first binds the strong man, and then he shall plunder his house. [28] Amen I say to you, that all sins will be forgiven the sons of men, and the blasphemies by which they will have blasphemed. [29] But he who will have blasphemed against the Holy Spirit shall not have forgiveness in eternity; instead he shall be guilty of an eternal offense." [30] For they said: "He has an unclean spirit." [31] And his mother and brothers arrived. And standing outside, they sent to him, calling him. [32] And the crowd was sitting around him. And they said to him, "Behold, your mother and your brothers are outside, seeking you." [33] And responding to them, he said, "Who is my mother and my brothers?" [34] And looking around at those who were sitting all around him, he said: "Behold, my mother and my brothers. [35] For whoever has done the will of God, the same is my brother, and my sister and mother."

CHAPTER 4

[1] And again, he began to teach by the sea. And a great crowd was gathered to him, so much so that, climbing into a boat, he was seated on the sea. And the entire crowd was on the land along the sea. [2] And he taught them many things in parables, and he said to them, in his doctrine: [3] "Listen. Behold, the sower went out to sow. [4] And while he was sowing, some fell along the way, and the birds of the air came and ate it. [5] Yet truly, others fell upon stony ground, where it did not have much soil. And it rose up quickly, because it had no depth of soil. [6] And when the sun was risen, it was scorched. And because it had no root, it withered away. [7] And some fell among thorns. And the thorns grew up and suffocated it, and it did not produce fruit. [8] And some fell on good soil. And it brought forth fruit that grew up, and increased, and yielded: some thirty, some sixty, and some one hundred." [9] And he said, "Whoever has ears to hear, let him hear." [10] And when he was alone, the twelve, who were with him, questioned him about the parable. [11] And he said to them: "To you, it has been given to know the mystery of the kingdom of God. But to those who are outside, everything is presented in parables: [12] 'so that, seeing, they may see, and not perceive; and hearing, they may hear, and not understand; lest at any time they may be converted, and their sins would be forgiven them.'" [13] And he said to them: "Do you not understand this parable? And so, how will you understand all the parables? [14] He who sows, sows the word. [15] Now there are those who are along the way, where the word is sown. And when they have heard it, Satan quickly comes and takes away the word, which was sown in their hearts. [16] And similarly, there are those who were sown upon stony ground. These, when they have heard the word, immediately accept it with gladness. [17] But they have no root in themselves, and so they are

for a limited time. And when next tribulation and persecution arises because of the word, they quickly fall away. [18] And there are others who are sown among thorns. These are those who hear the word, [19] but worldly tasks, and the deception of riches, and desires about other things enter in and suffocate the word, and it is effectively without fruit. [20] And there are those who are sown upon good soil, who hear the word and accept it; and these bear fruit: some thirty, some sixty, and some one hundred." [21] And he said to them: "Would someone enter with a lamp in order to place it under a basket or under a bed? Would it not be placed upon a lampstand? [22] For there is nothing hidden that will not be revealed. Neither was anything done in secret, except that it may be made public. [23] If anyone has ears to hear, let him hear." [24] And he said to them: "Consider what you hear. With whatever measure you have measured out, it shall be measured back to you, and more shall be added to you. [25] For whoever has, to him it shall be given. And whoever has not, from him even what he has shall be taken away." [26] And he said: "The kingdom of God is like this: it is as if a man were to cast seed on the land. [27] And he sleeps and he arises, night and day. And the seed germinates and grows, though he does not know it. [28] For the earth bears fruit readily: first the plant, then the ear, next the full grain in the ear. [29] And when the fruit has been produced, immediately he sends out the sickle, because the harvest has arrived." [30] And he said: "To what should we compare the kingdom of God? Or to what parable should we compare it? [31] It is like a grain of mustard seed which, when it has been sown in the earth, is less than all the seeds which are in the earth. [32] And when it is sown, it grows up and becomes greater than all the plants, and it produces great branches, so much so that the birds of the air are able to live under its shadow." [33] And with many such parables he spoke the word to them, as much as they were able to hear. [34] But he did not speak to them without a parable. Yet separately, he explained all things to his disciples. [35] And on that day, when evening had arrived, he said to them, "Let us cross over." [36] And dismissing the crowd, they brought him, so that he was in one boat, and other boats were with him. [37] And a great wind storm occurred, and the waves broke over the boat, so that the boat was being filled. [38] And he was in the stern of the boat, sleeping on a pillow. And they woke him and said to him, "Teacher, does it not concern you that we are perishing?" [39] And rising up, he rebuked the wind, and he said to the sea: "Silence. Be stilled." And the wind ceased. And a great tranquility occurred. [40] And he said to them: "Why are you afraid? Do you still lack faith?" And they were struck with a great fear. And they said to one another, "Who do you think this is, that both wind and sea obey him?"

CHAPTER 5

[1] And they went across the strait of the sea into the region of the Gerasenes. [2] And as he was departing from the boat, he was immediately met, from among the tombs, by a man with an unclean spirit, [3] who had his dwelling place with the tombs; neither had anyone been able to bind him, even with chains. [4] For having been bound often with shackles and chains, he had broken the chains and smashed the shackles; and no one had been able to tame him. [5] And he was always, day and night, among the tombs, or in the mountains, crying out and cutting himself with stones. [6] And seeing Jesus from afar, he ran and adored him. [7] And crying out with a loud voice, he said: "What am I to you, Jesus, the Son of the Most High God? I beseech you by God, that you not torment me." [8] For he said to him, "Depart from the man, you unclean spirit." [9] And he questioned him: "What is your name?" And he said to him, "My name is Legion, for we are many." [10] And he entreated him greatly, so that he would not expel him from the region. [11] And in that place, near the mountain, there was a great herd of swine, feeding. [12] And the spirits entreated him, saying: "Send us into the swine, so that we may enter into them." [13] And Jesus promptly gave them permission. And the unclean spirits, departing, entered into the swine. And the herd of about two thousand rushed down with great force into the sea, and they were drowned in the sea. [14] Then those who pastured them fled, and they reported it in the city and in the countryside. And they all went out to see what was happening. [15] And they came to Jesus. And they saw the man who had been troubled by the demon, sitting, clothed and with a sane mind, and they were afraid. [16] And those who had seen it explained to them how he had dealt with the man who had the demon, and about the swine. [17] And they began to petition him, so that he would withdraw from their borders. [18] And as he was climbing into the boat, the man who had been troubled by the demons began to beg him, so that he might be with him.

[19] And he did not permit him, but he said to him, "Go to your own people, in your own house, and announce to them how great are the things that the Lord has done for you, and how he has taken pity on you." [20] And he went away and began to preach in the Ten Cities, how great were the things that Jesus had done for him. And everyone wondered. [21] And when Jesus had crossed in the boat, over the strait again, a great crowd came together before him. And he was near the sea. [22] And one of the rulers of the synagogue, named Jairus, approached. And seeing him, he fell prostrate at his feet. [23] And he beseeched him greatly, saying: "For my daughter is near the end. Come and lay your hand on her, so that she may be healthy and may live." [24] And he went with him. And a great crowd followed him, and they pressed upon him. [25] And there was a woman who had a flow of blood for twelve years. [26] And she had endured much from several physicians, and she had spent everything she owned with no benefit at all, but instead she became worse. [27] Then, when she had heard of Jesus, she approached through the crowd behind him, and she touched his garment. [28] For she said: "Because if I touch even his garment, I will be saved." [29] And immediately, the source of her bleeding was dried up, and she sensed in her body that she had been healed from the wound. [30] And immediately Jesus, realizing within himself that power that had gone out from him, turning to the crowd, said, "Who touched my garments?" [31] And his disciples said to him, "You see that the crowd presses around you, and yet you say, 'Who touched me?'" [32] And he looked around to see the woman who had done this. [33] Yet truly, the woman, in fear and trembling, knowing what had happened within her, went and fell prostrate before him, and she told him the whole truth. [34] And he said to her: "Daughter, your faith has saved you. Go in peace, and be healed from your wound." [35] While he was still speaking, they arrived from the ruler of the synagogue, saying: "Your daughter is dead. Why trouble the Teacher any further?" [36] But Jesus, having heard the word that was spoken, said to the ruler of the synagogue: "Do not be afraid. You need only believe." [37] And he would not permit anyone to follow him, except Peter, and James, and John the brother of James. [38] And they went to the house of the ruler of the synagogue. And he saw a tumult, and weeping, and much wailing. [39] And entering, he said to them: "Why are you disturbed and weeping? The girl is not dead, but is asleep." [40] And they derided him. Yet truly, having put them all out, he took the father and mother of the girl, and those who were with him, and he entered to where the girl was lying. [41] And taking the girl by the hand, he said to her, "Talitha koumi," which means, "Little girl, (I say to you) arise." [42] And immediately the young girl rose up and walked. Now she was twelve years old. And they were suddenly struck with a great astonishment. [43] And he instructed them sternly, so that no one would know about it. And he told them to give her something to eat.

CHAPTER 6

[1] And departing from there, he went away to his own country; and his disciples followed him. [2] And when the Sabbath arrived, he began to teach in the synagogue. And many, upon hearing him, were amazed at his doctrine, saying: "Where did this one get all these things?" and, "What is this wisdom, which has been given to him?" and, "Such powerful deeds, which are wrought by his hands!" [3] "Is this not the carpenter, the son of Mary, the brother of James, and Joseph, and Jude, and Simon? Are not his sisters also here with us?" And they took great offense at him. [4] And Jesus said to them, "A prophet is not without honor, except in his own country, and in his own house, and among his own kindred." [5] And he was not able to perform any miracles there, except that he cured a few of the infirm by laying his hands on them. [6] And he wondered, because of their unbelief, and he traveled around in the villages, teaching. [7] And he called the twelve. And he began to send them out in twos, and he gave them authority over unclean spirits. [8] And he instructed them not to take anything for the journey, except a staff: no traveling bag, no bread, and no money belt, [9] but to wear sandals, and not to wear two tunics. [10] And he said to them: "Whenever you have entered into a house, stay there until you depart from that place. [11] And whoever will neither receive you, nor listen to you, as you go away from there, shake off the dust from your feet as a testimony against them." [12] And going out, they were preaching, so that people would repent. [13] And they cast out many demons, and they anointed many of the sick with oil and healed them. [14] And king Herod heard of it, (for his name had become well-known) and he said: "John the Baptist has risen again from the dead, and because of this, miracles are at work in him." [15] But others were saying, "Because it is Elijah." Still others were saying, "Because he is a prophet, like one

of the prophets." [16] When Herod had heard it, he said, "John whom I beheaded, the same has risen again from the dead." [17] For Herod himself had sent to capture John, and had chained him in prison, because of Herodias, the wife of his brother Philip; for he had married her. [18] For John was saying to Herod, "It is not lawful for you to have your brother's wife." [19] Now Herodias was devising treachery against him; and she wanted to kill him, but she was unable. [20] For Herod was apprehensive of John, knowing him to be a just and holy man, and so he guarded him. And he heard that he was accomplishing many things, and so he listened to him willingly. [21] And when an opportune time had arrived, Herod held a feast on his birthday, with the leaders, and the tribunes, and the first rulers of Galilee. [22] And when the daughter of the same Herodias had entered, and danced, and pleased Herod, along with those who were at table with him, the king said to the girl, "Request from me whatever you want, and I will give it to you." [23] And he swore to her, "Anything that you request, I will give to you, even up to half my kingdom." [24] And when she had gone out, she said to her mother, "What shall I request?" But her mother said, "The head of John the Baptist." [25] And immediately, when she had entered with haste to the king, she petitioned him, saying: "I want you to give me at once the head of John the Baptist on a platter." [26] And the king was greatly saddened. But because of his oath, and because of those who were sitting with him at table, he was not willing to disappoint her. [27] So, having sent an executioner, he instructed that his head be brought on a platter. [28] And he beheaded him in prison, and he brought his head on a platter. And he gave it to the girl, and the girl gave it her mother. [29] When his disciples heard about it, they came and took his body, and they placed it in a tomb. [30] And the Apostles, returning to Jesus, reported to him everything that they had done and taught. [31] And he said to them, "Go out alone, into a deserted place, and rest for a little while." For there were so many who were coming and going, that they did not even have time to eat. [32] And climbing into a boat, they went away to a deserted place alone. [33] And they saw them going away, and many knew about it. And together they ran by foot from all the cities, and they arrived before them. [34] And Jesus, going out, saw a great multitude. And he took pity on them, because they were like sheep without a shepherd, and he began to teach them many things. [35] And when many hours had now passed, his disciples drew near to him, saying: "This is a deserted place, and the hour is now late. [36] Send them away, so that by going out to nearby villages and towns, they might buy provisions for themselves to eat." [37] And responding, he said to them, "Give them something to eat yourselves." And they said to him, "Let us go out and buy bread for two hundred denarii, and then we will give them something to eat." [38] And he said to them: "How many loaves do you have? Go and see." And when they had found out, they said, "Five, and two fish." [39] And he instructed them to make them all sit down in groups on the green grass. [40] And they sat down in divisions by hundreds and by fifties. [41] And having received the five loaves and the two fish, gazing up to heaven, he blessed and broke the bread, and he gave it to his disciples to set before them. And the two fish he divided among them all. [42] And they all ate and were satisfied. [43] And they brought together the remainder: twelve baskets full of fragments and of fish. [44] Now those who ate were five thousand men. [45] And without delay he urged his disciples to climb into the boat, so that they might precede him across the sea to Bethsaida, while he dismissed the people. [46] And when he had dismissed them, he went to the mountain to pray. [47] And when it was late, the boat was in the midst of the sea, and he was alone on the land. [48] And seeing them struggling to row, (for the wind was against them,) and about the fourth watch of the night, he came to them, walking upon the sea. And he intended to pass by them. [49] But when they saw him walking upon the sea, they thought it was an apparition, and they cried out. [50] For they all saw him, and they were very disturbed. And immediately he spoke with them, and he said to them: "Be strengthened in faith. It is I. Do not be afraid." [51] And he climbed into the boat with them, and the wind ceased. And they became even more astonished within themselves. [52] For they did not understand about the bread. For their heart had been blinded. [53] And when they had crossed over, they arrived in the land of Genesaret, and they reached the shore. [54] And when they had disembarked from the boat, the people immediately recognized him. [55] And running throughout that entire region, they began to carry on beds those who had maladies, to where they heard that he would be. [56] And in whichever place he entered, in towns or villages or cities, they placed the infirm in the main streets, and they pleaded with him that they might touch even the hem of his garment. And as many as touched him were made healthy.

CHAPTER 7

[1] And the Pharisees and some of the scribes, arriving from Jerusalem, gathered together before him. [2] And when they had seen certain ones from his disciples eating bread with common hands, that is, with unwashed hands, they disparaged them. [3] For the Pharisees, and all the Jews, do not eat without repeatedly washing their hands, holding to the tradition of the elders. [4] And when returning from the market, unless they wash, they do not eat. And there are many other things which have been handed down to them to observe: the washings of cups, and pitchers, and bronze containers, and beds. [5] And so the Pharisees and the scribes questioned him: "Why do your disciples not walk according to the tradition of the elders, but they eat bread with common hands?" [6] But in response, he said to them: "So well did Isaiah prophesy about you hypocrites, just as it has been written: 'This people honors me with their lips, but their heart is far from me. [7] And in vain do they worship me, teaching the doctrines and precepts of men.' [8] For abandoning the commandment of God, you hold to the tradition of men, to the washing of pitchers and cups. And you do many other things similar to these." [9] And he said to them: "You effectively nullify the precept of God, so that you may observe your own tradition. [10] For Moses said: 'Honor your father and your mother,' and, 'Whoever will have cursed father or mother, let him die a death.' [11] But you say, 'If a man will have said to his father or mother: Korban, (which is a gift) whatever is from me will be to your benefit,' [12] then you do not release him to do anything for his father or mother, [13] rescinding the word of God through your tradition, which you have handed down. And you do many other similar things in this way." [14] And again, calling the crowd to him, he said to them: "Listen to me, all of you, and understand. [15] There is nothing from outside a man which, by entering into him, is able to defile him. But the things which proceed from a man, these are what pollute a man. [16] Whoever has ears to hear, let him hear." [17] And when he had entered into the house, away from the crowd, his disciples questioned him about the parable. [18] And he said to them: "So, are you also without prudence? Do you not understand that everything entering to a man from outside is not able to pollute him? [19] For it does not enter into his heart, but into the gut, and it exits into the sewer, purging all foods." [20] "But," he said "the things which go out from a man, these pollute a man. [21] For from within, from the heart of men, proceed evil thoughts, adulteries, fornications, murders, [22] thefts, avarice, wickedness, deceitfulness, homosexuality, an evil eye, blasphemy, self-exaltation, foolishness. [23] All these evils proceed from within and pollute a man." [24] And rising up, he went from there to the area of Tyre and Sidon. And entering into a house, he intended no one to know about it, but he was not able to remain hidden. [25] For a woman whose daughter had an unclean spirit, as soon as she heard about him, entered and fell prostrate at his feet. [26] For the woman was a Gentile, by birth a Syro-Phoenician. And she petitioned him, so that he would cast the demon from her daughter. [27] And he said to her: "First allow the sons to have their fill. For it is not good to take away the bread of the sons and throw it to the dogs." [28] But she responded by saying to him: "Certainly, Lord. Yet the young dogs also eat, under the table, from the crumbs of the children." [29] And he said to her, "Because of this saying, go; the demon has gone out of your daughter." [30] And when she had gone to her house, she found the girl lying on the bed; and the demon had gone away. [31] And again, departing from the borders of Tyre, he went by way of Sidon to the sea of Galilee, through the midst of the area of the Ten Cities. [32] And they brought someone who was deaf and mute to him. And they begged him, so that he would lay his hand upon him. [33] And taking him away from the crowd, he put his fingers into his ears; and spitting, he touched his tongue. [34] And gazing up to heaven, he groaned and said to him: "Ephphatha," which is, "Be opened." [35] And immediately his ears were opened, and the impediment of his tongue was released, and he spoke correctly. [36] And he instructed them not to tell anyone. But as much as he instructed them, so much more did they preach about it. [37] And so much more did they wonder, saying: "He has done all things well. He has caused both the deaf to hear and the mute to speak."

CHAPTER 8

[1] In those days, again, when there was a great crowd, and they did not have anything to eat, calling together his disciples, he said to them: [2] "I have compassion for the multitude, because, behold, they have persevered with me now for three days, and they do not have anything to eat. [3] And if I were to send them away fasting to

their home, they might faint on the way." For some of them came from far away. [4] And his disciples answered him, "From where would anyone be able to obtain enough bread for them in the wilderness?" [5] And he questioned them, "How many loaves do you have?" And they said, "Seven." [6] And he instructed the crowd to sit down to eat on the ground. And taking the seven loaves, giving thanks, he broke and gave it to his disciples in order to place before them. And they placed these before the crowd. [7] And they had a few small fish. And he blessed them, and he ordered them to be placed before them. [8] And they ate and were satisfied. And they took up what had been leftover from the fragments: seven baskets. [9] And those who ate were about four thousand. And he dismissed them. [10] And promptly climbing into a boat with his disciples, he went into the parts of Dalmanutha. [11] And the Pharisees went out and began to contend with him, seeking from him a sign from heaven, testing him. [12] And sighing deeply in spirit, he said: "Why does this generation seek a sign? Amen, I say to you, if only a sign will be given to this generation!" [13] And sending them away, he climbed into the boat again, and he went away across the sea. [14] And they forgot to take bread. And they did not have any with them in the boat, except one loaf. [15] And he instructed them, saying: "Consider and beware of the leaven of the Pharisees and of the leaven of Herod." [16] And they discussed this with one another, saying, "For we have no bread." [17] And Jesus, knowing this, said to them: "Why do you consider that it is because you have no bread? Do you not yet know or understand? Do you still have blindness in your heart? [18] Having eyes, do you not see? And having ears, do you not hear? Do you not remember, [19] when I broke the five loaves among the five thousand, how many baskets full of fragments you took up?" They said to him, "Twelve." [20] "And when the seven loaves were among the four thousand, how many baskets of fragments did you take up?" And they said to him, "Seven." [21] And he said to them, "How is it that you do not yet understand?" [22] And they went to Bethsaida. And they brought a blind man to him. And they petitioned him, so that he would touch him. [23] And taking the blind man by the hand, he led him beyond the village. And putting spit on his eyes, laying his hands on him, he asked him if he could see anything. [24] And looking up, he said, "I see men but they are like walking trees." [25] Next he placed his hands again over his eyes, and he began to see. And he was restored, so that he could see everything clearly. [26] And he sent him to his house, saying, "Go into your own house, and if you enter into the town, tell no one." [27] And Jesus departed with his disciples into the towns of Caesarea Philippi. And on the way, he questioned his disciples, saying to them, "Who do men say that I am?" [28] And they answered him by saying: "John the Baptist, others Elijah, still others perhaps one of the prophets." [29] Then he said to them, "Yet truly, who do you say that I am?" Peter responded by saying to him, "You are the Christ." [30] And he admonished them, not to tell anyone about him. [31] And he began to teach them that the Son of man must suffer many things, and be rejected by the elders, and by the high priests, and the scribes, and be killed, and after three days rise again. [32] And he spoke the word openly. And Peter, taking him aside, began to correct him. [33] And turning away and looking at his disciples, he admonished Peter, saying, "Get behind me, Satan, for you do not prefer the things that are of God, but the things that are of men." [34] And calling together the crowd with his disciples, he said to them, "If anyone chooses to follow me, let him deny himself, and take up his cross, and follow me. [35] For whoever will have chosen to save his life, will lose it. But whoever will have lost his life, for my sake and for the Gospel, shall save it. [36] For how does it benefit a man, if he gains the whole world, and yet causes harm to his soul? [37] Or, what will a man give in exchange for his soul? [38] For whoever has been ashamed of me and of my words, among this adulterous and sinful generation, the Son of man also will be ashamed of him, when he will arrive in the glory of his Father, with the holy Angels." [39] And he said to them, "Amen I say to you, that there are some among those standing here who shall not taste death until they see the kingdom of God arriving in power."

CHAPTER 9

[1] And after six days, Jesus took with him Peter, and James, and John; and he led them separately to a lofty mountain alone; and he was transfigured before them. [2] And his vestments became radiant and exceedingly white like snow, with such a brilliance as no fuller on earth is able to achieve. [3] And there appeared to them Elijah with Moses; and they were speaking with Jesus. [4] And in response, Peter said to Jesus: "Master, it is good for us to be here. And so let us make three

tabernacles, one for you, and one for Moses, and one for Elijah." [5] For he did not know what he was saying. For they were overwhelmed by fear. [6] And there was a cloud overshadowing them. And a voice came from the cloud, saying: "This is my most beloved Son. Listen to him." [7] And immediately, looking around, they no longer saw anyone, except Jesus alone with them. [8] And as they were descending from the mountain, he instructed them not to relate to anyone what they had seen, until after the Son of man will have risen again from the dead. [9] And they kept the word to themselves, arguing about what "after he will have risen from the dead" might mean. [10] And they questioned him, saying: "Then why do the Pharisees and the scribes say that Elijah must arrive first?" [11] And in response, he said to them: "Elijah, when he will arrive first, shall restore all things. And in the manner that it has been written about the Son of man, so must he suffer many things and be condemned. [12] But I say to you, that Elijah also has arrived, (and they have done to him whatever they wanted) just as it has been written about him." [13] And approaching his disciples, he saw a great crowd surrounding them, and the scribes were arguing with them. [14] And soon all the people, seeing Jesus, were astonished and struck with fear, and hurrying to him, they greeted him. [15] And he questioned them, "What are you arguing about among yourselves?" [16] And one from the crowd responded by saying: "Teacher, I have brought to you my son, who has a mute spirit. [17] And whenever it takes hold of him, it throws him down, and he foams and gnashes with his teeth, and he becomes unconscious. And I asked your disciples to cast him out, and they could not." [18] And answering them, he said: "O unbelieving generation, how long must I be with you? How long shall I endure you? Bring him to me." [19] And they brought him. And when he had seen him, immediately the spirit disturbed him. And having been thrown to the ground, he rolled around foaming. [20] And he questioned his father, "How long has this been happening to him?" But he said: "From infancy. [21] And often it casts him into fire or into water, in order to destroy him. But if you are able to do anything, help us and take pity on us." [22] But Jesus said to him, "If you are able to believe: all things are possible to one who believes." [23] And immediately the father of the boy, crying out with tears, said: "I do believe, Lord. Help my unbelief." [24] And when Jesus saw the crowd rushing together, he admonished the unclean spirit, saying to him, "Deaf and mute spirit, I command you, leave him; and do not enter into him anymore." [25] And crying out, and convulsing him greatly, he departed from him. And he became like one who is dead, so much so that many said, "He is dead." [26] But Jesus, taking him by the hand, lifted him up. And he arose. [27] And when he had entered into the house, his disciples questioned him privately, "Why were we unable to cast him out?" [28] And he said to them, "This kind is able to be expelled by nothing other than prayer and fasting." [29] And setting out from there, they passed through Galilee. And he intended that no one know about it. [30] Then he taught his disciples, and he said to them, "For the Son of man shall be delivered into the hands of men, and they will kill him, and having been killed, on the third day he will rise again." [31] But they did not understand the word. And they were afraid to question him. [32] And they went to Capernaum. And when they were in the house, he questioned them, "What did you discuss on the way?" [33] But they were silent. For indeed, on the way, they had disputed among themselves as to which of them was greater. [34] And sitting down, he called the twelve, and he said to them, "If anyone wants to be first, he shall be the last of all and the minister of all." [35] And taking a child, he set him in their midst. And when he had embraced him, he said to them: [36] "Whoever receives one such child in my name, receives me. And whoever receives me, receives not me, but him who sent me." [37] John responded to him by saying, "Teacher, we saw someone casting out demons in your name; he does not follow us, and so we prohibited him." [38] But Jesus said: "Do not prohibit him. For there is no one who can act with virtue in my name and soon speak evil about me. [39] For whoever is not against you is for you. [40] For whoever, in my name, will give you a cup of water to drink, because you belong to Christ: Amen I say to you, he shall not lose his reward. [41] And whoever will have scandalized one of these little ones who believe in me: it would be better for him if a great millstone were placed around his neck and he were thrown into the sea. [42] And if your hand causes you to sin, cut it off: it is better for you to enter into life disabled, than having two hands to go into Hell, into the unquenchable fire, [43] where their worm does not die, and the fire is not extinguished. [44] But if your foot causes you to sin, chop it off: it is better for you to enter into eternal life lame, than having two feet to be cast into the Hell of unquenchable fire, [45] where their worm does not die, and the fire is not extinguished. [46] But if your eye causes you to sin, pluck it out: it is better for you to enter into the kingdom of God with one eye, than having two eyes to be cast into the Hell of fire, [47] where their worm does not die, and the fire is not extinguished. [48] For all shall be salted with fire, and every victim shall be salted with salt. [49] Salt is good: but if the salt has become bland, with what will you season it? Have salt in yourselves, and have peace among yourselves."

CHAPTER 10

[1] And rising up, he went from there into the area of Judea beyond the Jordan. And again, the crowd came together before him. And just as he was accustomed to do, again he taught them. [2] And approaching, the Pharisees questioned him, testing him: "Is it lawful for a man to dismiss his wife?" [3] But in response, he said to them, "What did Moses instruct you?" [4] And they said, "Moses gave permission to write a bill of divorce and to dismiss her." [5] But Jesus responded by saying: "It was due to the hardness of your heart that he wrote that precept for you. [6] But from the beginning of creation, God made them male and female. [7] Because of this, a man shall leave behind his father and mother, and he shall cling to his wife. [8] And these two shall be one in flesh. And so, they are now, not two, but one flesh. [9] Therefore, what God has joined together, let no man separate." [10] And again, in the house, his disciples questioned him about the same thing. [11] And he said to them: "Whoever dismisses his wife, and marries another, commits adultery against her. [12] And if a wife dismisses her husband, and is married to another, she commits adultery." [13] And they brought to him the little children, so that he might touch them. But the disciples admonished those who brought them. [14] But when Jesus saw this, he took offense, and he said to them: "Allow the little ones to come to me, and do not prohibit them. For of such as these is the kingdom of God. [15] Amen I say to you, whoever will not accept the kingdom of God like a little child, will not enter into it." [16] And embracing them, and laying his hands upon them, he blessed them. [17] And when he had departed on the way, a certain one, running up and kneeling before him, asked him, "Good Teacher, what shall I do, so that I may secure eternal life?" [18] But Jesus said to him, "Why call me good? No one is good except the one God. [19] You know the precepts: "Do not commit adultery. Do not kill. Do not steal. Do not speak false testimony. Do not deceive. Honor your father and mother." [20] But in response, he said to him, "Teacher, all these I have observed from my youth." [21] Then Jesus, gazing at him, loved him, and he said to him: "One thing is lacking to you. Go, sell whatever you have, and give to the poor, and then you will have treasure in heaven. And come, follow me." [22] But he went away grieving, having been greatly saddened by the word. For he had many possessions. [23] And Jesus, looking around, said to his disciples, "How difficult it is for those who have riches to enter into the kingdom of God!" [24] And the disciples were astonished at his words. But Jesus, answering again, said to them: "Little sons, how difficult it is for those who trust in money to enter into the kingdom of God! [25] It is easier for a camel to pass through the eye of a needle, than for the rich to enter into the kingdom of God." [26] And they wondered even more, saying among themselves, "Who, then, can be saved?" [27] And Jesus, gazing at them, said: "With men it is impossible; but not with God. For with God all things are possible." [28] And Peter began to say to him, "Behold, we have left all things and have followed you." [29] In response, Jesus said: "Amen I say to you, There is no one who has left behind house, or brothers, or sisters, or father, or mother, or children, or land, for my sake and for the Gospel, [30] who will not receive one hundred times as much, now in this time: houses, and brothers, and sisters, and mothers, and children, and land, with persecutions, and in the future age eternal life. [31] But many of the first shall be last, and the last shall be first." [32] Now they were on the way ascending to Jerusalem. And Jesus went ahead of them, and they were astonished. And those following him were afraid. And again, taking aside the twelve, he began to tell them what was about to happen to him. [33] "For behold, we are going up to Jerusalem, and the Son of man will be handed over to the leaders of the priests, and to the scribes, and the elders. And they will condemn him to death, and they will hand him over to the Gentiles. [34] And they will mock him, and spit on him, and scourge him, and put him to death. And on the third day, he will rise again." [35] And James and John, the sons of Zebedee, drew near to him, saying, "Teacher, we wish that whatever we will ask, you would do for us." [36] But he said to them, "What do you want me to do for you?" [37] And they said, "Grant to us that we may sit, one at your right and the other at your left, in your glory." [38] But Jesus said to them: "You do not know what you are asking. Are you able to drink from the chalice from which I drink, or to

be baptized with the baptism with which I am to be baptized?" [39] But they said to him, "We can." Then Jesus said to them: "Indeed, you shall drink from the chalice, from which I drink; and you shall be baptized with the baptism, with which I am to be baptized. [40] But to sit at my right, or at my left, is not mine to give to you, but it is for those for whom it has been prepared." [41] And the ten, upon hearing this, began to be indignant toward James and John. [42] But Jesus, calling them, said to them: "You know that those who seem to be leaders among the Gentiles dominate them, and their leaders exercise authority over them. [43] But it is not to be this way among you. Instead, whoever would become greater shall be your minister; [44] and whoever will be first among you shall be the servant of all. [45] So, too, the Son of man has not come so that they would minister to him, but so that he would minister and would give his life as a redemption for many." [46] And they went to Jericho. And as he was setting out from Jericho with his disciples and a very numerous multitude, Bartimaeus, the son of Timaeus, a blind man, sat begging beside the way. [47] And when he had heard that it was Jesus of Nazareth, he began to cry out and to say, "Jesus, Son of David, take pity on me." [48] And many admonished him to be quiet. But he cried out all the more, "Son of David, take pity on me." [49] And Jesus, standing still, instructed him to be called. And they called the blind man, saying to him: "Be at peace. Arise. He is calling you." [50] And casting aside his garment, he leapt up and went to him. [51] And in response, Jesus said to him, "What do you want, that I should do for you?" And the blind man said to him, "Master, that I may see." [52] Then Jesus said to him, "Go, your faith has made you whole." And immediately he saw, and he followed him on the way.

CHAPTER 11

[1] And as they were approaching Jerusalem and Bethania, toward the mount of Olives, he sent two of his disciples, [2] and he said to them: "Go into the village that is opposite you, and immediately upon entering there, you will find a colt tied, on which no man has yet sat. Release him and bring him. [3] And if anyone will say to you: 'What are you doing?' Say that the Lord has need of him. And he will immediately send him here." [4] And going out, they found the colt tied before the outer gate, at the meeting of two ways. And they untied him. [5] And some of those who were standing there said to them, "What are you doing by releasing the colt?" [6] And they spoke to them just as Jesus had instructed them. And they permitted them. [7] And they led the colt to Jesus. And they placed their garments on it; and he sat upon it. [8] Then many spread their garments along the way; but others cut down leafy branches from trees and scattered them on the way. [9] And those who went ahead, and those who followed, cried out saying: "Hosanna! Blessed is he who has arrived in the name of the Lord. [10] Blessed is the advent of the kingdom of our father David. Hosanna in the highest!" [11] And he entered into Jerusalem, into the temple. And having looked around at everything, since it was now the evening hour, he went out to Bethania with the twelve. [12] And the next day, as they were departing from Bethania, he was hungry. [13] And when he had seen a fig tree with leaves in the distance, he went to it, in case he might find something on it. And when he had gone to it, he found nothing but leaves. For it was not the season for figs. [14] And in response, he said to it, "From now on and forever, may no one eat fruit from you again!" And his disciples heard this. [15] And they went to Jerusalem. And when he had entered into the temple, he began to cast out the sellers and the buyers in the temple. And he overturned the tables of the moneychangers and the chairs of the vendors of doves. [16] And he would not permit anyone to carry goods through the temple. [17] And he taught them, saying: "Is it not written: 'For my house shall be called the house of prayer for all nations?' But you have made it into a den of robbers." [18] And when the leaders of the priests, and the scribes, had heard this, they sought a means by which they might destroy him. For they feared him, because the entire multitude was in admiration over his doctrine. [19] And when evening had arrived, he departed from the city. [20] And when they passed by in the morning, they saw that the fig tree had dried up from the roots. [21] And Peter, remembering, said to him, "Master, behold, the fig tree that you cursed has withered." [22] And in response, Jesus said to them: "Have the faith of God. [23] Amen I say to you, that whoever will say to this mountain, 'Be taken up and cast into the sea,' and who will not have hesitated in his heart, but will have believed: then whatever he has said be done, it shall be done for him. [24] For this reason, I say to you, all things whatsoever that you ask for when praying: believe that you will receive them, and they will happen for you.

²⁵ And when you stand to pray, if you hold anything against anyone, forgive them, so that your Father, who is in heaven, may also forgive you your sins. ²⁶ But if you will not forgive, neither will your Father, who is in heaven, forgive you your sins."
²⁷ And they went again to Jerusalem. And when he was walking in the temple, the leaders of the priests, and the scribes, and the elders approached him. ²⁸ And they said to him: "By what authority do you do these things? And who has given you this authority, so that you would do these things?" ²⁹ But in response, Jesus said to them: "I also will ask you one word, and if you answer me, I will tell you by what authority I do these things. ³⁰ The baptism of John: was it from heaven or from men? Answer me." ³¹ But they discussed it among themselves, saying: "If we say, 'From heaven,' he will say, 'Then why did you not believe him?' ³² If we say, 'From men,' we fear the people. For they all hold that John was a true prophet." ³³ And answering, they said to Jesus, "We do not know." And in response, Jesus said to them, "Neither will I tell you by what authority I do these things."

CHAPTER 12

¹ And he began to speak to them in parables: "A man dug a vineyard, and surrounded it with a hedge, and dug a pit, and built a tower, and he loaned it out to farmers, and he set out on a long journey. ² And in time, he sent a servant to the farmers, in order to receive some of the fruit of the vineyard from the farmers. ³ But they, having apprehended him, beat him and sent him away empty. ⁴ And again, he sent another servant to them. And they wounded him on the head, and they treated him with contempt. ⁵ And again, he sent another, and him they killed, and many others: some they beat, but others they killed. ⁶ Therefore, having still one son, most dear to him, he sent him also to them, at the very end, saying, 'For they will reverence my son.' ⁷ But the settlers said one to another: 'This is the heir. Come, let us kill him. And then the inheritance will be ours.' ⁸ And apprehending him, they killed him. And they cast him out of the vineyard. ⁹ Therefore, what will the lord of the vineyard do?" "He will come and destroy the settlers. And he will give the vineyard to others." ¹⁰ "And so, have you not read this scripture?: 'The stone which the builders have rejected, the same has been made the head of the corner. ¹¹ By the Lord has this been done, and it is wondrous in our eyes.'" ¹² And they sought to take hold of him, but they feared the crowd. For they knew that he had spoken this parable about them. And leaving him behind, they went away. ¹³ And they sent some of the Pharisees and Herodians to him, so that they might trap him with words. ¹⁴ And these, arriving, said to him: "Teacher, we know that you are truthful and that you do not favor anyone; for you do not consider the appearance of men, but you teach the way of God in truth. Is it lawful to give the tribute to Caesar, or should we not give it?" ¹⁵ And knowing their skill in deception, he said to them: "Why do you test me? Bring me a denarius, so that I may see it." ¹⁶ And they brought it to him. And he said to them, "Whose image and inscription is this?" They said to him, "Caesar's." ¹⁷ So in response, Jesus said to them, "Then render to Caesar, the things that are of Caesar; and to God, the things that are of God." And they wondered over him. ¹⁸ And the Sadducees, who say there is no resurrection, approached him. And they questioned him, saying: ¹⁹ "Teacher, Moses wrote for us that if any man's brother will have died and left behind a wife, and not have left behind sons, his brother should take his wife to himself and should raise up offspring for his brother. ²⁰ So then, there were seven brothers. And the first took a wife, and he died without leaving behind offspring. ²¹ And the second took her, and he died. And neither did he leave behind offspring. And the third acted similarly. ²² And in like manner, each of the seven received her and did not leave behind offspring. Last of all, the woman also died. ²³ Therefore, in the resurrection, when they will rise again, to which of them will she be a wife? For each of the seven had her as wife." ²⁴ And Jesus responded by saying to them: "But have you not gone astray, by knowing neither the scriptures, nor the power of God? ²⁵ For when they will be resurrected from the dead, they shall neither marry, nor be given in marriage, but they are like the Angels in heaven. ²⁶ But concerning the dead who rise again, have you not read in the book of Moses, how God spoke to him from the bush, saying: 'I am the God of Abraham, and the God of Isaac, and the God of Jacob?' ²⁷ He is not the God of the dead, but of the living. Therefore, you have gone far astray." ²⁸ And one of the scribes, who had heard them arguing, drew near to him. And seeing that he had answered them well, he questioned him as to which was the first commandment of all. ²⁹ And Jesus answered him: "For the first commandment of all is this: 'Listen, O Israel. The Lord your God is one God. ³⁰ And you shall love

the Lord your God from your whole heart, and from your whole soul, and from your whole mind, and from your whole strength. This is the first commandment.' [31] But the second is similar to it: 'You shall love your neighbor as yourself.' There is no other commandment greater than these." [32] And the scribe said to him: Well said, Teacher. You have spoken the truth that there is one God, and there is no other beside him; [33] and that he should be loved from the whole heart, and from the whole understanding, and from the whole soul, and from the whole strength. And to love one's neighbor as one's self is greater than all holocausts and sacrifices." [34] And Jesus, seeing that he had responded wisely, said to him, "You are not far from the kingdom of God." And after that, no one dared to question him. [35] And while teaching in the temple, Jesus said in answer: "How is it that the scribes say that the Christ is the son of David? [36] For David himself said in the Holy Spirit: 'The Lord said to my Lord: Sit at my right hand, until I set your enemies as your footstool.' [37] Therefore, David himself calls him Lord, and so how can he be his son?" And a great multitude listened to him willingly. [38] And he said to them in his doctrine: "Beware of the scribes, who prefer to walk in long robes and to be greeted in the marketplace, [39] and to sit in the first chairs in the synagogues, and to have the first seats at feasts, [40] who devour the houses of widows under the pretense of long prayers. These shall receive the more extensive judgment." [41] And Jesus, sitting opposite the offertory box, considered the way in which the crowd cast coins into the offertory, and that many of the wealthy cast in a great deal. [42] But when one poor widow had arrived, she put in two small coins, which is a quarter. [43] And calling together his disciples, he said to them: "Amen I say to you, that this poor widow has put in more than all those who contributed to the offertory. [44] For they all gave from their abundance, yet truly, she gave from her scarcity, even all that she had, her entire living."

CHAPTER 13

[1] And as he was departing from the temple, one of his disciples said to him, "Teacher, observe these fine stones and fine structures." [2] And in response, Jesus said to him: "Do you see all these great buildings? There shall not be left stone upon stone, which is not torn down." [3] And as he sat at the Mount of Olives, opposite the temple, Peter, and James, and John, and Andrew questioned him privately. [4] "Tell us, when will these things be, and what will be the sign when all these things will begin to be fulfilled?" [5] And Jesus, answering, began to say to them: "See to it that no one leads you astray. [6] For many will come in my name, saying, 'For I am he,' and they will lead many astray. [7] But when you will have heard of wars and rumors of wars, you should not be afraid. For these things must be, but the end is not so soon. [8] For nation will rise up against nation, and kingdom over kingdom, and there shall be earthquakes in various places, and famines. These are but the beginning of the sorrows. [9] But see to yourselves. For they will hand you over to councils, and in the synagogues you will be beaten, and you shall stand before governors and kings because of me, as a testimony for them. [10] And the Gospel must first be preached to all nations. [11] And when they have seized you and handed you over, do not consider in advance what to say. But whatever will be given you in that hour, say that. For you will not be speaking, but the Holy Spirit. [12] Then brother will betray brother to death, and the father, a son; and children will rise up against their parents and will bring about their death. [13] And you will be hated by all for the sake of my name. But whoever will have persevered unto the end, the same will be saved. [14] Then, when you have seen the abomination of desolation, standing where it ought not to be, let the reader understand: then let those who are in Judea flee to the mountains. [15] And let whoever is on the rooftop not descend to the house, nor enter so as to take anything from the house. [16] And let whoever may be in the field not return to take his garment. [17] But woe to those who are pregnant or nursing in those days. [18] Truly, pray that these things may not happen in winter. [19] For those days shall have such tribulations as have not been since the beginning of the creation that God founded, even until now, and shall not be. [20] And unless the Lord had shortened the days, no flesh would be saved. But, for the sake of the elect, whom he has chosen, he has shortened the days. [21] And then, if anyone will have said to you: 'Behold, here is the Christ. Behold, in that place.' Do not believe it. [22] For false Christs and false prophets will rise up, and they will present signs and wonders, so as to lead astray, if it were possible, even the elect. [23] Therefore, you must take heed. Behold, I have foretold all to you. [24] But in those days, after that tribulation, the sun will be darkened, and the moon will not give her splendor.

25 And the stars of heaven will be falling down, and the powers that are in heaven will be moved. 26 And then they shall see the Son of man arriving on the clouds, with great power and glory. 27 And then he will send his Angels, and gather together his elect, from the four winds, from the limits of the earth, to the limits of heaven. 28 Now from the fig tree discern a parable. When its branch becomes tender and the foliage has been formed, you know that summer is very near. 29 So also, when you will have seen these things happen, know that it is very near, even at the doors. 30 Amen I say to you, that this lineage shall not pass away, until all these things have happened. 31 Heaven and earth shall pass away, but my word shall not pass away. 32 But concerning that day or hour, no one knows, neither the Angels in heaven, nor the Son, but only the Father. 33 Take heed, be vigilant, and pray. For you do not know when the time may be. 34 It is like a man who, setting out on a sojourn, left behind his house, and gave his servants authority over every work, and instructed the doorkeeper to stand watch. 35 Therefore, be vigilant, for you do not know when the lord of the house may arrive: in the evening, or in the middle of the night, or at first light, or in the morning. 36 Otherwise, when he will have arrived unexpectedly, he may find you sleeping. 37 But what I say to you, I say to all: Be vigilant."

CHAPTER 14

1 Now the feast of Passover and of Unleavened Bread was two days away. And the leaders of the priests, and the scribes, were seeking a means by which they might deceitfully seize him and kill him. 2 But they said, "Not on the feast day, lest perhaps there may be a tumult among the people." 3 And when he was in Bethania, in the house of Simon the leper, and was reclining to eat, a woman arrived having an alabaster container of ointment, of precious spikenard. And breaking open the alabaster container, she poured it over his head. 4 But there were some who became indignant within themselves and who were saying: "What is the reason for this waste of the ointment? 5 For this ointment could have been sold for more than three hundred denarii and been given to the poor." And they murmured against her. 6 But Jesus said: "Permit her. What is the reason that you trouble her? She has done a good deed for me. 7 For the poor, you have with you always. And whenever you wish, you are able to do good to them. But you do not have me always. 8 But she has done what she could. She has arrived in advance to anoint my body for burial. 9 Amen I say to you, wherever this Gospel shall be preached throughout the entire world, the things she has done also shall be told, in memory of her." 10 And Judas Iscariot, one of the twelve, went away, to the leaders of the priests, in order to betray him to them. 11 And they, upon hearing it, were gladdened. And they promised him that they would give him money. And he sought an opportune means by which he might betray him. 12 And on the first day of Unleavened Bread, when they immolate the Passover, the disciples said to him, "Where do you want us to go and prepare for you to eat the Passover?" 13 And he sent two of his disciples, and he said to them: "Go into the city. And you will meet a man carrying a pitcher of water; follow him. 14 And wherever he will have entered, say to the owner of the house, 'The Teacher says: Where is my dining room, where I may eat the Passover with my disciples?' 15 And he will show you a large cenacle, fully furnished. And there, you shall prepare it for us." 16 And his disciples departed and went into the city. And they found it just as he had told them. And they prepared the Passover. 17 Then, when evening came, he arrived with the twelve. 18 And while reclining and eating with them at table, Jesus said, "Amen I say to you, that one of you, who eats with me, will betray me." 19 But they began to be sorrowful and to say to him, one at a time: "Is it I?" 20 And he said to them: "It is one of the twelve, who dips his hand with me in the dish. 21 And indeed, the Son of man goes, just as it has been written of him. But woe to that man by whom the Son of man will be betrayed. It would be better for that man if he had never been born." 22 And while eating with them, Jesus took bread. And blessing it, he broke it and gave it to them, and he said: "Take. This is my body." 23 And having taken the chalice, giving thanks, he gave it to them. And they all drank from it. 24 And he said to them: "This is my blood of the new covenant, which shall be shed for many. 25 Amen I say to you, that I will no longer drink from this fruit of the vine, until that day when I will drink it new in the kingdom of God." 26 And having sung a hymn, they went out to the Mount of Olives. 27 And Jesus said to them: "You will all fall away from me in this night. For it has been written: 'I will strike the shepherd, and the sheep will be scattered.' 28 But after I have risen again, I will go before you to Galilee." 29 Then Peter said

to him, "Even if all will have fallen away from you, yet I will not." [30] And Jesus said to him, "Amen I say to you, that this day, in this night, before the rooster has uttered its voice twice, you will deny me three times." [31] But he spoke further, "Even if I must die along with you, I will not deny you." And they all spoke similarly also. [32] And they went to a country estate, by the name of Gethsemani. And he said to his disciples, "Sit here, while I pray." [33] And he took Peter, and James, and John with him. And he began to be afraid and wearied. [34] And he said to them: "My soul is sorrowful, even unto death. Remain here and be vigilant." [35] And when he had proceeded on a little ways, he fell prostrate on the ground. And he prayed that, if it were possible, the hour might pass away from him. [36] And he said: "Abba, Father, all things are possible to you. Take this chalice from me. But let it be, not as I will, but as you will." [37] And he went and found them sleeping. And he said to Peter: "Simon, are you sleeping? Were you not able to be vigilant for one hour? [38] Watch and pray, so that you may not enter into temptation. The spirit indeed is willing, but the flesh is weak." [39] And going away again, he prayed, saying the same words. [40] And upon returning, he found them sleeping yet again, (for their eyes were heavy) and they did not know how to respond to him. [41] And he arrived for the third time, and he said to them: "Sleep now, and take rest. It is enough. The hour has arrived. Behold, the Son of man will be betrayed into the hands of sinners. [42] Rise up, let us go. Behold, he who will betray me is near." [43] And while he was still speaking, Judas Iscariot, one of the twelve, arrived, and with him was a large crowd with swords and clubs, sent from the leaders of the priests, and the scribes, and the elders. [44] Now his betrayer had given them a sign, saying: "He whom I shall kiss, it is he. Take hold of him, and lead him away cautiously." [45] And when he had arrived, immediately drawing near to him, he said: "Hail, Master!" And he kissed him. [46] But they laid hands on him and held him. [47] Then a certain one of those standing near, drawing a sword, struck a servant of the high priest and cut off his ear. [48] And in response, Jesus said to them: "Have you set out to apprehend me, just as if to a robber, with swords and clubs? [49] Daily, I was with you in the temple teaching, and you did not take hold of me. But in this way, the scriptures are fulfilled." [50] Then his disciples, leaving him behind, all fled away. [51] Now a certain young man followed him, having nothing but a fine linen cloth over himself. And they took hold of him. [52] But he, rejecting the fine linen cloth, escaped from them naked. [53] And they led Jesus to the high priest. And all the priests and the scribes and the elders came together. [54] But Peter followed him from a distance, even into the court of the high priest. And he sat with the servants at the fire and warmed himself. [55] Yet truly, the leaders of the priests and the entire council sought testimony against Jesus, so that they might deliver him to death, and they found none. [56] For many spoke false testimony against him, but their testimony did not agree. [57] And certain ones, rising up, bore false witness against him, saying: [58] "For we heard him say, 'I will destroy this temple, made with hands, and within three days I will build another, not made with hands.'" [59] And their testimony did not agree. [60] And the high priest, rising up in their midst, questioned Jesus, saying, "Do you have nothing to say in answer to the things that are brought against you by these ones?" [61] But he was silent and gave no answer. Again, the high priest questioned him, and he said to him, "Are you the Christ, the Son of the Blessed God?" [62] Then Jesus said to him: "I am. And you shall see the Son of man sitting at the right hand of the power of God and arriving with the clouds of heaven." [63] Then the high priest, rending his garments, said: "Why do we still require witnesses? [64] You have heard the blasphemy. How does it seem to you?" And they all condemned him, as guilty unto death. [65] And some began to spit on him, and to cover his face and to strike him with fists, and to say to him, "Prophesy." And the servants struck him with the palms their hands. [66] And while Peter was in the court below, one of the maidservants of the high priest arrived. [67] And when she had seen Peter warming himself, she stared at him, and she said: "You also were with Jesus of Nazareth." [68] But he denied it, saying, "I neither know nor understand what you saying." And he went outside, in front of the court; and a rooster crowed. [69] Then again, when a maidservant had seen him, she began to say to the bystanders, "For this is one of them." [70] But he denied it again. And after a little while, again those standing near said to Peter: "In truth, you are one of them. For you, too, are a Galilean." [71] Then he began to curse and to swear, saying, "For I do not know this man, about whom you are speaking." [72] And immediately the rooster crowed again. And Peter remembered the word that Jesus had said to him, "Before the rooster crows twice, you will deny me three times." And he began to weep.

CHAPTER 15

[1] And immediately in the morning, after the leaders of the priests had taken counsel with the elders and the scribes and the entire council, binding Jesus, they led him away and delivered him to Pilate. [2] And Pilate questioned him, "You are the king of the Jews?" But in response, he said to him, "You are saying it." [3] And the leaders of the priests accused him in many things. [4] Then Pilate again questioned him, saying: "Do you not have any response? See how greatly they accuse you." [5] But Jesus continued to give no response, so that Pilate wondered. [6] Now on the feast day, he was accustomed to release to them one of the prisoners, whomever they requested. [7] But there was one called Barabbas, who had committed murder in the sedition, who was confined with those of the sedition. [8] And when the crowd had ascended, they began to petition him to do as he always did for them. [9] But Pilate answered them and said, "Do you want me to release to you the king of the Jews?" [10] For he knew that it was out of envy that the leaders of the priests had betrayed him. [11] Then the chief priests incited the crowd, so that he would release Barabbas to them instead. [12] But Pilate, responding again, said to them: "Then what do you want me to do with the king of the Jews?" [13] But again they cried out, "Crucify him." [14] Yet truly, Pilate said to them: "Why? What evil has he done?" But they cried out all the more, "Crucify him." [15] Then Pilate, wishing to satisfy the people, released Barabbas to them, and he delivered Jesus, having severely scourged him, to be crucified. [16] Then the soldiers led him away to the court of the praetorium. And they called together the entire cohort. [17] And they clothed him with purple. And platting a crown of thorns, they placed it on him. [18] And they began to salute him: "Hail, king of the Jews." [19] And they struck his head with a reed, and they spit on him. And kneeling down, they reverenced him. [20] And after they had mocked him, they stripped him of the purple, and they clothed him in his own garments. And they led him away, so that they might crucify him. [21] And they compelled a certain passerby, Simon the Cyrenian, who was arriving from the countryside, the father of Alexander and Rufus, to take up his cross. [22] And they led him through to the place called Golgotha, which means, 'the Place of Calvary.' [23] And they gave him wine with myrrh to drink. But he did not accept it. [24] And while crucifying him, they divided his garments, casting lots over them, to see who would take what. [25] Now it was the third hour. And they crucified him. [26] And the title of his case was written as: THE KING OF THE JEWS. [27] And with him they crucified two robbers: one at his right, and the other at his left. [28] And the scripture was fulfilled, which says: "And with the iniquitous he was reputed." [29] And the passersby blasphemed him, shaking their heads and saying, "Ah, you who would destroy the temple of God, and in three days rebuild it, [30] save yourself by descending from the cross." [31] And similarly the leaders of the priests, mocking him with the scribes, said to one another: "He saved others. He is not able to save himself. [32] Let the Christ, the king of Israel, descend now from the cross, so that we may see and believe." Those who were crucified with him also insulted him. [33] And when the sixth hour arrived, a darkness occurred over the entire earth, until the ninth hour. [34] And at the ninth hour, Jesus cried out with a loud voice, saying, "Eloi, Eloi, lamma sabacthani?" which means, "My God, My God, why have you forsaken me?" [35] And some of those standing near, upon hearing this, said, "Behold, he is calling Elijah." [36] Then one of them, running and filling a sponge with vinegar, and placing it around a reed, gave it to him to drink, saying: "Wait. Let us see if Elijah will come to take him down." [37] Then Jesus, having emitted a loud cry, expired. [38] And the veil of the temple was torn in two, from the top to the bottom. [39] Then the centurion who stood opposite him, seeing that he had expired while crying out in this way, said: "Truly, this man was the Son of God." [40] Now there were also women watching from a distance, among whom were Mary Magdalene, and Mary the mother of James the younger and of Joseph, and Salome, [41] (and while he was in Galilee, they followed him and ministered to him) and many other women, who had ascended along with him to Jerusalem. [42] And when evening had now arrived (because it was the Preparation Day, which is before the Sabbath) [43] there arrived Joseph of Arimathea, a noble council member, who himself was also awaiting the kingdom of God. And he boldly entered to Pilate and petitioned for the body of Jesus. [44] But Pilate wondered if he had already died. And summoning a centurion, he questioned him as to whether he was already dead. [45] And when he had been informed by the centurion, he gave the body to Joseph. [46] Then Joseph, having bought a fine linen cloth, and taking him down, wrapped him in the fine linen and laid him in a sepulcher, which was hewn from a rock. And he rolled a stone

to the entrance of the tomb. [47] Now Mary Magdalene and Mary the mother of Joseph observed where he was laid.

CHAPTER 16

[1] And when the Sabbath had passed, Mary Magdalene, and Mary the mother of James, and Salome bought aromatic spices, so that when they arrived they could anoint Jesus. [2] And very early in the morning, on the first of the Sabbaths, they went to the tomb, the sun having now risen. [3] And they said to one another, "Who will roll back the stone for us, away from the entrance of the tomb?" [4] And looking, they saw that the stone was rolled back. For certainly it was very large. [5] And upon entering the tomb, they saw a young man sitting on the right side, covered with a white robe, and they were astonished. [6] And he said to them, "Do not become frightened. You are seeking Jesus of Nazareth, the Crucified One. He has risen. He is not here. Behold, the place where they laid him. [7] But go, tell his disciples and Peter that he is going before you into Galilee. There you shall see him, just as he told you." [8] But they, going out, fled from the tomb. For trembling and fear had overwhelmed them. And they said nothing to anyone. For they were afraid. [9] But he, rising early on the first Sabbath, appeared first to Mary Magdalene, from whom he had cast out seven demons. [10] She went and announced it to those who had been with him, while they were mourning and weeping. [11] And they, upon hearing that he was alive and that he had been seen by her, did not believe it. [12] But after these events, he was shown in another likeness to two of them walking, as they were going out to the countryside. [13] And they, returning, reported it to the others; neither did they believe them. [14] Finally, he appeared to the eleven, as they sat at table. And he rebuked them for their incredulity and hardness of heart, because they did not believe those who had seen that he had risen again. [15] And he said to them: "Go forth to the whole world and preach the Gospel to every creature. [16] Whoever will have believed and been baptized will be saved. Yet truly, whoever will not have believed will be condemned. [17] Now these signs will accompany those who believe. In my name, they shall cast out demons. They will speak in new languages. [18] They will take up serpents, and, if they drink anything deadly, it will not harm them. They shall lay their hands upon the sick, and they will be well." [19] And indeed, the Lord Jesus, after he had spoken to them, was taken up into heaven, and he sits at the right hand of God. [20] Then they, setting out, preached everywhere, with the Lord cooperating and confirming the word by the accompanying signs.

THE SACRED BIBLE:
THE GOSPEL OF LUKE

CHAPTER 1

[1] Since, indeed, many have attempted to set in order a narrative of the things that have been completed among us, [2] just as they have been handed on to those of us who from the beginning saw the same and were ministers of the word, [3] so it seemed good to me also, having diligently followed everything from the beginning, to write to you, in an orderly manner, most excellent Theophilus, [4] so that you might know the truthfulness of those words by which you have been instructed. [5] There was, in the days of Herod, king of Judea, a certain priest named Zechariah, of the section of Abijah, and his wife was of the daughters of Aaron, and her name was Elizabeth. [6] Now they were both just before God, progressing in all of the commandments and the justifications of the Lord without blame. [7] And they had no child, because Elizabeth was barren, and they both had become advanced in years. [8] Then it happened that, when he was exercising the priesthood before God, in the order of his section, [9] according to the custom of the priesthood, the lot fell so that he would offer incense, entering into the temple of the Lord. [10] And the entire multitude of the people was praying outside, at the hour of incense. [11] Then there appeared to him an Angel of the Lord, standing at the right of the altar of incense. [12] And upon seeing him, Zechariah was disturbed, and fear fell over him. [13] But the Angel said to him: "Do not be afraid, Zechariah, for your prayer has been heard, and your wife Elizabeth shall bear a son to you. And you shall call his name John. [14] And there will be joy and exultation for you, and many will rejoice in his nativity. [15] For he will be great in the sight of the Lord, and he will not drink wine or strong drink, and he will be filled with the Holy Spirit, even from his mother's womb. [16] And he will convert many of the sons of Israel to the Lord their God. [17] And he will go before him with the spirit and power of Elijah, so that he may turn the hearts of the fathers to the sons, and the incredulous to the prudence of the just, so as to prepare for the Lord a completed people." [18] And Zechariah said to the Angel: "How may I know this? For I am elderly, and my wife is advanced in years." [19] And in response, the Angel said to him: "I am Gabriel, who stands before God, and I have been sent to speak to you, and to proclaim these things to you. [20] And behold, you will be silent and unable to speak, until the day on which these things shall be, because you have not believed my words, which will be fulfilled in their time." [21] And the people were waiting for Zechariah. And they wondered why he was being delayed in the temple. [22] Then, when he came out, he was unable to speak to them. And they realized that he had seen a vision in the temple. And he was making signs to them, but he remained mute. [23] And it happened that, after the days of his office were completed, he went away to his house. [24] Then, after those days, his wife Elizabeth conceived, and she hid herself for five months, saying: [25] "For the Lord did this for me, at the time when he decided to take away my reproach among men." [26] Then, in the sixth month, the Angel Gabriel was sent by God, to a city of Galilee named Nazareth, [27] to a virgin betrothed to a man whose name was Joseph, of the house of David; and the name of the virgin was Mary. [28] And upon entering, the Angel said to her: "Hail, full of grace. The Lord is with you. Blessed are you among women." [29] And when she had heard this, she was disturbed by his words, and she considered what kind of greeting this might be. [30] And the Angel said to her: "Do not be afraid, Mary, for you have found grace with God. [31] Behold, you shall conceive in your womb, and you shall bear a son, and you shall call his name: JESUS. [32] He will be great, and he will be called the Son of the Most High, and the Lord God will give him the throne of David his father. And he will reign in the house of Jacob for eternity. [33] And his kingdom shall have no end." [34] Then Mary said to the Angel, "How shall this be done, since I do not know man?" [35] And in response, the Angel said to her: "The Holy Spirit will pass over you, and the power of the Most High will overshadow you. And because of this also, the Holy One who will be born of you shall be called the Son of God. [36] And behold, your cousin Elizabeth has herself also conceived a son, in her old age. And this is the sixth month for her who is called barren. [37] For no word will be impossible with God." [38] Then Mary said: "Behold, I am the handmaid of the Lord. Let it be done to me according to your word." And the Angel departed from her. [39] And in those days, Mary, rising up, traveled quickly into the hill country, to a city of Judah. [40] And she entered into the house of Zechariah, and she greeted Elizabeth.

[41] And it happened that, as Elizabeth heard the greeting of Mary, the infant leaped in her womb, and Elizabeth was filled with the Holy Spirit. [42] And she cried out with a loud voice and said: "Blessed are you among women, and blessed is the fruit of your womb. [43] And how does this concern me, so that the mother of my Lord would come to me? [44] For behold, as the voice of your greeting came to my ears, the infant in my womb leaped for joy. [45] And blessed are you who believed, for the things that were spoken to you by the Lord shall be accomplished." [46] And Mary said: "My soul magnifies the Lord. [47] And my spirit leaps for joy in God my Savior. [48] For he has looked with favor on the humility of his handmaid. For behold, from this time, all generations shall call me blessed. [49] For he who is great has done great things for me, and holy is his name. [50] And his mercy is from generation to generations for those who fear him. [51] He has accomplished powerful deeds with his arm. He has scattered the arrogant in the intentions of their heart. [52] He has deposed the powerful from their seat, and he has exalted the humble. [53] He has filled the hungry with good things, and the rich he has sent away empty. [54] He has taken up his servant Israel, mindful of his mercy, [55] just as he spoke to our fathers: to Abraham and to his offspring forever." [56] Then Mary stayed with her for about three months. And she returned to her own house. [57] Now the time for Elizabeth to give birth arrived, and she brought forth a son. [58] And her neighbors and relatives heard that the Lord had magnified his mercy with her, and so they congratulated her. [59] And it happened that, on the eighth day, they arrived to circumcise the boy, and they called him by his father's name, Zechariah. [60] And in response, his mother said: "Not so. Instead, he shall be called John." [61] And they said to her, "But there is no one among your relatives who is called by that name." [62] Then they made signs to his father, as to what he wanted him to be called. [63] And requesting a writing tablet, he wrote, saying: "His name is John." And they all wondered. [64] Then, at once, his mouth was opened, and his tongue loosened, and he spoke, blessing God. [65] And fear fell upon all of their neighbors. And all these words were made known throughout all the hill country of Judea. [66] And all those who heard it stored it up in their heart, saying: "What do you think this boy will be?" And indeed, the hand of the Lord was with him. [67] And his father Zechariah was filled with the Holy Spirit. And he prophesied, saying: [68] "Blessed is the Lord God of Israel. For he has visited and has wrought the redemption of his people. [69] And he has raised up a horn of salvation for us, in the house of David his servant, [70] just as he spoke by the mouth of his holy Prophets, who are from ages past: [71] salvation from our enemies, and from the hand of all those who hate us, [72] to accomplish mercy with our fathers, and to call to mind his holy testament, [73] the oath, which he swore to Abraham, our father, that he would grant to us, [74] so that, having been freed from the hand of our enemies, we may serve him without fear, [75] in holiness and in justice before him, throughout all our days. [76] And you, child, shall be called the prophet of the Most High. For you will go before the face of the Lord: to prepare his ways, [77] to give knowledge of salvation to his people for the remission of their sins, [78] through the heart of the mercy of our God, by which, descending from on high, he has visited us, [79] to illuminate those who sit in darkness and in the shadow of death, and to direct our feet in the way of peace." [80] And the child grew, and he was strengthened in spirit. And he was in the wilderness, until the day of his manifestation to Israel.

CHAPTER 2

[1] And it happened in those days that a decree went out from Caesar Augustus, so that the whole world would be enrolled. [2] This was the first enrollment; it was made by the ruler of Syria, Quirinius. [3] And all went to be declared, each one to his own city. [4] Then Joseph also ascended from Galilee, from the city of Nazareth, into Judea, to the city of David, which is called Bethlehem, because he was of the house and family of David, [5] in order to be declared, with Mary his espoused wife, who was with child. [6] Then it happened that, while they were there, the days were completed, so that she would give birth. [7] And she brought forth her firstborn son. And she wrapped him in swaddling clothes and laid him in a manger, because there was no room for them at the inn. [8] And there were shepherds in the same region, being vigilant and keeping watch in the night over their flock. [9] And behold, an Angel of the Lord stood near them, and the brightness of God shone around them, and they were struck with a great fear. [10] And the Angel said to them: "Do not be afraid. For, behold, I proclaim to you a great joy, which will be for all the people. [11] For today a Savior has been born for you in the city of David: he is Christ the Lord. [12] And this will be a sign for

you: you will find the infant wrapped in swaddling clothes and lying in a manger." [13] And suddenly there was with the Angel a multitude of the celestial army, praising God and saying, [14] "Glory to God in the highest, and on earth peace to men of good will." [15] And it happened that, when the Angels had departed from them into heaven, the shepherds said to one another, "Let us cross over to Bethlehem and see this word, which has happened, which the Lord has revealed to us." [16] And they went quickly. And they found Mary and Joseph; and the infant was lying in a manger. [17] Then, upon seeing this, they understood the word that had been spoken to them about this boy. [18] And all who heard it were amazed by this, and by those things which were told to them by the shepherds. [19] But Mary kept all these words, pondering them in her heart. [20] And the shepherds returned, glorifying and praising God for all the things that they had heard and seen, just as it was told to them. [21] And after eight days were ended, so that the boy would be circumcised, his name was called JESUS, just as he was called by the Angel before he was conceived in the womb. [22] And after the days of her purification were fulfilled, according to the law of Moses, they brought him to Jerusalem, in order to present him to the Lord, [23] just as it is written in the law of the Lord, "For every male opening the womb shall be called holy to the Lord," [24] and in order to offer a sacrifice, according to what is said in the law of the Lord, "a pair of turtledoves or two young pigeons." [25] And behold, there was a man in Jerusalem, whose name was Simeon, and this man was just and God-fearing, awaiting the consolation of Israel. And the Holy Spirit was with him. [26] And he had received an answer from the Holy Spirit: that he would not see his own death before he had seen the Christ of the Lord. [27] And he went with the Spirit to the temple. And when the child Jesus was brought in by his parents, in order to act on his behalf according to the custom of the law, [28] he also took him up, into his arms, and he blessed God and said: [29] "Now you may dismiss your servant in peace, O Lord, according to your word. [30] For my eyes have seen your salvation, [31] which you have prepared before the face of all peoples: [32] the light of revelation to the nations and the glory of your people Israel." [33] And his father and mother were wondering over these things, which were spoken about him. [34] And Simeon blessed them, and he said to his mother Mary: "Behold, this one has been set for the ruin and for the resurrection of many in Israel, and as a sign which will be contradicted. [35] And a sword will pass through your own soul, so that the thoughts of many hearts may be revealed." [36] And there was a prophetess, Anna, a daughter of Phanuel, from the tribe of Asher. She was very advanced in years, and she had lived with her husband for seven years from her virginity. [37] And then she was a widow, even to her eighty-fourth year. And without departing from the temple, she was a servant to fasting and prayer, night and day. [38] And entering at the same hour, she confessed to the Lord. And she spoke about him to all who were awaiting the redemption of Israel. [39] And after they had performed all things according to the law of the Lord, they returned to Galilee, to their city, Nazareth. [40] Now the child grew, and he was strengthened with the fullness of wisdom. And the grace of God was in him. [41] And his parents went every year to Jerusalem, at the time of the solemnity of Passover. [42] And when he had become twelve years old, they ascended to Jerusalem, according to the custom of the feast day. [43] And having completed the days, when they returned, the boy Jesus remained in Jerusalem. And his parents did not realize this. [44] But, supposing that he was in the company, they went a day's journey, seeking him among their relatives and acquaintances. [45] And not finding him, they returned to Jerusalem, seeking him. [46] And it happened that, after three days, they found him in the temple, sitting in the midst of the doctors, listening to them and questioning them. [47] But all who listened to him were astonished over his prudence and his responses. [48] And upon seeing him, they wondered. And his mother said to him: "Son, why have you acted this way toward us? Behold, your father and I were seeking you in sorrow." [49] And he said to them: "How is it that you were seeking me? For did you not know that it is necessary for me to be in these things which are of my Father?" [50] And they did not understand the word that he spoke to them. [51] And he descended with them and went to Nazareth. And he was subordinate to them. And his mother kept all these words in her heart. [52] And Jesus advanced in wisdom, and in age, and in grace, with God and men.

CHAPTER 3

[1] Then, in the fifteenth year of the reign of Tiberius Caesar, Pontius Pilate being procurator of Judea, and Herod tetrarch of Galilee, and his brother Philip tetrarch

of Ituraea and of the region of Trachonitis, and Lysanias tetrarch of Abilene, [2] under the high priests Annas and Caiaphas: the word of the Lord came to John, the son of Zechariah, in the wilderness. [3] And he went into the entire region of the Jordan, preaching a baptism of repentance for the remission of sins, [4] just as it has been written in the book of the sermons of the prophet Isaiah: "The voice of one crying out in the wilderness: Prepare the way of the Lord. Make straight his paths. [5] Every valley shall be filled, and every mountain and hill shall be brought low. And what is crooked shall be made straight. And the rough paths shall be made into level ways. [6] And all flesh shall see the salvation of God." [7] Therefore, he said to the crowd that went out in order to be baptized by him: "You progeny of vipers! Who told you to flee from the approaching wrath? [8] So then, produce fruits worthy of repentance. And do not begin to say, 'We have Abraham as our father.' For I tell you that God has the power to raise up sons to Abraham from these stones. [9] For even now the axe has been placed at the root of the trees. Therefore, every tree that does not produce good fruit shall be cut down and cast into the fire." [10] And the crowed was questioning him, saying, "What then should we do?" [11] But in response, he said to them: "Whoever has two coats, let him give to those who do not have. And whoever has food, let him act similarly." [12] Now the tax collectors also came to be baptized, and they said to him, "Teacher, what should we do?" [13] But he said to them, "You should do nothing more than what has been appointed to you." [14] Then the soldiers also questioned him, saying, "And what should we do?" And he said to them: "You should strike no one, and you should not make false accusations. And be content with your pay." [15] Now all were thinking about John in their hearts, and the people were supposing that perhaps he might be the Christ. [16] John responded by saying to everyone: "Indeed, I baptize you with water. But there will arrive one stronger than me, the laces of whose shoes I am not worthy to loosen. He will baptize you in the Holy Spirit, and with fire. [17] His winnowing fan is in his hand. And he will purify his threshing floor. And he will gather the wheat into the barn. But the chaff he will burn with unquenchable fire." [18] Indeed, he also proclaimed many other things, exhorting the people. [19] But Herod the tetrarch, when he was corrected by him concerning Herodias, his brother's wife, and concerning all the evils that Herod had done, [20] added this also, above all else: that he confined John to prison. [21] Now it happened that, when all the people were being baptized, Jesus was baptized; and as he was praying, heaven was opened. [22] And the Holy Spirit, in a corporal appearance like a dove, descended upon him. And a voice came from heaven: "You are my beloved Son. In you, I am well pleased." [23] And Jesus himself was beginning to be about thirty years old, being (as it was supposed) the son of Joseph, who was of Heli, who was of Matthat, [24] who was of Levi, who was of Melchi, who was of Jannai, who was of Joseph, [25] who was of Mattathias, who was of Amos, who was of Nahum, who was of Esli, who was of Naggai, [26] who was of Maath, who was of Mattathias, who was of Semein, who was of Josech, who was of Joda, [27] who was of Joanan, who was of Rhesa, who was of Zerubbabel, who was of Shealtiel, who was of Neri, [28] who was of Melchi, who was of Addi, who was of Cosam, who was of Elmadam, who was of Er, [29] who was of Joshua, who was of Eliezer, who was of Jorim, who was of Matthat, who was of Levi, [30] who was of Simeon, who was of Judah, who was of Joseph, who was of Jonam, who was of Eliakim, [31] who was of Melea, who was of Menna, who was of Mattatha, who was of Nathan, who was of David, [32] who was of Jesse, who was of Obed, who was of Boaz, who was of Salmon, who was of Nahshon, [33] who was of Amminadab, who was of Aram, who was of Hezron, who was of Perez, who was of Judah, [34] who was of Jacob, who was of Isaac, who was of Abraham, who was of Terah, who was of Nahor, [35] who was of Serug, who was of Reu, who was of Peleg, who was of Eber, who was of Shelah, [36] who was of Cainan, who was of Arphaxad, who was of Shem, who was of Noah, who was of Lamech, [37] who was of Methuselah, who was of Enoch, who was of Jared, who was of Mahalalel, who was of Cainan, [38] who was of Enos, who was of Seth, who was of Adam, who was of God.

CHAPTER 4

[1] And Jesus, filled with the Holy Spirit, returned from the Jordan. And he was urged by the Spirit into the wilderness [2] for forty days, and he was tested by the devil. And he ate nothing in those days. And when they were completed, he was hungry. [3] Then the devil said to him, "If you are the Son of God, speak to this stone, so that it may be made into bread." [4] And Jesus answered him, "It is

written: 'Man shall not live by bread alone, but by every word of God.'" ⁵ And the devil led him onto a high mountain, and he showed him all the kingdoms of the world in a moment of time, ⁶ and he said to him: "To you, I will give all this power, and its glory. For they have been handed over to me, and I give them to whomever I wish. ⁷ Therefore, if you will worship before me, all will be yours." ⁸ And in response, Jesus said to him: "It is written: 'You shall worship the Lord your God, and you shall serve him alone.'" ⁹ And he brought him to Jerusalem, and he set him on the parapet of the temple, and he said to him: "If you are the Son of God, cast yourself down from here. ¹⁰ For it is written that he has given his Angels charge over you, so that they may guard you, ¹¹ and so that they may take you into their hands, lest perhaps you may hurt your foot against a stone." ¹² And in response, Jesus said to him, "It is said: 'You shall not tempt the Lord your God.'" ¹³ And when all the temptation was completed, the devil withdrew from him, until a time. ¹⁴ And Jesus returned, in the power of the Spirit, into Galilee. And his fame spread throughout the entire region. ¹⁵ And he taught in their synagogues, and he was magnified by everyone. ¹⁶ And he went to Nazareth, where he had been raised. And he entered into the synagogue, according to his custom, on the Sabbath day. And he rose up to read. ¹⁷ And the book of the prophet Isaiah was handed to him. And as he unrolled the book, he found the place where it was written: ¹⁸ "The Spirit of the Lord is upon me; because of this, he has anointed me. He has sent me to evangelize the poor, to heal the contrite of heart, ¹⁹ to preach forgiveness to captives and sight to the blind, to release the broken into forgiveness, to preach the acceptable year of the Lord and the day of retribution." ²⁰ And when he had rolled up the book, he returned it to the minister, and he sat down. And the eyes of everyone in the synagogue were fixed on him. ²¹ Then he began to say to them, "On this day, this scripture has been fulfilled in your hearing." ²² And everyone gave testimony to him. And they wondered at the words of grace that proceeded from his mouth. And they said, "Is this not the son of Joseph?" ²³ And he said to them: "Certainly, you will recite to me this saying, 'Physician, heal yourself.' The many great things that we have heard were done in Capernaum, do here also in your own country." ²⁴ Then he said: "Amen I say to you, that no prophet is accepted in his own country. ²⁵ In truth, I say to you, there were many widows in the days of Elijah in Israel, when the heavens were closed for three years and six months, when a great famine had occurred throughout the entire land. ²⁶ And to none of these was Elijah sent, except to Zarephath of Sidon, to a woman who was a widow. ²⁷ And there were many lepers in Israel under the prophet Elisha. And none of these was cleansed, except Naaman the Syrian." ²⁸ And all those in the synagogue, upon hearing these things, were filled with anger. ²⁹ And they rose up and drove him beyond the city. And they brought him all the way to the edge of the mount, upon which their city had been built, so that they might throw him down violently. ³⁰ But passing through their midst, he went away. ³¹ And he descended to Capernaum, a city of Galilee. And there he taught them on the Sabbaths. ³² And they were astonished at his doctrine, for his word was spoken with authority. ³³ And in the synagogue, there was a man who had an unclean demon, and he cried out with a loud voice, ³⁴ saying: "Let us alone. What are we to you, Jesus of Nazareth? Have you come to destroy us? I know you who you are: the Holy One of God." ³⁵ And Jesus rebuked him, saying, "Be silent and depart from him." And when the demon had thrown him into their midst, he departed from him, and he no longer harmed him. ³⁶ And fear fell over them all. And they discussed this among themselves, saying: "What is this word? For with authority and power he commands the unclean spirits, and they depart." ³⁷ And his fame spread to every place in the region. ³⁸ Then Jesus, rising up from the synagogue, entered into the house of Simon. Now Simon's mother-in-law was in the grip of a severe fever. And they petitioned him on her behalf. ³⁹ And standing over her, he commanded the fever, and it left her. And promptly rising up, she ministered to them. ⁴⁰ Then, when the sun had set, all those who had anyone afflicted with various diseases brought them to him. Then, laying his hands on each one of them, he cured them. ⁴¹ Now demons departed from many of them, crying out and saying, "You are the son of God." And rebuking them, he would not permit them to speak. For they knew him to be the Christ. ⁴² Then, when it was daytime, going out, he went to a deserted place. And the crowds sought him, and they went all the way to him. And they detained him, so that he would not depart from them. ⁴³ And he said to them, "I must also preach the kingdom of God to other cities, because it was for this reason that I was sent." ⁴⁴ And he was preaching in the synagogues of Galilee.

CHAPTER 5

[1] Now it happened that, when the crowds pressed toward him, so that they might hear the word of God, he was standing beside the lake of Genesaret. [2] And he saw two boats standing beside the lake. But the fishermen had climbed down, and they were washing their nets. [3] And so, climbing into one of the boats, which belonged to Simon, he asked him to draw back a little from the land. And sitting down, he taught the crowds from the boat. [4] Then, when he had ceased speaking, he said to Simon, "Lead us into deep water, and release your nets for a catch." [5] And in response, Simon said to him: "Teacher, working throughout the night, we caught nothing. But on your word, I will release the net." [6] And when they had done this, they enclosed such a copious multitude of fish that their net was rupturing. [7] And they signaled to their associates, who were in the other boat, so that they would come and help them. And they came and filled both boats, so that they were nearly submerged. [8] But when Simon Peter had seen this, he fell down at the knees of Jesus, saying, "Depart from me, Lord, for I am a sinful man." [9] For astonishment had enveloped him, and all who were with him, at the catch of fish that they had taken. [10] Now the same was true of James and John, the sons of Zebedee, who were associates of Simon. And Jesus said to Simon: "Do not be afraid. From now on, you will be catching men." [11] And having led their boats to land, leaving behind everything, they followed him. [12] And it happened that, while he was in a certain city, behold, there was a man full of leprosy who, upon seeing Jesus and falling to his face, petitioned him, saying: "Lord, if you are willing, you are able to cleanse me." [13] And extending his hand, he touched him, saying: "I am willing. Be cleansed." And at once, the leprosy departed from him. [14] And he instructed him that he should tell no one, "But go, show yourself to the priest, and make the offering for your cleansing, just as Moses has commanded, as a testimony for them." [15] Yet word of him traveled around all the more. And great crowds came together, so that they might listen and be cured by him from their infirmities. [16] And he withdrew into the desert and prayed. [17] And it happened, on a certain day, that he again sat down, teaching. And there were Pharisees and doctors of the law sitting nearby, who had come from every town of Galilee and Judea and Jerusalem. And the power of the Lord was present, to heal them. [18] And behold, some men were carrying in the bed of a man who was paralyzed. And they sought a way to bring him in, and to place him before him. [19] And not finding a way by which they might bring him in, because of the crowd, they climbed up to the roof, and they let him down through the roof tiles with his bed, into their midst, in front of Jesus. [20] And when he saw his faith, he said, "Man, your sins are forgiven you." [21] And the scribes and Pharisees began to think, saying: "Who is this, who is speaking blasphemies? Who is able to forgive sins, except God alone?" [22] But when Jesus realized their thoughts, responding, he said to them: "What are you thinking in your hearts? [23] Which is easier to say: 'Your sins are forgiven you,' or to say, 'Rise up and walk?' [24] But so that you may know that the Son of man has authority on earth to forgive sins," he said to the paralytic, "I say to you to: Rise up, take up your bed, and go into your house." [25] And at once, rising up in their sight, he took up the bed on which he was lying, and he went away to his own house, magnifying God. [26] And astonishment took hold of everyone, and they were magnifying God. And they were filled with fear, saying: "For we have seen miracles today." [27] And after these things, he went out, and he saw a tax collector named Levi, sitting at the customs office. And he said to him, "Follow me." [28] And leaving behind everything, rising up, he followed him. [29] And Levi made a great feast for him in his own house. And there was a large crowd of tax collectors and others, who were sitting at table with them. [30] But the Pharisees and scribes were murmuring, saying to his disciples, "Why do you eat and drink with tax collectors and sinners?" [31] And responding, Jesus said to them: "It is not those who are well who need a doctor, but those who have maladies. [32] I have not come to call the just, but sinners to repentance." [33] But they said to him, "Why do the disciples of John fast frequently, and make supplications, and those of the Pharisees act similarly, while yours eat and drink?" [34] And he said to them: "How can you cause the sons of the groom to fast, while the groom is still with them? [35] But the days will come when the groom will be taken away from them, and then they will fast, in those days." [36] Then he also made a comparison for them: "For no one sews a patch from a new garment onto an old garment. Otherwise, he both disrupts the new one, and the patch from the new one does not join together with the old one. [37] And no one puts new wine into old wineskins. Otherwise, the new wine ruptures the wineskins, and it will

be poured out, and the wineskins will be lost. ³⁸ Instead, the new wine is put into new wineskins, and both are preserved. ³⁹ And no one who is drinking the old, soon wishes for the new. For he says, 'The old is better.'"

CHAPTER 6

¹ Now it happened that, on the second first Sabbath, as he passed through the grain field, his disciples were separating the ears of grain and eating them, by rubbing them in their hands. ² Then certain Pharisees said to them, "Why are you doing what is not lawful on the Sabbaths?" ³ And responding to them, Jesus said: "Have you not read this, what David did when he was hungry, and those who were with him? ⁴ How he entered into the house of God, and took the bread of the Presence, and ate it, and gave it to those who were with him, though it is not lawful for anyone to eat it, except the priests alone?" ⁵ And he said to them, "For the Son of man is Lord, even of the Sabbath." ⁶ And it happened that, on another Sabbath, he entered into the synagogue, and he taught. And there was a man there, and his right hand was withered. ⁷ And the scribes and Pharisees observed whether he would heal on the Sabbath, so that they might thereby find an accusation against him. ⁸ Yet truly, he knew their thoughts, and so he said to the man who had the withered hand, "Rise up and stand in the middle." And rising up, he stood still. ⁹ Then Jesus said to them: "I ask you if it is lawful on the Sabbaths to do good, or to do evil? To give health to a life, or to destroy it?" ¹⁰ And looking around at everyone, he said to the man, "Extend your hand." And he extended it. And his hand was restored. ¹¹ Then they were filled with madness, and they discussed with one another, what, in particular, they might do about Jesus. ¹² And it happened that, in those days, he went out to a mountain to pray. And he was in the prayer of God throughout the night. ¹³ And when daylight had arrived, he called his disciples. And he chose twelve out of them (whom he also named Apostles): ¹⁴ Simon, whom he surnamed Peter, and Andrew his brother, James and John, Philip and Bartholomew, ¹⁵ Matthew and Thomas, James of Alphaeus, and Simon who is called the Zealot, ¹⁶ and Jude of James, and Judas Iscariot, who was a traitor. ¹⁷ And descending with them, he stood in a level place with a multitude of his disciples, and a copious multitude of people from all of Judea and Jerusalem and the seacoast, and Tyre and Sidon, ¹⁸ who had come so that they might listen to him and be healed of their diseases. And those who were troubled by unclean spirits were cured. ¹⁹ And the entire crowd was trying to touch him, because power went out from him and healed all. ²⁰ And lifting up his eyes to his disciples, he said: "Blessed are you poor, for yours is the kingdom of God. ²¹ Blessed are you who are hungry now, for you shall be satisfied. Blessed are you who are weeping now, for you shall laugh. ²² Blessed shall you be when men will have hated you, and when they will have separated you and reproached you, and thrown out your name as if evil, because of the Son of man. ²³ Be glad in that day and exult. For behold, your reward is great in heaven. For these same things their fathers did to the prophets. ²⁴ Yet truly, woe to you who are wealthy, for you have your consolation. ²⁵ Woe to you who are satisfied, for you will be hungry. Woe to you who laugh now, for you will mourn and weep. ²⁶ Woe to you when men will have blessed you. For these same things their fathers did to the false prophets. ²⁷ But I say to you who are listening: Love your enemies. Do good to those who hate you. ²⁸ Bless those who curse you, and pray for those who slander you. ²⁹ And to him who strikes you on the cheek, offer the other also. And from him who takes away your coat, do not withhold even your tunic. ³⁰ But distribute to all who ask of you. And do not ask again of him who takes away what is yours. ³¹ And exactly as you would want people to treat you, treat them also the same. ³² And if you love those who love you, what credit is due to you? For even sinners love those who love them. ³³ And if you will do good to those who do good to you, what credit is due to you? Indeed, even sinners behave this way. ³⁴ And if you will loan to those from whom you hope to receive, what credit is due to you? For even sinners lend to sinners, in order to receive the same in return. ³⁵ So truly, love your enemies. Do good, and lend, hoping for nothing in return. And then your reward will be great, and you will be sons of the Most High, for he himself is kind to the ungrateful and to the wicked. ³⁶ Therefore, be merciful, just as your Father is also merciful. ³⁷ Do not judge, and you will not be judged. Do not condemn, and you will not be condemned. Forgive, and you will be forgiven. ³⁸ Give, and it will be given to you: a good measure, pressed down and shaken together and overflowing, they will place upon your lap. Certainly, the same measure that you use to measure out, will be used to measure back to you

again." ³⁹ Now he told them another comparison: "How can the blind lead the blind? Would they not both fall into a pit? ⁴⁰ The disciple is not above his teacher. But each one will be perfected, if he is like his teacher. ⁴¹ And why do you see the straw that is in your brother's eye, while the log that is in your own eye, you do not consider? ⁴² Or how can you say to your brother, 'Brother, allow me to remove the straw from your eye,' while you yourself do not see the log in your own eye? Hypocrite, first remove the log from your own eye, and then will you see clearly, so that you may lead out the straw from your brother's eye. ⁴³ For there is no good tree which produces bad fruit, nor does an evil tree produce good fruit. ⁴⁴ For each and every tree is known by its fruit. For they do not gather figs from thorns, nor do they gather the grape from the bramble bush. ⁴⁵ A good man, from the good storehouse of his heart, offers what is good. And an evil man, from the evil storehouse, offers what is evil. For out of the abundance of the heart, the mouth speaks. ⁴⁶ But why do you call me, 'Lord, Lord,' and not do what I say? ⁴⁷ Anyone who comes to me, and listens to my words, and does them: I will reveal to you what he is like. ⁴⁸ He is like a man building a house, who has dug deep and has laid the foundation upon the rock. Then, when the floodwaters came, the river was rushing against that house, and it was not able to move it. For it was founded upon the rock. ⁴⁹ But whoever hears and does not do: he is like a man building his house upon the soil, without a foundation. The river rushed against it, and it soon fell down, and the ruin of that house was great."

CHAPTER 7

¹ And when he had completed all his words in the hearing of the people, he entered Capernaum. ² Now the servant of a certain centurion was dying, due to an illness. And he was very dear to him. ³ And when he had heard about Jesus, he sent elders of the Jews to him, petitioning him, so that he would come and heal his servant. ⁴ And when they had come to Jesus, they petitioned him anxiously, saying to him: "He is worthy that you should provide this to him. ⁵ For he loves our nation, and he has built a synagogue for us." ⁶ Then Jesus went with them. And when he was now not far from the house, the centurion sent friends to him, saying: "Lord, do not trouble yourself. For I am not worthy that you should enter under my roof. ⁷ Because of this, I also did not consider myself worthy to come to you. But say the word, and my servant shall be healed. ⁸ For I also am a man placed under authority, having soldiers under me. And I say to one, 'Go,' and he goes; and to another, 'Come,' and he comes; and to my servant, 'Do this,' and he does it." ⁹ And upon hearing this, Jesus was amazed. And turning to the multitude following him, he said, "Amen I say to you, not even in Israel have I found such great faith." ¹⁰ And those who had been sent, upon returning to the house, found that the servant, who had been sick, was now healthy. ¹¹ And it happened afterwards that he went to a city, which is called Nain. And his disciples, and an abundant crowd, went with him. ¹² Then, when he had drawn near to the gate of the city, behold, a deceased person was being carried out, the only son of his mother, and she was a widow. And a large crowd from the city was with her. ¹³ And when the Lord had seen her, being moved by mercy over her, he said to her, "Do not weep." ¹⁴ And he drew near and touched the coffin. Then those who carried it stood still. And he said, "Young man, I say to you, arise." ¹⁵ And the dead youth sat up and began to speak. And he gave him to his mother. ¹⁶ Then fear fell over all of them. And they magnified God, saying: "For a great prophet has risen up among us," and, "For God has visited his people." ¹⁷ And this word about him went out to all of Judea and to the entire surrounding region. ¹⁸ And the disciples of John reported to him concerning all these things. ¹⁹ And John called two of his disciples, and he sent them to Jesus, saying, "Are you he who is to come, or should we wait for another?" ²⁰ But when the men had come to him, they said: "John the Baptist has sent us to you, saying: 'Are you he who is to come, or should we wait for another?'" ²¹ Now in that same hour, he cured many of their diseases and wounds and evil spirits; and to many of the blind, he gave sight. ²² And responding, he said to them: "Go and report to John what you have heard and seen: that the blind see, the lame walk, the lepers are cleansed, the deaf hear, the dead rise again, the poor are evangelized. ²³ And blessed is anyone who has not taken offense at me." ²⁴ And when the messengers of John had withdrawn, he began to speak about John to the crowds. "What did you go out to the desert to see? A reed shaken by the wind? ²⁵ Then what did you go out to see? A man clothed in soft garments? Behold, those who are in costly apparel and finery are in the houses of kings. ²⁶ Then what did you go out to see? A prophet? Certainly,

I tell you, and more than a prophet. ²⁷This is he of whom it is written: "Behold, I send my Angel before your face, who shall prepare your way before you." ²⁸For I say to you, among those born of women, no one is greater than the prophet John the Baptist. But he who is least in the kingdom of God is greater than he." ²⁹And upon hearing this, all the people and the tax collectors justified God, by being baptized with the baptism of John. ³⁰But the Pharisees and the experts in the law despised the counsel of God concerning themselves, by not being baptized by him. ³¹Then the Lord said: "Therefore, to what shall I compare the men of this generation? And to what are they similar? ³²They are like children sitting in the marketplace, talking with one another, and saying: 'We sang to you, and you did not dance. We lamented, and you did not weep.' ³³For John the Baptist came, neither eating bread nor drinking wine, and you say, 'He has a demon.' ³⁴The Son of man came, eating and drinking, and you say, 'Behold, a voracious man and a drinker of wine, a friend of tax collectors and of sinners.' ³⁵But wisdom is justified by all her children." ³⁶Then certain Pharisees petitioned him, so that they might eat with him. And he went into the house of the Pharisee, and he reclined at table. ³⁷And behold, a woman who was in the city, a sinner, found out that he was reclining at table in the house of the Pharisee, so she brought an alabaster container of ointment. ³⁸And standing behind him, beside his feet, she began to wash his feet with tears, and she wiped them with the hair of her head, and she kissed his feet, and she anointed them with ointment. ³⁹Then the Pharisee, who had invited him, upon seeing this, spoke within himself, saying, "This man, if he were a prophet, would certainly know who and what kind of woman is this, who is touching him: that she is a sinner." ⁴⁰And in response, Jesus said to him, "Simon, I have something to say to you." So he said, "Speak, Teacher." ⁴¹"A certain creditor had two debtors: one owed five hundred denarii, and the other fifty. ⁴²And since they did not have the ability to repay him, he forgave them both. So then, which of them loves him more?" ⁴³In response, Simon said, "I suppose that it is he to whom he forgave the most." And he said to him, "You have judged correctly." ⁴⁴And turning to the woman, he said to Simon: "Do you see this woman? I entered into your house. You gave me no water for my feet. But she has washed my feet with tears, and has wiped them with her hair. ⁴⁵You gave no kiss to me. But she, from the time that she entered, has not ceased to kiss my feet. ⁴⁶You did not anoint my head with oil. But she has anointed my feet with ointment. ⁴⁷Because of this, I tell you: many sins are forgiven her, because she has loved much. But he who is forgiven less, loves less." ⁴⁸Then he said to her, "Your sins are forgiven you." ⁴⁹And those who sat at table with him began to say within themselves, "Who is this, who even forgives sins?" ⁵⁰Then he said to the woman: "Your faith has brought you salvation. Go in peace."

CHAPTER 8

¹And it happened afterwards that he was making a journey through the cities and towns, preaching and evangelizing the kingdom of God. And the twelve were with him, ²along with certain women who had been healed of evil spirits and infirmities: Mary, who is called Magdalene, from whom seven demons had departed, ³and Joanna, the wife of Chuza, Herod's steward, and Susanna, and many other women, who were ministering to him from their resources. ⁴Then, when a very numerous crowd was gathering together and hurrying from the cities to him, he spoke using a comparison: ⁵"The sower went out to sow his seed. And as he sowed, some fell beside the way; and it was trampled and the birds of the air devoured it. ⁶And some fell upon rock; and having sprung up, it withered away, because it had no moisture. ⁷And some fell among thorns; and the thorns, rising up with it, suffocated it. ⁸And some fell upon good soil; and having sprung up, it produced fruit one hundredfold." As he said these things, he cried out, "Whoever has ears to hear, let him hear." ⁹Then his disciples questioned him as to what this parable might mean. ¹⁰And he said to them: "To you it has been given to know the mystery of the kingdom of God. But to the rest, it is in parables, so that: seeing, they may not perceive, and hearing, they may not understand. ¹¹Now the parable is this: The seed is the word of God. ¹²And those beside the way are those who hear it, but then the devil comes and takes the word from their heart, lest by believing it they may be saved. ¹³Now those upon rock are those who, when they hear it, accept the word with joy, but these have no roots. So they believe for a time, but in a time of testing, they fall away. ¹⁴And those which fell among thorns are those who have heard it, but as they go along, they are suffocated by the concerns and riches and pleasures of this life, and so they

do not yield fruit. [15] But those which were on good soil are those who, upon hearing the word with a good and noble heart, retain it, and they bring forth fruit in patience. [16] Now no one, lighting a candle, covers it with a container, or sets it under a bed. Instead, he places it on a lampstand, so that those who enter may see the light. [17] For there is nothing secret, which will not be made clear, nor is there anything hidden, which will not be known and be brought into plain sight. [18] Therefore, take care how you listen. For whoever has, it will be given to him; and whoever does not have, even what he thinks he has will be taken away from him." [19] Then his mother and brothers came to him; but they were not able to go to him because of the crowd. [20] And it was reported to him, "Your mother and your brothers are standing outside, wanting to see you." [21] And in response, he said to them, "My mother and my brothers are those who hear the word of God and do it." [22] Now it happened, on a certain day, that he climbed into a little boat with his disciples. And he said to them, "Let us make a crossing over the lake." And they embarked. [23] And as they were sailing, he slept. And a windstorm descended over the lake. And they were taking on water and were in danger. [24] Then, drawing near, they awakened him, saying, "Teacher, we are perishing." But as he rose up, he rebuked the wind and the raging water, and they ceased. And a tranquility occurred. [25] Then he said to them, "Where is your faith?" And they, being afraid, were amazed, saying to one another, "Who do you think this is, so that he commands both wind and sea, and they obey him?" [26] And they sailed to the region of the Gerasenes, which is opposite Galilee. [27] And when he had gone out to the land, a certain man met him, who had now had a demon for a long time. And he did not wear clothes, nor did he stay in a house, but among the sepulchers. [28] And when he saw Jesus, he fell down before him. And crying out in a loud voice, he said: "What is there between me and you, Jesus, Son of the Most High God? I beg you not to torture me." [29] For he was ordering the unclean spirit to depart from the man. For on many occasions, it would seize him, and he was bound with chains and held by fetters. But breaking the chains, he was driven by the demon into deserted places. [30] Then Jesus questioned him, saying, "What is your name?" And he said, "Legion," because many demons had entered into him. [31] And they petitioned him not to order them to go into the abyss. [32] And in that place, there was a herd of many swine, pasturing on the mountain. And they petitioned him to permit them to enter into them. And he permitted them. [33] Therefore, the demons departed from the man, and they entered into the swine. And the herd rushed violently down a precipice into the lake, and they were drowned. [34] And when those who were pasturing them had seen this, they fled and reported it in the city and the villages. [35] Then they went out to see what was happening, and they came to Jesus. And they found the man, from whom the demons had departed, sitting at his feet, clothed as well as in a sane mind, and they were afraid. [36] Then those who had seen this also reported to them how he had been healed from the legion. [37] And the entire multitude from the region of the Gerasenes pleaded with him to depart from them. For they were seized by a great fear. Then, climbing into the boat, he went back again. [38] And the man from whom the demons had departed pleaded with him, so that he might be with him. But Jesus sent him away, saying, [39] "Return to your house and explain to them what great things God has done for you." And he traveled through the entire city, preaching about the great things that Jesus had done for him. [40] Now it happened that, when Jesus had returned, the crowd received him. For they were all waiting for him. [41] And behold, a man came, whose name was Jairus, and he was a leader of the synagogue. And he fell down at the feet of Jesus, asking him to enter into his house. [42] For he had an only daughter, nearly twelve years old, and she was dying. And it happened that, as he was going there, he was hemmed in by the crowd. [43] And there was a certain woman, with a flow of blood for twelve years, who had paid out all her substance on physicians, and she was unable to be cured by any of them. [44] She approached him from behind, and she touched the hem of his garment. And at once the flow of her blood stopped. [45] And Jesus said, "Who is it that touched me?" But as everyone was denying it, Peter, and those who were with him, said: "Teacher, the crowd hems you in and presses upon you, and yet you say, 'Who touched me?'" [46] And Jesus said: "Someone has touched me. For I know that power has gone out from me." [47] Then the woman, upon seeing that she was not hidden, came forward, trembling, and she fell down before his feet. And she declared before all the people the reason that she had touched him, and how she had been immediately healed. [48] But he said to her: "Daughter, your faith has saved you. Go in peace." [49] While he was still speaking, someone came to the ruler of the synagogue, saying to him: "Your daughter is dead. Do not trouble him." ⁵⁰ Then Jesus, upon hearing this word, replied to the father of the girl: "Do not be afraid. Only believe, and she will be saved." ⁵¹ And when he had arrived at the house, he would not permit anyone to enter with him, except Peter and James and John, and the father and mother of the girl. ⁵² Now all were weeping and mourning for her. But he said: "Do not weep. The girl is not dead, but only sleeping." ⁵³ And they derided him, knowing that she had died. ⁵⁴ But he, taking her by the hand, cried out, saying, "Little girl, arise." ⁵⁵ And her spirit returned, and she immediately rose up. And he ordered them to give her something to eat. ⁵⁶ And her parents were stupefied. And he instructed them not to tell anyone what had happened.

CHAPTER 9

¹ Then calling together the twelve Apostles, he gave them power and authority over all demons and to cure diseases. ² And he sent them to preach the kingdom of God and to heal the infirm. ³ And he said to them: "You should take nothing for the journey, neither staff, nor traveling bag, nor bread, nor money; and you should not have two tunics. ⁴ And into whatever house you shall enter, lodge there, and do not move away from there. ⁵ And whoever will not have received you, upon departing from that city, shake off even the dust on your feet, as a testimony against them." ⁶ And going forth, they traveled around, through the towns, evangelizing and curing everywhere. ⁷ Now Herod the tetrarch heard about all the things that were being done by him, but he doubted, because it was said ⁸ by some, "For John has risen from the dead," yet truly, by others, "For Elijah has appeared," and by still others, "For one of the prophets from of old has risen again." ⁹ And Herod said: "I beheaded John. So then, who is this, about whom I hear such things?" And he sought to see him. ¹⁰ And when the Apostles returned, they explained to him all the things that they had done. And taking them with him, he withdrew to a deserted place apart, which belongs to Bethsaida. ¹¹ But when the crowd had realized this, they followed him. And he received them and spoke to them about the kingdom of God. And those who were in need of cures, he healed. ¹² Then the day began to decline. And drawing near, the twelve said to him: "Dismiss the crowds, so that, by going into the surrounding towns and villages, they may separate and find food. For we are here in a deserted place." ¹³ But he said to them, "You give them something to eat." And they said, "There is with us no more than five loaves and two fish, unless perhaps we are to go and buy food for this entire multitude." ¹⁴ Now there were about five thousand men. So he said to his disciples, "Have them recline to eat in groups of fifty." ¹⁵ And they did so. And they caused them all to recline to eat. ¹⁶ Then, taking the five loaves and the two fish, he gazed up to heaven, and he blessed and broke and distributed them to his disciples, in order to set them before the crowd. ¹⁷ And they all ate and were satisfied. And twelve baskets of fragments were taken up, which were left over from them. ¹⁸ And it happened that, when he was praying alone, his disciples also were with him, and he questioned them, saying: "Who do the multitudes say that I am?" ¹⁹ But they answered by saying: "John the Baptist. But some say Elijah. Yet truly, others say that one of the prophets from before has risen again." ²⁰ Then he said to them, "But who do you say that I am?" In response, Simon Peter said, "The Christ of God." ²¹ But speaking sharply to them, he instructed them not to tell this to anyone, ²² saying, "For the Son of man must suffer many things, and be rejected by the elders and the leaders of the priests and the scribes, and be killed, and on the third day rise again." ²³ Then he said to everyone: "If anyone is willing to come after me: let him deny himself, and take up his cross every day, and follow me. ²⁴ For whoever will have saved his life, will lose it. Yet whoever will have lost his life for my sake, will save it. ²⁵ For how does it benefit a man, if he were to gain the whole world, yet lose himself, or cause himself harm? ²⁶ For whoever will be ashamed of me and of my words: of him the Son of man will be ashamed, when he will have arrived in his majesty and that of his Father and of the holy Angels. ²⁷ And yet, I tell you a truth: There are some standing here who shall not taste death, until they see the kingdom of God." ²⁸ And it happened that, about eight days after these words, he took Peter and James and John, and he ascended onto a mountain, so that he might pray. ²⁹ And while he was praying, the appearance of his countenance was altered, and his vestment became white and shining. ³⁰ And behold, two men were talking with him. And these were Moses and Elijah, appearing in majesty. ³¹ And they spoke of his departure, which he would accomplish at Jerusalem. ³² Yet truly, Peter and those who were with him were weighed down by sleep. And becoming alert, they

saw his majesty and the two men who were standing with him. ³³ And it happened that, as these were departing from him, Peter said to Jesus: "Teacher, it is good for us to be here. And so, let us make three tabernacles: one for you, and one for Moses, and one for Elijah." For he did not know what he was saying. ³⁴ Then, as he was saying these things, a cloud came and overshadowed them. And as these were entering into the cloud, they were afraid. ³⁵ And a voice came from the cloud, saying: "This is my beloved Son. Listen to him." ³⁶ And while the voice was being uttered, Jesus was found to be alone. And they were silent and told no one, in those days, any of these things, which they had seen. ³⁷ But it happened on the following day that, as they were descending from the mountain, a great crowd met him. ³⁸ And behold, a man from the crowd cried out, saying, "Teacher, I beg you, look kindly on my son, for he is my only son. ³⁹ And behold, a spirit takes hold of him, and he suddenly cries out, and it throws him down and convulses him, so that he foams. And though it tears him apart, it leaves him only with difficulty. ⁴⁰ And I asked your disciples to cast him out, and they were unable." ⁴¹ And in response, Jesus said: "O unfaithful and perverse generation! How long will I be with you and endure you? Bring your son here." ⁴² And as he was approaching him, the demon threw him down and convulsed him. ⁴³ And Jesus rebuked the unclean spirit, and he healed the boy, and he restored him to his father. ⁴⁴ And all were astonished at the greatness of God. And as everyone was wondering over all that he was doing, he said to his disciples: "You must set these words in your hearts. For it shall be that the Son of man will be delivered into the hands of men." ⁴⁵ But they did not understand this word, and it was concealed from them, so that they did not perceive it. And they were afraid to question him about this word. ⁴⁶ Now an idea entered into them, as to which of them was greater. ⁴⁷ But Jesus, perceiving the thoughts of their hearts, took a child and stood him beside him. ⁴⁸ And he said to them: "Whoever will receive this child in my name, receives me; and whoever receives me, receives him who sent me. For whoever is the lesser among you all, the same is greater." ⁴⁹ And responding, John said: "Teacher, we saw a certain one casting out demons in your name. And we prohibited him, for he does not follow with us." ⁵⁰ And Jesus said to him: "Do not prohibit him. For whoever is not against you, is for you." ⁵¹ Now it happened that, while the days of his dissipation were being completed, he steadfastly set his face to go to Jerusalem. ⁵² And he sent messengers before his face. And going on, they entered into a city of the Samaritans, to prepare for him. ⁵³ And they would not receive him, because his face was going toward Jerusalem. ⁵⁴ And when his disciples, James and John, had seen this, they said, "Lord, do you want us to call for fire to descend from heaven and consume them?" ⁵⁵ And turning, he rebuked them, saying: "Do you not know of whose spirit you are? ⁵⁶ The Son of man came, not to destroy lives, but to save them." And they went into another town. ⁵⁷ And it happened that, as they were walking along the way, someone said to him, "I will follow you, wherever you will go." ⁵⁸ Jesus said to him: "Foxes have dens, and the birds of the air have nests. But the Son of man has nowhere to lay his head." ⁵⁹ Then he said to another, "Follow me." But he said, "Lord, permit me first to go and bury my father." ⁶⁰ And Jesus said to him: "Let the dead bury their dead. But you go and announce the kingdom of God." ⁶¹ And another said: "I will follow you, Lord. But permit me first to explain this to those of my house." ⁶² Jesus said to him, "No one who puts his hand to the plow, and then looks back, is fit for the kingdom of God."

CHAPTER 10

¹ Then, after these things, the Lord also designated another seventy-two. And he sent them in pairs before his face, into every city and place where he was to arrive. ² And he said to them: "Certainly the harvest is great, but the workers are few. Therefore, ask the Lord of the harvest to send workers into his harvest. ³ Go forth. Behold, I send you out like lambs among wolves. ⁴ Do not choose to carry a purse, nor provisions, nor shoes; and you shall greet no one along the way. ⁵ Into whatever house you will have entered, first say, 'Peace to this house.' ⁶ And if a son of peace is there, your peace will rest upon him. But if not, it will return to you. ⁷ And remain in the same house, eating and drinking the things that are with them. For the worker is worthy of his pay. Do not choose to pass from house to house. ⁸ And into whatever city you have entered and they have received you, eat what they set before you. ⁹ And cure the sick who are in that place, and proclaim to them, 'The kingdom of God has drawn near to you.' ¹⁰ But into whatever city you have entered and they have not received you, going out into its main streets,

say: ¹¹'Even the dust which clings to us from your city, we wipe away against you. Yet know this: the kingdom of God has drawn near.' ¹²I say to you, that in that day, Sodom will be forgiven more than that city will be. ¹³Woe to you, Chorazin! Woe to you, Bethsaida! For if the miracles that have been wrought in you, had been wrought in Tyre and Sidon, they would have repented long ago, sitting in haircloth and ashes. ¹⁴Yet truly, Tyre and Sidon will be forgiven more in the judgment than you will be. ¹⁵And as for you, Capernaum, who would be exalted even up to Heaven: you shall be submerged into Hell. ¹⁶Whoever hears you, hears me. And whoever despises you, despises me. And whoever despises me, despises him who sent me." ¹⁷Then the seventy-two returned with gladness, saying, "Lord, even the demons are subject to us, in your name." ¹⁸And he said to them: "I was watching as Satan fell like lightning from heaven. ¹⁹Behold, I have given you authority to tread upon serpents and scorpions, and upon all the powers of the enemy, and nothing shall hurt you. ²⁰Yet truly, do not choose to rejoice in this, that the spirits are subject to you; but rejoice that your names are written in heaven." ²¹In the same hour, he exulted in the Holy Spirit, and he said: "I confess to you, Father, Lord of heaven and earth, because you have hidden these things from the wise and the prudent, and have revealed them to little ones. It is so, Father, because this way was pleasing before you. ²²All things have been delivered to me by my Father. And no one knows who the Son is, except the Father, and who the Father is, except the Son, and those to whom the Son has chosen to reveal him." ²³And turning to his disciples, he said: "Blessed are the eyes that see what you see. ²⁴For I say to you, that many prophets and kings wanted to see the things that you see, and they did not see them, and to hear the things that you hear, and they did not hear them." ²⁵And behold, a certain expert in the law rose up, testing him and saying, "Teacher, what must I do to possess eternal life?" ²⁶But he said to him: "What is written in the law? How do you read it?" ²⁷In response, he said: "You shall love the Lord your God from your whole heart, and from your whole soul, and from all your strength, and from all your mind, and your neighbor as yourself." ²⁸And he said to him: "You have answered correctly. Do this, and you will live." ²⁹But since he wanted to justify himself, he said to Jesus, "And who is my neighbor?" ³⁰Then Jesus, taking this up, said: "A certain man descended from Jerusalem to Jericho, and he happened upon robbers, who now also plundered him. And inflicting him with wounds, they went away, leaving him behind, half-alive. ³¹And it happened that a certain priest was descending along the same way. And seeing him, he passed by. ³²And similarly a Levite, when he was near the place, also saw him, and he passed by. ³³But a certain Samaritan, being on a journey, came near him. And seeing him, he was moved by mercy. ³⁴And approaching him, he bound up his wounds, pouring oil and wine on them. And setting him on his pack animal, he brought him to an inn, and he took care of him. ³⁵And the next day, he took out two denarii, and he gave them to the proprietor, and he said: 'Take care of him. And whatever extra you will have spent, I will repay to you at my return.' ³⁶Which of these three, does it seem to you, was a neighbor to him who fell among the robbers?" ³⁷Then he said, "The one who acted with mercy toward him." And Jesus said to him, "Go, and act similarly." ³⁸Now it happened that, while they were traveling, he entered into a certain town. And a certain woman, named Martha, received him into her home. ³⁹And she had a sister, named Mary, who, while sitting beside the Lord's feet, was listening to his word. ⁴⁰Now Martha was continually busying herself with serving. And she stood still and said: "Lord, is it not a concern to you that my sister has left me to serve alone? Therefore, speak to her, so that she may help me." ⁴¹And the Lord responded by saying to her: "Martha, Martha, you are anxious and troubled over many things. ⁴²And yet only one thing is necessary. Mary has chosen the best portion, and it shall not be taken away from her."

CHAPTER 11

¹And it happened that, while he was in a certain place praying, when he ceased, one of his disciples said to him, "Lord, teach us to pray, as John also taught his disciples." ²And he said to them: "When you are praying, say: Father, may your name be kept holy. May your kingdom come. ³Give us this day our daily bread. ⁴And forgive us our sins, since we also forgive all who are indebted to us. And lead us not into temptation." ⁵And he said to them: "Which of you will have a friend and will go to him in the middle of the night, and will say to him: 'Friend, lend me three loaves, ⁶because a friend of mine has arrived from a journey to me, and I do not have anything to set before him.' ⁷And from within, he would

answer by saying: 'Do not disturb me. The door is closed now, and my children and I are in bed. I cannot get up and give it to you.' ⁸ Yet if he will persevere in knocking, I tell you that, even though he would not get up and give it to him because he is a friend, yet due to his continued insistence, he will get up and give him whatever he needs. ⁹ And so I say to you: Ask, and it shall be given to you. Seek, and you shall find. Knock, and it shall be opened to you. ¹⁰ For everyone who asks, receives. And whoever seeks, finds. And whoever knocks, it shall be opened to him. ¹¹ So then, who among you, if he asks his father for bread, he would give him a stone? Or if he asks for a fish, he would give him a serpent, instead of a fish? ¹² Or if he will ask for an egg, he would offer to him a scorpion? ¹³ Therefore, if you, being evil, know how to give good things to your sons, how much more will your Father give, from heaven, a spirit of goodness to those who ask him?" ¹⁴ And he was casting out a demon, and the man was mute. But when he had cast out the demon, the mute man spoke, and so the crowds were amazed. ¹⁵ But some of them said, "It is by Beelzebub, the leader of demons, that he casts out demons." ¹⁶ And others, testing him, required a sign from heaven of him. ¹⁷ But when he perceived their thoughts, he said to them: "Every kingdom divided against itself will become desolate, and house will fall upon house. ¹⁸ So then, if Satan is also divided against himself, how will his kingdom stand? For you say that it is by Beelzebub that I cast out demons. ¹⁹ But if I cast out demons by Beelzebub, by whom do your own sons cast them out? Therefore, they shall be your judges. ²⁰ Moreover, if it is by the finger of God that I cast out demons, then certainly the kingdom of God has overtaken you. ²¹ When a strong armed man guards his entrance, the things that he possesses are at peace. ²² But if a stronger one, overwhelming him, has defeated him, he will take away all his weapons, in which he trusted, and he will distribute his spoils. ²³ Whoever is not with me, is against me. And whoever does not gather with me, scatters. ²⁴ When an unclean spirit has departed from a man, he walks through waterless places, seeking rest. And not finding any, he says: 'I will return to my house, from which I departed.' ²⁵ And when he has arrived, he finds it swept clean and decorated. ²⁶ Then he goes, and he takes in seven other spirits with him, more wicked than himself, and they enter and live there. And so, the end of that man is made worse than the beginning." ²⁷ And it happened that, when he was saying these things, a certain woman from the crowd, lifting up her voice, said to him, "Blessed is the womb that bore you and the breasts that nursed you." ²⁸ Then he said, "Yes, but moreover: blessed are those who hear the word of God and keep it." ²⁹ Then, as the crowds were quickly gathering, he began to say: "This generation is a wicked generation: it seeks a sign. But no sign will be given to it, except the sign of the prophet Jonah. ³⁰ For just as Jonah was a sign to the Ninevites, so also will the Son of man be to this generation. ³¹ The queen of the South will rise up, at the judgment, with the men of this generation, and she will condemn them. For she came from the ends of the earth to hear the wisdom of Solomon. And behold, more than Solomon is here. ³² The men of Nineveh will rise up, at the judgment, with this generation, and they will condemn it. For at the preaching of Jonah, they repented. And behold, more than Jonah is here. ³³ No one lights a candle and places it in hiding, nor under a bushel basket, but upon a lampstand, so that those who enter may see the light. ³⁴ Your eye is the light of your body. If your eye is wholesome, your entire body will be filled with light. But if it is wicked, then even your body will be darkened. ³⁵ Therefore, take care, lest the light that is within you become darkness. ³⁶ So then, if your entire body becomes filled with light, not having any part in darkness, then it will be entirely light, and, like a shining lamp, it will illuminate you." ³⁷ And as he was speaking, a certain Pharisee asked him to eat with him. And going inside, he sat down to eat. ³⁸ But the Pharisee began to say, thinking within himself: "Why might it be that he has not washed before eating?" ³⁹ And the Lord said to him: "You Pharisees today clean what is outside the cup and the plate, but what is inside of you is full of plunder and iniquity. ⁴⁰ Fools! Did not he who made what is outside, indeed also make what is inside? ⁴¹ Yet truly, give what is above as alms, and behold, all things are clean for you. ⁴² But woe to you, Pharisees! For you tithe mint and rue and every herb, but you ignore judgment and the charity of God. But these things you ought to have done, without omitting the others. ⁴³ Woe to you, Pharisees! For you love the first seats in the synagogues, and greetings in the marketplace. ⁴⁴ Woe to you! For you are like graves that are not noticeable, so that men walk over them without realizing it." ⁴⁵ Then one of the experts in the law, in response, said to him, "Teacher, in saying these things, you bring an insult against us as well." ⁴⁶ So he said: "And woe to you experts in the law! For you weigh men down with burdens which they are not able to bear, but you yourselves do not touch the weight with even one of your fingers. ⁴⁷Woe to you, who build the tombs of the prophets, while it is your fathers who killed them! ⁴⁸Clearly, you are testifying that you consent to the actions of your fathers, because even though they killed them, you build their sepulchers. ⁴⁹Because of this also, the wisdom of God said: I will send to them Prophets and Apostles, and some of these they will kill or persecute, ⁵⁰so that the blood of all the Prophets, which has been shed since the foundation of the world, may be charged against this generation: ⁵¹from the blood of Abel, even to the blood of Zachariah, who perished between the altar and the sanctuary. So I say to you: it will be required of this generation! ⁵²Woe to you, experts in the law! For you have taken away the key of knowledge. You yourselves do not enter, and those who were entering, you would have prohibited." ⁵³Then, while he was saying these things to them, the Pharisees and the experts in the law began to insist strongly that he restrain his mouth about many things. ⁵⁴And waiting to ambush him, they sought something from his mouth that they might seize upon, in order to accuse him.

CHAPTER 12

¹Then, as great crowds were standing so close that they were stepping on one another, he began to say to his disciples: "Beware of the leaven of the Pharisees, which is hypocrisy. ²For there is nothing covered, which will not be revealed, nor anything hidden, which will not be known. ³For the things that you have spoken in darkness will be declared in the light. And what you have said in the ear in bedrooms will be proclaimed from the housetops. ⁴So I say to you, my friends: Do not be fearful of those who kill the body, and afterwards have no more that they can do. ⁵But I will reveal to you whom you should fear. Fear him who, after he will have killed, has the power to cast into Hell. So I say to you: Fear him. ⁶Are not five sparrows sold for two small coins? And yet not one of these is forgotten in the sight of God. ⁷But even the very hairs of your head have all been numbered. Therefore, do not be afraid. You are worth more than many sparrows. ⁸But I say to you: Everyone who will have confessed me before men, the Son of man will also confess him before the Angels of God. ⁹But everyone who will have denied me before men, he will be denied before the Angels of God. ¹⁰And everyone who speaks a word against the Son of man, it will be forgiven of him. But of him who will have blasphemed against the Holy Spirit, it will not be forgiven. ¹¹And when they will lead you to the synagogues, and to magistrates and authorities, do not choose to be worried about how or what you will answer, or about what you might say. ¹²For the Holy Spirit will teach you, in the same hour, what you must say." ¹³And someone from the crowd said to him, "Teacher, tell my brother to share the inheritance with me." ¹⁴But he said to him, "Man, who has appointed me as judge or arbitrator over you?" ¹⁵So he said to them: "Be cautious and wary of all avarice. For a person's life is not found in the abundance of the things that he possesses." ¹⁶Then he spoke to them using a comparison, saying: "The fertile land of a certain wealthy man produced crops. ¹⁷And he thought within himself, saying: 'What should I do? For I have nowhere to gather together my crops.' ¹⁸And he said: 'This is what I will do. I will tear down my barns and build larger ones. And into these, I will gather all the things that have been grown for me, as well as my goods. ¹⁹And I will say to my soul: Soul, you have many goods, stored up for many years. Relax, eat, drink, and be cheerful.' ²⁰But God said to him: 'Foolish one, this very night they require your soul of you. To whom, then, will those things belong, which you have prepared?' ²¹So it is with him who stores up for himself, and is not wealthy with God." ²²And he said to his disciples: "And so I say to you: Do not choose to be anxious about your life, as to what you may eat, nor about your body, as to what you will wear. ²³Life is more than food, and the body is more than clothing. ²⁴Consider the ravens. For they neither sow nor reap; there is no storehouse or barn for them. And yet God pastures them. How much more are you, compared to them? ²⁵But which of you, by thinking, is able to add one cubit to his stature? ²⁶Therefore, if you are not capable, in what is so little, why be anxious about the rest? ²⁷Consider the lilies, how they grow. They neither work nor weave. But I say to you, not even Solomon, in all his glory, was clothed like one of these. ²⁸Therefore, if God so clothes the grass, which is in the field today and thrown into the furnace tomorrow, how much more you, O little in faith? ²⁹And so, do not choose to inquire as to what you will eat, or what you will drink. And do not choose to be lifted up on high. ³⁰For all these things are sought by the Gentiles of the world. And your Father knows that you have need of these

things. ³¹ Yet truly, seek first the kingdom of God, and his justice, and all these things shall be added to you. ³² Do not be afraid, little flock; for it has pleased your Father to give you the kingdom. ³³ Sell what you possess, and give alms. Make for yourselves purses that will not wear out, a treasure that will not fall short, in heaven, where no thief approaches, and no moth corrupts. ³⁴ For where your treasure is, there will your heart be also. ³⁵ Let your waists be girded, and let lamps be burning in your hands. ³⁶ And let you yourselves be like men awaiting their lord, when he will return from the wedding; so that, when he arrives and knocks, they may open to him promptly. ³⁷ Blessed are those servants whom the Lord, when he returns, will find being vigilant. Amen I say to you, that he will gird himself and have them sit down to eat, while he, continuing on, will minister to them. ³⁸ And if he will return in the second watch, or if in the third watch, and if he will find them to be so: then blessed are those servants. ³⁹ But know this: that if the father of the family knew at what hour the thief would arrive, he would certainly stand watch, and he would not permit his house to be broken into. ⁴⁰ You also must be prepared. For the Son of man will return at an hour that you will not realize." ⁴¹ Then Peter said to him, "Lord, are you telling this parable to us, or also to everyone?" ⁴² So the Lord said: "Who do you think is the faithful and prudent steward, whom his Lord has appointed over his family, in order to give them their measure of wheat in due time? ⁴³ Blessed is that servant if, when his Lord will return, he will find him acting in this manner. ⁴⁴ Truly I say to you, that he will appoint him over all that he possesses. ⁴⁵ But if that servant will have said in his heart, 'My Lord has made a delay in his return,' and if he has begun to strike the men and women servants, and to eat and drink, and to be inebriated, ⁴⁶ then the Lord of that servant will return on a day which he hoped not, and at an hour which he knew not. And he will separate him, and he will place his portion with that of the unfaithful. ⁴⁷ And that servant, who knew the will of his Lord, and who did not prepare and did not act according to his will, will be beaten many times over. ⁴⁸ Yet he who did not know, and who acted in a way that deserves a beating, will be beaten fewer times. So then, of all to whom much has been given, much will be required. And of those to whom much has been entrusted, even more will be asked. ⁴⁹ I have come to cast a fire upon the earth. And what should I desire, except that it may be kindled? ⁵⁰ And I have a baptism, with which I am to be baptized. And how I am constrained, even until it may be accomplished! ⁵¹ Do you think that I have come to give peace to the earth? No, I tell you, but division. ⁵² For from this time on, there will be five in one house: divided as three against two, and as two against three. ⁵³ A father will be divided against a son, and a son against his father; a mother against a daughter and a daughter against a mother; a mother-in-law against her daughter-in-law, and a daughter-in-law against her mother-in-law." ⁵⁴ And he also said to the crowds: "When you see a cloud rising from the setting of the sun, immediately you say, 'A rain cloud is coming.' And so it does. ⁵⁵ And when a south wind is blowing, you say, 'It will be hot.' And so it is. ⁵⁶ You hypocrites! You discern the face of the heavens, and of the earth, yet how is it that you do not discern this time? ⁵⁷ And why do you not, even among yourselves, judge what is just? ⁵⁸ So, when you are going with your adversary to the ruler, while you are on the way, make an effort to be freed from him, lest perhaps he may lead you to the judge, and the judge may deliver you to the officer, and the officer may cast you into prison. ⁵⁹ I tell you, you will not depart from there, until you have paid the very last coin."

CHAPTER 13

¹ And there were present, at that very time, some who were reporting about the Galileans, whose blood Pilate mixed with their sacrifices. ² And responding, he said to them: "Do you think that these Galileans must have sinned more than all other Galileans, because they suffered so much? ³ No, I tell you. But unless you repent, you will all perish similarly. ⁴ And those eighteen upon whom the tower of Siloam fell and killed them, do you think that they also were greater transgressors than all the men living in Jerusalem? ⁵ No, I tell you. But if you do not repent, you will all perish similarly." ⁶ And he also told this parable: "A certain man had a fig tree, which was planted in his vineyard. And he came seeking fruit on it, but found none. ⁷ Then he said to the cultivator of the vineyard: 'Behold, for these three years I came seeking fruit on this fig tree, and I have found none. Therefore, cut it down. For why should it even occupy the land?' ⁸ But in response, he said to him: 'Lord, let it be for this year also, during which time I will dig around it and add fertilizer. ⁹ And, indeed, it should bear fruit. But if not, in the future, you

shall cut it down.'" [10] Now he was teaching in their synagogue on the Sabbaths. [11] And behold, there was a woman who had a spirit of infirmity for eighteen years. And she was bent over; and she was unable to look upwards at all. [12] And when Jesus saw her, he called her to himself, and he said to her, "Woman, you are released from your infirmity." [13] And he laid his hands upon her, and immediately she was straightened, and she glorified God. [14] Then, as a result, the ruler of the synagogue became angry that Jesus had cured on the Sabbath, and he said to the crowd: "There are six days on which you ought to work. Therefore, come and be cured on those, and not on the day of the Sabbath." [15] Then the Lord said to him in response: "You hypocrites! Does not each one of you, on the Sabbath, release his ox or donkey from the stall, and lead it to water? [16] So then, should not this daughter of Abraham, whom Satan has bound for lo these eighteen years, be released from this restraint on the day of the Sabbath?" [17] And as he was saying these things, all his adversaries were ashamed. And all the people rejoiced in everything that was being done gloriously by him. [18] And so he said: "To what is the kingdom of God similar, and to what figure shall I compare it? [19] It is like a grain of mustard seed, which a man took and cast into his garden. And it grew, and it became a great tree, and the birds of the air rested in its branches." [20] And again, he said: "To what figure shall I compare the kingdom of God? [21] It is like leaven, which a woman took and hid in three measures of fine wheat flour, until it was entirely leavened." [22] And he was traveling through the cities and towns, teaching and making his way to Jerusalem. [23] And someone said to him, "Lord, are they few who are saved?" But he said to them: [24] "Strive to enter through the narrow gate. For many, I tell you, will seek to enter and not be able. [25] Then, when the father of the family will have entered and shut the door, you will begin to stand outside and to knock at the door, saying, 'Lord, open to us.' And in response, he will say to you, 'I do not know where you are from.' [26] Then you will begin to say, 'We ate and drank in your presence, and you taught in our streets.' [27] And he will say to you: 'I do not know where you are from. Depart from me, all you workers of iniquity!' [28] In that place, there will be weeping and gnashing of teeth, when you see Abraham, and Isaac, and Jacob, and all the prophets, in the kingdom of God, yet you yourselves are expelled outside. [29] And they will arrive from the East, and the West, and the North, and the South; and they will recline at table in the kingdom of God. [30] And behold, those who are last will be first, and those who are first will be last." [31] On the same day, some of the Pharisees approached, saying to him: "Depart, and go away from here. For Herod wishes to kill you." [32] And he said to them: "Go and tell that fox: 'Behold, I cast out demons and accomplish healings, today and tomorrow. And on the third day I reach the end.' [33] Yet truly, it is necessary for me to walk today and tomorrow and the following day. For it does not fall to a prophet to perish beyond Jerusalem. [34] Jerusalem, Jerusalem! You kill the prophets, and you stone those who are sent to you. Daily, I wanted to gather together your children, in the manner of a bird with her nest under her wings, but you were not willing! [35] Behold, your house will be left desolate for you. But I say to you, that you shall not see me, until it happens that you say: 'Blessed is he who has arrived in the name of the Lord.'"

CHAPTER 14

[1] And it happened that, when Jesus entered the house of a certain leader of the Pharisees on the Sabbath to eat bread, they were observing him. [2] And behold, a certain man before him was afflicted with edema. [3] And responding, Jesus spoke to the experts in the law and to the Pharisees, saying, "Is it lawful to cure on the Sabbath?" [4] But they kept silent. Yet truly, taking hold of him, he healed him and sent him away. [5] And responding to them, he said, "Which of you will have a donkey or an ox fall into a pit, and will not promptly pull him out, on the day of the Sabbath?" [6] And they were unable to respond to him about these things. [7] Then he also told a parable, to those who were invited, noticing how they chose the first seats at the table, saying to them: [8] "When you are invited to a wedding, do not sit down in the first place, lest perhaps someone more honored than yourself may have been invited by him. [9] And then he who called both you and him, approaching, may say to you, 'Give this place to him.' And then you would begin, with shame, to take the last place. [10] But when you are invited, go, sit down in the lowest place, so that, when he who invited you arrives, he may say to you, 'Friend, go up higher.' Then you will have glory in the sight of those who sit at table together with you. [11] For everyone who exalts himself shall be humbled, and whoever humbles himself shall be exalted." [12] Then he also said to the one

who had invited him: "When you prepare a lunch or dinner, do not choose to call your friends, or your brothers, or your relatives, or your wealthy neighbors, lest perhaps they might then invite you in return and repayment would made to you. ¹³ But when you prepare a feast, call the poor, the disabled, the lame, and the blind. ¹⁴ And you will be blessed because they do not have a way to repay you. So then, your recompense will be in the resurrection of the just." ¹⁵ When someone sitting at table with him had heard these things, he said to him, "Blessed is he who will eat bread in the kingdom of God." ¹⁶ So he said to him: "A certain man prepared a great feast, and he invited many. ¹⁷ And he sent his servant, at the hour of the feast, to tell the invited to come; for now everything was ready. ¹⁸ And at once they all began to make excuses. The first said to him: 'I bought a farm, and I need to go out and see it. I ask you to excuse me.' ¹⁹ And another said: 'I bought five yoke of oxen, and I am going to examine them. I ask you to excuse me.' ²⁰ And another said, 'I have taken a wife, and therefore I am not able to go.' ²¹ And returning, the servant reported these things to his lord. Then the father of the family, becoming angry, said to his servant: 'Go out quickly into the streets and neighborhoods of the city. And lead here the poor, and the disabled, and the blind, and the lame.' ²² And the servant said: 'It has been done, just as you ordered, lord, and there is still room.' ²³ And the lord said to the servant: 'Go out to the highways and hedges, and compel them to enter, so that my house may be filled. ²⁴ For I tell you, that none of those men who were invited will taste of my feast.' " ²⁵ Now great crowds traveled with him. And turning around, he said to them: ²⁶ "If anyone comes to me, and does not hate his father, and mother, and wife, and children, and brothers, and sisters, and yes, even his own life, he is not able to be my disciple. ²⁷ And whoever does not bear his cross and come after me, is not able to be my disciple. ²⁸ For who among you, wanting to build a tower, would not first sit down and determine the costs that are required, to see if he has the means to complete it? ²⁹ Otherwise, after he will have laid the foundation and not been able to finish it, everyone who sees it may begin to mock him, ³⁰ saying: 'This man began to build what he was not able to finish.' ³¹ Or, what king, advancing to engage in war against another king, would not first sit down and consider whether he may be able, with ten thousand, to meet one who comes against him with twenty thousand? ³² If not, then while the other is still far away, sending a delegation, he would ask him for terms of peace. ³³ Therefore, every one of you who does not renounce all that he possesses is not able to be my disciple. ³⁴ Salt is good. But if the salt has lost its flavor, with what will it be seasoned? ³⁵ It is useful neither in soil, nor in manure, so instead, it shall be thrown away. Whoever has ears to hear, let him hear."

CHAPTER 15

¹ Now tax collectors and sinners were drawing near to him, so that they might listen to him. ² And the Pharisees and the scribes murmured, saying, "This one accepts sinners and eats with them." ³ And he told this parable to them, saying: ⁴ "What man among you, who has one hundred sheep, and if he will have lost one of them, would not leave the ninety-nine in the desert and go after the one whom he had lost, until he finds it? ⁵ And when he has found it, he places it on his shoulders, rejoicing. ⁶ And returning home, he calls together his friends and neighbors, saying to them: 'Congratulate me! For I have found my sheep, which had been lost.' ⁷ I say to you, that there will be so much more joy in heaven over one sinner repenting, than over the ninety-nine just, who do not need to repent. ⁸ Or what woman, having ten drachmas, if she will have lost one drachma, would not light a candle, and sweep the house, and diligently search until she finds it? ⁹ And when she has found it, she calls together her friends and neighbors, saying: 'Rejoice with me! For I have found the drachma, which I had lost.' ¹⁰ So I say to you, there will be joy before the Angels of God over even one sinner who is repentant." ¹¹ And he said: "A certain man had two sons. ¹² And the younger of them said to the father, 'Father, give me the portion of your estate which would go to me.' And he divided the estate between them. ¹³ And after not many days, the younger son, gathering it all together, set out on a long journey to a distant region. And there, he dissipated his substance, living in luxury. ¹⁴ And after he had consumed it all, a great famine occurred in that region, and he began to be in need. ¹⁵ And he went and attached himself to one of the citizens of that region. And he sent him to his farm, in order to feed the swine. ¹⁶ And he wanted to fill his belly with the scraps that the swine ate. But no one would give it to him. ¹⁷ And returning to his senses, he said: 'How many hired hands in my father's

house have abundant bread, while I perish here in famine! ¹⁸ I shall rise up and go to my father, and I will say to him: Father, I have sinned against heaven and before you. ¹⁹ I am not worthy to be called your son. Make me one of your hired hands.' ²⁰ And rising up, he went to his father. But while he was still at a distance, his father saw him, and he was moved with compassion, and running to him, he fell upon his neck and kissed him. ²¹ And the son said to him: 'Father, I have sinned against heaven and before you. Now I am not worthy to be called your son.' ²² But the father said to his servants: 'Quickly! Bring out the best robe, and clothe him with it. And put a ring on his hand and shoes on his feet. ²³ And bring the fatted calf here, and kill it. And let us eat and hold a feast. ²⁴ For this son of mine was dead, and has revived; he was lost, and is found.' And they began to feast. ²⁵ But his elder son was in the field. And when he returned and drew near to the house, he heard music and dancing. ²⁶ And he called one of the servants, and he questioned him as to what these things meant. ²⁷ And he said to him: 'Your brother has returned, and your father has killed the fatted calf, because he has received him safely.' ²⁸ Then he became indignant, and he was unwilling to enter. Therefore, his father, going out, began to plead with him. ²⁹ And in response, he said to his father: 'Behold, I have been serving you for so many years. And I have never transgressed your commandment. And yet, you have never given me even a young goat, so that I might feast with my friends. ³⁰ Yet after this son of yours returned, who has devoured his substance with loose women, you have killed the fatted calf for him.' ³¹ But he said to him: 'Son, you are with me always, and all that I have is yours. ³² But it was necessary to feast and to rejoice. For this brother of yours was dead, and has revived; he was lost, and is found.'"

CHAPTER 16

¹ And he also said to his disciples: "A certain man was wealthy, and he had a steward of his estate. And this man was accused to him of having dissipated his goods. ² And he called him and said to him: 'What is this that I hear about you? Give an account of your stewardship. For you can no longer be my steward.' ³ And the steward said within himself: 'What shall I do? For my lord is taking the stewardship away from me. I am not strong enough to dig. I am too ashamed to beg. ⁴ I know what I will do so that, when I have been removed from the stewardship, they may receive me into their houses.' ⁵ And so, calling together each one of his lord's debtors, he said to the first, 'How much do you owe my lord?' ⁶ So he said, 'One hundred jars of oil.' And he said to him, 'Take your invoice, and quickly, sit down and write fifty.' ⁷ Next, he said to another, 'In truth, how much do you owe?' And he said, 'One hundred measures of wheat.' He said to him, 'Take your record books, and write eighty.' ⁸ And the lord praised the iniquitous steward, in that he had acted prudently. For the sons of this age are more prudent with their generation than are the sons of light. ⁹ And so I say to you, make friends for yourself using iniquitous mammon, so that, when you will have passed away, they may receive you into the eternal tabernacles. ¹⁰ Whoever is faithful in what is least, is also faithful in what is greater. And whoever is unjust in what is small, is also unjust in what is greater. ¹¹ So then, if you have not been faithful with iniquitous mammon, who will trust you with what is true? ¹² And if you have not been faithful with what belongs to another, who will give you what is yours? ¹³ No servant is able to serve two lords. For either he will hate the one and love the other, or he will cling to the one and despise the other. You cannot serve God and mammon." ¹⁴ But the Pharisees, who were greedy, were listening to all these things. And they ridiculed him. ¹⁵ And he said to them: "You are the ones who justify yourselves in the sight of men. But God knows your hearts. For what is lifted up by men is an abomination in the sight of God. ¹⁶ The law and the prophets were until John. Since then, the kingdom of God is being evangelized, and everyone acts with violence toward it. ¹⁷ But it is easier for heaven and earth to pass away, than for one dot of the law to fall away. ¹⁸ Everyone who divorces his wife and marries another commits adultery. And whoever marries her who has been divorced by her husband commits adultery. ¹⁹ A certain man was wealthy, and he was clothed in purple and in fine linen. And he feasted splendidly every day. ²⁰ And there was a certain beggar, named Lazarus, who lay at his gate, covered with sores, ²¹ wanting to be filled with the crumbs which were falling from the wealthy man's table. But no one gave it to him. And even the dogs came and licked his sores. ²² Then it happened that the beggar died, and he was carried by the Angels into the bosom of Abraham. Now the wealthy man also died, and he was entombed in Hell. ²³ Then lifting up his eyes, while

he was in torments, he saw Abraham far away, and Lazarus in his bosom. ²⁴ And crying out, he said: 'Father Abraham, take pity on me and send Lazarus, so that he may dip the tip of his finger in water to refresh my tongue. For I am tortured in this fire.' ²⁵ And Abraham said to him: 'Son, recall that you received good things in your life, and in comparison, Lazarus received bad things. But now he is consoled, and truly you are tormented. ²⁶ And besides all this, between us and you a great chasm has been established, so that those who might want to cross from here to you are not able, nor can someone cross from there to here.' ²⁷ And he said: 'Then, father, I beg you to send him to my father's house, for I have five brothers, ²⁸ so that he may testify to them, lest they also come into this place of torments.' ²⁹ And Abraham said to him: 'They have Moses and the prophets. Let them listen to them.' ³⁰ So he said: 'No, father Abraham. But if someone were to go to them from the dead, they would repent.' ³¹ But he said to him: 'If they will not listen to Moses and the prophets, neither will they believe even if someone has resurrected from the dead.'"

CHAPTER 17

¹ And he said to his disciples: "It is impossible for scandals not to occur. But woe to him through whom they come! ² It would be better for him if a millstone were placed around his neck and he were thrown into the sea, than to lead astray one of these little ones. ³ Be attentive to yourselves. If your brother has sinned against you, correct him. And if he has repented, forgive him. ⁴ And if he has sinned against you seven times a day, and seven times a day has turned back to you, saying, 'I am sorry,' then forgive him." ⁵ And the Apostles said to the Lord, "Increase our faith." ⁶ But the Lord said: "If you have faith like a grain of mustard seed, you may say to this mulberry tree, 'Be uprooted, and be transplanted into the sea.' And it would obey you. ⁷ But which of you, having a servant plowing or feeding cattle, would say to him, as he was returning from the field, 'Come in immediately; sit down to eat,' ⁸ and would not say to him: 'Prepare my dinner; gird yourself and minister to me, while I eat and drink; and after these things, you shall eat and drink?' ⁹ Would he be grateful to that servant, for doing what he commanded him to do? ¹⁰ I think not. So too, when you have done all these things that have been taught to you, you should say: 'We are useless servants. We have done what we should have done.'" ¹¹ And it happened that, while he was traveling to Jerusalem, he passed through the midst of Samaria and Galilee. ¹² And as he was entering a certain town, ten leprous men met him, and they stood at a distance. ¹³ And they lifted up their voice, saying, "Jesus, Teacher, take pity on us." ¹⁴ And when he saw them, he said, "Go, show yourselves to the priests." And it happened that, as they were going, they were cleansed. ¹⁵ And one of them, when he saw that he was cleansed, returned, magnifying God with a loud voice. ¹⁶ And he fell face down before his feet, giving thanks. And this one was a Samaritan. ¹⁷ And in response, Jesus said: "Were not ten made clean? And so where are the nine? ¹⁸ Was no one found who would return and give glory to God, except this foreigner?" ¹⁹ And he said to him: "Rise up, go forth. For your faith has saved you." ²⁰ Then he was questioned by the Pharisees: "When does the kingdom of God arrive?" And in response, he said to them: "The kingdom of God arrives unobserved. ²¹ And so, they will not say, 'Behold, it is here,' or 'Behold, it is there.' For behold, the kingdom of God is within you." ²² And he said to his disciples: "The time will come when you will desire to see one day of the Son of man, and you will not see it. ²³ And they will say to you, 'Behold, he is here,' and 'Behold, he is there.' Do not choose to go out, and do not follow them. ²⁴ For just as lightning flashes from under heaven and shines to whatever is under heaven, so also will the Son of man be in his day. ²⁵ But first he must suffer many things and be rejected by this generation. ²⁶ And just as it happened in the days of Noah, so also will it be in the days of the Son of man. ²⁷ They were eating and drinking; they were taking wives and being given in marriage, even until the day that Noah entered the ark. And the flood came and destroyed them all. ²⁸ It shall be similar to what happened in the days of Lot. They were eating and drinking; they were buying and selling; they were planting and building. ²⁹ Then, on the day that Lot departed from Sodom, it rained fire and brimstone from heaven, and it destroyed them all. ³⁰ According to these things, so shall it be in the day when the Son of man will be revealed. ³¹ In that hour, whoever will be on the rooftop, with his goods in the house, let him not descend to take them. And whoever will be in the field, similarly, let him not turn back. ³² Remember Lot's wife. ³³ Whoever has sought to save his life, will lose it; and whoever has lost it, will bring it back to

life. [34] I say to you, in that night, there will be two in one bed. One will be taken up, and the other will be left behind. [35] Two will be at the grindstone together. One will be taken up, and the other will be left behind. Two will be in the field. One will be taken up, and the other will be left behind." [36] Responding, they said to him, "Where, Lord?" [37] And he said to them, "Wherever the body will be, in that place also, the eagles shall be gathered together."

CHAPTER 18

[1] Now he also told them a parable, that we should continually pray and not cease, [2] saying: "There was a certain judge in a certain city, who did not fear God and did not respect man. [3] But there was a certain widow in that city, and she went to him, saying, 'Vindicate me from my adversary.' [4] And he refused to do so for a long time. But afterwards, he said within himself: 'Even though I do not fear God, nor respect man, [5] yet because this widow is pestering me, I will vindicate her, lest by returning, she may, in the end, wear me out.' " [6] Then the Lord said: "Listen to what the unjust judge said. [7] So then, will not God grant the vindication of his elect, who cry out to him day and night? Or will he continue to endure them? [8] I tell you that he will quickly bring vindication to them. Yet truly, when the Son of man returns, do you think that he will find faith on earth?" [9] Now about certain persons who consider themselves to be just, while disdaining others, he told also this parable: [10] "Two men ascended to the temple, in order to pray. One was a Pharisee, and the other was a tax collector. [11] Standing, the Pharisee prayed within himself in this way: 'O God, I give thanks to you that I am not like the rest of men: robbers, unjust, adulterers, even as this tax collector chooses to be. [12] I fast twice between Sabbaths. I give tithes from all that I possess.' [13] And the tax collector, standing at a distance, was not willing to even lift up his eyes to heaven. But he struck his chest, saying: 'O God, be merciful to me, a sinner.' [14] I say to you, this one descended to his house justified, but not the other. For everyone who exalts himself will be humbled; and whoever humbles himself will be exalted." [15] And they were bringing little children to him, so that he might touch them. And when the disciples saw this, they rebuked them. [16] But Jesus, calling them together, said: "Allow the children to come to me, and do not be an obstacle to them. For of such is the kingdom of God. [17] Amen, I say to you, whoever will not accept the kingdom of God like a child, will not enter into it." [18] And a certain leader questioned him, saying: "Good teacher, what should I do to possess eternal life?" [19] Then Jesus said to him: "Why do you call me good? No one is good except God alone. [20] You know the commandments: You shall not kill. You shall not commit adultery. You shall not steal. You shall not give false testimony. Honor your father and mother." [21] And he said, "I have kept all these things from my youth." [22] And when Jesus heard this, he said to him: "One thing is still lacking for you. Sell all the things that you have, and give to the poor. And then you will have treasure in heaven. And come, follow me." [23] When he heard this, he became very sorrowful. For he was very rich. [24] Then Jesus, seeing him brought to sorrow, said: "How difficult it is for those who have money to enter into the kingdom of God! [25] For it is easier for a camel to pass through the eye of a needle, than for a wealthy man to enter into the kingdom of God." [26] And those who were listening to this said, "Then who is able to be saved?" [27] He said to them, "Things that are impossible with men are possible with God." [28] And Peter said, "Behold, we have left everything, and we have followed you." [29] And he said to them: "Amen, I say to you, there is no one who has left behind home, or parents, or brothers, or a wife, or children, for the sake of the kingdom of God, [30] who will not receive much more in this time, and in the age to come eternal life." [31] Then Jesus took the twelve aside, and he said to them: "Behold, we are ascending to Jerusalem, and everything shall be completed which was written by the prophets about the Son of man. [32] For he will be handed over to the Gentiles, and he will be mocked and scourged and spit upon. [33] And after they have scourged him, they will kill him. And on the third day, he will rise again." [34] But they understood none of these things. For this word was concealed from them, and they did not understand the things that were said. [35] Now it happened that, as he was approaching Jericho, a certain blind man was sitting beside the way, begging. [36] And when he heard the multitude passing by, he asked what this was. [37] And they told him that Jesus of Nazareth was passing by. [38] And he cried out, saying, "Jesus, Son of David, take pity on me!" [39] And those who were passing by rebuked him, so that he would be silent. Yet truly, he cried out all the more, "Son of David, take pity on me!" [40] Then Jesus, standing still, ordered him to be brought to him.

And when he had drawn near, he questioned him, [41] saying, "What do you want, that I might do for you?" So he said, "Lord, that I may see." [42] And Jesus said to him: "Look around. Your faith has saved you." [43] And immediately he saw. And he followed him, magnifying God. And all the people, when they saw this, gave praise to God.

CHAPTER 19

[1] And having entered, he walked through Jericho. [2] And behold, there was a man named Zacchaeus. And he was the leader of the tax collectors, and he was wealthy. [3] And he sought to see Jesus, to see who he was. But he was unable to do so, because of the crowd, for he was small in stature. [4] And running ahead, he climbed up a sycamore tree, so that he might see him. For he was to pass near there. [5] And when he had arrived at the place, Jesus looked up and saw him, and he said to him: "Zacchaeus, hurry down. For today, I should lodge in your house." [6] And hurrying, he came down, and he received him joyfully. [7] And when they all saw this, they murmured, saying that he had turned aside to a sinful man. [8] But Zacchaeus, standing still, said to the Lord: "Behold, Lord, one half of my goods I give to the poor. And if I have cheated anyone in any matter, I will repay him fourfold." [9] Jesus said to him: "Today, salvation has come to this house; because of this, he too is a son of Abraham. [10] For the Son of man has come to seek and to save what had been lost." [11] As they were listening to these things, continuing on, he spoke a parable, because he was nearing Jerusalem, and because they guessed that the kingdom of God might be manifested without delay. [12] Therefore, he said: "A certain man of nobility traveled to a far away region, to receive for himself a kingdom, and to return. [13] And calling his ten servants, he gave them ten pounds, and he said to them: 'Do business until I return.' [14] But his citizens hated him. And so they sent a delegation after him, saying, 'We do not want this one to reign over us.' [15] And it happened that he returned, having received the kingdom. And he ordered the servants, to whom he had given the money, to be called so that he would know how much each one had earned by doing business. [16] Now the first approached, saying: 'Lord, your one pound has earned ten pounds.' [17] And he said to him: 'Well done, good servant. Since you have been faithful in a small matter, you will hold authority over ten cities.' [18] And the second came, saying: 'Lord, your one pound has earned five pounds.' [19] And he said to him, 'And so, you shall be over five cities.' [20] And another approached, saying: 'Lord, behold your one pound, which I kept stored in a cloth. [21] For I feared you, because you are an austere man. You take up what you did not lay down, and you reap what you did not sow.' [22] He said to him: 'By your own mouth, do I judge you, O wicked servant. You knew that I am an austere man, taking up what I did not lay down, and reaping what I did not sow. [23] And so, why did you not give my money to the bank, so that, upon my return, I might have withdrawn it with interest?' [24] And he said to the bystanders, 'Take the pound away from him, and give it to him who has ten pounds.' [25] And they said to him, 'Lord, he has ten pounds.' [26] So then, I say to you, that to all who have, it shall be given, and he will have in abundance. And from him who does not have, even what he has will be taken from him. [27] 'Yet truly, as for those enemies of mine, who did not want me to reign over them, bring them here, and put them to death before me.'" [28] And having said these things, he went ahead, ascending to Jerusalem. [29] And it happened that, when he had drawn near to Bethphage and Bethania, to the mount which is called Olivet, he sent two of his disciples, [30] saying: "Go into the town which is opposite you. Upon entering it, you will find the colt of a donkey, tied, on which no man has ever sat. Untie it, and lead it here. [31] And if anyone will ask you, 'Why are you untying it?' you shall say this to him: 'Because the Lord has requested its service.'" [32] And those who were sent went out, and they found the colt standing, just as he told them. [33] Then, as they were untying the colt, its owners said to them, "Why are you untying the colt?" [34] So they said, "Because the Lord has need of it." [35] And they led it to Jesus. And casting their garments on the colt, they helped Jesus onto it. [36] Then, as he was traveling, they were laying down their garments along the way. [37] And when he was now drawing near to the descent of Mount Olivet, the entire crowd of his disciples began to praise God joyfully, with a loud voice, over all the powerful works which they had seen, [38] saying: "Blessed is the king who has arrived in the name of the Lord! Peace in heaven and glory on high!" [39] And certain Pharisees within the crowd said to him, "Teacher, rebuke your disciples." [40] And he said to them, "I tell you, that if these will keep silent, the stones themselves will cry

out." [41] And when he drew near, seeing the city, he wept over it, saying: [42] "If only you had known, indeed even in this your day, which things are for your peace. But now they are hidden from your eyes. [43] For the days will overtake you. And your enemies will encircle you with a valley. And they will surround you and hem you in on every side. [44] And they will knock you down to the ground, with your sons who are in you. And they will not leave stone upon stone within you, because you did not recognize the time of your visitation." [45] And entering into the temple, he began to cast out those who sold in it, and those who bought, [46] saying to them: "It is written: 'My house is a house of prayer.' But you have made it into a den of robbers." [47] And he was teaching in the temple daily. And the leaders of the priests, and the scribes, and the leaders of the people were seeking to destroy him. [48] But they could not find what to do to him. For all the people were listening to him attentively.

CHAPTER 20

[1] And it happened that, on one of the days when he was teaching the people in the temple and preaching the Gospel, the leaders of the priests, and the scribes, gathered together with the elders, [2] and they spoke to him, saying: "Tell us, by what authority do you do these things? Or, who is it that has given you this authority?" [3] And in response, Jesus said to them: "I will also question you about one word. Respond to me: [4] The baptism of John, was it from heaven, or of men?" [5] So they discussed it among themselves, saying: "If we say, 'From heaven,' he will say, 'Then why did you not believe him?' [6] But if we say, 'Of men,' the whole people will stone us. For they are certain that John was a prophet." [7] And so they responded that they did not know where it was from. [8] And Jesus said to them, "Neither will I tell you by what authority I do these things." [9] Then he began to tell the people this parable: "A man planted a vineyard, and he loaned it to settlers, and he was on a sojourn for a long time. [10] And in due time, he sent a servant to the farmers, so that they would give to him from the fruit of the vineyard. And they beat him and drove him away, empty-handed. [11] And he continued to send another servant. But beating him and treating him with contempt, they likewise sent him away, empty-handed. [12] And he continued to send a third. And wounding him also, they drove him away. [13] Then the lord of the vineyard said: 'What shall I do? I will send my beloved son. Perhaps when they have seen him, they will respect him.' [14] And when the settlers had seen him, they discussed it among themselves, saying: 'This one is the heir. Let us kill him, so that the inheritance will be ours.' [15] And forcing him outside of the vineyard, they killed him. What, then, will the lord of the vineyard do to them?" [16] "He will come and destroy those settlers, and he will give the vineyard to others." And upon hearing this, they said to him, "Let it not be." [17] Then, gazing at them, he said: "Then what does this mean, which is written: 'The stone which the builders have rejected, the same has become the head of the corner?' [18] Everyone who falls on that stone will be shattered. And anyone upon whom it falls will be crushed." [19] And the leaders of the priests, and the scribes, were seeking to lay hands on him in that same hour, but they feared the people. For they realized that he had spoken this parable about them. [20] And being attentive, they sent traitors, who would pretend that they were just, so that they might catch him in his words and then hand him over to the power and authority of the procurator. [21] And they questioned him, saying: "Teacher, we know that you speak and teach correctly, and that you do not consider anyone's status, but you teach the way of God in truth. [22] Is it lawful for us to pay the tribute to Caesar, or not?" [23] But realizing their deceitfulness, he said to them: "Why do you test me? [24] Show me a denarius. Whose image and inscription does it have?" In response, they said to him, "Caesar's." [25] And so, he said to them: "Then repay the things that are Caesar's, to Caesar, and the things that are God's, to God." [26] And they were not able to contradict his word before the people. And being amazed at his answer, they were silent. [27] Now some of the Sadducees, who deny that there is a resurrection, approached him. And they questioned him, [28] saying: "Teacher, Moses wrote for us: If any man's brother will have died, having a wife, and if he does not have any children, then his brother should take her as his wife, and he should raise up offspring for his brother. [29] And so there were seven brothers. And the first took a wife, and he died without sons. [30] And the next one married her, and he also died without a son. [31] And the third married her, and similarly all seven, and none of them left behind any offspring, and they each died. [32] Last of all, the woman also died. [33] In the resurrection, then, whose wife will she be?

For certainly all seven had her as a wife." [34] And so, Jesus said to them: "The children of this age marry and are given in marriage. [35] Yet truly, those who shall be held worthy of that age, and of the resurrection from the dead, will neither be married, nor take wives. [36] For they can no longer die. For they are equal to the Angels, and they are children of God, since they are children of the resurrection. [37] For in truth, the dead do rise again, as Moses also showed beside the bush, when he called the Lord: 'The God of Abraham, and the God of Isaac, and the God of Jacob.' [38] And so he is not the God of the dead, but of the living. For all are alive to him." [39] Then some of the scribes, in response, said to him, "Teacher, you have spoken well." [40] And they no longer dared to question him about anything. [41] But he said to them: "How can they say that the Christ is the son of David? [42] Even David himself says, in the book of Psalms: 'The Lord said to my Lord, sit at my right hand, [43] until I set your enemies as your footstool.' [44] Therefore, David calls him Lord. So how can he be his son?" [45] Now in the hearing of all the people, he said to his disciples: [46] "Be cautious of the scribes, who choose to walk in long robes, and who love greetings in the marketplace, and the first chairs in the synagogues, and the first places at table during feasts, [47] who devour the houses of widows, feigning long prayers. These will receive the greater damnation."

CHAPTER 21

[1] And looking around, he saw the wealthy putting their donations into the offertory. [2] Then he also saw a certain widow, a pauper, putting in two small brass coins. [3] And he said: "Truly, I say to you, that this poor widow has put in more than all the others. [4] For all these, out of their abundance, have added to the gifts for God. But she, out of what she needed, has put in all that she had to live on." [5] And when some of them were saying, about the temple, that it was adorned with excellent stones and gifts, he said, [6] "These things that you see, the days will arrive when there will not be left behind stone upon stone, which is not thrown down." [7] Then they questioned him, saying: "Teacher, when will these things be? And what will be the sign when these things will happen?" [8] And he said: "Be cautious, lest you be seduced. For many will come in my name, saying: 'For I am he,' and, 'The time has drawn near.' And so, do not choose to go after them. [9] And when you will have heard of battles and seditions, do not be terrified. These things must happen first. But the end is not so soon." [10] Then he said to them: "People will rise up against people, and kingdom against kingdom. [11] And there will be great earthquakes in various places, and pestilences, and famines, and terrors from heaven; and there will be great signs. [12] But before all these things, they will lay their hands on you and persecute you, handing you over to synagogues and into custody, dragging you before kings and governors, because of my name. [13] And this will be an opportunity for you to give testimony. [14] Therefore, set this in your hearts: that you should not consider in advance how you might respond. [15] For I will give to you a mouth and wisdom, which all your adversaries will not be able to resist or contradict. [16] And you will be handed over by your parents, and brothers, and relatives, and friends. And they will bring about the death of some of you. [17] And you will be hated by all because of my name. [18] And yet, not a hair of your head will perish. [19] By your patience, you shall possess your souls. [20] Then, when you will have seen Jerusalem encircled by an army, know then that its desolation has drawn near. [21] Then let those who are in Judea flee to the mountains, and those who are in its midst withdraw, and those who are in the countryside not enter into it. [22] For these are the days of retribution, so that all things may be fulfilled, which have been written. [23] Then woe to those who are pregnant or nursing in those days. For there will be great distress upon the land and great wrath upon this people. [24] And they will fall by the edge of the sword. And they will be led away as captives into all nations. And Jerusalem will be trampled by the Gentiles, until the times of the nations are fulfilled. [25] And there will be signs in the sun and the moon and the stars. And there will be, on earth, distress among the Gentiles, out of confusion at the roaring of the sea and of the waves: [26] men withering away out of fear and out of apprehension over the things that will overwhelm the whole world. For the powers of the heavens will be moved. [27] And then they will see the Son of man coming on a cloud, with great power and majesty. [28] But when these things begin to happen, lift up your heads and look around you, because your redemption draws near." [29] And he told them a comparison: "Take notice of the fig tree and of all the trees. [30] When presently they produce fruit from themselves, you know that summer is near. [31] So you also,

when you will have seen these things happen, know that the kingdom of God is near. [32] Amen I say to you, this lineage shall not pass away, until all these things happen. [33] Heaven and earth shall pass away. But my words shall not pass away. [34] But be attentive to yourselves, lest perhaps your hearts may be weighed down by self-indulgence and inebriation and the cares of this life. And then that day may overwhelm you suddenly. [35] For like a snare it will overwhelm all those who sit upon the face of the entire earth. [36] And so, be vigilant, praying at all times, so that you may be held worthy to escape from all these things, which are in the future, and to stand before the Son of man." [37] Now in the daytime, he was teaching in the temple. But truly, departing in the evening, he lodged on the mount that is called Olivet. [38] And all the people arrived in the morning to listen to him in the temple.

CHAPTER 22

[1] Now the days of the Feast of Unleavened Bread, which is called Passover, were approaching. [2] And the leaders of the priests, and the scribes, were seeking a way to execute Jesus. Yet truly, they were afraid of the people. [3] Then Satan entered into Judas, who was surnamed Iscariot, one of the twelve. [4] And he went out and was speaking with the leaders of the priests, and the magistrates, as to how he might hand him over to them. [5] And they were glad, and so they made an agreement to give him money. [6] And he made a promise. And he was seeking an opportunity to hand him over, apart from the crowds. [7] Then the day of Unleavened Bread arrived, on which it was necessary to kill the Pascal lamb. [8] And he sent Peter and John, saying, "Go out, and prepare the Passover for us, so that we may eat." [9] But they said, "Where do you want us to prepare it?" [10] And he said to them: "Behold, as you are entering into the city, a certain man will meet you, carrying a pitcher of water. Follow him to the house into which he enters. [11] And you shall say to the father of the household: 'The Teacher says to you: Where is the guestroom, where I may eat the Passover with my disciples?' [12] And he will show you a large cenacle, fully furnished. And so, prepare it there." [13] And going out, they found it to be just as he had told them. And they prepared the Passover. [14] And when the hour had arrived, he sat down at table, and the twelve Apostles with him. [15] And he said to them: "With longing have I desired to eat this Passover with you, before I suffer. [16] For I say to you, that from this time, I will not eat it, until it is fulfilled in the kingdom of God." [17] And having taken the chalice, he gave thanks, and he said: "Take this and share it among yourselves. [18] For I say to you, that I will not drink from the fruit of the vine, until the kingdom of God arrives." [19] And taking bread, he gave thanks and broke it and gave it to them, saying: "This is my body, which is given for you. Do this as a commemoration of me." [20] Similarly also, he took the chalice, after he had eaten the meal, saying: "This chalice is the new covenant in my blood, which will be shed for you. [21] But in truth, behold, the hand of my betrayer is with me at table. [22] And indeed, the Son of man goes according to what has been determined. And yet, woe to that man by whom he will be betrayed." [23] And they began to inquire among themselves, as to which of them might do this. [24] Now there was also a contention among them, as to which of them seemed to be the greater. [25] And he said to them: "The kings of the Gentiles dominate them; and those who hold authority over them are called beneficent. [26] But it must not be so with you. Instead, whoever is greater among you, let him become the lesser. And whoever is the leader, let him become the server. [27] For who is greater: he who sits at table, or he who serves? Is not he who sits at table? Yet I am in your midst as one who serves. [28] But you are those who have remained with me during my trials. [29] And I dispose to you, just as my Father has disposed to me, a kingdom, [30] so that you may eat and drink at my table in my kingdom, and so that you may sit upon thrones, judging the twelve tribes of Israel." [31] And the Lord said: "Simon, Simon! Behold, Satan has asked for you, so that he may sift you like wheat. [32] But I have prayed for you, so that your faith may not fail, and so that you, once converted, may confirm your brothers." [33] And he said to him, "Lord, I am prepared to go with you, even to prison and to death." [34] And he said, "I say to you, Peter, the rooster will not crow this day, until you have three times denied that you know me." And he said to them, [35] "When I sent you without money or provisions or shoes, did you lack anything?" [36] And they said, "Nothing." Then he said to them: "But now, let whoever has money take it, and likewise with provisions. And whoever does not have these, let him sell his coat and buy a sword. [37] For I say to you, that what has been written must still

be fulfilled in me: 'And he was esteemed with the wicked.' Yet even these things about me have an end." [38] So they said, "Lord, behold, there are two swords here." But he said to them, "It is sufficient." [39] And departing, he went out, according to his custom, to the Mount of Olives. And his disciples also followed him. [40] And when he had arrived at the place, he said to them: "Pray, lest you enter into temptation." [41] And he was separated from them by about a stone's throw. And kneeling down, he prayed, [42] saying: "Father, if you are willing, take this chalice away from me. Yet truly, let not my will, but yours, be done." [43] Then an Angel appeared to him from heaven, strengthening him. And being in agony, he prayed more intensely; [44] and so his sweat became like drops of blood, running down to the ground. [45] And when he had risen up from prayer and had gone to his disciples, he found them sleeping out of sorrow. [46] And he said to them: "Why are you sleeping? Rise up, pray, lest you enter into temptation." [47] While he was still speaking, behold, a crowd arrived. And he who is called Judas, one of the twelve, went ahead of them and approached Jesus, in order to kiss him. [48] And Jesus said to him, "Judas, do you betray the Son of man with a kiss?" [49] Then those who were around him, realizing what was about to happen, said to him: "Lord, shall we strike with the sword?" [50] And one of them struck the servant of the high priest and cut off his right ear. [51] But in response, Jesus said, "Permit even this." And when he had touched his ear, he healed him. [52] Then Jesus said to the leaders of the priests, and the magistrates of the temple, and the elders, who had come to him: "Have you gone out, as if against a thief, with swords and clubs? [53] When I was with you each day in the temple, you did not extend your hands against me. But this is your hour and that of the power of darkness." [54] And apprehending him, they led him to the house of the high priest. Yet truly, Peter followed at a distance. [55] Now as they were sitting around a fire, which had been kindled in the middle of the atrium, Peter was in their midst. [56] And when a certain woman servant had seen him sitting in its light, and had looked at him intently, she said, "This one was also with him." [57] But he denied him by saying, "Woman, I do not know him." [58] And after a little while, another one, seeing him, said, "You also are one of them." Yet Peter said, "O man, I am not." [59] And after the interval of about one hour had passed, someone else affirmed it, saying: "Truly, this one also was with him. For he is also a Galilean." [60] And Peter said: "Man, I do not know what you are saying." And at once, while he was still speaking, the rooster crowed. [61] And the Lord turned around and looked at Peter. And Peter remembered the word of the Lord that he had said: "For before the rooster crows, you will deny me three times." [62] And going out, Peter wept bitterly. [63] And the men who were holding him ridiculed him and beat him. [64] And they blindfolded him and repeatedly struck his face. And they questioned him, saying: "Prophesy! Who is it that struck you?" [65] And blaspheming in many other ways, they spoke against him. [66] And when it was daytime, the elders of the people, and the leaders of the priests, and the scribes convened. And they led him into their council, saying, "If you are the Christ, tell us." [67] And he said to them: "If I tell you, you will not believe me. [68] And if I also question you, you will not answer me. Neither will you release me. [69] But from this time, the Son of man will be sitting at the right hand of the power of God." [70] Then they all said, "So you are the Son of God?" And he said. "You are saying that I am." [71] And they said: "Why do we still require testimony? For we have heard it ourselves, from his own mouth."

CHAPTER 23

[1] And the entire multitude of them, rising up, led him to Pilate. [2] Then they began to accuse him, saying, "We found this one subverting our nation, and prohibiting giving tribute to Caesar, and saying that he is Christ the king." [3] And Pilate questioned him, saying: "You are the king of the Jews?" But in response, he said: "You are saying it." [4] Then Pilate said to the leaders of the priests and to the crowds, "I find no case against this man." [5] But they continued more intensely, saying: "He has stirred up the people, teaching throughout all of Judea, beginning from Galilee, even to this place." [6] But Pilate, upon hearing Galilee, asked if the man were of Galilee. [7] And when he realized that he was under Herod's jurisdiction, he sent him away to Herod, who was himself also at Jerusalem in those days. [8] Then Herod, upon seeing Jesus, was very glad. For he had been wanting to see him for a long time, because he had heard so many things about him, and he was hoping to see some kind of sign wrought by him. [9] Then he questioned him with many words. But he gave him no response at all. [10] And the leaders of the priests, and the

scribes, stood firm in persistently accusing him. [11] Then Herod, with his soldiers, scorned him. And he ridiculed him, clothing him in a white garment. And he sent him back to Pilate. [12] And Herod and Pilate became friends on that day. For previously they were enemies to one another. [13] And Pilate, calling together the leaders of the priests, and the magistrates, and the people, [14] said to them: "You have brought before me this man, as one who disturbs the people. And behold, having questioned him before you, I find no case against this man, in those things about which you accuse him. [15] And neither did Herod. For I sent you all to him, and behold, nothing deserving of death was recorded about him. [16] Therefore, I will chastise him and release him." [17] Now he was required to release one person for them on the feast day. [18] But the entire crowd exclaimed together, saying: "Take this one, and release to us Barabbas!" [19] Now he had been cast into prison because of a certain sedition that occurred in the city and for murder. [20] Then Pilate spoke to them again, wanting to release Jesus. [21] But they shouted in response, saying: "Crucify him! Crucify him!" [22] Then he said to them a third time: "Why? What evil has he done? I find no case against him for death. Therefore, I will chastise him and release him." [23] But they persisted, with loud voices, in demanding that he be crucified. And their voices increased in intensity. [24] And so Pilate issued a judgment granting their petition. [25] Then he released for them the one who had been cast into prison for murder and sedition, whom they were requesting. Yet truly, Jesus he handed over to their will. [26] And as they were leading him away, they apprehended a certain one, Simon of Cyrene, as he was returning from the countryside. And they imposed the cross on him to carry after Jesus. [27] Then a great crowd of people followed him, with women who were mourning and lamenting him. [28] But Jesus, turning to them, said: "Daughters of Jerusalem, do not weep over me. Instead, weep over yourselves and over your children. [29] For behold, the days will arrive in which they will say, 'Blessed are the barren, and the wombs that have not borne, and the breasts that have not nursed.' [30] Then they will begin to say to the mountains, 'Fall over us,' and to the hills, 'Cover us.' [31] For if they do these things with green wood, what will be done with the dry?" [32] Now they also led out two other criminals with him, in order to execute them. [33] And when they arrived at the place that is called Calvary, they crucified him there, with the robbers, one to the right and the other to the left. [34] Then Jesus said, "Father, forgive them. For they know not what they do." And truly, dividing his garments, they cast lots. [35] And people were standing near, watching. And the leaders among them derided him, saying: "He saved others. Let him save himself, if this one is the Christ, the elect of God." [36] And the soldiers also ridiculed him, approaching him and offering him vinegar, [37] and saying, "If you are the king of the Jews, save yourself." [38] Now there was also an inscription written over him in letters of Greek, and Latin, and Hebrew: THIS IS THE KING OF THE JEWS. [39] And one of those robbers who were hanging blasphemed him, saying, "If you are the Christ, save yourself and us." [40] But the other responded by rebuking him, saying: "Do you have no fear of God, since you are under the same condemnation? [41] And indeed, it is just for us. For we are receiving what our deeds deserve. But truly, this one has done nothing wrong." [42] And he said to Jesus, "Lord, remember me when you come into your kingdom." [43] And Jesus said to him, "Amen I say to you, this day you shall be with me in Paradise." [44] Now it was nearly the sixth hour, and a darkness occurred over the entire earth, until the ninth hour. [45] And the sun was obscured. And the veil of the temple was torn down the middle. [46] And Jesus, crying out with a loud voice, said: "Father, into your hands I commend my spirit." And upon saying this, he expired. [47] Now, the centurion, seeing what had happened, glorified God, saying, "Truly, this man was the Just One." [48] And the entire crowd of those who came together to see this spectacle also saw what had happened, and they returned, striking their breasts. [49] Now all those who knew him, and the women who had followed him from Galilee, were standing at a distance, watching these things. [50] And behold, there was a man named Joseph, who was a councilman, a good and just man, [51] (for he had not consented to their decision or their actions). He was from Arimathea, a city of Judea. And he was himself also anticipating the kingdom of God. [52] This man approached Pilate and petitioned for the body of Jesus. [53] And taking him down, he wrapped him in a fine linen cloth, and he placed him in a tomb hewn from rock, in which no one had ever been placed. [54] And it was the day of Preparation, and the Sabbath was drawing near. [55] Now the women who had come with him from Galilee, by following, saw the tomb and the manner in which his body was placed. [56] And upon returning, they prepared aromatic spices and ointments. But on the Sabbath, indeed, they rested, according to the commandment.

CHAPTER 24

¹Then, on the first Sabbath, at very first light, they went to the tomb, carrying the aromatic spices that they had prepared. ²And they found the stone rolled back from the tomb. ³And upon entering, they did not find the body of the Lord Jesus. ⁴And it happened that, while their minds were still confused about this, behold, two men stood beside them, in shining apparel. ⁵Then, since they were afraid and were turning their faces toward the ground, these two said to them: "Why do you seek the living with the dead? ⁶He is not here, for he has risen. Recall how he spoke to you, when he was still in Galilee, ⁷saying: 'For the Son of man must be delivered into the hands of sinful men, and be crucified, and on the third day rise again.'" ⁸And they called to mind his words. ⁹And returning from the tomb, they reported all these things to the eleven, and to all the others. ¹⁰Now it was Mary Magdalene, and Joanna, and Mary of James, and the other women who were with them, who told these things to the Apostles. ¹¹But these words seemed to them a delusion. And so they did not believe them. ¹²But Peter, rising up, ran to the tomb. And stooping down, he saw the linen cloths positioned alone, and he went away wondering to himself about what had happened. ¹³And behold, two of them went out, on the same day, to a town named Emmaus, which was the distance of sixty stadia from Jerusalem. ¹⁴And they spoke to one another about all of these things that had occurred. ¹⁵And it happened that, while they were speculating and questioning within themselves, Jesus himself, drawing near, traveled with them. ¹⁶But their eyes were restrained, so that they would not recognize him. ¹⁷And he said to them, "What are these words, which you are discussing with one another, as you walk and are sad?" ¹⁸And one of them, whose name was Cleopas, responded by saying to him, "Are you the only one visiting Jerusalem who does not know the things that have happened there in these days?" ¹⁹And he said to them, "What things?" And they said, "About Jesus of Nazareth, who was a noble prophet, powerful in works and in words, before God and all the people. ²⁰And how our high priests and leaders handed him over to be condemned to death. And they crucified him. ²¹But we were hoping that he would be the Redeemer of Israel. And now, on top of all this, today is the third day since these things have happened. ²²Then, too, certain women from among us terrified us. For before daytime, they were at the tomb, ²³and, having not found his body, they returned, saying that they had even seen a vision of Angels, who said that he is alive. ²⁴And some of us went out to the tomb. And they found it just as the women had said. But truly, they did not find him." ²⁵And he said to them: "How foolish and reluctant in heart you are, to believe everything that has been spoken by the Prophets! ²⁶Was not the Christ required to suffer these things, and so enter into his glory?" ²⁷And beginning from Moses and all the Prophets, he interpreted for them, in all the Scriptures, the things that were about him. ²⁸And they drew near to the town where they were going. And he conducted himself so as to go on further. ²⁹But they were insistent with him, saying, "Remain with us, because it is toward evening and now daylight is declining." And so he entered with them. ³⁰And it happened that, while he was at table with them, he took bread, and he blessed and broke it, and he extended it to them. ³¹And their eyes were opened, and they recognized him. And he vanished from their eyes. ³²And they said to one another, "Was not our heart burning within us, while he was speaking on the way, and when he opened the Scriptures to us?" ³³And rising up at that same hour, they returned to Jerusalem. And they found the eleven gathered together, and those who were with them, ³⁴saying: "In truth, the Lord has risen, and he has appeared to Simon." ³⁵And they explained the things that were done on the way, and how they had recognized him at the breaking of the bread. ³⁶Then, while they were talking about these things, Jesus stood in their midst, And he said to them: "Peace be with you. It is I. Do not be afraid." ³⁷Yet truly, they were very disturbed and terrified, supposing that they saw a spirit. ³⁸And he said to them: "Why are you disturbed, and why do these thoughts rise up in your hearts? ³⁹See my hands and feet, that it is I myself. Look and touch. For a spirit does not have flesh and bones, as you see that I have." ⁴⁰And when he had said this, he showed them his hands and feet. ⁴¹Then, while they were still in disbelief and in wonder out of joy, he said, "Do you have anything here to eat?" ⁴²And they offered him a piece of roasted fish and a honeycomb. ⁴³And when he had eaten these in their sight, taking up what was left, he gave it to them. ⁴⁴And he said to them: "These are the words that I spoke to you when I was still with you, because all things must be fulfilled which are written in the law of Moses, and in the Prophets, and in the Psalms about me." ⁴⁵Then he opened their mind, so that they might

understand the Scriptures. ⁴⁶ And he said to them: "For so it is written, and so it was necessary, for the Christ to suffer and to rise up from the dead on the third day, ⁴⁷ and, in his name, for repentance and the remission of sins to be preached, among all the nations, beginning at Jerusalem. ⁴⁸ And you are witnesses of these things. ⁴⁹ And I am sending the Promise of my Father upon you. But you must stay in the city, until such time as you are clothed with power from on high." ⁵⁰Then he led them out as far as Bethania. And lifting up his hands, he blessed them. ⁵¹ And it happened that, while he was blessing them, he withdrew from them, and he was carried up into heaven. ⁵² And worshiping, they returned to Jerusalem with great joy. ⁵³ And they were always in the temple, praising and blessing God. Amen.

THE SACRED BIBLE: THE GOSPEL OF JOHN

CHAPTER 1

[1] In the beginning was the Word, and the Word was with God, and God was the Word. [2] He was with God in the beginning. [3] All things were made through Him, and nothing that was made was made without Him. [4] Life was in Him, and Life was the light of men. [5] And the light shines in the darkness, and the darkness did not comprehend it. [6] There was a man sent by God, whose name was John. [7] He arrived as a witness to offer testimony about the Light, so that all would believe through him. [8] He was not the Light, but he was to offer testimony about the Light. [9] The true Light, which illuminates every man, was coming into this world. [10] He was in the world, and the world was made through him, and the world did not recognize him. [11] He went to his own, and his own did not accept him. [12] Yet whoever did accept him, those who believed in his name, he gave them the power to become the sons of God. [13] These are born, not of blood, nor of the will of flesh, nor of the will of man, but of God. [14] And the Word became flesh, and he lived among us, and we saw his glory, glory like that of an only-begotten Son from the Father, full of grace and truth. [15] John offers testimony about him, and he cries out, saying: "This is the one about whom I said: 'He who is to come after me, has been placed ahead of me, because he existed before me.'" [16] And from his fullness, we all have received, even grace for grace. [17] For the law was given through Moses, but grace and truth came through Jesus Christ. [18] No one ever saw God; the only-begotten Son, who is in the bosom of the Father, he himself has described him. [19] And this is the testimony of John, when the Jews sent priests and Levites from Jerusalem to him, so that they might ask him, "Who are you?" [20] And he confessed it and did not deny it; and what he confessed was: "I am not the Christ." [21] And they questioned him: "Then what are you? Are you Elijah?" And he said, "I am not." "Are you the Prophet?" And he answered, "No." [22] Therefore, they said to him: "Who are you, so that we may give an answer to those who sent us? What do you say about yourself?" [23] He said, "I am a voice crying out in the desert, 'Make straight the way of the Lord,' just as the prophet Isaiah said." [24] And some of those who had been sent were from among the Pharisees. [25] And they questioned him and said to him, "Then why do you baptize, if you are not the Christ, and not Elijah, and not the Prophet?" [26] John answered them by saying: "I baptize with water. But in your midst stands one, whom you do not know. [27] The same is he who is to come after me, who has been placed ahead of me, the laces of whose shoes I am not worthy to loosen." [28] These things happened in Bethania, across the Jordan, where John was baptizing. [29] On the next day, John saw Jesus coming toward him, and so he said: "Behold, the Lamb of God. Behold, he who takes away the sin of the world. [30] This is the one about whom I said, 'After me arrives a man, who has been placed ahead of me, because he existed before me.' [31] And I did not know him. Yet it is for this reason that I come baptizing with water: so that he may be made manifest in Israel." [32] And John offered testimony, saying: "For I saw the Spirit descending from heaven like a dove; and he remained upon him. [33] And I did not know him. But he who sent me to baptize with water said to me: 'He over whom you will see the Spirit descending and remaining upon him, this is the one who baptizes with the Holy Spirit.' [34] And I saw, and I gave testimony: that this one is the Son of God." [35] The next day again, John was standing with two of his disciples. [36] And catching sight of Jesus walking, he said, "Behold, the Lamb of God." [37] And two disciples were listening to him speaking. And they followed Jesus. [38] Then Jesus, turning around and seeing them following him, said to them, "What are you seeking?" And they said to him, "Rabbi (which means in translation, Teacher), where do you live?" [39] He said to them, "Come and see." They went and saw where he was staying, and they stayed with him that day. Now it was about the tenth hour. [40] And Andrew, the brother of Simon Peter, was one of the two who had heard about him from John and had followed him. [41] First, he found his brother Simon, and he said to him, "We have found the Messiah," (which is translated as the Christ). [42] And he led him to Jesus. And Jesus, gazing at him, said: "You are Simon, son of Jonah. You shall be called Cephas," (which is translated as Peter). [43] On the next day, he wanted to go into Galilee, and he found Philip. And Jesus said to him, "Follow me." [44] Now Philip was from Bethsaida, the city of Andrew and Peter. [45] Philip found Nathanael, and he said to him, "We have found the one

about whom Moses wrote in the Law and the Prophets: Jesus, the son of Joseph, from Nazareth." ⁴⁶ And Nathanael said to him, "Can anything good be from Nazareth?" Philip said to him, "Come and see." ⁴⁷ Jesus saw Nathanael coming toward him, and he said about him, "Behold, an Israelite in whom truly there is no deceit." ⁴⁸ Nathanael said to him, "From where do you know me?" Jesus responded and said to him, "Before Philip called you, when you were under the fig tree, I saw you." ⁴⁹ Nathanael answered him and said: "Rabbi, you are the Son of God. You are the King of Israel." ⁵⁰ Jesus responded and said to him: "Because I told you that I saw you under the fig tree, you believe. Greater things than these, you will see." ⁵¹ And he said to him, "Amen, amen, I say to you, you will see heaven opened, and the Angels of God ascending and descending over the Son of man."

CHAPTER 2

¹ And on the third day, a wedding was held in Cana of Galilee, and the mother of Jesus was there. ² Now Jesus was also invited to the wedding, with his disciples. ³ And when the wine was failing, the mother of Jesus said to him, "They have no wine." ⁴ And Jesus said to her: "What is that to me and to you, woman? My hour has not yet arrived." ⁵ His mother said to the servants, "Do whatever he tells you." ⁶ Now in that place, there were six stone water jars, for the purification ritual of the Jews, containing two or three measures each. ⁷ Jesus said to them, "Fill the water jars with water." And they filled them to the very top. ⁸ And Jesus said to them, "Now draw from it, and carry it to the chief steward of the feast." And they took it to him. ⁹ Then, when the chief steward had tasted the water made into wine, since he did not know where it was from, for only the servants who had drawn the water knew, the chief steward called the groom, ¹⁰ and he said to him: "Every man offers the good wine first, and then, when they have become inebriated, he offers what is worse. But you have kept the good wine until now." ¹¹ This was the beginning of the signs that Jesus accomplished in Cana of Galilee, and it manifested his glory, and his disciples believed in him. ¹² After this, he descended to Capernaum, with his mother and his brothers and his disciples, but they did not remain there for many days. ¹³ And the Passover of the Jews was near, and so Jesus ascended to Jerusalem. ¹⁴ And he found, sitting in the temple, sellers of oxen and sheep and doves, and the moneychangers. ¹⁵ And when he had made something like a whip out of little cords, he drove them all out of the temple, including the sheep and the oxen. And he poured out the brass coins of the moneychangers, and he overturned their tables. ¹⁶ And to those who were selling doves, he said: "Take these things out of here, and do not make my Father's house into a house of commerce." ¹⁷ And truly, his disciples were reminded that it is written: "Zeal for your house consumes me." ¹⁸ Then the Jews responded and said to him, "What sign can you show to us, that you may do these things?" ¹⁹ Jesus responded and said to them, "Destroy this temple, and in three days I will raise it up." ²⁰ Then the Jews said, "This temple has been built up over forty-six years, and you will raise it up in three days?" ²¹ Yet he was speaking about the Temple of his body. ²² Therefore, when he had resurrected from the dead, his disciples were reminded that he had said this, and they believed in the Scriptures and in the word that Jesus had spoken. ²³ Now while he was at Jerusalem during the Passover, on the day of the feast, many trusted in his name, seeing his signs that he was accomplishing. ²⁴ But Jesus did not trust himself to them, because he himself had knowledge of all persons, ²⁵ and because he had no need of anyone to offer testimony about a man. For he knew what was within a man.

CHAPTER 3

¹ Now there was a man among the Pharisees, named Nicodemus, a leader of the Jews. ² He went to Jesus at night, and he said to him: "Rabbi, we know that you have arrived as a teacher from God. For no one would be able to accomplish these signs, which you accomplish, unless God were with him." ³ Jesus responded and said to him, "Amen, amen, I say to you, unless one has been reborn anew, he is not able to see the kingdom of God." ⁴ Nicodemus said to him: "How could a man be born when he is old? Surely, he cannot enter a second time into his mother's womb to be reborn?" ⁵ Jesus responded: "Amen, amen, I say to you, unless one has been reborn by water and the Holy Spirit, he is not able to enter into the kingdom of God. ⁶ What is born of the flesh is flesh, and what is born of the Spirit is spirit. ⁷ You should not be amazed that I said to you: You must be born anew. ⁸ The Spirit inspires where he wills. And you hear his voice, but you do not

know where he comes from, or where he is going. So it is with all who are born of the Spirit." [9] Nicodemus responded and said to him, "How are these things able to be accomplished?" [10] Jesus responded and said to him: "You are a teacher in Israel, and you are ignorant of these things? [11] Amen, amen, I say to you, that we speak about what we know, and we testify about what we have seen. But you do not accept our testimony. [12] If I have spoken to you about earthly things, and you have not believed, then how will you believe, if I will speak to you about heavenly things? [13] And no one has ascended to heaven, except the one who descended from heaven: the Son of man who is in heaven. [14] And just as Moses lifted up the serpent in the desert, so also must the Son of man be lifted up, [15] so that whoever believes in him may not perish, but may have eternal life. [16] For God so loved the world that he gave his only-begotten Son, so that all who believe in him may not perish, but may have eternal life. [17] For God did not send his Son into the world, in order to judge the world, but in order that the world may be saved through him. [18] Whoever believes in him is not judged. But whoever does not believe is already judged, because he does not believe in the name of the only-begotten Son of God. [19] And this is the judgment: that the Light has come into the world, and men loved darkness more than light. For their works were evil. [20] For everyone who does evil hates the Light and does not go toward the Light, so that his works may not be corrected. [21] But whoever acts in truth goes toward the Light, so that his works may be manifested, because they have been accomplished in God." [22] After these things, Jesus and his disciples went into the land of Judea. And he was living there with them and baptizing. [23] Now John was also baptizing, at Aenon near Salim, because there was much water in that place. And they were arriving and being baptized. [24] For John had not yet been cast into prison. [25] Then a dispute occurred between the disciples of John and the Jews, about purification. [26] And they went to John and said to him: "Rabbi, the one who was with you across the Jordan, about whom you offered testimony: behold, he is baptizing and everyone is going to him." [27] John responded and said: "A man is not able to receive anything, unless it has been given to him from heaven. [28] You yourselves offer testimony for me that I said, 'I am not the Christ,' but that I have been sent before him. [29] He who holds the bride is the groom. But the friend of the groom, who stands and listens to Him, rejoices joyfully at the voice of the groom. And so, this, my joy, has been fulfilled. [30] He must increase, while I must decrease. [31] He who comes from above, is above everything. He who is from below, is of the earth, and he speaks about the earth. He who comes from heaven is above everything. [32] And what he has seen and heard, about this he testifies. And no one accepts his testimony. [33] Whoever has accepted his testimony has certified that God is truthful. [34] For he whom God has sent speaks the words of God. For God does not give the Spirit by measure. [35] The Father loves the Son, and he has given everything into his hand. [36] Whoever believes in the Son has eternal life. But whoever is unbelieving toward the Son shall not see life; instead the wrath of God remains upon him."

CHAPTER 4

[1] And so, when Jesus realized that the Pharisees had heard that Jesus made more disciples and baptized more than John, [2] (though Jesus himself was not baptizing, but only his disciples) [3] he left behind Judea, and he traveled again to Galilee. [4] Now he needed to cross through Samaria. [5] Therefore, he went into a city of Samaria which is called Sychar, near the estate which Jacob gave to his son Joseph. [6] And Jacob's well was there. And so Jesus, being tired from the journey, was sitting in a certain way on the well. It was about the sixth hour. [7] A woman of Samaria arrived to draw water. Jesus said to her, "Give me to drink." [8] For his disciples had gone into the city in order to buy food. [9] And so, that Samaritan woman said to him, "How is it that you, being a Jew, are requesting a drink from me, though I am a Samaritan woman?" For the Jews do not associate with the Samaritans. [10] Jesus responded and said to her: "If you knew the gift of God, and who it is who is saying to you, 'Give me to drink,' perhaps you would have made a request of him, and he would have given you living water." [11] The woman said to him: "Lord, you do not have anything with which to draw water, and the well is deep. From where, then, do you have living water? [12] Surely, you are not greater than our father Jacob, who gave us the well and who drank from it, with his sons and his cattle?" [13] Jesus responded and said to her: "All who drink from this water will thirst again. But whoever shall drink from the water that I will give to him will not thirst for eternity. [14] Instead, the water that I will give to him will

become in him a fountain of water, springing up into eternal life." [15] The woman said to him, "Lord, give me this water, so that I may not thirst and may not come here to draw water." [16] Jesus said to her, "Go, call your husband, and return here." [17] The woman responded and said, "I have no husband." Jesus said to her: "You have spoken well, in saying, 'I have no husband.' [18] For you have had five husbands, but he whom you have now is not your husband. You have spoken this in truth." [19] The woman said to him: "Lord, I see that you are a Prophet. [20] Our fathers worshipped on this mountain, but you say that Jerusalem is the place where one ought to worship." [21] Jesus said to her: "Woman, believe me, the hour is coming when you shall worship the Father, neither on this mountain, nor in Jerusalem. [22] You worship what you do not know; we worship what we do know. For salvation is from the Jews. [23] But the hour is coming, and it is now, when true worshippers shall worship the Father in spirit and in truth. For the Father also seeks such persons who may worship him. [24] God is Spirit. And so, those who worship him must worship in spirit and in truth." [25] The woman said to him: "I know that the Messiah is coming (who is called the Christ). And then, when he will have arrived, he will announce everything to us." [26] Jesus said to her: "I am he, the one who is speaking with you." [27] And then his disciples arrived. And they wondered that he was speaking with the woman. Yet no one said: "What are you seeking?" or, "Why are you talking with her?" [28] And so the woman left behind her water jar and went into the city. And she said to the men there: [29] "Come and see a man who has told me all the things that I have done. Is he not the Christ?" [30] Therefore, they went out of the city and came to him. [31] Meanwhile, the disciples petitioned him, saying, "Rabbi, eat." [32] But he said to them, "I have food to eat which you do not know." [33] Therefore, the disciples said to one another, "Could someone have brought him something to eat?" [34] Jesus said to them: "My food is to do the will of the One who sent me, so that I may perfect his work. [35] Do you not say, 'There are still four months, and then the harvest arrives?' Behold, I say to you: Lift up your eyes and look at the countryside; for it is already ripe for the harvest. [36] For he who reaps, receives wages and gathers fruit unto eternal life, so that both he who sows and he who reaps may rejoice together. [37] For in this the word is true: that it is one who sows, and it is another who reaps. [38] I have sent you to reap that for which you did not labor. Others have labored, and you have entered into their labors." [39] Now many of the Samaritans from that city believed in him, because of the word of the woman who was offering testimony: "For he told me all the things that I have done." [40] Therefore, when the Samaritans had come to him, they petitioned him to lodge there. And he lodged there for two days. [41] And many more believed in him, because of his own word. [42] And they said to the woman: "Now we believe, not because of your speech, but because we ourselves have heard him, and so we know that he is truly the Savior of the world." [43] Then, after two days, he departed from there, and he traveled into Galilee. [44] For Jesus himself offered testimony that a Prophet has no honor in his own country. [45] And so, when he had arrived in Galilee, the Galileans received him, because they had seen all that he had done at Jerusalem, in the day of the feast. For they also went to the feast day. [46] Then he went again into Cana of Galilee, where he made water into wine. And there was a certain ruler, whose son was sick at Capernaum. [47] Since he had heard that Jesus came to Galilee from Judea, he sent to him and begged him to come down and heal his son. For he was beginning to die. [48] Therefore, Jesus said to him, "Unless you have seen signs and wonders, you do not believe." [49] The ruler said to him, "Lord, come down before my son dies." [50] Jesus said to him, "Go, your son lives." The man believed the word that Jesus spoke to him, and so he went away. [51] Then, as he was going down, his servants met him. And they reported to him, saying that his son was alive. [52] Therefore, he asked them at which hour he had become better. And they said to him, "Yesterday, at the seventh hour, the fever left him." [53] Then the father realized that it was at the same hour that Jesus said to him, "Your son lives." And both he and his entire household believed. [54] This next sign was the second that Jesus accomplished, after he had arrived in Galilee from Judea.

CHAPTER 5

[1] After these things, there was a feast day of the Jews, and so Jesus ascended to Jerusalem. [2] Now at Jerusalem is the Pool of Evidence, which in Hebrew is known as the Place of Mercy; it has five porticos. [3] Along these lay a great multitude of the sick, the blind, the lame, and the withered, waiting for the movement of the water. [4] Now at times an Angel of the Lord would descend into the pool, and

so the water was moved. And whoever descended first into the pool, after the motion of the water, he was healed of whatever infirmity held him. [5] And there was a certain man in that place, having been in his infirmity for thirty-eight years. [6] Then, when Jesus had seen him reclining, and when he realized that he had been afflicted for a long time, he said to him, "Do you want to be healed?" [7] The invalid answered him: "Lord, I do not have any man to put me in the pool, when the water has been stirred. For as I am going, another descends ahead of me." [8] Jesus said to him, "Rise, take up your stretcher, and walk." [9] And immediately the man was healed. And he took up his stretcher and walked. Now this day was the Sabbath. [10] Therefore, the Jews said to the one who had been healed: "It is the Sabbath. It is not lawful for you to take up your stretcher." [11] He answered them, "The one who healed me, he said to me, 'Take up your stretcher and walk.' " [12] Therefore, they questioned him, "Who is that man, who said to you, 'Take up your bed and walk?' " [13] But the one who had been given health did not know who it was. For Jesus had turned aside from the crowd gathered in that place. [14] Afterwards, Jesus found him in the temple, and he said to him: "Behold, you have been healed. Do not choose to sin further, otherwise something worse may happen to you." [15] This man went away, and he reported to the Jews that it was Jesus who had given him health. [16] Because of this, the Jews were persecuting Jesus, for he was doing these things on the Sabbath. [17] But Jesus answered them, "Even now, my Father is working, and I am working." [18] And so, because of this, the Jews were seeking to kill him even more so. For not only did he break the Sabbath, but he even said that God was his Father, making himself equal to God. [19] Then Jesus responded and said to them: "Amen, amen, I say to you, the Son is not able to do anything of himself, but only what he has seen the Father doing. For whatever he does, even this does the Son do, similarly. [20] For the Father loves the Son, and he shows him all that he himself does. And greater works than these will he show him, so much so that you shall wonder. [21] For just as the Father raises the dead and gives life, so also does the Son give life to whomever he wills. [22] For the Father does not judge anyone. But he has given all judgment to the Son, [23] so that all may honor the Son, just as they honor the Father. Whoever does not honor the Son, does not honor the Father who sent him. [24] Amen, amen, I say to you, that whoever hears my word, and believes in him who sent me, has eternal life, and he does not go into judgment, but instead he crosses from death into life. [25] Amen, amen, I say to you, that the hour is coming, and it is now, when the dead shall hear the voice of the Son of God; and those who hear it shall live. [26] For just as the Father has life in himself, so also has he granted to the Son to have life in himself. [27] And he has given him the authority to accomplish judgment. For he is the Son of man. [28] Do not be amazed at this. For the hour is coming in which all who are in the grave shall hear the voice of the Son of God. [29] And those who have done good shall go forth to the resurrection of life. Yet truly, those who have done evil shall go to the resurrection of judgment. [30] I am not able to do anything of myself. As I hear, so do I judge. And my judgment is just. For I do not seek my own will, but the will of him who sent me. [31] If I offer testimony about myself, my testimony is not true. [32] There is another who offers testimony about me, and I know that the testimony which he offers about me is true. [33] You sent to John, and he offered testimony to the truth. [34] But I do not accept testimony from man. Instead, I say these things, so that you may be saved. [35] He was a burning and shining light. So you were willing, at the time, to exult in his light. [36] But I hold a greater testimony than that of John. For the works which the Father has given to me, so that I may complete them, these works themselves that I do, offer testimony about me: that the Father has sent me. [37] And the Father who has sent me has himself offered testimony about me. And you have never heard his voice, nor have you beheld his appearance. [38] And you do not have his word abiding in you. For the one whom he sent, the same you would not believe. [39] Study the Scriptures. For you think that in them you have eternal life. And yet they also offer testimony about me. [40] And you are not willing to come to me, so that you may have life. [41] I do not accept glory from men. [42] But I know you, that you do not have the love of God within you. [43] I have come in the name of my Father, and you do not accept me. If another will arrive in his own name, him you will accept. [44] How are you able to believe, you who accept glory from one another and yet do not seek the glory that is from God alone? [45] Do not consider that I might accuse you with the Father. There is one who accuses you, Moses, in whom you hope. [46] For if you were believing in Moses, perhaps you would believe in me also. For he wrote about me. [47] But if you do not believe by his writings, how will you believe by my words?"

CHAPTER 6

[1] After these things, Jesus traveled across the sea of Galilee, which is the Sea of Tiberias. [2] And a great multitude was following him, for they saw the signs that he was accomplishing toward those who were infirm. [3] Therefore, Jesus went onto a mountain, and he sat down there with his disciples. [4] Now the Passover, the feast day of the Jews, was near. [5] And so, when Jesus had lifted up his eyes and had seen that a very great multitude came to him, he said to Philip, "From where should we buy bread, so that these may eat?" [6] But he said this to test him. For he himself knew what he would do. [7] Philip answered him, "Two hundred denarii of bread would not be sufficient for each of them to receive even a little." [8] One of his disciples, Andrew, the brother of Simon Peter, said to him: [9] "There is a certain boy here, who has five barley loaves and two fish. But what are these among so many?" [10] Then Jesus said, "Have the men sit down to eat." Now, there was much grass in that place. And so the men, in number about five thousand, sat down to eat. [11] Therefore, Jesus took the bread, and when he had given thanks, he distributed it to those who were sitting down to eat; similarly also, from the fish, as much as they wanted. [12] Then, when they were filled, he said to his disciples, "Gather the fragments that are left over, lest they be lost." [13] And so they gathered, and they filled twelve baskets with the fragments of the five barley loaves, which were left over from those who had eaten. [14] Therefore, those men, when they had seen that Jesus had accomplished a sign, they said, "Truly, this one is the Prophet who is to come into the world." [15] And so, when he realized that they were going to come and take him away and make him king, Jesus fled back to the mountain, by himself alone. [16] Then, when evening arrived, his disciples descended to the sea. [17] And when they had climbed into a boat, they went across the sea to Capernaum. And darkness had now arrived, and Jesus had not returned to them. [18] Then the sea was stirred up by a great wind that was blowing. [19] And so, when they had rowed about twenty-five or thirty stadia, they saw Jesus walking on the sea, and drawing near to the boat, and they were afraid. [20] But he said to them: "It is I. Do not be afraid." [21] Therefore, they were willing to receive him into the boat. But immediately the boat was at the land to which they were going. [22] On the next day, the crowd which was standing across the sea saw that there were no other small boats in that place, except one, and that Jesus had not entered into the boat with his disciples, but that his disciples had departed alone. [23] Yet truly, other boats came over from Tiberias, next to the place where they had eaten the bread after the Lord gave thanks. [24] Therefore, when the crowd had seen that Jesus was not there, nor his disciples, they climbed into the small boats, and they went to Capernaum, seeking Jesus. [25] And when they had found him across the sea, they said to him, "Rabbi, when did you come here?" [26] Jesus answered them and said: "Amen, amen, I say to you, you seek me, not because you have seen signs, but because you have eaten from the bread and were satisfied. [27] Do not work for food that perishes, but for that which endures to eternal life, which the Son of man will give to you. For God the Father has sealed him." [28] Therefore, they said to him, "What should we do, so that we may labor in the works of God?" [29] Jesus responded and said to them, "This is the work of God, that you believe in him whom he sent." [30] And so they said to him: "Then what sign will you do, so that we may see it and believe in you? What will you work? [31] Our fathers ate manna in the desert, just as it has been written, 'He gave them bread from heaven to eat.'" [32] Therefore, Jesus said to them: "Amen, amen, I say to you, Moses did not give you bread from heaven, but my Father gives you the true bread from heaven. [33] For the bread of God is he who descends from heaven and gives life to the world." [34] And so they said to him, "Lord, give us this bread always." [35] Then Jesus said to them: "I am the bread of life. Whoever comes to me shall not hunger, and whoever believes in me shall never thirst. [36] But I say to you, that even though you have seen me, you do not believe. [37] All that the Father gives to me shall come to me. And whoever comes to me, I will not cast out. [38] For I descended from heaven, not to do my own will, but the will of him who sent me. [39] Yet this is the will of the Father who sent me: that I should lose nothing out of all that he has given to me, but that I should raise them up on the last day. [40] So then, this is the will of my Father who sent me: that everyone who sees the Son and believes in him may have eternal life, and I will raise him up on the last day." [41] Therefore, the Jews murmured about him, because he had said: "I am the living bread, who descended from heaven." [42] And they said: "Is this not Jesus, the son of Joseph, whose father and mother we know? Then how can he say: 'For I descended from heaven?'" [43] And so Jesus responded and said to them: "Do not choose to murmur

among yourselves. ⁴⁴No one is able to come to me, unless the Father, who has sent me, has drawn him. And I will raise him up on the last day. ⁴⁵It has been written in the Prophets: 'And they shall all be taught by God.' Everyone who has listened and learned from the Father comes to me. ⁴⁶Not that anyone has seen the Father, except he who is from God; this one has seen the Father. ⁴⁷Amen, amen, I say to you, whoever believes in me has eternal life. ⁴⁸I am the bread of life. ⁴⁹Your fathers ate manna in the desert, and they died. ⁵⁰This is the bread which descends from heaven, so that if anyone will eat from it, he may not die. ⁵¹I am the living bread, who descended from heaven. ⁵²If anyone eats from this bread, he shall live in eternity. And the bread that I will give is my flesh, for the life of the world." ⁵³Therefore, the Jews debated among themselves, saying, "How can this man give us his flesh to eat?" ⁵⁴And so, Jesus said to them: "Amen, amen, I say to you, unless you eat the flesh of the Son of man and drink his blood, you will not have life in you. ⁵⁵Whoever eats my flesh and drinks my blood has eternal life, and I will raise him up on the last day. ⁵⁶For my flesh is true food, and my blood is true drink. ⁵⁷Whoever eats my flesh and drinks my blood abides in me, and I in him. ⁵⁸Just as the living Father has sent me and I live because of the Father, so also whoever eats me, the same shall live because of me. ⁵⁹This is the bread that descends from heaven. It is not like the manna that your fathers ate, for they died. Whoever eats this bread shall live forever." ⁶⁰He said these things when he was teaching in the synagogue at Capernaum. ⁶¹Therefore, many of his disciples, upon hearing this, said: "This saying is difficult," and, "Who is able to listen to it?" ⁶²But Jesus, knowing within himself that his disciples were murmuring about this, said to them: "Does this offend you? ⁶³Then what if you were to see the Son of man ascending to where he was before? ⁶⁴It is the Spirit who gives life. The flesh does not offer anything of benefit. The words that I have spoken to you are spirit and life. ⁶⁵But there are some among you who do not believe." For Jesus knew from the beginning who were unbelieving and which one would betray him. ⁶⁶And so he said, "For this reason, I said to you that no one is able to come to me, unless it has been given to him by my Father." ⁶⁷After this, many of his disciples went back, and they no longer walked with him. ⁶⁸Therefore, Jesus said to the twelve, "Do you also want to go away?" ⁶⁹Then Simon Peter answered him: "Lord, to whom would we go? You have the words of eternal life. ⁷⁰And we have believed, and we recognize that you are the Christ, the Son of God." ⁷¹Jesus answered them: "Have I not chosen you twelve? And yet one among you is a devil." ⁷²Now he was speaking about Judas Iscariot, the son of Simon. For this one, even though he was one of the twelve, was about to betray him.

CHAPTER 7

¹Then, after these things, Jesus was walking in Galilee. For he was not willing to walk in Judea, because the Jews were seeking to kill him. ²Now the feast day of the Jews, the Feast of Tabernacles, was near. ³And his brothers said to him: "Move away from here and go into Judea, so that your disciples there may also see your works that you do. ⁴Of course, no one does anything in secret, but he himself seeks to be in the public view. Since you do these things, manifest yourself to the world." ⁵For neither did his brothers believe in him. ⁶Therefore, Jesus said to them: "My time has not yet come; but your time is always at hand. ⁷The world cannot hate you. But it hates me, because I offer testimony about it, that its works are evil. ⁸You may go up to this feast day. But I am not going up to this feast day, because my time has not yet been fulfilled." ⁹When he had said these things, he himself remained in Galilee. ¹⁰But after his brothers went up, then he also went up to the feast day, not openly, but as if in secret. ¹¹Therefore, the Jews were seeking him on the feast day, and they were saying, "Where is he?" ¹²And there was much murmuring in the crowd concerning him. For certain ones were saying, "He is good." But others were saying, "No, for he seduces the crowds." ¹³Yet no one was speaking openly about him, out of fear of the Jews. ¹⁴Then, about the middle of the feast, Jesus ascended into the temple, and he was teaching. ¹⁵And the Jews wondered, saying: "How does this one know letters, though he has not been taught?" ¹⁶Jesus responded to them and said: "My doctrine is not of me, but of him who sent me. ¹⁷If anyone has chosen to do his will, then he will realize, about the doctrine, whether it is from God, or whether I am speaking from myself. ¹⁸Whoever speaks from himself seeks his own glory. But whoever seeks the glory of him who sent me, this one is true, and injustice is not in him. ¹⁹Did not Moses give you the law? And yet not one among you keeps the law! ²⁰Why are you seeking to kill me?" The crowd responded and said: "You must have a

demon. Who is seeking to kill you?" [21] Jesus responded and said to them: "One work have I done, and you all wonder. [22] For Moses gave you circumcision, (not that it is of Moses, but of the fathers) and on the Sabbath you circumcise a man. [23] If a man can receive circumcision on the Sabbath, so that the law of Moses may not be broken, why are you indignant toward me, because I have made a man whole on the Sabbath? [24] Do not judge according to appearances, but instead judge a just judgment." [25] Therefore, some of those from Jerusalem said: "Is he not the one whom they are seeking to kill? [26] And behold, he is speaking openly, and they say nothing to him. Could the leaders have decided that it is true this one is the Christ? [27] But we know him and where he is from. And when the Christ has arrived, no one will know where he is from." [28] Therefore, Jesus cried out in the temple, teaching and saying: "You know me, and you also know where I am from. And I have not arrived of myself, but he who sent me is true, and him you do not know. [29] I know him. For I am from him, and he has sent me." [30] Therefore, they were seeking to apprehend him, and yet no one laid hands on him, because his hour had not yet come. [31] But many among the crowd believed in him, and they were saying, "When the Christ arrives, will he perform more signs than this man does?" [32] The Pharisees heard the crowd murmuring these things about him. And the leaders and the Pharisees sent attendants to apprehend him. [33] Therefore, Jesus said to them: "For a brief time, I am still with you, and then I am going to him who sent me. [34] You shall seek me, and you will not find me. And where I am, you are not able to go." [35] And so the Jews said among themselves: "Where is this place to which he will go, such that we will not find him? Will he go to those dispersed among the Gentiles and teach the Gentiles? [36] What is this word that he spoke, 'You will seek me and you will not find me; and where I am, you are not able to go?'" [37] Then, on the last great day of the feast, Jesus was standing and crying out, saying: "If anyone thirsts, let him come to me and drink: [38] whoever believes in me, just as Scripture says, 'From his chest shall flow rivers of living water.'" [39] Now he said this about the Spirit, which those who believe in him would soon be receiving. For the Spirit had not yet been given, because Jesus had not yet been glorified. [40] Therefore, some from that crowd, when they had heard these words of his, were saying, "This one truly is the Prophet." [41] Others were saying, "He is the Christ." Yet certain ones were saying: "Does the Christ come from Galilee? [42] Does Scripture not say that the Christ comes from the offspring of David and from Bethlehem, the town where David was?" [43] And so there arose a dissension among the multitude because of him. [44] Now certain ones among them wanted to apprehend him, but no one laid hands upon him. [45] Therefore, the attendants went to the high priests and the Pharisees. And they said to them, "Why have you not brought him?" [46] The attendants responded, "Never has a man spoken like this man." [47] And so the Pharisees answered them: "Have you also been seduced? [48] Have any of the leaders believed in him, or any of the Pharisees? [49] But this crowd, which does not know the law, they are accursed." [50] Nicodemus, the one who came to him by night and who was one of them, said to them, [51] "Does our law judge a man, unless it has first heard him and has known what he has done?" [52] They responded and said to him: "Are you also a Galilean? Study the Scriptures, and see that a prophet does not arise from Galilee." [53] And each one returned to his own house.

CHAPTER 8

[1] But Jesus continued on to the Mount of Olives. [2] And early in the morning, he went again to the temple; and all the people came to him. And sitting down, he taught them. [3] Now the scribes and Pharisees brought forward a woman caught in adultery, and they stood her in front of them. [4] And they said to him: "Teacher, this woman was just now caught in adultery. [5] And in the law, Moses commanded us to stone such a one. Therefore, what do you say?" [6] But they were saying this to test him, so that they might be able to accuse him. Then Jesus bent down and wrote with his finger on the earth. [7] And then, when they persevered in questioning him, he stood upright and said to them, "Let whoever is without sin among you be the first to cast a stone at her." [8] And bending down again, he wrote on the earth. [9] But upon hearing this, they went away, one by one, beginning with the eldest. And Jesus alone remained, with the woman standing in front of him. [10] Then Jesus, raising himself up, said to her: "Woman, where are those who accused you? Has no one condemned you?" [11] And she said, "No one, Lord." Then Jesus said: "Neither will I condemn you. Go, and now do not choose to sin anymore." [12] Then Jesus spoke to them again, saying: "I am the light of the

world. Whoever follows me does not walk in darkness, but shall have the light of life." [13] And so the Pharisees said to him, "You offer testimony about yourself; your testimony is not true." [14] Jesus responded and said to them: "Even though I offer testimony about myself, my testimony is true, for I know where I came from and where I am going. [15] You judge according to the flesh. I do not judge anyone. [16] And when I do judge, my judgment is true. For I am not alone, but it is I and he who sent me: the Father. [17] And it is written in your law that the testimony of two men is true. [18] I am one who offers testimony about myself, and the Father who sent me offers testimony about me." [19] Therefore, they said to him, "Where is your Father?" Jesus answered: "You know neither me, nor my Father. If you did know me, perhaps you would know my Father also." [20] Jesus spoke these words at the treasury, while teaching in the temple. And no one apprehended him, because his hour had not yet come. [21] Therefore, Jesus again spoke to them: "I am going, and you shall seek me. And you will die in your sin. Where I am going, you are not able to go." [22] And so the Jews said, "Is he going to kill himself, for he said: 'Where I am going, you are not able to go?'" [23] And he said to them: "You are from below. I am from above. You are of this world. I am not of this world. [24] Therefore, I said to you, that you will die in your sins. For if you will not believe that I am, you will die in your sin." [25] And so they said to him, "Who are you?" Jesus said to them: "The Beginning, who is also speaking to you. [26] I have much to say about you and to judge. But he who sent me is true. And what I have heard from him, this I speak within the world." [27] And they did not realize that he was calling God his Father. [28] And so Jesus said to them: "When you will have lifted up the Son of man, then you shall realize that I am, and that I do nothing of myself, but just as the Father has taught me, so do I speak. [29] And he who sent me is with me, and he has not abandoned me alone. For I always do what is pleasing to him." [30] As he was speaking these things, many believed in him. [31] Therefore, Jesus said to those Jews who believed in him: "If you will abide in my word, you will truly be my disciples. [32] And you shall know the truth, and the truth shall set you free." [33] They answered him: "We are the offspring of Abraham, and we have never been a slave to anyone. How can you say, 'You shall be set free?'" [34] Jesus answered them: "Amen, amen, I say to you, that everyone who commits sin is a slave of sin. [35] Now the slave does not abide in the house for eternity. Yet the Son does abide in eternity. [36] Therefore, if the Son has set you free, then you will truly be free. [37] I know that you are sons of Abraham. But you are seeking to kill me, because my word has not taken hold in you. [38] I speak what I have seen with my Father. And you do what you have seen with your father." [39] They responded and said to him, "Abraham is our father." Jesus said to them: "If you are the sons of Abraham, then do the works of Abraham. [40] But now you are seeking to kill me, a man who has spoken the truth to you, which I have heard from God. This is not what Abraham did. [41] You do the works of your father." Therefore, they said to him: "We were not born out of fornication. We have one father: God." [42] Then Jesus said to them: "If God were your father, certainly you would love me. For I proceeded and came from God. For I did not come from myself, but he sent me. [43] Why do you not recognize my speech? It is because you are not able to hear my word. [44] You are of your father, the devil. And you will carry out the desires of your father. He was a murderer from the beginning. And he did not stand in the truth, because the truth is not in him. When he speaks a lie, he speaks it from his own self. For he is a liar, and the father of lies. [45] But if I speak the truth, you do not believe me. [46] Which of you can convict me of sin? If I speak the truth to you, why do you not believe me? [47] Whoever is of God, hears the words of God. For this reason, you do not hear them: because you are not of God." [48] Therefore, the Jews responded and said to him, "Are we not correct in saying that you are a Samaritan, and that you have a demon?" [49] Jesus responded: "I do not have a demon. But I honor my Father, and you have dishonored me. [50] But I am not seeking my own glory. There is One who seeks and judges. [51] Amen, amen, I say to you, if anyone will have kept my word, he will not see death for eternity." [52] Therefore, the Jews said: "Now we know that you have a demon. Abraham is dead, and the Prophets; and yet you say, 'If anyone will have kept my word, he shall not taste death for eternity.' [53] Are you greater than our father Abraham, who is dead? And the prophets are dead. So who do you make yourself to be?" [54] Jesus responded: "If I glorify myself, my glory is nothing. It is my Father who glorifies me. And you say about him that he is your God. [55] And yet you have not known him. But I know him. And if I were to say that I do not know him, then I would be like you, a liar. But I know him, and I keep his word. [56] Abraham, your father, rejoiced that he might see my day; he saw it and was glad." ⁵⁷ And so the Jews said to him, "You have not yet reached fifty years, and you have seen Abraham?" ⁵⁸ Jesus said to them, "Amen, amen, I say to you, before Abraham was made, I am." ⁵⁹ Therefore, they took up stones to cast at him. But Jesus hid himself, and he departed from the temple.

CHAPTER 9

¹ And Jesus, while passing by, saw a man blind from birth. ² And his disciples asked him, "Rabbi, who sinned, this man or his parents, that he would be born blind?" ³ Jesus responded: "Neither this man nor his parents sinned, but it was so that the works of God would be made manifest in him. ⁴ I must work the works of him who sent me, while it is day: the night is coming, when no one is able to work. ⁵ As long as I am in the world, I am the light of the world." ⁶ When he had said these things, he spat on the ground, and he made clay from the spittle, and he smeared the clay over his eyes. ⁷ And he said to him: "Go, wash in the pool of Siloam" (which is translated as: one who has been sent). Therefore, he went away and washed, and he returned, seeing. ⁸ And so the bystanders and those who had seen him before, when he was a beggar, said, "Is this not the one who was sitting and begging?" Some said, "This is he." ⁹ But others said, "Certainly not, but he is similar to him." Yet truly, he himself said, "I am he." ¹⁰ Therefore, they said to him, "How were your eyes opened?" ¹¹ He responded: "That man who is called Jesus made clay, and he anointed my eyes and said to me, 'Go to the pool of Siloam and wash.' And I went, and I washed, and I see." ¹² And they said to him, "Where is he?" He said, "I do not know." ¹³ They brought the one who had been blind to the Pharisees. ¹⁴ Now it was the Sabbath, when Jesus made the clay and opened his eyes. ¹⁵ Therefore, again the Pharisees questioned him as to how he had seen. And he said to them, "He placed clay over my eyes, and I washed, and I see." ¹⁶ And so certain Pharisees said: "This man, who does not keep the Sabbath, is not from God." But others said, "How could a sinful man accomplish these signs?" And there was a schism among them. ¹⁷ Therefore, they spoke again to the blind man, "What do you say about him who opened your eyes?" Then he said, "He is a Prophet." ¹⁸ Therefore, the Jews did not believe, about him, that he had been blind and had seen, until they called the parents of him who had seen. ¹⁹ And they questioned them, saying: "Is this your son, whom you say was born blind? Then how is it that he now sees?" ²⁰ His parents responded to them and said: "We know that this is our son and that he was born blind. ²¹ But how it is that he now sees, we do not know. And who opened his eyes, we do not know. Ask him. He is old enough. Let him speak for himself." ²² His parents said these things because they were afraid of the Jews. For the Jews had already conspired, so that if anyone were to confess him to be the Christ, he would be expelled from the synagogue. ²³ It was for this reason that his parents said: "He is old enough. Ask him." ²⁴ Therefore, they again called the man who had been blind, and they said to him: "Give glory to God. We know that this man is a sinner." ²⁵ And so he said to them: "If he is a sinner, I do not know it. One thing I do know, that although I was blind, now I see." ²⁶ Then they said to him: "What did he do to you? How did he open your eyes?" ²⁷ He answered them: "I have already told you, and you heard it. Why do you want to hear it again? Do you also want to become his disciples?" ²⁸ Therefore, they cursed him and said: "You be his disciple. But we are disciples of Moses. ²⁹ We know that God spoke to Moses. But this man, we do not know where he is from." ³⁰ The man responded and said to them: "Now in this is a wonder: that you do not know where he is from, and yet he has opened my eyes. ³¹ And we know that God does not hear sinners. But if anyone is a worshipper of God and does his will, then he heeds him. ³² From ancient times, it has not been heard that anyone has opened the eyes of someone born blind. ³³ Unless this man were of God, he would not be able to do any such thing." ³⁴ They responded and said to him, "You were born entirely in sins, and you would teach us?" And they cast him out. ³⁵ Jesus heard that they had cast him out. And when he had found him, he said to him, "Do you believe in the Son of God?" ³⁶ He responded and said, "Who is he, Lord, so that I may believe in him?" ³⁷ And Jesus said to him, "You have both seen him, and he is the one who is speaking with you." ³⁸ And he said, "I believe, Lord." And falling prostrate, he worshipped him. ³⁹ And Jesus said, "I came into this world in judgment, so that those who do not see, may see; and so that those who see, may become blind." ⁴⁰ And certain Pharisees, who were with him, heard this, and they said to him, "Are we also blind?" ⁴¹ Jesus said to them: "If you were blind, you would not have sin. Yet now you say, 'We see.' So your sin persists."

CHAPTER 10

[1] "Amen, amen, I say to you, he who does not enter through the door into the fold of the sheep, but climbs up by another way, he is a thief and a robber. [2] But he who enters through the door is the shepherd of the sheep. [3] To him the doorkeeper opens, and the sheep hear his voice, and he calls his own sheep by name, and he leads them out. [4] And when he has sent out his sheep, he goes before them, and the sheep follow him, because they know his voice. [5] But they do not follow a stranger; instead they flee from him, because they do not know the voice of strangers." [6] Jesus spoke this proverb to them. But they did not understand what he was saying to them. [7] Therefore, Jesus spoke to them again: "Amen, amen, I say to you, that I am the door of the sheep. [8] All others, as many as have come, are thieves and robbers, and the sheep did not listen to them. [9] I am the door. If anyone has entered through me, he will be saved. And he shall go in and go out, and he shall find pastures. [10] The thief does not come, except so that he may steal and slaughter and destroy. I have come so that they may have life, and have it more abundantly. [11] I am the good Shepherd. The good Shepherd gives his life for his sheep. [12] But the hired hand, and whoever is not a shepherd, to whom the sheep do not belong, he sees the wolf approaching, and he departs from the sheep and flees. And the wolf ravages and scatters the sheep. [13] And the hired hand flees, because he is a hired hand and there is no concern for the sheep within him. [14] I am the good Shepherd, and I know my own, and my own know me, [15] just as the Father knows me, and I know the Father. And I lay down my life for my sheep. [16] And I have other sheep that are not of this fold, and I must lead them. They shall hear my voice, and there shall be one sheepfold and one shepherd. [17] For this reason, the Father loves me: because I lay down my life, so that I may take it up again. [18] No one takes it away from me. Instead, I lay it down of my own accord. And I have the power to lay it down. And I have the power to take it up again. This is the commandment that I have received from my Father." [19] A dissension occurred again among the Jews because of these words. [20] Then many of them were saying: "He has a demon or he is insane. Why do you listen him?" [21] Others were saying: "These are not the words of someone who has a demon. How would a demon be able to open the eyes of the blind?" [22] Now it was the Feast of the Dedication at Jerusalem, and it was winter. [23] And Jesus was walking in the temple, in the portico of Solomon. [24] And so the Jews surrounded him and said to him: "How long will you hold our souls in suspense? If you are the Christ, tell us plainly." [25] Jesus answered them: "I speak to you, and you do not believe. The works that I do in the name of my Father, these offer testimony about me. [26] But you do not believe, because you are not of my sheep. [27] My sheep hear my voice. And I know them, and they follow me. [28] And I give them eternal life, and they shall not perish, for eternity. And no one shall seize them from my hand. [29] What my Father gave to me is greater than all, and no one is able to seize from the hand of my Father. [30] I and the Father are one." [31] Therefore, the Jews took up stones, in order to stone him. [32] Jesus answered them: "I have shown you many good works from my Father. For which of those works do you stone me?" [33] The Jews answered him: "We do not stone you for a good work, but for blasphemy and because, though you are a man, you make yourself God." [34] Jesus responded to them: "Is it not written in your law, 'I said: you are gods?' [35] If he called those to whom the word of God was given gods, and Scripture cannot be broken, [36] why do you say, about him whom the Father has sanctified and sent into the world, 'You have blasphemed,' because I said, 'I am the Son of God?' [37] If I do not do the works of my Father, do not believe in me. [38] But if I do them, even if you are not willing to believe in me, believe the works, so that you may know and believe that the Father is in me, and I am in the Father." [39] Therefore, they sought to apprehend him, but he escaped from their hands. [40] And he went again across the Jordan, to that place where John first was baptizing. And he lodged there. [41] And many went out to him. And they were saying: "Indeed, John accomplished no signs. [42] But all things whatsoever that John said about this man were true." And many believed in him.

CHAPTER 11

[1] Now there was a certain sick man, Lazarus of Bethania, from the town of Mary and her sister Martha. [2] And Mary was the one who anointed the Lord with ointment and wiped his feet with her hair; her brother Lazarus was sick. [3] Therefore, his sisters sent to him, saying: "Lord, behold, he whom you love is sick." [4] Then, upon hearing this, Jesus said to them: "This sickness is not unto

death, but for the glory of God, so that the Son of God may be glorified by it." [5] Now Jesus loved Martha, and her sister Mary, and Lazarus. [6] Even so, after he heard that he was sick, he then still remained in the same place for two days. [7] Then, after these things, he said to his disciples, "Let us go into Judea again." [8] The disciples said to him: "Rabbi, the Jews are even now seeking to stone you. And would you go there again?" [9] Jesus responded: "Are there not twelve hours in the day? If anyone walks in the daylight, he does not stumble, because he sees the light of this world. [10] But if he walks in the nighttime, he stumbles, because the light is not in him." [11] He said these things, and after this, he said to them: "Lazarus our friend is sleeping. But I am going, so that I may awaken him from sleep." [12] And so his disciples said, "Lord, if he is sleeping, he shall be healthy." [13] But Jesus had spoken about his death. Yet they thought that he spoke about the repose of sleep. [14] Therefore, Jesus then said to them plainly, "Lazarus has died. [15] And I am glad for your sake that I was not there, so that you may believe. But let us go to him." [16] And then Thomas, who is called the Twin, said to his fellow disciples, "Let us go, too, so that we may die with him." [17] And so Jesus went. And he found that he had already been in the tomb for four days. [18] (Now Bethania was near Jerusalem, about fifteen stadia.) [19] And many of the Jews had come to Martha and Mary, so as to console them over their brother. [20] Therefore, Martha, when she heard that Jesus was arriving, went out to meet him. But Mary was sitting at home. [21] And then Martha said to Jesus: "Lord, if you had been here, my brother would not have died. [22] But even now, I know that whatever you will request from God, God will give to you." [23] Jesus said to her, "Your brother shall rise again." [24] Martha said to him, "I know that he shall rise again, at the resurrection on the last day." [25] Jesus said to her: "I am the Resurrection and the Life. Whoever believes in me, even though he has died, he shall live. [26] And everyone who lives and believes in me shall not die for eternity. Do you believe this?" [27] She said to him: "Certainly, Lord. I have believed that you are the Christ, the Son of the living God, who has come into this world." [28] And when she had said these things, she went and called her sister Mary quietly, saying, "The Teacher is here, and he is calling you." [29] When she heard this, she rose up quickly and went to him. [30] For Jesus had not yet arrived in the town. But he was still at that place where Martha had met him. [31] Therefore, the Jews who were with her in the house and who were consoling her, when they had seen that Mary rose up quickly and went out, they followed her, saying, "She is going to the tomb, so that she may weep there." [32] Therefore, when Mary had arrived to where Jesus was, seeing him, she fell down at his feet, and she said to him. "Lord, if you had been here, my brother would not have died." [33] And then, when Jesus saw her weeping, and the Jews who had arrived with her weeping, he groaned in spirit and became troubled. [34] And he said, "Where have you laid him?" They said to him, "Lord, come and see." [35] And Jesus wept. [36] Therefore, the Jews said, "See how much he loved him!" [37] But some of them said, "Would not he who opened the eyes of one born blind have been able to cause this man not to die?" [38] Therefore, Jesus, again groaning from within himself, went to the tomb. Now it was a cave, and a stone had been placed over it. [39] Jesus said, "Take away the stone." Martha, the sister of him who had died, said to him, "Lord, by now it will smell, for this is the fourth day." [40] Jesus said to her, "Did I not say to you that if you believe, you shall see the glory of God?" [41] Therefore, they took away the stone. Then, lifting up his eyes, Jesus said: "Father, I give thanks to you because you have heard me. [42] And I know that you always hear me, but I have said this for the sake of the people who are standing nearby, so that they may believe that you have sent me." [43] When he had said these things, he cried in a loud voice, "Lazarus, come out." [44] And immediately, he who had been dead went forth, bound at the feet and hands with winding bands. And his face was bound with a separate cloth. Jesus said to them, "Release him and let him go." [45] Therefore, many of the Jews, who had come to Mary and Martha, and who had seen the things that Jesus did, believed in him. [46] But certain ones among them went to the Pharisees and told them the things that Jesus had done. [47] And so, the high priests and the Pharisees gathered a council, and they were saying: "What can we do? For this man accomplishes many signs. [48] If we leave him alone, in this way all will believe in him. And then the Romans will come and take away our place and our nation." [49] Then one of them, named Caiaphas, since he was the high priest that year, said to them: "You do not understand anything. [50] Nor do you realize that it is expedient for you that one man should die for the people, and that the entire nation should not perish." [51] Yet he did not say this from himself, but since he was the high priest that year, he prophesied that Jesus would die for the nation. ⁵²And not only for the nation, but in order to gather together as one the children of God who have been dispersed. ⁵³Therefore, from that day, they planned to put him to death. ⁵⁴And so, Jesus no longer walked in public with the Jews. But he went into a region near the desert, to a city which is called Ephraim. And he lodged there with his disciples. ⁵⁵Now the Passover of the Jews was near. And many from the countryside ascended to Jerusalem before the Passover, so that they might sanctify themselves. ⁵⁶Therefore, they were seeking Jesus. And they conferred with one another, while standing in the temple: "What do you think? Will he come to the feast day?" ⁵⁷And the high priests and Pharisees had given an order, so that if anyone would know where he may be, he should reveal it, so that they might apprehend him.

CHAPTER 12

¹Then six days before the Passover, Jesus went to Bethania, where Lazarus had died, whom Jesus raised up. ²And they made a dinner for him there. And Martha was ministering. And truly, Lazarus was one of those who were sitting at table with him. ³And then Mary took twelve ounces of pure spikenard ointment, very precious, and she anointed the feet of Jesus, and she wiped his feet with her hair. And the house was filled with the fragrance of the ointment. ⁴Then one of his disciples, Judas Iscariot, who was soon to betray him, said, ⁵"Why was this ointment not sold for three hundred denarii and given to the needy?" ⁶Now he said this, not out of concern for the needy, but because he was a thief and, since he held the purse, he used to carry what was put into it. ⁷But Jesus said: "Permit her, so that she may keep it against the day of my burial. ⁸For the poor, you have with you always. But me, you do always not have." ⁹Now a great multitude of the Jews knew that he was in that place, and so they came, not so much because of Jesus, but so that they might see Lazarus, whom he had raised from the dead. ¹⁰And the leaders of the priests planned to put Lazarus to death also. ¹¹For many of the Jews, because of him, were going away and were believing in Jesus. ¹²Then, on the next day, the great crowd that had come to the feast day, when they had heard that Jesus was coming to Jerusalem, ¹³took branches of palm trees, and they went ahead to meet him. And they were crying out: "Hosanna! Blessed is he who arrives in the name of the Lord, the king of Israel!" ¹⁴And Jesus found a small donkey, and he sat upon it, just as it is written: ¹⁵"Do not be afraid, daughter of Zion. Behold, your king arrives, sitting on the colt of a donkey." ¹⁶At first, his disciples did not realize these things. But when Jesus was glorified, then they remembered that these things were written about him, and that these things happened to him. ¹⁷And so the crowd that had been with him, when he called Lazarus from the tomb and raised him from the dead, offered testimony. ¹⁸Because of this, too, the crowd went out to meet him. For they heard that he had accomplished this sign. ¹⁹Therefore, the Pharisees said among themselves: "Do you see that we are accomplishing nothing? Behold, the entire world has gone after him." ²⁰Now there were certain Gentiles among those who went up so that they might worship on the feast day. ²¹Therefore, these approached Philip, who was from Bethsaida of Galilee, and they petitioned him, saying: "Sir, we want to see Jesus." ²²Philip went and told Andrew. Next, Andrew and Philip told Jesus. ²³But Jesus answered them by saying: "The hour arrives when the Son of man shall be glorified. ²⁴Amen, amen, I say to you, unless the grain of wheat falls to the ground and dies, ²⁵it remains alone. But if it dies, it yields much fruit. Whoever loves his life, will lose it. And whoever hates his life in this world, preserves it unto eternal life. ²⁶If anyone serves me, let him follow me. And where I am, there too my minister shall be. If anyone has served me, my Father will honor him. ²⁷Now my soul is troubled. And what should I say? Father, save me from this hour? But it is for this reason that I came to this hour. ²⁸Father, glorify your name!" And then a voice came from heaven, "I have glorified it, and I will glorify it again." ²⁹Therefore, the crowd, which was standing near and had heard it, said that it was like thunder. Others were saying, "An Angel was speaking with him." ³⁰Jesus responded and said: "This voice came, not for my sake, but for your sakes. ³¹Now is the judgment of the world. Now will the prince of this world be cast out. ³²And when I have been lifted up from the earth, I will draw all things to myself." ³³(Now he said this, signifying what kind of death he would die.) ³⁴The crowd answered him: "We have heard, from the law, that the Christ remains forever. And so how can you say, 'The Son of man must be lifted up?' Who is this Son of man?" ³⁵Therefore, Jesus said to them: "For a brief time, the Light is among you. Walk while you have the Light, so that the darkness may not

overtake you. But whoever walks in darkness does not know where is he going. [36] While you have the Light, believe in the Light, so that you may be sons of the Light." Jesus spoke these things, and then he went away and hid himself from them. [37] And although he had done such great signs in their presence, they did not believe in him, [38] so that the word of the prophet Isaiah might be fulfilled, which says: "Lord, who has believed in our hearing? And to whom has the arm of the Lord been revealed?" [39] Because of this, they were not able to believe, for Isaiah said again: [40] "He has blinded their eyes, and hardened their heart, so that they may not see with their eyes, and understand with their heart, and be converted: and then I would heal them." [41] These things Isaiah said, when he saw his glory and was speaking about him. [42] Yet truly, many of the leaders also believed in him. But because of the Pharisees, they did not confess him, so that they would not be cast out of the synagogue. [43] For they loved the glory of men more than the glory of God. [44] But Jesus cried out and said: "Whoever believes in me, does not believe in me, but in him who sent me. [45] And whoever sees me, sees him who sent me. [46] I have arrived as a light to the world, so that all who believe in me might not remain in darkness. [47] And if anyone has heard my words and not kept them, I do not judge him. For I did not come so that I may judge the world, but so that I may save the world. [48] Whoever despises me and does not accept my words has one who judges him. The word that I have spoken, the same shall judge him on the last day. [49] For I am not speaking from myself, but from the Father who sent me. He gave a commandment to me as to what I should say and how I should speak. [50] And I know that his commandment is eternal life. Therefore, the things that I speak, just as the Father has said to me, so also do I speak."

CHAPTER 13

[1] Before the feast day of the Passover, Jesus knew that the hour was approaching when he would pass from this world to the Father. And since he had always loved his own who were in the world, he loved them unto the end. [2] And when the meal had taken place, when the devil had now put it into the heart of Judas Iscariot, the son of Simon, to betray him, [3] knowing that the Father had given all things into his hands and that he came from God and was going to God, [4] he rose up from the meal, and he set aside his vestments, and when he had received a towel, he wrapped it around himself. [5] Next he put water into a shallow bowl, and he began to wash the feet of the disciples and to wipe them with the towel with which he was wrapped. [6] And then he came to Simon Peter. And Peter said to him, "Lord, would you wash my feet?" [7] Jesus responded and said to him: "What I am doing, you do not now understand. But you shall understand it afterward." [8] Peter said to him, "You shall never wash my feet!" Jesus answered him, "If I do not wash you, you will have no place with me." [9] Simon Peter said to him, "Then Lord, not only my feet, but also my hands and my head!" [10] Jesus said to him: "He who is washed need only wash his feet, and then he will be entirely clean. And you are clean, but not all." [11] For he knew which one would betray him. For this reason, he said, "You are not all clean." [12] And so, after he washed their feet and received his vestments, when he had sat down at table again, he said to them: "Do you know what I have done for you? [13] You call me Teacher and Lord, and you speak well: for so I am. [14] Therefore, if I, your Lord and Teacher, have washed your feet, you also ought to wash the feet of one another. [15] For I have given you an example, so that just as I have done for you, so also should you do. [16] Amen, amen, I say to you, the servant is not greater than his Lord, and the apostle is not greater than he who sent him. [17] If you understand this, you shall be blessed if you will do it. [18] I am not speaking about all of you. I know those whom I have chosen. But this is so that the Scripture may be fulfilled, 'He who eats bread with me shall lift up his heel against me.' [19] And I tell you this now, before it happens, so that when it has happened, you may believe that I am. [20] Amen, amen, I say to you, whoever receives anyone whom I send, receives me. And whoever receives me, receives him who sent me." [21] When Jesus had said these things, he was troubled in spirit. And he bore witness by saying: "Amen, amen, I say to you, that one among you shall betray me." [22] Therefore, the disciples looked around at one another, uncertain about whom he spoke. [23] And leaning against the bosom of Jesus was one of his disciples, the one whom Jesus loved. [24] Therefore, Simon Peter motioned to this one and said to him, "Who is it that he is speaking about?" [25] And so, leaning against the chest of Jesus, he said to him, "Lord, who is it?" [26] Jesus responded, "It is he to whom I shall extend the dipped bread." And when he had dipped the bread, he gave it to Judas Iscariot, son of

Simon. ²⁷ And after the morsel, Satan entered into him. And Jesus said to him, "What you are going to do, do quickly." ²⁸ Now none of those sitting at table knew why he had said this to him. ²⁹ For some were thinking that, because Judas held the purse, that Jesus had told him, "Buy those things which are needed by us for the feast day," or that he might give something to the needy. ³⁰ Therefore, having accepted the morsel, he went out immediately. And it was night. ³¹ Then, when he had gone out, Jesus said: "Now the Son of man has been glorified, and God has been glorified in him. ³² If God has been glorified in him, then God will also glorify him in himself, and he will glorify him without delay. ³³ Little sons, for a brief while, I am with you. You shall seek me, and just as I said to the Jews, 'Where I am going, you are not able to go,' so also I say to you now. ³⁴ I give you a new commandment: Love one another. Just as I have loved you, so also must you love one another. ³⁵ By this, all shall recognize that you are my disciples: if you will have love for one another." ³⁶ Simon Peter said to him, "Lord, where are you going?" Jesus responded: "Where I am going, you are not able to follow me now. But you shall follow afterward." ³⁷ Peter said to him: "Why am I unable to follow you now? I will lay down my life for you!" ³⁸ Jesus answered him: "You will lay down your life for me? Amen, amen, I say to you, the rooster will not crow, until you deny me three times."

CHAPTER 14

¹ "Do not let your heart be troubled. You believe in God. Believe in me also. ² In my Father's house, there are many dwelling places. If there were not, I would have told you. For I go to prepare a place for you. ³ And if I go and prepare a place for you, I will return again, and then I will take you to myself, so that where I am, you also may be. ⁴ And you know where I am going. And you know the way." ⁵ Thomas said to him, "Lord, we do not know where you are going, so how can we know the way?" ⁶ Jesus said to him: "I am the Way, and the Truth, and the Life. No one comes to the Father, except through me. ⁷ If you had known me, certainly you would also have known my Father. And from now on, you shall know him, and you have seen him." ⁸ Philip said to him, "Lord, reveal the Father to us, and it is enough for us." ⁹ Jesus said to him: "Have I been with you for so long, and you have not known me? Philip, whoever sees me, also sees the Father. How can you say, 'Reveal the Father to us?' ¹⁰ Do you not believe that I am in the Father and the Father is in me? The words that I am speaking to you, I do not speak from myself. But the Father abiding in me, he does these works. ¹¹ Do you not believe that I am in the Father and the Father is in me? ¹² Or else, believe because of these same works. Amen, amen, I say to you, whoever believes in me shall also do the works that I do. And greater things than these shall he do, for I go to the Father. ¹³ And whatever you shall ask the Father in my name, that I will do, so that the Father may be glorified in the Son. ¹⁴ If you shall ask anything of me in my name, that I will do. ¹⁵ If you love me, keep my commandments. ¹⁶ And I will ask the Father, and he will give another Advocate to you, so that he may abide with you for eternity: ¹⁷ the Spirit of Truth, whom the world is not able to accept, because it neither perceives him nor knows him. But you shall know him. For he will remain with you, and he will be in you. ¹⁸ I will not leave you orphans. I will return to you. ¹⁹ Yet a little while and the world will not see me any longer. But you will see me. For I live, and you shall live. ²⁰ In that day, you shall know that I am in my Father, and you are in me, and I am in you. ²¹ Whoever holds to my commandments and keeps them: it is he who loves me. And whoever loves me shall be loved by my Father. And I will love him, and I will manifest myself to him." ²² Judas, not the Iscariot, said to him: "Lord, how does it happen that you will manifest yourself to us and not to the world?" ²³ Jesus responded and said to him: "If anyone loves me, he shall keep my word. And my Father will love him, and we will come to him, and we will make our dwelling place with him. ²⁴ Whoever does not love me, does not keep not my words. And the word that you have heard is not of me, but it is of the Father who sent me. ²⁵ These things I have spoken to you, while abiding with you. ²⁶ But the Advocate, the Holy Spirit, whom the Father will send in my name, will teach you all things and will suggest to you everything whatsoever that I have said to you. ²⁷ Peace I leave for you; my Peace I give to you. Not in the way that the world gives, do I give to you. Do not let your heart be troubled, and let it not fear. ²⁸ You have heard that I said to you: I am going away, and I am returning to you. If you loved me, certainly you would be gladdened, because I am going to the Father. For the Father is greater than I. ²⁹ And now I have told you this, before it happens, so that, when it will happen, you may believe. ³⁰ I will not now speak

at length with you. For the prince of this world is coming, but he does not have anything in me. [31] Yet this is so that the world may know that I love the Father, and that I am acting according to the commandment that the Father has given to me. Rise up, let us go from here."

CHAPTER 15

[1] "I am the true vine, and my Father is the vinedresser. [2] Every branch in me that does not bear fruit, he will take away. And each one that does bear fruit, he will cleanse, so that it may bring forth more fruit. [3] You are clean now, because of the word that I have spoken to you. [4] Abide in me, and I in you. Just as the branch is not able to bear fruit of itself, unless it abides in the vine, so also are you unable, unless you abide in me. [5] I am the vine; you are the branches. Whoever abides in me, and I in him, bears much fruit. For without me, you are able to do nothing. [6] If anyone does not abide in me, he will be cast away, like a branch, and he will wither, and they will gather him and cast him into the fire, and he burns. [7] If you abide in me, and my words abide in you, then you may ask for whatever you will, and it shall be done for you. [8] In this, my Father is glorified: that you should bring forth very much fruit and become my disciples. [9] As the Father has loved me, so I have loved you. Abide in my love. [10] If you keep my precepts, you shall abide in my love, just as I also have kept my Father's precepts and I abide in his love. [11] These things I have spoken to you, so that my joy may be in you, and your joy may be fulfilled. [12] This is my precept: that you love one another, just as I have loved you. [13] No one has a greater love than this: that he lay down his life for his friends. [14] You are my friends, if you do what I instruct you. [15] I will no longer call you servants, for the servant does not know what his Lord is doing. But I have called you friends, because everything whatsoever that I have heard from my Father, I have made known to you. [16] You have not chosen me, but I have chosen you. And I have appointed you, so that you may go forth and bear fruit, and so that your fruit may last. Then whatever you have asked of the Father in my name, he shall give to you. [17] This I command you: that you love one another. [18] If the world hates you, know that it has hated me before you. [19] If you had been of the world, the world would love what is its own. Yet truly, you are not of the world, but I have chosen you out of the world; because of this, the world hates you. [20] Remember my saying that I told you: The servant is not greater than his Lord. If they have persecuted me, they will persecute you also. If they have kept my word, they will keep yours also. [21] But all these things they will do to you because of my name, for they do not know him who sent me. [22] If I had not come and had not spoken to them, they would not have sin. But now they have no excuse for their sin. [23] Whoever hates me, hates my Father also. [24] If I had not accomplished among them works that no other person has accomplished, they would not have sin. But now they have both seen me, and they have hated me and my Father. [25] But this is so that the word may be fulfilled which was written in their law: 'For they hated me without cause.' [26] But when the Advocate has arrived, whom I will send to you from the Father, the Spirit of truth who proceeds from the Father, he will offer testimony about me. [27] And you shall offer testimony, because you are with me from the beginning."

CHAPTER 16

[1] "These things I have spoken to you, so that you would not stumble. [2] They will put you out of the synagogues. But the hour is coming when everyone who puts you to death will consider that he is offering an excellent service to God. [3] And they will do these things to you because they have not known the Father, nor me. [4] But these things I have spoken to you, so that, when the hour for these things will have arrived, you may remember that I told you. [5] But I did not tell you these things from the beginning, because I was with you. And now I am going to him who sent me. And no one among you has asked me, 'Where are you going?' [6] But because I have spoken these things to you, sorrow has filled your heart. [7] But I tell you the truth: it is expedient for you that I am going. For if I do not go, the Advocate will not come to you. But when I will have gone away, I will send him to you. [8] And when he has arrived, he will argue against the world, about sin and about justice and about judgment: [9] about sin, indeed, because they have not believed in me; [10] about justice, truly, because I am going to the Father, and you will not see me any longer; [11] about judgment, then, because the prince of this world has already been judged. [12] I still have many things to say to you, but

you are not able to bear them now. [13] But when the Spirit of truth has arrived, he will teach the whole truth to you. For he will not be speaking from himself. Instead, whatever he will hear, he will speak. And he will announce to you the things that are to come. [14] He shall glorify me. For he will receive from what is mine, and he will announce it to you. [15] All things whatsoever that the Father has are mine. For this reason, I said that he will receive from what is mine and that he will announce it to you. [16] A little while, and then you will not see me. And again a little while, and you will see me. For I am going to the Father." [17] Then some of his disciples said to one another: "What is this, that he is saying to us: 'A little while, and you will not see me,' and 'Again a little while, and you will see me,' and, 'For I am going to the Father?'" [18] And they said: "What is this, that he is saying, 'A little while?' We do not understand what he is saying." [19] But Jesus realized that they wanted to question him, and so he said to them: "Are you inquiring among yourselves about this, that I said: 'A little while, and you will not see me, and again a little while, and you will see me?' [20] Amen, amen, I say to you, that you shall mourn and weep, but the world will rejoice. And you shall be greatly saddened, yet your sorrow shall be turned into joy. [21] A woman, when she is giving birth, has sorrow, because her hour has arrived. But when she has given birth to the child, then she no longer remembers the difficulties, because of the joy: for a man has been born into the world. [22] Therefore, you also, indeed, have sorrow now. But I will see you again, and your heart shall rejoice. And no one will take away your joy from you. [23] And, in that day, you will not petition me for anything. Amen, amen, I say to you, if you ask the Father for anything in my name, he will give it to you. [24] Until now, you have not requested anything in my name. Ask, and you shall receive, so that your joy may be full. [25] I have spoken these things to you in proverbs. The hour is coming when I will no longer speak to you in proverbs; instead, I will announce to you plainly from the Father. [26] In that day, you shall ask in my name, and I do not say to you that I will ask the Father for you. [27] For the Father himself loves you, because you have loved me, and because you have believed that I went forth from God. [28] I went forth from the Father, and I have come into the world. Next I am leaving the world, and I am going to the Father." [29] His disciples said to him: "Behold, now you are speaking plainly and not reciting a proverb. [30] Now we know that you know all things, and that you have no need for anyone to question you. By this, we believe that you went forth from God." [31] Jesus answered them: "Do you believe now? [32] Behold, the hour is coming, and it has now arrived, when you will be scattered, each one on his own, and you will leave me behind, alone. And yet I am not alone, for the Father is with me. [33] These things I have spoken to you, so that you may have peace in me. In the world, you will have difficulties. But have confidence: I have overcome the world."

CHAPTER 17

[1] Jesus said these things, and then, lifting up his eyes toward heaven, he said: "Father, the hour has arrived: glorify your Son, so that your Son may glorify you, [2] just as you have given authority over all flesh to him, so that he may give eternal life to all those whom you have given to him. [3] And this is eternal life: that they may know you, the only true God, and Jesus Christ, whom you have sent. [4] I have glorified you on earth. I have completed the work that you gave me to accomplish. [5] And now Father, glorify me within yourself, with the glory that I had with you before the world ever was. [6] I have manifested your name to the men whom you have given to me from the world. They were yours, and you gave them to me. And they have kept your word. [7] Now they realize that all the things that you have given me are from you. [8] For I have given them the words that you gave to me. And they have accepted these words, and they have truly understood that I went forth from you, and they have believed that you sent me. [9] I pray for them. I do not pray for the world, but for those whom you have given to me. For they are yours. [10] And all that is mine is yours, and all that is yours is mine, and I am glorified in this. [11] And though I am not in the world, these are in the world, and I am coming to you. Father most holy, preserve them in your name, those whom you have given to me, so that they may be one, even as we are one. [12] While I was with them, I preserved them in your name. I have guarded those whom you have given to me, and not one of them is lost, except the son of perdition, so that the Scripture may be fulfilled. [13] And now I am coming to you. But I am speaking these things in the world, so that they may have the fullness of my joy within themselves. [14] I have given them your word, and the world has hated

them. For they are not of the world, just as I, too, am not of the world. [15] I am not praying that you would take them out of the world, but that you would preserve them from evil. [16] They are not of the world, just as I also am not of the world. [17] Sanctify them in truth. Your word is truth. [18] Just as you have sent me into the world, I also have sent them into the world. [19] And it is for them that I sanctify myself, so that they, too, may be sanctified in truth. [20] But I am not praying for them only, but also for those who through their word shall believe in me. [21] So may they all be one. Just as you, Father, are in me, and I am in you, so also may they be one in us: so that the world may believe that you have sent me. [22] And the glory that you have given to me, I have given to them, so that they may be one, just as we also are one. [23] I am in them, and you are in me. So may they be perfected as one. And may the world know that you have sent me and that you have loved them, just as you have also loved me. [24] Father, I will that where I am, those whom you have given to me may also be with me, so that they may see my glory which you have given to me. For you loved me before the founding of the world. [25] Father most just, the world has not known you. But I have known you. And these have known that you sent me. [26] And I have made known your name to them, and I will make it known, so that the love in which you have loved me may be in them, and so that I may be in them."

CHAPTER 18

[1] When Jesus had said these things, he departed with his disciples across the Torrent of Kidron, where there was a garden, into which he entered with his disciples. [2] But Judas, who betrayed him, also knew the place, for Jesus had frequently met with his disciples there. [3] Then Judas, when he had received a cohort from both the high priests and the attendants of the Pharisees, approached the place with lanterns and torches and weapons. [4] And so Jesus, knowing all that was about to happen to him, advanced and said to them, "Who are you seeking?" [5] They answered him, "Jesus the Nazarene." Jesus said to them, "I am he." Now Judas, who betrayed him, was also standing with them. [6] Then, when he said to them, "I am he," they moved back and fell to the ground. [7] Then again he questioned them: "Who are you seeking?" And they said, "Jesus the Nazarene." [8] Jesus responded: "I told you that I am he. Therefore, if you are seeking me, permit these others to go away." [9] This was so that the word might be fulfilled, which he said, "Of those whom you have given to me, I have not lost any of them." [10] Then Simon Peter, having a sword, drew it, and he struck the servant of the high priest, and he cut off his right ear. Now the name of the servant was Malchus. [11] Therefore, Jesus said to Peter: "Set your sword into the scabbard. Should I not drink the chalice which my Father has given to me?" [12] Then the cohort, and the tribune, and the attendants of the Jews apprehended Jesus and bound him. [13] And they led him away, first to Annas, for he was the father-in-law of Caiaphas, who was the high priest that year. [14] Now Caiaphas was the one who had given counsel to the Jews that it was expedient for one man to die for the people. [15] And Simon Peter was following Jesus with another disciple. And that disciple was known to the high priest, and so he entered with Jesus into the court of the high priest. [16] But Peter was standing outside at the entrance. Therefore, the other disciple, who was known to the high priest, went out and spoke to the woman who was the doorkeeper, and he led in Peter. [17] Therefore, the woman servant keeping the door said to Peter, "Are you not also among the disciples of this man?" He said, "I am not." [18] Now the servants and attendants were standing before burning coals, for it was cold, and they were warming themselves. And Peter was standing with them also, warming himself. [19] Then the high priest questioned Jesus about his disciples and about his doctrine. [20] Jesus responded to him: "I have spoken openly to the world. I have always taught in the synagogue and in the temple, where all the Jews meet. And I have said nothing in secret. [21] Why do you question me? Question those who heard what I said to them. Behold, they know these things that I have said." [22] Then, when he had said this, one of the attendants standing nearby struck Jesus, saying: "Is this the way you answer the high priest?" [23] Jesus answered him: "If I have spoken wrongly, offer testimony about the wrong. But if I have spoken correctly, then why do you strike me?" [24] And Annas sent him bound to Caiaphas, the high priest. [25] Now Simon Peter was standing and warming himself. Then they said to him, "Are you not also one of his disciples?" He denied it and said, "I am not." [26] One of the servants of the high priest (a relative of him whose ear Peter had cut off) said to him, "Did I not see you in the garden with him?" [27] Therefore, again, Peter denied it. And

immediately the rooster crowed. [28] Then they led Jesus from Caiaphas into the praetorium. Now it was morning, and so they did not enter into the praetorium, so that they would not be defiled, but might eat the Passover. [29] Therefore, Pilate went outside to them, and he said, "What accusation are you bringing against this man?" [30] They responded and said to him, "If he were not an evil-doer, we would not have handed him over to you." [31] Therefore, Pilate said to them, "Take him yourselves and judge him according to your own law." Then the Jews said to him, "It is not lawful for us to execute anyone." [32] This was so that the word of Jesus would be fulfilled, which he spoke signifying what kind of death he would die. [33] Then Pilate entered the praetorium again, and he called Jesus and said to him, "You are the king of the Jews?" [34] Jesus responded, "Are you saying this of yourself, or have others spoken to you about me?" [35] Pilate responded: "Am I a Jew? Your own nation and the high priests have handed you over to me. What have you done?" [36] Jesus responded: "My kingdom is not of this world. If my kingdom were of this world, my ministers would certainly strive so that I would not be handed over to the Jews. But my kingdom is not now from here." [37] And so Pilate said to him, "You are a king, then?" Jesus answered, "You are saying that I am a king. For this I was born, and for this I came into the world: so that I may offer testimony to the truth. Everyone who is of the truth hears my voice." [38] Pilate said to him, "What is truth?" And when he had said this, he went out again to the Jews, and he said to them, "I find no case against him. [39] But you have a custom, that I should release someone to you at the Passover. Therefore, do you want me to release to you the king of the Jews?" [40] Then they all cried out repeatedly, saying: "Not this one, but Barabbas." Now Barabbas was a robber.

CHAPTER 19

[1] Therefore, Pilate then took Jesus into custody and scourged him. [2] And the soldiers, plaiting a crown of thorns, imposed it on his head. And they put a purple garment around him. [3] And they were approaching him and saying, "Hail, king of the Jews!" And they struck him repeatedly. [4] Then Pilate went outside again, and he said to them: "Behold, I am bringing him out to you, so that you may realize that I find no case against him." [5] (Then Jesus went out, bearing the crown of thorns and the purple garment.) And he said to them, "Behold the man." [6] Therefore, when the high priests and the attendants had seen him, they cried out, saying: "Crucify him! Crucify him!" Pilate said to them: "Take him yourselves and crucify him. For I find no case against him." [7] The Jews answered him, "We have a law, and according to the law, he ought to die, for he has made himself the Son of God." [8] Therefore, when Pilate had heard this word, he was more fearful. [9] And he entered into the praetorium again. And he said to Jesus. "Where are you from?" But Jesus gave him no response. [10] Therefore, Pilate said to him: "Will you not speak to me? Do you not know that I have authority to crucify you, and I have authority to release you?" [11] Jesus responded, "You would not have any authority over me, unless it were given to you from above. For this reason, he who has handed me over to you has the greater sin." [12] And from then on, Pilate was seeking to release him. But the Jews were crying out, saying: "If you release this man, you are no friend of Caesar. For anyone who makes himself a king contradicts Caesar." [13] Now when Pilate had heard these words, he brought Jesus outside, and he sat down in the seat of judgment, in a place which is called the Pavement, but in Hebrew, it is called the Elevation. [14] Now it was the preparation day of the Passover, about the sixth hour. And he said to the Jews, "Behold your king." [15] But they were crying out: "Take him away! Take him away! Crucify him!" Pilate said to them, "Shall I crucify your king?" The high priests responded, "We have no king except Caesar." [16] Therefore, he then handed him over to them to be crucified. And they took Jesus and led him away. [17] And carrying his own cross, he went forth to the place which is called Calvary, but in Hebrew it is called the Place of the Skull. [18] There they crucified him, and with him two others, one on each side, with Jesus in the middle. [19] Then Pilate also wrote a title, and he set it above the cross. And it was written: JESUS THE NAZARENE, KING OF THE JEWS. [20] Therefore, many of the Jews read this title, for the place where Jesus was crucified was close to the city. And it was written in Hebrew, in Greek, and in Latin. [21] Then the high priests of the Jews said to Pilate: Do not write, 'King of the Jews,' but that he said, 'I am King of the Jews.' [22] Pilate responded, "What I have written, I have written." [23] Then the soldiers, when they had crucified him, took his garments, and they made four parts, one part to each soldier, and the tunic. But the tunic was seamless, woven

from above throughout the whole. ²⁴Then they said to one another, "Let us not cut it, but instead let us cast lots over it, to see whose it will be." This was so that the Scripture would be fulfilled, saying: "They have distributed my garments among themselves, and for my vesture they have cast lots." And indeed, the soldiers did these things. ²⁵And standing beside the cross of Jesus were his mother, and his mother's sister, and Mary of Cleophas, and Mary Magdalene. ²⁶Therefore, when Jesus had seen his mother and the disciple whom he loved standing near, he said to his mother, "Woman, behold your son." ²⁷Next, he said to the disciple, "Behold your mother." And from that hour, the disciple accepted her as his own. ²⁸After this, Jesus knew that all had been accomplished, so in order that the Scripture might be completed, he said, "I thirst." ²⁹And there was a container placed there, full of vinegar. Then, placing a sponge full of vinegar around hyssop, they brought it to his mouth. ³⁰Then Jesus, when he had received the vinegar, said: "It is consummated." And bowing down his head, he surrendered his spirit. ³¹Then the Jews, because it was the preparation day, so that the bodies would not remain upon the cross on the Sabbath (for that Sabbath was a great day), they petitioned Pilate in order that their legs might be broken, and they might be taken away. ³²Therefore, the soldiers approached, and, indeed, they broke the legs of the first one, and of the other who was crucified with him. ³³But after they had approached Jesus, when they saw that he was already dead, they did not break his legs. ³⁴Instead, one of the soldiers opened his side with a lance, and immediately there went out blood and water. ³⁵And he who saw this has offered testimony, and his testimony is true. And he knows that he speaks the truth, so that you also may believe. ³⁶For these things happened so that the Scripture would be fulfilled: "You shall not break a bone of him." ³⁷And again, another Scripture says: "They shall look upon him, whom they have pierced." ³⁸Then, after these things, Joseph from Arimathea, (because he was a disciple of Jesus, but a secret one for fear of the Jews) petitioned Pilate so that he might take away the body of Jesus. And Pilate gave permission. Therefore, he went and took away the body of Jesus. ³⁹Now Nicodemus also arrived, (who had gone to Jesus at first by night) bringing a mixture of myrrh and aloe, weighing about seventy pounds. ⁴⁰Therefore, they took the body of Jesus, and they bound it with linen cloths and the aromatic spices, just as it is the manner of the Jews to bury. ⁴¹Now in the place where he was crucified there was a garden, and in the garden there was a new tomb, in which no one had yet been laid. ⁴²Therefore, because of the preparation day of the Jews, since the tomb was nearby, they placed Jesus there.

CHAPTER 20

¹Then on the first Sabbath, Mary Magdalene went to the tomb early, while it was still dark, and she saw that the stone had been rolled away from the tomb. ²Therefore, she ran and went to Simon Peter, and to the other disciple, whom Jesus loved, and she said to them, "They have taken the Lord away from the tomb, and we do not know where they have laid him." ³Therefore, Peter departed with the other disciple, and they went to the tomb. ⁴Now they both ran together, but the other disciple ran more quickly, ahead of Peter, and so he arrived at the tomb first. ⁵And when he bowed down, he saw the linen cloths lying there, but he did not yet enter. ⁶Then Simon Peter arrived, following him, and he entered the tomb, and he saw the linen cloths lying there, ⁷and the separate cloth which had been over his head, not placed with the linen cloths, but in a separate place, wrapped up by itself. ⁸Then the other disciple, who had arrived first at the tomb, also entered. And he saw and believed. ⁹For as yet they did not understand the Scripture, that it was necessary for him to rise again from the dead. ¹⁰Then the disciples went away again, each by himself. ¹¹But Mary was standing outside the tomb, weeping. Then, while she was weeping, she bowed down and gazed into the tomb. ¹²And she saw two Angels in white, sitting where the body of Jesus had been placed, one at the head, and one at the feet. ¹³They said to her, "Woman, why are you weeping?" She said to them, "Because they have taken away my Lord, and I do not know where they have placed him." ¹⁴When she had said this, she turned around and saw Jesus standing there, but she did not know that it was Jesus. ¹⁵Jesus said to her: "Woman, why are you weeping? Who are you seeking?" Considering that it was the gardener, she said to him, "Sir, if you have moved him, tell me where you have placed him, and I will take him away." ¹⁶Jesus said to her, "Mary!" And turning, she said to him, "Rabboni!" (which means, Teacher). ¹⁷Jesus said to her: "Do not touch me. For I have not yet ascended to my Father. But go to my brothers and tell them: 'I am ascending to my Father and to your

Father, to my God and to your God.'" ¹⁸ Mary Magdalene went, announcing to the disciples, "I have seen the Lord, and these are the things that he said to me." ¹⁹ Then, when it was late on the same day, on the first of the Sabbaths, and the doors were closed where the disciples were gathered, for fear of the Jews, Jesus came and stood in their midst, and he said to them: "Peace to you." ²⁰ And when he had said this, he showed them his hands and side. And the disciples were gladdened when they saw the Lord. ²¹ Therefore, he said to them again: "Peace to you. As the Father has sent me, so I send you." ²² When he had said this, he breathed on them. And he said to them: "Receive the Holy Spirit. ²³ Those whose sins you shall forgive, they are forgiven them, and those whose sins you shall retain, they are retained." ²⁴ Now Thomas, one of the twelve, who is called the Twin, was not with them when Jesus arrived. ²⁵ Therefore, the other disciples said to him, "We have seen the Lord." But he said to them, "Unless I will see in his hands the mark of the nails and place my finger into the place of the nails, and place my hand into his side, I will not believe." ²⁶ And after eight days, again his disciples were within, and Thomas was with them. Jesus arrived, though the doors had been closed, and he stood in their midst and said, "Peace to you." ²⁷ Next, he said to Thomas: "Look at my hands, and place your finger here; and bring your hand close, and place it at my side. And do not choose to be unbelieving, but faithful." ²⁸ Thomas responded and said to him, "My Lord and my God." ²⁹ Jesus said to him: "You have seen me, Thomas, so you have believed. Blessed are those who have not seen and yet have believed." ³⁰ Jesus also accomplished many other signs in the sight of his disciples. These have not been written in this book. ³¹ But these things have been written, so that you may believe that Jesus is the Christ, the Son of God, and so that, in believing, you may have life in his name.

CHAPTER 21

¹ After this, Jesus manifested himself again to the disciples at the Sea of Tiberias. And he manifested himself in this way. ² These were together: Simon Peter and Thomas, who is called the Twin, and Nathanael, who was from Cana of Galilee, and the sons of Zebedee, and two others of his disciples. ³ Simon Peter said to them, "I am going fishing." They said to him, "And we are going with you." And they went and climbed into the ship. And in that night, they caught nothing. ⁴ But when morning arrived, Jesus stood on the shore. Yet the disciples did not realize that it was Jesus. ⁵ Then Jesus said to them, "Children, do you have any food?" They answered him, "No." ⁶ He said to them, "Cast the net to the right side of the ship, and you will find some." Therefore, they cast it out, and then they were not able to draw it in, because of the multitude of fish. ⁷ Therefore, the disciple whom Jesus loved said to Peter, "It is the Lord." Simon Peter, when he had heard that it was the Lord, wrapped his tunic around himself, (for he was naked) and he cast himself into the sea. ⁸ Then the other disciples arrived in a boat, (for they were not far from the land, only about two hundred cubits) dragging the net with the fish. ⁹ Then, when they climbed down to the land they saw burning coals prepared, and fish already placed above them, and bread. ¹⁰ Jesus said to them, "Bring some of the fish that you have just now caught." ¹¹ Simon Peter climbed up and drew in the net to land: full of large fish, one hundred and fifty-three of them. And although there were so many, the net was not torn. ¹² Jesus said to them, "Approach and dine." And not one of them sitting down to eat dared to ask him, "Who are you?" For they knew that it was the Lord. ¹³ And Jesus approached, and he took bread, and he gave it to them, and similarly with the fish. ¹⁴ This was now the third time that Jesus was manifested to his disciples, after he had resurrected from the dead. ¹⁵ Then, when they had dined, Jesus said to Simon Peter, "Simon, son of John, do you love me more than these?" He said to him, "Yes, Lord, you know that I love you." He said to him, "Feed my lambs." ¹⁶ He said to him again: "Simon, son of John, do you love me?" He said to him, "Yes, Lord, you know that I love you." He said to him, "Feed my lambs." ¹⁷ He said to him a third time, "Simon, son of John, do you love me?" Peter was very grieved that he had asked him a third time, "Do you love me?" And so he said to him: "Lord, you know all things. You know that I love you." He said to him, "Feed my sheep. ¹⁸ Amen, amen, I say to you, when you were younger, you girded yourself and walked wherever you wanted. But when you are older, you will extend your hands, and another shall gird you and lead you where you do not want to go." ¹⁹ Now he said this to signify by what kind of death he would glorify God. And when he had said this, he said to him, "Follow me." ²⁰ Peter, turning around, saw the disciple whom Jesus loved following, the one who also had leaned on his chest at supper and said, "Lord, who is it who shall betray you?" ²¹ Therefore, when Peter had seen him, he said to Jesus, "Lord, but what about this one?" ²² Jesus said to him: "If I want him to remain until I return, what is that to you? You follow me." ²³ Therefore, the saying went out among the brothers that this disciple would not die. But Jesus did not say to him that he would not die, but only, "If I want him to remain until I return, what is that to you?" ²⁴ This is the same disciple who offers testimony about these things, and who has written these things. And we know that his testimony is true. ²⁵ Now there are also many other things that Jesus did, which, if each of these were written down, the world itself, I suppose, would not be able to contain the books that would be written.

Acts

THE SACRED BIBLE:
THE ACTS OF THE APOSTLES

CHAPTER 1

[1] Certainly, O Theophilus, I composed the first discourse about everything that Jesus began to do and to teach, [2] instructing the Apostles, whom he had chosen through the Holy Spirit, even until the day on which he was taken up. [3] He also presented himself alive to them, after his Passion, appearing to them throughout forty days and speaking about the kingdom of God with many elucidations. [4] And dining with them, he instructed them that they should not depart from Jerusalem, but that they should wait for the Promise of the Father, "about which you have heard," he said, "from my own mouth. [5] For John, indeed, baptized with water, but you shall be baptized with the Holy Spirit, not many days from now." [6] Therefore, those who had assembled together questioned him, saying, "Lord, is this the time when you will restore the kingdom of Israel?" [7] But he said to them: "It is not yours to know the times or the moments, which the Father has set by his own authority. [8] But you shall receive the power of the Holy Spirit, passing over you, and you shall be witnesses for me in Jerusalem, and in all Judea and Samaria, and even to the ends of the earth." [9] And when he had said these things, while they were watching, he was lifted up, and a cloud took him from their sight. [10] And while they were watching him going up to heaven, behold, two men stood near them in white vestments. [11] And they said: "Men of Galilee, why do you stand here looking up toward heaven? This Jesus, who has been taken up from you into heaven, shall return in just the same way that you have seen him going up to heaven." [12] Then they returned to Jerusalem from the mountain, which is called Olivet, which is next to Jerusalem, within a Sabbath day's journey. [13] And when they had entered into the cenacle, they ascended to the place where Peter and John, James and Andrew, Philip and Thomas, Bartholomew and Matthew, James of Alphaeus and Simon the Zealot, and Jude of James, were staying. [14] All these were persevering with one accord in prayer with the women, and with Mary, the mother of Jesus, and with his brothers. [15] In those days, Peter, rising up in the midst of the brothers, said (now the crowd of men altogether was about one hundred and twenty): [16] "Noble brothers, the Scripture must be fulfilled, which the Holy Spirit predicted by the mouth of David about Judas, who was the leader of those who apprehended Jesus. [17] He had been numbered among us, and he was chosen by lot for this ministry. [18] And this man certainly possessed an estate from the wages of iniquity, and so, having been hanged, he burst open in the middle and all his internal organs poured out. [19] And this became known to all the inhabitants of Jerusalem, so that this field was called in their language, Akeldama, that is, 'Field of Blood.' [20] For it has been written in the book of Psalms: 'Let their dwelling place be desolate and may there be no one who dwells within it,' and 'Let another take his episcopate.' [21] Therefore, it is necessary that, out of these men who have been assembling with us throughout the entire time that the Lord Jesus went in and out among us, [22] beginning from the baptism of John, until the day when he was taken up from us, one of these be made a witness with us of his Resurrection." [23] And they appointed two: Joseph, who was called Barsabbas, who was surnamed Justus, and Matthias. [24] And praying, they said: "May you, O Lord, who knows the heart of everyone, reveal which one of these two you have chosen, [25] to take a place in this ministry and apostleship, from which Judas prevaricated, so that he might go to his own place." [26] And they cast lots concerning them, and the lot fell upon Matthias. And he was numbered with the eleven Apostles.

CHAPTER 2

[1] And when the days of Pentecost were completed, they were all together in the same place. [2] And suddenly, there came a sound from heaven, like that of a wind approaching violently, and it filled the entire house where they were sitting. [3] And there appeared to them separate tongues, as if of fire, which settled upon each one of them. [4] And they were all filled with the Holy Spirit. And they began to speak in various languages, just as the Holy Spirit bestowed eloquence to them. [5] Now there were Jews staying in Jerusalem, pious men from every nation that is under heaven. [6] And when this sound occurred, the multitude came together and

was confused in mind, because each one was listening to them speaking in his own language. ⁷Then all were astonished, and they wondered, saying: "Behold, are not all of these who are speaking Galileans? ⁸And how is it that we have each heard them in our own language, into which we were born? ⁹Parthians and Medes and Elamites, and those who inhabit Mesopotamia, Judea and Cappadocia, Pontus and Asia, ¹⁰Phrygia and Pamphylia, Egypt and the parts of Libya which are around Cyrene, and new arrivals of the Romans, ¹¹likewise Jews and new converts, Cretans and Arabs: we have heard them speaking in our own languages the mighty deeds of God." ¹²And they were all astonished, and they wondered, saying to one another: "But what does this mean?" ¹³But others mockingly said, "These men are full of new wine." ¹⁴But Peter, standing up with the eleven, lifted up his voice, and he spoke to them: "Men of Judea, and all those who are staying in Jerusalem, let this be known to you, and incline your ears to my words. ¹⁵For these men are not inebriated, as you suppose, for it is the third hour of the day. ¹⁶But this is what was spoken of by the prophet Joel: ¹⁷'And this shall be: in the last days, says the Lord, I will pour out, from my Spirit, upon all flesh. And your sons and your daughters shall prophesy. And your youths shall see visions, and your elders shall dream dreams. ¹⁸And certainly, upon my men and women servants in those days, I will pour out from my Spirit, and they shall prophesy. ¹⁹And I will bestow wonders in heaven above, and signs on earth below: blood and fire and the vapor of smoke. ²⁰The sun shall be turned into darkness and the moon into blood, before the great and manifest day of the Lord arrives. ²¹And this shall be: whoever shall invoke the name of the Lord will be saved.' ²²Men of Israel, hear these words: Jesus the Nazarene is a man confirmed by God among you through the miracles and wonders and signs that God accomplished through him in your midst, just as you also know. ²³This man, under the definitive plan and foreknowledge of God, was delivered by the hands of the unjust, afflicted, and put to death. ²⁴And he whom God has raised up has broken the sorrows of Hell, for certainly it was impossible for him to be held by it. ²⁵For David said about him: 'I foresaw the Lord always in my sight, for he is at my right hand, so that I may not be moved. ²⁶Because of this, my heart has rejoiced, and my tongue has exulted. Moreover, my flesh shall also rest in hope. ²⁷For you will not abandon my soul to Hell, nor will you allow your Holy One to see corruption. ²⁸You have made known to me the ways of life. You will completely fill me with happiness by your presence.' ²⁹Noble brothers, permit me to speak freely to you about the Patriarch David: for he passed away and was buried, and his sepulcher is with us, even to this very day. ³⁰Therefore, he was a prophet, for he knew that God had sworn an oath to him about the fruit of his loins, about the One who would sit upon his throne. ³¹Foreseeing this, he was speaking about the Resurrection of the Christ. For he was neither left behind in Hell, nor did his flesh see corruption. ³²This Jesus, God raised up again, and of this we are all witnesses. ³³Therefore, being exalted to the right hand of God, and having received from the Father the Promise of the Holy Spirit, he poured this out, just as you now see and hear. ³⁴For David did not ascend into heaven. But he himself said: 'The Lord said to my Lord: Sit at my right hand, ³⁵until I make your enemies your footstool.' ³⁶Therefore, may the entire house of Israel know most certainly that God has made this same Jesus, whom you crucified, both Lord and Christ." ³⁷Now when they had heard these things, they were contrite in heart, and they said to Peter and to the other Apostles: "What should we do, noble brothers?" ³⁸Yet truly, Peter said to them: "Do penance; and be baptized, each one of you, in the name of Jesus Christ, for the remission of your sins. And you shall receive the gift of the Holy Spirit. ³⁹For the Promise is for you and for your sons, and for all who are far away: for whomever the Lord our God will have called." ⁴⁰And then, with very many other words, he testified and he exhorted them, saying, "Save yourselves from this depraved generation." ⁴¹Therefore, those who accepted his discourse were baptized. And about three thousand souls were added on that day. ⁴²Now they were persevering in the doctrine of the Apostles, and in the communion of the breaking of the bread, and in the prayers. ⁴³And fear developed in every soul. Also, many miracles and signs were accomplished by the Apostles in Jerusalem. And there was a great awe in everyone. ⁴⁴And then all who believed were together, and they held all things in common. ⁴⁵They were selling their possessions and belongings, and dividing them to all, just as any of them had need. ⁴⁶Also, they continued, daily, to be of one accord in the temple and to break bread among the houses; and they took their meals with exultation and simplicity of heart, ⁴⁷praising God greatly, and holding favor with all the people. And every day, the Lord increased those who were being saved among them.

CHAPTER 3

[1] Now Peter and John went up to the temple at the ninth hour of prayer. [2] And a certain man, who was lame from his mother's womb, was being carried in. They would lay him every day at the gate of the temple, which is called the Beautiful, so that he might request alms from those entering into the temple. [3] And this man, when he had seen Peter and John beginning to enter the temple, was begging, so that he might receive alms. [4] Then Peter and John, gazing at him, said, "Look at us." [5] And he looked intently at them, hoping that he might receive something from them. [6] But Peter said: "Silver and gold is not mine. But what I have, I give to you. In the name of Jesus Christ the Nazarene, rise up and walk." [7] And taking him by the right hand, he lifted him up. And immediately his legs and feet were strengthened. [8] And leaping up, he stood and walked around. And he entered with them into the temple, walking and leaping and praising God. [9] And all the people saw him walking and praising God. [10] And they recognized him, that he was the same one who was sitting for alms at the Beautiful Gate of the temple. And they were filled with awe and amazement at what had happened to him. [11] Then, as he held on to Peter and John, all the people ran to them at the portico, which is called Solomon's, in astonishment. [12] But Peter, seeing this, responded to the people: "Men of Israel, why do you wonder at this? Or why do you stare at us, as if it were by our own strength or power that we caused this man to walk? [13] The God of Abraham and the God of Isaac and the God of Jacob, the God of our fathers, has glorified his Son Jesus, whom you, indeed, handed over and denied before the face of Pilate, when he was giving judgment to release him. [14] Then you denied the Holy and Just One, and petitioned for a murderous man to be given to you. [15] Truly, it was the Author of Life whom you put to death, whom God raised from the dead, to whom we are witnesses. [16] And by faith in his name, this man, whom you have seen and known, has confirmed his name. And faith through him has given this man complete health in the sight of you all. [17] And now, brothers, I know that you did this through ignorance, just as your leaders also did. [18] But in this way God has fulfilled the things that he announced beforehand through the mouth of all the Prophets: that his Christ would suffer. [19] Therefore, repent and be converted, so that your sins may be wiped away. [20] And then, when the time of consolation will have arrived from the presence of the Lord, he will send the One who was foretold to you, Jesus Christ, [21] whom heaven certainly must take up, until the time of the restoration of all things, which God has spoken of by the mouth of his holy prophets, from ages past. [22] Indeed, Moses said: 'For the Lord your God shall raise up a Prophet for you from your brothers, one like me; the same shall you listen to according to everything whatsoever that he shall speak to you. [23] And this shall be: every soul who will not listen to that Prophet shall be exterminated from the people.' [24] And all the prophets who have spoken, from Samuel and thereafter, have announced these days. [25] You are sons of the prophets and of the testament which God has appointed for our fathers, saying to Abraham: 'And by your offspring all the families of the earth shall be blessed.' [26] God raised up his Son and sent him first to you, to bless you, so that each one may turn himself away from his wickedness."

CHAPTER 4

[1] But while they were speaking to the people, the priests and the magistrate of the temple and the Sadducees overwhelmed them, [2] being grieved that they were teaching the people and announcing in Jesus the resurrection from the dead. [3] And they laid hands on them, and they placed them under guard until the next day. For it was now evening. [4] But many of those who had heard the word believed. And the number of men became five thousand. [5] And it happened on the next day that their leaders and elders and scribes gathered together in Jerusalem, [6] including Annas, the high priest, and Caiaphas, and John and Alexander, and as many as were of the priestly family. [7] And stationing them in the middle, they questioned them: "By what power, or in whose name, have you done this?" [8] Then Peter, filled with the Holy Spirit, said to them: "Leaders of the people and elders, listen. [9] If we today are judged by a good deed done to an infirm man, by which he has been made whole, [10] let it be known to all of you and to all of the people of Israel, that in the name of our Lord Jesus Christ the Nazarene, whom you crucified, whom God has raised from the dead, by him, this man stands before you, healthy. [11] He is the stone, which was rejected by you, the builders, which has become the head of the corner. [12] And there is no salvation in any other. For there is no other name under heaven given to men, by which it is necessary for us to be saved." [13] Then,

seeing the constancy of Peter and John, having verified that they were men without letters or learning, they wondered. And they recognized that they had been with Jesus. ¹⁴ Also, seeing the man who had been cured standing with them, they were unable to say anything to contradict them. ¹⁵ But they ordered them to withdraw outside, away from the council, and they conferred among themselves, ¹⁶ saying: "What shall we do to these men? For certainly a public sign has been done through them, before all the inhabitants of Jerusalem. It is manifest, and we cannot deny it. ¹⁷ But lest it spread further among the people, let us threaten them not to speak anymore in this name to any man." ¹⁸ And calling them in, they warned them not to speak or teach at all in the name of Jesus. ¹⁹ Yet truly, Peter and John said in response to them: "Judge whether it is just in the sight of God to listen to you, rather than to God. ²⁰ For we are unable to refrain from speaking the things that we have seen and heard." ²¹ But they, threatening them, sent them away, having not found a way that they might punish them because of the people. For all were glorifying the things that had been done in these events. ²² For the man in whom this sign of a cure had been accomplished was more than forty years old. ²³ Then, having been released, they went to their own, and they reported in full what the leaders of the priests and the elders had said to them. ²⁴ And when they had heard it, with one accord, they lifted up their voice to God, and they said: "Lord, you are the One who made heaven and earth, the sea and all that is in them, ²⁵ who, by the Holy Spirit, through the mouth of our father David, your servant, said: 'Why have the Gentiles been seething, and why have the people been pondering nonsense? ²⁶ The kings of the earth have stood up, and the leaders have joined together as one, against the Lord and against his Christ.' ²⁷ For truly Herod and Pontius Pilate, with the Gentiles and the people of Israel, joined together in this city against your holy servant Jesus, whom you anointed ²⁸ to do what your hand and your counsel had decreed would be done. ²⁹ And now, O Lord, look upon their threats, and grant to your servants that they may speak your word with all confidence, ³⁰ by extending your hand in cures and signs and miracles, to be done through the name of your holy Son, Jesus." ³¹ And when they had prayed, the place in which they were gathered was moved. And they were all filled with the Holy Spirit. And they were speaking the Word of God with confidence. ³² Then the multitude of believers were of one heart and one soul. Neither did anyone say that any of the things that he possessed were his own, but all things were common to them. ³³ And with great power, the Apostles were rendering testimony to the Resurrection of Jesus Christ our Lord. And great grace was in them all. ³⁴ And neither was anyone among them in need. For as many as were owners of fields or houses, selling these, were bringing the proceeds of the things that they were selling, ³⁵ and were placing it before the feet of the Apostles. Then it was divided to each one, just as he had need. ³⁶ Now Joseph, who the Apostles surnamed Barnabas (which is translated as 'son of consolation'), who was a Levite of Cyprian descent, ³⁷ since he had land, he sold it, and he brought the proceeds and placed these at the feet of the Apostles.

CHAPTER 5

¹ But a certain man named Ananias, with his wife Sapphira, sold a field, ² and he was deceitful about the price of the field, with his wife's consent. And bringing only part of it, he placed it at the feet of the Apostles. ³ But Peter said: "Ananias, why has Satan tempted your heart, so that you would lie to the Holy Spirit and be deceitful about the price of the land? ⁴ Did it not belong to you while you retained it? And having sold it, was it not in your power? Why have you set this thing in your heart? You have not lied to men, but to God!" ⁵ Then Ananias, upon hearing these words, fell down and expired. And a great fear overwhelmed all who heard of it. ⁶ And the young men rose up and removed him; and carrying him out, they buried him. ⁷ Then about the space of three hours passed, and his wife entered, not knowing what had happened. ⁸ And Peter said to her, "Tell me, woman, if you sold the field for this amount?" And she said, "Yes, for that amount." ⁹ And Peter said to her: "Why have you agreed together to test the Spirit of the Lord? Behold, the feet of those who have buried your husband are at the door, and they shall carry you out!" ¹⁰ Immediately, she fell down before his feet and expired. Then the young men entered and found her dead. And they carried her out and buried her next to her husband. ¹¹ And a great fear came over the entire Church and over all who heard these things. ¹² And through the hands of the Apostles many signs and wonders were accomplished among the people. And they all met with one accord at Solomon's portico. ¹³ And among the others, no one dared to join

himself to them. But the people magnified them. [14] Now the multitude of men and women who believed in the Lord was ever increasing, [15] so much so that they laid the infirm in the streets, placing them on beds and stretchers, so that, as Peter arrived, at least his shadow might fall upon any one of them, and they would be freed from their infirmities. [16] But a multitude also hurried to Jerusalem from the neighboring cities, carrying the sick and those troubled by unclean spirits, who were all healed. [17] Then the high priest and all those who were with him, that is, the heretical sect of the Sadducees, rose up and were filled with jealousy. [18] And they laid hands on the Apostles, and they placed them in the common prison. [19] But in the night, an Angel of the Lord opened the doors of the prison and led them out, saying, [20] "Go and stand in the temple, speaking to the people all these words of life." [21] And when they had heard this, they entered the temple at first light, and they were teaching. Then the high priest, and those who were with him, approached, and they called together the council and all the elders of the sons of Israel. And they sent to the prison to have them brought. [22] But when the attendants had arrived, and, upon opening the prison, had not found them, they returned and reported to them, [23] saying: "We found the prison certainly locked up with all diligence, and the guards standing before the door. But upon opening it, we found no one within." [24] Then, when the magistrate of the temple and the chief priests heard these words, they were uncertain about them, as to what should happen. [25] But someone arrived and reported to them, "Behold, the men whom you placed in prison are in the temple, standing and teaching the people." [26] Then the magistrate, with the attendants, went and brought them without force. For they were afraid of the people, lest they be stoned. [27] And when they had brought them, they stood them before the council. And the high priest questioned them, [28] and said: "We strongly order you not to teach in this name. For behold, you have filled Jerusalem with your doctrine, and you wish to bring the blood of this man upon us." [29] But Peter and the Apostles responded by saying: "It is necessary to obey God, more so than men. [30] The God of our fathers has raised up Jesus, whom you put to death by hanging him on a tree. [31] It is he whom God has exalted at his right hand as Ruler and Savior, so as to offer repentance and the remission of sins to Israel. [32] And we are witnesses of these things, with the Holy Spirit, whom God has given to all who are obedient to him." [33] When they had heard these things, they were deeply wounded, and they were planning to put them to death. [34] But someone in the council, a Pharisee named Gamaliel, a teacher of the law honored by all the people, rose up and ordered the men to be put outside briefly. [35] And he said to them: "Men of Israel, you should be careful in your intentions about these men. [36] For before these days, Theudas stepped forward, asserting himself to be someone, and a number of men, about four hundred, joined with him. But he was killed, and all who believed in him were scattered, and they were reduced to nothing. [37] After this one, Judas the Galilean stepped forward, in the days of the enrollment, and he turned the people toward himself. But he also perished, and all of them, as many as had joined with him, were dispersed. [38] And now therefore, I say to you, withdraw from these men and leave them alone. For if this counsel or work is of men, it will be broken. [39] Yet truly, if it is of God, you will not be able to break it, and perhaps you might be found to have fought against God." And they agreed with him. [40] And calling in the Apostles, having beaten them, they warned them not to speak at all in the name of Jesus. And they dismissed them. [41] And indeed, they went forth from the presence of the council, rejoicing that they were considered worthy to suffer insult on behalf of the name of Jesus. [42] And every day, in the temple and among the houses, they did not cease to teach and to evangelize Christ Jesus.

CHAPTER 6

[1] In those days, as the number of disciples was increasing, there occurred a murmuring of the Greeks against the Hebrews, because their widows were treated with disdain in the daily ministration. [2] And so the twelve, calling together the multitude of the disciples, said: "It is not fair for us to leave behind the Word of God to serve at tables also. [3] Therefore, brothers, search among yourselves for seven men of good testimony, filled with the Holy Spirit and with wisdom, whom we may appoint over this work. [4] Yet truly, we will be continually in prayer and in the ministry of the Word." [5] And the plan pleased the entire multitude. And they chose Stephen, a man filled with faith and with the Holy Spirit, and Philip and Prochorus and Nicanor and Timon and Parmenas and Nicolas, a new arrival from Antioch. [6] These they set before the sight of the Apostles, and

while praying, they imposed hands on them. [7] And the Word of the Lord was increasing, and the number of disciples in Jerusalem was multiplied exceedingly. And even a large group of the priests were obedient to the faith. [8] Then Stephen, filled with grace and fortitude, wrought great signs and miracles among the people. [9] But certain ones, from the synagogue of the so-called Libertines, and of the Cyrenians, and of the Alexandrians, and of those who were from Cilicia and Asia rose up and were disputing with Stephen. [10] But they were not able to resist the wisdom and the Spirit with which he was speaking. [11] Then they suborned men who were to claim that they had heard him speaking words of blasphemy against Moses and against God. [12] And thus did they stir up the people and the elders and the scribes. And hurrying together, they seized him and brought him to the council. [13] And they set up false witnesses, who said: "This man does not cease to speak words against the holy place and the law. [14] For we have heard him saying that this Jesus the Nazarene will destroy this place and will change the traditions, which Moses handed down to us." [15] And all those who were sitting in the council, gazing at him, saw his face, as if it had become the face of an Angel.

CHAPTER 7

[1] Then the high priest said, "Are these things so?" [2] And Stephen said: "Noble brothers and fathers, listen. The God of glory appeared to our father Abraham, when he was in Mesopotamia, before he stayed in Haran. [3] And God said to him, 'Depart from your country and from your kindred, and go into the land that I will show to you.' [4] Then he went away from the land of the Chaldeans, and he lived at Haran. And later, after his father was dead, God brought him into this land, in which you now dwell. [5] And he gave him no inheritance in it, not even the space of one step. But he promised to give it to him as a possession, and to his offspring after him, though he did not have a son. [6] Then God told him that his offspring would be a settler in a foreign land, and that they would subjugate them, and treat them badly, for four hundred years. [7] 'And the nation whom they will serve, I will judge,' said the Lord. 'And after these things, they shall depart and shall serve me in this place.' [8] And he gave him the covenant of circumcision. And so he conceived Isaac and circumcised him on the eighth day. And Isaac conceived Jacob, and Jacob, the twelve Patriarchs. [9] And the Patriarchs, being jealous, sold Joseph into Egypt. But God was with him. [10] And he rescued him from all his tribulations. And he gave him grace and wisdom in the sight of Pharaoh, the king of Egypt. And he appointed him as governor over Egypt and over all his house. [11] Then a famine occurred in all of Egypt and Canaan, and a great tribulation. And our fathers did not find food. [12] But when Jacob had heard that there was grain in Egypt, he sent our fathers first. [13] And on the second occasion, Joseph was recognized by his brothers, and his ancestry was made manifest to Pharaoh. [14] Then Joseph sent for and brought his father Jacob, with all his kindred, seventy-five souls. [15] And Jacob descended into Egypt, and he passed away, and so did our fathers. [16] And they crossed over into Shechem, and they were placed in the sepulcher which Abraham bought for a sum of money from the sons of Hamor, the son of Shechem. [17] And when the time of the Promise that God had revealed to Abraham drew near, the people increased and were multiplied in Egypt, [18] even until another king, who did not know Joseph, rose up in Egypt. [19] This one, encompassing our kindred, afflicted our fathers, so that they would expose their infants, lest they be kept alive. [20] In the same time, Moses was born. And he was in the grace of God, and he was nourished for three months in the house of his father. [21] Then, having been abandoned, the daughter of Pharaoh took him in, and she raised him as her own son. [22] And Moses was instructed in all the wisdom of the Egyptians. And he was mighty in his words and in his deeds. [23] But when forty years of age were completed in him, it rose up in his heart that he should visit his brothers, the sons of Israel. [24] And when he had seen a certain one suffering injury, he defended him. And striking the Egyptian, he wrought a retribution for him who was enduring the injury. [25] Now he supposed that his brothers would understand that God would grant them salvation through his hand. But they did not understand it. [26] So truly, on the following day, he appeared before those who were arguing, and he would have reconciled them in peace, saying, 'Men, you are brothers. So why would you harm one another?' [27] But he who was causing the injury to his neighbor rejected him, saying: 'Who has appointed you as leader and judge over us? [28] Could it be that you want to kill me, in the same way that you killed the Egyptian yesterday?' [29] Then, at this word, Moses fled. And he became a foreigner in the land of Midian, where he produced

two sons. ³⁰And when forty years were completed, there appeared to him, in the desert of Mount Sinai, an Angel, in a flame of fire in a bush. ³¹And upon seeing this, Moses was amazed at the sight. And as he drew near in order to gaze at it, the voice of the Lord came to him, saying: ³²'I am the God of your fathers: the God of Abraham, the God of Isaac, and the God of Jacob.' And Moses, being made to tremble, did not dare to look. ³³But the Lord said to him: 'Loosen the shoes from your feet. For the place in which you stand is holy ground. ³⁴Certainly, I have seen the affliction of my people who are in Egypt, and I have heard their groaning. And so, I am coming down to free them. And now, go forth and I will send you into Egypt.' ³⁵This Moses, whom they rejected by saying, 'Who has appointed you as leader and judge?' is the one God sent to be leader and redeemer, by the hand of the Angel who appeared to him in the bush. ³⁶This man led them out, accomplishing signs and wonders in the land of Egypt, and at the Red Sea, and in the desert, for forty years. ³⁷This is Moses, who said to the sons of Israel: 'God will raise up for you a prophet like me from your own brothers. You shall listen to him.' ³⁸This is he who was in the Church in the wilderness, with the Angel who was speaking to him on Mount Sinai, and with our fathers. It is he who received the words of life to give to us. ³⁹It is he whom our fathers were not willing to obey. Instead, they rejected him, and in their hearts they turned away toward Egypt, ⁴⁰saying to Aaron: 'Make gods for us, which may go before us. For this Moses, who led us away from the land of Egypt, we do not know what has happened to him.' ⁴¹And so they fashioned a calf in those days, and they offered sacrifices to an idol, and they rejoiced in the works of their own hands. ⁴²Then God turned, and he handed them over, to subservience to the armies of heaven, just as it was written in the Book of the Prophets: 'Did you not offer victims and sacrifices to me for forty years in the desert, O house of Israel? ⁴³And yet you took up for yourselves the tabernacle of Moloch and the star of your god Rephan, figures which you yourselves formed in order to adore them. And so I will carry you away, beyond Babylon.' ⁴⁴The tabernacle of the testimony was with our fathers in the desert, just as God ordained for them, speaking to Moses, so that he would make it according to the form that he had seen. ⁴⁵But our fathers, receiving it, also brought it, with Joshua, into the land of the Gentiles, whom God expelled before the face of our fathers, even until the days of David, ⁴⁶who found grace before God and who asked that he might obtain a tabernacle for the God of Jacob. ⁴⁷But it was Solomon who built a house for him. ⁴⁸Yet the Most High does not live in houses built by hands, just as he said through the prophet: ⁴⁹'Heaven is my throne, and the earth is my footstool. What kind of house would you build for me? says the Lord. And which is my resting place? ⁵⁰Has not my hand made all these things?' ⁵¹Stiff-necked and uncircumcised in heart and ears, you ever resist the Holy Spirit. Just as your fathers did, so also do you do. ⁵²Which of the Prophets have your fathers not persecuted? And they killed those who foretold the advent of the Just One. And you have now become the betrayers and murderers of him. ⁵³You received the law by the actions of Angels, and yet you have not kept it." ⁵⁴Then, upon hearing these things, they were deeply wounded in their hearts, and they gnashed their teeth at him. ⁵⁵But he, being filled with the Holy Spirit, and gazing intently toward heaven, saw the glory of God and Jesus standing at the right hand of God. And he said, "Behold, I see the heavens opened, and the Son of man standing at the right hand of God." ⁵⁶Then they, crying out with a loud voice, blocked their ears and, with one accord, rushed violently toward him. ⁵⁷And driving him out, beyond the city, they stoned him. And witnesses placed their garments beside the feet of a youth, who was called Saul. ⁵⁸And as they were stoning Stephen, he called out and said, "Lord Jesus, receive my spirit." ⁵⁹Then, having been brought to his knees, he cried out with a loud voice, saying, "Lord, do not hold this sin against them." And when he had said this, he fell asleep in the Lord. And Saul was consenting to his murder.

CHAPTER 8

¹Now in those days, there occurred a great persecution against the Church at Jerusalem. And they were all dispersed throughout the regions of Judea and Samaria, except the Apostles. ²But God-fearing men arranged for Stephen's funeral, and they made a great mourning over him. ³Then Saul was laying waste to the Church by entering throughout the houses, and dragging away men and women, and committing them to prison. ⁴Therefore, those who had been dispersed were traveling around, evangelizing the Word of God. ⁵Now Philip, descending to a city of Samaria, was preaching Christ to them. ⁶And the crowd was listening

intently and with one accord to those things which were being said by Philip, and they were watching the signs which he was accomplishing. ⁷For many of them had unclean spirits, and, crying out with a loud voice, these departed from them. ⁸And many of the paralytics and the lame were cured. ⁹Therefore, there was great gladness in that city. Now there was a certain man named Simon, who formerly had been a magician in that city, seducing the people of Samaria, claiming himself to be someone great. ¹⁰And to all those who would listen, from the least even to the greatest, he was saying: "Here is the power of God, which is called great." ¹¹And they were attentive to him because, for a long time, he had deluded them with his magic. ¹²Yet truly, once they had believed Philip, who was evangelizing the kingdom of God, both men and women were baptized in the name of Jesus Christ. ¹³Then Simon himself also believed and, when he had been baptized, he adhered to Philip. And now, seeing also the greatest signs and miracles being wrought, he was amazed and stupefied. ¹⁴Now when the Apostles who were in Jerusalem had heard that Samaria had received the Word of God, they sent Peter and John to them. ¹⁵And when they had arrived, they prayed for them, so that they might receive the Holy Spirit. ¹⁶For he had not yet come to any among them, since they were only baptized in the name of the Lord Jesus. ¹⁷Then they laid their hands on them, and they received the Holy Spirit. ¹⁸But when Simon had seen that, by the imposition of the hands of the Apostles, the Holy Spirit was given, he offered them money, ¹⁹saying, "Give this power to me also, so that on whomever I will lay my hands, he may receive the Holy Spirit." But Peter said to him: ²⁰"Let your money be with you in perdition, for you have supposed that a gift of God might be possessed by money. ²¹There is no part or place for you in this matter. For your heart is not upright in the sight of God. ²²And so, repent from this, your wickedness, and beg God, so that perhaps this plan of your heart might be forgiven you. ²³For I perceive you to be in the gall of bitterness and in the bond of iniquity." ²⁴Then Simon responded by saying, "Pray for me to the Lord, so that nothing of what you have said may happen to me." ²⁵And indeed, after testifying and speaking the Word of the Lord, they returned to Jerusalem, and they evangelized the many regions of the Samaritans. ²⁶Now an Angel of the Lord spoke to Philip, saying, "Rise up and go toward the south, to the way which descends from Jerusalem into Gaza, where there is a desert." ²⁷And rising up, he went. And behold, an Ethiopian man, a eunuch, powerful under Candace, the queen of the Ethiopians, who was over all her treasures, had arrived in Jerusalem to worship. ²⁸And while returning, he was sitting upon his chariot and reading from the prophet Isaiah. ²⁹Then the Spirit said to Philip, "Draw near and join yourself to this chariot." ³⁰And Philip, hurrying, heard him reading from the prophet Isaiah, and he said, "Do you think that you understand what you are reading?" ³¹And he said, "But how can I, unless someone will have revealed it to me?" And he asked Philip to climb up and sit with him. ³²Now the place in Scripture that he was reading was this: "Like a sheep he was led to the slaughter. And like a lamb silent before his shearer, so he opened not his mouth. ³³He endured his judgment with humility. Who of his generation shall describe how his life was taken away from the earth?" ³⁴Then the eunuch responded to Philip, saying: "I beg you, about whom is the prophet saying this? About himself, or about someone else?" ³⁵Then Philip, opening his mouth and beginning from this Scripture, evangelized Jesus to him. ³⁶And while they were going along the way, they arrived at a certain water source. And the eunuch said: "There is water. What would prevent me from being baptized?" ³⁷Then Philip said, "If you believe from your whole heart, it is permitted." And he responded by saying, "I believe the Son of God to be Jesus the Christ." ³⁸And he ordered the chariot to stand still. And both Philip and the eunuch descended into the water. And he baptized him. ³⁹And when they had ascended from the water, the Spirit of the Lord took Philip away, and the eunuch did not see him anymore. Then he went on his way, rejoicing. ⁴⁰Now Philip was found in Azotus. And continuing on, he evangelized all the cities, until he arrived in Caesarea.

CHAPTER 9

¹Now Saul, still breathing threats and beatings against the disciples of the Lord, went to the high priest, ²and he petitioned him for letters to the synagogues in Damascus, so that, if he found any men or women belonging to this Way, he could lead them as prisoners to Jerusalem. ³And as he made the journey, it happened that he was approaching Damascus. And suddenly, a light from heaven shone around him. ⁴And falling to the ground, he heard a voice saying to him,

"Saul, Saul, why are you persecuting me?" [5] And he said, "Who are you, Lord?" And he: "I am Jesus, whom you are persecuting. It is hard for you to kick against the goad." [6] And he, trembling and astonished, said, "Lord, what do you want me to do?" [7] And the Lord said to him, "Rise up and go into the city, and there you will be told what you ought to do." Now the men who were accompanying him were standing stupefied, hearing indeed a voice, but seeing no one. [8] Then Saul rose up from the ground. And upon opening his eyes, he saw nothing. So leading him by the hand, they brought him into Damascus. [9] And in that place, he was without sight for three days, and he neither ate nor drank. [10] Now there was a certain disciple at Damascus, named Ananias. And the Lord said to him in a vision, "Ananias!" And he said, "Here I am, Lord." [11] And the Lord said to him: "Rise up and go into the street that is called Straight, and seek, in the house of Judas, the one named Saul of Tarsus. For behold, he is praying." [12] (And Paul saw a man named Ananias entering and imposing hands upon him, so that he might receive his sight.) [13] But Ananias responded: "Lord, I have heard from many about this man, how much harm he has done to your saints in Jerusalem. [14] And he has authority here from the leaders of the priests to bind all who invoke your name." [15] Then the Lord said to him: "Go, for this one is an instrument chosen by me to convey my name before nations and kings and the sons of Israel. [16] For I will reveal to him how much he must suffer on behalf of my name." [17] And Ananias departed. And he entered the house. And laying his hands upon him, he said: "Brother Saul, the Lord Jesus, he who appeared to you on the way by which you arrived, sent me so that you would receive your sight and be filled with the Holy Spirit." [18] And immediately, it was as if scales had fallen from his eyes, and he received his sight. And rising up, he was baptized. [19] And when he had taken a meal, he was strengthened. Now he was with the disciples who were at Damascus for some days. [20] And he was continuously preaching Jesus in the synagogues: that he is the Son of God. [21] And all who heard him were astonished, and they said, "Is this not the one who, in Jerusalem, was fighting against those invoking this name, and who came here for this: so that he might lead them away to the leaders of the priests?" [22] But Saul was increasing to a greater extent in ability, and so he was confounding the Jews who lived at Damascus, by affirming that he is the Christ. [23] And when many days were completed, the Jews took counsel as one, so that they might put him to death. [24] But their treachery became known to Saul. Now they were also watching the gates, day and night, so that they might put him to death. [25] But the disciples, taking him away by night, sent him over the wall by letting him down in a basket. [26] And when he had arrived in Jerusalem, he attempted to join himself to the disciples. And they were all afraid of him, not believing that he was a disciple. [27] But Barnabas took him aside and led him to the Apostles. And he explained to them how he had seen the Lord, and that he had spoken to him, and how, in Damascus, he had acted faithfully in the name of Jesus. [28] And he was with them, entering and departing Jerusalem, and acting faithfully in the name of the Lord. [29] He also was speaking with the Gentiles and disputing with the Greeks. But they were seeking to kill him. [30] And when the brothers had realized this, they brought him to Caesarea and sent him away to Tarsus. [31] Certainly, the Church had peace throughout all of Judea and Galilee and Samaria, and it was being built up, while walking in the fear of the Lord, and it was being filled with the consolation of the Holy Spirit. [32] Then it happened that Peter, as he traveled around everywhere, came to the saints who were living at Lydda. [33] But he found there a certain man, named Aeneas, who was a paralytic, who had lain in bed for eight years. [34] And Peter said to him: "Aeneas, the Lord Jesus Christ heals you. Rise up and arrange your bed." And immediately he rose up. [35] And all who were living in Lydda and Sharon saw him, and they were converted to the Lord. [36] Now in Joppa there was a certain disciple named Tabitha, which in translation is called Dorcas. She was filled with the good works and almsgiving that she was accomplishing. [37] And it happened that, in those days, she became ill and died. And when they had washed her, they laid her in an upper room. [38] Now since Lydda was close to Joppa, the disciples, upon hearing that Peter was there, sent two men to him, asking him: "Do not be slow in coming to us." [39] Then Peter, rising up, went with them. And when he had arrived, they led him to an upper room. And all the widows were standing around him, weeping and showing him the tunics and garments that Dorcas had made for them. [40] And when they had all been sent outside, Peter, kneeling down, prayed. And turning to the body, he said: "Tabitha, arise." And she opened her eyes and, upon seeing Peter, sat up again. [41] And offering her his hand, he lifted her up. And when he had called in the saints and the widows, he presented her alive. ⁴²Now this became known throughout all of Joppa. And many believed in the Lord. ⁴³And it happened that he resided for many days in Joppa, with a certain Simon, a tanner.

CHAPTER 10

¹Now there was a certain man in Caesarea, named Cornelius, a centurion of the cohort which is called Italian, ²a devout man, fearing God with all his house, giving many alms to the people, and praying to God continually. ³This man saw in a vision clearly, at about the ninth hour of the day, the Angel of God entering to him and saying to him: "Cornelius!" ⁴And he, gazing at him, was seized by fear, and he said, "What is it, lord?" And he said to him: "Your prayers and your almsgiving have ascended as a memorial in the sight of God. ⁵And now, send men to Joppa and summon a certain Simon, who is surnamed Peter. ⁶This man is a guest with a certain Simon, a tanner, whose house is beside the sea. He will tell you what you must do." ⁷And when the Angel who was speaking to him had departed, he called, out of those who were subject to him, two of his household servants and a soldier who feared the Lord. ⁸And when he had explained everything to them, he sent them to Joppa. ⁹Then, on the following day, while they were making the journey and approaching the city, Peter ascended to the upper rooms, so that he might pray, at about the sixth hour. ¹⁰And since he was hungry, he wanted to enjoy some food. Then, as they were preparing it, an ecstasy of mind fell over him. ¹¹And he saw heaven opened, and a certain container descending, as if a great linen sheet were let down, by its four corners, from heaven to earth, ¹²on which were all four-footed beasts, and the crawling things of the earth and the flying things of the air. ¹³And a voice came to him: "Rise up, Peter! Kill and eat." ¹⁴But Peter said: "Far be it from me, lord. For I have never eaten anything common or unclean." ¹⁵And the voice, again a second time to him: "What God has purified, you shall not call common." ¹⁶Now this was done three times. And immediately the container was taken up to heaven. ¹⁷Now while Peter was still hesitant within himself as to what the vision, which he had seen, might mean, behold, the men who had been sent from Cornelius stood at the gate, inquiring about Simon's house. ¹⁸And when they had called out, they asked if Simon, who is surnamed Peter, was a guest in that place. ¹⁹Then, as Peter was thinking about the vision, the Spirit said to him, "Behold, three men seek you. ²⁰And so, rise up, descend, and go with them, doubting nothing. For I have sent them." ²¹Then Peter, descending to the men, said: "Behold, I am the one whom you seek. What is the reason for which you have arrived?" ²²And they said: "Cornelius, a centurion, a just and God-fearing man, who has good testimony from the entire nation of the Jews, received a message from a holy Angel to summon you to his house and to listen to words from you." ²³Therefore, leading them in, he received them as guests. Then, on following the day, rising up, he set out with them. And some of the brothers from Joppa accompanied him. ²⁴And on the next day, he entered Caesarea. And truly, Cornelius was waiting for them, having called together his family and closest friends. ²⁵And it happened that, when Peter had entered, Cornelius went to meet him. And falling before his feet, he reverenced. ²⁶Yet truly, Peter, lifting him up, said: "Rise up, for I also am only a man." ²⁷And speaking with him, he entered, and he found many who had gathered together. ²⁸And he said to them: "You know how abominable it would be for a Jewish man to be joined with, or to be added to, a foreign people. But God has revealed to me to call no man common or unclean. ²⁹Because of this and without doubt, I came when summoned. Therefore, I ask you, for what reason have you summoned me?" ³⁰And Cornelius said: "It is now the fourth day, to this very hour, since I was praying in my house at the ninth hour, and behold, a man stood before me in a white vestment, and he said: ³¹'Cornelius, your prayer has been heard and your almsgiving has been remembered in the sight of God. ³²Therefore, send to Joppa and summon Simon, who is surnamed Peter. This man is a guest in the house of Simon, a tanner, near the sea.' ³³And so, I promptly sent for you. And you have done well in coming here. Therefore, all of us are now present in your sight to hear all the things that were taught to you by the Lord." ³⁴Then, Peter, opening his mouth, said: "I have concluded in truth that God is not a respecter of persons. ³⁵But within every nation, whoever fears him and works justice is acceptable to him. ³⁶God sent the Word to the sons of Israel, announcing the peace through Jesus Christ, for he is the Lord of all. ³⁷You know that the Word has been made known throughout all

Judea. For beginning from Galilee, after the baptism which John preached, [38] Jesus of Nazareth, whom God anointed with the Holy Spirit and with power, traveled around doing good and healing all those oppressed by the devil. For God was with him. [39] And we are witnesses of all that he did in the region of Judea and in Jerusalem, he whom they killed by hanging him on a tree. [40] God raised him up on the third day and permitted him to be made manifest, [41] not to all the people, but to the witnesses preordained by God, to those of us who ate and drank with him after he rose again from the dead. [42] And he instructed us to preach to the people, and to testify that he is the One who was appointed by God to be the judge of the living and of the dead. [43] To him all the Prophets offer testimony that through his name all who believe in him receive the remission of sins." [44] While Peter was still speaking these words, the Holy Spirit fell over all of those who were listening to the Word. [45] And the faithful of the circumcision, who had arrived with Peter, were astonished that the grace of the Holy Spirit was also poured out upon the Gentiles. [46] For they heard them speaking in tongues and magnifying God. [47] Then Peter responded, "How could anyone prohibit water, so that those who have received the Holy Spirit would not be baptized, just as we also have been?" [48] And he ordered them to be baptized in the name of the Lord Jesus Christ. Then they begged him to remain with them for some days.

CHAPTER 11

[1] Now the Apostles and brothers who were in Judea heard that the Gentiles had also received the Word of God. [2] Then, when Peter had gone up to Jerusalem, those who were of the circumcision argued against him, [3] saying, "Why did you enter to uncircumcised men, and why did you eat with them?" [4] And Peter began to explain to them, in an orderly manner, saying: [5] "I was in the city of Joppa praying, and I saw, in an ecstasy of mind, a vision: a certain container descending, like a great linen sheet being let down from heaven by its four corners. And it drew near to me. [6] And looking into it, I considered and saw the four-footed beasts of the earth, and the wild beasts, and the reptiles, and the flying things of the air. [7] Then I also heard a voice saying to me: 'Rise up, Peter. Kill and eat.' [8] But I said: 'Never, lord! For what is common or unclean has never entered into my mouth.' [9] Then the voice responded a second time from heaven, 'What God has cleansed, you shall not call common.' [10] Now this was done three times. And then everything was taken up again into heaven. [11] And behold, immediately there were three men standing near the house where I was, having been sent to me from Caesarea. [12] Then the Spirit told me that I should go with them, doubting nothing. And these six brothers went with me also. And we entered into the house of the man. [13] And he described for us how he had seen an Angel in his house, standing and saying to him: 'Send to Joppa and summon Simon, who is surnamed Peter. [14] And he shall speak to you words, by which you shall be saved with your whole house.' [15] And when I had begun to speak, the Holy Spirit fell upon them, just as upon us also, in the beginning. [16] Then I remembered the words of the Lord, just as he himself said: 'John, indeed, baptized with water, but you shall be baptized with the Holy Spirit.' [17] Therefore, if God gave them the same grace, as also to us, who have believed in the Lord Jesus Christ, who was I, that I would be able to prohibit God?" [18] Having heard these things, they were silent. And they glorified God, saying: "So has God also given to the Gentiles repentance unto life." [19] And some of them, having been dispersed by the persecution that had occurred under Stephen, traveled around, even to Phoenicia and Cyprus and Antioch, speaking the Word to no one, except to Jews only. [20] But some of these men from Cyprus and Cyrene, when they had entered into Antioch, were speaking also to the Greeks, announcing the Lord Jesus. [21] And the hand of the Lord was with them. And a great number believed and were converted to the Lord. [22] Now the news came to the ears of the Church at Jerusalem about these things, and they sent Barnabas as far as Antioch. [23] And when he had arrived there and had seen the grace of God, he was gladdened. And he exhorted them all to continue in the Lord with a resolute heart. [24] For he was a good man, and he was filled with the Holy Spirit and with faith. And a great multitude was added to the Lord. [25] Then Barnabas set out for Tarsus, so that he might seek Saul. And when he had found him, he brought him to Antioch. [26] And they were conversing there in the Church for an entire year. And they taught such a great multitude, that it was at Antioch that the disciples were first known by the name of Christian. [27] Now in these days, prophets from Jerusalem went over to Antioch. [28] And one of them,

named Agabus, rising up, signified through the Spirit that there was going to be a great famine over the entire world, which did happen under Claudius. ²⁹Then the disciples declared, according to what each one possessed, what they would offer to be sent to the brothers living in Judea. ³⁰And so they did, sending it to the elders by the hands of Barnabas and Saul.

CHAPTER 12

¹Now at the same time, king Herod extended his hand, in order to afflict some from the Church. ²Then he killed James, the brother of John, with the sword. ³And seeing that it pleased the Jews, he set out next to apprehend Peter also. Now it was the days of Unleavened Bread. ⁴So when he had apprehended him, he sent him into prison, handing him over into the custody of four groups of four soldiers, intending to produce him to the people after the Passover. ⁵And so Peter was detained in prison. But prayers were being made without ceasing, by the Church, to God on his behalf. ⁶And when Herod was ready to produce him, in that same night, Peter was sleeping between two soldiers, and was bound with two chains. And there were guards in front of the door, guarding the prison. ⁷And behold, an Angel of the Lord stood near, and a light shined forth in the cell. And tapping Peter on the side, he awakened him, saying, "Rise up, quickly." And the chains fell from his hands. ⁸Then the Angel said to him: "Dress yourself, and put on your boots." And he did so. And he said to him, "Wrap your garment around yourself and follow me." ⁹And going out, he followed him. And he did not know this truth: that this was being done by an Angel. For he thought that he was seeing a vision. ¹⁰And passing by the first and second guards, they came to the iron gate which leads into the city; and it opened for them by itself. And departing, they continued on along a certain side street. And suddenly the Angel withdrew from him. ¹¹And Peter, returning to himself, said: "Now I know, truly, that the Lord sent his Angel, and that he rescued me from the hand of Herod and from all that the people of the Jews were anticipating." ¹²And as he was considering this, he arrived at the house of Mary, the mother of John, who was surnamed Mark, where many were gathered and were praying. ¹³Then, as he knocked at the door of the gate, a girl went out to answer, whose name was Rhoda. ¹⁴And when she recognized the voice of Peter, out of joy, she did not open the gate, but instead, running in, she reported that Peter stood before the gate. ¹⁵But they said to her, "You are crazy." But she reaffirmed that this was so. Then they were saying, "It is his angel." ¹⁶But Peter was persevering in knocking. And when they had opened, they saw him and were astonished. ¹⁷But motioning to them with his hand to be silent, he explained how the Lord had led him away from prison. And he said, "Inform James and those brothers." And going out, he went away to another place. ¹⁸Then, when daylight came, there was no small commotion among the soldiers, as to what had happened concerning Peter. ¹⁹And when Herod had requested him and did not obtain him, having had the guards interrogated, he ordered them led away. And descending from Judea into Caesarea, he lodged there. ²⁰Now he was angry with those of Tyre and Sidon. But they came to him with one accord, and, having persuaded Blastus, who was over the bedchamber of the king, they petitioned for peace, because their regions were supplied with food by him. ²¹Then, on the appointed day, Herod was clothed in kingly apparel, and he sat in the judgment seat, and he gave a speech to them. ²²Then the people were crying out, "The voice of a god, and not of a man!" ²³And immediately, an Angel of the Lord struck him down, because he had not given honor to God. And having been consumed by worms, he expired. ²⁴But the word of the Lord was increasing and multiplying. ²⁵Then Barnabas and Saul, having completed the ministry, returned from Jerusalem, bringing with them John, who was surnamed Mark.

CHAPTER 13

¹Now there were, in the Church at Antioch, prophets and teachers, among whom were Barnabas, and Simon, who was called the Black, and Lucius of Cyrene, and Manahen, who was the foster brother of Herod the tetrarch, and Saul. ²Now as they were ministering for the Lord and fasting, the Holy Spirit said to them: "Separate Saul and Barnabas for me, for the work for which I have selected them." ³Then, fasting and praying and imposing their hands upon them, they sent them away. ⁴And having been sent by the Holy Spirit, they went to Seleucia. And from there they sailed to Cyprus. ⁵And when they had arrived at Salamis,

they were preaching the Word of God in the synagogues of the Jews. And they also had John in the ministry. [6] And when they had traveled throughout the entire island, even to Paphos, they found a certain man, a magician, a false prophet, a Jew, whose name was Bar-Jesu. [7] And he was with the proconsul, Sergius Paulus, a prudent man. This man, summoning Barnabas and Saul, wanted to hear the Word of God. [8] But Elymas the magician (for so his name is translated) stood against them, seeking to turn the proconsul away from the Faith. [9] Then Saul, who is also called Paul, having been filled with the Holy Spirit, looked intently at him, [10] and he said: "So full of every deceit and of all falsehoods, son of the devil, enemy of all justice, you never cease to subvert the righteous ways of the Lord! [11] And now, behold, the hand of the Lord is upon you. And you will be blinded, not seeing the sun for a length of time." And immediately a fog and a darkness fell over him. And wandering around, he was seeking someone who might lead him by the hand. [12] Then the proconsul, when he had seen what was done, believed, being in wonder over the doctrine of the Lord. [13] And when Paul and those who were with him had sailed from Paphos, they arrived at Perga in Pamphylia. Then John departed from them and returned to Jerusalem. [14] Yet truly, they, traveling on from Perga, arrived at Antioch in Pisidia. And upon entering the synagogue on the Sabbath day, they sat down. [15] Then, after the reading from the Law and the Prophets, the leaders of the synagogue sent to them, saying: "Noble brothers, if there is in you any word of exhortation to the people, speak." [16] Then Paul, rising up and motioning for silence with his hand, said: "Men of Israel and you who fear God, listen closely. [17] The God of the people of Israel chose our fathers, and exalted the people, when they were settlers in the land of Egypt. And with an exalted arm, he led them away from there. [18] And throughout a time of forty years, he endured their behavior in the desert. [19] And by destroying seven nations in the land of Canaan, he divided their land among them by lot, [20] after about four hundred and fifty years. And after these things, he gave them judges, even until the prophet Samuel. [21] And later on, they petitioned for a king. And God gave them Saul, the son of Kish, a man from the tribe of Benjamin, for forty years. [22] And having removed him, he raised up for them king David. And offering testimony about him, he said, 'I have found David, the son of Jesse, to be a man according to my own heart, who will accomplish all that I will.' [23] From his offspring, according to the Promise, God has brought Jesus the Savior to Israel. [24] John was preaching, before the face of his advent, a baptism of repentance to all the people of Israel. [25] Then, when John completed his course, he was saying: 'I am not the one you consider me to be. For behold, one arrives after me, the shoes of whose feet I am not worthy to loosen.' [26] Noble brothers, sons of the stock of Abraham, and those among you who fear God, it is to you the Word of this salvation has been sent. [27] For those who were living in Jerusalem, and its rulers, heeding neither him, nor the voices of the Prophets that are read on every Sabbath, fulfilled these by judging him. [28] And although they found no case for death against him, they petitioned Pilate, so that they might put him to death. [29] And when they had fulfilled everything that had been written about him, taking him down from the tree, they placed him in a tomb. [30] Yet truly, God raised him up from the dead on the third day. [31] And he was seen for many days by those who went up with him from Galilee to Jerusalem, who even now are his witnesses to the people. [32] And we are announcing to you that the Promise, which was made to our fathers, [33] has been fulfilled by God for our children by raising up Jesus, just as it has been written in the second Psalm also: 'You are my Son. This day I have begotten you.' [34] Now, since he raised him from the dead, so as to no longer return to corruption, he has said this: 'I will give to you the holy things of David, the faithful one.' [35] And also then, in another place, he says: 'You will not allow your Holy One to see corruption.' [36] For David, when he had ministered to his generation in accordance with the will of God, fell asleep, and he was placed next to his fathers, and he saw corruption. [37] Yet truly, he whom God has raised from the dead has not seen corruption. [38] Therefore, let it be known to you, noble brothers, that through him is announced to you remission from sins and from everything by which you were not able to be justified in the law of Moses. [39] In him, all who believe are justified. [40] Therefore, be careful, lest what was said by the Prophets may overwhelm you: [41] 'You despisers! Look, and wonder, and be scattered! For I am working a deed in your days, a deed which you would not believe, even if someone were to explain it to you.'" [42] Then, as they were departing, they asked them if, on the following Sabbath, they might speak these words to them. [43] And when the synagogue had been dismissed, many among the Jews and the new worshipers were following Paul and Barnabas. And they, speaking to them, persuaded them to continue in the grace of God. ⁴⁴Yet truly, on the following Sabbath, nearly the entire city came together to hear the Word of God. ⁴⁵Then the Jews, seeing the crowds, were filled with envy, and they, blaspheming, contradicted the things that were being said by Paul. ⁴⁶Then Paul and Barnabas said firmly: "It was necessary to speak the Word of God first to you. But because you reject it, and so judge yourselves unworthy of eternal life, behold, we turn to the Gentiles. ⁴⁷For so has the Lord instructed us: 'I have set you as a light to the Gentiles, so that you may bring salvation to the ends of the earth.' " ⁴⁸Then the Gentiles, upon hearing this, were gladdened, and they were glorifying the Word of the Lord. And as many as believed were preordained to eternal life. ⁴⁹Now the word of the Lord was disseminated throughout the entire region. ⁵⁰But the Jews incited some devout and honest women, and the leaders of the city. And they stirred up a persecution against Paul and Barnabas. And they drove them away from their parts. ⁵¹But they, shaking the dust from their feet against them, went on to Iconium. ⁵²The disciples were likewise filled with gladness and with the Holy Spirit.

CHAPTER 14

¹Now it happened in Iconium that they entered together into the synagogue of the Jews, and they spoke in such a way that a copious multitude of both Jews and Greeks believed. ²Yet truly, the Jews who were unbelieving had incited and enflamed the souls of the Gentiles against the brothers. ³And so, they remained for a long time, acting faithfully in the Lord, offering testimony to the Word of his grace, providing signs and wonders done by their hands. ⁴Then the multitude of the city was divided. And certainly, some were with the Jews, yet truly others were with the Apostles. ⁵Now when an assault had been planned by the Gentiles and the Jews with their leaders, so that they might treat them with contempt and stone them, ⁶they, realizing this, fled together to Lystra and Derbe, cities of Lycaonia, and to the entire surrounding region. And they were evangelizing in that place. ⁷And a certain man was sitting at Lystra, disabled in his feet, lame from his mother's womb, who had never walked. ⁸This man heard Paul speaking. And Paul, gazing at him intently, and perceiving that he had faith, so that he might be healed, ⁹said with a loud voice, "Stand upright upon your feet!" And he leaped up and walked around. ¹⁰But when the crowds had seen what Paul had done, they lifted up their voice in the Lycaonian language, saying, "The gods, having taken the likenesses of men, have descended to us!" ¹¹And they called Barnabas, 'Jupiter,' yet truly they called Paul, 'Mercury,' because he was the lead speaker. ¹²Also, the priest of Jupiter, who was outside the city, in front of the gate, bringing in oxen and garlands, was willing to offer sacrifice with the people. ¹³And as soon as the Apostles, Barnabas and Paul, had heard this, tearing their tunics, they leapt into the crowd, crying out ¹⁴and saying: "Men, why would you do this? We also are mortals, men like yourselves, preaching to you to be converted, from these vain things, to the living God, who made heaven and earth and the sea and all that is in them. ¹⁵In previous generations, he permitted all nations to walk in their own ways. ¹⁶But certainly, he did not leave himself without testimony, doing good from heaven, giving rains and fruitful seasons, filling their hearts with food and gladness." ¹⁷And by saying these things, they were barely able to restrain the crowds from immolating to them. ¹⁸Now certain Jews from Antioch and Iconium arrived there. And having persuaded the crowd, they stoned Paul and dragged him outside of the city, thinking him to be dead. ¹⁹But as the disciples were standing around him, he got up and entered the city. And the next day, he set out with Barnabas for Derbe. ²⁰And when they had evangelized that city, and had taught many, they returned again to Lystra and to Iconium and to Antioch, ²¹strengthening the souls of the disciples, and exhorting them that they should remain always in the faith, and that it is necessary for us to enter into the kingdom of God through many tribulations. ²²And when they had established priests for them in each church, and had prayed with fasting, they commended them to the Lord, in whom they believed. ²³And traveling by way of Pisidia, they arrived in Pamphylia. ²⁴And having spoken the word of the Lord in Perga, they went down into Attalia. ²⁵And from there, they sailed to Antioch, where they had been commended to the grace of God for the work which they had now accomplished. ²⁶And when they had arrived and had gathered together the church, they related what great things God had done with them, and how he had opened the door of faith to the Gentiles. ²⁷And they remained for no small amount of time with the disciples.

CHAPTER 15

[1] And certain ones, descending from Judea, were teaching the brothers, "Unless you are circumcised according to the custom of Moses, you cannot be saved." [2] Therefore, when Paul and Barnabas made no small uprising against them, they decided that Paul and Barnabas, and some from the opposing side, should go up to the Apostles and priests in Jerusalem concerning this question. [3] Therefore, being led by the church, they traveled through Phoenicia and Samaria, describing the conversion of the Gentiles. And they caused great joy among all the brothers. [4] And when they had arrived in Jerusalem, they were received by the church and the Apostles and the elders, reporting what great things God had done with them. [5] But some from the sect of the Pharisees, those who were believers, rose up saying, "It is necessary for them to be circumcised and to be instructed to keep the Law of Moses." [6] And the Apostles and elders came together to take care of this matter. [7] And after a great contention had taken place, Peter rose up and said to them: "Noble brothers, you know that, in recent days, God has chosen from among us, by my mouth, Gentiles to hear the word of the Gospel and to believe. [8] And God, who knows hearts, offered testimony, by giving the Holy Spirit to them, just as to us. [9] And he distinguished nothing between us and them, purifying their hearts by faith. [10] Now therefore, why do you tempt God to impose a yoke upon the necks of the disciples, which neither our fathers nor we have been able to bear? [11] But by the grace of the Lord Jesus Christ, we believe in order to be saved, in the same manner also as them." [12] Then the entire multitude was silent. And they were listening to Barnabas and Paul, describing what great signs and wonders God had wrought among the Gentiles through them. [13] And after they had been silent, James responded by saying: "Noble brothers, listen to me. [14] Simon has explained in what manner God first visited, so as to take from the Gentiles a people to his name. [15] And the words of the Prophets are in agreement with this, just as it was written: [16] 'After these things, I will return, and I will rebuild the tabernacle of David, which has fallen down. And I will rebuild its ruins, and I will raise it up, [17] so that the rest of men may seek the Lord, along with all the nations over whom my name has been invoked, says the Lord, who does these things.' [18] To the Lord, his own work has been known from eternity. [19] Because of this, I judge that those who were converted to God from among the Gentiles are not to be disturbed, [20] but instead that we write to them, that they should keep themselves from the defilement of idols, and from fornication, and from whatever has been suffocated, and from blood. [21] For Moses, from ancient times, has had in each city those who preach him in the synagogues, where he is read on every Sabbath." [22] Then it pleased the Apostles and elders, with the whole Church, to choose men from among them, and to send to Antioch, with Paul and Barnabas, and Judas, who was surnamed Barsabbas, and Silas, preeminent men among the brothers, [23] what was written by their own hands: "The Apostles and elders, brothers, to those who are at Antioch and Syria and Cilicia, brothers from the Gentiles, greetings. [24] Since we have heard that some, going out from among us, have troubled you with words, subverting your souls, to whom we gave no commandment, [25] it pleased us, being assembled as one, to choose men and to send them to you, with our most beloved Barnabas and Paul: [26] men who have handed over their lives on behalf of the name of our Lord Jesus Christ. [27] Therefore, we have sent Judas and Silas, who themselves also will, with the spoken word, reaffirm to you the same things. [28] For it has seemed good to the Holy Spirit and to us to impose no further burden upon you, other than these necessary things: [29] that you abstain from things immolated to idols, and from blood, and from what has been suffocated, and from fornication. You will do well to keep yourselves from these things. Farewell." [30] And so, having been dismissed, they went down to Antioch. And gathering the multitude together, they delivered the epistle. [31] And when they had read it, they were gladdened by this consolation. [32] But Judas and Silas, being also prophets themselves, consoled the brothers with many words, and they were strengthened. [33] Then, after spending some more time there, they were dismissed with peace, by the brothers, to those who had sent them. [34] But it seemed good to Silas to remain there. So Judas alone departed to Jerusalem. [35] And Paul and Barnabas remained at Antioch, with many others, teaching and evangelizing the Word of the Lord. [36] Then, after some days, Paul said to Barnabas, "Let us return to visit the brothers throughout all the cities in which we have preached the Word of the Lord, to see how they are." [37] And Barnabas wanted to take John, who was surnamed Mark, with them also. [38] But Paul was saying that he ought not to be received, since he withdrew from them at

Pamphylia, and he had not gone with them in the work. ³⁹ And there occurred a dissension, to such an extent that they departed from one another. And Barnabas, indeed taking Mark, sailed to Cyprus. ⁴⁰ Yet truly, Paul, choosing Silas, set out, being delivered by the brothers to the grace of God. ⁴¹ And he traveled through Syria and Cilicia, confirming the Churches, instructing them to keep the precepts of the Apostles and the elders.

CHAPTER 16

¹ Then he arrived at Derbe and Lystra. And behold, a certain disciple named Timothy was there, the son of a faithful Jewish woman, his father a Gentile. ² The brothers who were at Lystra and Iconium rendered good testimony to him. ³ Paul wanted this man to travel with him, and taking him, he circumcised him, because of the Jews who were in those places. For they all knew that his father was a Gentile. ⁴ And as they were traveling through the cities, they delivered to them the dogmas to be kept, which were decreed by the Apostles and elders who were at Jerusalem. ⁵ And certainly, the Churches were being strengthened in faith and were increasing in number every day. ⁶ Then, while crossing through Phrygia and the region of Galatia, they were prevented by the Holy Spirit from speaking the Word in Asia. ⁷ But when they had arrived in Mysia, they attempted to go into Bithynia, but the Spirit of Jesus would not permit them. ⁸ Then, when they had crossed through Mysia, they descended to Troas. ⁹ And a vision in the night was revealed to Paul of a certain man of Macedonia, standing and pleading with him, and saying: "Cross into Macedonia and help us!" ¹⁰ Then, after he saw the vision, immediately we sought to set out for Macedonia, having been assured that God had called us to evangelize to them. ¹¹ And sailing from Troas, taking a direct path, we arrived at Samothrace, and on the following day, at Neapolis, ¹² and from there to Philippi, which is the preeminent city in the area of Macedonia, a colony. Now we were in this city some days, conferring together. ¹³ Then, on the Sabbath day, we were walking outside the gate, beside a river, where there seemed to be a prayer gathering. And sitting down, we were speaking with the women who had assembled. ¹⁴ And a certain woman, named Lydia, a seller of purple in the city of Thyatira, a worshiper of God, listened. And the Lord opened her heart to be receptive to what Paul was saying. ¹⁵ And when she had been baptized, with her household, she pleaded with us, saying: "If you have judged me to be faithful to the Lord, enter into my house and lodge there." And she convinced us. ¹⁶ Then it happened that, as we were going out to prayer, a certain girl, having a spirit of divination, met with us. She was a source of great profit to her masters, through her divining. ¹⁷ This girl, following Paul and us, was crying out, saying: "These men are servants of the Most High God! They are announcing to you the way of salvation!" ¹⁸ Now she behaved in this way for many days. But Paul, being grieved, turned and said to the spirit, "I command you, in the name of Jesus Christ, to go out from her." And it went away in that same hour. ¹⁹ But her masters, seeing that the hope of their profit went away, apprehended Paul and Silas, and they brought them to the rulers at the courthouse. ²⁰ And presenting them to the magistrates, they said: "These men are disturbing our city, since they are Jews. ²¹ And they are announcing a way which is not lawful for us to accept or to observe, since we are Romans." ²² And the people rushed together against them. And the magistrates, tearing their tunics, ordered them to be beaten with staffs. ²³ And when they had inflicted many scourges on them, they cast them into prison, instructing the guard to watch them diligently. ²⁴ And since he had received this kind of order, he cast them into the interior prison cell, and he restricted their feet with stocks. ²⁵ Then, in the middle of the night, Paul and Silas were praying and praising God. And those who were also in custody were listening to them. ²⁶ Yet truly, there was a sudden earthquake, so great that the foundations of the prison were moved. And immediately all the doors were opened, and the bindings of everyone were released. ²⁷ Then the prison guard, having been jarred awake, and seeing the doors of the prison open, drew his sword and intended to kill himself, supposing that the prisoners had fled. ²⁸ But Paul cried out with a loud voice, saying: "Do no harm to yourself, for we are all here!" ²⁹ Then calling for a light, he entered. And trembling, he fell before the feet of Paul and Silas. ³⁰ And bringing them outside, he said, "Sirs, what must I do, so that I may be saved?" ³¹ So they said, "Believe in the Lord Jesus, and then you will be saved, with your household." ³² And they spoke the Word of the Lord to him, along with all those who were in his house. ³³ And he, taking them in the same hour of the night, washed their scourges. And he was baptized, and next his entire household. ³⁴ And when

he had brought them into his own house, he set a table for them. And he was joyous, with his entire household, believing in God. [35] And when daylight had arrived, the magistrates sent the attendants, saying, "Release those men." [36] But the prison guard reported these words to Paul: "The magistrates have sent to have you released. Now therefore, depart. Go in peace." [37] But Paul said to them: "They have beaten us publicly, though we were not condemned. They have cast men who are Romans into prison. And now they would drive us away secretly? Not so. Instead, let them come forward, [38] and let us drive them away." Then the attendants reported these words to the magistrates. And upon hearing that they were Romans, they were afraid. [39] And arriving, they pleaded with them, and leading them out, they begged them to depart from the city. [40] And they went away from the prison and entered into the house of Lydia. And having seen the brothers, they consoled them, and then they set out.

CHAPTER 17

[1] Now when they had walked through Amphipolis and Apollonia, they arrived at Thessalonica, where there was a synagogue of the Jews. [2] Then Paul, according to custom, entered to them. And for three Sabbaths he disputed with them about the Scriptures, [3] interpreting and concluding that it was necessary for the Christ to suffer and to rise again from the dead, and that "this is the Jesus Christ, whom I am announcing to you." [4] And some of them believed and were joined to Paul and Silas, and a great number of these were from the worshipers and the Gentiles, and not a few were noble women. [5] But the Jews, being jealous, and joining with certain evildoers among the common men, caused a disturbance, and they stirred up the city. And taking up a position near the house of Jason, they sought to lead them out to the people. [6] And when they had not found them, they dragged Jason and certain brothers to the rulers of the city, crying out: "For these are the ones who have stirred up the city. And they came here, [7] and Jason has received them. And all these men act contrary to the decrees of Caesar, saying that there is another king, Jesus." [8] And they incited the people. And the rulers of the city, upon hearing these things, [9] and having received an explanation from Jason and the others, released them. [10] Yet truly, the brothers promptly sent Paul and Silas away by night to Beroea. And when they had arrived, they entered the synagogue of the Jews. [11] But these were more noble than those who were at Thessalonica. They received the Word with all enthusiasm, daily examining the Scriptures to see if these things were so. [12] And indeed, many believed among them, as well as not a few among the honorable Gentile men and women. [13] Then, when the Jews of Thessalonica had realized that the Word of God was also preached by Paul at Beroea, they went there also, stirring up and disturbing the multitude. [14] And then the brothers quickly sent Paul away, so that he might travel by sea. But Silas and Timothy remained there. [15] Then those who were leading Paul brought him as far as Athens. And having received an order from him to Silas and Timothy, that they should come to him quickly, they set out. [16] Now while Paul waited for them at Athens, his spirit was stirred up within him, seeing the city given over to idolatry. [17] And so, he was disputing with the Jews in the synagogue, and with the worshipers, and in public places, throughout each day, with whomever was there. [18] Now certain Epicurean and Stoic philosophers were arguing with him. And some were saying, "What does this sower of the Word want to say?" Yet others were saying, "He seems to be an announcer for new demons." For he was announcing to them Jesus and the Resurrection. [19] And apprehending him, they brought him to the Areopagus, saying: "Are we able to know what this new doctrine is, about which you speak? [20] For you bring certain new ideas to our ears. And so we would like to know what these things mean." [21] (Now all the Athenians, and arriving visitors, were occupying themselves with nothing other than speaking or hearing various new ideas.) [22] But Paul, standing in the middle of the Areopagus, said: "Men of Athens, I perceive that in all things you are rather superstitious. [23] For as I was passing by and noticing your idols, I also found an altar, on which was written: TO THE UNKNOWN GOD. Therefore, what you worship in ignorance, this is what I am preaching to you: [24] the God who made the world and all that is in it, the One who is the Lord of heaven and earth, who does not live in temples made with hands. [25] Neither is he served by the hands of men, as if in need of anything, since it is he who gives to all things life and breath and all else. [26] And he has made, out of one, every family of man: to live upon the face of the entire earth, determining the appointed seasons and the limits of their habitation, [27] so

as to seek God, if perhaps they may consider him or find him, though he is not far from each one of us. ²⁸ 'For in him we live, and move, and exist.' Just as some of your own poets have said. 'For we are also of his family.' ²⁹ Therefore, since we are of the family of God, we must not consider gold or silver or precious stones, or the engravings of art and of the imagination of man, to be a representation of what is Divine. ³⁰ And indeed, God, having looked down to see the ignorance of these times, has now announced to men that everyone everywhere should do penance. ³¹ For he has appointed a day on which he will judge the world in equity, through the man whom he has appointed, offering faith to all, by raising him from the dead." ³² And when they had heard about the Resurrection of the dead, indeed, some were derisive, while others said, "We will listen to you about this again." ³³ So Paul departed from their midst. ³⁴ Yet truly, certain men, adhering to him, did believe. Among these were also Dionysius the Areopagite, and a woman named Damaris, and others with them.

CHAPTER 18

¹ After these things, having departed from Athens, he arrived at Corinth. ² And upon finding a certain Jew named Aquila, born in Pontus, who had recently arrived from Italy with Priscilla his wife, (because Claudius had ordered all Jews to depart from Rome,) he met with them. ³ And because he was of the same trade, he lodged with them and was working. (Now they were tentmakers by trade.) ⁴ And he was arguing in the synagogue on every Sabbath, introducing the name of the Lord Jesus. And he was persuading Jews and Greeks. ⁵ And when Silas and Timothy had arrived from Macedonia, Paul stood firm in the Word, testifying to the Jews that Jesus is the Christ. ⁶ But since they were contradicting him and blaspheming, he shook out his garments and said to them: "Your blood is on your own heads. I am clean. From now on, I will go to the Gentiles." ⁷ And moving from that place, he entered into the house of a certain man, named Titus the Just, a worshiper of God, whose house was adjoined to the synagogue. ⁸ Now Crispus, a leader of the synagogue, believed in the Lord, with his entire house. And many of the Corinthians, upon hearing, believed and were baptized. ⁹ Then the Lord said to Paul, through a vision in the night: "Do not be afraid. Instead, speak out and do not be silent. ¹⁰ For I am with you. And no one will take hold of you, so as to do you harm. For many of the people in this city are with me." ¹¹ Then he settled there for a year and six months, teaching the Word of God among them. ¹² But when Gallio was proconsul of Achaia, the Jews rose up with one accord against Paul. And they brought him to the tribunal, ¹³ saying, "He persuades men to worship God contrary to the law." ¹⁴ Then, when Paul was beginning to open his mouth, Gallio said to the Jews: "If this were some matter of injustice, or a wicked deed, O noble Jews, I would support you, as is proper. ¹⁵ Yet if truly these are questions about a word and names and your law, you should see to it yourselves. I will not be the judge of such things." ¹⁶ And he ordered them from the tribunal. ¹⁷ But they, apprehending Sosthenes, a leader of the synagogue, beat him in front of the tribunal. And Gallio showed no concern for these things. ¹⁸ Yet truly, Paul, after he had remained for many more days, having said goodbye to the brothers, sailed into Syria, and with him were Priscilla and Aquila. Now he had shaved his head in Cenchreae, for he had made a vow. ¹⁹ And he arrived at Ephesus, and he left them behind there. Yet truly, he himself, entering into the synagogue, was disputing with the Jews. ²⁰ Then, although they were asking him to remain for a longer time, he would not agree. ²¹ Instead, saying goodbye and telling them, "I will return to you again, God willing," he set out from Ephesus. ²² And after going down to Caesarea, he went up to Jerusalem, and he greeted the Church there, and then he descended to Antioch. ²³ And having spent some length of time there, he set out, and he walked in order through the region of Galatia and Phrygia, strengthening all the disciples. ²⁴ Now a certain Jew named Apollo, born at Alexandria, an eloquent man who was powerful with the Scriptures, arrived at Ephesus. ²⁵ He was learned in the Way of the Lord. And being fervent in spirit, he was speaking and teaching the things that are of Jesus, but knowing only the baptism of John. ²⁶ And so, he began to act faithfully in the synagogue. And when Priscilla and Aquila had heard him, they took him aside and expounded the Way of the Lord to him more thoroughly. ²⁷ Then, since he wanted to go to Achaia, the brothers wrote an exhortation to the disciples, so that they might accept him. And when he had arrived, he held many discussions with those who had believed. ²⁸ For he was vehemently and publicly reproving the Jews, by revealing through the Scriptures that Jesus is the Christ.

CHAPTER 19

¹ Now it happened that, while Apollo was at Corinth, Paul, after he had journeyed through the upper regions, arrived at Ephesus. And he met with certain disciples. ² And he said to them, "After believing, have you received the Holy Spirit?" But they said to him, "We have not even heard that there is a Holy Spirit." ³ Yet truly, he said, "Then with what have you been baptized?" And they said, "With the baptism of John." ⁴ Then Paul said: "John baptized the people with the baptism of repentance, saying that they should believe in the One who is to come after him, that is, in Jesus." ⁵ Upon hearing these things, they were baptized in the name of the Lord Jesus. ⁶ And when Paul had imposed his hands on them, the Holy Spirit came over them. And they were speaking in tongues and prophesying. ⁷ Now the men were about twelve in all. ⁸ Then, upon entering the synagogue, he was speaking faithfully for three months, disputing and persuading them about the kingdom of God. ⁹ But when certain ones became hardened and would not believe, cursing the Way of the Lord in the presence of the multitude, Paul, withdrawing from them, separated the disciples, disputing daily in a certain school of Tyrannus. ¹⁰ Now this was done throughout two years, so that all who were living in Asia listened to the Word of the Lord, both Jews and Gentiles. ¹¹ And God was accomplishing powerful and uncommon miracles by the hand of Paul, ¹² so much so that even when small cloths and wrappings were brought from his body to the sick, the illnesses withdrew from them and the wicked spirits departed. ¹³ Then, even some of the traveling Jewish exorcists had attempted to invoke the name of the Lord Jesus over those who had evil spirits, saying, "I bind you by oath through Jesus, whom Paul preaches." ¹⁴ And there were certain Jews, the seven sons of Sceva, leaders among the priests, who were acting in this way. ¹⁵ But a wicked spirit responded by saying to them: "Jesus I know, and Paul I know. But who are you?" ¹⁶ And the man, in whom there was a wicked spirit, leaping at them and getting the better of them both, prevailed against them, so that they fled from that house, naked and wounded. ¹⁷ And so, this became known to all the Jews and Gentiles who were living at Ephesus. And a fear fell over them all. And the name of the Lord Jesus was magnified. ¹⁸ And many believers were arriving, confessing, and announcing their deeds. ¹⁹ Then many of those who had followed odd sects brought together their books, and they burned them in the sight of all. And after determining the value of these, they found the price to be fifty thousand denarii. ²⁰ In this way, the Word of God was increasing strongly and was being confirmed. ²¹ Then, when these things were completed, Paul decided in the Spirit, after crossing through Macedonia and Achaia, to go to Jerusalem, saying, "Then, after I have been there, it is necessary for me to see Rome also." ²² But sending two of those who were ministering to him, Timothy and Erastus, into Macedonia, he himself remained for a time in Asia. ²³ Now at that time, there occurred no small disturbance concerning the Way of the Lord. ²⁴ For a certain man named Demetrius, a silversmith making silver shrines for Diana, was providing no small profit to craftsmen. ²⁵ And calling them together, with those who were employed in the same way, he said: "Men, you know that our income is from this craft. ²⁶ And you are seeing and hearing that this man Paul, by persuasion, has turned away a great multitude, not only from Ephesus, but from nearly all of Asia, saying, 'These things are not gods which have been made by hands.' ²⁷ Thus, not only is this, our occupation, in danger of being brought into repudiation, but also the temple of the great Diana will be reputed as nothing! Then even her majesty, whom all of Asia and the world worships, will begin to be destroyed." ²⁸ Upon hearing this, they were filled with anger, and they cried out, saying, "Great is Diana of the Ephesians!" ²⁹ And the city was filled with confusion. And having seized Gaius and Aristarchus of Macedonia, companions of Paul, they rushed violently, with one accord, into the amphitheater. ³⁰ Then, when Paul wanted to enter to the people, the disciples would not permit him. ³¹ And some of the leaders from Asia, who were his friends, also sent to him, requesting that he not present himself in the amphitheater. ³² But others were crying out various things. For the assembly was in confusion, and most did not know the reason they had been called together. ³³ So they dragged Alexander from the crowd, while the Jews were propelling him forward. And Alexander, gesturing with his hand for silence, wanted to give the people an explanation. ³⁴ But as soon as they realized him to be a Jew, all with one voice, for about two hours, were crying out, "Great is Diana of the Ephesians!" ³⁵ And when the scribe had calmed the crowds, he said: "Men of Ephesus, now what man is there who does not know that the city of the Ephesians is in the service of the great

Diana and of the offspring of Jupiter? ³⁶Therefore, since these things are not able to be contradicted, it is necessary for you to be calm and to do nothing rash. ³⁷For you have brought forward these men, who are neither sacrilegious nor blasphemers against your goddess. ³⁸But if Demetrius and the craftsmen who are with him have a case against anyone, they can convene in the courts, and there are proconsuls. Let them accuse one another. ³⁹But if you would inquire about other things, this can be decided in a lawful assembly. ⁴⁰For now we are in peril of being convicted of sedition over today's events, since there is no one guilty (against whom we are able to provide evidence) in this gathering." And when he had said this, he dismissed the assembly.

CHAPTER 20

¹Then, after the tumult ceased, Paul, calling the disciples to himself and exhorting them, said farewell. And he set out, so that he might go into Macedonia. ²And when he had walked through those areas and had exhorted them with many sermons, he went into Greece. ³After he had spent three months there, treacheries were planned against him by the Jews, just as he was about to sail into Syria. And having been advised of this, he return through Macedonia. ⁴Now those accompanying him were Sopater, the son of Pyrrhus from Beroea; and also the Thessalonians, Aristarchus and Secundus; and Gaius of Derbe, and Timothy; and also Tychicus and Trophimus from Asia. ⁵These, after they had gone ahead, waited for us at Troas. ⁶Yet truly, we sailed from Philippi, after the days of Unleavened Bread, and in five days we went to them at Troas, where we stayed for seven days. ⁷Then, on the first Sabbath, when we had assembled together to break bread, Paul discoursed with them, intending to set out the next day. But he prolonged his sermon into the middle of the night. ⁸Now there were plenty of lamps in the upper room, where we were gathered. ⁹And a certain adolescent named Eutychus, sitting on the window sill, was being weighed down by a heavy drowsiness (for Paul was preaching at length). Then, as he went to sleep, he fell from the third floor room downward. And when he was lifted up, he was dead. ¹⁰When Paul had gone down to him, he laid himself over him and, embracing him, said, "Do not worry, for his soul is still within him." ¹¹And so, going up, and breaking bread, and eating, and having spoken well on until daylight, he then set out. ¹²Now they had brought the boy in alive, and they were more than a little consoled. ¹³Then we climbed aboard the ship and sailed to Assos, where we were to take in Paul. For so he himself had decided, since he was making the journey by land. ¹⁴And when he had joined us at Assos, we took him in, and we went to Mitylene. ¹⁵And sailing from there, on the following day, we arrived opposite Chios. And next we landed at Samos. And on the following day we went to Miletus. ¹⁶For Paul had decided to sail past Ephesus, so that he would not be delayed in Asia. For he was hurrying so that, if it were possible for him, he might observe the day of Pentecost at Jerusalem. ¹⁷Then, sending from Miletus to Ephesus, he called those greater by birth in the church. ¹⁸And when they had come to him and were together, he said to them: "You know that from the first day when I entered into Asia, I have been with you, for the entire time, in this manner: ¹⁹serving the Lord, with all humility and despite the tears and trials which befell me from the treacheries of the Jews, ²⁰how I held back nothing that was of value, how well I have preached to you, and that I have taught you publicly and throughout the houses, ²¹testifying both to Jews and to Gentiles about repentance in God and faith in our Lord Jesus Christ. ²²And now, behold, being obliged in spirit, I am going to Jerusalem, not knowing what will happen to me there, ²³except that the Holy Spirit, throughout every city, has cautioned me, saying that chains and tribulations await me at Jerusalem. ²⁴But I dread none of these things. Neither do I consider my life to be more precious because it is my own, provided that in some way I may complete my own course and that of the ministry of the Word, which I received from the Lord Jesus, to testify to the Gospel of the grace of God. ²⁵And now, behold, I know that you will no longer see my face, all of you among whom I have traveled, preaching the kingdom of God. ²⁶For this reason, I call you as witnesses on this very day: that I am clean from the blood of all. ²⁷For I have not turned aside in the least from announcing every counsel of God to you. ²⁸Take care of yourselves and of the entire flock, over which the Holy Spirit has stationed you as Bishops to rule the Church of God, which he has purchased by his own blood. ²⁹I know that after my departure ravenous wolves will enter among you, not sparing the flock. ³⁰And from among yourselves, men will rise up, speaking perverse things in order to entice disciples

after them. [31] Because of this, be vigilant, retaining in memory that throughout
three years I did not cease, night and day, with tears, to admonish each and every
one of you. [32] And now, I commend you to God and to the Word of his grace. He
has the power to build up, and to give an inheritance to all who are sanctified.
[33] I have coveted neither silver and gold, nor apparel, [34] as you yourselves know.
For that which was needed by me and by those who are with me, these hands
have provided. [35] I have revealed all things to you, because by laboring in this way,
it is necessary to support the weak and to remember the words of the Lord Jesus,
how he said, 'It is more blessed to give than to receive.'" [36] And when he had said
these things, kneeling down, he prayed with all of them. [37] Then a great weeping
occurred among them all. And, falling upon the neck of Paul, they kissed him,
[38] being grieved most of all over the word which he had said, that they would
never see his face again. And they brought him to the ship.

CHAPTER 21

[1] And after these things had happened, having reluctantly parted from them, we
sailed a direct course, arriving at Cos, and on following the day at Rhodes, and
from there to Patara. [2] And when we had found a ship sailing across to Phoenicia,
climbing aboard, we set sail. [3] Then, after we had caught sight of Cyprus, keeping
it to the left, we sailed on to Syria, and we arrived at Tyre. For the ship was going
to unload its cargo there. [4] Then, having found the disciples, we lodged there for
seven days. And they were saying to Paul, through the Spirit, that he should
not go up to Jerusalem. [5] And when the days were completed, setting out, we
went on; and they all accompanied us with their wives and children, until we
were outside of the city. And we kneeled down at the shore and prayed. [6] And
when we had said farewell to one another, we climbed aboard the ship. And they
returned to their own. [7] Yet truly, having completed our journey by boat from
Tyre, we descended to Ptolemais. And greeting the brothers, we lodged with
them for one day. [8] Then, after setting out the next day, we arrived at Caesarea.
And upon entering into the house of Philip the evangelist, who was one of the
seven, we stayed with him. [9] Now this man had four daughters, virgins, who were
prophesying. [10] And while we were delayed for some days, a certain prophet from
Judea, named Agabus, arrived. [11] And he, when he had come to us, took Paul's
belt, and binding his own feet and hands, he said: "Thus says the Holy Spirit: The
man whose belt this is, the Jews will bind in this way at Jerusalem. And they will
deliver him into the hands of the Gentiles." [12] And when we had heard this, both
we and those who were from that place begged him not to go up to Jerusalem.
[13] Then Paul responded by saying: "What do you accomplish by weeping and
afflicting my heart? For I am prepared, not only to be bound, but also to die
in Jerusalem, for the name of the Lord Jesus." [14] And since we were not able to
persuade him, we quieted, saying: "May the will of the Lord be done." [15] Then,
after those days, having made preparations, we ascended to Jerusalem. [16] Now
some of the disciples from Caesarea also went with us, bringing with them a
certain Cypriot named Mnason, a very old disciple, whose guests we would
be. [17] And when we had arrived at Jerusalem, the brothers received us willingly.
[18] Then, on the following day, Paul entered with us to James. And all the elders
were assembled. [19] And when he had greeted them, he explained each thing that
God had accomplished among the Gentiles through his ministry. [20] And they,
upon hearing it, magnified God and said to him: "You understand, brother, how
many thousands there are among the Jews who have believed, and they are all
zealous for the law. [21] Now they have heard about you, that you are teaching
those Jews who are among the Gentiles to withdraw from Moses, telling them
that they should not circumcise their sons, nor act according to custom. [22] What
is next? The multitude ought to be convened. For they will hear that you have
arrived. [23] Therefore, do this thing that we ask of you: We have four men, who
are under a vow. [24] Take these and sanctify yourself with them, and require them
to shave their heads. And then everyone will know that the things that they
have heard about you are false, but that you yourself walk in keeping with the
law. [25] But, about those Gentiles who have believed, we have written a judgment
that they should keep themselves from what has been immolated to idols, and
from blood, and from what has been suffocated, and from fornication." [26] Then
Paul, taking the men on the next day, was purified with them, and he entered
the temple, announcing the process of the days of purification, until an oblation
would be offered on behalf of each one of them. [27] But when the seven days were
reaching completion, those Jews who were from Asia, when they had seen him

in the temple, incited all the people, and they laid hands on him, crying out: ²⁸"Men of Israel, help! This is the man who is teaching, everyone, everywhere, against the people and the law and this place. Furthermore, he has even brought Gentiles into the temple, and he has violated this holy place." ²⁹(For they had seen Trophimus, an Ephesian, in the city with him, and they supposed that Paul had brought him into the temple.) ³⁰And the entire city was stirred up. And it happened that the people ran together. And apprehending Paul, they dragged him outside of the temple. And immediately the doors were closed. ³¹Then, as they were seeking to kill him, it was reported to the tribune of the cohort: "All Jerusalem is in confusion." ³²And so, immediately taking soldiers and centurions, he rushed down to them. And when they had seen the tribune and the soldiers, they ceased to strike Paul. ³³Then the tribune, drawing near, apprehended him and ordered that he be bound with two chains. And he was asking who he was and what he had done. ³⁴Then they were crying out various things within the crowd. And since he could not understand anything clearly because of the noise, he ordered him to be brought into the fortress. ³⁵And when he had arrived at the stairs, it happened that he was carried up by the soldiers, because of the threat of violence from the people. ³⁶For the multitude of the people were following and crying out, "Take him away!" ³⁷And as Paul was beginning to be brought into the fortress, he said to the tribune, "Is it permissible for me to say something to you?" And he said, "You know Greek? ³⁸So then, are you not that Egyptian who before these days incited a rebellion and led out into the desert four thousand murderous men?" ³⁹But Paul said to him: "I am a man, indeed a Jew, from Tarsus in Cilicia, a citizen of a well-known city. So I petition you, permit me to speak to the people." ⁴⁰And when he had given him permission, Paul, standing on the stairs, motioned with his hand to the people. And when a great silence occurred, he spoke to them in the Hebrew language, saying:

CHAPTER 22

¹"Noble brothers and fathers, listen to the explanation that I now give to you." ²And when they heard him speaking to them in the Hebrew language, they offered a greater silence. ³And he said: "I am a Jewish man, born at Tarsus in Cilicia, but raised in this city beside the feet of Gamaliel, taught according to the truth of the law of the fathers, zealous for the law, just as all of you also are to this day. ⁴I persecuted this Way, even unto death, binding and delivering into custody both men and women, ⁵just as the high priest and all those greater by birth bear witness to me. Having received letters from them to the brothers, I journeyed to Damascus, so that I might lead them bound from there to Jerusalem, so that they might be punished. ⁶But it happened that, as I was traveling and was approaching Damascus at midday, suddenly from heaven a great light shone around me. ⁷And falling to the ground, I heard a voice saying to me, 'Saul, Saul, why are you persecuting me?' ⁸And I responded, 'Who are you, Lord?' And he said to me, 'I am Jesus the Nazarene, whom you are persecuting.' ⁹And those who were with me, indeed, saw the light, but they did not hear the voice of him who was speaking with me. ¹⁰And I said, 'What should I do, Lord?' Then the Lord said to me: 'Rise up, and go to Damascus. And there, you shall be told all that you must do.' ¹¹And since I could not see, because of the brightness of that light, I was led by the hand by my companions, and I went to Damascus. ¹²Then a certain Ananias, a man in accord with the law, having the testimony of all the Jews who were living there, ¹³drawing near to me and standing close by, said to me, 'Brother Saul, see!' And in that same hour, I looked upon him. ¹⁴But he said: 'The God of our fathers has preordained you, so that you would come to know his will and would see the Just One, and would hear the voice from his mouth. ¹⁵For you shall be his witness to all men about those things which you have seen and heard. ¹⁶And now, why do you delay? Rise up, and be baptized, and wash away your sins, by invoking his name.' ¹⁷Then it happened that, when I returned to Jerusalem and was praying in the temple, a mental stupor came over me, ¹⁸and I saw him saying to me: 'Hurry! Depart quickly from Jerusalem! For they will not accept your testimony about me.' ¹⁹And I said: 'Lord, they know that I am beating and enclosing in prison, throughout every synagogue, those who have believed in you. ²⁰And when the blood of your witness Stephen was poured out, I stood nearby and was consenting, and I watched over the garments of those who put him to death.' ²¹And he said to me, 'Go forth. For I am sending you to far away nations.'" ²²Now they were listening to him, until this word, and then they lifted up their voice, saying: "Take this kind away from the earth! For it is not

fitting for him to live!" ²³ And while they were shouting, and tossing aside their garments, and casting dust into the air, ²⁴ the tribune ordered him to be brought into the fortress, and to be scourged and tortured, in order to discover the reason that they were crying out in this way against him. ²⁵ And when they had tied him with straps, Paul said to the centurion who was standing near him, "Is it lawful for you to scourge a man who is a Roman and has not been condemned?" ²⁶ Upon hearing this, the centurion went to the tribune and reported it to him, saying: "What do you intend to do? For this man is a Roman citizen." ²⁷ And the tribune, approaching, said to him: "Tell me. Are you a Roman?" So he said, "Yes." ²⁸ And the tribune responded, "I obtained this citizenship at great cost." And Paul said, "But I was born to it." ²⁹ Therefore, those who were going to torture him, immediately withdrew from him. The tribune was similarly afraid, after he realized that he was a Roman citizen, for he had bound him. ³⁰ But on the next day, wanting to discover more diligently what the reason was that he was accused by the Jews, he released him, and he ordered the priests to convene, with the entire council. And, producing Paul, he stationed him among them.

CHAPTER 23

¹ Then Paul, gazing intently at the council, said, "Noble brothers, I have spoken with all good conscience before God, even to this present day." ² And the high priest, Ananias, instructed those who were standing nearby to strike him on the mouth. ³ Then Paul said to him: "God shall strike you, you whitewashed wall! For would you sit and judge me according to the law, when, contrary to the law, you order me to be struck?" ⁴ And those who were standing nearby said, "Are you speaking evil about the high priest of God?" ⁵ And Paul said: "I did not know, brothers, that he is the high priest. For it is written: 'You shall not speak evil of the leader of your people.'" ⁶ Now Paul, knowing that one group were Sadducees and the other were Pharisees, exclaimed in the council: "Noble brothers, I am a Pharisee, the son of Pharisees! It is over the hope and resurrection of the dead that I am being judged." ⁷ And when he had said this, a dissension occurred between the Pharisees and the Sadducees. And the multitude was divided. ⁸ For the Sadducees claim that there is no resurrection, and neither angels, nor spirits. But the Pharisees confess both of these. ⁹ Then there occurred a great clamor. And some of the Pharisees, rising up, were fighting, saying: "We find nothing evil in this man. What if a spirit has spoken to him, or an angel?" ¹⁰ And since a great dissension had been made, the tribune, fearing that Paul might be torn apart by them, ordered the soldiers to descend and to seize him from their midst, and to bring him into the fortress. ¹¹ Then, on the following night, the Lord stood near him and said: "Be constant. For just as you have testified about me in Jerusalem, so also it is necessary for you to testify at Rome." ¹² And when daylight arrived, some of the Jews gathered together and bound themselves with an oath, saying that they would neither eat nor drink until they had killed Paul. ¹³ Now there were more than forty men who had taken this oath together. ¹⁴ And they approached the leaders of the priests, and the elders, and they said: "We have sworn ourselves by an oath, so that we will taste nothing, until we have killed Paul. ¹⁵ Therefore, with the council, you should now give notice to the tribune, so that he may bring him to you, as if you intended to determine something else about him. But before he approaches, we have made preparations to put him to death." ¹⁶ But when Paul's sister's son had heard of this, about their treachery, he went and entered into the fortress, and he reported it to Paul. ¹⁷ And Paul, calling to him one of the centurions, said: "Lead this young man to the tribune. For he has something to tell him." ¹⁸ And indeed, he took him and led him to the tribune, and he said, "Paul, the prisoner, asked me to lead this young man to you, since he has something to say to you." ¹⁹ Then the tribune, taking him by the hand, withdrew with him by themselves, and he asked him: "What is it that you have to tell me?" ²⁰ Then he said: "The Jews have met to ask you to bring Paul tomorrow to the council, as if they intended to question him about something else. ²¹ But truly, you should not believe them, for they would ambush him with more than forty men from among them, who have bound themselves by an oath neither to eat, nor to drink, until they have put him to death. And they are now prepared, hoping for an affirmation from you." ²² And then the tribune dismissed the young man, instructing him not to tell anyone that he had made known these things to him. ²³ Then, having called two centurions, he said to them: "Prepare two hundred soldiers, so that they may go as far as Caesarea, and seventy horsemen, and two hundred spearmen, for the third hour of the night. ²⁴ And prepare beasts

of burden to carry Paul, so that they may lead him safely to Felix, the governor." [25] For he was afraid, lest perhaps the Jews might seize him and kill him, and that afterwards he would be falsely accused, as if he had accepted a bribe. And so he wrote a letter containing the following: [26] "Claudius Lysias, to the most excellent governor, Felix: greetings. [27] This man, having been apprehended by the Jews and being about to be put to death by them, I rescued, overwhelming them with soldiers, since I realized that he is a Roman. [28] And wanting to know the reason that they objected to him, I brought him into their council. [29] And I discovered him to be accused about questions of their law. Yet truly, nothing deserving of death or imprisonment was within the accusation. [30] And when I had been given news of ambushes, which they had prepared against him, I sent him to you, notifying his accusers also, so that they may plead their accusations before you. Farewell." [31] Therefore the soldiers, taking Paul according to their orders, brought him by night to Antipatris. [32] And the next day, sending the horsemen to go with him, they returned to the fortress. [33] And when they had arrived at Caesarea and had delivered the letter to the governor, they also presented Paul before him. [34] And when he had read it and had asked which province he was from, realizing that he was from Cilicia, he said: [35] "I will hear you, when your accusers have arrived." And he ordered him to be kept in the praetorium of Herod.

CHAPTER 24

[1] Then, after five days, the high priest Ananias came down with some of the elders and a certain Tertullus, a speaker. And they went to the governor against Paul. [2] And having summoned Paul, Tertullus began to accuse him, saying: "Most excellent Felix, since we have much peace through you, and many things may be corrected by your providence, [3] we acknowledge this, always and everywhere, with acts of thanksgiving for everything. [4] But lest I speak at too great a length, I beg you, by your clemency, to listen to us briefly. [5] We have found this man to be pestilent, to be inciting seditions among all the Jews in the entire world, and to be the author of the sedition of the sect of the Nazarenes. [6] And he has even been attempting to violate the temple. And having apprehended him, we wanted him to be judged according to our law. [7] But Lysias, the tribune, overwhelming us with great violence, snatched him away from our hands, [8] ordering his accusers to come to you. From them, you yourself will be able, by judging about all these things, to understand the reason that we accuse him." [9] And then the Jews interjected, saying that these things were so. [10] Then, since the governor had motioned for him to speak, Paul responded: "Knowing that you have been the judge over this nation for many years, I will give an explanation of myself with an honest soul. [11] For, as you may realize, it has only been twelve days since I went up to worship in Jerusalem. [12] And they did not find me in the temple arguing with anyone, nor causing a rally of the people: neither in the synagogues, nor in the city. [13] And they are not able to prove to you the things about which they now accuse me. [14] But I confess this to you, that according to that sect, which they call a heresy, so do I serve my God and Father, believing all that is written in the Law and the Prophets, [15] having a hope in God, which these others themselves also expect, that there will be a future resurrection of the just and the unjust. [16] And in this, I myself always strive to have a conscience that is lacking in any offense toward God and toward men. [17] Then, after many years, I went to my nation, bringing alms and offerings and vows, [18] through which I obtained purification in the temple: neither with a crowd, nor with a commotion. [19] But certain Jews out of Asia are the ones who should have appeared before you to accuse me, if they have anything against me. [20] Or let these ones here say if they have found in me any iniquity, while standing before the council. [21] For while standing among them, I spoke out solely about this one matter: about the resurrection of the dead. It is about this that I am being judged today by you." [22] Then Felix, after having ascertained much knowledge about this Way, kept them waiting, by saying, "When Lysias the tribune has arrived, I will give you a hearing." [23] And he ordered a centurion to guard him, and to take rest, and not to prohibit any of his own from ministering to him. [24] Then, after some days, Felix, arriving with his wife Drusilla who was a Jew, called for Paul and listened to him about the faith that is in Christ Jesus. [25] And after he discoursed about justice and chastity, and about the future judgment, Felix was trembling, and he responded: "For now, go, but remain under guard. Then, at an opportune time, I will summon you." [26] He was also hoping that money might be given to him by Paul, and because of this, he frequently summoned him and spoke with him. [27] Then, when two years had

passed, Felix was succeeded by Portius Festus. And since Felix wanted to show particular favor to the Jews, he left Paul behind as a prisoner.

CHAPTER 25

[1] And so, when Festus had arrived in the province, after three days, he ascended to Jerusalem from Caesarea. [2] And the leaders of the priests, and those first among the Jews, went to him against Paul. And they were petitioning him, [3] asking for favor against him, so that he would order him to be led to Jerusalem, where they were maintaining an ambush in order to kill him along the way. [4] But Festus responded that Paul was to be kept in Caesarea, and that he himself would soon go there. [5] "Therefore," he said, "let those among you who are able, descend at the same time, and if there is any guilt in the man, they may accuse him." [6] Then, having stayed among them no more than eight or ten days, he descended to Caesarea. And on the next day, he sat in the judgment seat, and he ordered Paul to be led in. [7] And when he had been brought, the Jews who had come down from Jerusalem stood around him, throwing out many serious accusations, none of which they were able to prove. [8] Paul offered this defense: "Neither against the law of the Jews, nor against the temple, nor against Caesar, have I offended in any matter." [9] But Festus, wanting to show greater favor to the Jews, responded to Paul by saying: "Are you willing to ascend to Jerusalem and to be judged there about these things before me?" [10] But Paul said: "I stand in Caesar's tribunal, which is where I ought to be judged. I have done no harm to the Jews, as you well know. [11] For if I have harmed them, or if I have done anything deserving of death, I do not object to dying. But if there is nothing to these things about which they accuse me, no one is able to deliver me to them. I appeal to Caesar." [12] Then Festus, having spoken with the council, responded: "You have appealed to Caesar, to Caesar you shall go." [13] And when some days had passed, king Agrippa and Bernice descended to Caesarea, to greet Festus. [14] And since they remained there for many days, Festus spoke to the king about Paul, saying: "A certain man was left behind as a prisoner by Felix. [15] When I was at Jerusalem, the leaders of the priests and the elders of the Jews came to me about him, asking for condemnation against him. [16] I answered them that it is not the custom of the Romans to condemn any man, before he who is being accused has been confronted by his accusers and has received the opportunity to defend himself, so as to clear himself of the charges. [17] Therefore, when they had arrived here, without any delay, on the following day, sitting in the judgment seat, I ordered the man to be brought. [18] But when the accusers had stood up, they did not present any accusation about him from which I would suspect evil. [19] Instead, they brought against him certain disputes about their own superstition and about a certain Jesus, who had died, but whom Paul asserted to be alive. [20] Therefore, being in doubt about this kind of question, I asked him if he was willing go to Jerusalem and to be judged there about these things. [21] But since Paul was appealing to be kept for a decision before Augustus, I ordered him to be kept, until I might send him to Caesar." [22] Then Agrippa said to Festus: "I myself also want to hear the man." "Tomorrow," he said, "you shall hear him." [23] And on the next day, when Agrippa and Bernice had arrived with great ostentation and had entered into the auditorium with the tribunes and the principal men of the city, Paul was brought in, at the order of Festus. [24] And Festus said: "King Agrippa, and all who are present together with us, you see this man, about whom all the multitude of the Jews disturbed me at Jerusalem, petitioning and clamoring that he should not be allowed to live any longer. [25] Truly, I have discovered nothing brought forth against him that is worthy of death. But since he himself has appealed to Augustus, it was my judgment to send him. [26] But I have not determined what to write to the emperor about him. Because of this, I have brought him before you all, and especially before you, O king Agrippa, so that, once an inquiry has occurred, I may have something to write. [27] For it seems to me unreasonable to send a prisoner and not to indicate the accusations set against him."

CHAPTER 26

[1] Yet truly, Agrippa said to Paul, "It is permitted for you to speak for yourself." Then Paul, extending his hand, began to offer his defense. [2] "I consider myself blessed, O king Agrippa, that I am to give my defense today before you, about everything of which I am accused by the Jews, [3] especially since you know everything that pertains to the Jews, both customs and questions. Because of this,

I beg you to listen to me patiently. [4] And certainly, all the Jews know about my life from my youth, which had its beginning among my own people in Jerusalem. [5] They knew me well from the beginning, (if they would be willing to offer testimony) for I lived according to the most determined sect of our religion: as a Pharisee. [6] And now, it is in the hope of the Promise which was made by God to our fathers that I stand subject to judgment. [7] It is the Promise that our twelve tribes, worshiping night and day, hope to see. About this hope, O king, I am accused by the Jews. [8] Why should it be judged so unbelievable with you all that God might raise the dead? [9] And certainly, I myself formerly considered that I ought to act in many ways which are contrary to the name of Jesus the Nazarene. [10] This is also how I acted at Jerusalem. And so, I enclosed many holy persons in prison, having received authority from the leaders of the priests. And when they were to be killed, I brought the sentence. [11] And in every synagogue, frequently while punishing them, I compelled them to blaspheme. And being all the more maddened against them, I persecuted them, even to foreign cities. [12] Thereafter, as I was going to Damascus, with authority and permission from the high priest, [13] at midday, O king, I and those who were also with me, saw along the way a light from heaven shining around me with a splendor greater than that of the sun. [14] And when we had all fallen down to the ground, I heard a voice speaking to me in the Hebrew language: 'Saul, Saul, why are you persecuting me? It is hard for you to kick against the goad.' [15] Then I said, 'Who are you, Lord?' And the Lord said, 'I am Jesus, whom you are persecuting. [16] But rise up and stand on your feet. For I appeared to you for this reason: so that I may establish you as a minister and a witness concerning the things that you have seen, and concerning the things that I will show to you: [17] rescuing you from the people and the nations to which I am now sending you, [18] in order to open their eyes, so that they may be converted from darkness to light, and from the power of Satan to God, so that they may receive the remission of sins and a place among the saints, through the faith that is in me.' [19] From then on, O king Agrippa, I was not unbelieving to the heavenly vision. [20] But I preached, first to those who are at Damascus and at Jerusalem, and then to the entire region of Judea, and to the Gentiles, so that they would repent and convert to God, doing the works that are worthy of repentance. [21] It was for this reason that the Jews, having apprehended me when I was in the temple, attempted to kill me. [22] But having been aided by the help of God, even to this day, I stand witnessing to the small and the great, saying nothing beyond what the Prophets and Moses have said would be in the future: [23] that the Christ would suffer, and that he would be the first from the resurrection of the dead, and that he would bring light to the people and to the nations." [24] While he was speaking these things and presenting his defense, Festus said with a loud voice: "Paul, you are insane! Too much studying has turned you to insanity." [25] And Paul said: "I am not insane, most excellent Festus, but rather I am speaking words of truth and sobriety. [26] For the king knows about these things. To him also, I am speaking with constancy. For I think that none of these things are unknown to him. And neither were these things done in a corner. [27] Do you believe the Prophets, O king Agrippa? I know that you believe." [28] Then Agrippa said to Paul, "To some extent, you persuade me to become a Christian." [29] And Paul said, "I hope to God that, both to a small extent and to a great extent, not only you, but also all those who hear me this day will become just as I also am, except for these chains." [30] And the king rose up, and the governor, and Bernice, and those who were sitting with them. [31] And when they had withdrawn, they were speaking among themselves, saying, "This man has done nothing worthy of death, nor of imprisonment." [32] Then Agrippa said to Festus, "This man could have been released, if he had not appealed to Caesar."

CHAPTER 27

[1] Then it was decided to send him by ship to Italy, and that Paul, with the others in custody, should be delivered to a centurion named Julius, of the cohort of Augusta. [2] After climbing aboard a ship from Adramyttium, we set sail and began to navigate along the ports of Asia, with Aristarchus, the Macedonian from Thessalonica, joining us. [3] And on the following day, we arrived at Sidon. And Julius, treating Paul humanely, permitted him to go to his friends and to look after himself. [4] And when we had set sail from there, we navigated below Cyprus, because the winds were contrary. [5] And navigating though the sea of Cilicia and Pamphylia, we arrived at Lystra, which is in Lycia. [6] And there the centurion found a ship from Alexandria sailing to Italy, and he transferred us to

it. ⁷ And when we had sailed slowly for many days and had barely arrived opposite Cnidus, for the wind was hindering us, we sailed to Crete, near Salmone. ⁸ And barely being able to sail past it, we arrived at a certain place, which is called Good Shelter, next to which was the city of Lasea. ⁹ Then, after much time had passed, and since sailing would no longer be prudent because the Fast Day had now passed, Paul consoled them, ¹⁰ and he said to them: "Men, I perceive that the voyage is now in danger of injury and much damage, not only to the cargo and the ship, but also to our own lives." ¹¹ But the centurion put more trust in the captain and the navigator of the ship, than in the things being said by Paul. ¹² And since it was not a fitting port in which to winter, the majority opinion was to sail from there, so that somehow they might be able to arrive at Phoenicia, in order to winter there, at a port of Crete, which looks out toward the southwest and northwest. ¹³ And since the south wind was blowing gently, they thought that they might reach their goal. And after they had set out from Asson, they weighed anchor at Crete. ¹⁴ But not long afterward, a violent wind came against them, which is called the Northeast Wind. ¹⁵ And once the ship had been caught in it and was not able to strive against the wind, giving over the ship to the winds, we were driven along. ¹⁶ Then, being forced along a certain island, which is called the Tail, we were barely able to hold on to the ship's lifeboat. ¹⁷ When this was taken up, they used it to assist in securing the ship. For they were afraid that they might run aground. And having lowered the sails, they were being driven along in this way. ¹⁸ Then, since we were being tossed about strongly by the tempest, on the following day, they threw the heavy items overboard. ¹⁹ And on the third day, with their own hands, they threw the equipment of the ship overboard. ²⁰ Then, when neither sun nor stars appeared for many days, and no end to the storm was imminent, all hope for our safety was now taken away. ²¹ And after they had fasted for a long time, Paul, standing in their midst, said: "Certainly, men, you should have listened to me and not set out from Crete, so as to cause this injury and loss. ²² And now, let me persuade you to be courageous in soul. For there shall be no loss of life among you, but only of the ship. ²³ For an Angel of God, who is assigned to me and whom I serve, stood beside me this night, ²⁴ saying: 'Do not be afraid, Paul! It is necessary for you to stand before Caesar. And behold, God has given to you all those who are sailing with you.' ²⁵ Because of this, men, be courageous in soul. For I trust God that this will happen in the same way that it has been told to me. ²⁶ But it is necessary for us to arrive at a certain island." ²⁷ Then, after the fourteenth night arrived, as we were navigating in the sea of Adria, about the middle of the night, the sailors believed that they saw some portion of the land. ²⁸ And upon dropping a weight, they found a depth of twenty paces. And some distance from there, they found a depth of fifteen paces. ²⁹ Then, fearing that we might happen upon rough places, they cast four anchors out of the stern, and they were hoping for daylight to arrive soon. ³⁰ Yet truly, the sailors were seeking a way to flee from the ship, for they had lowered a lifeboat into the sea, on the pretext that they were attempting to cast anchors from the bow of the ship. ³¹ So Paul said to the centurion and to the soldiers, "Unless these men remain in the ship, you will not be able to be saved." ³² Then the soldiers cut the ropes to the lifeboat, and they allowed it to fall. ³³ And when it began to be light, Paul requested that they all take food, saying: "This is the fourteenth day that you have been waiting and continuing to fast, taking nothing. ³⁴ For this reason, I beg you to accept food for the sake of your health. For not a hair from the head of any of you shall perish." ³⁵ And when he had said these things, taking bread, he gave thanks to God in the sight of them all. And when he had broken it, he began to eat. ³⁶ Then they all became more peaceful in soul. And they also took food. ³⁷ Truly, we were two hundred and seventy-six souls on the ship. ³⁸ And having been nourished with food, they lightened the ship, casting the wheat into the sea. ³⁹ And when day had arrived, they did not recognize the landscape. Yet truly, they caught sight of a certain narrow inlet having a shore, into which they thought it might be possible to force the ship. ⁴⁰ And when they had taken up the anchors, they committed themselves to the sea, at the same time loosing the restraints of the rudders. And so, raising the mainsail to the gusting wind, they pressed on toward the shore. ⁴¹ And when we happened upon a place open to two seas, they ran the ship aground. And indeed, the bow, being immobilized, remained fixed, but truly the stern was broken by the violence of the sea. ⁴² Then the soldiers were in agreement that they should kill the prisoners, lest anyone, after escaping by swimming, might flee. ⁴³ But the centurion, wanting to save Paul, prohibited it from being done. And he ordered those who were able to swim to jump in first, and to escape, and to get to the land. ⁴⁴ And as for the others, some they carried on boards, and others on those things that belonged to the ship. And so it happened that every soul escaped to the land.

CHAPTER 28

[1] And after we had escaped, we then realized that the island was called Malta. Yet truly, the natives offered us no small amount of humane treatment. [2] For they refreshed us all by kindling a fire, because rain was imminent and because of the cold. [3] But when Paul had gathered together a bundle of twigs, and had placed them on the fire, a viper, which had been drawn to the heat, fastened itself to his hand. [4] And truly, when the natives saw the beast hanging from his hand, they were saying to one another: "Certainly, this man must be a murderer, for though he escaped from the sea, vengeance will not permit him to live." [5] But shaking off the creature into the fire, he indeed suffered no ill effects. [6] But they were supposing that he would soon swell up, and then would suddenly fall down and die. But having waited a long time, and seeing no ill effects in him, they changed their minds and were saying that he was a god. [7] Now among these places were estates owned by the ruler of the island, named Publius. And he, taking us in, showed us kind hospitality for three days. [8] Then it happened that the father of Publius lay ill with a fever and with dysentery. Paul entered to him, and when he had prayed and had laid his hands on him, he saved him. [9] When this had been done, all who had diseases on the island approached and were cured. [10] And then they also presented us with many honors. And when we were ready to set sail, they gave us whatever we needed. [11] And so, after three months, we sailed in a ship from Alexandria, whose name was 'the Castors,' and which had wintered at the island. [12] And when we had arrived at Syracuse, we were delayed there for three days. [13] From there, sailing close to the shore, we arrived at Rhegium. And after one day, with the south wind blowing, we arrived on the second day at Puteoli. [14] There, after locating the brothers, we were asked to remain with them for seven days. And then we went on to Rome. [15] And there, when the brothers had heard of us, they went to meet us as far as the Forum of Appius and the Three Taverns. And when Paul had seen them, giving thanks to God, he took courage. [16] And when we had arrived at Rome, Paul was given permission to stay by himself, with a soldier to guard him. [17] And after the third day, he called together the leaders of the Jews. And when they had convened, he said to them: "Noble brothers, I have done nothing against the people, nor against the customs of the fathers, yet I was delivered as a prisoner from Jerusalem into the hands of the Romans. [18] And after they held a hearing about me, they would have released me, because there was no case for death against me. [19] But with the Jews speaking against me, I was constrained to appeal to Caesar, though it was not as if I had any kind of accusation against my own nation. [20] And so, because of this, I requested to see you and to speak to you. For it is because of the hope of Israel that I am encircled with this chain." [21] But they said to him: "We have not received letters about you from Judea, nor have any of the other new arrivals among the brothers reported or spoken anything evil against you. [22] But we are asking to hear your opinions from you, for concerning this sect, we know that it is being spoken against everywhere." [23] And when they had appointed a day for him, very many persons went to him at his guest quarters. And he discoursed, testifying to the kingdom of God, and persuading them about Jesus, using the law of Moses and the Prophets, from morning until evening. [24] And some believed the things that he was saying, yet others did not believe. [25] And when they could not agree among themselves, they departed, while Paul was speaking this one word: "How well did the Holy Spirit speak to our fathers through the prophet Isaiah, [26] saying: 'Go to this people and say to them: Hearing, you shall hear and not understand, and seeing, you shall see and not perceive. [27] For the heart of this people has grown dull, and they have listened with reluctant ears, and they have closed their eyes tightly, lest perhaps they might see with the eyes, and hear with the ears, and understand with the heart, and so be converted, and I would heal them.' [28] Therefore, let it be known to you, that this salvation of God has been sent to the Gentiles, and they shall listen to it." [29] And when he had said these things, the Jews went away from him, though they still had many questions among themselves. [30] Then he remained for two whole years in his own rented lodgings. And he received all who went in to him, [31] preaching the kingdom of God and teaching the things which are from the Lord Jesus Christ, with all faithfulness, without prohibition.

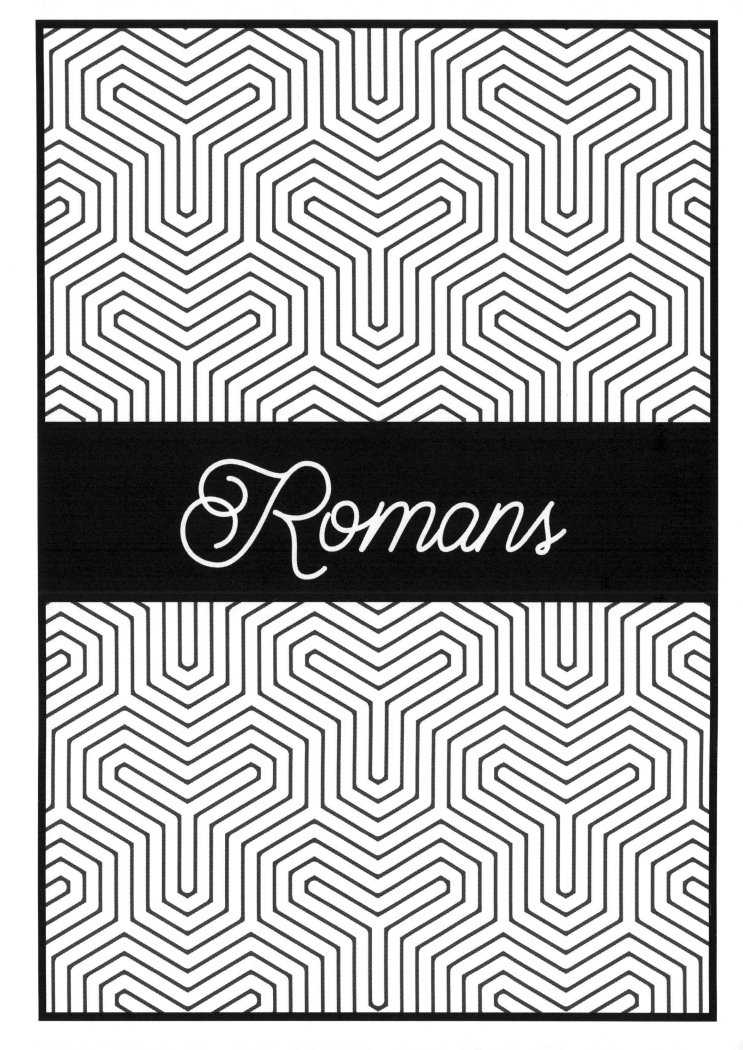

Romans

THE SACRED BIBLE:
THE LETTER TO THE ROMANS

CHAPTER 1

[1] Paul, a servant of Jesus Christ, called as an Apostle, separated for the Gospel of God, [2] which he had promised beforehand, through his Prophets, in the Holy Scriptures, [3] about his Son, who was made for him from the offspring of David according to the flesh, [4] the Son of God, who was predestined in virtue according to the Spirit of sanctification from the resurrection of the dead, our Lord Jesus Christ, [5] through whom we have received grace and Apostleship, for the sake of his name, for the obedience of faith among all the Gentiles, [6] from whom you also have been called by Jesus Christ: [7] To all who are at Rome, the beloved of God, called as saints. Grace to you, and peace, from God our Father and from the Lord Jesus Christ. [8] Certainly, I give thanks to my God, through Jesus Christ, first for all of you, because your faith is being announced throughout the entire world. [9] For God is my witness, whom I serve in my spirit by the Gospel of his Son, that without ceasing I have kept a remembrance of you [10] always in my prayers, pleading that in some way, at some time, I may have a prosperous journey, within the will of God, to come to you. [11] For I long to see you, so that I may impart to you a certain spiritual grace to strengthen you, [12] specifically, to be consoled together with you through that which is mutual: your faith and mine. [13] But I want you to know, brothers, that I have often intended to come to you, (though I have been hindered even to the present time) so that I might obtain some fruit among you also, just as also among the other Gentiles. [14] To the Greeks and to the uncivilized, to the wise and to the foolish, I am in debt. [15] So within me there is a prompting to evangelize to you also who are at Rome. [16] For I am not ashamed of the Gospel. For it is the power of God unto salvation for all believers, the Jew first, and the Greek. [17] For the justice of God is revealed within it, by faith unto faith, just as it was written: "For the just one lives by faith." [18] For the wrath of God is revealed from heaven over every impiety and injustice among those men who fend off the truth of God with injustice. [19] For what is known about God is manifest in them. For God has manifested it to them. [20] For unseen things about him have been made conspicuous, since the creation of the world, being understood by the things that were made; likewise his everlasting virtue and divinity, so much so that they have no excuse. [21] For although they had known God, they did not glorify God, nor give thanks. Instead, they became weakened in their thoughts, and their foolish heart was obscured. [22] For, while proclaiming themselves to be wise, they became foolish. [23] And they exchanged the glory of the incorruptible God for the likeness of an image of corruptible man, and of flying things, and of four-legged beasts, and of serpents. [24] For this reason, God handed them over to the desires of their own heart for impurity, so that they afflicted their own bodies with indignities among themselves. [25] And they exchanged the truth of God for a lie. And they worshipped and served the creature, rather than the Creator, who is blessed for all eternity. Amen. [26] Because of this, God handed them over to shameful passions. For example, their females have exchanged the natural use of the body for a use which is against nature. [27] And similarly, the males also, abandoning the natural use of females, have burned in their desires for one another: males doing with males what is disgraceful, and receiving within themselves the recompense that necessarily results from their error. [28] And since they did not prove to have God by knowledge, God handed them over to a morally depraved way of thinking, so that they might do those things which are not fitting: [29] having been completely filled with all iniquity, malice, fornication, avarice, wickedness; full of envy, murder, contention, deceit, spite, gossiping; [30] slanderous, hateful toward God, abusive, arrogant, self-exalting, devisers of evil, disobedient to parents, [31] foolish, disorderly; without affection, without fidelity, without mercy. [32] And these, though they had known the justice of God, did not understand that those who act in such a manner are deserving of death, and not only those who do these things, but also those who consent to what is done.

CHAPTER 2

[1] For this reason, O man, each one of you who judges is inexcusable. For by that which you judge another, you condemn yourself. For you do the same things

that you judge. ²For we know that the judgment of God is in accord with truth against those who do such things. ³But, O man, when you judge those who do such things as you yourself also do, do you think that you will escape the judgment of God? ⁴Or do you despise the riches of his goodness and patience and forbearance? Do you not know that the kindness of God is calling you to repentance? ⁵But in accord with your hard and impenitent heart, you store up wrath for yourself, unto the day of wrath and of revelation by the just judgment of God. ⁶For he will render to each one according to his works: ⁷To those who, in accord with patient good works, seek glory and honor and incorruption, certainly, he will render eternal life. ⁸But to those who are contentious and who do not acquiesce to the truth, but instead trust in iniquity, he will render wrath and indignation. ⁹Tribulation and anguish are upon every soul of man that works evil: the Jew first, and also the Greek. ¹⁰But glory and honor and peace are for all who do what is good: the Jew first, and also the Greek. ¹¹For there is no favoritism with God. ¹²For whoever had sinned without the law, will perish without the law. And whoever had sinned in the law, will be judged by the law. ¹³For it is not the hearers of the law who are just before God, but rather it is the doers of the law who shall be justified. ¹⁴For when the Gentiles, who do not have the law, do by nature those things which are of the law, such persons, not having the law, are a law unto themselves. ¹⁵For they reveal the work of the law written in their hearts, while their conscience renders testimony about them, and their thoughts within themselves also accuse or even defend them, ¹⁶unto the day when God shall judge the hidden things of men, through Jesus Christ, according to my Gospel. ¹⁷But if you are called by name a Jew, and you rest upon the law, and you find glory in God, ¹⁸and you have known his will, and you demonstrate the more useful things, having been instructed by the law: ¹⁹you become confident within yourself that you are a guide to the blind, a light to those who are in darkness, ²⁰an instructor to the foolish, a teacher to children, because you have a type of knowledge and truth in the law. ²¹As a result, you teach others, but you do not teach yourself. You preach that men should not steal, but you yourself steal. ²²You speak against adultery, but you commit adultery. You abominate idols, but you commit sacrilege. ²³You would glory in the law, but through a betrayal of the law you dishonor God. ²⁴(For because of you the name of God is being blasphemed among the Gentiles, just as it was written.) ²⁵Certainly, circumcision is beneficial, if you observe the law. But if you are a betrayer of the law, your circumcision becomes uncircumcision. ²⁶And so, if the uncircumcised keep the justices of the law, shall not this lack of circumcision be counted as circumcision? ²⁷And that which is by nature uncircumcised, if it fulfills the law, should it not judge you, who by the letter and by circumcision are a betrayer of the law? ²⁸For a Jew is not he who seems so outwardly. Neither is circumcision that which seems so outwardly, in the flesh. ²⁹But a Jew is he who is so inwardly. And circumcision of the heart is in the spirit, not in the letter. For its praise is not of men, but of God.

CHAPTER 3

¹So then, what more is the Jew, or what is the usefulness of circumcision? ²Much in every way: First of all, certainly, because the eloquence of God was entrusted to them. ³But what if some of them have not believed? Shall their unbelief nullify the faith of God? Let it not be so! ⁴For God is truthful, but every man is deceitful; just as it was written: "Therefore, you are justified in your words, and you will prevail when you give judgment." ⁵But if even our injustice points to the justice of God, what shall we say? Could God be unfair for inflicting wrath? ⁶(I am speaking in human terms.) Let it not be so! Otherwise, how would God judge this world? ⁷For if the truth of God has abounded, through my falseness, unto his glory, why should I still be judged as such a sinner? ⁸And should we not do evil, so that good may result? For so we have been slandered, and so some have claimed we said; their condemnation is just. ⁹What is next? Should we try to excel ahead of them? By no means! For we have accused all Jews and Greeks to be under sin, ¹⁰just as it was written: "There is no one who is just. ¹¹There is no one who understands. There is no one who seeks God. ¹²All have gone astray; together they have become useless. There is no one who does good; there is not even one. ¹³Their throat is an open sepulcher. With their tongues, they have been acting deceitfully. The venom of asps is under their lips. ¹⁴Their mouth is full of curses and bitterness. ¹⁵Their feet are swift to shed blood. ¹⁶Grief and unhappiness are in their ways. ¹⁷And the way of peace they have not known. ¹⁸There is no fear of God before their eyes." ¹⁹But we know that whatever the law

speaks, it speaks to those who are in the law, so that every mouth may be silenced and the entire world may be subject to God. [20] For in his presence no flesh shall be justified by the works of the law. For knowledge of sin is through the law. [21] But now, without the law, the justice of God, to which the law and the prophets have testified, has been made manifest. [22] And the justice of God, through the faith of Jesus Christ, is in all those and over all those who believe in him. For there is no distinction. [23] For all have sinned and all are in need of the glory of God. [24] We have been justified freely by his grace through the redemption that is in Christ Jesus, [25] whom God has offered as a propitiation, through faith in his blood, to reveal his justice for the remission of the former offenses, [26] and by the forbearance of God, to reveal his justice in this time, so that he himself might be both the Just One and the Justifier of anyone who is of the faith of Jesus Christ. [27] So then, where is your self-exaltation? It is excluded. Through what law? That of works? No, but rather through the law of faith. [28] For we judge a man to be justified by faith, without the works of the law. [29] Is God of the Jews only and not also of the Gentiles? On the contrary, of the Gentiles also. [30] For One is the God who justifies circumcision by faith and uncircumcision through faith. [31] Are we then destroying the law through faith? Let it not be so! Instead, we are making the law stand.

CHAPTER 4

[1] So then, what shall we say that Abraham had achieved, who is our father according to the flesh? [2] For if Abraham was justified by works, he would have glory, but not with God. [3] For what does Scripture say? "Abram believed God, and it was reputed to him unto justice." [4] But for he who works, wages are not accounted according to grace, but according to debt. [5] Yet truly, for he who does not work, but who believes in him who justifies the impious, his faith is reputed unto justice, according to the purpose of the grace of God. [6] Similarly, David also declares the blessedness of a man, to whom God brings justice without works: [7] "Blessed are they whose iniquities have been forgiven and whose sins have been covered. [8] Blessed is the man to whom the Lord has not imputed sin." [9] Does this blessedness, then, remain only in the circumcised, or is it even in the uncircumcised? For we say that faith was reputed to Abraham unto justice. [10] But then how was it reputed? In circumcision or in uncircumcision? Not in circumcision, but in uncircumcision. [11] For he received the sign of circumcision as a symbol of the justice of that faith which exists apart from circumcision, so that he might be the father of all those who believe while uncircumcised, so that it might also be reputed to them unto justice, [12] and he might be the father of circumcision, not only for those who are of circumcision, but even for those who follow the footsteps of that faith which is in the uncircumcision of our father Abraham. [13] For the Promise to Abraham, and to his posterity, that he would inherit the world, was not through the law, but through the justice of faith. [14] For if those who are of the law are the heirs, then faith becomes empty and the Promise is abolished. [15] For the law works unto wrath. And where there is no law, there is no law-breaking. [16] Because of this, it is from faith according to grace that the Promise is ensured for all posterity, not only for those who are of the law, but also for those who are of the faith of Abraham, who is the father of us all before God, [17] in whom he believed, who revives the dead and who calls those things that do not exist into existence. For it is written: "I have established you as the father of many nations." [18] And he believed, with a hope beyond hope, so that he might become the father of many nations, according to what was said to him: "So shall your posterity be." [19] And he was not weakened in faith, nor did he consider his own body to be dead (though he was then almost one hundred years old), nor the womb of Sarah to be dead. [20] And then, in the Promise of God, he did not hesitate out of distrust, but instead he was strengthened in faith, giving glory to God, [21] knowing most fully that whatever God has promised, he is also able to accomplish. [22] And for this reason, it was reputed to him unto justice. [23] Now this has been written, that it was reputed to him unto justice, not only for his sake, [24] but also for our sake. For the same shall be reputed to us, if we believe in him who raised up our Lord Jesus Christ from the dead, [25] who was handed over because of our offenses, and who rose again for our justification.

CHAPTER 5

[1] Therefore, having been justified by faith, let us be at peace with God, through our Lord Jesus Christ. [2] For through him we also have access by faith to this

grace, in which we stand firm, and to glory, in the hope of the glory of the sons of God. ³ And not only that, but we also find glory in tribulation, knowing that tribulation exercises patience, ⁴ and patience leads to proving, yet truly proving leads to hope, ⁵ but hope is not unfounded, because the love of God is poured forth in our hearts through the Holy Spirit, who has been given to us. ⁶ Yet why did Christ, while we were still infirm, at the proper time, suffer death for the impious? ⁷ Now someone might barely be willing to die for the sake of justice, for example, perhaps someone might dare to die for the sake of a good man. ⁸ But God demonstrates his love for us in that, while we were yet sinners, at the proper time, ⁹ Christ died for us. Therefore, having been justified now by his blood, all the more so shall we be saved from wrath through him. ¹⁰ For if we were reconciled to God through the death of his Son, while we were still enemies, all the more so, having been reconciled, shall we be saved by his life. ¹¹ And not only that, but we also glory in God through our Lord Jesus Christ, through whom we have now received reconciliation. ¹² Therefore, just as through one man sin entered into this world, and through sin, death; so also death was transferred to all men, to all who have sinned. ¹³ For even before the law, sin was in the world, but sin was not imputed while the law did not exist. ¹⁴ Yet death reigned from Adam until Moses, even in those who have not sinned, in the likeness of the transgression of Adam, who is a figure of him who was to come. ¹⁵ But the gift is not entirely like the offense. For though by the offense of one, many died, yet much more so, by the grace of one man, Jesus Christ, has the grace and gift of God abounded to many. ¹⁶ And the sin through one is not entirely like the gift. For certainly, the judgment of one was unto condemnation, but the grace toward many offenses is unto justification. ¹⁷ For though, by the one offense, death reigned through one, yet so much more so shall those who receive an abundance of grace, both of the gift and of justice, reign in life through the one Jesus Christ. ¹⁸ Therefore, just as through the offense of one, all men fell under condemnation, so also through the justice of one, all men fall under justification unto life. ¹⁹ For, just as through the disobedience of one man, many were established as sinners, so also through the obedience of one man, many shall be established as just. ²⁰ Now the law entered in such a way that offenses would abound. But where offenses were abundant, grace was superabundant. ²¹ So then, just as sin has reigned unto death, so also may grace reign through justice unto eternal life, through Jesus Christ our Lord.

CHAPTER 6

¹ So what shall we say? Should we remain in sin, so that grace may abound? ² Let it not be so! For how can we who have died to sin still live in sin? ³ Do you not know that those of us who have been baptized in Christ Jesus have been baptized into his death? ⁴ For through baptism we have been buried with him into death, so that, in the manner that Christ rose from the dead, by the glory of the Father, so may we also walk in the newness of life. ⁵ For if we have been planted together, in the likeness of his death, so shall we also be, in the likeness of his resurrection. ⁶ For we know this: that our former selves have been crucified together with him, so that the body which is of sin may be destroyed, and moreover, so that we may no longer serve sin. ⁷ For he who has died has been justified from sin. ⁸ Now if we have died with Christ, we believe that we shall also live together with Christ. ⁹ For we know that Christ, in rising up from the dead, can no longer die: death no longer has dominion over him. ¹⁰ For in as much as he died for sin, he died once. But in as much as he lives, he lives for God. ¹¹ And so, you should consider yourselves to be certainly dead to sin, and to be living for God in Christ Jesus our Lord. ¹² Therefore, let not sin reign in your mortal body, such that you would obey its desires. ¹³ Nor should you offer the parts of your body as instruments of iniquity for sin. Instead, offer yourselves to God, as if you were living after death, and offer the parts of your body as instruments of justice for God. ¹⁴ For sin should not have dominion over you. For you are not under the law, but under grace. ¹⁵ What is next? Should we sin because we are not under the law, but under grace? Let it not be so! ¹⁶ Do you not know to whom you are offering yourselves as servants under obedience? You are the servants of whomever you obey: whether of sin, unto death, or of obedience, unto justice. ¹⁷ But thanks be to God that, though you used to be the servants of sin, now you have been obedient from the heart to the very form of the doctrine into which you have been received. ¹⁸ And having been freed from sin, we have become servants of justice. ¹⁹ I am speaking in human terms because of the infirmity of your flesh. For just as you offered the parts of your body to serve impurity and iniquity, for

the sake of iniquity, so also have you now yielded the parts of your body to serve justice, for the sake of sanctification. [20] For though you were once the servants of sin, you have become the children of justice. [21] But what fruit did you hold at that time, in those things about which you are now ashamed? For the end of those things is death. [22] Yet truly, having been freed now from sin, and having been made servants of God, you hold your fruit in sanctification, and truly its end is eternal life. [23] For the wages of sin is death. But the free gift of God is eternal life in Christ Jesus our Lord.

CHAPTER 7

[1] Or do you not know, brothers, (now I am speaking to those who know the law) that the law has dominion over a man only so long as he lives? [2] For example, a woman who is subject to a husband is obligated by the law while her husband lives. But when her husband has died, she is released from the law of her husband. [3] Therefore, while her husband lives, if she has been with another man, she should be called an adulteress. But when her husband has died, she is freed from the law of her husband, such that, if she has been with another man, she is not an adulteress. [4] And so, my brothers, you also have become dead to the law, through the body of Christ, so that you may be another one who has risen from the dead, in order that we may bear fruit for God. [5] For when we were in the flesh, the passions of sins, which were under the law, operated within our bodies, so as to bear fruit unto death. [6] But now we have been released from the law of death, by which we were being held, so that now we may serve with a renewed spirit, and not in the old way, by the letter. [7] What should we say next? Is the law sin? Let it not be so! But I do not know sin, except through the law. For example, I would not have known about coveting, unless the law said: "You shall not covet." [8] But sin, receiving an opportunity through the commandment, wrought in me all manner of coveting. For apart from the law, sin was dead. [9] Now I lived for some time apart from the law. But when the commandment had arrived, sin was revived, [10] and I died. And the commandment, which was unto life, was itself found to be unto death for me. [11] For sin, receiving an opportunity through the commandment, seduced me, and, through the law, sin killed me. [12] And so, the law itself is indeed holy, and the commandment is holy and just and good. [13] Then was what is good made into death for me? Let it not be so! But rather sin, in order that it might be known as sin by what is good, wrought death in me; so that sin, through the commandment, might become sinful beyond measure. [14] For we know that the law is spiritual. But I am carnal, having been sold under sin. [15] For I do things that I do not understand. For I do not do the good that I want to do. But the evil that I hate is what I do. [16] So, when I do what I do not want to do, I am in agreement with the law, that the law is good. [17] But I am then acting not according to the law, but according to the sin which lives within me. [18] For I know that what is good does not live within me, that is, within my flesh. For the willingness to do good lies close to me, but the carrying out of that good, I cannot reach. [19] For I do not do the good that I want to do. But instead, I do the evil that I do not want to do. [20] Now if I do what I am not willing to do, it is no longer I who am doing it, but the sin which lives within me. [21] And so, I discover the law, by wanting to do good within myself, though evil lies close beside me. [22] For I am delighted with the law of God, according to the inner man. [23] But I perceive another law within my body, fighting against the law of my mind, and captivating me with the law of sin which is in my body. [24] Unhappy man that I am, who will free me from this body of death? [25] The grace of God, by Jesus Christ our Lord! Therefore, I serve the law of God with my own mind; but with the flesh, the law of sin.

CHAPTER 8

[1] Therefore, there is now no condemnation for those who are in Christ Jesus, who are not walking according to the flesh. [2] For the law of the Spirit of life in Christ Jesus has freed me from the law of sin and death. [3] For though this was impossible under the law, because it was weakened by the flesh, God sent his own Son in the likeness of sinful flesh and because of sin, in order to condemn sin in the flesh, [4] so that the justification of the law might be fulfilled in us. For we are not walking according to the flesh, but according to the spirit. [5] For those who are in agreement with the flesh are mindful of the things of the flesh. But those who are in agreement with the spirit are mindful of the things of the spirit.

⁶ For the prudence of the flesh is death. But the prudence of the spirit is life and peace. ⁷ And the wisdom of the flesh is inimical to God. For it is not subject to the law of God, nor can it be. ⁸ So those who are in the flesh are not able to please God. ⁹ And you are not in the flesh, but in the spirit, if it is true that the Spirit of God lives within you. But if anyone does not have the Spirit of Christ, he does not belong to him. ¹⁰ But if Christ is within you, then the body is indeed dead, concerning sin, but the spirit truly lives, because of justification. ¹¹ But if the Spirit of him who raised up Jesus from the dead lives within you, then he who raised up Jesus Christ from the dead shall also enliven your mortal bodies, by means of his Spirit living within you. ¹² Therefore, brothers, we are not debtors to the flesh, so as to live according to the flesh. ¹³ For if you live according to the flesh, you will die. But if, by the Spirit, you mortify the deeds of the flesh, you shall live. ¹⁴ For all those who are led by the Spirit of God are the sons of God. ¹⁵ And you have not received, again, a spirit of servitude in fear, but you have received the Spirit of the adoption of sons, in whom we cry out: "Abba, Father!" ¹⁶ For the Spirit himself renders testimony to our spirit that we are the sons of God. ¹⁷ But if we are sons, then we are also heirs: certainly heirs of God, but also co-heirs with Christ, yet in such a way that, if we suffer with him, we shall also be glorified with him. ¹⁸ For I consider that the sufferings of this time are not worthy to be compared with that future glory which shall be revealed in us. ¹⁹ For the anticipation of the creature anticipates the revelation of the sons of God. ²⁰ For the creature was made subject to emptiness, not willingly, but for the sake of the One who made it subject, unto hope. ²¹ For the creature itself shall also be delivered from the servitude of corruption, into the liberty of the glory of the sons of God. ²² For we know that every creature groans inwardly, as if giving birth, even until now; ²³ and not only these, but also ourselves, since we hold the first-fruits of the Spirit. For we also groan within ourselves, anticipating our adoption as the sons of God, and the redemption of our body. ²⁴ For we have been saved by hope. But a hope which is seen is not hope. For when a man sees something, why would he hope? ²⁵ But since we hope for what we do not see, we wait with patience. ²⁶ And similarly, the Spirit also helps our weakness. For we do not know how to pray as we ought, but the Spirit himself asks on our behalf with ineffable sighing. ²⁷ And he who examines hearts knows what the Spirit seeks, because he asks on behalf of the saints in accordance with God. ²⁸ And we know that, for those who love God, all things work together unto good, for those who, in accordance with his purpose, are called to be saints. ²⁹ For those whom he foreknew, he also predestined, in conformity with the image of his Son, so that he might be the Firstborn among many brothers. ³⁰ And those whom he predestined, he also called. And those whom he called, he also justified. And those whom he justified, he also glorified. ³¹ So, what should we say about these things? If God is for us, who is against us? ³² He who did not spare even his own Son, but handed him over for the sake of us all, how could he not also, with him, have given us all things? ³³ Who will make an accusation against the elect of God? God is the One who justifies; ³⁴ who is the one who condemns? Christ Jesus who has died, and who has indeed also risen again, is at the right hand of God, and even now he intercedes for us. ³⁵ Then who will separate us from the love of Christ? Tribulation? Or anguish? Or famine? Or nakedness? Or peril? Or persecution? Or the sword? ³⁶ For it is as it has been written: "For your sake, we are being put to death all day long. We are being treated like sheep for the slaughter." ³⁷ But in all these things we overcome, because of him who has loved us. ³⁸ For I am certain that neither death, nor life, nor Angels, nor Principalities, nor Powers, nor the present things, nor the future things, nor strength, ³⁹ nor the heights, nor the depths, nor any other created thing, will be able to separate us from the love of God, which is in Christ Jesus our Lord.

CHAPTER 9

¹ I am speaking the truth in Christ; I am not lying. My conscience offers testimony to me in the Holy Spirit, ² because the sadness within me is great, and there is a continuous sorrow in my heart. ³ For I was desiring that I myself might be anathemized from Christ, for the sake of my brothers, who are my kinsmen according to the flesh. ⁴ These are the Israelites, to whom belongs adoption as sons, and the glory and the testament, and the giving and following of the law, and the promises. ⁵ Theirs are the fathers, and from them, according to the flesh, is the Christ, who is over all things, blessed God, for all eternity. Amen. ⁶ But it is not that the Word of God has perished. For not all those who are Israelites

are of Israel. [7] And not all sons are the offspring of Abraham: "For your offspring will be invoked in Isaac." [8] In other words, those who are the sons of God are not those who are sons of the flesh, but those who are sons of the Promise; these are considered to be the offspring. [9] For the word of promise is this: "I will return at the proper time. And there shall be a son for Sarah." [10] And she was not alone. For Rebecca also, having conceived by Isaac our father, from one act, [11] when the children had not yet been born, and had not yet done anything good or bad (such that the purpose of God might be based on their choice), [12] and not because of deeds, but because of a calling, it was said to her: "The elder shall serve the younger." [13] So also it was written: "I have loved Jacob, but I have hated Esau." [14] What should we say next? Is there unfairness with God? Let it not be so! [15] For to Moses he says: "I will pity whomever I pity. And I will offer mercy to whomever I will pity." [16] Therefore, it is not based on those who choose, nor on those who excel, but on God who takes pity. [17] For Scripture says to the Pharaoh: "I have raised you up for this purpose, so that I may reveal my power by you, and so that my name may be announced to all the earth." [18] Therefore, he takes pity on whomever he wills, and he hardens whomever he wills. [19] And so, you would say to me: "Then why does he still find fault? For who can resist his will?" [20] O man, who are you to question God? How can the thing that has been formed say to the One who formed him: "Why have you made me this way?" [21] And does not the potter have the authority over the clay to make, from the same material, indeed, one vessel unto honor, yet truly another unto disgrace? [22] What if God, wanting to reveal his wrath and to make his power known, endured, with much patience, vessels deserving wrath, fit to be destroyed, [23] so that he might reveal the wealth of his glory, within these vessels of mercy, which he has prepared unto glory? [24] And so it is with those of us whom he has also called, not only from among the Jews, but even from among the Gentiles, [25] just as he says in Hosea: "I will call those who were not my people, 'my people,' and she who was not beloved, 'beloved,' and she who had not obtained mercy, 'one who has obtained mercy.' [26] And this shall be: in the place where it was said to them, 'You are not my people,' there they shall be called the sons of the living God." [27] And Isaiah cried out on behalf of Israel: "When the number of the sons of Israel is like the sand of the sea, a remnant shall be saved. [28] For he shall complete his word, while abbreviating it out of equity. For the Lord shall accomplish a brief word upon the earth." [29] And it is just as Isaiah predicted: "Unless the Lord of hosts had bequeathed offspring, we would have become like Sodom, and we would have been made similar to Gomorrah." [30] What should we say next? That the Gentiles who did not follow justice have attained justice, even the justice that is of faith. [31] Yet truly, Israel, though following the law of justice, has not arrived at the law of justice. [32] Why is this? Because they did not seek it from faith, but as if it were from works. For they stumbled over a stumbling block, [33] just as it was written: "Behold, I am placing a stumbling block in Zion, and a rock of scandal. But whoever believes in him shall not be confounded."

CHAPTER 10

[1] Brothers, certainly the will of my heart, and my prayer to God, is for them unto salvation. [2] For I offer testimony to them, that they have a zeal for God, but not according to knowledge. [3] For, being ignorant of the justice of God, and seeking to establish their own justice, they have not subjected themselves to the justice of God. [4] For the end of the law, Christ, is unto justice for all who believe. [5] And Moses wrote, about the justice that is of the law, that the man who will have done justice shall live by justice. [6] But the justice that is of faith speaks in this way: Do not say in your heart: "Who shall ascend into heaven?" (that is, to bring Christ down); [7] "Or who shall descend into the abyss?" (that is, to call back Christ from the dead). [8] But what does Scripture say? "The word is near, in your mouth and in your heart." This is the word of faith, which we are preaching. [9] For if you confess with your mouth the Lord Jesus, and if you believe in your heart that God has raised him up from the dead, you shall be saved. [10] For with the heart, we believe unto justice; but with the mouth, confession is unto salvation. [11] For Scripture says: "All those who believe in him shall not be confounded." [12] For there is no distinction between Jew and Greek. For the same Lord is over all, richly in all who call upon him. [13] For all those who have called upon the name of the Lord shall be saved. [14] Then in what way will those who have not believed in him call upon him? Or in what way will those who have not heard of him believe in him? And in what way will they hear of him without preaching? [15] And truly, in what

way will they preach, unless they have been sent, just as it has been written: "How beautiful are the feet of those who evangelize peace, of those who evangelize what is good!" [16] But not all are obedient to the Gospel. For Isaiah says: "Lord, who has believed our report?" [17] Therefore, faith is from hearing, and hearing is through the Word of Christ. [18] But I say: Have they not heard? For certainly: "Their sound has gone forth throughout all the earth, and their words unto the limits of the whole world." [19] But I say: Has Israel not known? First, Moses says: "I will lead you into a rivalry with those who are not a nation; in the midst of a foolish nation, I will send you into wrath." [20] And Isaiah dares to say: "I was discovered by those who were not seeking me. I appeared openly to those who were not asking about me." [21] Then to Israel he says: "All day long I have stretched out my hands to a people who do not believe and who contradict me."

CHAPTER 11

[1] Therefore, I say: Has God driven away his people? Let it not be so! For I, too, am an Israelite of the offspring of Abraham, from the tribe of Benjamin. [2] God has not driven away his people, whom he foreknew. And do you not know what Scripture says in Elijah, how he calls upon God against Israel? [3] "Lord, they have slain your Prophets. They have overturned your altars. And I alone remain, and they are seeking my life." [4] But what is the Divine response to him? "I have retained for myself seven thousand men, who have not bent their knees before Baal." [5] Therefore, in the same way, again in this time, there is a remnant that has been saved in accord with the choice of grace. [6] And if it is by grace, then it is not now by works; otherwise grace is no longer free. [7] What is next? What Israel was seeking, he has not obtained. But the elect have obtained it. And truly, these others have been blinded, [8] just as it was written: "God has given them a spirit of reluctance: eyes that do not perceive, and ears that do not hear, even until this very day." [9] And David says: "Let their table become like a snare, and a deception, and a scandal, and a retribution for them. [10] Let their eyes be obscured, so that they may not see, and so that they may bow down their backs always." [11] Therefore, I say: Have they stumbled in such a way that they should fall? Let it not be so! Instead, by their offense, salvation is with the Gentiles, so that they may be a rival to them. [12] Now if their offense is the riches of the world, and if their diminution is the riches of the Gentiles, how much more is their fullness? [13] For I say to you Gentiles: Certainly, as long as I am an Apostle to the Gentiles, I will honor my ministry, [14] in such a way that I might provoke to rivalry those who are my own flesh, and so that I may save some of them. [15] For if their loss is for the reconciliation of the world, what could their return be for, except life out of death? [16] For if the first-fruit has been sanctified, so also has the whole. And if the root is holy, so also are the branches. [17] And if some of the branches are broken, and if you, being a wild olive branch, are grafted on to them, and you become a partaker of the root and of the fatness of the olive tree, [18] do not glorify yourself above the branches. For though you glory, you do not support the root, but the root supports you. [19] Therefore, you would say: The branches were broken off, so that I might be grafted on. [20] Well enough. They were broken off because of unbelief. But you stand on faith. So do not choose to savor what is exalted, but instead be afraid. [21] For if God has not spared the natural branches, perhaps also he might not spare you. [22] So then, notice the goodness and the severity of God. Certainly, toward those who have fallen, there is severity; but toward you, there is the goodness of God, if you remain in goodness. Otherwise, you also will be cut off. [23] Moreover, if they do not remain in unbelief, they will be grafted on. For God is able to graft them on again. [24] So if you have been cut off from the wild olive tree, which is natural to you, and, contrary to nature, you are grafted on to the good olive tree, how much more shall those who are the natural branches be grafted on to their own olive tree? [25] For I do not want you to be ignorant, brothers, of this mystery (lest you seem wise only to yourselves) that a certain blindness has occurred in Israel, until the fullness of the Gentiles has arrived. [26] And in this way, all of Israel may be saved, just as it was written: "From Zion shall arrive he who delivers, and he shall turn impiety away from Jacob. [27] And this will be my covenant for them, when I will take away their sins." [28] Certainly, according to the Gospel, they are enemies for your sake. But according to the election, they are most beloved for the sake of the fathers. [29] For the gifts and the call of God are without regret. [30] And just as you also, in times past, did not believe in God, but now you have obtained mercy because of their unbelief, [31] so also have these now not believed, for your mercy, so that they might obtain mercy

also. ³²For God has enclosed everyone in unbelief, so that he may have mercy on everyone. ³³Oh, the depths of the richness of the wisdom and knowledge of God! How incomprehensible are his judgments, and how unsearchable are his ways! ³⁴For who has known the mind of the Lord? Or who has been his counselor? ³⁵Or who first gave to him, so that repayment would be owed? ³⁶For from him, and through him, and in him are all things. To him is glory, for all eternity. Amen.

CHAPTER 12

¹And so, I beg you, brothers, by the mercy of God, that you offer your bodies as a living sacrifice, holy and pleasing to God, with the subservience of your mind. ²And do not choose to be conformed to this age, but instead choose to be reformed in the newness of your mind, so that you may demonstrate what is the will of God: what is good, and what is well-pleasing, and what is perfect. ³For I say, through the grace that has been given to me, to all who are among you: Taste no more than it is necessary to taste, but taste unto sobriety and just as God has distributed a share of the faith to each one. ⁴For just as, within one body, we have many parts, though all the parts do not have the same role, ⁵so also we, being many, are one body in Christ, and each one is a part, the one of the other. ⁶And we each have different gifts, according to the grace that has been given to us: whether prophecy, in agreement with the reasonableness of faith; ⁷or ministry, in ministering; or he who teaches, in doctrine; ⁸he who exhorts, in exhortation; he who gives, in simplicity; he who governs, in solicitude; he who shows mercy, in cheerfulness. ⁹Let love be without falseness: hating evil, clinging to what is good, ¹⁰loving one another with fraternal charity, surpassing one another in honor: ¹¹in solicitude, not lazy; in spirit, fervent; serving the Lord; ¹²in hope, rejoicing; in tribulation, enduring; in prayer, ever-willing; ¹³in the difficulties of the saints, sharing; in hospitality, attentive. ¹⁴Bless those who are persecuting you: bless, and do not curse. ¹⁵Rejoice with those who are rejoicing. Weep with those who are weeping. ¹⁶Be of the same mind toward one another: not savoring what is exalted, but consenting in humility. Do not choose to seem wise to yourself. ¹⁷Render to no one harm for harm. Provide good things, not only in the sight of God, but also in the sight of all men. ¹⁸If it is possible, in so far as you are able, be at peace with all men. ¹⁹Do not defend yourselves, dearest ones. Instead, step aside from wrath. For it is written: "Vengeance is mine. I shall give retribution, says the Lord." ²⁰So if an enemy is hungry, feed him; if he is thirsty, give him a drink. For in doing so, you will heap burning coals upon his head. ²¹Do not allow evil to prevail, instead prevail over evil by means of goodness.

CHAPTER 13

¹Let every soul be subject to higher authorities. For there is no authority except from God and those who have been ordained by God. ²And so, whoever resists authority, resists what has been ordained by God. And those who resist are acquiring damnation for themselves. ³For leaders are not a source of fear to those who work good, but to those who work evil. And would you prefer not to be afraid of authority? Then do what is good, and you shall have praise from them. ⁴For he is a minister of God for you unto good. But if you do what is evil, be afraid. For it is not without reason that he carries a sword. For he is a minister of God; an avenger to execute wrath upon whomever does evil. ⁵For this reason, it is necessary to be subject, not solely because of wrath, but also because of conscience. ⁶Therefore, you must also offer tribute. For they are the ministers of God, serving him in this. ⁷Therefore, render to all whatever is owed. Taxes, to whom taxes is due; revenue, to whom revenue is due; fear, to whom fear is due; honor, to whom honor is due. ⁸You should owe nothing to anyone, except so as to love one another. For whoever loves his neighbor has fulfilled the law. ⁹For example: You shall not commit adultery. You shall not kill. You shall not steal. You shall not speak false testimony. You shall not covet. And if there is any other commandment, it is summed up in this word: You shall love your neighbor as yourself. ¹⁰The love of neighbor does no harm. Therefore, love is the plenitude of the law. ¹¹And we know the present time, that now is the hour for us to rise up from sleep. For already our salvation is closer than when we first believed. ¹²The night has passed, and the day draws near. Therefore, let us cast aside the works of darkness, and be clothed with the armor of light. ¹³Let us walk honestly, as in the daylight, not in carousing and drunkenness, not in promiscuity and sexual immorality, not in contention and envy. ¹⁴Instead, be clothed with the Lord Jesus Christ, and make no provision for the flesh in its desires.

CHAPTER 14

[1] But accept those who are weak in faith, without disputing about ideas. [2] For one person believes that he may eat all things, but if another is weak, let him eat plants. [3] He who eats should not despise him who does not eat. And he who does not eat should not judge him who eats. For God has accepted him. [4] Who are you to judge the servant of another? He stands or falls by his own Lord. But he shall stand. For God is able to make him stand. [5] For one person discerns one age from the next. But another discerns unto every age. Let each one increase according to his own mind. [6] He who understands the age, understands for the Lord. And he who eats, eats for the Lord; for he gives thanks to God. And he who does not eat, does not eat for the Lord, and he gives thanks to God. [7] For none of us lives for himself, and none of us dies for himself. [8] For if we live, we live for the Lord, and if we die, we die for the Lord. Therefore, whether we live or die, we belong to the Lord. [9] For Christ died and rose again for this purpose: that he might be the ruler of both the dead and the living. [10] So then, why do you judge your brother? Or why do you despise your brother? For we shall all stand before the judgment seat of Christ. [11] For it is written: "As I live, says the Lord, every knee shall bend to me, and every tongue shall confess to God." [12] And so, each one of us shall offer an explanation of himself to God. [13] Therefore, we should no longer judge one another. Instead, judge this to a greater extent: that you should not place an obstacle before your brother, nor lead him astray. [14] I know, with confidence in the Lord Jesus, that nothing is unclean in and of itself. But to him who considers anything to be unclean, it is unclean to him. [15] For if your brother is grieved because of your food, you are not now walking according to love. Do not allow your food to destroy him for whom Christ died. [16] Therefore, what is good for us should not be a cause of blasphemy. [17] For the kingdom of God is not food and drink, but rather justice and peace and joy, in the Holy Spirit. [18] For he who serves Christ in this, pleases God and is proven before men. [19] And so, let us pursue the things that are of peace, and let us keep to the things that are for the edification of one another. [20] Do not be willing to destroy the work of God because of food. Certainly, all things are clean. But there is harm for a man who offends by eating. [21] It is good to refrain from eating meat and from drinking wine, and from anything by which your brother is offended, or led astray, or weakened. [22] Do you have faith? It belongs to you, so hold it before God. Blessed is he who does not judge himself in that by which he is tested. [23] But he who discerns, if he eats, is condemned, because it is not of faith. For all that is not of faith is sin.

CHAPTER 15

[1] But we who are stronger must bear with the feebleness of the weak, and not so as to please ourselves. [2] Each one of you should please his neighbor unto good, for edification. [3] For even Christ did not please himself, but as it was written: "The reproaches of those who reproached you fell upon me." [4] For whatever was written, was written to teach us, so that, through patience and the consolation of the Scriptures, we might have hope. [5] So may the God of patience and solace grant you to be of one mind toward one another, in accord with Jesus Christ, [6] so that, together with one mouth, you may glorify the God and Father of our Lord Jesus Christ. [7] For this reason, accept one another, just as Christ also has accepted you, in the honor of God. [8] For I declare that Christ Jesus was the minister of circumcision because of the truth of God, so as to confirm the promises to the fathers, [9] and that the Gentiles are to honor God because of his mercy, just as it was written: "Because of this, I will confess you among the Gentiles, O Lord, and I will sing to your name." [10] And again, he says: "Rejoice, O Gentiles, along with his people." [11] And again: "All Gentiles, praise the Lord; and all peoples, magnify him." [12] And again, Isaiah says: "There shall be a root of Jesse, and he shall rise up to rule the Gentiles, and in him the Gentiles shall hope." [13] So may the God of hope fill you with every joy and with peace in believing, so that you may abound in hope and in the virtue of the Holy Spirit. [14] But I am also certain about you, my brothers, that you also have been filled with love, completed with all knowledge, so that you are able to admonish one another. [15] But I have written to you, brothers, more boldly than to the others, as if calling you to mind again, because of the grace which has been given to me from God, [16] so that I may be a minister of Christ Jesus among the Gentiles, sanctifying the Gospel of God, in order that the oblation of the Gentiles may be made acceptable and may be sanctified in the Holy Spirit. [17] Therefore, I have glory in Christ Jesus before God. [18] So I dare not speak of any of those things which Christ does not effect through me, unto

the obedience of the Gentiles, in word and deed, [19] with the power of signs and wonders, by power of the Holy Spirit. For in this way, from Jerusalem, throughout its surroundings, as far as Illyricum, I have replenished the Gospel of Christ. [20] And so I have preached this Gospel, not where Christ was known by name, lest I build upon the foundation of another, [21] but just as it was written: "Those to whom he was not announced shall perceive, and those who have not heard shall understand." [22] Because of this also, I was greatly hindered in coming to you, and I have been prevented until the present time. [23] Yet truly now, having no other destination in these regions, and having already had a great desire to come to you over the past many years, [24] when I begin to set out on my journey to Spain, I hope that, as I pass by, I may see you, and I may be guided from there by you, after first having borne some fruit among you. [25] But next I will set out for Jerusalem, to minister to the saints. [26] For those of Macedonia and Achaia have decided to make a collection for those of the poor among the saints who are at Jerusalem. [27] And this has pleased them, because they are in their debt. For, since the Gentiles have become partakers of their spiritual things, they also ought to minister to them in worldly things. [28] Therefore, when I have completed this task, and have consigned to them this fruit, I shall set out, by way of you, to Spain. [29] And I know that when I come to you I shall arrive with an abundance of the blessings of the Gospel of Christ. [30] Therefore, I beg you, brothers, through our Lord Jesus Christ and through the love of the Holy Spirit, that you assist me with your prayers to God on my behalf, [31] so that I may be freed from the unfaithful who are in Judea, and so that the oblation of my service may be acceptable to the saints in Jerusalem. [32] So may I come to you with joy, through the will of God, and so may I be refreshed with you. [33] And may the God of peace be with you all. Amen.

CHAPTER 16

[1] Now I commend to you our sister Phoebe, who is in the ministry of the church, which is at Cenchreae, [2] so that you may receive her in the Lord with the worthiness of the saints, and so that you may be of assistance to her in whatever task she will have need of you. For she herself has also assisted many, and myself also. [3] Greet Prisca and Aquila, my helpers in Christ Jesus, [4] who have risked their own necks on behalf of my life, for whom I give thanks, not I alone, but also all the churches of the Gentiles; [5] and greet the church at their house. Greet Epaenetus, my beloved, who is among the first-fruits of Asia in Christ. [6] Greet Mary, who has labored much among you. [7] Greet Andronicus and Junias, my kinsmen and fellow captives, who are noble among the Apostles, and who were in Christ prior to me. [8] Greet Ampliatus, most beloved to me in the Lord. [9] Greet Urbanus, our helper in Christ Jesus, and Stachys, my beloved. [10] Greet Apelles, who has been tested in Christ. [11] Greet those who are from the household of Aristobulus. Greet Herodian, my kinsman. Greet those who are of the household of Narcissus, who are in the Lord. [12] Greet Tryphaena and Tryphosa, who labor in the Lord. Greet Persis, most beloved, who has labored much in the Lord. [13] Greet Rufus, elect in the Lord, and his mother and mine. [14] Greet Asyncritus, Phlegon, Hermas, Patrobas, Hermes, and the brothers who are with them. [15] Greet Philologus and Julia, Nereus and his sister, and Olympas, and all the saints who are with them. [16] Greet one another with a holy kiss. All the churches of Christ greet you. [17] But I beg you, brothers, to take note of those who cause dissensions and offenses contrary to the doctrine that you have learned, and to turn away from them. [18] For ones such as these do not serve Christ our Lord, but their inner selves, and, through pleasing words and skillful speaking, they seduce the hearts of the innocent. [19] But your obedience has been made known in every place. And so, I rejoice in you. But I want you to be wise in what is good, and simple in what is evil. [20] And may the God of peace quickly crush Satan under your feet. The grace of our Lord Jesus Christ be with you. [21] Timothy, my fellow laborer, greets you, and Lucius and Jason and Sosipater, my kinsmen. [22] I, Tertius, who wrote this epistle, greet you in the Lord. [23] Gaius, my host, and the entire church, greets you. Erastus, the treasurer of the city, greets you, and Quartus, a brother. [24] The grace of our Lord Jesus Christ be with you all. Amen. [25] But to him who is able to confirm you according to my Gospel and the preaching of Jesus Christ, in accord with the revelation of the mystery which has been hidden from time immemorial, [26] (which now has been made clear through the Scriptures of the Prophets, in accord with the precept of the eternal God, unto the obedience of faith) which has been made known among all the Gentiles: [27] to God, who alone is wise, through Jesus Christ, to him be honor and glory forever and ever. Amen.

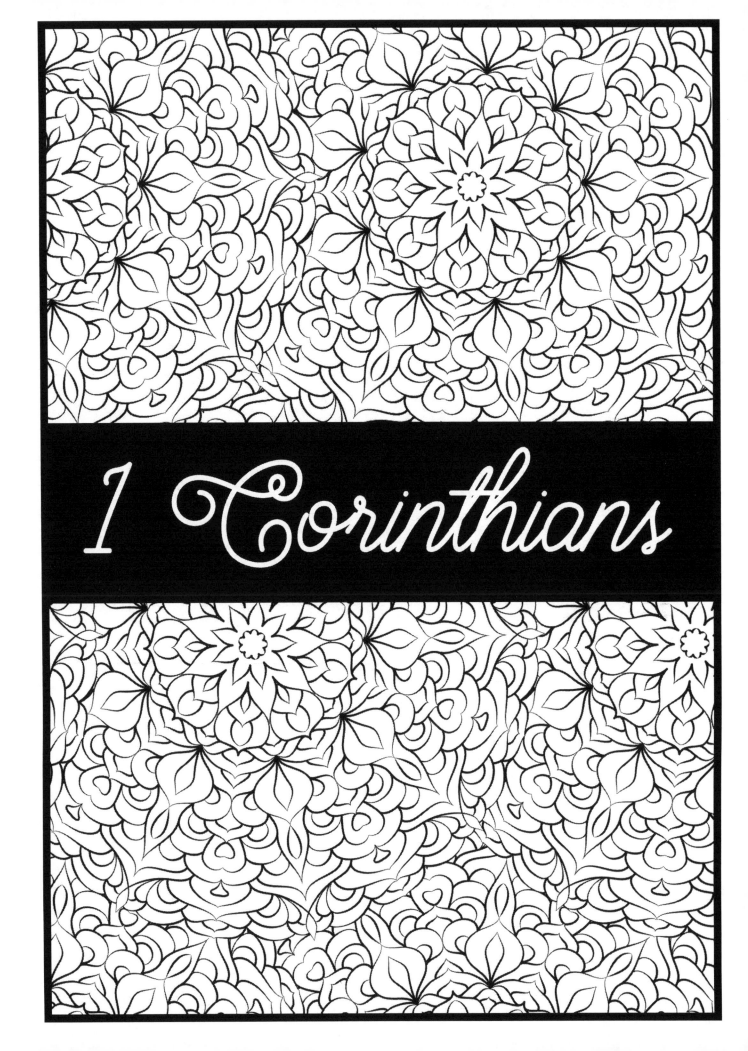

1 Corinthians

THE SACRED BIBLE:
THE FIRST LETTER TO THE CORINTHIANS

1 CORINTHIANS 1

[1] Paul, called as an Apostle of Jesus Christ by the will of God; and Sosthenes, a brother: [2] to the Church of God which is at Corinth, to those sanctified in Christ Jesus, called to be saints with all who are invoking the name of our Lord Jesus Christ in every place of theirs and of ours. [3] Grace and peace to you from God our Father and from the Lord Jesus Christ. [4] I give thanks to my God continuously for you because of the grace of God that has been given to you in Christ Jesus. [5] By that grace, in all things, you have become wealthy in him, in every word and in all knowledge. [6] And so, the testimony of Christ has been strengthened in you. [7] In this way, nothing is lacking to you in any grace, as you await the revelation of our Lord Jesus Christ. [8] And he, too, will strengthen you, even until the end, without guilt, until the day of the advent of our Lord Jesus Christ. [9] God is faithful. Through him, you have been called into the fellowship of his Son, Jesus Christ our Lord. [10] And so, I beg you, brothers, by the name of our Lord Jesus Christ, that every one of you speak in the same way, and that there be no schisms among you. So may you become perfect, with the same mind and with the same judgment. [11] For it has been indicated to me, about you, my brothers, by those who are with Chloes, that there are contentions among you. [12] Now I say this because each of you is saying: "Certainly, I am of Paul;" "But I am of Apollo;" "Truly, I am of Cephas;" as well as: "I am of Christ." [13] Has Christ been divided? Was Paul crucified for you? Or were you baptized in the name of Paul? [14] I give thanks to God that I have baptized none of you, except Crispus and Gaius, [15] lest anyone say that you have been baptized in my name. [16] And I also baptized the household of Stephanus. Other than these, I do not recall if I baptized any others. [17] For Christ did not send me to baptize, but to evangelize: not through the wisdom of words, lest the cross of Christ become empty. [18] For the Word of the Cross is certainly foolishness to those who are perishing. But to those who have been saved, that is, to us, it is the power of God. [19] For it has been written: "I will perish the wisdom of the wise, and I will reject the discernment of the prudent." [20] Where are the wise? Where are the scribes? Where are the truth-seekers of this age? Has not God made the wisdom of this world into foolishness? [21] For the world did not know God through wisdom, and so, in the wisdom of God, it pleased God to accomplish the salvation of believers, through the foolishness of our preaching. [22] For the Jews ask for signs, and the Greeks seek wisdom. [23] But we are preaching Christ crucified. Certainly, to the Jews, this is a scandal, and to the Gentiles, this is foolishness. [24] But to those who have been called, Jews as well as Greeks, the Christ is the virtue of God and the wisdom of God. [25] For what is foolishness to God is considered wise by men, and that which is weakness to God is considered strong by men. [26] So take care of your vocation, brothers. For not many are wise according to the flesh, not many are powerful, not many are noble. [27] But God has chosen the foolish of the world, so that he may confound the wise. And God has chosen the weak of the world, so that he may confound the strong. [28] And God has chosen the ignoble and contemptible of the world, those who are nothing, so that he may reduce to nothing those who are something. [29] So then, nothing that is of the flesh should glory in his sight. [30] But you are of him in Christ Jesus, who was made by God to be our wisdom and justice and sanctification and redemption. [31] And so, in the same way, it was written: "Whoever glories, should glory in the Lord."

1 CORINTHIANS 2

[1] And so, brothers, when I came to you, announcing to you the testimony of Christ, I did not bring exalted words or lofty wisdom. [2] For I did not judge myself to know anything among you, except Jesus Christ, and him crucified. [3] And I was with you in weakness, and in fear, and with much trembling. [4] And my words and preaching were not the persuasive words of human wisdom, but were a manifestation of the Spirit and of virtue, [5] so that your faith would not be based on the wisdom of men, but on the virtue of God. [6] Now, we do speak wisdom among the perfect, yet truly, this is not the wisdom of this age, nor that of the leaders of this age, which shall be reduced to nothing. [7] Instead, we speak of the

wisdom of God in a mystery which has been hidden, which God predestined before this age for our glory, [8] something that none of the leaders of this world have known. For if they had known it, they would never have crucified the Lord of glory. [9] But this is just as it has been written: "The eye has not seen, and the ear has not heard, nor has it entered into the heart of man, what things God has prepared for those who love him." [10] But God has revealed these things to us through his Spirit. For the Spirit searches all things, even the depths of God. [11] And who can know the things that are of a man, except the spirit which is within that man? So also, no one knows the things which are of God, except the Spirit of God. [12] But we have not received the spirit of this world, but the Spirit who is of God, so that we may understand the things that have been given to us by God. [13] And we are also speaking of these things, not in the learned words of human wisdom, but in the doctrine of the Spirit, bringing spiritual things together with spiritual things. [14] But the animal nature of man does not perceive these things that are of the Spirit of God. For it is foolishness to him, and he is not able to understand it, because it must be examined spiritually. [15] But the spiritual nature of man judges all things, and he himself may be judged by no man. [16] For who has known the mind of the Lord, so that he may instruct him? But we have the mind of Christ.

1 CORINTHIANS 3

[1] And so, brothers, I was not able to speak to you as if to those who are spiritual, but rather as if to those who are carnal. For you are like infants in Christ. [2] I gave you milk to drink, not solid food. For you were not yet able. And indeed, even now, you are not able; for you are still carnal. [3] And since there is still envy and contention among you, are you not carnal, and are you not walking according to man? [4] For if one says, "Certainly, I am of Paul," while another says, "I am of Apollo," are you not men? But what is Apollo, and what is Paul? [5] We are only the ministers of him in whom you have believed, just as the Lord has granted to each of you. [6] I planted, Apollo watered, but God provided the growth. [7] And so, neither he who plants, nor he who waters, is anything, but only God, who provides the growth. [8] Now he who plants, and he who waters, are one. But each shall receive his proper reward, according to his labors. [9] For we are God's assistants. You are God's cultivation; you are God's construction. [10] According to the grace of God, which has been given to me, I have laid the foundation like a wise architect. But another builds upon it. So then, let each one be careful how he builds upon it. [11] For no one is able to lay any other foundation, in place of that which has been laid, which is Christ Jesus. [12] But if anyone builds upon this foundation, whether gold, silver, precious stones, wood, hay, or stubble, [13] each one's work shall be made manifest. For the day of the Lord shall declare it, because it will be revealed by fire. And this fire will test each one's work, as to what kind it is. [14] If anyone's work, which he has built upon it, remains, then he will receive a reward. [15] If anyone's work is burned up, he will suffer its loss, but he himself will still be saved, but only as through fire. [16] Do you not know that you are the Temple of God, and that the Spirit of God lives within you? [17] But if anyone violates the Temple of God, God will destroy him. For the Temple of God is holy, and you are that Temple. [18] Let no one deceive himself. If anyone among you seems to be wise in this age, let him become foolish, so that he may be truly wise. [19] For the wisdom of this world is foolishness with God. And so it has been written: "I will catch the wise in their own astuteness." [20] And again: "The Lord knows the thoughts of the wise, that they are vain." [21] And so, let no one glory in men. [22] For all is yours: whether Paul, or Apollo, or Cephas, or the world, or life, or death, or the present, or the future. Yes, all is yours. [23] But you are Christ's, and Christ is God's.

1 CORINTHIANS 4

[1] Accordingly, let man consider us to be ministers of Christ and attendants of the mysteries of God. [2] Here and now, it is required of attendants that each one be found to be faithful. [3] But as for me, it is such a small thing to be judged by you, or by the age of mankind. And neither do I judge myself. [4] For I have nothing on my conscience. But I am not justified by this. For the Lord is the One who judges me. [5] And so, do not choose to judge before the time, until the Lord returns. He will illuminate the hidden things of the darkness, and he will make manifest the decisions of hearts. And then each one shall have praise from God. [6] And so, brothers, I have presented these things in myself and in Apollo, for your sakes, so that you may learn, through us, that no one should be inflated against one person

and for another, not beyond what has been written. ⁷For what distinguishes you from another? And what do you have that you have not received? But if you have received it, why do you glory, as if you had not received it? ⁸So, now you have been filled, and now you have been made wealthy, as if to reign without us? But I wish that you would reign, so that we, too, might reign with you! ⁹For I think that God has presented us as the last Apostles, as those destined for death. For we have been made into a spectacle for the world, and for Angels, and for men. ¹⁰So we are fools because of Christ, but you are discerning in Christ? We are weak, but you are strong? You are noble, but we are ignoble? ¹¹Even to this very hour, we hunger and thirst, and we are naked and repeatedly beaten, and we are unsteady. ¹²And we labor, working with our own hands. We are slandered, and so we bless. We suffer and endure persecution. ¹³We are cursed, and so we pray. We have become like the refuse of this world, like the reside of everything, even until now. ¹⁴I am not writing these things in order to confound you, but in order to admonish you, as my dearest sons. ¹⁵For you might have ten thousand instructors in Christ, but not so many fathers. For in Christ Jesus, through the Gospel, I have begotten you. ¹⁶Therefore, I beg you, be imitators of me, just as I am of Christ. ¹⁷For this reason, I have sent you Timothy, who is my dearest son, and who is faithful in the Lord. He will remind you of my ways, which are in Christ Jesus, just as I teach everywhere, in every church. ¹⁸Certain persons have become inflated in thinking that I would not return to you. ¹⁹But I will return to you soon, if the Lord is willing. And I will consider, not the words of those who are inflated, but the virtue. ²⁰For the kingdom of God is not in words, but in virtue. ²¹What would you prefer? Should I return to you with a rod, or with charity and a spirit of meekness?

1 CORINTHIANS 5

¹Above all else, it is being said that there is fornication among you, even fornication of a such kind that is not among the Gentiles, so that someone would have the wife of his father. ²And yet you are inflated, and you have not instead been grieved, so that he who has done this thing would be taken away from your midst. ³Certainly, though absent in body, I am present in spirit. Thus, I have already judged, as if I were present, him who has done this. ⁴In the name of our Lord Jesus Christ, you have been gathered together with my spirit, in the power of our Lord Jesus, ⁵to hand over such a one as this to Satan, for the destruction of the flesh, so that the spirit may be saved in the day of our Lord Jesus Christ. ⁶It is not good for you to glory. Do you not know that a little leaven corrupts the entire mass? ⁷Purge the old leaven, so that you may become the new bread, for you are unleavened. For Christ, our Passover, has now been immolated. ⁸And so, let us feast, not with the old leaven, not with the leaven of malice and wickedness, but with the unleavened bread of sincerity and truth. ⁹As I have written to you in an epistle: "Do not associate with fornicators," ¹⁰certainly not with the fornicators of this world, nor with the greedy, nor with robbers, nor with the servants of idolatry. Otherwise, you ought to depart from this world. ¹¹But now I have written to you: do not associate with anyone who is called a brother and yet is a fornicator, or greedy, or a servant of idolatry, or a slanderer, or inebriated, or a robber. With such a one as this, do not even take food. ¹²For what have I to do with judging those who are outside? But do not even you yourselves judge those who are inside? ¹³For those who are outside, God will judge. But send this evil person away from yourselves.

1 CORINTHIANS 6

¹How is it that anyone of you, having a dispute against another, would dare to be judged before the iniquitous, and not before the saints? ²Or do you not know that the saints from this age shall judge it? And if the world is to be judged by you, are you unworthy, then, to judge even the smallest matters? ³Do you not know that we shall judge angels? How much more the things of this age? ⁴Therefore, if you have matters to judge concerning this age, why not appoint those who are most contemptible in the Church to judge these things! ⁵But I am speaking so as to shame you. Is there no one among you wise enough, so that he might be able to judge between his brothers? ⁶Instead, brother contends against brother in court, and this before the unfaithful! ⁷Now there is certainly an offense among you, beyond everything else, when you have court cases against one another. Should you not accept injury instead? Should you not endure being cheated instead? ⁸But you are doing the injuring and the cheating, and this toward brothers! ⁹Do

you not know that the iniquitous will not possess the kingdom of God? Do not choose to wander astray. For neither fornicators, nor servants of idolatry, nor adulterers, ⁹ nor the effeminate, nor males who sleep with males, nor thieves, nor the avaricious, nor the inebriated, nor slanderers, nor the rapacious shall possess the kingdom of God. ¹¹ And some of you were like this. But you have been absolved, but you have been sanctified, but you have been justified: all in the name of our Lord Jesus Christ and in the Spirit of our God. ¹² All is lawful to me, but not all is expedient. All is lawful to me, but I will not be driven back by the authority of anyone. ¹³ Food is for the stomach, and the stomach is for food. But God shall destroy both the stomach and food. And the body is not for fornication, but rather for the Lord; and the Lord is for the body. ¹⁴ Truly, God has raised up the Lord, and he will raise us up by his power. ¹⁵ Do you not know that your bodies are a part of Christ? So then, should I take a part of Christ and make it a part of a harlot? Let it not be so! ¹⁶ And do you not know that whoever is joined to a harlot becomes one body? "For the two," he said, "shall be as one flesh." ¹⁷ But whoever is joined to the Lord is one spirit. ¹⁸ Flee from fornication. Every sin whatsoever that a man commits is outside of the body, but whoever fornicates, sins against his own body. ¹⁹ Or do you not know that your bodies are the Temple of the Holy Spirit, who is in you, whom you have from God, and that you are not your own? ²⁰ For you have been bought at a great price. Glorify and carry God in your body.

1 CORINTHIANS 7

¹ Now concerning the things about which you wrote to me: It is good for a man not to touch a woman. ² But, because of fornication, let each man have his own wife, and let each woman have her own husband. ³ A husband should fulfill his obligation to his wife, and a wife should also act similarly toward her husband. ⁴ It is not the wife, but the husband, who has power over her body. But, similarly also, it is not the husband, but the wife, who has power over his body. ⁵ So, do not fail in your obligations to one another, except perhaps by consent, for a limited time, so that you may empty yourselves for prayer. And then, return together again, lest Satan tempt you by means of your abstinence. ⁶ But I am saying this, neither as an indulgence, nor as a commandment. ⁷ For I would prefer it if you were all like myself. But each person has his proper gift from God: one in this way, yet another in that way. ⁸ But I say to the unmarried and to widows: It is good for them, if they would remain as they are, just as I also am. ⁹ But if they cannot restrain themselves, they should marry. For it is better to marry, than to be burned. ¹⁰ But to those who have been joined in matrimony, it is not I who commands you, but the Lord: a wife is not to separate from her husband. ¹¹ But if she has separated from him, she must remain unmarried, or be reconciled to her husband. And a husband should not divorce his wife. ¹² Concerning the rest, I am speaking, not the Lord. If any brother has an unbelieving wife, and she consents to live with him, he should not divorce her. ¹³ And if any woman has an unbelieving husband, and he consents to live with her, she should not divorce her husband. ¹⁴ For the unbelieving husband has been sanctified through the believing wife, and the unbelieving wife has been sanctified through the believing husband. Otherwise, your children would be unclean, whereas instead they are holy. ¹⁵ But if the unbeliever departs, let him depart. For a brother or sister cannot be made subject to servitude in this way. For God has called us to peace. ¹⁶ And how do you know, wife, whether you will save your husband? Or how do you know, husband, whether you will save your wife? ¹⁷ However, let each one walk just as the Lord has distributed to him, each one just as God has called him. And thus do I teach in all the churches. ¹⁸ Has any circumcised man been called? Let him not cover his circumcision. Has any uncircumcised man been called? Let him not be circumcised. ¹⁹ Circumcision is nothing, and uncircumcision is nothing; there is only the observance of the commandments of God. ²⁰ Let each and every one remain in the same calling to which he was called. ²¹ Are you a servant who has been called? Do not be concerned about it. But if you ever have the ability to be free, make use of it. ²² For any servant who has been called in the Lord is free in the Lord. Similarly, any free person who has been called is a servant in Christ. ²³ You have been bought with a price. Do not be willing to become the servants of men. ²⁴ Brothers, let each one, in whatever state he was called, remain in that state with God. ²⁵ Now, concerning virgins, I have no commandment from the Lord. But I give counsel, as one who has obtained the mercy of the Lord, so as to be faithful. ²⁶ Therefore, I consider this to be good, because of the present necessity:

that it is good for a man to be such as I am. ²⁷ Are you bound to a wife? Do not seek to be freed. Are you free of a wife? Do not seek a wife. ²⁸ But if you take a wife, you have not sinned. And if a virgin has married, she has not sinned. Even so, such as these will have the tribulation of the flesh. But I would spare you from this. ²⁹ And so, this is what I say, brothers: The time is short. What remains of it is such that: those who have wives should be as if they had none; ³⁰ and those who weep, as though they were not weeping; and those who rejoice, as if they were not rejoicing; and those who buy, as if they possessed nothing; ³¹ and those who use the things of this world, as if they were not using them. For the figure of this world is passing away. ³² But I would prefer you to be without worry. Whoever is without a wife is worried about the things of the Lord, as to how he may please God. ³³ But whoever is with a wife is worried about the things of the world, as to how he may please his wife. And so, he is divided. ³⁴ And the unmarried woman and the virgin think about the things that are of the Lord, so that she may be holy in body and in spirit. But she who is married thinks about the things that are of the world, as to how she may please her husband. ³⁵ Furthermore, I am saying this for your own benefit, not in order to cast a snare over you, but toward whatever is honest and whatever may provide you with the ability to be without hindrance, so as to worship the Lord. ³⁶ But if any man considers himself to seem dishonorable, concerning a virgin who is of adult age, and so it ought to be, he may do as he wills. If he marries her, he does not sin. ³⁷ But if he has decided firmly in his heart, and he does not have any obligation, but only the power of his free will, and if he has judged this in his heart, to let her remain a virgin, he does well. ³⁸ And so, he who joins with his virgin in matrimony does well, and he who does not join with her does better. ³⁹ A woman is bound under the law for as long as her husband lives. But if her husband has died, she is free. She may marry whomever she wishes, but only in the Lord. ⁴⁰ But she will be more blessed, if she remains in this state, in accord with my counsel. And I think that I, too, have the Spirit of God.

1 CORINTHIANS 8

¹ Now concerning those things that are sacrificed to idols: we know that we all have knowledge. Knowledge puffs up, but charity builds up. ² But if anyone considers himself to know anything, he does not yet know in the way that he ought to know. ³ For if anyone loves God, he is known by him. ⁴ But as to the foods that are immolated to idols, we know that an idol in the world is nothing, and that no one is God, except One. ⁵ For although there are things that are called gods, whether in heaven or on earth, (if one even considers there to be many gods and many lords) ⁶ yet we know that there is only one God, the Father, from whom all things are, and in whom we are, and one Lord Jesus Christ, through whom all things are, and by whom we are. ⁷ But knowledge is not in everyone. For some persons, even now, with consent to an idol, eat what has been sacrificed to an idol. And their conscience, being infirm, becomes polluted. ⁸ Yet food does not commend us to God. For if we eat, we will not have more, and if we do not eat, we will not have less. ⁹ But be careful not to let your liberty become a cause of sin to those who are weak. ¹⁰ For if anyone sees someone with knowledge sitting down to eat in idolatry, will not his own conscience, being infirm, be emboldened to eat what has been sacrificed to idols? ¹¹ And should an infirm brother perish by your knowledge, even though Christ died for him? ¹² So when you sin in this way against the brothers, and you harm their weakened conscience, then you sin against Christ. ¹³ Because of this, if food leads my brother to sin, I will never eat meat, lest I lead my brother to sin.

1 CORINTHIANS 9

¹ Am I not free? Am I not an Apostle? Have I not seen Christ Jesus our Lord? Are you not my work in the Lord? ² And if I am not an Apostle to others, yet still I am to you. For you are the seal of my Apostleship in the Lord. ³ My defense with those who question me is this: ⁴ Do we not have the authority to eat and to drink? ⁵ Do we not have the authority to travel around with a woman who is a sister, just as do the other Apostles, and the brothers of the Lord, and Cephas? ⁶ Or is it only myself and Barnabas who do not have the authority to act in this way? ⁷ Who has ever served as a soldier and paid his own stipend? Who plants a vineyard and does not eat from its produce? Who pastures a flock and does not drink from the milk of the flock? ⁸ Am I saying these things according to man? Or does the law not also say these things? ⁹ For it is written in the law of Moses:

"You shall not bind the mouth of an ox, while it is treading out the grain." Is God here concerned with the oxen? [10] Or is he saying this, indeed, for our sake? These things were written specifically for us, because he who plows, ought to plow in hope, and he who threshes, too, in hope of receiving the produce. [11] If we have sown spiritual things in you, is it important if we harvest from your worldly things? [12] If others are sharers in this authority over you, why are we not more entitled? And yet we have not used this authority. Instead, we bear all things, lest we give any hindrance to the Gospel of Christ. [13] Do you not know that those who work in the holy place eat the things that are for the holy place, and that those who serve at the altar also share with the altar? [14] So, too, has the Lord ordained that those who announce the Gospel should live by the Gospel. [15] Yet I have used none of these things. And I have not written so that these things may be done for me. For it is better for me to die, rather than to let anyone empty out my glory. [16] For if I preach the Gospel, it is not glory for me. For an obligation has been laid upon me. And woe to me, if I do not preach the Gospel. [17] For if I do this willingly, I have a reward. But if I do this reluctantly, a dispensation is granted to me. [18] And what, then, would be my reward? So, when preaching the Gospel, I should give the Gospel without taking, so that I may not misuse my authority in the Gospel. [19] For when I was a free man to all, I made myself the servant of all, so that I might gain all the more. [20] And so, to the Jews, I became like a Jew, so that I might gain the Jews. [21] To those who are under the law, I became as if I were under the law, (though I was not under the law) so that I might gain those who were under the law. To those who were without the law, I became as if I were without the law, (though I was not without the law of God, being in the law of Christ) so that I might gain those who were without the law. [22] To the weak, I became weak, so that I might gain the weak. To all, I became all, so that I might save all. [23] And I do everything for the sake of the Gospel, so that I may become its partner. [24] Do you not know that, of those who run in a race, all of them, certainly, are runners, but only one achieves the prize. Similarly, you must run, so that you may achieve. [25] And one who competes in a contest abstains from all things. And they do this, of course, so that they may achieve a corruptible crown. But we do this, so that we may achieve what is incorruptible. [26] And so I run, but not with uncertainty. And so I fight, but not by flailing in the air. [27] Instead, I chastise my body, so as to redirect it into servitude. Otherwise, I might preach to others, but become myself an outcast.

1 CORINTHIANS 10

[1] For I do not want you to be ignorant, brothers, that our fathers were all under the cloud, and they all went across the sea. [2] And in Moses, they all were baptized, in the cloud and in the sea. [3] And they all ate of the same spiritual food. [4] And they all drank of the same spiritual drink. And so, they all were drinking of the spiritual rock seeking to obtain them; and that rock was Christ. [5] But with most of them, God was not well-pleased. For they were struck down in the desert. [6] Now these things were done as an example for us, so that we might not desire evil things, just as they desired. [7] And so, do not take part in idolatry, as some of them did, just as it was written: "The people sat down to eat and to drink, and then they rose up to amuse themselves." [8] And let us not commit fornication, as some of them fornicated, and so twenty-three thousand fell on one day. [9] And let us not tempt Christ, as some of them tempted, and so they perished by serpents. [10] And you should not murmur, as some of them murmured, and so they perished by the destroyer. [11] Now all of these things happened to them as an example, and so they have been written for our correction, because the final age has fallen upon us. [12] And so, whosoever considers himself to be standing, let him be careful not to fall. [13] Temptation should not take hold of you, except what is human. For God is faithful, and he will not permit you to be tempted beyond your ability. Instead, he will effect his Providence, even during temptation, so that you may be able to bear it. [14] Because of this, most beloved of mine, flee from the worship of idols. [15] Since I am speaking to those who are prudent, judge what I say for yourselves. [16] The cup of benediction that we bless, is it not a communion in the Blood of Christ? And the bread that we break, is it not a participation in the Body of the Lord? [17] Through the one bread, we, though many, are one body: all of us who are partakers of the one bread. [18] Consider Israel, according to the flesh. Are not those who eat from the sacrifices partakers of the altar? [19] What is next? Should I say that what is immolated to idols is anything? Or that the idol is anything? [20] But the things that the Gentiles immolate, they immolate to demons, and not

to God. And I do not want you to become partakers with demons. [21] You cannot drink the cup of the Lord, and the cup of demons. You cannot be partakers of the table of the Lord, and partakers of the table of demons. [22] Or should we provoke the Lord to jealousy? Are we stronger than he is? All is lawful to me, but not all is expedient. [23] All is lawful to me, but not all is edifying. [24] Let no one seek for himself, but for others. [25] Whatever is sold in the market, you may eat, without asking questions for the sake of conscience. [26] "The earth and all its fullness belong to the Lord." [27] If you are invited by any unbelievers, and you are willing to go, you may eat whatever is set before you, without asking questions for the sake of conscience. [28] But if anyone says, "This has been sacrificed to idols," do not eat it, for the sake of the one who told you, and for the sake of conscience. [29] But I am referring to the conscience of the other person, not to yours. For why should my liberty be judged by the conscience of another? [30] If I partake with thanksgiving, why should I be slandered over that for which I give thanks? [31] Therefore, whether you eat or drink, or whatever else you may do, do everything for the glory of God. [32] Be without offense toward the Jews, and toward the Gentiles, and toward the Church of God, [33] just as I also, in all things, please everyone, not seeking what is best for myself, but what is best for many others, so that they may be saved.

1 CORINTHIANS 11

[1] Be imitators of me, as I also am of Christ. [2] Now I praise you, brothers, because you are mindful of me in everything, in such a way as to hold to my precepts as I have handed them down to you. [3] So I want you to know that the head of every man is Christ. But the head of woman is man. Yet truly, the head of Christ is God. [4] Every man praying or prophesying with his head covered disgraces his head. [5] But every woman praying or prophesying with her head not covered disgraces her head. For it is the same as if her head were shaven. [6] So if a woman is not veiled, let her hair be cut off. Truly then, if it is a disgrace for a woman to have her hair cut off, or to have her head shaven, then she should cover her head. [7] Certainly, a man ought not to cover his head, for he is the image and glory of God. But woman is the glory of man. [8] For man is not of woman, but woman is of man. [9] And indeed, man was not created for woman, but woman was created for man. [10] Therefore, a woman ought to have a sign of authority on her head, because of the Angels. [11] Yet truly, man would not exist without woman, nor would woman exist without man, in the Lord. [12] For just as woman came into existence from man, so also does man exist through woman. But all things are from God. [13] Judge for yourselves. Is it proper for a woman to pray to God unveiled? [14] Does not even nature herself teach you that, indeed, if a man grows his hair long, it is a disgrace for him? [15] Yet truly, if a woman grows her hair long, it is a glory for her, because her hair has been given to her as a covering. [16] But if anyone has a mind to be contentious, we have no such custom, nor does the Church of God. [17] Now I caution you, without praising, about this: that you assemble together, and not for better, but for worse. [18] First of all, indeed, I hear that when you assemble together in the church, there are schisms among you. And I believe this, in part. [19] For there must also be heresies, so that those who have been tested may be made manifest among you. [20] And so, when you assemble together as one, it is no longer in order to eat the Lord's supper. [21] For each one first takes his own supper to eat. And as a result, one person is hungry, while another is inebriated. [22] Do you not have houses, in which to eat and drink? Or do you have such contempt for the Church of God that you would confound those who do not have such contempt? What should I say to you? Should I praise you? I am not praising you in this. [23] For I have received from the Lord what I have also delivered to you: that the Lord Jesus, on the same night that he was handed over, took bread, [24] and giving thanks, he broke it, and said: "Take and eat. This is my body, which shall be given up for you. Do this in remembrance of me." [25] Similarly also, the cup, after he had eaten supper, saying: "This cup is the new covenant in my blood. Do this, as often as you drink it, in remembrance of me." [26] For whenever you eat this bread and drink this cup, you proclaim the death of the Lord, until he returns. [27] And so, whoever eats this bread, or drinks from the cup of the Lord, unworthily, shall be liable of the body and blood of the Lord. [28] But let a man examine himself, and, in this way, let him eat from that bread, and drink from that cup. [29] For whoever eats and drinks unworthily, eats and drinks a sentence against himself, not discerning it to be the body of the Lord. [30] As a result, many are weak and sick among you, and many have fallen asleep. [31] But if we ourselves were discerning, then certainly we would not be judged. [32] Yet when we are judged, we are being corrected by

the Lord, so that we might not be condemned along with this world. ³³ And so, my brothers, when you assemble together to eat, be attentive to one another. ³⁴ If anyone is hungry, let him eat at home, so that you may not assemble together unto judgment. As for the rest, I will set it in order when I arrive.

1 CORINTHIANS 12

¹ Now concerning spiritual things, I do not want you to be ignorant, brothers. ² You know that when you were Gentiles, you approached mute idols, doing what you were led to do. ³ Because of this, I would have you know that no one speaking in the Spirit of God utters a curse against Jesus. And no one is able to say that Jesus is Lord, except in the Holy Spirit. ⁴ Truly, there are diverse graces, but the same Spirit. ⁵ And there are diverse ministries, but the same Lord. ⁶ And there are diverse works, but the same God, who works everything in everyone. ⁷ However, the manifestation of the Spirit is given to each one toward what is beneficial. ⁸ Certainly, to one, through the Spirit, is given words of wisdom; but to another, according to the same Spirit, words of knowledge; ⁹ to another, in the same Spirit, faith; to another, in the one Spirit, the gift of healing; ¹⁰ to another, miraculous works; to another, prophecy; to another, the discernment of spirits; to another, different kinds of languages; to another, the interpretation of words. ¹¹ But one and the same Spirit works all these things, distributing to each one according to his will. ¹² For just as the body is one, and yet has many parts, so all the parts of the body, though they are many, are only one body. So also is Christ. ¹³ And indeed, in one Spirit, we were all baptized into one body, whether Jews or Gentiles, whether servant or free. And we all drank in the one Spirit. ¹⁴ For the body, too, is not one part, but many. ¹⁵ If the foot were to say, "Because I am not the hand, I am not of the body," would it then not be of the body? ¹⁶ And if the ear were to say, "Because I am not the eye, I am not of the body," would it then not be of the body? ¹⁷ If the whole body were the eye, how would it hear? If the whole were hearing, how would it smell? ¹⁸ But instead, God has placed the parts, each one of them, in the body, just as it has pleased him. ¹⁹ So if they were all one part, how would it be a body? ²⁰ But instead, there are many parts, indeed, yet one body. ²¹ And the eye cannot say to the hand, "I have no need for your works." And again, the head cannot say to the feet, "You are of no use to me." ²² In fact, so much more necessary are those parts of the body which seem to be weaker. ²³ And though we consider certain parts of the body to be less noble, we surround these with more abundant dignity, and so, those parts which are less presentable end up with more abundant respect. ²⁴ However, our presentable parts have no such need, since God has tempered the body together, distributing the more abundant honor to that which has the need, ²⁵ so that there might be no schism in the body, but instead the parts themselves might take care of one another. ²⁶ And so, if one part suffers anything, all the parts suffer with it. Or, if one part finds glory, all the parts rejoice with it. ²⁷ Now you are the body of Christ, and parts like any part. ²⁸ And indeed, God has established a certain order in the Church: first Apostles, second Prophets, third Teachers, next miracle-workers, and then the grace of healing, of helping others, of governing, of different kinds of languages, and of the interpretation of words. ²⁹ Are all Apostles? Are all Prophets? Are all Teachers? ³⁰ Are all workers of miracles? Do all have the grace of healing? Do all speak in tongues? Do all interpret? ³¹ But be zealous for the better charisms. And I reveal to you a yet more excellent way.

1 CORINTHIANS 13

¹ If I were to speak in the language of men, or of Angels, yet not have charity, I would be like a clanging bell or a crashing cymbal. ² And if I have prophecy, and learn every mystery, and obtain all knowledge, and possess all faith, so that I could move mountains, yet not have charity, then I am nothing. ³ And if I distribute all my goods in order to feed the poor, and if I hand over my body to be burned, yet not have charity, it offers me nothing. ⁴ Charity is patient, is kind. Charity does not envy, does not act wrongly, is not inflated. ⁵ Charity is not ambitious, does not seek for itself, is not provoked to anger, devises no evil. ⁶ Charity does not rejoice over iniquity, but rejoices in truth. ⁷ Charity suffers all, believes all, hopes all, endures all. ⁸ Charity is never torn away, even if prophecies pass away, or languages cease, or knowledge is destroyed. ⁹ For we know only in part, and we prophesy only in part. ¹⁰ But when the perfect arrives, the imperfect passes away. ¹¹ When I was a child, I spoke like a child, I understood like a child, I thought like a child. But when I became a man, I put aside the things of a child.

12 Now we see through a glass darkly. But then we shall see face to face. Now I know in part, but then I shall know, even as I am known. 13 But for now, these three continue: faith, hope, and charity. And the greatest of these is charity.

1 CORINTHIANS 14

1 Pursue charity. Be zealous for spiritual things, but only so that you may prophesy. 2 For whoever speaks in tongues, speaks not to men, but to God. For no one understands. Yet by the Spirit, he speaks mysteries. 3 But whoever prophesies speaks to men for edification and exhortation and consolation. 4 Whoever speaks in tongues edifies himself. But whoever prophesies edifies the Church. 5 Now I want you all to speak in tongues, but more so to prophesy. For he who prophesies is greater than he who speaks in tongues, unless perhaps he interprets, so that the Church may receive edification. 6 But now, brothers, if I were to come to you speaking in tongues, how would it benefit you, unless instead I speak to you in revelation, or in knowledge, or in prophecy, or in doctrine? 7 Even those things that are without a soul can make sounds, whether it is a wind or a stringed instrument. But unless they present a distinction within the sounds, how will it be known which is from the pipe and which is from the string? 8 For example, if the trumpet made an uncertain sound, who would prepare himself for battle? 9 So it is with you also, for unless you utter with the tongue in plain speech, how will it be known what is said? For then you would be speaking into the air. 10 Consider that there are so many different kinds of languages in this world, and yet none is without a voice. 11 Therefore, if I do not understand the nature of the voice, then I shall be like a foreigner to the one with whom I am speaking; and he who is speaking will be like a foreigner to me. 12 So it is with you also. And since you are zealous for what is spiritual, seek the edification of the Church, so that you may abound. 13 For this reason, too, whoever speaks in tongues, let him pray for the interpretation. 14 So, if I pray in tongues, my spirit prays, but my mind is without fruit. 15 What is next? I should pray with the spirit, and also pray with the mind. I should sing psalms with the spirit, and also recite psalms with the mind. 16 Otherwise, if you have blessed only with the spirit, how can someone, in a state of ignorance, add an "Amen" to your blessing? For he does not know what you are saying. 17 In this case, certainly, you give thanks well, but the other person is not edified. 18 I thank my God that I speak in tongues for all of you. 19 But in the Church, I prefer to speak five words from my mind, so that I may instruct others also, rather than ten thousand words in tongues. 20 Brothers, do not choose to have the minds of children. Instead, be free of malice like infants, but be mature in your minds. 21 It is written in the law: "I will speak to this people with other tongues and other lips, and even so, they will not heed me, says the Lord." 22 And so, tongues are a sign, not for believers, but for unbelievers; and prophecies are not for unbelievers, but for believers. 23 If then, the entire Church were to gather together as one, and if all were to speak in tongues, and then ignorant or unbelieving persons were to enter, would they not say that you were insane? 24 But if everyone prophesies, and one who is ignorant or unbelieving enters, he may be convinced by it all, because he understands it all. 25 The secrets of his heart are then made manifest. And so, falling to his face, he would adore God, proclaiming that God is truly among you. 26 What is next, brothers? When you gather together, each one of you may have a psalm, or a doctrine, or a revelation, or a language, or an interpretation, but let everything be done for edification. 27 If anyone is speaking in tongues, let there be only two, or at most three, and then in turn, and let someone interpret. 28 But if there is no one to interpret, he should remain silent in the church, then he may speak when he is alone with God. 29 And let the prophets speak, two or three, and let the others discern. 30 But then, if something is revealed to another who is sitting, let the first one become silent. 31 For you are all able to prophesy one at a time, so that all may learn and all may be encouraged. 32 For the spirits of the prophets are subject to the prophets. 33 And God is not of dissension, but of peace, just as I also teach in all the churches of the saints. 34 Women should be silent in the churches. For it is not permitted for them to speak; but instead, they should be subordinate, as the law also says. 35 And if they want to learn anything, let them ask their husbands at home. For it is disgraceful for a woman to speak in church. 36 So now, did the Word of God proceed from you? Or was it sent to you alone? 37 If anyone seems to be a prophet or a spiritual person, he should understand these things which I am writing to you, that these things are the commandments of the Lord. 38 If anyone does not recognize these things, he should not be recognized. 39 And so,

brothers, be zealous to prophesy, and do not prohibit speaking in tongues. [40] But let everything be done respectfully and according to proper order.

1 CORINTHIANS 15

[1] And so I make known to you, brothers, the Gospel that I preached to you, which you also received, and on which you stand. [2] By the Gospel, too, you are being saved, if you hold to the understanding that I preached to you, lest you believe in vain. [3] For I handed on to you, first of all, what I also received: that Christ died for our sins, according to the Scriptures; [4] and that he was buried; and that he rose again on the third day, according to the Scriptures; [5] and that he was seen by Cephas, and after that by the eleven. [6] Next he was seen by more than five hundred brothers at one time, many of whom remain, even to the present time, although some have fallen asleep. [7] Next, he was seen by James, then by all the Apostles. [8] And last of all, he was seen also by me, as if I were someone born at the wrong time. [9] For I am the least of the Apostles. I am not worthy to be called an Apostle, because I persecuted the Church of God. [10] But, by the grace of God, I am what I am. And his grace in me has not been empty, since I have labored more abundantly than all of them. Yet it is not I, but the grace of God within me. [11] For whether it is I or they: so we preach, and so you have believed. [12] Now if Christ is preached, that he rose again from the dead, how is it that some among you say that there is no resurrection of the dead? [13] For if there is no resurrection of the dead, then Christ has not risen. [14] And if Christ has not risen, then our preaching is useless, and your faith is also useless. [15] Then, too, we would be found to be false witnesses of God, because we would have given testimony against God, saying that he had raised up Christ, when he had not raised him up, if, indeed, the dead do not rise again. [16] For if the dead do not rise again, then neither has Christ risen again. [17] But if Christ has not risen, then your faith is vain; for you would still be in your sins. [18] Then, too, those who have fallen asleep in Christ would have perished. [19] If we have hope in Christ for this life only, then we are more miserable than all men. [20] But now Christ has risen again from the dead, as the first-fruits of those who sleep. [21] For certainly, death came through a man. And so, the resurrection of the dead came through a man [22] And just as in Adam all die, so also in Christ all will be brought to life, [23] but each one in his proper order: Christ, as the first-fruits, and next, those who are of Christ, who have believed in his advent. [24] Afterwards is the end, when he will have handed over the kingdom to God the Father, when he will have emptied all principality, and authority, and power. [25] For it is necessary for him to reign, until he has set all his enemies under his feet. [26] Lastly, the enemy called death shall be destroyed. For he has subjected all things under his feet. And although he says, [27] "All things have been subjected to him," without doubt he does not include the One who has subjected all things to him. [28] And when all things will have been subjected to him, then even the Son himself will be subjected to the One who subjected all things to him, so that God may be all in all. [29] Otherwise, what will those who are being baptized for the dead do, if the dead do not rise again at all? Why then are they being baptized for them? [30] Why also do we endure trials every hour? [31] Daily I die, by means of your boasting, brothers: you whom I have in Christ Jesus our Lord. [32] If, according to man, I fought with the beasts at Ephesus, how would that benefit me, if the dead do not rise again? "Let us eat and drink, for tomorrow we shall die." [33] Do not be led astray. Evil communication corrupts good morals. [34] Be vigilant, you just ones, and do not be willing to sin. For certain persons have an ignorance of God. I say this to you with respect. [35] But someone may say, "How do the dead rise again?" or, "What type of body do they return with?" [36] How foolish! What you sow cannot be brought back to life, unless it first dies. [37] And what you sow is not the body that will be in the future, but a bare grain, such as of wheat, or of some other grain. [38] For God gives it a body according to his will, and according to each seed's proper body. [39] Not all flesh is the same flesh. But one is indeed of men, another truly is of beasts, another is of birds, and another is of fish. [40] Also, there are heavenly bodies and earthly bodies. But while the one, certainly, has the glory of heaven, the other has the glory of earth. [41] One has the brightness of the sun, another the brightness of the moon, and another the brightness of the stars. For even star differs from star in brightness. [42] So it is also with the resurrection of the dead. What is sown in corruption shall rise to incorruption. [43] What is sown in dishonor shall rise to glory. What is sown in weakness shall rise to power. [44] What is sown with an animal body shall rise with a spiritual body. If there is an animal body, there is also a spiritual one. [45] Just as it was written that the first man,

Adam, was made with a living soul, so shall the last Adam be made with a spirit brought back to life. [46] So what is, at first, not spiritual, but animal, next becomes spiritual. [47] The first man, being earthly, was of the earth; the second man, being heavenly, will be of heaven. [48] Such things as are like the earth are earthly; and such things as are like the heavens are heavenly. [49] And so, just as we have carried the image of what is earthly, let us also carry the image of what is heavenly. [50] Now I say this, brothers, because flesh and blood is not able to possess the kingdom of God; neither will what is corrupt possess what is incorrupt. [51] Behold, I tell you a mystery. Certainly, we shall all rise again, but we shall not all be transformed: [52] in a moment, in the twinkling of an eye, at the last trumpet. For the trumpet will sound, and the dead will rise up, incorruptible. And we shall be transformed. [53] Thus, it is necessary for this corruptibility to be clothed with incorruptibility, and for this mortality to be clothed with immortality. [54] And when this mortality has been clothed with immortality, then the word that was written shall occur: "Death is swallowed up in victory." [55] "O death, where is your victory? O death, where is your sting?" [56] Now the sting of death is sin, and the power of sin is the law. [57] But thanks be to God, who has given us victory through our Lord Jesus Christ. [58] And so, my beloved brothers, be steadfast and unmovable, abounding always in the work of the Lord, knowing that your labor is not useless in the Lord.

1 CORINTHIANS 16

[1] Now concerning the collections which are made for the saints: just as I have arranged for the churches of Galatia, so should it also be done with you. [2] On the first day of the week, the Sabbath, let each one of you take from himself, setting aside what will be well-pleasing to him, so that when I arrive, the collections will not have to be made then. [3] And when I am present, whomever you shall approve through letters, these I shall send to bear your gifts to Jerusalem. [4] And if it is fitting for me to go too, they shall go with me. [5] Now I will visit you after I have passed through Macedonia. For I will pass through Macedonia. [6] And perhaps I will stay with you, and even spend the winter, so that you may lead me on my way, whenever I depart. [7] For I am not willing to see you now only in passing, since I hope that I may remain with you for some length of time, if the Lord permits. [8] But I must remain at Ephesus, even until Pentecost. [9] For a door, great and unavoidable, has opened to me, as well as many adversaries. [10] Now if Timothy arrives, see to it that he may be among you without fear. For he is doing the work of the Lord, just as I also do. [11] Therefore, let no one despise him. Instead, lead him on his way in peace, so that he may come to me. For I am awaiting him with the brothers. [12] But concerning our brother, Apollo, I am letting you know that I pleaded with him greatly to go to you with the brothers, and clearly it was not his will to go at this time. But he will arrive when there is a space of time for him. [13] Be vigilant. Stand with faith. Act manfully and be strengthened. [14] Let all that is yours be immersed in charity. [15] And I beg you, brothers: You know the house of Stephanus, and of Fortunatus, and of Achaicus, that they are the first-fruits of Achaia, and that they have dedicated themselves to the ministry of the saints. [16] So you should be subject also to persons such as this, as well as to all who are cooperating and working with them. [17] Now I rejoice in the presence of Stephanus and Fortunatus and Achaicus, because what was lacking in you, they have supplied. [18] For they have refreshed my spirit and yours. Therefore, recognize persons such as this. [19] The churches of Asia greet you. Aquila and Priscilla greet you greatly in the Lord, with the church of their household, where I also am a guest. [20] All the brothers greet you. Greet one another with a holy kiss. [21] This is a greeting from my own hand, Paul. [22] If anyone does not love our Lord Jesus Christ, let him be anathema! Maran Atha. [23] May the grace of our Lord Jesus Christ be with you all. [24] My charity is with all of you in Christ Jesus. Amen.

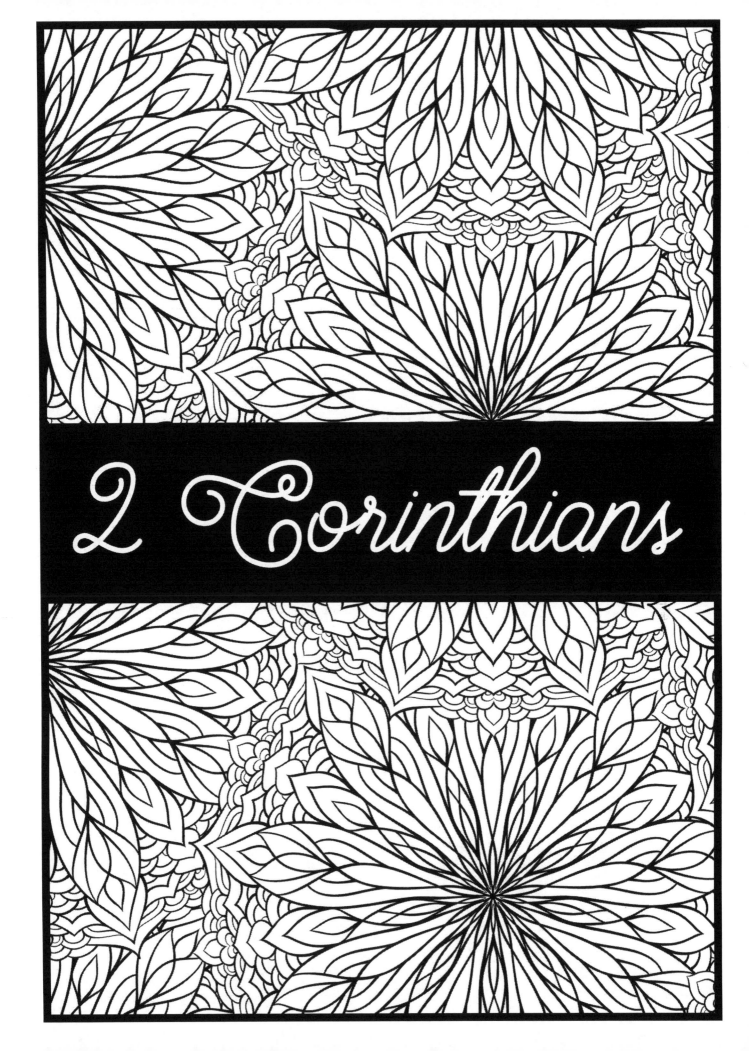

2 Corinthians

THE SACRED BIBLE:
THE SECOND LETTER TO THE CORINTHIANS

2 CORINTHIANS 1

[1] Paul, an Apostle of Jesus Christ by the will of God, and Timothy, a brother, to the church of God which is at Corinth, with all the saints who are in all of Achaia: [2] Grace and peace to you from God our Father and from the Lord Jesus Christ. [3] Blessed be the God and Father of our Lord Jesus Christ, the Father of mercies and the God of all consolation. [4] He consoles us in all our tribulation, so that we too may be able to console those who are in any kind of distress, through the exhortation by which we also are being exhorted by God. [5] For just as the Passion of Christ abounds in us, so also, through Christ, does our consolation abound. [6] So, if we are in tribulation, it is for your exhortation and salvation, or if we are in consolation, it is for your consolation, or if we are exhorted, it is for your exhortation and salvation, which results in the patient endurance of the same passion which we also endure. [7] So may our hope for you be made firm, knowing that, just as you are participants in the suffering, so also shall you be participants in the consolation. [8] For we do not want you to be ignorant, brothers, about our tribulation, which happened to us in Asia. For we were weighed down beyond measure, beyond our strength, so that we became weary, even of life itself. [9] But we had within ourselves the response to death, so that we would not have faith in ourselves, but in God, who raises the dead. [10] He has rescued us, and he is rescuing us, from great peril. In him, we hope that he will continue to rescue us. [11] And you are assisting, with your prayers for us, so that from many persons, by that which is a gift in us, thanks may be given through many persons, because of us. [12] For our glory is this: the testimony of our conscience, which is found in simplicity of heart and in sincerity toward God. And it is not with worldly wisdom, but in the grace of God, that we have conversed with this world, and more abundantly toward you. [13] For we write nothing else to you other than what you have read and understood. And I hope that you will continue to understand, even unto the end. [14] And just as you have acknowledged us in our role, that we are your glory, so also you are ours, unto the day of our Lord Jesus Christ. [15] And with this confidence, I wanted to come to you sooner, so that you might have a second grace, [16] and through you to pass into Macedonia, and to return to you again from Macedonia, and so be led by you on my way to Judea. [17] Then, although I had intended this, did I act lightly? Or in the things that I consider, do I consider according to the flesh, so that there would be, with me, both Yes and No? [18] But God is faithful, so our word, which was set before you, was not, in him, both Yes and No. [19] For the Son of God, Jesus Christ, who was preached among you through us, through myself and Sylvanus and Timothy, was not Yes, and No; but was simply Yes in him. [20] For whatever promises are of God are, in him, Yes. For this reason, too, through him: Amen to God for our glory. [21] Now the One who confirms us with you in Christ, and who has anointed us, is God. [22] And he has sealed us, and he has placed the pledge of the Spirit in our hearts. [23] But I call God as a witness to my soul, that I was lenient with you, in that I did not return to Corinth: [24] not because we have dominion over your faith, but because we are assistants of your joy. For by faith you stand.

2 CORINTHIANS 2

[1] But I determined this within myself, not to return again to you in sorrow. [2] For if I make you sorrowful, then who is it that can make me glad, except the one who is made sorrowful by me? [3] And so, I wrote this same thing to you, so that I might not, when I arrive, add sorrow to sorrow for those with whom I ought to rejoice, having confidence in you in all things, so that my joy may be entirely yours. [4] For with much tribulation and anguish of heart, I wrote to you with many tears: not so that you would be sorrowful, but so that you might know the charity that I have more abundantly toward you. [5] But if anyone has brought sorrow, he has not sorrowed me. Yet, for my part, this is so that I might not burden all of you. [6] Let this rebuke be sufficient for someone like this, for it has been brought by many. [7] So then, to the contrary, you should be more forgiving and consoling, lest perhaps someone like this may be overwhelmed with excessive sorrow. [8] Because of this, I beg you to confirm your charity toward him. [9] It was for this reason, also, that I wrote, so that I might know, by testing you, whether you would be obedient

in all things. ¹⁰But anyone whom you have forgiven of anything, I also forgive. And then, too, anyone I have forgiven, if I have forgiven anything, it was done in the person of Christ for your sakes, ¹¹so that we would not be circumvented by Satan. For we are not ignorant of his intentions. ¹²And when I had arrived at Troas, because of the Gospel of Christ, and a door had opened to me in the Lord, ¹³I had no rest within my spirit, because I was not able to find Titus, my brother. So, saying goodbye to them, I set out for Macedonia. ¹⁴But thanks be to God, who always brings triumph to us in Christ Jesus, and who manifests the fragrance of his knowledge through us in every place. ¹⁵For we are the sweet fragrance of Christ for God, both with those who are being saved and with those who are perishing. ¹⁶To the one, certainly, the fragrance is of death unto death. But to the other, the fragrance is of life unto life. And concerning these things, who is so suitable? ¹⁷For we are not like many others, adulterating the Word of God. But instead, we speak with sincerity: from God, before God, and in Christ.

2 CORINTHIANS 3

¹Must we begin again to commend ourselves? Or are we in need (as some are) of epistles of commendation for you, or from you? ²You are our Epistle, written in our hearts, which is known and read by all men. ³It has been made manifest that you are the Epistle of Christ, ministered by us, and written down, not with ink, but with the Spirit of the living God, and not on tablets of stone, but on the fleshly tablets of the heart. ⁴And we have such faith, through Christ, toward God. ⁵It is not that we are adequate to think anything of ourselves, as if anything was from us. But our adequacy is from God. ⁶And he has made us suitable ministers of the New Testament, not in the letter, but in the Spirit. For the letter kills, but the Spirit gives life. ⁷But if the ministration of death, engraved with letters upon stones, was in glory, (so much so that the sons of Israel were not able to gaze intently upon the face of Moses, because of the glory of his countenance) even though this ministration was ineffective, ⁸how could the ministration of the Spirit not be in greater glory? ⁹For if the ministration of condemnation is with glory, so much more is the ministration of justice abundant in glory. ¹⁰And neither was it glorified by means of an excellent glory, though it was made illustrious in its own way. ¹¹For if even what was temporary has its glory, then what is lasting has an even greater glory. ¹²Therefore, having such a hope, we act with much confidence, ¹³and not as Moses did, in placing a veil over his face, so that the sons of Israel would not gaze intently at his face. This was ineffective, ¹⁴for their minds were obtuse. And, even until this present day, the very same veil, in the readings from the Old Testament, remains not taken away (though, in Christ, it is taken away). ¹⁵But even until today, when Moses is read, a veil is still set over their hearts. ¹⁶But when they will have been converted to the Lord, then the veil shall be taken away. ¹⁷Now the Spirit is Lord. And wherever the Spirit of the Lord is, there is liberty. ¹⁸Yet truly, all of us, as we gaze upon the unveiled glory of the face of the Lord, are transfigured into the same image, from one glory to another. And this is done by the Spirit of the Lord.

2 CORINTHIANS 4

¹Therefore, since we have this ministry, and in as much as we have obtained mercy for ourselves, we are not inadequate. ²For we renounce dishonorable and hidden acts, not walking by craftiness, nor by adulterating the Word of God. Instead, by the manifestation of truth, we commend ourselves to the conscience of each man before God. ³But if our Gospel is in some way hidden, it is hidden to those who are perishing. ⁴As for them, the god of this age has blinded the minds of unbelievers, so that the light of the Gospel of the glory of Christ, who is the image of God, would not shine in them. ⁵For we are not preaching about ourselves, but about Jesus Christ our Lord. We are merely your servants through Jesus. ⁶For God, who told the light to shine out of darkness, has shined a light into our hearts, to illuminate the knowledge of the splendor of God, in the person of Christ Jesus. ⁷But we hold this treasure in earthen vessels, so that what is sublime may be of the power of God, and not of us. ⁸In all things, we endure tribulation, yet we are not in anguish. We are constrained, yet we are not destitute. ⁹We suffer persecution, yet we have not been abandoned. We are thrown down, yet we do not perish. ¹⁰We ever carry around the mortification of Jesus in our bodies, so that the life of Jesus may also be manifested in our bodies. ¹¹For we who live are ever handed over unto death for the sake of Jesus, so that the life of Jesus may also be manifested in our mortal flesh. ¹²Therefore, death is at work

in us, and life is at work in you. [13] But we have the same Spirit of faith. And just as it is written, "I believed, and for that reason I spoke," so we also believe, and for that reason, we also speak. [14] For we know that the One who raised up Jesus will raise us up also with Jesus and will place us with you. [15] Thus, all is for you, so that grace, abounding through many in thanksgiving, may abound to the glory of God. [16] For this reason, we are not insufficient. But it is as though our outer man is corrupted, while our inner man is renewed from day to day. [17] For though our tribulation is, at the present time, brief and light, it accomplishes in us the weight of a sublime eternal glory, beyond measure. [18] And we are contemplating, not the things that are seen, but the things that are unseen. For the things that are seen are temporal, whereas the things that are not seen are eternal.

2 CORINTHIANS 5

[1] For we know that, when our earthly house of this habitation is dissolved, we have a building of God, a house not made with hands, eternal in heaven. [2] And for this reason also, we groan, desiring to be clothed from above with our habitation from heaven. [3] If we are so clothed, then we will not be found to be naked. [4] Then too, we who are in this tabernacle groan under the burden, because we do not want to be stripped, but rather to be clothed from above, so that what is mortal may be absorbed by life. [5] Now the One who accomplishes this very thing in us is God, who has given us the pledge of the Spirit. [6] Therefore, we are ever confident, knowing that, while we are in the body, we are on a pilgrimage in the Lord. [7] For we walk by means of faith, and not by sight. [8] So we are confident, and we have the good will to be on a pilgrimage in the body, so as to be present to the Lord. [9] And thus we struggle, whether absent or present, to please him. [10] For it is necessary for us to be manifested before the judgment seat of Christ, so that each one may receive the proper things of the body, according to his behavior, whether it was good or evil. [11] Therefore, having knowledge of the fear of the Lord, we appeal to men, but we are made manifest before God. Yet I hope, too, that we may be made manifest in your consciences. [12] We are not commending ourselves again to you, but rather we are presenting you with an opportunity to glory because of us, when you deal with those who glory in face, and not in heart. [13] For if we are excessive in mind, it is for God; but if we are sober, it is for you. [14] For the charity of Christ urges us on, in consideration of this: that if one died for all, then all have died. [15] And Christ died for all, so that even those who live might not now live for themselves, but for him who died for them and who rose again. [16] And so, from now on, we know no one according to the flesh. And though we have known Christ according to the flesh, yet now we know him in this way no longer. [17] So if anyone is a new creature in Christ, what is old has passed away. Behold, all things have been made new. [18] But all is of God, who has reconciled us to himself through Christ, and who has given us the ministry of reconciliation. [19] For certainly God was in Christ, reconciling the world to himself, not charging them with their sins. And he has placed in us the Word of reconciliation. [20] Therefore, we are ambassadors for Christ, so that God is exhorting through us. We beseech you for Christ: be reconciled to God. [21] For God made him who did not know sin to be sin for us, so that we might become the justice of God in him.

2 CORINTHIANS 6

[1] But, as a help to you, we exhort you not to receive the grace of God in vain. [2] For he says: "In a favorable time, I heeded you; and on the day of salvation, I helped you." Behold, now is the favorable time; behold, now is the day of salvation. [3] May we never give offense to anyone, so that our ministry may not be disparaged. [4] But in all things, let us exhibit ourselves as ministers of God with great patience: through tribulation, difficulties, and distress; [5] despite wounds, imprisonment, and rebellion; with hard work, vigilance, and fasting; [6] by chastity, knowledge, and longsuffering; in pleasantness, in the Holy Spirit, and in unfeigned charity; [7] with the Word of truth, with the power of God, and with the armor of justice to the right and to the left; [8] through honor and dishonor, despite good reports and bad, whether seen as deceivers or truth-tellers, whether ignored or acknowledged; [9] as if dying and yet truly alive; as if chastised and yet not subdued; [10] as if sorrowful and yet always rejoicing; as if needy and yet enriching many; as if having nothing and possessing everything. [11] Our mouth is open to you, O Corinthians; our heart is enlarged. [12] You are not narrowed by us, but it is by your own inner selves that you are narrowed. [13] But since we have the same recompense, (I am speaking as if to my own sons), you, too, should be enlarged. [14] Do not choose to bear the yoke

with unbelievers. For how can justice be a participant with iniquity? Or how can the fellowship of light be a participant with darkness? [15] And how can Christ join together with Belial? Or what part do the faithful have with the unfaithful? [16] And what consensus does the temple of God have with idols? For you are the temple of the living God, just as God says: "I will dwell with them, and I will walk among them. And I will be their God, and they shall be my people. [17] Because of this, you must depart from their midst and be separate, says the Lord. And do not touch what is unclean. [18] Then I will accept you. And I will be a Father to you, and you shall be sons and daughters to me, says the Lord Almighty."

2 CORINTHIANS 7

[1] Therefore, having these promises, most beloved, let us cleanse ourselves from all defilement of the flesh and of the spirit, perfecting sanctification in the fear of God. [2] Consider us. We have injured no one; we have corrupted no one; we have defrauded no one. [3] I am not saying this to your condemnation. For we have told you before that you are in our hearts: to die together and to live together. [4] Great is my confidence in you. Great is my glorying over you. I have been filled with consolation. I have a superabundant joy throughout all our tribulation. [5] Then, too, when we had arrived in Macedonia, our flesh had no rest. Instead, we suffered every tribulation: exterior conflicts, interior fears. [6] But God, who consoles the humble, consoled us by the arrival of Titus, [7] and not only by his arrival, but also by the consolation with which he was consoled among you. For he brought to us your desire, your weeping, your zeal for me, so that I rejoiced all the more. [8] For though I made you sorrowful by my epistle, I do not repent. And if I did repent, but only for a time, having realized that the same epistle made you sorrowful, [9] now I am glad: not because you were sorrowful, but because you were sorrowful unto repentance. For you became sorrowful for God, so that you might not suffer any harm from us. [10] For the sorrow that is according to God accomplishes a repentance which is steadfast unto salvation. But the sorrow that is of the world accomplishes death. [11] So consider this same idea, being sorrowful according to God, and what great solicitude it accomplishes in you: including protection, and indignation, and fear, and desire, and zeal, and vindication. In all things, you have shown yourselves to be uncorrupted by this sorrow. [12] And so, though I wrote to you, it was not because of him who caused the injury, nor because of him who suffered from it, but so as to manifest our solicitude, which we have for you before God. [13] Therefore, we have been consoled. But in our consolation, we have rejoiced even more abundantly over the joy of Titus, because his spirit was refreshed by all of you. [14] And if I have gloried in anything to him about you, I have not been put to shame. But, just as we have spoken all things to you in truth, so also our glorying before Titus has been the truth. [15] And his feelings are now more abundant toward you, since he remembers the obedience of you all, and how you received him with fear and trembling. [16] I rejoice that in all things I have confidence in you.

2 CORINTHIANS 8

[1] And so we are making known to you, brothers, the grace of God that has been given in the churches of Macedonia. [2] For within a great experience of tribulation, they have had an abundance of joy, and their profound poverty has only increased the richness of their simplicity. [3] And I bear witness to them, that they were willing to accept what was in accord with their ability, and even what was beyond their ability. [4] For they were begging us, with great exhortation, for the grace and the communication of the ministry that is with the saints. [5] And this is beyond what we had hoped, since they gave themselves, first of all to the Lord, and then also to us, through the will of God, [6] so much so that we petitioned Titus, that in the same manner as he had begun, he would also complete in you this same grace. [7] But, just as in all things you abound in faith and in word and in knowledge and in all solicitude, and even more so in your charity toward us, so also may you abound in this grace. [8] I am speaking, not commanding. But through the solicitude of others, I approve of the good character of your charity. [9] For you know the grace of our Lord Jesus Christ, that though he was rich, he became poor for your sakes, so that through his poverty, you might become rich. [10] And about this, I give my counsel. For this is useful to those of you who, only a year earlier, had just begun to act, or even to be willing to act. [11] So, truly now, accomplish this in deed, so that, in the same manner as your willing mind is prompted, you may also act, out of that which you have. [12] For when the will is

prompted, it receives according to what that person has, not according to what that person does not have. [13] And it is not that others should be relieved, while you are troubled, but that there should be an equality. [14] In this present time, let your abundance supply their need, so that their abundance may also supply your need, in order that there may be an equality, just as it was written: [15] "He with more did not have too much; and he with less did not have too little." [16] But thanks be to God, who has granted to the heart of Titus, this same solicitude for you. [17] For certainly, he accepted the exhortation. But since he was more solicitous, he went to you of his own free will. [18] And we have even sent with him a brother whose praise accompanies the Gospel throughout all the churches. [19] And not only that, but he was also chosen by the churches to be a companion for our sojourn in this grace, which is ministered by us with our determined will, to the glory of the Lord. [20] So let us avoid this, lest anyone disparage us over the abundance that is ministered by us. [21] For we provide for what is good, not only in the sight of God, but also in the sight of men. [22] And we have also sent with them our brother, whom we have proven to be frequently solicitous in many matters. But now there is a greater solicitousness, which is greatly entrusted to you; [23] and whether it concerns Titus, who is a companion to me and a helper to you, or whether it concerns our brothers, the Apostles of the churches, it is to the glory of Christ. [24] Therefore, in the sight of the churches, show them the proof of your charity and of our glorying about you.

2 CORINTHIANS 9

[1] Now, concerning the ministry that is done toward the saints, it is not necessary for me to write to you. [2] For I know your willing mind. I glory about you, concerning this, to the Macedonians. For Achaia has also been prepared, for the past year. And your example has inspired very many others. [3] Now I have sent the brothers, so that what we glory about concerning you might not be empty in this matter, in order that (as I have explained) you may be prepared. [4] Otherwise, if the Macedonians arrive with me and find you unprepared, we (not to mention you) would be ashamed in this matter. [5] Therefore, I considered it necessary to ask the brothers to go to you in advance and to prepare this blessing as promised, and in this way, you may be ready as a blessing, not as an excess. [6] But I say this: Whoever sows sparingly will also reap sparingly. And whoever sows with blessings shall also reap from blessings: [7] each one giving, just as he has determined in his heart, neither out of sadness, nor out of obligation. For God loves a cheerful giver. [8] And God is able to make every grace abound in you, so that, always having what you need in all things, you may abound unto every good work, [9] just as it was written: "He has distributed widely, he has given to the poor; his justice remains from age to age." [10] And he who ministers seed to the sower will offer you bread to eat, and will multiply your seed, and will increase the growth of the fruits of your justice. [11] So then, having been enriched in all things, you may abound in all simplicity, which works thanksgiving to God through us. [12] For the ministration of this office not only supplies whatever the saints need, but also abounds through many thanksgivings in the Lord. [13] And so, through the evidence of this ministry, you glorify God by the obedience of your confession in the Gospel of Christ, and by the simplicity of your communion with them and with everyone, [14] and they offer prayers for you, being solicitous about you, because of the excellent grace of God within you. [15] Thanks be to God for his ineffable gift.

2 CORINTHIANS 10

[1] But I myself, Paul, am begging you, through the meekness and modesty of Christ. I am certainly, by appearances, lowly among you, yet I have confidence in you, even while I am absent. [2] So I am petitioning you, lest I be bold, when present, with that bold confidence that I am considered to have by certain ones who judge us as if we were walking according to the flesh. [3] For though we walk in the flesh, we do not battle according to the flesh. [4] For the weapons of our battles are not carnal, yet still they are powerful with God, unto the destruction of fortifications: tearing down every counsel [5] and height that extols itself contrary to the wisdom of God, and leading every intellect into the captivity of obedience to Christ, [6] and standing ready to repudiate every disobedience, when your own obedience has been fulfilled. [7] Consider the things that are in accord with appearances. If anyone trusts that by these things he belongs to Christ, let him reconsider this within himself. For just as he belongs to Christ, so also do

we. ⁸ And if I were even to glory somewhat more about our authority, which the Lord has given to us for your edification, and not for your destruction, I should not be ashamed. ⁹ But let it not be said that I am scaring you by means of epistles. ¹⁰ For they say: "His epistles, indeed, are weighty and strong. But his bodily presence is weak, and his speech is contemptible." ¹¹ Let someone like this realize that whatever we are in word through epistles, while absent: we are much the same in deed, while present. ¹² For we would not dare to interpose or compare ourselves with certain ones who commend themselves. But we measure ourselves by ourselves, and we compare ourselves with ourselves. ¹³ Thus, we will not glory beyond our measure, but rather according to the measure of the limit which God has measured out to us, a measure which extends even to you. ¹⁴ For we are not overextending ourselves, as if we are not able to reach as far as you are able. For we have gone even as far as you have in the Gospel of Christ. ¹⁵ We are not glorying immeasurably over the labors of others. Instead, we hold on to the hope of your growing faith, so as to be magnified in you, according to our own limits, but in abundance, ¹⁶ and even so as to evangelize in those places that are beyond you, not in order to glory in the measure of others, but rather in those things which have already been prepared. ¹⁷ But whoever glories, let him glory in the Lord. ¹⁸ For it is not he who commends himself who is approved, but rather he whom God commends.

2 CORINTHIANS 11

¹ I wish that you would endure a small amount of my foolishness, so as to bear with me. ² For I am jealous toward you, with the jealousy of God. And I have espoused you to one husband, offering you as a chaste virgin to Christ. ³ But I am afraid lest, as the serpent led astray Eve by his cleverness, so your minds might be corrupted and might fall away from the simplicity which is in Christ. ⁴ For if anyone arrives preaching another Christ, one whom we have not preached; or if you receive another Spirit, one whom you have not received; or another Gospel, one which you have not been given: you might permit him to guide you. ⁵ For I consider that I have done nothing less than the great Apostles. ⁶ For although I may be unskilled in speech, yet I am not so in knowledge. But, in all things, we have been made manifest to you. ⁷ Or did I commit a sin by humbling myself so that you would be exalted? For I preached the Gospel of God to you freely. ⁸ I have taken from other churches, receiving a stipend from them to the benefit of your ministry. ⁹ And when I was with you and in need, I was burdensome to no one. For the brothers who came from Macedonia supplied whatever was lacking to me. And in all things, I have kept myself, and I will keep myself, from being burdensome to you. ¹⁰ The truth of Christ is in me, and so this glorying shall not be broken away from me in the regions of Achaia. ¹¹ Why so? Is it because I do not love you? God knows I do. ¹² But what I am doing, I will continue to do, so that I may take away an opportunity from those who desire an opportunity by which they may glory, so as to be considered to be like us. ¹³ For false apostles, such as these deceitful workers, are presenting themselves as if they were Apostles of Christ. ¹⁴ And no wonder, for even Satan presents himself as if he were an Angel of light. ¹⁵ Therefore, it is no great thing if his ministers present themselves as if they were ministers of justice, for their end shall be according to their works. ¹⁶ I say again. And let no one consider me to be foolish. Or, at least, accept me as if I were foolish, so that I also may glory a small amount. ¹⁷ What I am saying is not said according to God, but as if in foolishness, in this matter of glorying. ¹⁸ Since so many glory according to the flesh, I will glory also. ¹⁹ For you freely accept the foolish, though you yourselves claim to be wise. ²⁰ For you permit it when someone guides you into servitude, even if he devours you, even if he takes from you, even if he is extolled, even if he strikes you repeatedly on the face. ²¹ I speak according to disgrace, as if we had been weak in this regard. In this matter, (I speak in foolishness) if anyone dares, I dare also. ²² They are Hebrews; so am I. They are Israelites; so am I. They are the offspring of Abraham; so am I. ²³ They are the ministers of Christ (I speak as if I were less wise); more so am I: with many more labors, with numerous imprisonments, with wounds beyond measure, with frequent mortifications. ²⁴ On five occasions, I received forty stripes, less one, from the Jews. ²⁵ Three times, I was beaten with rods. One time, I was stoned. Three times, I was shipwrecked. For a night and a day, I was in the depths of the sea. ²⁶ I have made frequent journeys, through dangerous waters, in danger of robbers, in danger from my own nation, in danger from the Gentiles, in danger in the city, in danger in the wilderness, in danger in the sea, in danger from

false brothers, ²⁷ with hardships and difficulties, with much vigilance, in hunger and thirst, with frequent fasts, in cold and nakedness, ²⁸ and, in addition to these things, which are external: there is my daily earnestness and solicitude for all the churches. ²⁹ Who is weak, and I am not weak? Who is scandalized, and I am not being burned? ³⁰ If it is necessary to glory, I will glory of the things that concern my weaknesses. ³¹ The God and Father of our Lord Jesus Christ, who is blessed forever, knows that I am not lying. ³² At Damascus, the governor of the nation under Aretas the king, watched over the city of the Damascenes, so as to apprehend me. ³³ And, through a window, I was let down along the wall in a basket; and so I escaped his hands.

2 CORINTHIANS 12

¹ If it is necessary (though certainly not expedient) to glory, then I will next tell of visions and revelations from the Lord. ² I know a man in Christ, who, more than fourteen years ago (whether in the body, I do not know, or out of the body, I do not know: God knows), was enraptured to the third heaven. ³ And I know a certain man (whether in the body, or out of the body, I do not know: God knows), ⁴ who was enraptured into Paradise. And he heard words of mystery, which it is not permitted for man to speak. ⁵ On behalf of someone like this, I will glory. But on behalf of myself, I will not glory about anything, except my infirmities. ⁶ For even though I am willing to glory, I will not be foolish. But I will speak the truth. Yet I will do so sparingly, lest anyone may consider me to be anything more than what he sees in me, or anything more than what he hears from me. ⁷ And lest the greatness of the revelations should extol me, there was given to me a prodding in my flesh: an angel of Satan, who struck me repeatedly. ⁸ Because of this, three times I petitioned the Lord that it might be taken away from me. ⁹ And he said to me: "My grace is sufficient for you. For virtue is perfected in weakness." And so, willingly shall I glory in my weaknesses, so that the virtue of Christ may live within me. ¹⁰ Because of this, I am pleased in my infirmity: in reproaches, in difficulties, in persecutions, in distresses, for the sake of Christ. For when I am weak, then I am powerful. ¹¹ I have become foolish; you have compelled me. For I ought to have been commended by you. For I have been nothing less than those who claim to be above the measure of Apostles, even though I am nothing. ¹² And the seal of my Apostleship has been set over you, with all patience, with signs and wonders and miracles. ¹³ For what is there that you have had which is less than the other churches, except that I myself did not burden you? Forgive me this injury. ¹⁴ Behold, this is the third time I have prepared to come to you, and yet I will not be a burden to you. For I am seeking not the things that are yours, but you yourselves. And neither should the children store up for the parents, but the parents for the children. ¹⁵ And so, very willingly, I will spend and exhaust myself for the sake of your souls, loving you more, while being loved less. ¹⁶ And so be it. I have not burdened you, but instead, being astute, I obtained you by guile. ¹⁷ And yet, did I defraud you by means of any of those whom I sent to you? ¹⁸ I asked for Titus, and I sent a brother with him. Did Titus defraud you? Did we not walk with the same spirit? Did we not walk in the same steps? ¹⁹ Have you ever thought that we should explain ourselves to you? We speak in the sight of God, in Christ. But all things, most beloved, are for your edification. ²⁰ Yet I fear, lest perhaps, when I have arrived, I might not find you such as I would want, and I might be found by you, such as you would not want. For perhaps there may be among you: contention, envy, animosity, dissension, detraction, whispering, self-exaltation, and rebellion. ²¹ If so, then, when I have arrived, God may again humble me among you. And so, I mourn for the many who sinned beforehand, and did not repent, over the lust and fornication and homosexuality, which they have committed.

2 CORINTHIANS 13

¹ Behold, this is the third time that I am coming to you. By the mouth of two or three witnesses, every word shall stand. ² I have preached when present, and I will preach now while absent, to those who sinned before, and to all the others, because, when I arrive again, I will not be lenient with you. ³ Do you seek evidence that it is Christ who speaks in me, who is not weak with you, but is powerful with you? ⁴ For although he was crucified in weakness, yet he lives by the power of God. And yes, we are weak in him. But we shall live with him by the power of God among you. ⁵ Test yourselves as to whether you are in the faith. Examine yourselves. Or do you yourselves not know whether Christ Jesus is in you? But perhaps you are reprobates. ⁶ But I hope you know that we ourselves are not reprobates. ⁷ Now we pray to God that you shall do nothing evil, not so that we may seem to be approved, but so that you may do what is good, even if we seem like reprobates. ⁸ For we cannot do anything against the truth, but only for the truth. ⁹ For we rejoice that we are weak, while you are strong. This is also what we pray for: your perfection. ¹⁰ Therefore, I write these things while absent, so that, when present, I may not have to act more harshly, according to the authority which the Lord has given to me, for edification and not for destruction. ¹¹ As to the rest, brothers, rejoice, be perfect, be encouraged, have the same mind, have peace. And so the God of peace and love will be with you. ¹² Greet one another with a holy kiss. All the saints greet you. ¹³ The grace of our Lord Jesus Christ, and the charity of God, and the communion of the Holy Spirit be with you all. Amen.

Galatians

THE SACRED BIBLE:
THE LETTER TO THE GALATIANS

CHAPTER 1

[1] Paul, an Apostle, not from men and not through man, but through Jesus Christ, and God the Father, who raised him from the dead, [2] and all the brothers who are with me: to the churches of Galatia. [3] Grace and peace to you from God the Father, and from our Lord Jesus Christ, [4] who gave himself on behalf of our sins, so that he might deliver us from this present wicked age, according to the will of God our Father. [5] To him is glory forever and ever. Amen. [6] I wonder that you have been so quickly transferred, from him who called you into the grace of Christ, over to another gospel. [7] For there is no other, except that there are some persons who disturb you and who want to overturn the Gospel of Christ. [8] But if anyone, even we ourselves or an Angel from Heaven, were to preach to you a gospel other than the one that we have preached to you, let him be anathema. [9] Just as we have said before, so now I say again: If anyone has preached a gospel to you, other than that which you have received, let him be anathema. [10] For am I now persuading men, or God? Or, am I seeking to please men? If I still were pleasing men, then I would not be a servant of Christ. [11] For I would have you understand, brothers, that the Gospel which has been preached by me is not according to man. [12] And I did not receive it from man, nor did I learn it, except through the revelation of Jesus Christ. [13] For you have heard of my former behavior within Judaism: that, beyond measure, I persecuted the Church of God and fought against Her. [14] And I advanced in Judaism beyond many of my equals among my own kind, having proven to be more abundant in zeal toward the traditions of my fathers. [15] But, when it pleased him who, from my mother's womb, had set me apart, and who has called me by his grace, [16] to reveal his Son within me, so that I might evangelize him among the Gentiles, I did not next seek the consent of flesh and blood. [17] Neither did I go to Jerusalem, to those who were Apostles before me. Instead, I went into Arabia, and next I returned to Damascus. [18] And then, after three years, I went to Jerusalem to see Peter; and I stayed with him for fifteen days. [19] But I saw none of the other Apostles, except James, the brother of the Lord. [20] Now what I am writing to you: behold, before God, I am not lying. [21] Next, I went into the regions of Syria and Cilicia. [22] But I was unknown by face to the churches of Judea, which were in Christ. [23] For they had only heard that: "He, who formerly persecuted us, now evangelizes the faith which he once fought." [24] And they glorified God in me.

CHAPTER 2

[1] Next, after fourteen years, I went up again to Jerusalem, taking with me Barnabas and Titus. [2] And I went up according to revelation, and I debated with them about the Gospel that I am preaching among the Gentiles, but away from those who were pretending to be something, lest perhaps I might run, or have run, in vain. [3] But even Titus, who was with me, though he was a Gentile, was not compelled to be circumcised, [4] but only because of false brothers, who were brought in unknowingly. They entered secretly to spy on our liberty, which we have in Christ Jesus, so that they might reduce us to servitude. [5] We did not yield to them in subjection, even for an hour, in order that the truth of the Gospel would remain with you, [6] and away from those who were pretending to be something. (Whatever they might have been once, it means nothing to me. God does not accept the reputation of a man.) And those who were claiming to be something had nothing to offer me. [7] But it was to the contrary, since they had seen that the Gospel to the uncircumcised was entrusted to me, just as the Gospel to the circumcised was entrusted to Peter. [8] For he who was working the Apostleship to the circumcised in Peter, was also working in me among the Gentiles. [9] And so, when they had acknowledged the grace that was given to me, James and Cephas and John, who seemed like pillars, gave to me and to Barnabas the right hand of fellowship, so that we would go to the Gentiles, while they went to the circumcised, [10] asking only that we should be mindful of the poor, which was the very thing that I also was solicitous to do. [11] But when Cephas had arrived at Antioch, I stood against him to his face, because he was blameworthy. [12] For before certain ones arrived from James, he ate with the Gentiles. But when

they had arrived, he drew apart and separated himself, fearing those who were of the circumcision. ¹³And the other Jews consented to his pretense, so that even Barnabas was led by them into that falseness. ¹⁴But when I had seen that they were not walking correctly, by the truth of the Gospel, I said to Cephas in front of everyone: "If you, while you are a Jew, are living like the Gentiles and not the Jews, how is it that you compel the Gentiles to keep the customs of the Jews?" ¹⁵By nature, we are Jews, and not of the Gentiles, sinners. ¹⁶And we know that man is not justified by the works of the law, but only by the faith of Jesus Christ. And so we believe in Christ Jesus, in order that we may be justified by the faith of Christ, and not by the works of the law. For no flesh will be justified by the works of the law. ¹⁷But if, while seeking to be justified in Christ, we ourselves are also found to be sinners, would then Christ be the minister of sin? Let it not be so! ¹⁸For if I rebuild the things that I have destroyed, I establish myself as a prevaricator. ¹⁹For through the law, I have become dead to the law, so that I may live for God. I have been nailed to the cross with Christ. ²⁰I live; yet now, it is not I, but truly Christ, who lives in me. And though I live now in the flesh, I live in the faith of the Son of God, who loved me and who delivered himself for me. ²¹I do not reject the grace of God. For if justice is through the law, then Christ died in vain.

CHAPTER 3

¹O senseless Galatians, who has so fascinated you that you would not obey the truth, even though Jesus Christ has been presented before your eyes, crucified among you? ²I wish to know only this from you: Did you receive the Spirit by the works of the law, or by the hearing of faith? ³Are you so foolish that, though you began with the Spirit, you would now end with the flesh? ⁴Have you been suffering so much without a reason? If so, then it is in vain. ⁵Therefore, does he who distributes the Spirit to you, and who works miracles among you, act by the works of the law, or by the hearing of the faith? ⁶It is just as it was written: "Abraham believed God, and it was reputed to him unto justice." ⁷Therefore, know that those who are of faith, these are the sons of Abraham. ⁸Thus Scripture, foreseeing that God would justify the Gentiles by faith, foretold to Abraham: "All nations shall be blessed in you." ⁹And so, those who are of faith shall be blessed with faithful Abraham. ¹⁰For as many as are of the works of the law are under a curse. For it has been written: "Cursed is everyone who does not continue in all the things that have been written in the book of the Law, so as to do them." ¹¹And, since in the law no one is justified with God, this is manifest: "For the just man lives by faith." ¹²But the law is not of faith; instead, "he who does these things shall live by them." ¹³Christ has redeemed us from the curse of the law, since he became a curse for us. For it is written: "Cursed is anyone who hangs from a tree." ¹⁴This was so that the blessing of Abraham might reach the Gentiles through Christ Jesus, in order that we might receive the promise of the Spirit through faith. ¹⁵Brothers (I speak according to man), if a man's testament has been confirmed, no one would reject it or add to it. ¹⁶The promises were made to Abraham and to his offspring. He did not say, "and to descendents," as if to many, but instead, as if to one, he said, "and to your offspring," who is Christ. ¹⁷But I say this: the testament confirmed by God, which, after four hundred and thirty years became the Law, does not nullify, so as to make the promise empty. ¹⁸For if the inheritance is of the law, then it is no longer of the promise. But God bestowed it to Abraham through the promise. ¹⁹Why, then, was there a law? It was established because of transgressions, until the offspring would arrive, to whom he made the promise, ordained by Angels through the hand of a mediator. ²⁰Now a mediator is not of one, yet God is one. ²¹So then, was the law contrary to the promises of God? Let it not be so! For if a law had been given, which was able to give life, truly justice would be of the law. ²²But Scripture has enclosed everything under sin, so that the promise, by the faith of Jesus Christ, might be given to those who believe. ²³But before the faith arrived, we were preserved by being enclosed under the law, unto that faith which was to be revealed. ²⁴And so the law was our guardian in Christ, in order that we might be justified by faith. ²⁵But now that faith has arrived, we are no longer under a guardian. ²⁶For you are all sons of God, through the faith which is in Christ Jesus. ²⁷For as many of you as have been baptized in Christ have become clothed with Christ. ²⁸There is neither Jew nor Greek; there is neither servant nor free; there is neither male nor female. For you are all one in Christ Jesus. ²⁹And if you are Christ's, then are you the offspring of Abraham, heirs according to the promise.

CHAPTER 4

[1] But I say that, during the time an heir is a child, he is no different from a servant, even though he is the owner of everything. [2] For he is under tutors and caretakers, until the time which was predetermined by the father. [3] So also we, when we were children, were subservient to the influences of the world. [4] But when the fullness of time arrived, God sent his Son, formed from a woman, formed under the law, [5] so that he might redeem those who were under the law, in order that we might receive the adoption of sons. [6] Therefore, because you are sons, God has sent the Spirit of his Son into your hearts, crying out: "Abba, Father." [7] And so now he is not a servant, but a son. But if he is a son, then he is also an heir, through God. [8] But then, certainly, while ignorant of God, you served those who, by nature, are not gods. [9] But now, since you have known God, or rather, since you have been known by God: how can you turn away again, to weak and destitute influences, which you desire to serve anew? [10] You serve the days, and months, and times, and years. [11] I am afraid for you, lest perhaps I may have labored in vain among you. [12] Brothers, I beg you. Be as I am. For I, too, am like you. You have not injured me at all. [13] But you know that, in the weakness of the flesh, I have preached the Gospel to you for a long time, and that your trials are in my flesh. [14] You did not despise or reject me. But instead, you accepted me like an Angel of God, even like Christ Jesus. [15] Therefore, where is your happiness? For I offer to you testimony that, if it could be done, you would have plucked out your own eyes and would have given them to me. [16] So then, have I become your enemy by telling you the truth? [17] They are not imitating you well. And they are willing to exclude you, so that you might imitate them. [18] But be imitators of what is good, always in a good way, and not only when I am present with you. [19] My little sons, I am giving birth to you again, until Christ is formed in you. [20] And I would willingly be present with you, even now. But I would alter my voice: for I am ashamed of you. [21] Tell me, you who desire to be under the law, have you not read the law? [22] For it is written that Abraham had two sons: one by a servant woman, and one by a free woman. [23] And he who was of the servant was born according to the flesh. But he who was of the free woman was born by the promise. [24] These things are said through an allegory. For these represent the two testaments. Certainly the one, on Mount Sinai, gives birth unto servitude, which is Hagar. [25] For Sinai is a mountain in Arabia, which is related to the Jerusalem of the present time, and it serves with her sons. [26] But that Jerusalem which is above is free; the same is our mother. [27] For it was written: "Rejoice, O barren one, though you do not conceive. Burst forth and cry out, though you do not give birth. For many are the children of the desolate, even more than of her who has a husband." [28] Now we, brothers, like Isaac, are sons of the promise. [29] But just as then, he who was born according to the flesh persecuted him who was born according to the Spirit, so also it is now. [30] And what does Scripture say? "Cast out the woman servant and her son. For the son of a servant women shall not be an heir with the son of a free woman." [31] And so, brothers, we are not the sons of the servant woman, but rather of the free woman. And this is the freedom with which Christ has set us free.

CHAPTER 5

[1] Stand firm, and do not be willing to be again held by the yoke of servitude. [2] Behold, I, Paul, say to you, that if you have been circumcised, Christ will be of no benefit to you. [3] For I again testify, about every man circumcising himself, that he is obligated to act according to the entire law. [4] You are being emptied of Christ, you who are being justified by the law. You have fallen from grace. [5] For in spirit, by faith, we await the hope of justice. [6] For in Christ Jesus, neither circumcision nor uncircumcision prevails over anything, but only faith which works through charity. [7] You have run well. So what has impeded you, that you would not obey the truth? [8] This kind of influence is not from him who is calling you. [9] A little leaven corrupts the whole mass. [10] I have confidence in you, in the Lord, that you will accept nothing of the kind. However, he who disturbs you shall bear the judgment, whomever he may be. [11] And as for me, brothers, if I still preach circumcision, why am I still suffering persecution? For then the scandal of the Cross would be made empty. [12] And I wish that those who disturb you would be torn away. [13] For you, brothers, have been called to liberty. Only you must not make liberty into an occasion for the flesh, but instead, serve one another through the charity of the Spirit. [14] For the entire law is fulfilled by one word: "You shall love your neighbor as yourself." [15] But if you bite and devour one another, be careful that you are not consumed by one another! [16] So then, I say: Walk in

the spirit, and you will not fulfill the desires of the flesh. ¹⁷ For the flesh desires against the spirit, and the spirit against the flesh. And since these are against one another, you may not do whatever you want. ¹⁸ But if you are led by the Spirit, you are not under the law. ¹⁹ Now the works of the flesh are manifest; they are: fornication, lust, homosexuality, self-indulgence, ²⁰ the serving of idols, drug use, hostility, contentiousness, jealousy, wrath, quarrels, dissensions, divisions, ²¹ envy, murder, inebriation, carousing, and similar things. About these things, I continue to preach to you, as I have preached to you: that those who act in this way shall not obtain the kingdom of God. ²² But the fruit of the Spirit is charity, joy, peace, patience, kindness, goodness, forbearance, ²³ meekness, faith, modesty, abstinence, chastity. There is no law against such things. ²⁴ For those who are Christ's have crucified their flesh, along with its vices and desires. ²⁵ If we live by the Spirit, we should also walk by the Spirit. ²⁶ Let us not become desirous of empty glory, provoking one another, envying one another.

CHAPTER 6

¹ And, brothers, if a man has been overtaken by any offense, you who are spiritual should instruct someone like this with a spirit of leniency, considering that you yourselves might also be tempted. ² Carry one another's burdens, and so shall you fulfill the law of Christ. ³ For if anyone considers himself to be something, though he may be nothing, he deceives himself. ⁴ So let each one prove his own work. And in this way, he shall have glory in himself only, and not in another. ⁵ For each one shall carry his own burden. ⁶ And let him who is being taught the Word discuss it with him who is teaching it to him, in every good way. ⁷ Do not choose to wander astray. God is not to be ridiculed. ⁸ For whatever a man will have sown, that also shall he reap. For whoever sows in his flesh, from the flesh he shall also reap corruption. But whoever sows in the Spirit, from the Spirit he shall reap eternal life. ⁹ And so, let us not be deficient in doing good. For in due time, we shall reap without fail. ¹⁰ Therefore, while we have time, we should do good works toward everyone, and most of all toward those who are of the household of the faith. ¹¹ Consider what kind of letters I have written to you with my own hand. ¹² For as many of you as they desire to please in the flesh, they compel to be circumcised, but only so that they might not suffer the persecution of the cross of Christ. ¹³ And yet, neither do they themselves, who are circumcised, keep the law. Instead, they want you to be circumcised, so that they may glory in your flesh. ¹⁴ But far be it from me to glory, except in the cross of our Lord Jesus Christ, through whom the world is crucified to me, and I to the world. ¹⁵ For in Christ Jesus, neither circumcision nor uncircumcision prevails in any way, but instead there is a new creature. ¹⁶ And whoever follows this rule: may peace and mercy be upon them, and upon the Israel of God. ¹⁷ Concerning other matters, let no one trouble me. For I carry the stigmata of the Lord Jesus in my body. ¹⁸ May the grace of our Lord Jesus Christ be with your spirit, brothers. Amen.

THE SACRED BIBLE:
THE LETTER TO THE EPHESIANS

CHAPTER 1

¹ Paul, an Apostle of Jesus Christ through the will of God, to all the saints who are at Ephesus and to the faithful in Christ Jesus. ² Grace and peace to you from God the Father, and from the Lord Jesus Christ. ³ Blessed be the God and Father of our Lord Jesus Christ, who has blessed us with every spiritual blessing in the heavens, in Christ, ⁴ just as he chose us in him before the foundation of the world, so that we would be holy and immaculate in his sight, in charity. ⁵ He has predestined us to adoption as sons, through Jesus Christ, in himself, according to the purpose of his will, ⁶ for the praise of the glory of his grace, with which he has gifted us in his beloved Son. ⁷ In him, we have redemption through his blood: the remission of sins in accord with the riches of his grace, ⁸ which is superabundant in us, with all wisdom and prudence. ⁹ So does he make known to us the mystery of his will, which he has set forth in Christ, in a manner well-pleasing to him, ¹⁰ in the dispensation of the fullness of time, so as to renew in Christ everything that exists through him in heaven and on earth. ¹¹ In him, we too are called to our portion, having been predestined in accord with the plan of the One who accomplishes all things by the counsel of his will. ¹² So may we be, to the praise of his glory, we who have hoped beforehand in Christ. ¹³ In him, you also, after you heard and believed the Word of truth, which is the Gospel of your salvation, were sealed with the Holy Spirit of the Promise. ¹⁴ He is the pledge of our inheritance, unto the acquisition of redemption, to the praise of his glory. ¹⁵ Because of this, and hearing of your faith that is in the Lord Jesus, and of your love toward all the saints, ¹⁶ I have not ceased giving thanks for you, calling you to mind in my prayers, ¹⁷ so that the God of our Lord Jesus Christ, the Father of glory, may give a spirit of wisdom and of revelation to you, in knowledge of him. ¹⁸ May the eyes of your heart be illuminated, so that you may know what is the hope of his calling, and the wealth of the glory of his inheritance with the saints, ¹⁹ and the preeminent magnitude of his virtue toward us, toward we who believe in accord with the work of his powerful virtue, ²⁰ which he wrought in Christ, raising him from the dead and establishing him at his right hand in the heavens, ²¹ above every principality and power and virtue and dominion, and above every name that is given, not only in this age, but even in the future age. ²² And he has subjected all things under his feet, and he has made him the head over the entire Church, ²³ which is his body and which is the fullness of him who accomplishes everything in everyone.

CHAPTER 2

¹ And you were once dead in your sins and offenses, ² in which you walked in times past, according to the age of this world, according to the prince of the power of this sky, the spirit who now works in the sons of distrust. ³ And we too were all conversant in these things, in times past, by the desires of our flesh, acting according to the will of the flesh and according to our own thoughts. And so we were, by nature, sons of wrath, even like the others. ⁴ Yet still, God, who is rich in mercy, for the sake of his exceedingly great charity with which he loved us, ⁵ even when we were dead in our sins, has enlivened us together in Christ, by whose grace you have been saved. ⁶ And he has raised us up together, and he has caused us to sit down together in the heavens, in Christ Jesus, ⁷ so that he may display, in the ages soon to arrive, the abundant wealth of his grace, by his goodness toward us in Christ Jesus. ⁸ For by grace, you have been saved through faith. And this is not of yourselves, for it is a gift of God. ⁹ And this is not of works, so that no one may glory. ¹⁰ For we are his handiwork, created in Christ Jesus for the good works which God has prepared and in which we should walk. ¹¹ Because of this, be mindful that, in times past, you were Gentiles in the flesh, and that you were called uncircumcised by those who are called circumcised in the flesh, something done by man, ¹² and that you were, in that time, without Christ, being foreign to the way of life of Israel, being visitors to the testament, having no hope of the promise, and being without God in this world. ¹³ But now, in Christ Jesus, you, who were in times past far away, have been brought near by the blood of Christ. ¹⁴ For he is our peace. He made the two into one, by dissolving the

intermediate wall of separation, of opposition, by his flesh, [15] emptying the law of commandments by decree, so that he might join these two, in himself, into one new man, making peace [16] and reconciling both to God, in one body, through the cross, destroying this opposition in himself. [17] And upon arriving, he evangelized peace to you who were far away, and peace to those who were near. [18] For by him, we both have access, in the one Spirit, to the Father. [19] Now, therefore, you are no longer visitors and new arrivals. Instead, you are citizens among the saints in the household of God, [20] having been built upon the foundation of the Apostles and of the Prophets, with Jesus Christ himself as the preeminent cornerstone. [21] In him, all that has been built is framed together, rising up into a holy temple in the Lord. [22] In him, you also have been built together into a habitation of God in the Spirit.

CHAPTER 3

[1] By reason of this grace, I, Paul, am a prisoner of Jesus Christ, for the sake of you Gentiles. [2] Now certainly, you have heard of the dispensation of the grace of God, which has been given to me among you: [3] that, by means of revelation, the mystery was made known to me, just as I have written above in a few words. [4] Yet, by reading this closely, you might be able to understand my prudence in the mystery of Christ. [5] In other generations, this was unknown to the sons of men, even as it has now been revealed to his holy Apostles and Prophets in the Spirit, [6] so that the Gentiles would be co-heirs, and of the same body, and partners together, by his promise in Christ Jesus, through the Gospel. [7] Of this Gospel, I have been made a minister, according to the gift of the grace of God, which has been given to me by means of the operation of his virtue. [8] Although I am the least of all the saints, I have been given this grace: to evangelize among the Gentiles the unsearchable riches of Christ, [9] and to enlighten everyone concerning the dispensation of the mystery, hidden before the ages in God who created all things, [10] so that the manifold wisdom of God may become well-known to the principalities and powers in the heavens, through the Church, [11] according to that timeless purpose, which he has formed in Christ Jesus our Lord. [12] In him we trust, and so we approach with confidence, through his faith. [13] Because of this, I ask you not to be weakened by my tribulations on your behalf; for this is your glory. [14] By reason of this grace, I bend my knees to the Father of our Lord Jesus Christ, [15] from whom all paternity in heaven and on earth takes its name. [16] And I ask him to grant to you to be strengthened in virtue by his Spirit, in accord with the wealth of his glory, in the inner man, [17] so that Christ may live in your hearts through a faith rooted in, and founded on, charity. [18] So may you be able to embrace, with all the saints, what is the width and length and height and depth [19] of the charity of Christ, and even be able to know that which surpasses all knowledge, so that you may be filled with all the fullness of God. [20] Now to him who is able to do all things, more abundantly than we could ever ask or understand, by means of the virtue which is at work in us: [21] to him be glory, in the Church and in Christ Jesus, throughout every generation, forever and ever. Amen.

CHAPTER 4

[1] And so, as a prisoner in the Lord, I beg you to walk in a manner worthy of the vocation to which you have been called: [2] with all humility and meekness, with patience, supporting one another in charity. [3] Be anxious to preserve the unity of the Spirit within the bonds of peace. [4] One body and one Spirit: to this you have been called by the one hope of your calling: [5] one Lord, one faith, one baptism, [6] one God and Father of all, who is over all, and through all, and in us all. [7] Yet to each one of us there has been given grace according to the measure allotted by Christ. [8] Because of this, he says: "Ascending on high, he took captivity itself captive; he gave gifts to men." [9] Now that he has ascended, what is left except for him also to descend, first to the lower parts of the earth? [10] He who descended is the same one who also ascended above all the heavens, so that he might fulfill everything. [11] And the same one granted that some would be Apostles, and some Prophets, yet truly others evangelists, and others pastors and teachers, [12] for the sake of the perfection of the saints, by the work of the ministry, in the edification of the body of Christ, [13] until we all meet in the unity of faith and in the knowledge of the Son of God, as a perfect man, in the measure of the age of the fullness of Christ. [14] So may we then no longer be little children, disturbed

and carried about by every wind of doctrine, by the wickedness of men, and by the craftiness which deceives unto error. [15]Instead, acting according to truth in charity, we should increase in everything, in him who is the head, Christ himself. [16]For in him, the whole body is joined closely together, by every underlying joint, through the function allotted to each part, bringing improvement to the body, toward its edification in charity. [17]And so, I say this, and I testify in the Lord: that from now on you should walk, not as the Gentiles also walk, in the vanity of their mind, [18]having their intellect obscured, being alienated from the life of God, through the ignorance that is within them, because of the blindness of their hearts. [19]Such as these, despairing, have given themselves over to sexual immorality, carrying out every impurity with rapacity. [20]But this is not what you have learned in Christ. [21]For certainly, you have listened to him, and you have been instructed in him, according to the truth that is in Jesus: [22]to set aside your earlier behavior, the former man, who was corrupted, by means of desire, unto error, [23]and so be renewed in the spirit of your mind, [24]and so put on the new man, who, in accord with God, is created in justice and in the holiness of truth. [25]Because of this, setting aside lying, speak the truth, each one with his neighbor. For we are all part of one another. [26]"Be angry, but do not be willing to sin." Do not let the sun set over your anger. [27]Provide no place for the devil. [28]Whoever was stealing, let him now not steal, but rather let him labor, working with his hands, doing what is good, so that he may have something to distribute to those who suffer need. [29]Let no evil words proceed from your mouth, but only what is good, toward the edification of faith, so as to bestow grace upon those who listen. [30]And do not be willing to grieve the Holy Spirit of God, in whom you have been sealed, unto the day of redemption. [31]Let all bitterness and anger and indignation and outcry and blasphemy be taken away from you, along with all malice. [32]And be kind and merciful to one another, forgiving one another, just as God has forgiven you in Christ.

CHAPTER 5

[1]Therefore, as most beloved sons, be imitators of God. [2]And walk in love, just as Christ also loved us and delivered himself for us, as an oblation and a sacrifice to God, with a fragrance of sweetness. [3]But let not any kind of fornication, or impurity, or rapacity so much as be named among you, just as is worthy of the saints, [4]nor any indecent, or foolish, or abusive talk, for this is without purpose; but instead, give thanks. [5]For know and understand this: no one who is a fornicator, or lustful, or rapacious (for these are a kind of service to idols) holds an inheritance in the kingdom of Christ and of God. [6]Let no one seduce you with empty words. For because of these things, the wrath of God was sent upon the sons of unbelief. [7]Therefore, do not choose to become participants with them. [8]For you were darkness, in times past, but now you are light, in the Lord. So then, walk as sons of the light. [9]For the fruit of the light is in all goodness and justice and truth, [10]affirming what is well-pleasing to God. [11]And so, have no fellowship with the unfruitful works of darkness, but instead, refute them. [12]For the things that are done by them in secret are shameful, even to mention. [13]But all things that are disputed are made manifest by the light. For all that is made manifest is light. [14]Because of this, it is said: "You who are sleeping: awaken, and rise up from the dead, and so shall the Christ enlighten you." [15]And so, brothers, see to it that you walk cautiously, not like the foolish, [16]but like the wise: atoning for this age, because this is an evil time. [17]For this reason, do not choose to be imprudent. Instead, understand what is the will of God. [18]And do not choose to be inebriated by wine, for this is self-indulgence. Instead, be filled with the Holy Spirit, [19]speaking among yourselves in psalms and hymns and spiritual canticles, singing and reciting psalms to the Lord in your hearts, [20]giving thanks always for everything, in the name of our Lord Jesus Christ, to God the Father. [21]Be subject to one another in the fear of Christ. [22]Wives should be submissive to their husbands, as to the Lord. [23]For the husband is the head of the wife, just as Christ is the head of the Church. He is the Savior of his body. [24]Therefore, just as the Church is subject to Christ, so also should wives be subject to their husbands in all things. [25]Husbands, love your wives, just as Christ also loved the Church and handed himself over for her, [26]so that he might sanctify her, washing her clean by water and the Word of life, [27]so that he might offer her to himself as a glorious Church, not having any spot or wrinkle or any such thing, so that she would be holy and immaculate. [28]So, too, husbands should love their wives as their own bodies. He who loves his wife loves himself. [29]For no man has ever

hated his own flesh, but instead he nourishes and cherishes it, as Christ also does to the Church. [30] For we are a part of his body, of his flesh and of his bones. [31] "For this reason, a man shall leave behind his father and mother, and he shall cling to his wife; and the two shall be as one flesh." [32] This is a great Sacrament. And I am speaking in Christ and in the Church. [33] Yet truly, each and every one of you should love his wife as himself. And a wife should fear her husband.

CHAPTER 6

[1] Children, obey your parents in the Lord, for this is just. [2] Honor your father and your mother. This is the first commandment with a promise: [3] so that it may be well with you, and so that you may have a long life upon the earth. [4] And you, fathers, do not provoke your children to anger, but educate them with the discipline and correction of the Lord. [5] Servants, be obedient to your lords according to the flesh, with fear and trembling, in the simplicity of your heart, as to Christ. [6] Do not serve only when seen, as if to please men, but act as servants of Christ, doing the will of God from the heart. [7] Serve with good will, as to the Lord, and not to men. [8] For you know that whatever good each one will do, the same will he receive from the Lord, whether he is servant or free. [9] And you, lords, act similarly toward them, setting aside threats, knowing that the Lord of both you and them is in heaven. For with him there is no favoritism toward anyone. [10] Concerning the rest, brothers, be strengthened in the Lord, by the power of his virtue. [11] Be clothed in the armor of God, so that you may be able to stand against the treachery of the devil. [12] For our struggle is not against flesh and blood, but against principalities and powers, against the directors of this world of darkness, against the spirits of wickedness in high places. [13] Because of this, take up the armor of God, so that you may be able to withstand the evil day and remain perfect in all things. [14] Therefore, stand firm, having been girded about your waist with truth, and having been clothed with the breastplate of justice, [15] and having feet which have been shod by the preparation of the Gospel of peace. [16] In all things, take up the shield of faith, with which you may be able to extinguish all the fiery darts of the most wicked one. [17] And take up the helmet of salvation and the sword of the Spirit (which is the Word of God). [18] Through every kind of prayer and supplication, pray at all times in spirit, and so be vigilant with every kind of earnest supplication, for all the saints, [19] and also for me, so that words may be given to me, as I open my mouth with faith to make known the mystery of the Gospel, [20] in such a manner that I may dare to speak exactly as I ought to speak. For I act as an ambassador in chains for the Gospel. [21] Now, so that you also may know the things that concern me and what I am doing, Tychicus, a most beloved brother and a faithful minister in the Lord, will make known everything to you. [22] I have sent him to you for this very reason, so that you may know the things that concern us, and so that he may console your hearts. [23] Peace to the brothers, and charity with faith, from God the Father and the Lord Jesus Christ. [24] May grace be with all those who love our Lord Jesus Christ, unto incorruption. Amen.

Philippians

THE SACRED BIBLE:
THE LETTER TO THE PHILIPPIANS

CHAPTER 1

[1] Paul and Timothy, servants of Jesus Christ, to all the saints in Christ Jesus who are at Philippi, with the bishops and deacons. [2] Grace and peace to you, from God our Father and from the Lord Jesus Christ. [3] I give thanks to my God, with every remembrance of you, [4] always, in all my prayers, making supplication for all of you with joy, [5] because of your communion in the Gospel of Christ, from the first day even until now. [6] I am confident of this very thing: that he who has begun this good work in you will perfect it, unto the day of Christ Jesus. [7] So then, it is right for me to feel this way about all of you, because I hold you in my heart, and because, in my chains and in the defense and confirmation of the Gospel, you all are partakers of my joy. [8] For God is my witness how, within the heart of Jesus Christ, I long for all of you. [9] And this I pray: that your charity may abound more and more, with knowledge and with all understanding, [10] so that you may be confirmed in what is better, in order that you may be sincere and without offense on the day of Christ: [11] filled with the fruit of justice, through Jesus Christ, in the glory and praise of God. [12] Now, brothers, I want you to know that the things concerning me happened for the advancement of the Gospel, [13] in such a way that my chains have become manifest in Christ in every place of judgment and in all other such places. [14] And many from among the brothers in the Lord, becoming confident through my chains, are now much bolder in speaking the Word of God without fear. [15] Certainly, some do so even because of envy and contention; and others, too, do so because of a good will to preach Christ. [16] Some act out of charity, knowing that I have been appointed for the defense of the Gospel. [17] But others, out of contention, announce Christ insincerely, claiming that their difficulties lift them up to my chains. [18] But what does it matter? As long as, by every means, whether under pretext or in truthfulness, Christ is announced. And about this, I rejoice, and moreover, I will continue to rejoice. [19] For I know that this will bring me to salvation, through your prayers and under the ministration of the Spirit of Jesus Christ, [20] by means of my own expectation and hope. For in nothing shall I be confounded. Instead, with all confidence, now just as always, Christ shall be magnified in my body, whether by life or by death. [21] For to me, to live is Christ, and to die is gain. [22] And while I live in the flesh, for me, there is the fruit of works. But I do not know which I would choose. [23] For I am constrained between the two: having a desire to be dissolved and to be with Christ, which is the far better thing, [24] but then to remain in the flesh is necessary for your sake. [25] And having this confidence, I know that I shall remain and that I shall continue to remain with all of you, for your advancement and for your joy in the faith, [26] so that your rejoicing may abound in Christ Jesus for me, through my return to you again. [27] Only let your behavior be worthy of the Gospel of Christ, so that, whether I return and see you, or whether, being absent, I hear about you, still you may stand firm with one spirit, with one mind, laboring together for the faith of the Gospel. [28] And in nothing be terrified by the adversaries. For what is to them an occasion of perdition, is to you an occasion of salvation, and this is from God. [29] For this has been given to you on behalf of Christ, not only so that you may believe in him, but even so that you may suffer with him, [30] engaging in the same struggle, of a kind which you also have seen in me, and which you now have heard from me.

CHAPTER 2

[1] Therefore, if there is any consolation in Christ, any solace of charity, any fellowship of the Spirit, any feelings of commiseration: [2] complete my joy by having the same understanding, holding to the same charity, being of one mind, with the same sentiment. [3] Let nothing be done by contention, nor in vain glory. Instead, in humility, let each of you esteem others to be better than himself. [4] Let each of you not consider anything to be your own, but rather to belong to others. [5] For this understanding in you was also in Christ Jesus: [6] who, though he was in the form of God, did not consider equality with God something to be seized. [7] Instead, he emptied himself, taking the form of a servant, being made in the likeness of men, and accepting the state of a man. [8] He humbled himself,

becoming obedient even unto death, even the death of the Cross. [9] Because of this, God has also exalted him and has given him a name which is above every name, [10] so that, at the name of Jesus, every knee would bend, of those in heaven, of those on earth, and of those in hell, [11] and so that every tongue would confess that the Lord Jesus Christ is in the glory of God the Father. [12] And so, my most beloved, just as you have always obeyed, not only in my presence, but even more so now in my absence: work toward your salvation with fear and trembling. [13] For it is God who works in you, both so as to choose, and so as to act, in accord with his good will. [14] And do everything without murmuring or hesitation. [15] So may you be without blame, simple sons of God, without reproof, in the midst of a depraved and perverse nation, among whom you shine like lights in the world, [16] holding to the Word of Life, until my glory in the day of Christ. For I have not run in vain, nor have I labored in vain. [17] Moreover, if I am to be immolated because of the sacrifice and service of your faith, I rejoice and give thanks with all of you. [18] And over this same thing, you also should rejoice and give thanks, together with me. [19] Now I hope in the Lord Jesus to send Timothy to you soon, in order that I may be encouraged, when I know the things concerning you. [20] For I have no one else with such an agreeable mind, who, with sincere affection, is solicitous for you. [21] For they all seek the things that are of themselves, not the things that are of Jesus Christ. [22] So know this evidence of him: that like a son with a father, so has he served with me in the Gospel. [23] Therefore, I hope to send him to you immediately, as soon as I see what will happen concerning me. [24] But I trust in the Lord that I myself will also return to you soon. [25] Now I have considered it necessary to send to you Epaphroditus, my brother, and co-worker, and fellow soldier, and an attendant to my needs, but your Apostle. [26] For certainly, he has desired all of you, and he was saddened because you had heard that he was sick. [27] For he was sick, even unto death, but God took pity on him, and not only on him, but truly on myself also, so that I would not have sorrow upon sorrow. [28] Therefore, I sent him more readily, in order that, by seeing him again, you may rejoice, and I may be without sorrow. [29] And so, receive him with every joy in the Lord, and treat all those like him with honor. [30] For he was brought close even to death, for the sake of the work of Christ, handing over his own life, so that he might fulfill what was lacking from you concerning my service.

CHAPTER 3

[1] Concerning other things, my brothers, rejoice in the Lord. It is certainly not tiresome for me to write the same things to you, but for you, it is not necessary. [2] Beware of dogs; beware of those who work evil; beware of those who are divisive. [3] For we are the circumcised, we who serve God in the Spirit and who glory in Christ Jesus, having no confidence in the flesh. [4] Nevertheless, I might have confidence also in the flesh, for if anyone else seems to have confidence in the flesh, more so do I. [5] For I was circumcised on the eighth day, of the stock of Israel, from the tribe of Benjamin, a Hebrew among Hebrews. According to the law, I was a Pharisee; [6] according to zeal, I persecuted the Church of God; according to the justice that is in the law, I lived without blame. [7] But the things which had been to my gain, the same have I considered a loss, for the sake of Christ. [8] Yet truly, I consider everything to be a loss, because of the preeminent knowledge of Jesus Christ, my Lord, for whose sake I have suffered the loss of everything, considering it all to be like dung, so that I may gain Christ, [9] and so that you may be found in him, not having my justice, which is of the law, but that which is of the faith of Christ Jesus, the justice within faith, which is of God. [10] So shall I know him, and the power of his resurrection, and the fellowship of his Passion, having been fashioned according to his death, [11] if, by some means, I might attain to the resurrection which is from the dead. [12] It is not as though I have already received this, or were already perfect. But rather I pursue, so that by some means I might attain, that in which I have already been attained by Christ Jesus. [13] Brothers, I do not consider that I have already attained this. Instead, I do one thing: forgetting those things that are behind, and extending myself toward those things that are ahead, [14] I pursue the destination, the prize of the heavenly calling of God in Christ Jesus. [15] Therefore, as many of us as are being perfected, let us agree about this. And if in anything you disagree, God will reveal this to you also. [16] Yet truly, whatever point we reach, let us be of the same mind, and let us remain in the same rule. [17] Be imitators of me, brothers, and observe those who are walking similarly, just as you have seen by our example. [18] For many persons, about whom I have often told you (and now tell you, weeping,) are walking as

enemies of the cross of Christ. [19]Their end is destruction; their god is their belly; and their glory is in their shame: for they are immersed in earthly things. [20]But our way of life is in heaven. And from heaven, too, we await the Savior, our Lord Jesus Christ, [21]who will transform the body of our lowliness, according to the form of the body of his glory, by means of that power by which he is even able to subject all things to himself.

CHAPTER 4

[1]And so, my most beloved and most desired brothers, my joy and my crown: stand firm in this way, in the Lord, most beloved. [2]I ask Euodia, and I beg Syntyche, to have the same understanding in the Lord. [3]And I also ask you, as my genuine companion, to assist those women who have labored with me in the Gospel, with Clement and the rest of my assistants, whose names are in the Book of Life. [4]Rejoice in the Lord always. Again, I say, rejoice. [5]Let your modesty be known to all men. The Lord is near. [6]Be anxious about nothing. But in all things, with prayer and supplication, with acts of thanksgiving, let your petitions be made known to God. [7]And so shall the peace of God, which exceeds all understanding, guard your hearts and minds in Christ Jesus. [8]Concerning the rest, brothers, whatever is true, whatever is chaste, whatever is just, whatever is holy, whatever is worthy to be loved, whatever is of good repute, if there is any virtue, if there is any praiseworthy discipline: meditate on these. [9]All the things that you have learned and accepted and heard and seen in me, do these. And so shall the God of peace be with you. [10]Now I rejoice in the Lord exceedingly, because finally, after some time, your feelings for me have flourished again, just as you formerly felt. For you had been preoccupied. [11]I am not saying this as if out of need. For I have learned that, in whatever state I am, it is sufficient. [12]I know how to be humbled, and I know how to abound. I am prepared for anything, anywhere: either to be full or to be hungry, either to have abundance or to endure scarcity. [13]Everything is possible in him who has strengthened me. [14]Yet truly, you have done well by sharing in my tribulation. [15]But you also know, O Philippians, that at the beginning of the Gospel, when I set out from Macedonia, not a single church shared with me in the plan of giving and receiving, except you alone. [16]For you even sent to Thessalonica, once, and then a second time, for what was useful to me. [17]It is not that I am seeking a gift. Instead, I seek the fruit that abounds to your benefit. [18]But I have everything in abundance. I have been filled up, having received from Epaphroditus the things that you sent; this is an odor of sweetness, an acceptable sacrifice, pleasing to God. [19]And may my God fulfill all your desires, according to his riches in glory in Christ Jesus. [20]And to God our Father be glory forever and ever. Amen. [21]Greet every saint in Christ Jesus. [22]The brothers who are with me greet you. All the saints greet you, but especially those who are of Caesar's household. [23]May the grace of our Lord Jesus Christ be with your spirit. Amen.

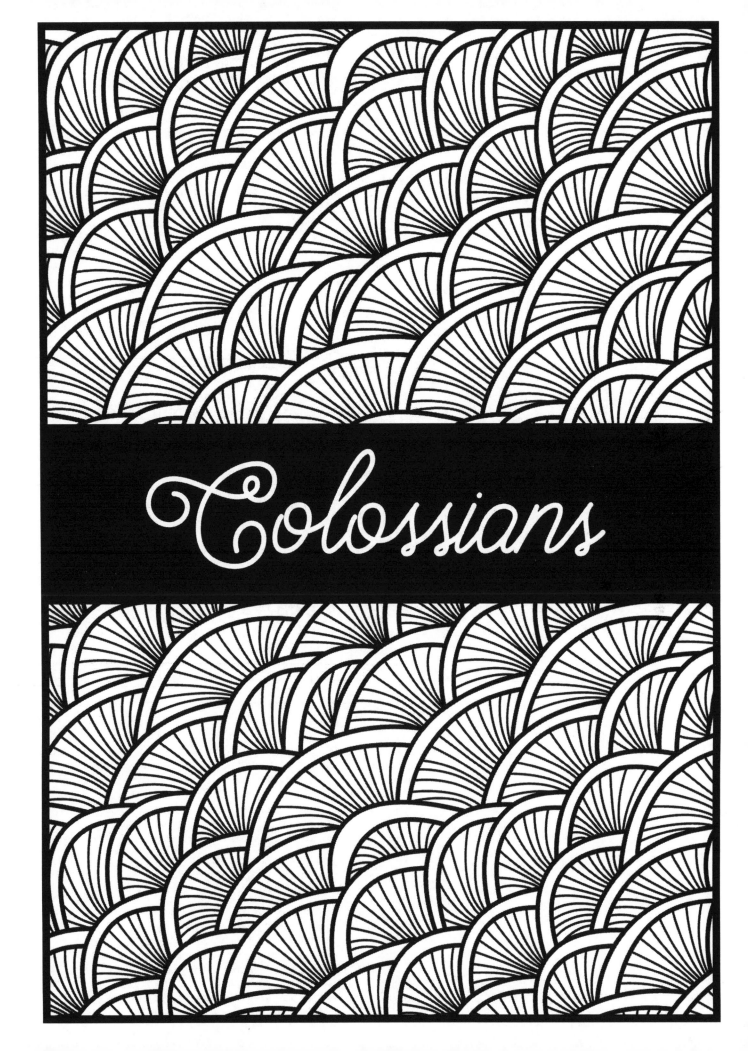

Colossians

THE SACRED BIBLE:
THE LETTER TO THE COLOSSIANS

CHAPTER 1

[1] Paul, an Apostle of Jesus Christ by the will of God, and Timothy, a brother, [2] to the saints and faithful brothers in Christ Jesus who are at Colossae. [3] Grace and peace to you, from God our Father and from the Lord Jesus Christ. We give thanks to God, the Father of our Lord Jesus Christ, praying for you always. [4] For we have heard of your faith in Christ Jesus, and of the love that you have toward all the saints, [5] because of the hope that has been stored up for you in heaven, which you have heard through the Word of Truth in the Gospel. [6] This has reached you, just as it is present in the whole world, where it grows and bears fruit, as it has also done in you, since the day when you first heard and knew the grace of God in truth, [7] just as you learned it from Epaphras, our most beloved fellow servant, who is for you a faithful minister of Christ Jesus. [8] And he has also manifested to us your love in the Spirit. [9] Then, too, from the day when we first heard it, we have not ceased praying for you and requesting that you be filled with the knowledge of his will, with all wisdom and spiritual understanding, [10] so that you may walk in a manner worthy of God, being pleasing in all things, being fruitful in every good work, and increasing in the knowledge of God, [11] being strengthened in every virtue, in accord with the power of his glory, with all patience and longsuffering, with joy, [12] giving thanks to God the Father, who has made us worthy to have a share in the portion of the saints, in the light. [13] For he has rescued us from the power of darkness, and he has transferred us into the kingdom of the Son of his love, [14] in whom we have redemption through his blood, the remission of sins. [15] He is the image of the invisible God, the first-born of every creature. [16] For in him was created everything in heaven and on earth, visible and invisible, whether thrones, or dominations, or principalities, or powers. All things were created through him and in him. [17] And he is before all, and in him all things continue. [18] And he is the head of his body, the Church. He is the beginning, the first-born from the dead, so that in all things he may hold primacy. [19] For the Father is well-pleased that all fullness reside in him, [20] and that, through him, all things be reconciled to himself, making peace through the blood of his cross, for the things that are on earth, as well as the things that are in heaven. [21] And you, though you had been, in times past, understood to be foreigners and enemies, with works of evil, [22] yet now he has reconciled you, by his body of flesh, through death, so as to offer you, holy and immaculate and blameless, before him. [23] So then, continue in the faith: well-founded and steadfast and immovable, by the hope of the Gospel that you have heard, which has been preached throughout all creation under heaven, the Gospel of which I, Paul, have become a minister. [24] For now I rejoice in my passion on your behalf, and I complete in my flesh the things that are lacking in the Passion of Christ, for the sake of his body, which is the Church. [25] For I have become a minister of the Church, according to the dispensation of God that has been given to me among you, so that I may fulfill the Word of God, [26] the mystery which had remained hidden to past ages and generations, but which now is manifested to his saints. [27] To them, God willed to make known the riches of the glory of this mystery among the Gentiles, which is Christ and the hope of his glory within you. [28] We are announcing him, correcting every man and teaching every man, with all wisdom, so that we may offer every man perfect in Christ Jesus. [29] In him, too, I labor, striving according to his action within me, which he works in virtue.

CHAPTER 2

[1] For I want you to know the kind of solicitude that I have for you, and for those who are at Laodicea, as well as for those who have not seen my face in the flesh. [2] May their hearts be consoled and instructed in charity, with all the riches of a plenitude of understanding, with knowledge of the mystery of God the Father and of Christ Jesus. [3] For in him are hidden all treasures of wisdom and knowledge. [4] Now I say this, so that no one may deceive you with grandiose words. [5] For though I may be absent in body, yet I am with you in spirit. And I rejoice as I gaze upon your order and its foundation, which is in Christ, your faith. [6] Therefore, just as you have received the Lord Jesus Christ, walk in him.

⁷ Be rooted and continually built up in Christ. And be confirmed in the faith, just as you have also learned it, increasing in him with acts of thanksgiving. ⁸ See to it that no one deceives you through philosophy and empty falsehoods, as found in the traditions of men, in accord with the influences of the world, and not in accord with Christ. ⁹ For in him, all the fullness of the Divine Nature dwells bodily. ¹⁰ And in him, you have been filled; for he is the head of all principality and power. ¹¹ In him also, you have been circumcised with a circumcision not made by hand, not by the despoiling of the body of flesh, but by the circumcision of Christ. ¹² You have been buried with him in baptism. In him also, you have risen again through faith, by the work of God, who raised him up from the dead. ¹³ And when you were dead in your transgressions and in the uncircumcision of your flesh, he enlivened you, together with him, forgiving you of all transgressions, ¹⁴ and wiping away the handwriting of the decree which was against us, which was contrary to us. And he has taken this away from your midst, affixing it to the Cross. ¹⁵ And so, despoiling principalities and powers, he has led them away confidently and openly, triumphing over them in himself. ¹⁶ Therefore, let no one judge you as concerns food or drink, or a particular feast day, or feast days of new moons, or of Sabbaths. ¹⁷ For these are a shadow of the future, but the body is of Christ. ¹⁸ Let no one seduce you, preferring base things and a religion of Angels, walking according to what he has not seen, being vainly inflated by the sensations of his flesh, ¹⁹ and not holding up the head, with which the whole body, by its underlying joints and ligaments, is joined together and grows with an increase that is of God. ²⁰ So then, if you have died with Christ to the influences of this world, why do you still make decisions as if you were living in the world? ²¹ Do not touch, do not taste, do not handle these things, ²² which all lead to destruction by their very use, in accord with the precepts and doctrines of men. ²³ Such ideas have at least an intention to attain to wisdom, but through superstition and debasement, not sparing the body, and they are without any honor in satiating the flesh.

CHAPTER 3

¹ Therefore, if you have risen together with Christ, seek the things that are above, where Christ is seated at the right hand of God. ² Consider the things that are above, not the things that are upon the earth. ³ For you have died, and so your life is hidden with Christ in God. ⁴ When Christ, your life, appears, then you also will appear with him in glory. ⁵ Therefore, mortify your body, while it is upon the earth. For because of fornication, impurity, lust, evil desires, and avarice, which are a kind of service to idols, ⁶ the wrath of God has overwhelmed the sons of unbelief. ⁷ You, too, walked in these things, in times past, when you were living among them. ⁸ But now you must set aside all these things: anger, indignation, malice, blasphemy, and indecent speech from your mouth. ⁹ Do not lie to one another. Strip yourselves of the old man, with his deeds, ¹⁰ and clothe yourself with the new man, who has been renewed by knowledge, in accord with the image of the One who created him, ¹¹ where there is neither Gentile nor Jew, circumcision nor uncircumcision, Barbarian nor Scythian, servant nor free. Instead, Christ is everything, in everyone. ¹² Therefore, clothe yourselves like the elect of God: holy and beloved, with hearts of mercy, kindness, humility, modesty, and patience. ¹³ Support one another, and, if anyone has a complaint against another, forgive one another. For just as the Lord has forgiven you, so also must you do. ¹⁴ And above all these things have charity, which is the bond of perfection. ¹⁵ And let the peace of Christ lift up your hearts. For in this peace, you have been called, as one body. And be thankful. ¹⁶ Let the word of Christ live in you in abundance, with all wisdom, teaching and correcting one another, with psalms, hymns, and spiritual canticles, singing to God with the grace in your hearts. ¹⁷ Let everything whatsoever that you do, whether in word or in deed, be done all in the name of the Lord Jesus Christ, giving thanks to God the Father through him. ¹⁸ Wives, be submissive to your husbands, as is proper in the Lord. ¹⁹ Husbands, love your wives, and do not be bitter toward them. ²⁰ Children, obey your parents in all things. For this is well-pleasing to the Lord. ²¹ Fathers, do not provoke your children to indignation, lest they lose heart. ²² Servants, obey, in all things, your lords according to the flesh, not serving only when seen, as if to please men, but serving in simplicity of heart, fearing God. ²³ Whatever you do, do it from the heart, as for the Lord, and not for men. ²⁴ For you know that you will receive from the Lord the repayment of an inheritance. Serve Christ the Lord. ²⁵ For whoever causes injury shall be repaid for what he has wrongfully done. And there no favoritism with God.

CHAPTER 4

¹You masters, supply your servants with what is just and equitable, knowing that you, too, have a Master in heaven. ²Pursue prayer. Be watchful in prayer with acts of thanksgiving. ³Pray together, for us also, so that God may open a door of speech to us, so as to speak the mystery of Christ, (because of which, even now, I am in chains) ⁴so that I may manifest it in the manner that I ought to speak. ⁵Walk in wisdom toward those who are outside, redeeming this age. ⁶Let your speech be ever graceful, seasoned with salt, so that you may know how you ought to respond to each person. ⁷As for the things that concern me, Tychicus, a most beloved brother and faithful minister and fellow servant in the Lord, will make everything known to you. ⁸I have sent him to you for this very purpose, so that he may know the things that concern you, and may console your hearts, ⁹with Onesimus, a most beloved and faithful brother, who is from among you. They shall make known to you everything that is happening here. ¹⁰Aristarchus, my fellow prisoner, greets you, as does Mark, the near cousin of Barnabas, about whom you have received instructions, (if he comes to you, receive him) ¹¹and Jesus, who is called Justus, and those who are of the circumcision. These alone are my assistants, unto the kingdom of God; they have been a consolation to me. ¹²Epaphras greets you, who is from among you, a servant of Christ Jesus, ever solicitous for you in prayer, so that you may stand, perfect and complete, in the entire will of God. ¹³For I offer testimony to him, that he has labored greatly for you, and for those who are at Laodicea, and for those at Hierapolis. ¹⁴Luke, a most beloved physician, greets you, as does Demas. ¹⁵Greet the brothers who are at Laodicea, and Nymphas, and those who are at his house, a church. ¹⁶And when this epistle has been read among you, cause it to be read also in the church of the Laodiceans, and you should read that which is from the Laodiceans. ¹⁷And tell Archippus: "See to the ministry that you have received in the Lord, in order to fulfill it." ¹⁸The greeting of Paul by my own hand. Remember my chains. May grace be with you. Amen.

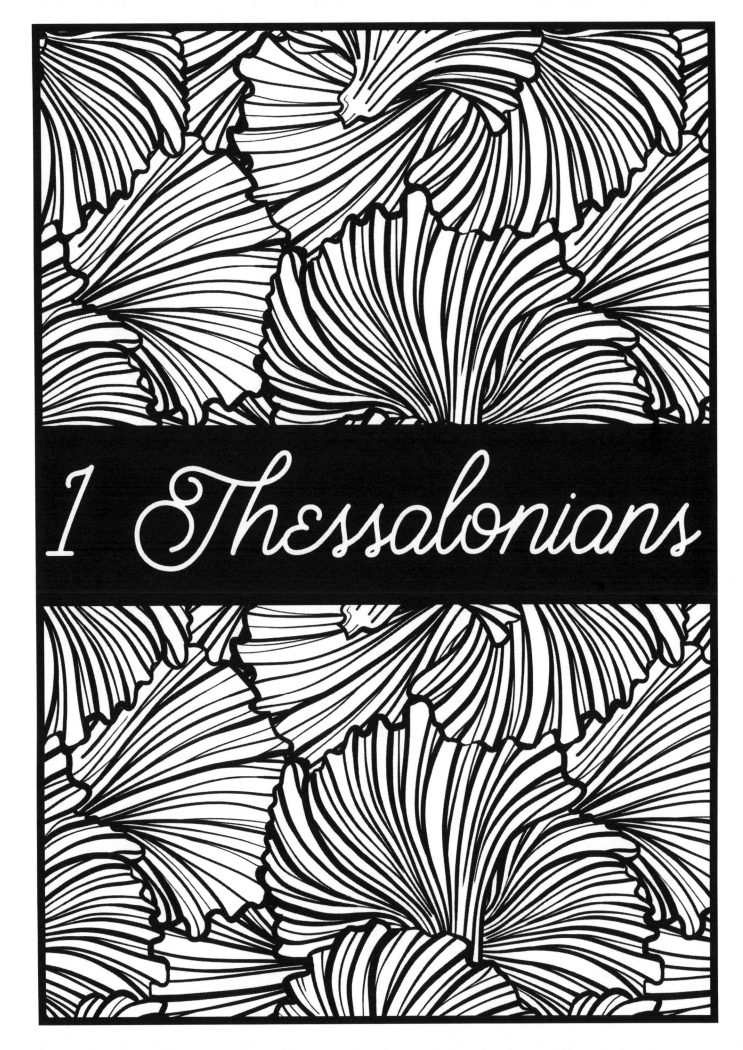

1 Thessalonians

THE SACRED BIBLE:
THE FIRST LETTER TO THE THESSALONIANS

1 THESSALONIANS 1

[1] Paul and Sylvanus and Timothy, to the church of the Thessalonians, in God the Father and the Lord Jesus Christ. [2] Grace and peace to you. We give thanks to God always for all of you, keeping the memory of you in our prayers without ceasing, [3] remembering your work of faith, and hardship, and charity, and enduring hope, in our Lord Jesus Christ, before God our Father. [4] For we know, brothers, beloved of God, of your election. [5] For our Gospel has not been among you in word alone, but also in virtue, and in the Holy Spirit, and with a great fullness, in the same manner as you know we have acted among you for your sake. [6] And so, you became imitators of us and of the Lord, accepting the Word in the midst of great tribulation, but with the joy of the Holy Spirit. [7] So have you become a pattern for all who believe in Macedonia and in Achaia. [8] For from you, the Word of the Lord was spread, not only in Macedonia and in Achaia, but also in every place. Your faith, which is toward God, has advanced so much so that we do not need to speak to you about anything. [9] For others are reporting among us of the kind of acceptance we had among you, and how you were converted from idols to God, to the service of the living and true God, [10] and to the expectation of his Son from heaven (whom he raised up from the dead), Jesus, who has rescued us from the approaching wrath.

1 THESSALONIANS 2

[1] For you yourselves know, brothers, that our acceptance among you was not empty. [2] Instead, having previously suffered and been treated shamefully, as you know, at Philippi, we had confidence in our God, so as to speak the Gospel of God to you with much solicitude. [3] For our exhortation was not in error, nor from impurity, nor with deception. [4] But, just as we have been tested by God, so that the Gospel would be entrusted to us, so also did we speak, not so as to please men, but rather to please God, who tests our hearts. [5] And neither did we, at any time, become flattering in speech, as you know, nor did we seek an opportunity for avarice, as God is witness. [6] Nor did we seek the glory of men, neither from you, nor from others. [7] And although we could have been a burden to you, as Apostles of Christ, instead we became like little ones in your midst, like a nurse cherishing her children. [8] So desirous were we for you that we were willing to hand over to you, not only the Gospel of God, but even our own souls. For you have become most beloved to us. [9] For you remember, brothers, our hardship and weariness. We preached the Gospel of God among you, working night and day, so that we would not be burdensome to any of you. [10] You are witnesses, as is God, of how holy and just and blameless we were with you who have believed. [11] And you know the manner, with each one of you, like a father with his sons, [12] in which we were pleading with you and consoling you, bearing witness, so that you would walk in a manner worthy of God, who has called you into his kingdom and glory. [13] For this reason also, we give thanks to God without ceasing: because, when you had accepted from us the Word of the hearing of God, you accepted it not as the word of men, but (as it truly is) as the Word of God, who is working in you who have believed. [14] For you, brothers, have become imitators of the churches of God which are at Judea, in Christ Jesus. For you, too, have suffered the same things from your fellow countrymen as they have suffered from the Jews, [15] who also killed both the Lord Jesus, and the Prophets, and who have persecuted us. But they do not please God, and so they are adversaries to all men. [16] They prohibit us to speak to the Gentiles, so that they may be saved, and thus do they continually add to their own sins. But the wrath of God will overtake them in the very end. [17] And we, brothers, having been deprived of you for a short time, in sight, but not in heart, have hurried all the more to see your face, with a great desire. [18] For we wanted to come to you, (indeed, I, Paul, attempted to do so once, and then again,) but Satan impeded us. [19] For what is our hope, and our joy, and our crown of glory? Is it not you, before our Lord Jesus Christ at his return? [20] For you are our glory and our joy.

1 THESSALONIANS 3

[1] Because of this, willing to wait no longer, it was pleasing to us to remain at Athens, alone. [2] And we sent Timothy, our brother and a minister of God in the

Gospel of Christ, to confirm you and to exhort you, on behalf of your faith, ³ so that no one would be disturbed during these tribulations. For you yourselves know that we have been appointed to this. ⁴ For even while we were with you, we predicted to you that we would suffer tribulations, even as it has happened, and as you know. ⁵ For this reason also, I was not willing to wait any longer, and I sent to find out about your faith, lest perhaps he who tempts may have tempted you, and our labor might have been in vain. ⁶ But then, when Timothy arrived to us from you, he reported to us your faith and charity, and that you keep a good remembrance of us always, desiring to see us, just as we likewise desire to see you. ⁷ As a result, we were consoled in you, brothers, in the midst of all our difficulties and tribulations, through your faith. ⁸ For we now live so that you may stand firm in the Lord. ⁹ For what thanks would we be able to repay to God because of you, for all the joy with which we rejoice over you before our God? ¹⁰ For night and day, ever more abundantly, we are praying that we may see your face, and that we may complete those things that are lacking in your faith. ¹¹ But may God our Father himself, and our Lord Jesus Christ, direct our way to you. ¹² And may the Lord multiply you, and make you abound in your charity toward one another and toward all, just as we also do toward you, ¹³ in order to confirm your hearts without blame, in sanctity, before God our Father, unto the return of our Lord Jesus Christ, with all his saints. Amen.

1 THESSALONIANS 4

¹ Therefore, concerning other things, brothers, we ask and beg you, in the Lord Jesus, that, just as you have received from us the way in which you ought to walk and to please God, so also may you walk, in order that you may abound all the more. ² For you know what precepts I have given to you through the Lord Jesus. ³ For this is the will of God, your sanctification: that you should abstain from fornication, ⁴ that each one of you should know how to possess his vessel in sanctification and honor, ⁵ not in passions of lust, like the Gentiles who do not know God, ⁶ and that no one should overwhelm or circumvent his brother in business. For the Lord is the vindicator of all these things, just as we have preached and testified to you. ⁷ For God has not called us to impurity, but to sanctification. ⁸ And so, whoever despises these teachings, does not despise man, but God, who has even provided his Holy Spirit within us. ⁹ But concerning the charity of brotherhood, we have no need to write to you. For you yourselves have learned from God that you should love one another. ¹⁰ For indeed, you act in this way with all the brothers in all of Macedonia. But we petition you, brothers, so that you may abound all the more, ¹¹ to choose work that allows you to be tranquil, and to carry out your business and to do your work with your own hands, just as we have instructed you, ¹² and to walk honestly with those who are outside, and to desire nothing belonging to another. ¹³ And we do not want you to be ignorant, brothers, concerning those who are sleeping, so as not to be sorrowful, like these others who do not have hope. ¹⁴ For if we believe that Jesus has died and risen again, so also will God bring back with Jesus those who sleep in him. ¹⁵ For we say this to you, in the Word of the Lord: that we who are alive, who remain until the return of the Lord, will not precede those who have fallen asleep. ¹⁶ For the Lord himself, with a command and with the voice of an Archangel and with a trumpet of God, shall descend from heaven. And the dead, who are in Christ, shall rise up first. ¹⁷ Next, we who are alive, who are remaining, shall be taken up quickly together with them into the clouds to meet Christ in the air. And in this way, we shall be with the Lord always. ¹⁸ Therefore, console one another with these words.

1 THESSALONIANS 5

¹ But concerning dates and times, brothers, you do not need us to write to you. ² For you yourselves thoroughly understand that the day of the Lord shall arrive much like a thief in the night. ³ For when they will say, "Peace and security!" then destruction will suddenly overwhelm them, like the labor pains of a woman with child, and they will not escape. ⁴ But you, brothers, are not in darkness, so that you would be overtaken by that day as by a thief. ⁵ For all of you are sons of light and sons of daytime; we are not of nighttime, nor of darkness. ⁶ Therefore, let us not sleep, as the rest do. Instead, we should be vigilant and sober. ⁷ For those who sleep, sleep in the night; and those who are inebriated, are inebriated in the night. ⁸ But we, who are of the daylight, should be sober, being clothed with the breastplate of faith and of charity and having, as a helmet, the hope of salvation. ⁹ For God has not appointed us for wrath, but for the acquisition of salvation

through our Lord Jesus Christ, ¹⁰ who died for us, so that, whether we watch, or whether we sleep, we may live in union with him. ¹¹ Because of this, console one another and build up one another, just as you are doing. ¹² And we ask you, brothers, to recognize those who labor among you, and who preside over you in the Lord, and who admonish you, ¹³ so that you may consider them with an abundance of charity, for the sake of their work. Be at peace with them. ¹⁴ And we ask you, brothers: correct the disruptive, console the weak-minded, support the sick, be patient with everyone. ¹⁵ See to it that no one repays evil for evil to anyone. Instead, always pursue whatever is good, with one another and with all. ¹⁶ Rejoice always. ¹⁷ Pray without ceasing. ¹⁸ Give thanks in everything. For this is the will of God in Christ Jesus for all of you. ¹⁹ Do not choose to extinguish the Spirit. ²⁰ Do not spurn prophecies. ²¹ But test all things. Hold on to whatever is good. ²² Abstain from every kind of evil. ²³ And may the God of peace himself sanctify you through all things, so that your whole spirit and soul and body may be preserved without blame unto the return of our Lord Jesus Christ. ²⁴ He who has called you is faithful. He shall act even now. ²⁵ Brothers, pray for us. ²⁶ Greet all the brothers with a holy kiss. ²⁷ I bind you, through the Lord, that this epistle is to be read to all the holy brothers. ²⁸ May the grace of our Lord Jesus Christ be with you. Amen.

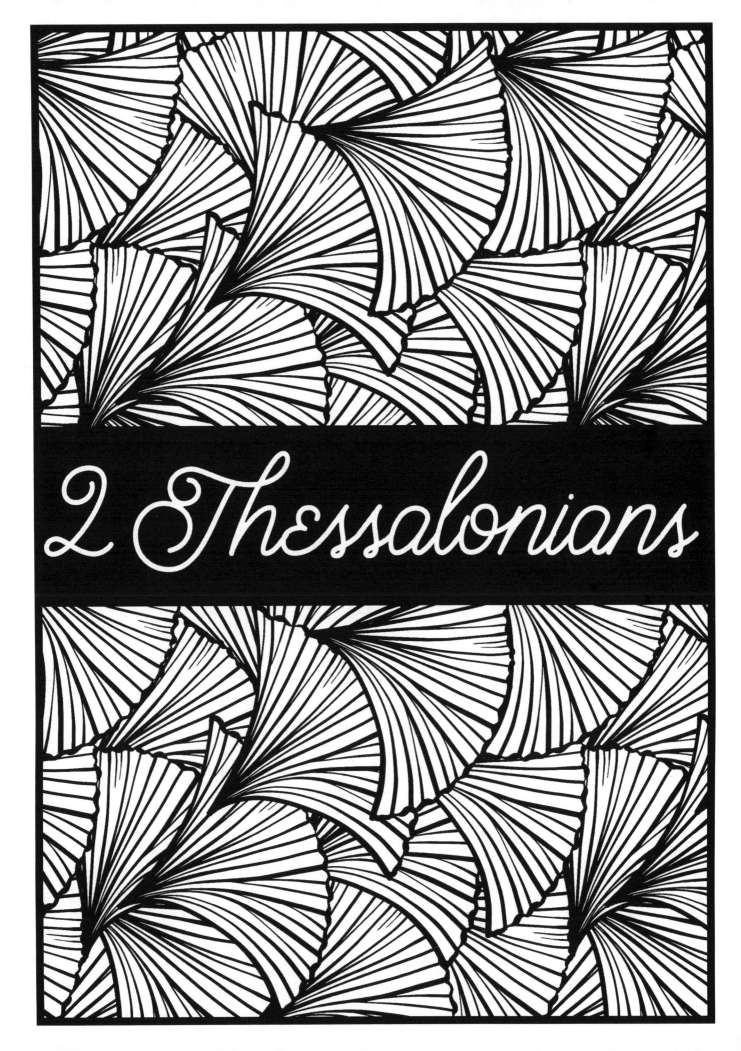

2 Thessalonians

THE SACRED BIBLE:
THE SECOND LETTER TO THE THESSALONIANS

2 THESSALONIANS 1

[1] Paul and Sylvanus and Timothy, to the church of the Thessalonians, in God our Father and the Lord Jesus Christ. [2] Grace and peace to you, from God our Father and from the Lord Jesus Christ. [3] We ought to give thanks always to God for you, brothers, in a fitting manner, because your faith is increasing greatly, and because the charity of each of you toward one another is abundant, [4] so much so that we ourselves even glory in you among the churches of God, because of your patience and faith in all of your persecutions and tribulations that you endure, [5] which are a sign of the just judgment of God, so that you may be held worthy of the kingdom of God, for which you also suffer. [6] For certainly, it is just for God to repay trouble to those who trouble you, [7] and to repay you, who are being troubled, with a repose with us, when the Lord Jesus is revealed from heaven with the Angels of his virtue, [8] granting vindication, by a flame of fire, against those who do not know God and who are not obedient to the Gospel of our Lord Jesus Christ. [9] These shall be given the eternal punishment of destruction, apart from the face of the Lord and apart from the glory of his virtue, [10] when he arrives to be glorified in his saints, and to become a wonder in all those who have believed, in that day, because our testimony has been believed by you. [11] Because of this, too, we pray always for you, so that our God may make you worthy of his calling and may complete every act of his goodness, as well as his work of faith in virtue, [12] in order that the name of our Lord Jesus may be glorified in you, and you in him, in accord with the grace of our God and of the Lord Jesus Christ.

2 THESSALONIANS 2

[1] But we ask you, brothers, concerning the advent of our Lord Jesus Christ and of our gathering to him, [2] that you not be readily disturbed or terrified in your minds, by any spirit, or word, or epistle, supposedly sent from us, claiming that the day of the Lord is close by. [3] Let no one deceive you in any way. For this cannot be, unless the apostasy will have arrived first, and the man of sin will have been revealed, the son of perdition, [4] who is an adversary to, and who is lifted up above, all that is called God or that is worshipped, so much so that he sits in the temple of God, presenting himself as if he were God. [5] Do you not recall that, when I was still with you, I told you these things? [6] And now you know what it is that holds him back, so that he may be revealed in his own time. [7] For the mystery of iniquity is already at work. And only one now holds back, and will continue to hold back, until he is taken from our midst. [8] And then that iniquitous one shall be revealed, the one whom the Lord Jesus shall bring to ruin with the spirit of his mouth, and shall destroy at the brightness of his return: [9] him whose advent is accompanied by the works of Satan, with every kind of power and signs and false miracles, [10] and with every seduction of iniquity, toward those who are perishing because they have not accepted the love of truth, so that they may be saved. For this reason, God will send to them works of deception, so that they may believe in lies, [11] in order that all those who have not believed in the truth, but who have consented to iniquity, may be judged. [12] Yet we must always give thanks to God for you, brothers, beloved of God, because God has chosen you as first-fruits for salvation, by the sanctification of the Spirit and by faith in the truth. [13] He has also called you into truth through our Gospel, unto the acquisition of the glory of our Lord Jesus Christ. [14] And so, brothers, stand firm, and hold to the traditions that you have learned, whether by word or by our epistle. [15] So may our Lord Jesus Christ himself, and God our Father, who has loved us and who has given us an everlasting consolation and good hope in grace, [16] exhort your hearts and confirm you in every good word and deed.

2 THESSALONIANS 3

[1] Concerning other things, brothers, pray for us, so that the Word of God may advance and be glorified, just as it is among you, [2] and so that we may be freed from pertinacious and evil men. For not everyone is faithful. [3] But God is faithful. He will strengthen you, and he will guard you from evil. [4] And we have confidence about you in the Lord, that you are doing, and will continue to do, just as we have instructed. [5] And may the Lord direct your hearts, in the charity of God and with the patience of Christ. [6] But we strongly caution you, brothers, in the name of our Lord Jesus Christ, to draw yourselves away from every brother who is walking in disorder and not according to the tradition that they received from us. [7] For you yourselves know the manner in which you ought to imitate us. For we were not disorderly among you. [8] Nor did we eat bread from anyone for free, but rather, we worked night and day, in hardship and weariness, so as not to be burdensome to you. [9] It was not as if we had no authority, but this was so that we might present ourselves as an example to you, in order to imitate us. [10] Then, too, while we were with you, we insisted on this to you: that if anyone was not willing to work, neither should he eat. [11] For we have heard that there are some among you who act disruptively, not working at all, but eagerly meddling. [12] Now we charge those who act in this way, and we beg them in the Lord Jesus Christ, that they work in silence and eat their own bread. [13] And you, brothers, do not grow weak in doing good. [14] But if anyone does not obey our word by this epistle, take note of him and do not keep company with him, so that he may be ashamed. [15] But do not be willing to consider him as an enemy; instead, correct him as a brother. [16] Then may the Lord of peace himself give you an everlasting peace, in every place. May the Lord be with all of you. [17] The greeting of Paul with my own hand, which is the seal in every epistle. So do I write. [18] May the grace of our Lord Jesus Christ be with you all. Amen.

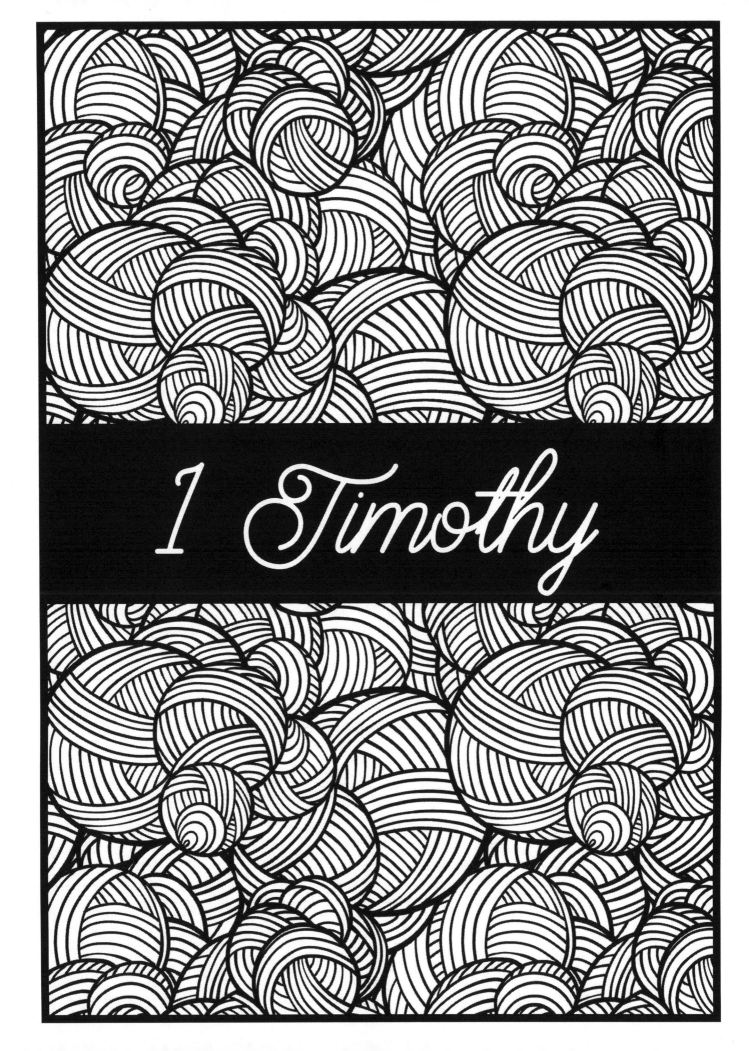

THE SACRED BIBLE:
THE FIRST LETTER TO TIMOTHY

1 TIMOTHY 1

[1] Paul, an Apostle of Jesus Christ by the authority of God our Savior and Christ Jesus our hope, [2] to Timothy, beloved son in the faith. Grace, mercy, and peace, from God the Father and from Christ Jesus our Lord. [3] Now I asked you to remain at Ephesus, while I went into Macedonia, so that you would speak strongly against certain ones who have been teaching a different way, [4] against those who have been paying attention to fables and endless genealogies. These things present questions as if they were greater than the edification that is of God, which is in faith. [5] Now the goal of instruction is charity from a pure heart, and a good conscience, and an unfeigned faith. [6] Certain persons, wandering away from these things, have been turned aside to empty babbling, [7] desiring to be teachers of the law, but understanding neither the things that they themselves are saying, nor what they are affirming about these things. [8] But we know that the law is good, if one makes use of it properly. [9] Knowing this, that the law was not set in place for the just, but for the unjust and the insubordinate, for the impious and sinners, for the wicked and the defiled, for those who commit patricide, matricide, or homicide, [10] for fornicators, for males who sleep with males, for kidnappers, for liars, for perjurers, and whatever else is contrary to sound doctrine, [11] which is in accord with the Gospel of the glory of the blessed God, the Gospel which has been entrusted to me. [12] I give thanks to him who has strengthened me, Christ Jesus our Lord, because he has considered me faithful, placing me in the ministry, [13] though previously I was a blasphemer, and a persecutor, and contemptuous. But then I obtained the mercy of God. For I had been acting ignorantly, in unbelief. [14] And so the grace of our Lord has abounded greatly, with the faith and love that is in Christ Jesus. [15] It is a faithful saying, and worthy of acceptance by everyone, that Christ Jesus came into this world to bring salvation to sinners, among whom I am first. [16] But it was for this reason that I obtained mercy, so that in me as first, Christ Jesus would display all patience, for the instruction of those who would believe in him unto eternal life. [17] So then, to the King of ages, to the immortal, invisible, solitary God, be honor and glory forever and ever. Amen. [18] This precept I commend to you, my son Timothy, in accord with the prophets who preceded you: that you serve among them like a soldier in a good war, [19] holding to faith and good conscience, against those who, by rejecting these things, have made a shipwreck of the faith. [20] Among these are Hymenaeus and Alexander, whom I have handed over to Satan, so that they may learn not to blaspheme.

1 TIMOTHY 2

[1] And so I beg you, first of all, to make supplications, prayers, petitions, and thanksgivings for all men, [2] for kings, and for all who are in high places, so that we may lead a quiet and tranquil life in all piety and chastity. [3] For this is good and acceptable in the sight of God our Savior, [4] who wants all men to be saved and to arrive at an acknowledgment of the truth. [5] For there is one God, and one mediator of God and of men, the man Christ Jesus, [6] who gave himself as a redemption for all, as a testimony in its proper time. [7] Of this testimony, I have been appointed a preacher and an Apostle, (I speak the truth, I do not lie) as a teacher of the Gentiles, in faith and in truth. [8] Therefore, I want men to pray in every place, lifting up pure hands, without anger or dissension. [9] Similarly also, women should be dressed fittingly, adorning themselves with compunction and restraint, and not with plaited hair, nor gold, nor pearls, nor costly attire, [10] but in a manner proper for women who are professing piety by means of good works. [11] Let a woman learn in silence with all subjection. [12] For I do not permit a woman to teach, nor to be in authority over a man, but to be in silence. [13] For Adam was formed first, then Eve. [14] And Adam was not seduced, but the woman, having been seduced, was in transgression. [15] Yet she will be saved by bearing children, if she has continued in faith and love, and in sanctification accompanied by self-restraint.

1 TIMOTHY 3

[1] It is a faithful saying: if a man desires the episcopate, he desires a good work. [2] Therefore, it is necessary for a bishop to be beyond reproach, the husband of one

wife, sober, prudent, gracious, chaste, hospitable, a teacher, ³not a drunkard, not combative but restrained, not quarrelsome, not covetous; ⁴but a man who leads his own house well, having children who are subordinate with all chastity. ⁵For if a man does not know how to lead his own house, how will he take care of the Church of God? ⁶He must not be a new convert, lest, being elated by pride, he may fall under the sentence of the devil. ⁷And it is necessary for him also to have good testimony from those who are outside, so that he may not fall into disrepute and the snare of the devil. ⁸Similarly, deacons must be chaste, not double-tongued, not given to much wine, not pursuing tainted profit, ⁹holding to the mystery of the faith with a pure conscience. ¹⁰And these things should be proven first, and then they may minister, being without offense. ¹¹Similarly, the women must be chaste, not slanderers, sober, faithful in all things. ¹²Deacons should be the husband of one wife, men who lead their own children and their own houses well. ¹³For those who have ministered well will acquire for themselves a good position, and much confidence in the faith which is in Christ Jesus. ¹⁴I am writing these things to you, with the hope that I will come to you soon. ¹⁵But, if I am delayed, you should know the manner in which it is necessary to conduct yourself in the house of God, which is the Church of the living God, the pillar and the foundation of truth. ¹⁶And it is clearly great, this mystery of piety, which was manifested in the flesh, which was justified in the Spirit, which has appeared to Angels, which has been preached to the Gentiles, which is believed in the world, which has been taken up in glory.

1 TIMOTHY 4

¹Now the Spirit has clearly said that, in the end times, some persons will depart from the faith, paying attention to spirits of error and the doctrines of devils, ²speaking lies in hypocrisy, and having their consciences seared, ³prohibiting marriage, abstaining from foods, which God has created to be accepted with thanksgiving by the faithful and by those who have understood the truth. ⁴For every creature of God is good, and nothing is to be rejected which is received with thanksgiving; ⁵for it has been sanctified by the Word of God and by prayer. ⁶By proposing these things to the brothers, you will be a good minister of Christ Jesus, nourished by words of faith, and by the good doctrine that you have secured. ⁷But avoid the silly fables of old women. And exercise yourself so as to advance in piety. ⁸For the exercise of the body is somewhat useful. But piety is useful in all things, holding the promise of life, in the present and in the future. ⁹This is a faithful saying and worthy of full acceptance. ¹⁰For this reason we labor and are maligned: because we hope in the living God, who is the Savior of all men, most especially of the faithful. ¹¹Instruct and teach these things. ¹²Let no one despise your youth, but be an example among the faithful in word, in behavior, in charity, in faith, in chastity. ¹³Until I arrive, attend to reading, to exhortation, and to doctrine. ¹⁴Do not be willing to neglect the grace that is within you, which was given to you through prophecy, with the imposition of the hands of the priesthood. ¹⁵Meditate on these things, so that your progress may be manifest to all. ¹⁶Pay attention to yourself and to doctrine. Pursue these things. For in doing so, you will save both yourself and those who listen to you.

1 TIMOTHY 5

¹You should not rebuke an old man, but rather plead with him, as if he were your father; with young men, like brothers; ²with old women, like mothers; with young women, in all chastity, like sisters. ³Honor those widows who are true widows. ⁴But if any widow has children or grandchildren, let her first learn to manage her own household, and to fulfill, in turn, her own obligation to her parents; for this is acceptable before God. ⁵But she who is truly a widow and is destitute, let her hope in God, and let her be urgent in supplications and prayers, night and day. ⁶For she who is living in pleasures is dead, while living. ⁷And give instruction in this, so that they may be beyond reproach. ⁸But if anyone has no concern for his own, and especially for those of his own household, he has denied the faith, and he is worse than an unbeliever. ⁹Let a widow be chosen who is no less than sixty years of age, who was the wife of one husband, ¹⁰who has testimony of her good works: whether she has educated children, or has provided hospitality, or has washed the feet of the saints, or has ministered to those suffering tribulation, or has pursued any kind of good work. ¹¹But avoid the younger widows. For once they have flourished in Christ, they will want to marry, ¹²resulting in damnation, because they have disregarded the primacy

of faith. [13] And being at the same time also idle, they learn to go from house to house, being not only idle, but also talkative and curious, speaking of things which do not concern them. [14] Therefore, I want the younger women to marry, to procreate children, to be mothers of families, to provide no ready opportunity for the adversary to speak evil. [15] For certain ones have already been turned back to Satan. [16] If any among the faithful have widows, let him minister to them and not burden the Church, so that there may be enough for those who are true widows. [17] Let priests who lead well be held worthy of twice the honor, especially those who labor in the Word and in doctrine. [18] For Scripture says: "You shall not muzzle an ox as it is treading out the grain," and, "The worker is worthy of his pay." [19] Do not be willing to accept an accusation against a priest, except under two or three witnesses. [20] Reprove sinners in the sight of everyone, so that the others may have fear. [21] I testify before God and Christ Jesus and the elect Angels, that you should observe these things without prejudgment, doing nothing which shows favoritism to either side. [22] You should not be quick to impose hands on anyone, nor should you take part in the sins of outsiders. Keep yourself chaste. [23] Do not continue to drink only water, but make use of a little wine, for the sake of your stomach and your frequent infirmities. [24] The sins of some men have been made manifest, preceding them to judgment, but those of others are manifested later. [25] Similarly, too, good deeds have been made manifest, but even when they are not, they cannot remain hidden.

1 TIMOTHY 6

[1] Whoever are servants under the yoke, let them consider their masters to be worthy of every honor, lest the name and doctrine of the Lord be blasphemed. [2] But those who have believing masters, let them not despise them because they are brothers, but rather serve them all the more because they are believing and beloved, participants of the same service. Teach and exhort these things. [3] If anyone teaches otherwise, and does not consent to the sound words of our Lord Jesus Christ, and to that doctrine which is in accord with piety, [4] then he is arrogant, knowing nothing, yet languishing amid the questions and quarrels of words. From these arise envy, contention, blasphemy, evil suspicions: [5] the conflicts of men who have been corrupted in mind and deprived of truth, who consider profit to be piety. [6] But piety with sufficiency is great gain. [7] For we brought nothing into this world, and there is no doubt that we can take nothing away. [8] But, having nourishment and some kind of covering, we should be content with these. [9] For those who want to become rich fall into temptation and into the snare of the devil and into many useless and harmful desires, which submerge men in destruction and in perdition. [10] For desire is the root of all evils. Some persons, hungering in this way, have strayed from the faith and have entangled themselves in many sorrows. [11] But you, O man of God, flee from these things, and truly pursue justice, piety, faith, charity, patience, meekness. [12] Fight the good fight of faith. Take hold of the eternal life to which you have been called, and make a good profession of faith in the sight of many witnesses. [13] I charge you, in the sight of God, who enlivens all things, and in the sight of Christ Jesus, who gave the testimony of a good profession under Pontius Pilate, [14] to observe the commandment, immaculately, irreproachably, unto the return of our Lord Jesus Christ. [15] For at the proper time, he shall reveal the blessed and only Power, the King of kings and the Lord of lords, [16] who alone holds immortality, and who inhabits the inaccessible light, whom no man has seen, nor even is able to see, to whom is honor and everlasting dominion. Amen. [17] Instruct the wealthy of this age not to have a superior attitude, nor to hope in the uncertainty of riches, but in the living God, who offers us everything in abundance to enjoy, [18] and to do good, to become rich in good works, to donate readily, to share, [19] to gather for themselves the treasure of a good foundation for the future, so that they may obtain true life. [20] O Timothy, guard what has been deposited with you, avoiding the voice of profane novelties and of opposing ideas, which are falsely called knowledge. [21] Certain persons, promising these things, have perished from the faith. May grace be with you. Amen.

2 Timothy

THE SACRED BIBLE:
THE SECOND LETTER TO TIMOTHY

2 TIMOTHY 1

[1] Paul, an Apostle of Jesus Christ through the will of God, in accord with the promise of the life which is in Christ Jesus, [2] to Timothy, most beloved son. Grace, mercy, peace, from God the Father and from Christ Jesus our Lord. [3] I give thanks to God, whom I serve, as my forefathers did, with a pure conscience. For without ceasing I hold the remembrance of you in my prayers, night and day, [4] desiring to see you, recalling your tears so as to be filled with joy, [5] calling to mind the same faith, which is in you unfeigned, which also first dwelt in your grandmother, Lois, and in your mother, Eunice, and also, I am certain, in you. [6] Because of this, I admonish you to revive the grace of God, which is in you by the imposition of my hands. [7] For God has not given us a spirit of fear, but of virtue, and of love, and of self-restraint. [8] And so, do not be ashamed of the testimony of our Lord, nor of me, his prisoner. Instead, collaborate with the Gospel in accord with the virtue of God, [9] who has freed us and has called us to his holy vocation, not according to our works, but according to his own purpose and grace, which was given to us in Christ Jesus, before the ages of time. [10] And this has now been made manifest by the illumination of our Savior Jesus Christ, who certainly has destroyed death, and who has also illuminated life and incorruption through the Gospel. [11] Of this Gospel, I have been appointed a preacher, and an Apostle, and a teacher of the Gentiles. [12] For this reason, I also suffer these things. But I am not confounded. For I know in whom I have believed, and I am certain that he has the power to preserve what was entrusted to me, unto that day. [13] Hold to the kind of sound words that you have heard from me in the faith and love which is in Christ Jesus. [14] Guard the good entrusted to you through the Holy Spirit, who lives within us. [15] Know this: that all those who are in Asia have turned away from me, among whom are Phigellus and Hermogenes. [16] May the Lord have mercy on the house of Onesiphorus, because he has often refreshed me, and he has not been ashamed of my chains. [17] Instead, when he had arrived in Rome, he anxiously sought me and found me. [18] May the Lord grant to him to obtain mercy from the Lord in that day. And you know well in how many ways he has ministered to me at Ephesus.

2 TIMOTHY 2

[1] And as for you, my son, be strengthened by the grace which is in Christ Jesus, [2] and by the things which you have heard from me through many witnesses. These things encourage faithful men, who shall then be suitable to teach others also. [3] Labor like a good soldier of Christ Jesus. [4] No man, acting as a soldier for God, entangles himself in worldly matters, so that he may be pleasing to him for whom he has proven himself. [5] Then, too, whoever strives in a competition is not crowned, unless he has competed lawfully. [6] The farmer who labors ought to be the first to share in the produce. [7] Understand what I am saying. For the Lord will give you understanding in all things. [8] Be mindful that the Lord Jesus Christ, who is the offspring of David, has risen again from the dead, according to my Gospel. [9] I labor in this Gospel, even while chained like an evildoer. But the Word of God is not bound. [10] I endure all things for this reason: for the sake of the elect, so that they, too, may obtain the salvation which is in Christ Jesus, with heavenly glory. [11] It is a faithful saying: that if we have died with him, we will also live with him. [12] If we suffer, we will also reign with him. If we deny him, he will also deny us. [13] If we are unfaithful, he remains faithful: he is not able to deny himself. [14] Insist on these things, testifying before the Lord. Do not be contentious about words, for this is useful for nothing but the subversion of listeners. [15] Be solicitous in the task of presenting yourself before God as a proven and unashamed worker who has handled the Word of Truth correctly. [16] But avoid profane or empty talk. For these things advance one greatly in impiety. [17] And their word spreads like a cancer: among these are Hymenaeus and Philetus, [18] who have fallen away from the truth by saying that the resurrection is already complete. And so they have subverted the faith of certain persons. [19] But the firm foundation of God remains standing, having this seal: the Lord knows those who are his own, and all who know the name of the

Lord depart from iniquity. [20] But, in a large house, there are not only vessels of gold and of silver, but also those of wood and of clay; and certainly some are held in honor, but others in dishonor. [21] If anyone, then, will have cleansed himself from these things, he shall be a vessel held in honor, sanctified and useful to the Lord, prepared for every good work. [22] So then, flee from the desires of your youth, yet truly, pursue justice, faith, hope, charity, and peace, along with those who call upon the Lord from a pure heart. [23] But avoid foolish and undisciplined questions, for you know that these produce strife. [24] For the servant of the Lord must not be contentious, but instead he must be meek toward everyone, teachable, patient, [25] correcting with self-restraint those who resist the truth. For at any time God may give them repentance, so as to recognize the truth, [26] and then they may recover from the snares of the devil, by whom they are held captive at his will.

2 TIMOTHY 3

[1] And know this: that in the last days perilous times will press near. [2] Men will be lovers of themselves, greedy, self-exalting, arrogant, blasphemers, disobedient to parents, ungrateful, wicked, [3] without affection, without peace, false accusers, unchaste, cruel, without kindness, [4] traitorous, reckless, self-important, loving pleasure more than God, [5] even having the appearance of piety while rejecting its virtue. And so, avoid them. [6] For among these are ones who penetrate houses and lead away, like captives, foolish women burdened with sins, who are led away by means of various desires, [7] always learning, yet never achieving knowledge of the truth. [8] And in the same manner that Jannes and Jambres resisted Moses, so also will these resist the truth, men corrupted in mind, reprobates from the faith. [9] But they will not advance beyond a certain point. For the folly of the latter shall be made manifest to all, just as that of the former. [10] But you have fully comprehended my doctrine, instruction, purpose, faith, longsuffering, love, patience, [11] persecutions, afflictions; such things as happened to me at Antioch, at Iconium, and at Lystra; how I endured persecutions, and how the Lord rescued me from everything. [12] And all those who willingly live the piety in Christ Jesus will suffer persecution. [13] But evil men and deceivers will advance in evil, erring and sending into error. [14] Yet truly, you should remain in those things which you have learned and which have been entrusted to you. For you know from whom you have learned them. [15] And, from your infancy, you have known the Sacred Scriptures, which are able to instruct you toward salvation, through the faith which is in Christ Jesus. [16] All Scripture, having been divinely inspired, is useful for teaching, for reproof, for correction, and for instruction in justice, [17] so that the man of God may be perfect, having been trained for every good work.

2 TIMOTHY 4

[1] I testify before God, and before Jesus Christ, who shall judge the living and the dead through his return and his kingdom: [2] that you should preach the word urgently, in season and out of season: reprove, entreat, rebuke, with all patience and doctrine. [3] For there shall be a time when they will not endure sound doctrine, but instead, according to their own desires, they will gather to themselves teachers, with itching ears, [4] and certainly, they will turn their hearing away from the truth, and they will be turned toward fables. [5] But as for you, truly, be vigilant, laboring in all things. Do the work of an Evangelist, fulfilling your ministry. Show self-restraint. [6] For I am already being worn away, and the time of my dissolution presses close. [7] I have fought the good fight. I have completed the course. I have preserved the faith. [8] As for the remainder, a crown of justice has been reserved for me, one which the Lord, the just judge, will render to me in that day, and not only to me, but also to those who look forward to his return. Hurry to return to me soon. [9] For Demas has abandoned me, out of love for this age, and he has departed for Thessalonica. [10] Crescens has gone to Galatia; Titus to Dalmatia. [11] Luke alone is with me. Take Mark and bring him with you; for he is useful to me in the ministry. [12] But Tychicus I have sent to Ephesus. [13] When you return, bring with you the supplies that I left with Carpus at Troas, and the books, but especially the parchments. [14] Alexander the coppersmith has shown me much evil; the Lord will repay him according to his works. [15] And you should also avoid him; for he has strongly resisted our words. [16] At my first defense, no one stood by me, but everyone

abandoned me. May it not be counted against them! [17] But the Lord stood with me and strengthened me, so that through me the preaching would be accomplished, and so that all the Gentiles would hear. And I was freed from the mouth of the lion. [18] The Lord has freed me from every evil work, and he will accomplish salvation by his heavenly kingdom. To him be glory forever and ever. Amen. [19] Greet Prisca, and Aquila, and the household of Onesiphorus. [20] Erastus remained at Corinth. And Trophimus I left sick at Miletus. [21] Hurry to arrive before winter. Eubulus, and Pudens, and Linus, and Claudia, and all the brothers greet you. [22] May the Lord Jesus Christ be with your spirit. May grace be with you. Amen.

THE SACRED BIBLE: THE LETTER TO TITUS

CHAPTER 1

[1] Paul, a servant of God and an Apostle of Jesus Christ, in accord with the faith of God's elect and in acknowledgment of the truth which is accompanied by piety, [2] in the hope of the eternal life that God, who does not lie, promised before the ages of time, [3] which, at the proper time, he has manifested by his Word, in the preaching that has been entrusted to me by the command of God our Savior; [4] to Titus, beloved son according to the common faith. Grace and peace, from God the Father and from Christ Jesus our Savior. [5] For this reason, I left you behind in Crete: so that those things which are lacking, you would correct, and so that you would ordain, throughout the communities, priests, (just as I also ordained you) [6] if such a man is without offense, the husband of one wife, having faithful children, not accused of self-indulgence, nor of insubordination. [7] And a bishop, as a steward of God, must be without offense: not arrogant, not short-tempered, not a drunkard, not violent, not desiring tainted profit, [8] but instead: hospitable, kind, sober, just, holy, chaste, [9] embracing faithful speech which is in agreement with doctrine, so that he may be able to exhort in sound doctrine and to argue against those who contradict. [10] For there are, indeed, many who are disobedient, who speak empty words, and who deceive, especially those who are of the circumcision. [11] These must be reproved, for they subvert entire houses, teaching things which should not be taught, for the favor of shameful gain. [12] A certain one of these, a prophet of their own kind, said: "The Cretans are ever liars, evil beasts, lazy gluttons." [13] This testimony is true. Because of this, rebuke them sharply, so that they may be sound in the faith, [14] not paying attention to Jewish fables, nor to the rules of men who have turned themselves away from the truth. [15] All things are clean to those who are clean. But to those who are defiled, and to unbelievers, nothing is clean; for both their mind and their conscience have been polluted. [16] They claim that they know God. But, by their own works, they deny him, since they are abominable, and unbelieving, and reprobate, toward every good work.

CHAPTER 2

[1] But you are to speak the things that befit sound doctrine. [2] Old men should be sober, chaste, prudent, sound in faith, in love, in patience. [3] Old women, similarly, should be in holy attire, not false accusers, not given to much wine, teaching well, [4] so that they may teach prudence to the young women, so that they may love their husbands, love their children, [5] be sensible, chaste, restrained, have concern for the household, be kind, be subordinate to their husbands: so that the Word of God may be not blasphemed. [6] Exhort young men similarly, so that they may show self-restraint. [7] In all things, present yourself as an example of good works: in doctrine, with integrity, with seriousness, [8] with sound words, irreproachably, so that he who is an opponent may dread that he has nothing evil to say about us. [9] Exhort servants to be submissive to their masters, in all things pleasing, not contradicting, [10] not cheating, but in all things showing good fidelity, so that they may adorn the doctrine of God our Savior in all things. [11] For the grace of God our Savior has appeared to all men, [12] instructing us to reject impiety and worldly desires, so that we may live soberly and justly and piously in this age, [13] looking forward to the blessed hope and the advent of the glory of the great God and of our Savior Jesus Christ. [14] He gave himself for our sake, so that he might redeem us from all iniquity, and might cleanse for himself an acceptable people, pursuers of good works. [15] Speak and exhort and argue these things with all authority. Let no one despise you.

CHAPTER 3

[1] Admonish them to be subordinate to the rulers and authorities, to obey their dictates, to be prepared for every good work, [2] to speak evil of no one, not to be litigious, but to be reserved, displaying all meekness toward all men. [3] For, in times past, we ourselves were also unwise, unbelieving, erring, servants of various desires and pleasures, acting with malice and envy, being hateful and hating one another. [4] But then the kindness and humanity of God our Savior appeared. [5] And he saved us, not by works of justice that we had done, but, in accord with his mercy, by the washing of regeneration and by the renovation of the Holy Spirit, [6] whom he has poured out upon us in abundance, through Jesus Christ our Savior, [7] so that, having been justified by his grace, we may become heirs according to the hope of eternal life. [8] This is a faithful saying. And I want you to confirm these things, so that those who believe in God may take care to excel in good works. These things are good and useful to men. [9] But avoid foolish questions, and genealogies, and contentions, as well as arguments against the law. For these are useless and empty. [10] Avoid a man who is a heretic, after the first and second correction, [11] knowing that one who is like this has been subverted, and that he offends; for he has been condemned by his own judgment. [12] When I send Artemas or Tychicus to you, hurry to return to me at Nicopolis. For I have decided to winter there. [13] Send Zenas the lawyer and Apollo ahead with care, and let nothing be lacking to them. [14] But let our men also learn to excel in good works pertaining to the necessities of life, so that they may not be unfruitful. [15] All those who are with me greet you. Greet those who love us in the faith. May the grace of God be with you all. Amen.

Philemon

THE SACRED BIBLE:
THE LETTER TO PHILEMON

CHAPTER 1

[1] Paul, a prisoner of Christ Jesus, and Timothy, a brother, to Philemon, our beloved fellow laborer, [2] and to Apphia, most beloved sister, and to Archippus, our fellow soldier, and to the church which is in your house. [3] Grace and peace to you, from God our Father and from the Lord Jesus Christ. [4] I give thanks to my God, always keeping remembrance of you in my prayers, [5] (for I am hearing of your charity and faith, which you have in the Lord Jesus and with all the saints) [6] so that the participation of your faith may become evident by the recognition of every good work which is in you in Christ Jesus. [7] For I have found great joy and consolation in your charity, because the hearts of the saints have been refreshed by you, brother. [8] Because of this, I have enough confidence in Christ Jesus to command you concerning certain things, [9] but I beg you instead, for the sake of charity, since you are so much like Paul: an old man and now also a prisoner of Jesus Christ. [10] I beg you, on behalf of my son, whom I have begotten in my chains, Onesimus. [11] In times past, he was useless to you, but now he is useful both to me and to you. [12] So I have sent him back to you. And may you receive him like my own heart. [13] I myself wanted to retain him with me, so that he might minister to me, on your behalf, while I am in the chains of the Gospel. [14] But I was willing to do nothing without your counsel, so as not to make use of your good deed as if out of necessity, but only willingly. [15] So perhaps, then, he departed from you for a time, so that you might receive him again for eternity, [16] no longer as a servant, but, in place of a servant, a most beloved brother, especially to me: but how much more to you, both in the flesh and in the Lord! [17] Therefore, if you hold me to be a companion, receive him as you would me. [18] But if he has harmed you in any way, or if he is in your debt, charge it to me. [19] I, Paul, have written this with my own hand: I will repay. And I need not tell you, that you are also in debt yourself, to me. [20] So it is, brother. May I delight with you in the Lord! Refresh my heart in Christ. [21] I have written to you, trusting in your obedience, knowing, too, that you will do even more than what I say. [22] But also, at once, prepare a lodging for me. For I am hoping, through your prayers, to present myself to you. [23] Greet Epaphras, my fellow captive in Christ Jesus, [24] and Mark, Aristarchus, Demas, and Luke, my helpers. [25] May the grace of our Lord Jesus Christ be with your spirit. Amen.

THE SACRED BIBLE: THE LETTER
TO THE HEBREWS

CHAPTER 1

¹In many places and in many ways, in past times, God spoke to the fathers through the Prophets; ²lastly, in these days, he has spoken to us through the Son, whom he appointed as the heir of all things, and through whom he made the world. ³And since the Son is the brightness of his glory, and the figure of his substance, and is carrying all things by the Word of his virtue, thereby accomplishing a purging of sins, he sits at the right hand of Majesty on high. ⁴And having been made so much better than the Angels, he has inherited a name so much greater than theirs. ⁵For to which of the Angels has he ever said: "You are my Son; today have I begotten you?" Or again: "I will be a Father to him, and he shall be a Son to me?" ⁶And again, when he brings the only-begotten Son into the world, he says: "And let all the Angels of God adore him." ⁷And about the Angels, certainly, he says: "He makes his Angels spirits, and his ministers a flame of fire." ⁸But about the Son: "Your throne, O God, is forever and ever. The scepter of your kingdom is a scepter of equity. ⁹You have loved justice, and you have hated iniquity. Because of this, God, your God, has anointed you with the oil of exultation, above your companions." ¹⁰And: "In the beginning, O Lord, you founded the earth. And the heavens are the work of your hands. ¹¹These shall pass away, but you will remain. And all will grow old like a garment. ¹²And you will change them like a cloak, and they shall be changed. Yet you are ever the same, and your years will not diminish." ¹³But to which of the Angels has he ever said: "Sit at my right hand, until I make your enemies your footstool?" ¹⁴Are they not all spirits of ministration, sent to minister for the sake of those who shall receive the inheritance of salvation?

CHAPTER 2

¹For this reason, it is necessary for us to observe more thoroughly the things that we have heard, lest we let them slip away. ²For if a word that was spoken through the Angels has been made firm, and every transgression and disobedience has received the recompense of a just retribution, ³in what way might we escape, if we neglect such a great salvation? For though initially it had begun to be described by the Lord, it was confirmed among us by those who heard him, ⁴with God testifying to it by signs and wonders, and by various miracles, and by the pouring out of the Holy Spirit, in accord with his own will. ⁵For God did not subject the future world, about which we are speaking, to the Angels. ⁶But someone, in a certain place, has testified, saying: "What is man, that you are mindful of him, or the Son of man, that you visit him? ⁷You have reduced him to a little less than the Angels. You have crowned him with glory and honor, and you have set him over the works of your hands. ⁸You have subjected all things under his feet." For in as much as he has subjected all things to him, he has left nothing not subject to him. But in the present time, we do not yet perceive that all things have been made subject to him. ⁹Yet we understand that Jesus, who was reduced to a little less than the Angels, was crowned with glory and honor because of his Passion and death, in order that, by the grace of God, he might taste death for all. ¹⁰For it was fitting for him, because of whom and through whom all things exist, who had led many children into glory, to complete the authorship of their salvation through his Passion. ¹¹For he who sanctifies, and those who are sanctified, are all from One. For this reason, he is not ashamed to call them brothers, saying: ¹²"I will announce your name to my brothers. In the midst of the Church, I will praise you." ¹³And again: "I will be faithful in him." And again: "Behold, I and my children, whom God has given to me." ¹⁴Therefore, because children have a common flesh and blood, he himself also, in like manner, has shared in the same, so that through death, he might destroy him who held the dominion of death, that is, the devil, ¹⁵and so that he might free those who, through the fear of death, had been condemned to servitude throughout their entire life. ¹⁶For at no time did he take hold of the Angels, but instead he took hold of the offspring of Abraham. ¹⁷Therefore, it is fitting for him to be made similar to his brothers in all things, so that he might become a merciful and faithful High Priest before God,

in order that he might bring forgiveness to the offenses of the people. [18] For in as much as he himself has suffered and has been tempted, he also is able to assist those who are tempted.

CHAPTER 3

[1] Therefore, holy brothers, sharers in the heavenly calling, consider the Apostle and High Priest of our confession: Jesus. [2] He is faithful to the One who made him, just as Moses also was, with his entire house. [3] For this Jesus was considered worthy of greater glory than Moses, so much so that the house which he has built holds a greater honor than the former one. [4] For every house is built by someone, but God is the One who has created all things. [5] And certainly Moses was faithful, with his entire house, like any servant, as a testimony to those things that would soon be said. [6] Yet truly, Christ is like a Son in his own house. We are that house, if we firmly retain the faithfulness and the glory of hope, even unto the end. [7] Because of this, it is just as the Holy Spirit says: "If today you hear his voice, [8] harden not your hearts, as in the provocation, the very day of temptation, in the desert, [9] where your fathers tested me, even though they had seen and examined my works for forty years. [10] For this reason, I was enraged against this generation, and I said: They always wander astray in heart. For they have not known my ways. [11] So it is as I swore in my wrath: They shall not enter into my rest!" [12] Be cautious, brothers, lest perhaps there may be, in any of you, an evil heart of unbelief, turning aside from the living God. [13] Instead, exhort one another every day, while it is still called 'today,' so that none of you may become hardened through the falseness of sin. [14] For we have been made participants in Christ. This is only so, if we firmly retain the beginning of his substance, even unto the end. [15] For it has been said: "If today you hear his voice, harden not your hearts, in the same manner as in the former provocation." [16] For some of those listening did provoke him. But not all of these had set forth from Egypt through Moses. [17] So against whom was he angry for forty years? Was it not those who had sinned, whose dead bodies lay prostrate in the desert? [18] But to whom did he swear that they would not enter into his rest, except to those who were incredulous? [19] And so, we perceive that they were not able to enter because of unbelief.

CHAPTER 4

[1] Therefore, we should be afraid, lest the promise of entering into his rest may be relinquished, and some of you may be judged to be lacking. [2] For this was announced to us in a similar manner as to them. But the mere hearing of the word did not benefit them, since it was not joined together with a faith in those things that they heard. [3] For we who have believed shall enter into rest, in the same manner as he said: "So it is as I have sworn in my wrath: They shall not enter into my rest!" And certainly, this is when the works from the foundation of the world have been finished. [4] For, in a certain place, he spoke about the seventh day in this manner: "And God rested on the seventh day from all his works." [5] And in this place again: "They shall not enter into my rest!" [6] Therefore, this is because certain ones remain who are to enter into it, and those to whom it was announced first did not enter into it, because of unbelief. [7] Again, he defines a certain day, after so much time, saying in David, "Today," just as it was stated above, "If today you hear his voice, harden not your hearts." [8] For if Jesus had offered them rest, he would never have spoken, afterward, about another day. [9] And so, there remains a Sabbath of rest for the people of God. [10] For whoever has entered into his rest, the same has also rested from his works, just as God did from his. [11] Therefore, let us hasten to enter into that rest, so that no one may fall into the same example of unbelief. [12] For the Word of God is living and effective: more piercing than any two-edged sword, reaching to the division even between the soul and the spirit, even between the joints and the marrow, and so it discerns the thoughts and intentions of the heart. [13] And there is no created thing that is invisible to his sight. For all things are naked and open to the eyes of him, about whom we are speaking. [14] Therefore, since we have a great High Priest, who has pierced the heavens, Jesus the Son of God, we should hold to our confession. [15] For we do not have a high priest who is unable to have compassion on our infirmities, but rather one who was tempted in all things, just as we are, yet without sin. [16] Therefore, let us go forth with confidence toward the throne of grace, so that we may obtain mercy, and find grace, in a helpful time.

CHAPTER 5

[1] For every high priest, having been taken from among men, is appointed on behalf of men toward the things which pertain to God, so that he may offer gifts and sacrifices on behalf of sins; [2] he is able to commiserate with those who are ignorant and who wander astray, because he himself is also encompassed by infirmity. [3] And because of this, he also must make such offerings for sins even for himself, in the same manner as for the people. [4] Neither does anyone take up this honor himself, but rather he who is called by God, just as Aaron was. [5] Thus, even Christ did not glorify himself, so as to become High Priest, but instead, it was God who said to him: "You are my Son. Today I have begotten you." [6] And similarly, he says in another place: "You are a priest forever, according to the order of Melchizedek." [7] It is Christ who, in the days of his flesh, with a strong cry and tears, offered prayers and supplications to the One who was able to save him from death, and who was heard because of his reverence. [8] And although, certainly, he is the Son of God, he learned obedience by the things that he suffered. [9] And having reached his consummation, he was made, for all who are obedient to him, the cause of eternal salvation, [10] having been called by God to be the High Priest, according to the order of Melchizedek. [11] Our message about him is great, and difficult to explain when speaking, because you have been made feeble when listening. [12] For even though it is the time when you ought to be teachers, you are still lacking, so that you must be taught the things that are the basic elements of the Word of God, and so you have been made like those who are in need of milk, and not of solid food. [13] For anyone who is still feeding on milk is still unskillful in the Word of Justice; for he is like an infant. [14] But solid food is for those who are mature, for those who, by practice, have sharpened their mind, so as to discern good from evil.

CHAPTER 6

[1] Therefore, interrupting an explanation of the basics of Christ, let us consider what is more advanced, not presenting again the fundamentals of repentance from dead works, and of faith toward God, [2] of the doctrine of baptism, and also of the imposition of hands, and of the resurrection of the dead, and of eternal judgment. [3] And we shall do this, if indeed God permits it. [4] For it is impossible for those who were once illuminated, and have even tasted of the heavenly gift, and have become sharers in the Holy Spirit, [5] who, despite having tasted the good Word of God and the virtues of the future age, have yet fallen away, [6] to be renewed again to penance, since they are crucifying again in themselves the Son of God and are still maintaining pretenses. [7] For the earth accepts a blessing from God, by drinking in the rain that often falls upon it, and by producing plants that are useful to those by whom it is cultivated. [8] But whatever brings forth thorns and briers is rejected, and is closest to what is accursed; their consummation is in combustion. [9] But from you, most beloved, we are confident that there will be things better and closer to salvation; even though we speak in this way. [10] For God is not unjust, such that he would forget your work and the love that you have shown in his name. For you have ministered, and you continue to minister, to the saints. [11] Yet we desire that each one of you display the same solicitude toward the fulfillment of hope, even unto the end, [12] so that you may not be slow to act, but instead may be imitators of those who, through faith and patience, shall inherit the promises. [13] For God, in making promises to Abraham, swore by himself, (because he had no one greater by whom he might swear), [14] saying: "Blessing, I shall bless you, and multiplying, I shall multiply you." [15] And in this way, by enduring patiently, he secured the promise. [16] For men swear by what is greater than themselves, and an oath as confirmation is the end of all their controversy. [17] In this matter, God, wanting to reveal more thoroughly the immutability of his counsel to the heirs of the promise, interposed an oath, [18] so that by two immutable things, in which it is impossible for God to lie, we may have the strongest solace: we who have fled together so as to hold fast to the hope set before us. [19] This we have as an anchor of the soul, safe and sound, which advances even to the interior of the veil, [20] to the place where the forerunner Jesus has entered on our behalf, so as to become the High Priest for eternity, according to the order of Melchizedek.

CHAPTER 7

[1] For this Melchizedek, king of Salem, priest of the Most High God, met Abraham, as he was returning from the slaughter of the kings, and blessed him. [2] And Abraham divided to him a tenth part of everything. And in translation his

name is first, indeed, king of justice, and next also king of Salem, that is, king of peace. ³Without father, without mother, without genealogy, having neither beginning of days, nor end of life, he is thereby likened to the Son of God, who remains a priest continuously. ⁴Next, consider how great this man is, since the Patriarch Abraham even gave tithes to him from the principal things. ⁵And indeed, those who are from the sons of Levi, having received the priesthood, hold a commandment to take tithes from the people in accord with the law, that is, from their brothers, even though they also went forth from the loins of Abraham. ⁶But this man, whose lineage is not enumerated with them, received tithes from Abraham, and he blessed even the one who held the promises. ⁷Yet this is without any contradiction, for what is less should be blessed by what is better. ⁸And certainly, here, men who receive tithes still die; but there, he bears witness that he lives. ⁹And so it may be said that even Levi, who received tithes, was himself a tithe through Abraham. ¹⁰For he was still in the loins of his father, when Melchizedek met him. ¹¹Therefore, if consummation had occurred through the Levitical priesthood (for under it the people received the law), then what further need would there be for another Priest to rise up according to the order of Melchizedek, one who was not called according to the order of Aaron? ¹²For since the priesthood has been transferred, it is necessary that the law also be transferred. ¹³For he about whom these things have been spoken is from another tribe, in which no one attends before the altar. ¹⁴For it is evident that our Lord arose out of Judah, a tribe about which Moses said nothing concerning priests. ¹⁵And yet it is far more evident that, according to the likeness of Melchizedek, there rises up another priest, ¹⁶who was made, not according to the law of a carnal commandment, but according to the virtue of an indissoluble life. ¹⁷For he testifies: "You are a priest forever, according to the order of Melchizedek." ¹⁸Certainly, there is a setting aside of the former commandment, because of its weakness and lack of usefulness. ¹⁹For the law led no one to perfection, yet truly it introduced a better hope, through which we draw near to God. ²⁰Moreover, it is not without an oath. For certainly, the others were made priests without an oath. ²¹But this man was made a priest with an oath, by the One who said to him: "The Lord has sworn and he will not repent. You are a priest forever." ²²By so much, Jesus has been made the sponsor of a better testament. ²³And certainly, so many of the others became priests because, due to death, they were prohibited from continuing. ²⁴But this man, because he continues forever, has an everlasting priesthood. ²⁵And for this reason, he is able, continuously, to save those who approach God through him, since he is ever alive to make intercession on our behalf. ²⁶For it was fitting that we should have such a High Priest: holy, innocent, undefiled, set apart from sinners, and exalted higher than the heavens. ²⁷And he has no need, daily, in the manner of other priests, to offer sacrifices, first for his own sins, and then for those of the people. For he has done this once, by offering himself. ²⁸For the law appoints men as priests, though they have infirmities. But, by the word of the oath that is after the law, the Son has been perfected for eternity.

CHAPTER 8

¹Now the main point in the things that have been stated is this: that we have so great a High Priest, who is seated at the right hand of the throne of Majesty in the heavens, ²who is the minister of holy things, and of the true tabernacle, which was established by the Lord, not by man. ³For every high priest is appointed to offer gifts and sacrifices. Therefore, it is necessary for him also to have something to offer. ⁴And so, if he were upon the earth, he would not be a priest, since there would be others to offer gifts according to the law, ⁵gifts which serve as mere examples and shadows of the heavenly things. And so it was answered to Moses, when he was about to complete the tabernacle: "See to it," he said, "that you make everything according to the example which was revealed to you on the mountain." ⁶But now he has been granted a better ministry, so much so that he is also the Mediator of a better testament, which has been confirmed by better promises. ⁷For if the former one had been entirely without fault, then a place certainly would not have been sought for a subsequent one. ⁸For, finding fault with them, he says: "Behold, the days shall arrive, says the Lord, when I will consummate a New Testament over the house of Israel and the house of Judah, ⁹not according to the testament which I made with their fathers, on the day when I took them by the hand, so that I might lead them away from the land of Egypt. For they did not remain in my testament, and so I disregarded them, says the Lord. ¹⁰For

this is the testament which I will set before the house of Israel, after those days, says the Lord. I will instill my laws in their minds, and I will inscribe my laws on their hearts. And so, I will be their God, and they shall be my people. [11] And they will not teach, each one his neighbor, and each one his brother, saying: 'Know the Lord.' For all shall know me, from the least, even to the greatest of them. [12] For I will forgive their iniquities, and I will no longer remember their sins." [13] Now in saying something new, he has made the former old. But that which decays and grows old is close to passing away.

CHAPTER 9

[1] Certainly, the former also had the justifications of worship and a holy place for that age. [2] For a tabernacle was made at first, in which were the lampstand, and the table, and the bread of the Presence, which is called Holy. [3] Then, beyond the second veil, was the tabernacle, which is called the Holy of Holies, [4] having a golden censer, and the ark of the testament, covered all around and on every part with gold, in which was a golden urn containing manna, and the rod of Aaron which had blossomed, and the tablets of the testament. [5] And over the ark were the Cherubim of glory, overshadowing the propitiatory. There is not enough time to speak about each of these things. [6] Yet truly, once such things were placed together, in the first part of the tabernacle, the priests were, indeed, continually entering, so as to carry out the duties of the sacrifices. [7] But into the second part, once a year, the high priest alone entered, not without blood, which he offered on behalf of the neglectful offenses of himself and of the people. [8] In this way, the Holy Spirit is signifying that the way to what is most holy was not yet made manifest, not while the first tabernacle was still standing. [9] And this is a parable for the present time. Accordingly, those gifts and sacrifices that are offered are not able, as concerns the conscience, to make perfect those things that serve only as food and drink, [10] as well as the various washings and justices of the flesh, which were imposed upon them until the time of correction. [11] But Christ, standing as the High Priest of future good things, through a greater and more perfect tabernacle, one not made by hand, that is, not of this creation, [12] entered once into the Holy of Holies, having obtained eternal redemption, neither by the blood of goats, nor of calves, but by his own blood. [13] For if the blood of goats and oxen, and the ashes of a calf, when these are sprinkled, sanctify those who have been defiled, in order to cleanse the flesh, [14] how much more will the blood of Christ, who through the Holy Spirit has offered himself, immaculate, to God, cleanse our conscience from dead works, in order to serve the living God? [15] And thus he is the Mediator of the new testament, so that, by his death, he intercedes for the redemption of those transgressions which were under the former testament, so that those who have been called may receive the promise of an eternal inheritance. [16] For where there is a testament, it is necessary for the death of the one who testifies to intervene. [17] For a testament is confirmed by death. Otherwise, it as yet has no force, as long as the one who testifies lives. [18] Therefore, indeed, the first was not dedicated without blood. [19] For when every commandment of the law had been read by Moses to the entire people, he took up the blood of calves and goats, with water and with scarlet wool and hyssop, and he sprinkled both the book itself and the entire people, [20] saying: "This is the blood of the testament which God has commanded for you." [21] And even the tabernacle, and all the vessels for the ministry, he similarly sprinkled with blood. [22] And nearly everything, according to the law, is to be cleansed with blood. And without the shedding of blood, there is no remission. [23] Therefore, it is necessary for the examples of heavenly things to be cleansed, just as, indeed, these things were. Yet the heavenly things are themselves better sacrifices than these. [24] For Jesus did not enter by means of holy things made with hands, mere examples of the true things, but he entered into Heaven itself, so that he may appear now before the face of God for us. [25] And he did not enter so as to offer himself repeatedly, as the high priest enters into the Holy of Holies each year, with the blood of another. [26] Otherwise, he would need to have suffered repeatedly since the beginning of the world. But now, one time, at the consummation of the ages, he has appeared in order to destroy sin though his own sacrifice. [27] And in the same manner as it has been appointed for men to die one time, and after this, to be judged, [28] so also Christ was offered, one time, in order to empty the sins of so many. He shall appear a second time without sin, for those who await him, unto salvation.

CHAPTER 10

¹For the law contains the shadow of future good things, not the very image of these things. So, by the very same sacrifices which they offer ceaselessly each year, they can never cause these to approach perfection. ²Otherwise, they would have ceased to be offered, because the worshipers, once cleansed, would no longer be conscious of any sin. ³Instead, in these things, a commemoration of sins is made every year. ⁴For it is impossible for sins to be taken away by the blood of oxen and goats. ⁵For this reason, as Christ enters into the world, he says: "Sacrifice and oblation, you did not want. But you have fashioned a body for me. ⁶Holocausts for sin were not pleasing to you. ⁷Then I said, 'Behold, I draw near.' At the head of the book, it has been written of me that I should do your will, O God." ⁸In the above, by saying, "Sacrifices, and oblations, and holocausts for sin, you did not want, nor are those things pleasing to you, which are offered according to the law; ⁹then I said, 'Behold, I have come to do your will, O God,'" he takes away the first, so that he may establish what follows. ¹⁰For by this will, we have been sanctified, through the one time oblation of the body of Jesus Christ. ¹¹And certainly, every priest stands by, ministering daily, and frequently offering the same sacrifices, which are never able to take away sins. ¹²But this man, offering one sacrifice for sins, sits at the right hand of God forever, ¹³awaiting that time when his enemies will be made his footstool. ¹⁴For, by one oblation, he has brought to fulfillment, for all time, those who are sanctified. ¹⁵Now the Holy Spirit also testifies for us about this. For afterward, he said: ¹⁶"And this is the testament which I will commit to them after those days, says the Lord. I will instill my laws in their hearts, and I will inscribe my laws on their minds. ¹⁷And I will no longer remember their sins and iniquities." ¹⁸Now, when there is a remission of these things, there is no longer an oblation for sin. ¹⁹And so, brothers, have faith in the entrance into the Holy of Holies by the blood of Christ, ²⁰and in the new and living Way, which he has initiated for us by the veil, that is, by his flesh, ²¹and in the Great Priest over the house of God. ²²So, let us draw near with a true heart, in the fullness of faith, having hearts cleansed from an evil conscience, and bodies absolved with clean water. ²³Let us hold fast to the confession of our hope, without wavering, for he who has promised is faithful. ²⁴And let us be considerate of one another, so as to prompt ourselves to charity and to good works, ²⁵not deserting our assembly, as some are accustomed to do, but consoling one another, and even more so as you see that the day is approaching. ²⁶For if we sin willingly, after receiving knowledge of the truth, there is no sacrifice remaining for sins, ²⁷but instead, a certain terrible expectation of judgment, and the rage of a fire that shall consume its adversaries. ²⁸If someone dies for acting against the law of Moses, and is shown no compassion because of two or three witnesses, ²⁹how much more, do you think, someone would deserve worse punishments, if he has tread upon the Son of God, and has treated the blood of the testament, by which he was sanctified, as unclean, and has acted with disgrace toward the Spirit of grace? ³⁰For we know that he has said: "Vengeance is mine, and I will repay," and again, "The Lord will judge his people." ³¹It is dreadful to fall into the hands of the living God. ³²But call to mind the former days, in which, after being enlightened, you endured a great struggle of afflictions. ³³And certainly, in one way, by insults and tribulations, you were made a spectacle, but in another way, you became the companions of those who were the object of such behavior. ³⁴For you even had compassion on those who were imprisoned, and you accepted with gladness being deprived of your goods, knowing that you have a better and more lasting substance. ³⁵And so, do not lose your confidence, which has a great reward. ³⁶For it is necessary for you to be patient, so that, by doing the will of God, you may receive the promise. ³⁷"For, in a little while, and somewhat longer, he who is to come will return, and he will not delay. ³⁸For my just man lives by faith. But if he were to draw himself back, he would not please my soul." ³⁹So then, we are not sons who are drawn away to perdition, but we are sons of faith toward the securing of the soul.

CHAPTER 11

¹Now, faith is the substance of things hoped for, the evidence of things not apparent. ²For this reason, the ancients were given testimony. ³By faith, we understand the world to be fashioned by the Word of God, so that the visible might be made by the invisible. ⁴By faith, Abel offered to God a much better sacrifice than that of Cain, through which he obtained testimony that he was

just, in that God offered testimony to his gifts. And through that sacrifice, he still speaks to us, though he is dead. ⁵ By faith, Enoch was transferred, so that he would not see death, and he was not found because God had transferred him. For before he was transferred, he had testimony that he pleased God. ⁶ But without faith, it is impossible to please God. For whoever approaches God must believe that he exists, and that he rewards those who seek him. ⁷ By faith, Noah, having accepted an answer about those things which were not yet seen, being afraid, fashioned an ark for the salvation of his house. Through the ark, he condemned the world, and was established as the heir of the justice that occurs through faith. ⁸ By faith, the one called Abraham obeyed, going out to the place that he was to receive as an inheritance. And he went out, not knowing where he was going. ⁹ By faith, he stayed in the Land of the Promise as if in a foreign land, dwelling in cottages, with Isaac and Jacob, co-heirs of the same promise. ¹⁰ For he was awaiting a city having firm foundations, whose designer and builder is God. ¹¹ By faith also, Sarah herself, being barren, received the ability to conceive offspring, even though she was past that age in life. For she believed him to be faithful, who had promised. ¹² Because of this, there were also born, from one who himself was as if dead, a multitude like the stars of heaven, who are, like the sand of the seashore, innumerable. ¹³ All of these passed away, adhering to faith, not having received the promises, yet beholding them from afar and saluting them, and confessing themselves to be sojourners and guests upon the earth. ¹⁴ For those who speak in this way are themselves indicating that they seek a homeland. ¹⁵ And if, indeed, they had been mindful of the very place from which they departed, they certainly would have returned in time. ¹⁶ But now they hunger for a better place, that is, Heaven. For this reason, God is not ashamed to be called their God. For he has prepared a city for them. ¹⁷ By faith, Abraham, when he was tested, offered Isaac, so that he who had received the promises was offering up his only son. ¹⁸ To him, it was said, "Through Isaac, shall your offspring be summoned," ¹⁹ indicating that God is even able to raise up from the dead. And thus, he also established him as a parable. ²⁰ By faith, also, Isaac blessed Jacob and Esau, concerning future events. ²¹ By faith, Jacob, as he was dying, blessed each of the sons of Joseph; and he reverenced the summit of his rod. ²² By faith, Joseph, as he was dying, recalled the departure of the sons of Israel, and gave a commandment concerning his bones. ²³ By faith, Moses, after being born, was hidden for three months by his parents, because they had seen that he was a graceful infant, and they did not fear the king's edict. ²⁴ By faith, Moses, after growing up, denied himself a place as the son of Pharaoh's daughter, ²⁵ choosing to be afflicted with the people of God, rather than to have the pleasantness of sin for a time, ²⁶ valuing the reproach of Christ to be a greater wealth than the treasures of the Egyptians. For he looked forward to his reward. ²⁷ By faith, he abandoned Egypt, not dreading the animosity of the king. For he pressed on, as if seeing him who is unseen. ²⁸ By faith, he celebrated the Passover and the shedding of the blood, so that he who destroyed the firstborn might not touch them. ²⁹ By faith, they crossed the Red Sea, as if on dry land, yet when the Egyptians attempted it, they were swallowed up. ³⁰ By faith, the walls of Jericho collapsed, after being encircled for seven days. ³¹ By faith, Rahab, the harlot, did not perish with the unbelievers, after receiving the spies with peace. ³² And what should I say next? For time is not sufficient for me to give an account of Gideon, Barak, Samson, Jephthah, David, Samuel, and the Prophets: ³³ those who, by faith, conquered kingdoms, accomplished justice, obtained promises, closed the mouths of lions, ³⁴ extinguished the violence of fire, escaped the edge of the sword, recovered from infirmities, showed strength in battle, turned back the armies of foreigners. ³⁵ Women received their dead by means of resurrection. But others suffered severe punishment, not yet receiving redemption, so that they would find a better resurrection. ³⁶ Truly, others were tested by mocking and lashes, and moreover by chains and imprisonment. ³⁷ They were stoned; they were cut; they were tempted. With the slaughter of the sword, they were killed. They wandered about in sheepskin and in goatskin, in dire need, in anguish afflicted. ³⁸ Of them, the world was not worthy, wandering in solitude on mountains, in the caves and caverns of the earth. ³⁹ And all these, having been proven by the testimony of faith, did not receive the Promise. ⁴⁰ God's Providence holds something better for us, so that not without us would they be perfected.

CHAPTER 12

¹ Furthermore, since we also have so great a cloud of witnesses over us, let us set aside every burden and sin which may surround us, and advance, through

patience, to the struggle offered to us. ² Let us gaze upon Jesus, as the Author and the completion of our faith, who, having joy laid out before him, endured the cross, disregarding the shame, and who now sits at the right hand of the throne of God. ³ So then, meditate upon him who endured such adversity from sinners against himself, so that you may not become weary, failing in your souls. ⁴ For you have not yet resisted unto blood, while striving against sin. ⁵ And you have forgotten the consolation which speaks to you like sons, saying: "My son, do not be willing to neglect the discipline of the Lord. Neither should you become weary, while being rebuked by him." ⁶ For whomever the Lord loves, he chastises. And every son whom he accepts, he scourges. ⁷ Persevere in discipline. God presents you to himself as sons. But what son is there, whom his father does not correct? ⁸ But if you are without that discipline in which all have become sharers, then you are of adultery, and you are not sons. ⁹ Then, too, we have certainly had the fathers of our flesh as instructors, and we reverenced them. Should we not obey the Father of spirits all the more, and so live? ¹⁰ And indeed, for a few days and according to their own wishes, they instructed us. But he does so to our benefit, so that we may receive his sanctification. ¹¹ Now every discipline, in the present time, does not seem a gladness, of course, but a grief. But afterwards, it will repay a most peaceful fruit of justice to those who become trained in it. ¹² Because of this, lift up your lazy hands and your lax knees, ¹³ and straighten the path of your feet, so that no one, being lame, may wander astray, but instead may be healed. ¹⁴ Pursue peace with everyone. Pursue sanctity, without which no one shall see God. ¹⁵ Be contemplative, lest anyone lack the grace of God, lest any root of bitterness spring up and impede you, and by it, many might be defiled, ¹⁶ lest any fornicator or worldly person be like Esau, who, for the sake of one meal, sold his birthright. ¹⁷ For you know that afterwards, when he desired to inherit the benediction, he was rejected. For he found no place for repentance, even though he had sought it with tears. ¹⁸ But you have not drawn near to a tangible mountain, or a burning fire, or a whirlwind, or a mist, or a storm, ¹⁹ or the sound of a trumpet, or a voice of words. Those who had experienced these things excused themselves, lest the Word be spoken to them. ²⁰ For they could not bear what was said, and so, if even a beast would have touched the mountain, it would have been stoned. ²¹ And what was seen was so terrible that even Moses said: "I am terrified, and so, I tremble." ²² But you have drawn near to mount Zion, and to the city of the living God, to the heavenly Jerusalem, and to the company of many thousands of Angels, ²³ and to the Church of the first-born, those who have been inscribed in the heavens, and to God, the judge of all, and to the spirits of the just made perfect, ²⁴ and to Jesus, the Mediator of the New Testament, and to a sprinkling of blood, which speaks better than the blood of Abel. ²⁵ Be careful not to reject the One who is speaking. For if those who rejected him who was speaking upon the earth were not able to escape, so much more we who might turn away from the One who is speaking to us from heaven. ²⁶ Then, his voice moved the earth. But now, he makes a promise, saying: "There is still one more time, and then I will move, not only the earth, but also heaven itself." ²⁷ And so, in saying, "There is still one more time," he declares the transfer of the moveable things of creation, so that those things which are immoveable may remain. ²⁸ Thus, in receiving an immoveable kingdom, we have grace. So, through grace, let us be of service, by pleasing God with fear and reverence. ²⁹ For our God is a consuming fire.

CHAPTER 13

¹ May fraternal charity remain in you. ² And do not be willing to forget hospitality. For by it, certain persons, without realizing it, have received Angels as guests. ³ Remember those who are prisoners, just as if you were imprisoned with them, and those who endure hardships, just as if you were in their place. ⁴ May marriage be honorable in every way, and may the marriage bed be immaculate. For God will judge fornicators and adulterers. ⁵ Let your behavior be without avarice; be content with what you are offered. For he himself has said, "I will not abandon you, and I will not neglect you." ⁶ So then, we may confidently say, "The Lord is my helper. I will not fear what man can do to me." ⁷ Remember your leaders, who have spoken the Word of God to you, whose faith you imitate, by observing the goal of their way of life: ⁸ Jesus Christ, yesterday and today; Jesus Christ forever. ⁹ Do not be led away by changing or strange doctrines. And it is best for the heart to be sustained by grace, not by foods. For the latter have not been as useful to those who walked by them. ¹⁰ We have an altar: those who serve in the tabernacle have no authority to eat from it. ¹¹ For the bodies of those animals whose blood

is carried into the Holy of holies by the high priest, on behalf of sin, are burned outside the camp. [12] Because of this, Jesus, too, in order to sanctify the people by his own blood, suffered outside the gate. [13] And so, let us go forth to him, outside the camp, bearing his reproach. [14] For in this place, we have no everlasting city; instead, we seek one in the future. [15] Therefore, through him, let us offer the sacrifice of continual praise to God, which is the fruit of lips confessing his name. [16] But do not be willing to forget good works and fellowship. For God is deserving of such sacrifices. [17] Obey your leaders and be subject to them. For they watch over you, as if to render an account of your souls. So then, may they do this with joy, and not with grief. Otherwise, it would not be as helpful to you. [18] Pray for us. For we trust that we have a good conscience, being willing to conduct ourselves well in all things. [19] And I beg you, all the more, to do this, so that I may be quickly returned to you. [20] Then may the God of peace, who led back from the dead that great Pastor of sheep, our Lord Jesus Christ, with the blood of the eternal testament, [21] equip you with all goodness, so that you may do his will. May he accomplish in you whatever is pleasing in his sight, through Jesus Christ, to whom is glory forever and ever. Amen. [22] And I beg you, brothers, that you may permit this word of consolation, especially since I have written to you with few words. [23] Know that our brother Timothy has been set free. If he arrives soon, then I will see you with him. [24] Greet all your leaders and all the saints. The brothers from Italy greet you. [25] Grace be with you all. Amen.

THE SACRED BIBLE:
THE LETTER OF JAMES

CHAPTER 1

[1] James, servant of God and of our Lord Jesus Christ, to the twelve tribes of the dispersion, greetings. [2] My brothers, when you have fallen into various trials, consider everything a joy, [3] knowing that the proving of your faith exercises patience, [4] and patience brings a work to perfection, so that you may be perfect and whole, deficient in nothing. [5] But if anyone among you is in need of wisdom, let him petition God, who gives abundantly to all without reproach, and it shall be given to him. [6] But he should ask with faith, doubting nothing. For he who doubts is like a wave on the ocean, which is moved about by the wind and carried away; [7] then a man should not consider that he would receive anything from the Lord. [8] For a man who is of two minds is inconstant in all his ways. [9] Now a humble brother should glory in his exaltation, [10] and a rich one, in his humiliation, for he will pass away like the flower of the grass. [11] For the sun has risen with a scorching heat, and has dried the grass, and its flower has fallen off, and the appearance of its beauty has perished. So also will the rich one wither away, according to his paths. [12] Blessed is the man who suffers temptation. For when he has been proven, he shall receive the crown of life which God has promised to those who love him. [13] No one should say, when he is tempted, that he was tempted by God. For God does not entice toward evils, and he himself tempts no one. [14] Yet truly, each one is tempted by his own desires, having been enticed and drawn away. [15] Thereafter, when desire has conceived, it gives birth to sin. Yet truly sin, when it has been consummated, produces death. [16] And so, do not choose to go astray, my most beloved brothers. [17] Every excellent gift and every perfect gift is from above, descending from the Father of lights, with whom there is no change, nor any shadow of alteration. [18] For by his own will he produced us through the Word of truth, so that we might be a kind of beginning among his creatures. [19] You know this, my most beloved brothers. So let every man be quick to listen, but slow to speak and slow to anger. [20] For the anger of man does not accomplish the justice of God. [21] Because of this, having cast away all uncleanness and an abundance of malice, receive with meekness the newly-grafted Word, which is able to save your souls. [22] So be doers of the Word, and not listeners only, deceiving yourselves. [23] For if anyone is a listener of the Word, but not also a doer, he is comparable to a man gazing into a mirror upon the face that he was born with; [24] and after considering himself, he went away and promptly forgot what he had seen. [25] But he who gazes upon the perfect law of liberty, and who remains in it, is not a forgetful hearer, but instead a doer of the work. He shall be blessed in what he does. [26] But if anyone considers himself to be religious, but he does not restrain his tongue, but instead seduces his own heart: such a one's religion is vanity. [27] This is religion, clean and undefiled before God the Father: to visit orphans and widows in their tribulations, and to keep yourself immaculate, apart from this age.

CHAPTER 2

[1] My brothers, within the glorious faith of our Lord Jesus Christ, do not choose to show favoritism toward persons. [2] For if a man has entered your assembly having a gold ring and splendid apparel, and if a poor man has also entered, in dirty clothing, [3] and if you are then attentive to the one who is clothed in excellent apparel, so that you say to him, "You may sit in this good place," but you say to the poor man, "You stand over there," or, "Sit below my footstool," [4] are you not judging within yourselves, and have you not become judges with unjust thoughts? [5] My most beloved brothers, listen. Has not God chosen the poor in this world to be rich in faith and heirs of the kingdom that God has promised to those who love him? [6] But you have dishonored the poor. Are not the rich the ones who oppress you through power? And are not they the ones who drag you to judgment? [7] Are not they the ones who blaspheme the good name which has been invoked over you? [8] So if you perfect the regal law, according to the Scriptures, "You shall love your neighbor as yourself," then you do well. [9] But if you show favoritism to persons, then you commit a sin, having been convicted again by the law as transgressors. [10] Now whoever has observed the whole law,

yet who offends in one matter, has become guilty of all. [11] For he who said, "You shall not commit adultery," also said, "You shall not kill." So if you do not commit adultery, but you kill, you have become a transgressor of the law. [12] So speak and act just as you are beginning to be judged, by the law of liberty. [13] For judgment is without mercy toward him who has not shown mercy. But mercy exalts itself above judgment. [14] My brothers, what benefit is there if someone claims to have faith, but he does not have works? How would faith be able to save him? [15] So if a brother or sister is naked and daily in need of food, [16] and if anyone of you were to say to them: "Go in peace, keep warm and nourished," and yet not give them the things that are necessary for the body, of what benefit is this? [17] Thus even faith, if it does not have works, is dead, in and of itself. [18] Now someone may say: "You have faith, and I have works." Show me your faith without works! But I will show you my faith by means of works. [19] You believe that there is one God. You do well. But the demons also believe, and they tremble greatly. [20] So then, are you willing to understand, O foolish man, that faith without works is dead? [21] Was not our father Abraham justified by means of works, by offering his son Isaac upon the altar? [22] Do you see that faith was cooperating with his works, and that by means of works faith was brought to fulfillment? [23] And so the Scripture was fulfilled which says: "Abraham believed God, and it was reputed to him unto justice." And so he was called the friend of God. [24] Do you see that a man is justified by means of works, and not by faith alone? [25] Similarly also, Rahab, the harlot, was she not justified by works, by receiving the messengers and sending them out through another way? [26] For just as the body without the spirit is dead, so also faith without works is dead.

CHAPTER 3

[1] My brothers, not many of you should choose to become teachers, knowing that you shall receive a stricter judgment. [2] For we all offend in many ways. If anyone does not offend in word, he is a perfect man. And he is then able, as if with a bridle, to lead the whole body around. [3] For so we put bridles into the mouths of horses, in order to submit them to our will, and so we turn their whole body around. [4] Consider also the ships, which, though they are great and may be driven by strong winds, yet they are turned around with a small rudder, to be directed to wherever the strength of the pilot might will. [5] So also the tongue certainly is a small part, but it moves great things. Consider that a small fire can set ablaze a great forest. [6] And so the tongue is like a fire, comprising all iniquity. The tongue, stationed in the midst of our body, can defile the entire body and inflame the wheel of our nativity, setting a fire from Hell. [7] For the nature of all beasts and birds and serpents and others is ruled over, and has been ruled over, by human nature. [8] But no man is able to rule over the tongue, a restless evil, full of deadly poison. [9] By it we bless God the Father, and by it we speak evil of men, who have been made in the likeness of God. [10] From the same mouth proceeds blessing and cursing. My brothers, these things ought not to be so! [11] Does a fountain emit, out of the same opening, both sweet and bitter water? [12] My brothers, can the fig tree yield grapes? Or the vine, figs? Then neither is salt water able to produce fresh water. [13] Who is wise and well-taught among you? Let him show, by means of good conversation, his work in the meekness of wisdom. [14] But if you hold a bitter zeal, and if there is contention in your hearts, then do not boast and do not be liars against the truth. [15] For this is not wisdom, descending from above, but rather it is earthly, beastly, and diabolical. [16] For wherever envy and contention is, there too is inconstancy and every depraved work. [17] But within the wisdom that is from above, certainly, chastity is first, and next peacefulness, meekness, openness, consenting to what is good, a plenitude of mercy and good fruits, not judging, without falseness. [18] And so the fruit of justice is sown in peace by those who make peace.

CHAPTER 4

[1] Where do wars and contentions among you come from? Is it not from this: from your own desires, which battle within your members? [2] You desire, and you do not have. You envy and you kill, and you are unable to obtain. You argue and you fight, and you do not have, because you do not ask. [3] You ask and you do not receive, because you ask badly, so that you may use it toward your own desires. [4] You adulterers! Do you not know that the friendship of this world is hostile to God? Therefore, whoever has chosen to be a friend of this world has been made into an enemy of God. [5] Or do you think that Scripture says in vain: "The spirit which

lives within you desires unto envy?" [6] But he gives a greater grace. Therefore he says: "God resists the arrogant, but he gives grace to the humble." [7] Therefore, be subject to God. But resist the devil, and he will flee from you. [8] Draw near to God, and he will draw near to you. Cleanse your hands, you sinners! And purify your hearts, you duplicitous souls! [9] Be afflicted: mourn and weep. Let your laughter be turned into mourning, and your gladness into sorrow. [10] Be humbled in the sight of the Lord, and he will exalt you. [11] Brothers, do not choose to slander one another. Whoever slanders his brother, or whoever judges his brother, slanders the law and judges the law. But if you judge the law, you are not a doer of the law, but a judge. [12] There is one lawgiver and one judge. He is able to destroy, and he is able to set free. [13] But who are you to judge your neighbor? Consider this, you who say, "Today or tomorrow we will go into that city, and certainly we will spend a year there, and we will do business, and we will make our profit," [14] consider that you do not know what will be tomorrow. [15] For what is your life? It is a mist that appears for a brief time, and afterwards will vanish away. So what you ought to say is: "If the Lord wills," or, "If we live," we will do this or that. [16] But now you exult in your arrogance. All such exultation is wicked. [17] Therefore, he who knows that he ought to do a good thing, and does not do it, for him it is a sin.

CHAPTER 5

[1] Act now, you who are wealthy! Weep and wail in your miseries, which will soon come upon you! [2] Your riches have been corrupted, and your garments have been eaten by moths. [3] Your gold and silver have rusted, and their rust will be a testimony against you, and it will eat away at your flesh like fire. You have stored up wrath for yourselves unto the last days. [4] Consider the pay of the workers who reaped your fields: it has been misappropriated by you; it cries out. And their cry has entered into the ears of the Lord of hosts. [5] You have feasted upon the earth, and you have nourished your hearts with luxuries, unto the day of slaughter. [6] You led away and killed the Just One, and he did not resist you. [7] Therefore, be patient, brothers, until the advent of the Lord. Consider that the farmer anticipates the precious fruit of the earth, waiting patiently, until he receives the early and the late rains. [8] Therefore, you too should be patient and should strengthen your hearts. For the advent of the Lord draws near. [9] Brothers, do not complain against one another, so that you may not be judged. Behold, the judge stands before the door. [10] My brothers, consider the Prophets, who spoke in the name of the Lord, as an example of departing from evil, of labor, and of patience. [11] Consider that we beatify those who have endured. You have heard of the patient suffering of Job. And you have seen the end of the Lord, that the Lord is merciful and compassionate. [12] But before all things, my brothers, do not choose to swear, neither by heaven, nor by the earth, nor in any other oath. But let your word 'Yes' be yes, and your word 'No' be no, so that you may not fall under judgment. [13] Is any of you sad? Let him pray. Is he even-tempered? Let him sing psalms. [14] Is anyone ill among you? Let him bring in the priests of the Church, and let them pray over him, anointing him with oil in the name of the Lord. [15] And a prayer of faith will save the infirm, and the Lord will alleviate him. And if he has sins, these will be forgiven him. [16] Therefore, confess your sins to one another, and pray for one another, so that you may be saved. For the unremitting prayer of a just person prevails over many things. [17] Elijah was a mortal man like us, and in prayer he prayed that it would not rain upon the earth. And it did not rain for three years and six months. [18] And he prayed again. And the heavens gave rain, and the earth brought forth her fruit. [19] My brothers, if anyone of you strays from the truth, and if someone converts him, [20] he ought to know that whoever causes a sinner to be converted from the error of his ways will save his soul from death and will cover a multitude of sins.

1 Peter

THE SACRED BIBLE: THE FIRST LETTER OF PETER

1 PETER 1

¹Peter, Apostle of Jesus Christ, to the newly-arrived elect of the dispersion in Pontus, Galatia, Cappadocia, Asia, and Bithynia, ²in accord with the foreknowledge of God the Father, in the sanctification of the Spirit, with the obedience and the sprinkling of the blood of Jesus Christ: May grace and peace be multiplied for you. ³Blessed be the God and Father of our Lord Jesus Christ, who according to his great mercy has regenerated us into a living hope, through the resurrection of Jesus Christ from the dead: ⁴unto an incorruptible and undefiled and unfading inheritance, which is reserved for you in heaven. ⁵By the power of God, you are guarded through faith for a salvation which is ready to be revealed in the end time. ⁶In this, you should exult, if now, for a brief time, it is necessary to be made sorrowful by various trials, ⁷so that the testing of your faith, which is much more precious than gold tested by fire, may be found in praise and glory and honor at the revelation of Jesus Christ. ⁸For though you have not seen him, you love him. In him also, though you do not see him, you now believe. And in believing, you shall exult with an inexpressible and glorious joy, ⁹returning with the goal of your faith, the salvation of souls. ¹⁰About this salvation, the prophets inquired and diligently searched, those who prophesied about the future grace in you, ¹¹inquiring as to what type of condition was signified to them by the Spirit of Christ, when foretelling those sufferings that are in Christ, as well as the subsequent glories. ¹²To them, it was revealed that they were ministering, not for themselves, but for you those things which have now been announced to you through those who have preached the Gospel to you, through the Holy Spirit, who was sent down from heaven to the One upon whom the Angels desire to gaze. ¹³For this reason, gird the waist of your mind, be sober, and hope perfectly in the grace that is offered to you in the revelation of Jesus Christ. ¹⁴Be like sons of obedience, not conforming to the desires of your former ignorance, ¹⁵but in accord with him who has called you: the Holy One. And in every behavior, you yourself must be holy, ¹⁶for it is written: "You shall be holy, for I am Holy." ¹⁷And if you invoke as Father him who, without showing favoritism to persons, judges according to each one's work, then act in fear during the time of your sojourning here. ¹⁸For you know that it was not with corruptible gold or silver that you were redeemed away from your useless behavior in the traditions of your fathers, ¹⁹but it was with the precious blood of Christ, an immaculate and undefiled lamb, ²⁰foreknown, certainly, before the foundation of the world, and made manifest in these latter times for your sake. ²¹Through him, you have been faithful to God, who raised him up from the dead and gave him glory, so that your faith and hope would be in God. ²²So chastise your souls with the obedience of charity, in fraternal love, and love one another from a simple heart, attentively. ²³For you have been born again, not from corruptible seed, but from what is incorruptible, from the Word of God, living and remaining for all eternity. ²⁴For all flesh is like the grass and all its glory is like the flower of the grass. The grass withers and its flower falls away. ²⁵But the Word of the Lord endures for eternity. And this is the Word that has been evangelized to you.

1 PETER 2

¹Therefore, set aside all malice and all deceitfulness, as well as falseness and envy and every detraction. ²Like newborn infants, desire the milk of reasonableness without guile, so that by this you may increase unto salvation, ³if it is true that you have tasted that the Lord is sweet. ⁴And approaching him as if he were a living stone, rejected by men, certainly, but elect and honored by God, ⁵be also yourselves like living stones, built upon him, a spiritual house, a holy priesthood, so as to offer up spiritual sacrifices, acceptable to God through Jesus Christ. ⁶Because of this, Scripture asserts: "Behold, I am setting in Zion a chief cornerstone, elect, precious. And whoever will have believed in him will not be confounded." ⁷Therefore, to you who believe, he is honor. But to those who do not believe, the stone which the builders have rejected, the same has been made into the head of the corner, ⁸and a stone of offense, and a rock of scandal, to those who are offended by the Word; neither do they believe, though they also have been built upon him. ⁹But you are a chosen generation, a royal priesthood,

a holy nation, an acquired people, so that you may announce the virtues of him who has called you out of darkness into his marvelous light. ¹⁰Though in past times you were not a people, yet now you are the people of God. Though you had not obtained mercy, yet now you have obtained mercy. ¹¹Most beloved, I beg you, as new arrivals and sojourners, to abstain from carnal desires, which battle against the soul. ¹²Keep your behavior among the Gentiles to what is good, so that, when they slander you as if you were evildoers, they may, by the good works that are seen in you, glorify God on the day of visitation. ¹³Therefore, be subject to every human creature because of God, whether it is to the king as preeminent, ¹⁴or to leaders as having been sent from him for vindication over evildoers, it is truly for the praise of what is good. ¹⁵For such is the will of God, that by doing good you may bring about the silence of imprudent and ignorant men, ¹⁶in an open manner, and not as if cloaking malice with liberty, but like servants of God. ¹⁷Honor everyone. Love brotherhood. Fear God. Honor the king. ¹⁸Servants, be subject to your masters with all fear, not only to the good and meek, but also to the unruly. ¹⁹For this is grace: when, because of God, a man willingly endures sorrows, suffering injustice. ²⁰For what glory is there, if you sin and then suffer a beating? But if you do well and suffer patiently, this is grace with God. ²¹For you have been called to this because Christ also suffered for us, leaving you an example, so that you would follow in his footsteps. ²²He committed no sin, neither was deceit found in his mouth. ²³And when evil was spoken against him, he did not speak evil. When he suffered, he did not threaten. Then he handed himself over to him who judged him unjustly. ²⁴He himself bore our sins in his body upon the tree, so that we, having died to sin, would live for justice. By his wounds, you have been healed. ²⁵For you were like wandering sheep. But now you have been turned back toward the Pastor and the Bishop of your souls.

1 PETER 3

¹Similarly also, wives should be subject to their husbands, so that, even if some do not believe the Word, they may benefit without the Word, through the behavior of these wives, ²as they consider with fear your chaste behavior. ³For you, there should be no unnecessary adornment of the hair, or surrounding with gold, or the wearing of ornate clothing. ⁴Instead, you should be a hidden person of the heart, with the incorruptibility of a quiet and meek spirit, rich in the sight of God. ⁵For in this way, in past times also, holy women adorned themselves, hoping in God, being subject to their own husbands. ⁶For so Sarah obeyed Abraham, calling him lord. You are her daughters, well-behaved and unafraid of any disturbance. ⁷Similarly, you husbands should live with them in accord with knowledge, bestowing honor on the female as the weaker vessel and as co-heirs of the life of grace, so that your prayers may not be hindered. ⁸And finally, may you all be of one mind: compassionate, loving brotherhood, merciful, meek, humble, ⁹not repaying evil with evil, nor slander with slander, but, to the contrary, repaying with blessings. For to this you have been called, so that you may possess the inheritance of a blessing. ¹⁰For whoever wants to love life and to see good days should restrain his tongue from evil, and his lips, so that they utter no deceit. ¹¹Let him turn away from evil, and do good. Let him seek peace, and pursue it. ¹²For the eyes of the Lord are upon the just, and his ears are with their prayers, but the countenance of the Lord is upon those who do evil. ¹³And who is it who can harm you, if you are zealous in what is good? ¹⁴And yet, even when you suffer something for the sake of justice, you are blessed. So then, do not be afraid with their fear, and do not be disturbed. ¹⁵But sanctify Christ the Lord in your hearts, being always ready to give an explanation to all who ask you the reason for that hope which is in you. ¹⁶But do so with meekness and fear, having a good conscience, so that, in whatever matter they may slander you, they shall be confounded, since they falsely accuse your good behavior in Christ. ¹⁷For it is better to suffer for doing good, if it is the will of God, than for doing evil. ¹⁸For Christ also died once for our sins, the Just One on behalf of the unjust, so that he might offer us to God, having died, certainly, in the flesh, but having been enlivened by the Spirit. ¹⁹And in the Spirit, he preached to those who were in prison, going to those souls ²⁰who had been unbelieving in past times, while they waited for the patience of God, as in the days of Noah, when the ark was being built. In that ark, a few, that is, eight souls, were saved by water. ²¹And now you also are saved, in a similar manner, by baptism, not by the testimony of sordid flesh, but by the examination of a good conscience in God, through the resurrection of Jesus Christ. ²²He is at the right hand of God, devouring death, so

that we may be made heirs to eternal life. And since he has journeyed to heaven, the Angels and powers and virtues are subject to him.

1 PETER 4

[1] Since Christ has suffered in the flesh, you also should be armed with the same intention. For he who suffers in the flesh desists from sin, [2] so that now he may live, for the remainder of his time in the flesh, not by the desires of men, but by the will of God. [3] For the time that has passed is sufficient to have fulfilled the will of the Gentiles, those who have walked in luxuries, lusts, intoxication, feasting, drinking, and the illicit worship of idols. [4] About this, they wonder why you do not rush with them into the same confusion of indulgences, blaspheming. [5] But they must render an account to him who is prepared to judge the living and the dead. [6] For because of this, the Gospel was also preached to the dead, so that they might be judged, certainly, just like men in the flesh, yet also, so that they might live according to God, in the Spirit. [7] But the end of everything draws near. And so, be prudent, and be vigilant in your prayers. [8] But, before all things, have a constant mutual charity among yourselves. For love covers a multitude of sins. [9] Show hospitality to one another without complaining. [10] Just as each of you has received grace, minister in the same way to one another, as good stewards of the manifold grace of God. [11] When anyone speaks, it should be like words of God. When anyone ministers, it should be from the virtue that God provides, so that in all things God may be honored through Jesus Christ. To him is glory and dominion forever and ever. Amen. [12] Most beloved, do not choose to sojourn in the passion which is a temptation to you, as if something new might happen to you. [13] But instead, commune in the Passion of Christ, and be glad that, when his glory will be revealed, you too may rejoice with exultation. [14] If you are reproached for the name of Christ, you will be blessed, because that which is of the honor, glory, and power of God, and that which is of his Spirit, rests upon you. [15] But let none of you suffer for being a murderer, or a thief, or a slanderer, or one who covets what belongs to another. [16] But if one of you suffers for being a Christian, he should not be ashamed. Instead, he should glorify God in that name. [17] For it is time that judgment begin at the house of God. And if it is first from us, what shall be the end of those who do not believe the Gospel of God? [18] And if the just man will scarcely be saved, where will the impious and the sinner appear? [19] Therefore, too, let those who suffer according to the will of God commend their souls by good deeds to the faithful Creator.

1 PETER 5

[1] Therefore, I beg the elders who are among you, as one who is also an elder and a witness of the Passion of Christ, who also shares in that glory which is to be revealed in the future: [2] pasture the flock of God that is among you, providing for it, not as a requirement, but willingly, in accord with God, and not for the sake of tainted profit, but freely, [3] not so as to dominate by means of the clerical state, but so as to be formed into a flock from the heart. [4] And when the Leader of pastors will have appeared, you shall secure an unfading crown of glory. [5] Similarly, young persons, be subject to the elders. And infuse all humility among one another, for God resists the arrogant, but to the humble he gives grace. [6] And so, be humbled under the powerful hand of God, so that he may exalt you in the time of visitation. [7] Cast all your cares upon him, for he takes care of you. [8] Be sober and vigilant. For your adversary, the devil, is like a roaring lion, traveling around and seeking those whom he might devour. [9] Resist him by being strong in faith, being aware that the same passions afflict those who are your brothers in the world. [10] But the God of all grace, who has called us to his eternal glory in Christ Jesus, will himself perfect, confirm, and establish us, after a brief time of suffering. [11] To him be glory and dominion forever and ever. Amen. [12] I have written briefly, through Sylvanus, whom I consider to be a faithful brother to you, begging and testifying that this is the true grace of God, in which you have been established. [13] The Church which is in Babylon, elect together with you, greets you, as does my son, Mark. [14] Greet one another with a holy kiss. Grace be to all of you who are in Christ Jesus. Amen.

2 Peter

THE SACRED BIBLE:
THE SECOND LETTER OF PETER

2 PETER 1

¹Simon Peter, servant and Apostle of Jesus Christ, to those who have been allotted an equal faith with us in the justice of our God and in our Savior Jesus Christ. ²Grace to you. And may peace be fulfilled according to the plan of God and of Christ Jesus our Lord, ³in the same manner that all things which are for life and piety have been given to us by his Divine virtue, through the plan of him who has called us to our own glory and virtue. ⁴Through Christ, he has given us the greatest and most precious promises, so that by these things you may become sharers in the Divine Nature, fleeing from the corruption of that desire which is in the world. ⁵But as for you, taking up every concern, minister virtue in your faith; and in virtue, knowledge; ⁶and in knowledge, moderation; and in moderation, patience; and in patience, piety; ⁷and in piety, love of brotherhood; and in love of brotherhood, charity. ⁸For if these things are with you, and if they abound, they will cause you to be neither empty, nor without fruit, within the plan of our Lord Jesus Christ. ⁹For he who does not have these things at hand is blind and groping, being forgetful of his purification from his former offenses. ¹⁰Because of this, brothers, be all the more diligent, so that by good works you may make certain your calling and election. For in doing these things, you do not sin at any time. ¹¹For in this way, you shall be provided abundantly with an entrance into the eternal kingdom of our Lord and Savior Jesus Christ. ¹²For this reason, I will always begin to admonish you about these things, even though, certainly, you know them and are confirmed in the present truth. ¹³But I consider it just, as long as I am in this tabernacle, to stir you up with admonishments. ¹⁴For it is certain that the laying to rest of this, my tabernacle, is approaching swiftly, just as our Lord Jesus Christ has also indicated to me. ¹⁵Therefore, I will present a work for you to have, so that, frequently after my passing, you may call to mind these things. ¹⁶For it was not by following fanciful doctrines that we made known to you the power and presence of our Lord Jesus Christ, but we were made eyewitnesses of his greatness. ¹⁷For he received honor and glory from God the Father, whose voice descended to him from the magnificent glory: "This is my beloved Son, in whom I am well pleased. Listen to him." ¹⁸We also heard this voice conveyed from heaven, when we were with him on the holy mountain. ¹⁹And so, we have an even firmer prophetic word, to which you would do well to listen, as to a light shining within a dark place, until the day dawns, and the daystar rises, in your hearts. ²⁰Understand this first: that every prophecy of Scripture does not result from one's own interpretation. ²¹For prophecy was not conveyed by human will at any time. Instead, holy men were speaking about God while inspired by the Holy Spirit.

2 PETER 2

¹But there were also false prophets among the people, just as there will be among you lying teachers, who will introduce divisions of perdition, and they will deny him who bought them, the Lord, bringing upon themselves swift destruction. ²And many persons will follow their indulgences; through such persons, the way of truth will be blasphemed. ³And in avarice, they will negotiate about you with false words. Their judgment, in the near future, is not delayed, and their perdition does not sleep. ⁴For God did not spare those Angels who sinned, but instead delivered them, as if dragged down by infernal ropes, into the torments of the underworld, to be reserved unto judgment. ⁵And he did not spare the original world, but he preserved the eighth one, Noah, the herald of justice, bringing the flood upon the world of the impious. ⁶And he reduced the cities of Sodom and Gomorrah to ashes, condemning them to be overthrown, setting them as an example to anyone who might act impiously. ⁷And he rescued a just man, Lot, who was oppressed by the unjust and lewd behavior of the wicked. ⁸For in seeing and in hearing, he was just, though he lived with those who, from day to day, crucified the just soul with works of iniquity. ⁹Thus, the Lord knows how to rescue the pious from trials, and how to reserve the iniquitous for torments on the day of judgment; ¹⁰even more so, those who walk after the flesh in unclean desires, and who despise proper authority. Boldly pleasing themselves, they do

not dread to introduce divisions by blaspheming; [11] whereas the Angels, who are greater in strength and virtue, did not bring against themselves such a deplorable judgment. [12] Yet truly, these others, like irrational beasts, naturally fall into traps and into ruin by blaspheming whatever they do not understand, and so they shall perish in their corruption, [13] receiving the reward of injustice, the fruition of valuing the delights of the day: defilements and stains, overflowing with self-indulgences, taking pleasure in their feasts with you, [14] having eyes full of adultery and of incessant offenses, luring unstable souls, having a heart well-trained in avarice, sons of curses! [15] Abandoning the straight path, they wandered astray, having followed the way of Balaam, the son of Beor, who loved the wages of iniquity. [16] Yet truly, he had a correction of his madness: the mute animal under the yoke, which, by speaking with a human voice, forbid the folly of the prophet. [17] These ones are like fountains without water, and like clouds stirred up by whirlwinds. For them, the mist of darkness is reserved. [18] For, speaking with the arrogance of vanity, they lure, by the desires of fleshly pleasures, those who are fleeing to some extent, who are being turned from error, [19] promising them freedoms, while they themselves are the servants of corruption. For by whatever a man is overcome, of this also is he the servant. [20] For if, after taking refuge from the defilements of the world in the understanding of our Lord and Savior Jesus Christ, they again become entangled and overcome by these things, then the latter state becomes worse than the former. [21] For it would have been better for them not to have known the way of justice than, after acknowledging it, to turn away from that holy commandment which was handed on to them. [22] For the truth of the proverb has happened to them: The dog has returned to his own vomit, and the washed sow has returned to her wallowing in the mud.

2 PETER 3

[1] Consider, most beloved, this second epistle which I am writing to you, in which I stir up, by admonition, your sincere mind, [2] so that you may be mindful of those words that I preached to you from the holy prophets, and of the precepts of the Apostles of your Lord and Savior. [3] Know this first: that in the last days there will arrive deceitful mockers, walking according to their own desires, [4] saying: "Where is his promise or his advent? For from the time that the fathers have slept, all things have continued just as they were from the beginning of creation." [5] But they willfully ignore this: that the heavens existed first, and that the earth, from water and through water, was established by the Word of God. [6] By water, the former world then, having been inundated with water, perished. [7] But the heavens and the earth that exist now were restored by the same Word, being reserved unto fire on the day of judgment, and unto the perdition of impious men. [8] Yet truly, let this one thing not escape notice, most beloved, that with the Lord one day is like a thousand years, and a thousand years is like one day. [9] The Lord is not delaying his promise, as some imagine, but he does act patiently for your sake, not wanting anyone to perish, but wanting all to be turned back to penance. [10] Then the day of the Lord shall arrive like a thief. On that day, the heavens shall pass away with great violence, and truly the elements shall be dissolved with heat; then the earth, and the works that are within it, shall be completely burned up. [11] Therefore, since all these things will be dissolved, what kind of people ought you to be? In behavior and in piety, be holy, [12] waiting for, and hurrying toward, the advent of the day of the Lord, by which the burning heavens shall be dissolved, and the elements shall melt from the heat of the fire. [13] Yet truly, in accord with his promises, we are looking forward to the new heavens and the new earth, in which justice lives. [14] Therefore, most beloved, while awaiting these things, be diligent, so that you may be found to be immaculate and unassailable before him, in peace. [15] And let the longsuffering of our Lord be considered salvation, as also our most beloved brother Paul, according to the wisdom given to him, has written to you, [16] just as he also spoke in all of his epistles about these things. In these, there are certain things which are difficult to understand, which the unlearned and the unsteady distort, as they also do the other Scriptures, to their own destruction. [17] But since you, brothers, know these things beforehand, be cautious, lest by being drawn into the error of the foolish, you may fall away from your own steadfastness. [18] Yet truly, increase in grace and in the knowledge of our Lord and Savior Jesus Christ. To him be glory, both now and in the day of eternity. Amen.

THE SACRED BIBLE: THE FIRST LETTER OF JOHN

1 JOHN 1

[1] He who was from the beginning, whom we have heard, whom we have seen with our eyes, upon whom we have gazed, and whom our hands have certainly touched: He is the Word of Life. [2] And that Life has been made manifest. And we have seen, and we testify, and we announce to you: the Eternal Life, who was with the Father, and who appeared to us. [3] He whom we have seen and heard, we announce to you, so that you, too, may have fellowship with us, and so that our fellowship may be with the Father and with his Son Jesus Christ. [4] And this we write to you, so that you may rejoice, and so that your joy may be full. [5] And this is the announcement which we have heard from him, and which we announce to you: that God is light, and in him there is no darkness. [6] If we claim that we have fellowship with him, and yet we walk in darkness, then we are lying and not telling the truth. [7] But if we walk in the light, just as he also is in the light, then we have fellowship with one another, and the blood of Jesus Christ, his Son, cleanses us from all sin. [8] If we claim that we have no sin, then we are deceiving ourselves and the truth is not in us. [9] If we confess our sins, then he is faithful and just, so as to forgive us our sins and to cleanse us from all iniquity. [10] If we claim that we have not sinned, then we make him a liar, and his Word is not in us.

1 JOHN 2

[1] My little sons, this I write to you, so that you may not sin. But if anyone has sinned, we have an Advocate with the Father, Jesus Christ, the Just One. [2] And he is the propitiation for our sins. And not only for our sins, but also for those of the whole world. [3] And we can be sure that we have known him by this: if we observe his commandments. [4] Whoever claims that he knows him, and yet does not keep his commandments, is a liar, and the truth is not in him. [5] But whoever keeps his word, truly in him the charity of God is perfected. And by this we know that we are in him. [6] Whoever declares himself to remain in him, ought to walk just as he himself walked. [7] Most beloved, I am not writing to you a new commandment, but the old commandment, which you had from the beginning. The old commandment is the Word, which you have heard. [8] Then too, I am writing to you a new commandment, which is the Truth in him and in you. For the darkness has passed away, and the true Light is now shining. [9] Whoever declares himself to be in the light, and yet hates his brother, is in the darkness even now. [10] Whoever loves his brother abides in the light, and there is no cause of offense in him. [11] But whoever hates his brother is in the darkness, and in darkness he walks, and he does not know where he is going. For the darkness has blinded his eyes. [12] I am writing to you, little sons, because your sins are forgiven for the sake of his name. [13] I am writing to you, fathers, because you have known him who is from the beginning. I am writing to you, adolescents, because you have overcome the evil one. [14] I am writing to you, little children, because you have known the Father. I am writing to you, young men, because you are strong, and the Word of God abides in you, and you have overcome the evil one. [15] Do not choose to love the world, nor the things that are in the world. If anyone loves the world, the charity of the Father is not in him. [16] For all that is in the world is the desire of the flesh, and the desire of the eyes, and the arrogance of a life which is not of the Father, but is of the world. [17] And the world is passing away, with its desire. But whoever does the will of God abides unto eternity. [18] Little sons, it is the last hour. And, as you have heard that the Antichrist is coming, so now many antichrists have arrived. By this, we know that it is the last hour. [19] They went out from among us, but they were not of us. For, if they had been of us, certainly they would have remained with us. But in this way, it is made manifest that none of them are of us. [20] Yet you have the anointing of the Holy One, and you know everything. [21] I have not written to you as to ones who are ignorant of the truth, but as to ones who know the truth. For no lie is of the truth. [22] Who is a liar, other than he who denies that Jesus is the Christ? This one is the Antichrist, who denies the Father and the Son. [23] No one who denies the Son also has the Father. Whoever confesses the Son, also has the Father. [24] As for you, let what you have heard from the beginning remain in you. If what you have heard from the beginning remains in you, then you, too, shall abide in the Son

and in the Father. [25] And this is the Promise, which he himself has promised to us: Eternal Life. [26] I have written these things to you, because of those who would seduce you. [27] But as for you, let the Anointing that you have received from him abide in you. And so, you have no need of anyone to teach you. For his Anointing teaches you about everything, and it is the truth, and it is not a lie. And just as his Anointing has taught you, abide in him. [28] And now, little sons, abide in him, so that when he appears, we may have faith, and we may not be confounded by him at his advent. [29] If you know that he is just, then know, too, that all who do what is just are born of him.

1 JOHN 3

[1] See what kind of love the Father has given to us, that we would be called, and would become, the sons of God. Because of this, the world does not know us, for it did not know him. [2] Most beloved, we are now the sons of God. But what we shall be then has not yet appeared. We know that when he does appear, we shall be like him, for we shall see him as he is. [3] And everyone who holds this hope in him, keeps himself holy, just as he also is holy. [4] Everyone who commits a sin, also commits iniquity. For sin is iniquity. [5] And you know that he appeared in order that he might take away our sins. For in him there is no sin. [6] Everyone who abides in him does not sin. For whoever sins has not seen him, and has not known him. [7] Little sons, let no one deceive you. Whoever does justice is just, even as he also is just. [8] Whoever commits sin is of the devil. For the devil sins from the beginning. For this reason, the Son of God appeared, so that he might eradicate the works of the devil. [9] All those who have been born of God do not commit sin. For the offspring of God abides in them, and he is not able to sin, because he was born of God. [10] In this way, the sons of God are made manifest, and also the sons of the devil. Everyone who is not just, is not of God, as also anyone who does not love his brother. [11] For this is the announcement that you heard from the beginning: that you should love one another. [12] Do not be like Cain, who was of the evil one, and who killed his brother. And why did he kill him? Because his own works were wicked, but his brother's works were just. [13] If the world hates you, brothers, do not be surprised. [14] We know that we have passed from death to life. For we love as brothers. Whoever does not love, abides in death. [15] Everyone who hates his brother is a murderer. And you know that no murderer has eternal life abiding within him. [16] We know the love of God in this way: because he laid down his life for us. And so, we must lay down our lives for our brothers. [17] Whoever possesses the goods of this world, and sees his brother to be in need, and yet closes his heart to him: in what way does the love of God abide in him? [18] My little sons, let us not love in words only, but in works and in truth. [19] In this way, we will know that we are of the truth, and we will commend our hearts in his sight. [20] For even if our heart reproaches us, God is greater than our heart, and he knows all things. [21] Most beloved, if our heart does not reproach us, we can have confidence toward God; [22] and whatever we shall request of him, we shall receive from him. For we keep his commandments, and we do the things that are pleasing in his sight. [23] And this is his commandment: that we should believe in the name of his Son, Jesus Christ, and love one another, just as he has commanded us. [24] And those who keep his commandments abide in him, and he in them. And we know that he abides in us by this: by the Spirit, whom he has given to us.

1 JOHN 4

[1] Most beloved, do not be willing to believe every spirit, but test the spirits to see if they are of God. For many false prophets have gone out into the world. [2] The Spirit of God may be known in this way. Every spirit who confesses that Jesus Christ has arrived in the flesh is of God; [3] and every spirit who contradicts Jesus is not of God. And this one is the Antichrist, the one that you have heard is coming, and even now he is in the world. [4] Little sons, you are of God, and so you have overcome him. For he who is in you is greater than he who is in the world. [5] They are of the world. Therefore, they speak about the world, and the world listens to them. [6] We are of God. Whoever knows God, listens to us. Whoever is not of God, does not listen to us. In this way, we know the Spirit of truth from the spirit of error. [7] Most beloved, let us love one another. For love is of God. And everyone who loves is born of God and knows God. [8] Whoever does not love, does not know God. For God is love. [9] The love of God was made apparent to us in this way: that God sent his only-begotten Son into the world, so that we might live

through him. ¹⁰ In this is love: not as if we had loved God, but that he first loved us, and so he sent his Son as a propitiation for our sins. ¹¹ Most beloved, if God has so loved us, we also ought to love one another. ¹² No one has ever seen God. But if we love one another, God abides in us, and his love is perfected in us. ¹³ In this way, we know that we abide in him, and he in us: because he has given to us from his Spirit. ¹⁴ And we have seen, and we testify, that the Father has sent his Son to be the Savior of the world. ¹⁵ Whoever has confessed that Jesus is the Son of God, God abides in him, and he in God. ¹⁶ And we have known and believed the love that God has for us. God is love. And he who abides in love, abides in God, and God in him. ¹⁷ In this way, the love of God is perfected with us, so that we may have confidence on the day of judgment. For as he is, so also are we, in this world. ¹⁸ Fear is not in love. Instead, perfect love casts out fear, for fear pertains to punishment. And whoever fears is not perfected in love. ¹⁹ Therefore, let us love God, for God first loved us. ²⁰ If anyone says that he loves God, but hates his brother, then he is a liar. For he who does not love his brother, whom he does see, in what way can he love God, whom he does not see? ²¹ And this is the commandment that we have from God, that he who loves God must also love his brother.

1 JOHN 5

¹ Everyone who believes that Jesus is the Christ, is born of God. And everyone who loves God, who provides that birth, also loves him who has been born of God. ² In this way, we know that we love those born of God: when we love God and do his commandments. ³ For this is the love of God: that we keep his commandments. And his commandments are not heavy. ⁴ For all that is born of God overcomes the world. And this is the victory that overcomes the world: our faith. ⁵ Who is it that overcomes the world? Only he who believes that Jesus is the Son of God! ⁶ This is the One who came by water and blood: Jesus Christ. Not by water only, but by water and blood. And the Spirit is the One who testifies that the Christ is the Truth. ⁷ For there are Three who give testimony in heaven: the Father, the Word, and the Holy Spirit. And these Three are One. ⁸ And there are three who give testimony on earth: the Spirit, and the water, and the blood. And these three are one. ⁹ If we accept the testimony of men, then the testimony of God is greater. For this is the testimony of God, which is greater: that he has testified about his Son. ¹⁰ Whoever believes in the Son of God, holds the testimony of God within himself. Whoever does not believe in the Son, makes him a liar, because he does not believe in the testimony which God has testified about his Son. ¹¹ And this is the testimony which God has given to us: Eternal Life. And this Life is in his Son. ¹² Whoever has the Son, has Life. Whoever does not have the Son, does not have Life. ¹³ I am writing this to you, so that you may know that you have Eternal Life: you who believe in the name of the Son of God. ¹⁴ And this is the confidence which we have toward God: that no matter what we shall request, in accord with his will, he hears us. ¹⁵ And we know that he hears us, no matter what we request; so we know that we can obtain the things that we request of him. ¹⁶ Anyone who realizes that his brother has sinned, with a sin that is not unto death, let him pray, and life shall be given to him who has sinned not unto death. There is a sin which is unto death. I am not saying that anyone should ask on behalf of that sin. ¹⁷ All that is iniquity is sin. But there is a sin unto death. ¹⁸ We know that everyone who is born of God does not sin. Instead, rebirth in God preserves him, and the evil one cannot touch him. ¹⁹ We know that we are of God, and that the entire world is established in wickedness. ²⁰ And we know that the Son of God has arrived, and that he has given us understanding, so that we may know the true God, and so that we may remain in his true Son. This is the true God, and this is Eternal Life. ²¹ Little sons, keep yourselves from false worship. Amen.

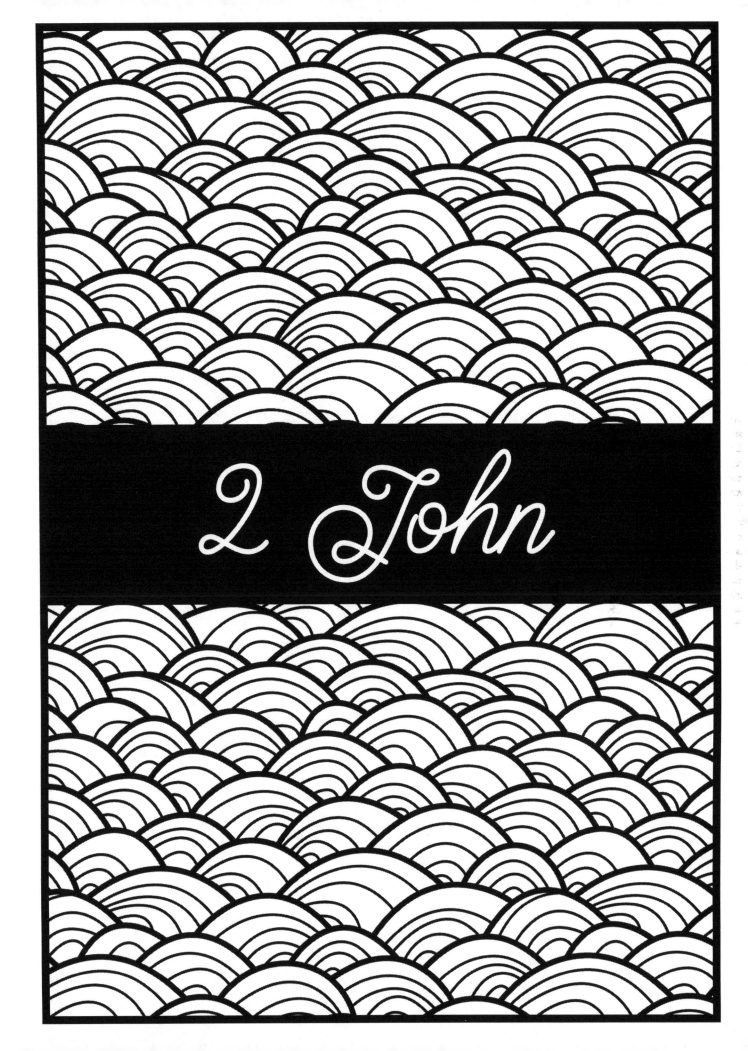

2 John

THE SACRED BIBLE: THE SECOND LETTER OF JOHN

2 JOHN 1

[1] The Elder to the Elect Lady, and those born of her, whom I love in the truth: and not I alone, but also all those who have known the truth, [2] because the truth which dwells in us shall be with us for eternity. [3] May grace, mercy, and peace be with you from God the Father, and from Christ Jesus, the Son of the Father, in truth and in love. [4] I was very glad because I discovered some of your sons walking in the truth, just as we received the commandment from the Father. [5] And now I petition you, Lady, not as if writing a new commandment to you, but instead that commandment which we have had from the beginning: that we love one another. [6] And this is love: that we walk according to his commandments. For this is the commandment that you have heard in the same way from the beginning, and in which you should walk. [7] For many deceivers have gone out into the world, those who do not confess that Jesus Christ has arrived in the flesh. Such a one as this is a deceiver and an antichrist. [8] Be cautious for yourselves, lest you lose what you have accomplished, and so that, instead, you may receive a full reward. [9] Everyone who withdraws and does not remain in the doctrine of Christ, does not have God. Whoever remains in the doctrine, such a one as this has both the Father and the Son. [10] If anyone comes to you, and does not bring this doctrine, do not be willing to receive him into the house, and do not speak a greeting to him. [11] For whoever speaks a greeting to him, is speaking with his evil works. [12] I have much more to write to you, but I am not willing to do so through paper and ink. For I hope that I may be with you in the future, and that I may speak face to face, so that your joy may be full. [13] The sons of your Elect Sister greet you.

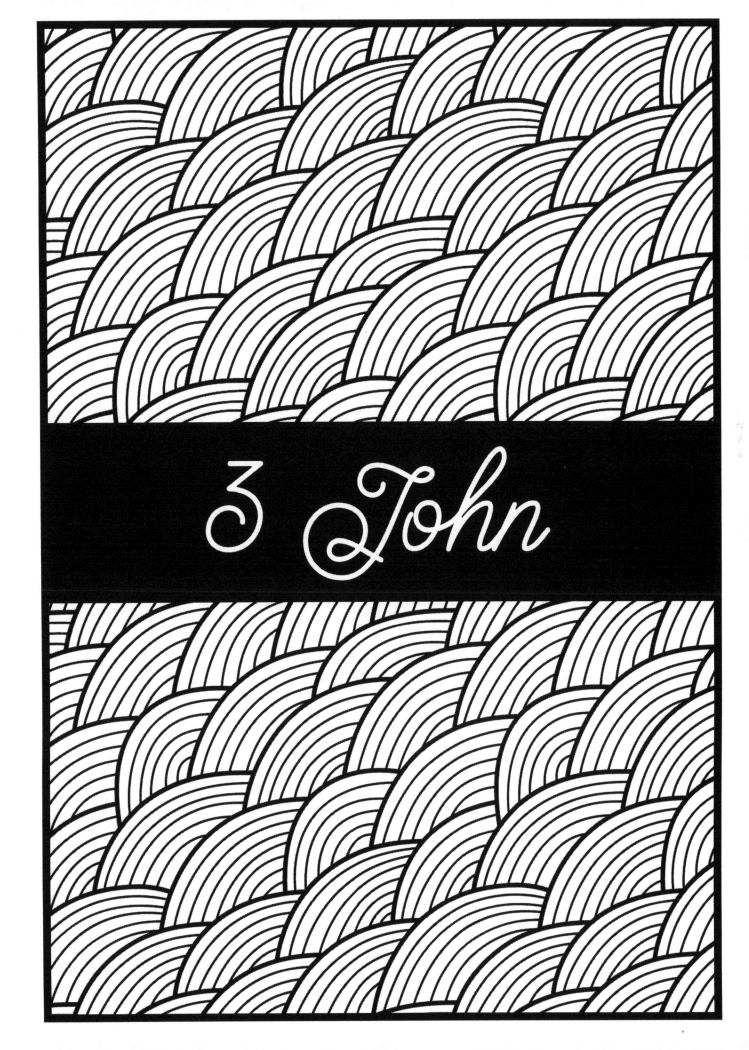

3 John

THE SACRED BIBLE:
THE THIRD LETTER OF JOHN

3 JOHN 1

[1] The Elder, to Gaius, most beloved, whom I love in the truth. [2] Most beloved, concerning everything, I make it my prayer that you may benefit by advancing and succeeding in whatever may be to the benefit of your soul. [3] I was very glad when the brothers arrived, and when they offered testimony to the truth in you, that you are walking in the truth. [4] I have no greater grace than this, when I hear that my sons are walking in the truth. [5] Most beloved, you should act faithfully in whatever you do for the brothers, and those who are sojourners; [6] they have given testimony to your charity in the sight of the Church. You would do well to lead these ones worthily to God. [7] For they set out, on behalf of his name, accepting nothing from the unbelievers. [8] Therefore, we must accept such as these, in order that we may cooperate with the truth. [9] As it happens, I had written to the church. But Diotrephes, who loves to bear the highest rank among them, would not accept us. [10] Because of this, when I come, I will admonish his works which he does, babbling against us with malicious words. And as if this were not sufficient for him, he himself does not receive the brothers. And those who do receive them, he hinders, and he ejects them from the church. [11] Most beloved, do not be willing to imitate what is evil; instead imitate what is good. Whoever does good is of God. Whoever does evil has not seen God. [12] Testimony is being given for Demetrius by everyone, and by the truth itself. And we also offer testimony. And you know that our testimony is true. [13] I had many things to write to you, but I am not willing, through ink and pen, to write to you. [14] Yet I hope to see you soon, and then we will speak face to face. Peace to you. The friends greet you. Greet the friends by name.

Jude

THE SACRED BIBLE: THE LETTER OF JUDE

CHAPTER 1

[1] Jude, a servant of Jesus Christ, and brother of James, to those who are beloved in God the Father, and who are guarded and called in Jesus Christ: [2] May mercy, and peace, and love be fulfilled in you. [3] Most beloved, taking all care to write to you about your common salvation, I found it necessary to write to you in order to beg you to contend earnestly for the faith that was handed down once to the saints. [4] For certain men entered unnoticed, who were written of beforehand unto this judgment: impious persons who are transforming the grace of our God into self-indulgence, and who are denying both the sole Ruler and our Lord Jesus Christ. [5] So I want to caution you. Those who once knew everything that Jesus did, in saving the people from the land of Egypt, afterwards perished because they did not believe. [6] And truly, the Angels, who did not keep to their first place, but instead abandoned their own domiciles, he has reserved with perpetual chains under darkness, unto the great day of judgment. [7] And also Sodom and Gomorrah, and the adjoining cities, in similar ways, having given themselves over to fornication and to the pursuing of other flesh, were made an example, suffering the punishment of eternal fire. [8] Similarly also, these ones certainly defile the flesh, and they despise proper authority, and they blaspheme against majesty. [9] When Michael the Archangel, disputing with the devil, contended about the body of Moses, he did not dare to bring against him a judgment of blasphemy, so instead he said: "The Lord commands you." [10] But these men certainly blaspheme against whatever they do not understand. And yet, whatever they, like mute animals, know from nature, in these things they are corrupted. [11] Woe to them! For they have gone after the way of Cain, and they have poured out the error of Balaam for profit, and they have perished in the sedition of Korah. [12] These ones are defiled within their banquets, enjoying themselves and feeding themselves without fear; waterless clouds, which are tossed about by winds; autumn trees, unfruitful, twice dead, uprooted; [13] raging waves of the sea, foaming from their own confusion; wandering stars, for whom the whirlwind of darkness has been reserved forever! [14] And about these, Enoch, the seventh from Adam, also prophesied, saying: "Behold, the Lord is arriving with thousands of his saints, [15] to execute judgment against everyone, and to reprove all the impious concerning all the works of their impiety, by which they have acted impiously, and concerning all the harsh things that impious sinners have spoken against God." [16] These ones are complaining murmurers, walking according to their own desires. And their mouth is speaking arrogance, admiring persons for the sake of gain. [17] But as for you, most beloved, be mindful of the words which have been foretold by the Apostles of our Lord Jesus Christ, [18] who declared to you that, in the end time, there would arrive mockers, walking according to their own desires, in impieties. [19] These are the ones who segregate themselves; they are animals, not having the Spirit. [20] But you, most beloved, are building yourselves up by your most holy faith, praying in the Holy Spirit, [21] keeping yourselves in the love of God, and anticipating the mercy of our Lord Jesus Christ unto eternal life. [22] So certainly, reprove them, after they have been judged. [23] Yet truly, save them, seizing them from the fire. And have mercy on others: in fear, hating even that which is of the flesh, the defiled garment. [24] Then, to him who has the power to keep you free from sin and to present you, immaculate, with exultation, before the presence of his glory at the advent of our Lord Jesus Christ, [25] to the only God, our Savior, through Jesus Christ our Lord: to him be glory and magnificence, dominion and power, before all ages, and now, and in every age, forever. Amen.

Revelation

THE SACRED BIBLE:
THE REVELATION OF JESUS CHRIST

CHAPTER 1

[1] The Revelation of Jesus Christ, which God gave to him, in order to make known to his servants the things that must soon occur, and which he signified by sending his Angel to his servant John; [2] he has offered testimony to the Word of God, and whatever he saw is the testimony of Jesus Christ. [3] Blessed is he who reads or hears the words of this Prophecy, and who keeps the things that have been written in it. For the time is near. [4] John, to the seven Churches, which are in Asia. Grace and peace to you, from him who is, and who was, and who is to come, and from the seven spirits who are in the sight of his throne, [5] and from Jesus Christ, who is the faithful witness, the first-born of the dead, and the leader over the kings of the earth, who has loved us and has washed us from our sins with his blood, [6] and who has made us into a kingdom and into priests for God and for his Father. To him be glory and dominion forever and ever. Amen. [7] Behold, he arrives with the clouds, and every eye shall see him, even those who pierced him. And all the tribes of the earth shall lament for themselves over him. Even so. Amen. [8] "I am the Alpha and the Omega, the Beginning and the End," says the Lord God, who is, and who was, and who is to come, the Almighty. [9] I, John, your brother, and a sharer in the tribulation and in the kingdom and in patient endurance for Christ Jesus, was on the island which is called Patmos, because of the Word of God and the testimony to Jesus. [10] I was in the Spirit on the Lord's day, and I heard behind me a great voice, like that of a trumpet, [11] saying, "What you see, write in a book, and send it to the seven Churches, which are in Asia: to Ephesus, and to Smyrna, and to Pergamus, and to Thyatira, and to Sardis, and to Philadelphia, and to Laodicea." [12] And I turned around, so as to see the voice which was speaking with me. And having turned around, I saw seven golden lampstands. [13] And in the midst of the seven golden lampstands was one resembling the Son of man, clothed to the feet with a vestment, and wrapped to the breast with a wide belt of gold. [14] But his head and hair were bright, like white wool, or like snow; and his eyes were like a flame of fire; [15] and his feet resembled shining brass, just as in a burning furnace; and his voice was like the voice of many waters. [16] And in his right hand, he held the seven stars; and from his mouth went out a sharp two-edged sword; and his face was like the sun, shining with all its might. [17] And when I had seen him, I fell at his feet, like one who is dead. And he laid his right hand upon me, saying: "Do not be afraid. I am the First and the Last. [18] And I am alive, though I was dead. And, behold, I live forever and ever. And I hold the keys of death and of Hell. [19] Therefore, write the things which you have seen, and which are, and which must occur afterward: [20] the mystery of the seven stars, which you have seen in my right hand, and of the seven golden lampstands. The seven stars are the Angels of the seven Churches, and the seven lampstands are the seven Churches."

CHAPTER 2

[1] "And to the Angel of the Church of Ephesus write: Thus says the One who holds the seven stars in his right hand, who walks in the midst of the seven golden lampstands: [2] I know your works, and your hardship and patient endurance, and that you cannot stand those who are evil. And so, you have tested those who declare themselves to be Apostles and are not, and you have found them to be liars. [3] And you have patient endurance for the sake of my name, and you have not fallen away. [4] But I have this against you: that you have relinquished your first charity. [5] And so, call to mind the place from which you have fallen, and do penance, and do the first works. Otherwise, I will come to you and remove your lampstand from its place, unless you repent. [6] But this you have, that you hate the deeds of the Nicolaitans, which I also hate. [7] Whoever has an ear, let him hear what the Spirit says to the Churches. To him who prevails, I will give to eat from the Tree of Life, which is in the Paradise of my God. [8] And to the Angel of the Church of Smyrna write: Thus says the First and the Last, he who was dead and now lives: [9] I know your tribulation and your poverty, but you are rich, and that you are blasphemed by those who declare themselves to be Jews and are not, but who are a synagogue of Satan. [10] You should fear nothing amid those things which you will suffer. Behold, the devil will cast some of you into prison, so that you may

be tested. And you will have tribulation for ten days. Be faithful even unto death, and I will give to you the crown of life. ¹¹ Whoever has an ear, let him hear what the Spirit says to the Churches. Whoever will prevail, he shall not be harmed by the second death. ¹² And to the Angel of the Church of Pergamus write: Thus says he who holds the sharp two-edged spear: ¹³ I know where you dwell, where the seat of Satan is, and that you hold to my name and have not denied my faith, even in those days when Antipas was my faithful witness, who was slain among you, where Satan dwells. ¹⁴ But I have a few things against you. For you have, in that place, those who hold to the doctrine of Balaam, who instructed Balak to cast a stumbling block before the sons of Israel, to eat and to commit fornication. ¹⁵ And you also have those who hold to the doctrine of the Nicolaitans. ¹⁶ So do penance to the same extent. If you do less, I will come to you quickly and I will fight against these ones with the sword of my mouth. ¹⁷ Whoever has an ear, let him hear what the Spirit says to the Churches. To him who prevails, I will give the hidden manna. And I will give to him a white emblem, and on the emblem, a new name has been written, which no one knows, except the one who receives it. ¹⁸ And to the Angel of the Church of Thyatira write: Thus says the Son of God, who has eyes like a flame of fire, and his feet are like shining brass. ¹⁹ I know your works, and your faith and charity, and your ministry and patient endurance, and that your more recent works are greater than the earlier ones. ²⁰ But I have a few things against you. For you permit the woman Jezebel, who calls herself a prophetess, to teach and to seduce my servants, to commit fornication and to eat the food of idolatry. ²¹ And I gave her a time, so that she might do penance, but she is not willing to repent from her fornication. ²² Behold, I will cast her onto a bed, and those who commit adultery with her shall be in a very great tribulation, unless they repent from their works. ²³ And I will put her sons to death, and all the Churches shall know that I am the one who examines temperaments and hearts. And I will give to each one of you according to your works. But I say to you, ²⁴ and to the others who are at Thyatira: Whoever does not hold to this doctrine, and who has not 'known the depths of Satan,' as they say, I will not set any other weight upon you. ²⁵ Even so, that which you have, hold on to it until I return. ²⁶ And whoever will prevail and will observe my works even unto the end, I will give to him authority over the nations. ²⁷ And he shall rule them with an iron rod, and they shall be broken like the earthenware of a potter. ²⁸ The same I also have received from my Father. And I will give to him the morning star. ²⁹ Whoever has an ear, let him hear what the Spirit says to the Churches."

CHAPTER 3

¹ "And to the Angel of the Church of Sardis write: Thus says he who has the seven spirits of God and the seven stars: I know your works, that you have a name which is alive, but you are dead. ² Be vigilant, and confirm the things that remain, lest they soon die out. For I do not find your works to be full in the sight of my God. ³ Therefore, keep in mind the way that you have received and heard, and then observe it and repent. But if you will not be vigilant, I will come to you like a thief, and you will not know at what hour I will come to you. ⁴ But you have a few names in Sardis who have not defiled their garments. And these shall walk with me in white, because they are worthy. ⁵ Whoever prevails, so shall he be clothed in white vestments. And I will not delete his name from the Book of Life. And I will confess his name in the presence of my Father and in the presence of his Angels. ⁶ Whoever has an ear, let him hear what the Spirit says to the Churches. ⁷ And to the Angel of the Church of Philadelphia write: Thus says the Holy One, the True One, he who holds the key of David. He opens and no one closes. He closes and no one opens. ⁸ I know your works. Behold, I have set an open door before you, which no one is able to close. For you have little power, and you have observed my word, and you have not denied my name. ⁹ Behold, I will take from the synagogue of Satan those who declare themselves to be Jews and are not, for they are lying. Behold, I will cause them to approach and to reverence before your feet. And they shall know that I have loved you. ¹⁰ Since you have kept the word of my patient endurance, I also will keep you from the hour of temptation, which shall overcome the whole world in order to test those living upon the earth. ¹¹ Behold, I am approaching quickly. Hold on to what you have, so that no one may take your crown. ¹² Whoever prevails, I will set him as a column in the temple of my God, and he shall not depart from it anymore. And I will write upon him the name of my God, and the name of the city of my God, the new Jerusalem that descends out of heaven from my God, and my new

name. ¹³Whoever has an ear, let him hear what the Spirit says to the Churches. ¹⁴And to the Angel of the Church of Laodicea write: Thus says the Amen, the faithful and true Witness, who is the Beginning of the creation of God: ¹⁵I know your works: that you are neither cold, nor hot. I wish that you were either cold or hot. ¹⁶But because you are lukewarm and are neither cold nor hot, I will begin to vomit you out of my mouth. ¹⁷For you declare, 'I am wealthy, and I have been enriched further, and I have need of nothing.' And you do not know that you are wretched, and miserable, and poor, and blind, and naked. ¹⁸I urge you to buy from me gold, tested by fire, so that you may be enriched and may be clothed in white vestments, and so that the shame of your nakedness may disappear. And anoint your eyes with an eye salve, so that you may see. ¹⁹Those whom I love, I rebuke and chastise. Therefore, be zealous and do penance. ²⁰Behold, I stand at the door and knock. If anyone will hear my voice and will open the door to me, I will enter to him, and I will dine with him, and he with me. ²¹Whoever prevails, I will grant to him to sit with me on my throne, just as I also have overcome and have sat down with my Father on his throne. ²²Whoever has an ear, let him hear what the Spirit says to the Churches."

CHAPTER 4

¹After these things, I saw, and behold, a door was opened in heaven, and the voice that I heard speaking with me first was like a trumpet, saying: "Ascend to here, and I will reveal to you what must occur after these things." ²And immediately I was in the Spirit. And behold, a throne had been placed in heaven, and there was One sitting upon the throne. ³And the One who was sitting there was similar in appearance to a stone of jasper and sardius. And there was an iridescence surrounding the throne, in aspect similar to an emerald. ⁴And surrounding the throne were twenty-four smaller thrones. And upon the thrones, twenty-four elders were sitting, clothed entirely in white vestments, and on their heads were gold crowns. ⁵And from the throne, lightnings and voices and thunders went forth. And there were seven burning lamps before the throne, which are the seven spirits of God. ⁶And in view of the throne, there was something that seemed like a sea of glass, similar to crystal. And in the middle of the throne, and all around the throne, there were four living creatures, full of eyes in front and in back. ⁷And the first living creature resembled a lion, and the second living creature resembled a calf, and the third living creature had a face like a man, and the fourth living creature resembled a flying eagle. ⁸And each of the four living creatures had upon them six wings, and all around and within they are full of eyes. And they took no rest, day or night, from saying: "Holy, Holy, Holy is the Lord God Almighty, who was, and who is, and who is to come." ⁹And while those living creatures were giving glory and honor and blessings to the One sitting upon the throne, who lives forever and ever, ¹⁰the twenty-four elders fell prostrate before the One sitting upon the throne, and they adored him who lives forever and ever, and they cast their crowns before the throne, saying: ¹¹"You are worthy, O Lord our God, to receive glory and honor and power. For you have created all things, and they became and were created because of your will."

CHAPTER 5

¹And in the right hand of the One sitting upon the throne, I saw a book, written inside and out, sealed with seven seals. ²And I saw a strong Angel, proclaiming with a great voice, "Who is worthy to open the book and to break its seals?" ³And no one was able, neither in heaven, nor on earth, nor under the earth, to open the book, nor to gaze upon it. ⁴And I wept greatly because no one was found worthy to open the book, nor to see it. ⁵And one of the elders said to me: "Weep not. Behold, the lion from the tribe of Judah, the root of David, has prevailed to open the book and to break its seven seals." ⁶And I saw, and behold, in the midst of the throne and the four living creatures, and in the midst of the elders, a Lamb was standing, as if it were slain, having seven horns and seven eyes, which are the seven spirits of God, sent forth to all the earth. ⁷And he approached and received the book from the right hand of the One sitting upon the throne. ⁸And when he had opened the book, the four living creatures and the twenty-four elders fell down before the Lamb, each having stringed instruments, as well as golden bowls full of fragrances, which are the prayers of the saints. ⁹And they were singing a new canticle, saying: "O Lord, you are worthy to receive the book and to open its seals, because you were slain and have redeemed us for God, by your blood, from every tribe and language and people and nation. ¹⁰And you have made us into a

kingdom and into priests for our God, and we shall reign over the earth." ¹¹ And I saw, and I heard the voice of many Angels surrounding the throne and the living creatures and the elders, (and their number was thousands of thousands) ¹² saying with a great voice: "The Lamb who was slain is worthy to receive power, and divinity, and wisdom, and strength, and honor, and glory, and blessing." ¹³ And every creature that is in heaven, and on earth, and under the earth, and all that is within the sea: I heard them all saying: "To the One sitting upon the throne and to the Lamb be blessing, and honor, and glory, and authority, forever and ever." ¹⁴ And the four living creatures were saying, "Amen." And the twenty-four elders fell down on their faces, and they adored the One who lives forever and ever.

CHAPTER 6

¹ And I saw that the Lamb had opened one of the seven seals. And I heard one of the four living creatures saying, in a voice like thunder: "Draw near and see." ² And I saw, and behold, a white horse. And he who was sitting upon it was holding a bow, and a crown was given to him, and he went forth conquering, so that he might prevail. ³ And when he had opened the second seal, I heard the second living creature saying: "Draw near and see." ⁴ And another horse went forth, which was red. And it was granted to him who was sitting upon it that he would take peace from the earth, and that they would kill one another. And a great sword was given to him. ⁵ And when he had opened the third seal, I heard the third living creature saying: "Draw near and see." And behold, a black horse. And he who was sitting upon it was holding a balance in his hand. ⁶ And I heard something like a voice in the midst of the four living creatures saying, "A double measure of wheat for a denarius, and three double measures of barley for a denarius, but do no harm to wine and oil." ⁷ And when he had opened the fourth seal, I heard the voice of the fourth living creature saying: "Draw near and see." ⁸ And behold, a pale horse. And he who was sitting upon it, his name was Death, and Hell was following him. And authority was given to him over the four parts of the earth, to destroy by the sword, by famine, and by death, and by the creatures of the earth. ⁹ And when he had opened the fifth seal, I saw, under the altar, the souls of those who had been slain because of the Word of God and because of the testimony that they held. ¹⁰ And they were crying out with a loud voice, saying: "How long, O Holy and True Lord, will you not judge and not vindicate our blood against those who dwell upon the earth?" ¹¹ And white robes were given to each of them. And they were told that they should rest for a brief time, until their fellow servants and their brothers, who were to be slain even as they were slain, would be completed. ¹² And when he had opened the sixth seal, I saw, and behold, a great earthquake occurred. And the sun became black, like a haircloth sack, and the entire moon became like blood. ¹³ And the stars from heaven fell upon the earth, just as when a fig tree, shaken by a great wind, drops its immature figs. ¹⁴ And heaven receded, like a scroll being rolled up. And every mountain, and the islands, were moved from their places. ¹⁵ And the kings of the earth, and the rulers, and the military leaders, and the wealthy, and the strong, and everyone, servant and free, hid themselves in caves and among the rocks of the mountains. ¹⁶ And they said to the mountains and the rocks: "Fall over us and hide us from the face of the One sitting upon the throne, and from the wrath of the Lamb. ¹⁷ For the great day of their wrath has arrived. And who will be able to stand?"

CHAPTER 7

¹ After these things, I saw four Angels standing above the four corners of the earth, holding the four winds of the earth, so that they would not blow upon the earth, nor upon the sea, nor upon any tree. ² And I saw another Angel ascending from the rising of the sun, having the Seal of the living God. And he cried out, in a great voice, to the four Angels to whom it was given to harm the earth and the sea, ³ saying: "Do no harm to the earth, nor to the sea, nor to the trees, until we seal the servants of our God on their foreheads." ⁴ And I heard the number of those who were sealed: one hundred and forty-four thousand sealed, out of every tribe of the sons of Israel. ⁵ From the tribe of Judah, twelve thousand were sealed. From the tribe of Reuben, twelve thousand were sealed. From the tribe of Gad, twelve thousand were sealed. ⁶ From the tribe of Asher, twelve thousand were sealed. From the tribe of Naphtali, twelve thousand were sealed. From the tribe of Manasseh, twelve thousand were sealed. ⁷ From the tribe of Simeon, twelve thousand were sealed. From the tribe of Levi, twelve thousand were sealed. From the tribe of Issachar, twelve thousand were sealed. ⁸ From the tribe of Zebulun,

twelve thousand were sealed. From the tribe of Joseph, twelve thousand were sealed. From the tribe of Benjamin, twelve thousand were sealed. [9] After these things, I saw a great crowd, which no one could number, from all the nations and tribes and peoples and languages, standing before the throne and in sight of the Lamb, clothed in white robes, with palm branches in their hands. [10] And they cried out, with a great voice, saying: "Salvation is from our God, who sits upon the throne, and from the Lamb." [11] And all the Angels were standing around the throne, with the elders and the four living creatures. And they fell upon their faces in view of the throne, and they worshipped God, [12] saying: "Amen. Blessing and glory and wisdom and thanksgiving, honor and power and strength to our God, forever and ever. Amen." [13] And one of the elders responded and said to me: "These ones who are clothed in white robes, who are they? And where did they come from?" [14] And I said to him, "My lord, you know." And he said to me: "These are the ones who have come out of the great tribulation, and they have washed their robes and have made them white by the blood of the Lamb. [15] Therefore, they are before the throne of God, and they serve him, day and night, in his temple. And the One who sits upon the throne shall dwell over them. [16] They shall not hunger, nor shall they thirst, anymore. Neither shall the sun beat down upon them, nor any heat. [17] For the Lamb, who is in the midst of the throne, will rule over them, and he will lead them to the fountains of the waters of life. And God will wipe away every tear from their eyes."

CHAPTER 8

[1] And when he had opened the seventh seal, there was silence in heaven for about half an hour. [2] And I saw seven Angels standing in the sight of God. And seven trumpets were given to them. [3] And another Angel approached, and he stood before the altar, holding a golden censer. And much incense was given to him, so that he might offer upon the golden altar, which is before the throne of God, the prayers of all the saints. [4] And the smoke of the incense of the prayers of the saints ascended, in the presence of God, from the hand of the Angel. [5] And the Angel received the golden censer, and he filled it from the fire of the altar, and he cast it down upon the earth, and there were thunders and voices and lightnings and a great earthquake. [6] And the seven Angels who hold the seven trumpets prepared themselves, in order to sound the trumpet. [7] And the first Angel sounded the trumpet. And there came hail and fire, mixed with blood; and it was cast down upon the earth. And a third part of the earth was burned, and a third part of the trees was entirely burned up, and all the green plants were burned. [8] And the second Angel sounded the trumpet. And something like a great mountain, burning with fire, was cast down into the sea. And a third part of the sea became like blood. [9] And a third part of the creatures that were living in the sea died. And a third part of the ships were destroyed. [10] And the third Angel sounded the trumpet. And a great star fell from heaven, burning like a torch. And it fell upon a third part of the rivers and upon the sources of water. [11] And the name of the star is called Wormwood. And a third part of the waters were turned into wormwood. And many men died from the waters, because they were made bitter. [12] And the fourth Angel sounded the trumpet. And a third part of the sun, and a third part of the moon, and a third part of the stars were struck, in such a way that a third part of them was obscured. And a third part of the day did not shine, and similarly the night. [13] And I saw, and I heard the voice of a lone eagle flying through the midst of heaven, calling with a great voice: "Woe, Woe, Woe, to the inhabitants of the earth, from the remaining voices of the three Angels, who will soon sound the trumpet!"

CHAPTER 9

[1] And the fifth Angel sounded the trumpet. And I saw upon the earth, a star that had fallen from heaven, and the key to the well of the abyss was given to him. [2] And he opened the well of the abyss. And the smoke of the well ascended, like the smoke of a great furnace. And the sun and the air were obscured by the smoke of the well. [3] And locusts went forth from the smoke of the well into the earth. And power was given to them, like the power that the scorpions of the earth have. [4] And it was commanded of them that they must not harm the plants of the earth, nor anything green, nor any tree, but only those men who do not have the Seal of God upon their foreheads. [5] And it was given to them that they would not kill them, but that they would torture them for five months. And their torture was like the torture of a scorpion, when he strikes a man. [6] And in those days, men

will seek death and they will not find it. And they will desire to die, and death will flee from them. [7] And the likenesses of the locusts resembled horses prepared for battle. And upon their heads were something like crowns similar to gold. And their faces were like the faces of men. [8] And they had hair like the hair of women. And their teeth were like the teeth of lions. [9] And they had breastplates like iron breastplates. And the noise of their wings was like the noise of many running horses, rushing to battle. [10] And they had tails similar to scorpions. And there were stingers in their tails, and these had the power to harm men for five months. [11] And they had over them a king, the Angel of the abyss, whose name in Hebrew is Doom; in Greek, Destroyer; in Latin, Exterminator. [12] One woe has gone out, but behold, there are still two woes approaching afterward. [13] And the sixth Angel sounded the trumpet. And I heard a lone voice from the four horns of the golden altar, which is before the eyes of God, [14] saying to the sixth Angel who had the trumpet: "Release the four Angels who were bound at the great river Euphrates." [15] And the four Angels were released, who had been prepared for that hour, and day, and month, and year, in order to kill one third part of men. [16] And the number of the army of horsemen was two hundred million. For I heard their number. [17] And I also saw the horses in the vision. And those who were sitting upon them had breastplates of fire and hyacinth and sulphur. And the heads of the horses were like the heads of lions. And from their mouths proceeded fire and smoke and sulphur. [18] And one third part of men were slain by these three afflictions: by the fire and by the smoke and by the sulphur, which proceeded from their mouths. [19] For the power of these horses is in their mouths and in their tails. For their tails resemble serpents, having heads; and it is with these that they cause harm. [20] And the rest of men, who were not slain by these afflictions, did not repent from the works of their hands, so that they would not worship demons, or idols of gold and silver and brass and stone and wood, which can neither see, nor hear, nor walk. [21] And they did not repent from their murders, nor from their drugs, nor from their fornication, nor from their thefts.

CHAPTER 10

[1] And I saw another strong Angel, descending from heaven, clothed with a cloud. And a rainbow was upon his head, and his face was like the sun, and his feet were like columns of fire. [2] And he held in his hand a small open book. And he stationed his right foot upon the sea, and his left foot upon the land. [3] And he cried out with a great voice, in the manner of a lion roaring. And when he had cried out, seven thunders uttered their voices. [4] And when the seven thunders had uttered their voices, I was about to write. But I heard a voice from heaven, saying to me: "Seal the things that the seven thunders have spoken, and do not write them." [5] And the Angel, whom I saw standing upon the sea and upon the land, lifted up his hand toward heaven. [6] And he swore by the One who lives forever and ever, who created heaven, and the things that are in it; and the earth, and the things that are in it; and the sea, and the things that are in it: that the time will not be any longer, [7] but in the days of the voice of the seventh Angel, when he shall begin to sound the trumpet, the mystery of God will be completed, just as he has proclaimed in the Gospel, through his servants the Prophets. [8] And again, I heard a voice from heaven speaking with me and saying: "Go and receive the open book from the hand of the Angel who stands upon the sea and upon the land." [9] And I went to the Angel, saying to him that he should give the book to me. And he said to me: "Receive the book and consume it. And it shall cause bitterness in your stomach, but in your mouth it shall be sweet like honey." [10] And I received the book from the hand of the Angel, and I consumed it. And it was sweet like honey in my mouth. And when I had consumed it, my stomach was made bitter. [11] And he said to me, "It is necessary for you to prophesy again about many nations and peoples and languages and kings."

CHAPTER 11

[1] And a reed, similar to a staff, was given to me. And it was said to me: "Rise up and measure the temple of God, and those who are worshiping in it, and the altar. [2] But the atrium, which is outside of the temple, set it aside and do not measure it, because it has been given over to the Gentiles. And they shall trample upon the Holy City for forty-two months. [3] And I will present my two witnesses, and they shall prophesy for one thousand two hundred and sixty days, clothed in sackcloth. [4] These are the two olive trees and the two lampstands, standing in the sight of the lord of the earth. [5] And if anyone will want to harm them, fire shall

go forth from their mouths, and it shall devour their enemies. And if anyone will want to wound them, so must he be slain. ⁶These have the power to close up the heavens, so that it may not rain during the days of their prophesying. And they have power over the waters, to convert them into blood, and to strike the earth with every kind of affliction as often as they will. ⁷And when they will have finished their testimony, the beast that ascended from the abyss will make war against them, and will overcome them, and will kill them. ⁸And their bodies shall lie in the streets of the Great City, which is figuratively called 'Sodom' and 'Egypt,' the place where their Lord also was crucified. ⁹And those from the tribes and peoples and languages and nations shall be watching their bodies for three and one half days. And they shall not permit their bodies to be placed in tombs. ¹⁰And the inhabitants of the earth will rejoice over them, and they will celebrate, and they will send gifts to one another, because these two prophets tortured those who were living upon the earth. ¹¹And after three and one half days, the spirit of life from God entered into them. And they stood upright on their feet. And a great fear fell over those who saw them. ¹²And they heard a great voice from heaven, saying to them, "Ascend to here!" And they ascended into heaven on a cloud. And their enemies saw them. ¹³And at that hour, a great earthquake occurred. And one tenth part of the City fell. And the names of the men slain in the earthquake were seven thousand. And the remainder were thrown into fear, and they gave glory to the God of heaven. ¹⁴The second woe has gone out, but behold, the third woe approaches quickly. ¹⁵And the seventh Angel sounded the trumpet. And there were great voices in heaven, saying: "The kingdom of this world has become our Lord's and his Christ's, and he shall reign forever and ever. Amen." ¹⁶And the twenty-four elders, who sit on their thrones in the sight of God, fell upon their faces, and they adored God, saying: ¹⁷"We give thanks to you, Lord God Almighty, who is, and who was, and who is to come. For you have taken your great power, and you have reigned. ¹⁸And the nations became angry, but your wrath arrived, and the time for the dead to be judged, and to render a reward to your servants the prophets, and to the saints, and to those who fear your name, small and great, and to exterminate those who have corrupted the earth." ¹⁹And the temple of God was opened in heaven. And the Ark of his Testament was seen in his temple. And there were lightnings and voices and thunders, and an earthquake, and great hail.

CHAPTER 12

¹And a great sign appeared in heaven: a woman clothed with the sun, and the moon was under her feet, and on her head was a crown of twelve stars. ²And being with child, she cried out while giving birth, and she was suffering in order to give birth. ³And another sign was seen in heaven. And behold, a great red dragon, having seven heads and ten horns, and on his heads were seven diadems. ⁴And his tail drew down a third part of the stars of heaven and cast them to the earth. And the dragon stood before the woman, who was about to give birth, so that, when she had brought forth, he might devour her son. ⁵And she brought forth a male child, who was soon to rule all the nations with an iron rod. And her son was taken up to God and to his throne. ⁶And the woman fled into solitude, where a place was being held ready by God, so that they might pasture her in that place for one thousand two hundred and sixty days. ⁷And there was a great battle in heaven. Michael and his Angels were battling with the dragon, and the dragon was fighting, and so were his angels. ⁸But they did not prevail, and a place for them was no longer found in heaven. ⁹And he was thrown out, that great dragon, that ancient serpent, who is called the devil and Satan, who seduces the whole world. And he was thrown down to the earth, and his angels were cast down with him. ¹⁰And I heard a great voice in heaven, saying: "Now have arrived salvation and virtue and the kingdom of our God and the power of his Christ. For the accuser of our brothers has been cast down, he who accused them before our God day and night. ¹¹And they overcame him by the blood of the Lamb and by the word of his testimony. And they loved not their own lives, even unto death. ¹²Because of this, rejoice, O heavens, and all who dwell within it. Woe to the earth and to the sea! For the devil has descended to you, holding great anger, knowing that he has little time." ¹³And after the dragon saw that he had been thrown down to the earth, he pursued the woman who brought forth the male child. ¹⁴And the two wings of a great eagle were given to the woman, so that she might fly away, into the desert, to her place, where she is being nourished for a time, and times, and half a time, from the face of the serpent. ¹⁵And the serpent

sent out from his mouth, after the woman, water like a river, so that he might cause her to be carried away by the river. ¹⁶ But the earth assisted the woman. And the earth opened her mouth and absorbed the river, which the dragon sent out from his mouth. ¹⁷ And the dragon was angry at the woman. And so he went away to do battle with the remainder of her offspring, those who keep the commandments of God and who hold to the testimony of Jesus Christ. ¹⁸ And he stood upon the sand of the sea.

CHAPTER 13

¹ And I saw a beast ascending from the sea, having seven heads and ten horns, and upon its horns were ten diadems, and upon its heads were names of blasphemy. ² And the beast that I saw was similar to a leopard, and its feet were like the feet of a bear, and its mouth was like the mouth of a lion. And the dragon gave his own power and great authority to it. ³ And I saw that one of its heads seemed to be slain unto death, but his deadly wound was healed. And the entire world was in wonder following the beast. ⁴ And they worshiped the dragon, who gave authority to the beast. And they worshiped the beast, saying: "Who is like the beast? And who would be able to fight with it?" ⁵ And there was given to it a mouth, speaking great things and blasphemies. And authority was given to him to act for forty-two months. ⁶ And he opened his mouth in blasphemies against God, to blaspheme his name and his tabernacle and those who dwell in heaven. ⁷ And it was given to him to make war with the saints and to overcome them. And authority was given to him over every tribe and people and language and nation. ⁸ And all who inhabit the earth worshiped the beast, those whose names have not been written, from the origin of the world, in the Book of Life of the Lamb who was slain. ⁹ If anyone has an ear, let him hear. ¹⁰ Whoever will be led into captivity, into captivity he goes. Whoever will kill with the sword, with the sword he must be killed. Here is the patient endurance and faith of the Saints. ¹¹ And I saw another beast ascending from the land. And she had two horns like the Lamb, but she was speaking like the dragon. ¹² And she acted with all the authority of the first beast in his sight. And she caused the earth, and those dwelling in it, to worship the first beast, whose deadly wound was healed. ¹³ And she accomplished great signs, even so that she would cause fire to descend from the sky to the earth in the sight of men. ¹⁴ And she seduced those living on the earth, by means of the signs that were given to her to perform in the sight of the beast, saying to those dwelling on the earth that they should make an image of the beast who had a wound of the sword and yet lived. ¹⁵ And it was given to her to give a spirit to the image of the beast, so that the image of the beast would speak. And she acted so that whoever would not worship the image of the beast would be slain. ¹⁶ And she will cause everyone, small and great, wealthy and poor, free and servant, to have a character on their right hand or on their foreheads, ¹⁷ so that no one may buy or sell, unless he has the character, or the name of the beast, or the number of his name. ¹⁸ Here is wisdom. Whoever has intelligence, let him determine the number of the beast. For it is the number of a man, and his number is six hundred and sixty-six.

CHAPTER 14

¹ And I saw, and behold, the Lamb was standing above mount Zion, and with him were one hundred and forty-four thousand, having his name and the name of his Father written on their foreheads. ² And I heard a voice from heaven, like the voice of many waters, and like the voice of a great thunder. And the voice that I heard was like that of singers, while playing on their stringed instruments. ³ And they were singing what seemed like a new canticle before the throne and before the four living creatures and the elders. And no one was able to recite the canticle, except those one hundred and forty-four thousand, who were redeemed from the earth. ⁴ These are the ones who were not defiled with women, for they are Virgins. These follow the Lamb wherever he will go. These were redeemed from men as the first-fruits for God and for the Lamb. ⁵ And in their mouth, no lie was found, for they are without flaw before the throne of God. ⁶ And I saw another Angel, flying through the midst of heaven, holding the eternal Gospel, so as to evangelize those sitting upon the earth and those of every nation and tribe and language and people, ⁷ saying with a loud voice: "Fear the Lord, and give honor to him, for the hour of his judgment has arrived. And worship him who made heaven and earth, the sea and the sources of water." ⁸ And another

Angel followed, saying: "Fallen, fallen is Babylon the great, who inebriated all nations with the wine of her wrath and of fornication." [9] And the third Angel followed them, saying with a great voice: "If anyone has worshiped the beast, or his image, or has received his character on his forehead or on his hand, [10] he shall drink also from the wine of the wrath of God, which has been mixed with strong wine in the cup of his wrath, and he shall be tortured with fire and sulphur in the sight of the holy Angels and before the sight of the Lamb. [11] And the smoke of their torments shall ascend forever and ever. And they shall have no rest, day or night, those who have worshiped the beast or his image, or who have received the character of his name." [12] Here is the patient endurance of the Saints, those who keep the commandments of God and the faith of Jesus. [13] And I heard a voice from heaven, saying to me: "Write: Blessed are the dead, who die in the Lord, now and hereafter, says the Spirit, so that they may find rest from their labors. For their works follow them." [14] And I saw, and behold, a white cloud. And upon the cloud was one sitting, resembling a son of man, having a crown of gold on his head, and a sharp sickle in his hand. [15] And another Angel went forth from the temple, crying out in a great voice to the one sitting upon the cloud: "Send out your sickle and reap! For the hour of reaping has arrived, because the harvest of the earth has ripened." [16] And the one who was sitting upon the cloud sent out his sickle to the earth, and the earth was reaped. [17] And another Angel went forth from the temple that is in heaven; he also had a sharp sickle. [18] And another Angel went forth from the altar, who held power over fire. And he cried out in a great voice to him who held the sharp sickle, saying: "Send out your sharp sickle, and harvest the clusters of grapes from the vineyard of the earth, because its grapes have matured." [19] And the Angel sent out his sharp sickle to the earth, and he harvested the vineyard of the earth, and he cast it into the great basin of the wrath of God. [20] And the basin was trodden beyond the city, and blood went forth from the basin, even as high as the harnesses of horses, out to one thousand six hundred stadia.

CHAPTER 15

[1] And I saw another sign in heaven, great and wondrous: seven Angels, holding the seven last afflictions. For with them, the wrath of God is completed. [2] And I saw something like a sea of glass mixed with fire. And those who had overcome the beast and his image and the number of his name, were standing upon the sea of glass, holding the harps of God, [3] and singing the canticle of Moses, the servant of God, and the canticle of the Lamb, saying: "Great and wondrous are your works, Lord God Almighty. Just and true are your ways, King of all ages. [4] Who shall not fear you, O Lord, and magnify your name? For you alone are blessed. For all nations shall approach and adore in your sight, because your judgments are manifest." [5] And after these things, I saw, and behold, the temple of the tabernacle of the testimony in heaven was opened. [6] And the seven Angels went forth from the temple, holding the seven afflictions, clothed with clean white linen, and girded around the chest with wide golden belts. [7] And one of the four living creatures gave to the seven Angels seven golden bowls, filled with the wrath of God, of the One who lives forever and ever. [8] And the temple was filled with smoke from the majesty of God and from his power. And no one was able to enter into the temple, until the seven afflictions of the seven Angels were completed.

CHAPTER 16

[1] And I heard a great voice from the temple, saying to the seven Angels: "Go forth and pour out the seven bowls of the wrath of God upon the earth." [2] And the first Angel went forth and poured out his bowl upon the earth. And a severe and most grievous wound occurred upon the men who had the character of the beast, and upon those who adored the beast or its image. [3] And the second Angel poured out his bowl upon the sea. And it became like the blood of the dead, and every living creature in the sea died. [4] And the third Angel poured out his bowl upon the rivers and the sources of water, and these became blood. [5] And I heard the Angel of the waters saying: "You are just, O Lord, who is and who was: the Holy One who has judged these things. [6] For they have shed the blood of the Saints and the Prophets, and so you have given them blood to drink. For they deserve this." [7] And from the altar, I heard another one, saying, "Even now, O Lord God Almighty, your judgments are true and just." [8] And the fourth Angel poured out his bowl upon the sun. And it was given to him

to afflict men with heat and fire. [9] And men were scorched by the great heat, and they blasphemed the name of God, who holds power over these afflictions, but they did not repent, so as to give him glory. [10] And the fifth Angel poured out his bowl upon the throne of the beast. And his kingdom became darkened, and they gnawed at their tongues out of anguish. [11] And they blasphemed the God of heaven, because of their anguish and wounds, but they did not repent from their works. [12] And the sixth Angel poured out his bowl upon that great river Euphrates. And its water dried up, so that a way might be prepared for the kings from the rising of the sun. [13] And I saw, from the mouth of the dragon, and from the mouth of the beast, and from the mouth of the false prophetess, three unclean spirits go out in the manner of frogs. [14] For these are the spirits of the demons that were causing the signs. And they advanced to the kings of the entire earth, to gather them for battle on the great day of Almighty God. [15] "Behold, I arrive like a thief. Blessed is he who is vigilant and who preserves his vestment, lest he walk naked and they see his disgrace." [16] And he shall gather them together at a place which is called, in Hebrew, Armageddon. [17] And the seventh Angel poured out his bowl upon the air. And a great voice went out of the temple from the throne, saying: "It is done." [18] And there were lightnings and voices and thunders. And a great earthquake occurred, of a kind such as has never happened since men have been upon the earth, so great was this kind of earthquake. [19] And the Great City became divided into three parts. And the cities of the Gentiles fell. And Babylon the great came to mind before God, to give her the cup of the wine of the indignation of his wrath. [20] And every island fled away, and the mountains were not found. [21] And hail as heavy as a talent descended from the sky upon men. And men blasphemed God, because of the affliction of the hail, for it was exceedingly great.

CHAPTER 17

[1] And one of the seven Angels, those who hold the seven bowls, approached and spoke with me, saying: "Come, I will show you the condemnation of the great harlot, who sits upon many waters. [2] With her, the kings of the earth have fornicated. And those who inhabit the earth have been inebriated by the wine of her prostitution." [3] And he carried me away in spirit to the desert. And I saw a woman sitting upon a scarlet beast, filled with names of blasphemy, having seven heads and ten horns. [4] And the woman was clothed all around with purple and scarlet, and adorned with gold and precious stones and pearls, holding a golden cup in her hand, filled with the abomination and with the filth of her fornication. [5] And a name was written upon her forehead: Mystery, Babylon the great, the mother of the fornications and the abominations of the earth. [6] And I saw that the woman was inebriated from the blood of the saints and from the blood of the martyrs of Jesus. And I was amazed, when I had seen her, with a great wonder. [7] And the Angel said to me: "Why do you wonder? I will tell you the mystery of the woman, and of the beast that carries her, which has seven heads and ten horns. [8] The beast that you saw, was, and is not, and is soon to ascend from the abyss. And he goes forth unto destruction. And the inhabitants upon the earth (those whose names have not been written in the Book of Life from the foundation of the world) shall be amazed upon seeing the beast who was and is not. [9] And this is for one who understands, who has wisdom: the seven heads are seven mountains, upon which the woman sits, and they are seven kings. [10] Five have fallen, one is, and the other has not yet arrived. And when he arrives, he must remain for a brief time. [11] And the beast who was, and is not, the same is also the eighth, and he is of the seven, and he goes forth unto destruction. [12] And the ten horns that you saw are ten kings; these have not yet received a kingdom, but they shall receive authority, as if they were kings, for one hour, after the beast. [13] These hold to one plan, and they shall hand over their power and authority to the beast. [14] These shall fight against the Lamb, and the Lamb shall conquer them. For he is the Lord of lords and the King of kings. And those who are with him are called, and chosen, and faithful." [15] And he said to me: "The waters that you saw, where the harlot sits, are peoples and nations and languages. [16] And the ten horns that you saw on the beast, these shall hate the woman who fornicates, and they shall make her desolate and naked, and they shall chew her flesh, and they shall burn her completely with fire. [17] For God has granted to their hearts that they may do to her whatever is pleasing, so that they may give their kingdom to the beast, until the words of God may be completed. [18] And the woman that you saw is the great City, which holds a kingdom above that of the kings of the earth."

CHAPTER 18

[1] And after these things, I saw another Angel, descending from heaven, having great authority. And the earth was illuminated by his glory. [2] And he cried out with strength, saying: "Fallen, fallen is Babylon the great. And she has become the habitation of demons, and the keepsake of every unclean spirit, and the possession of every unclean and hateful flying thing. [3] For all the nations have imbibed the wine of the wrath of her fornication. And the kings of the earth have fornicated with her. And the merchants of the earth have become wealthy by the power of her pleasures." [4] And I heard another voice from heaven, saying: "Go away from her, my people, so that you may not be participants in her pleasures, and so that you may not be recipients of her afflictions. [5] For her sins have pierced through even to heaven, and the Lord has remembered her iniquities. [6] Render to her, as she has also rendered to you. And repay her doubly, according to her works. Mix for her a double portion, in the cup with which she mixed. [7] As much as she has glorified herself and lived in pleasure, so much so give to her torment and grief. For in her heart, she has said: 'I am enthroned as queen,' and, 'I am not a widow,' and, 'I shall not see sorrow.' [8] For this reason, her afflictions shall arrive in one day: death and grief and famine. And she shall be burned with fire. For God, who will judge her, is strong. [9] And the kings of the earth, who have fornicated with her and lived in luxury, shall weep and mourn for themselves over her, when they see the smoke of her conflagration, [10] standing far away, out of fear of her torments, saying: 'Woe! Woe! to Babylon, that great city, that strong city. For in one hour, your judgment has arrived.' [11] And the businessmen of the earth shall weep and mourn over her, because no one will buy their merchandise anymore: [12] merchandise of gold and silver and precious stones and pearls, and of fine linen and purple and silk and scarlet, and of every citrus tree wood, and of every tool of ivory, and of every tool from precious stone and brass and iron and marble, [13] and of cinnamon and black cardamom, and of fragrances and ointments and incense, and of wine and oil and fine flour and wheat, and of beasts of burden and sheep and horses and four-wheeled wagons, and of slaves and the souls of men. [14] And the fruits of the desires of your soul have gone away from you. And all things fat and splendid have perished from you. And they shall never find these things again. [15] The merchants of these things, who were made wealthy, shall stand far away from her, out of fear of her torments, weeping and mourning, [16] and saying: 'Woe! Woe! to that great city, which was clothed with fine linen and purple and scarlet, and which was adorned with gold and precious stones and pearls.' [17] For such great wealth was brought to destitution in one hour. And every shipmaster, and all who navigate on lakes, and mariners, and those who work at sea, stood far away. [18] And they cried out, seeing the place of her conflagration, saying: 'What city resembles this great city?' [19] And they cast dust upon their heads. And they cried out, weeping and mourning, saying: 'Woe! Woe! to that great city, by which all who had ships at sea were made rich from her treasures. For she has been made desolate in one hour. [20] Exult over her, O heaven, O holy Apostles and Prophets. For God has judged your judgment upon her.'" [21] And a certain strong Angel took up a stone, similar to a great millstone, and he cast it into the sea, saying: "With this force shall Babylon, that great city, be cast down. And she shall never be found again. [22] And the sound of singers, and musicians, and flute and trumpet players shall not be heard in you again. And every artisan of every art shall not be found in you again. And the sound of the mill shall not be heard in you again. [23] And the light of the lamp shall not shine in you again. And the voice of the groom and of the bride shall not be heard in you anymore. For your merchants were the leaders of the earth. For all the nations were led astray by your drugs. [24] And in her was found the blood of the Prophets and of the Saints, and of all who were slain upon the earth."

CHAPTER 19

[1] After these things, I heard something like the voice of many multitudes in heaven, saying: "Alleluia! Praise and glory and power is for our God. [2] For true and just are his judgments, he who has judged the great harlot that corrupted the earth by her prostitution. And he has vindicated the blood of his servants from her hands." [3] And again, they said: "Alleluia! For her smoke ascends forever and ever." [4] And the twenty-four elders and the four living creatures fell down and worshiped God, sitting upon the throne, saying: "Amen! Alleluia!" [5] And a voice went out from the throne, saying: "Express praise to our God, all you his

servants, and you who fear him, small and great." ⁶ And I heard something like the voice of a great multitude, and like the voice of many waters, and like the voice of great thunders, saying: "Alleluia! For the Lord our God, the Almighty, has reigned. ⁷ Let us be glad and exult. And let us give glory to him. For the marriage feast of the Lamb has arrived, and his wife has prepared herself." ⁸ And it was granted to her that she should cover herself with fine linen, splendid and white. For the fine linen is the justifications of the Saints. ⁹ And he said to me: "Write: Blessed are those who have been called to the wedding feast of the Lamb." And he said to me, "These words of God are true." ¹⁰ And I fell down before his feet, to adore him. And he said to me: "Be careful not to do so. I am your fellow servant, and I am among your brothers, who hold to the testimony of Jesus. Adore God. For the testimony of Jesus is a spirit of prophecy." ¹¹ And I saw heaven opened, and behold, a white horse. And he who was sitting upon it was called Faithful and True. And with justice does he judge and fight. ¹² And his eyes are like a flame of fire, and on his head are many diadems, having a name written, which no one knows except himself. ¹³ And he was clothed with a vestment sprinkled with blood. And his name is called: THE WORD OF GOD. ¹⁴ And the armies that are in heaven were following him on white horses, clothed in fine linen, white and clean. ¹⁵ And from his mouth proceeded a sharp two-edged sword, so that with it he may strike the nations. And he shall rule them with an iron rod. And he treads the winepress of the fury of the wrath of God Almighty. ¹⁶ And he has on his garment and on his thigh written: KING OF KINGS AND LORD OF LORDS. ¹⁷ And I saw a certain Angel, standing in the sun. And he cried out with a great voice, saying to all the birds that were flying through the midst of the sky, "Come and gather together for the great supper of God, ¹⁸ so that you may eat the flesh of kings, and the flesh of tribunes, and the flesh of the strong, and the flesh of horses and those sitting on them, and the flesh of all: free and servant, small and great." ¹⁹ And I saw the beast and the kings of the earth and their armies, having been gathered together to do battle against him who was sitting upon the horse, and against his army. ²⁰ And the beast was apprehended, and with him the false prophetess, who in his presence caused the signs, by which she seduced those who accepted the character of the beast and who worshiped his image. These two were cast alive into the pool of fire burning with sulphur. ²¹ And the others were slain by the sword that proceeds from the mouth of him who was sitting upon the horse. And all the birds were sated with their flesh.

CHAPTER 20

¹ And I saw an Angel, descending from heaven, holding in his hand the key of the abyss and a great chain. ² And he apprehended the dragon, the ancient serpent, who is the devil and Satan, and he bound him for a thousand years. ³ And he cast him into the abyss, and he closed and sealed it, so that he would no longer seduce the nations, until the thousand years are completed. And after these things, he must be released for a brief time. ⁴ And I saw thrones. And they sat upon them. And judgment was given to them. And the souls of those beheaded because of the testimony of Jesus and because of the Word of God, and who did not adore the beast, nor his image, nor accept his character on their foreheads or on their hands: they lived and they reigned with Christ for a thousand years. ⁵ The rest of the dead did not live, until the thousand years are completed. This is the First Resurrection. ⁶ Blessed and holy is he who takes part in the First Resurrection. Over these the second death has no power. But they shall be priests of God and of Christ, and they shall reign with him for a thousand years. ⁷ And when the thousand years will have been completed, Satan shall be released from his prison, and he will go out and seduce the nations which are upon the four quarters of the earth, Gog and Magog. And he will gather them together for battle, those whose number is like the sand of the sea. ⁸ And they climbed across the breadth of the earth, and they encompassed the camp of the Saints and the Beloved City. ⁹ And fire from God descended from heaven and devoured them. And the devil, who seduced them, was cast into the pool of fire and sulphur, ¹⁰ where both the beast and the false prophetess shall be tortured, day and night, forever and ever. ¹¹ And I saw a great white throne, and One sitting upon it, from whose sight earth and heaven fled, and no place was found for them. ¹² And I saw the dead, great and small, standing in view of the throne. And books were opened. And another Book was opened, which is the Book of Life. And the dead were judged by those things that had been written

in the books, according to their works. ¹³ And the sea gave up the dead who were in it. And death and Hell gave up their dead who were in them. And they were judged, each one according to his works. ¹⁴ And Hell and death were cast into the pool of fire. This is the second death. ¹⁵ And whoever was not found written in the Book of Life was cast into the pool of fire.

CHAPTER 21

¹ I saw the new heaven and the new earth. For the first heaven and the first earth passed away, and the sea is no more. ² And I, John, saw the Holy City, the New Jerusalem, descending out of heaven from God, prepared like a bride adorned for her husband. ³ And I heard a great voice from the throne, saying: "Behold the tabernacle of God with men. And he will dwell with them, and they will be his people. And God himself will be their God with them. ⁴ And God will wipe away every tear from their eyes. And death shall be no more. And neither mourning, nor crying out, nor grief shall be anymore. For the first things have passed away." ⁵ And the One who was sitting upon the throne, said, "Behold, I make all things new." And he said to me, "Write, for these words are entirely faithful and true." ⁶ And he said to me: "It is done. I am the Alpha and the Omega, the Beginning and the End. To those who thirst, I will give freely from the fountain of the water of life. ⁷ Whoever prevails shall possess these things. And I will be his God, and he shall be my son. ⁸ But the fearful, and the unbelieving, and the abominable, and murderers, and fornicators, and drug users, and idolaters, and all liars, these shall be a part of the pool burning with fire and sulphur, which is the second death." ⁹ And one of the seven Angels, those holding the bowls filled with the seven last afflictions, approached and spoke with me, saying: "Come, and I will show you the bride, the wife of the Lamb." ¹⁰ And he took me up in spirit to a great and high mountain. And he showed me the Holy City Jerusalem, descending out of heaven from God, ¹¹ having the glory of God. And its light was like that of a precious stone, even like that of the jasper stone or like crystal. ¹² And it had a wall, great and high, having twelve gates. And at the gates were twelve Angels. And names were written upon them, which are the names of the twelve tribes of the sons of Israel. ¹³ On the East were three gates, and on the North were three gates, and on the South were three gates, and on the West were three gates. ¹⁴ And the wall of the City had twelve foundations. And upon them were the twelve names of the twelve Apostles of the Lamb. ¹⁵ And he who was speaking with me was holding a golden measuring reed, in order to measure the City, and its gates and wall. ¹⁶ And the city is laid out as a square, and so its length is as great as the width. And he measured the city with the golden reed for twelve thousand stadia, and its length and height and breadth were equal. ¹⁷ And he measured its wall as one hundred and forty-four cubits, the measure of a man, which is of an Angel. ¹⁸ And the structure of its wall was of jasper stone. Yet truly, the city itself was of pure gold, similar to pure glass. ¹⁹ And the foundations of the wall of the city were adorned with every kind of precious stone. The first foundation was of jasper, the second was of sapphire, the third was of chalcedony, the fourth was of emerald, ²⁰ the fifth was of sardonyx, the sixth was of sardius, the seventh was of chrysolite, the eighth was of beryl, the ninth was of topaz, the tenth was of chrysoprasus, the eleventh was of jacinth, the twelfth was of amethyst. ²¹ And the twelve gates are twelve pearls, one for each, so that each gate was made from a single pearl. And the main street of the city was of pure gold, similar to transparent glass. ²² And I saw no temple in it. For the Lord God Almighty is its temple, and the Lamb. ²³ And the city has no need of sun or moon to shine in it. For the glory of God has illuminated it, and the Lamb is its lamp. ²⁴ And the nations shall walk by its light. And the kings of the earth shall bring their glory and honor into it. ²⁵ And its gates shall not be closed throughout the day, for there shall be no night in that place. ²⁶ And they shall bring the glory and honor of the nations into it. ²⁷ There shall not enter into it anything defiled, nor anything causing an abomination, nor anything false, but only those who have been written in the Book of Life of the Lamb.

CHAPTER 22

¹ And he showed me the river of the water of life, shining like crystal, proceeding from the throne of God and of the Lamb. ² In the midst of its main street, and on both sides of the river, was the Tree of Life, bearing twelve fruits, offering one fruit for each month, and the leaves of gthe tree are for the health of the nations.

³ And every curse shall be no more. But the throne of God and of the Lamb will be in it, and his servants shall serve him. ⁴ And they shall see his face. And his name shall be on their foreheads. ⁵ And night shall be no more. And they will not need the light of a lamp, nor the light of the sun, because the Lord God will illuminate them. And they shall reign forever and ever. ⁶ And he said to me: "These words are entirely faithful and true." And the Lord, the God of the spirits of the prophets, sent his Angel to reveal to his servant what must occur soon: ⁷ "For behold, I am approaching quickly! Blessed is he who keeps the words of the prophecy of this book." ⁸ And I, John, heard and saw these things. And, after I had heard and seen, I fell down, so as to adore before the feet of the Angel, who was revealing these things to me. ⁹ And he said to me: "Be careful not to do so. For I am your fellow servant, and I am among your brothers the prophets, and among those who keep the words of the prophecy of this book. Adore God." ¹⁰ And he said to me: "Do not seal the words of the prophecy of this book. For the time is near. ¹¹ Whoever does harm, he might still do harm. And whoever is filthy, he might still be filthy. And whoever is just, he may still be just. And one who is holy, he may still be holy." ¹² "Behold, I am approaching quickly! And my repayment is with me, to render to each one according to his works. ¹³ I am the Alpha and the Omega, the First and the Last, the Beginning and the End." ¹⁴ Blessed are those who wash their robes in the blood of the Lamb. So may they have a right to the tree of life; so may they enter through the gates into the City. ¹⁵ Outside are dogs, and drug users, and homosexuals, and murderers, and those who serve idols, and all who love and do what is false. ¹⁶ "I, Jesus, have sent my Angel, to testify to these things for you among the Churches. I am the Root and the Origin of David, the bright morning Star." ¹⁷ And the Spirit and the Bride say: "Draw near." And whoever hears, let him say: "Draw near." And whoever thirsts, let him draw near. And whoever is willing, let him accept the water of life, freely. ¹⁸ For I call as witnesses all listeners of the words of the prophecy of this book. If anyone will have added to these, God will add upon him the afflictions written in this book. ¹⁹ And if anyone will have taken away from the words of the book of this prophecy, God will take away his portion from the Book of Life, and from the Holy City, and from these things which have been written in this book. ²⁰ He who offers testimony to these things, says: "Even now, I am approaching quickly." Amen. Come, Lord Jesus. ²¹ The grace of our Lord Jesus Christ be with you all. Amen.

BE SURE TO FOLLOW US
ON SOCIAL MEDIA FOR THE
LATEST NEWS, SNEAK
PEEKS, & GIVEAWAYS

@drawntofaith

Drawn To Faith

@drawntofaith

ADD YOURSELF TO OUR MONTHLY
NEWSLETTER FOR FREE DIGITAL
DOWNLOADS AND DISCOUNT CODES
www.drawntofaith.com/newsletter

CHECK OUT OUR OTHER BOOKS!

www.drawntofaith.com

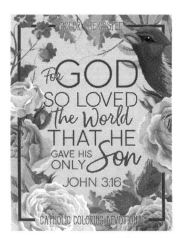

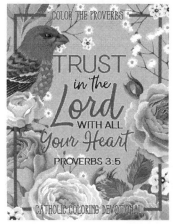

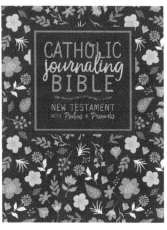

Made in the USA
Lexington, KY
29 May 2018